Many therapists express a desire to move into a spiritually integrated treatment with clients but are unsure of the new territory, both in conceptualization and technique. This handbook presents a much-awaited clear, actionable guide for therapists. Cases and treatment approaches are drawn from clinical science as much as the wise experience of long-time spiritually integrated therapists. Increasingly, patients in deep suffering are looking to engage spiritually with their therapist. It's time for us to embrace this expanded opportunity.

—Lisa Miller, PhD, Professor, Columbia University, New York, NY, and author of *The Awakened Brain: The New Science of Spirituality and Our Quest for an Inspired Life*

Authoritative, evidence-based, and a proven learning resource: What more could you ask for? I have no doubt that *Handbook of Spiritually Integrated Psychotherapies* will be the essential resource for educating the current and future generations of mental health professionals in integrating spiritual and religious issues in mental health practice.

—Len Sperry, MD, PhD, Professor, Florida Atlantic University, Boca Raton, FL, and author of *Spirituality in Clinical Practice: Theory and Practice of Spiritually Oriented Psychotherapy, Second Edition*

In *Handbook of Spiritually Integrated Psychotherapies*, we get a state-of-the-art, comprehensive, engaging, and scholarly yet practical book on the important area of spiritually integrated psychotherapies. It highlights multiple faith traditions, patient populations, and techniques, and it is multicultural in focus. Most of the contributors are superstars in this area, so the reader is learning from those who have shaped the field as well. The book should be on the desk of every mental health professional who is engaged with spiritually and religiously informed psychotherapies and will surely become a classic in the field. I'm sure that my copy will be well-worn rather soon.

—Thomas G. Plante, PhD, ABPP, Augustin Cardinal Bea, S.J. University Professor, Santa Clara University, Santa Clara, CA, and Adjunct Clinical Professor, Department of Psychiatry & Behavioral Sciences at Stanford University School of Medicine, Palo Alto, CA

HANDBOOK OF
Spiritually Integrated Psychotherapies

HANDBOOK OF
Spiritually Integrated Psychotherapies

EDITED BY

P. Scott Richards • G. E. Kawika Allen
Daniel K Judd

AMERICAN PSYCHOLOGICAL ASSOCIATION

Copyright © 2023 by the American Psychological Association. All rights reserved. Except as permitted under the United States Copyright Act of 1976, no part of this publication may be reproduced or distributed in any form or by any means, including, but not limited to, the process of scanning and digitization, or stored in a database or retrieval system, without the prior written permission of the publisher.

The opinions and statements published are the responsibility of the authors, and such opinions and statements do not necessarily represent the policies of the American Psychological Association.

Published by
American Psychological Association
750 First Street, NE
Washington, DC 20002
https://www.apa.org

Order Department
https://www.apa.org/pubs/books
order@apa.org

In the U.K., Europe, Africa, and the Middle East, copies may be ordered from Eurospan
https://www.eurospanbookstore.com/apa
info@eurospangroup.com

Typeset in Meridien and Ortodoxa by Circle Graphics, Inc., Reisterstown, MD

Printer: Gasch Printing, Odenton, MD
Cover Designer: Anthony D. Paular, Anthony Paular Design, Newbury Park, CA

Library of Congress Cataloging-in-Publication Data

Names: Richards, P. Scott, editor. | Allen, G. E. Kawika, editor. | Judd,
    Daniel K, editor.
Title: Handbook of spiritually integrated psychotherapies / edited by
    P. Scott Richards, G. E. Kawika Allen, and Daniel K Judd.
Description: Washington, DC : American Psychological Association, [2023] |
    Includes bibliographical references and index.
Identifiers: LCCN 2022044287 (print) | LCCN 2022044288 (ebook) |
    ISBN 9781433835926 (paperback) | ISBN 9781433835933 (ebook)
Subjects: LCSH: Psychotherapy--Religious aspects. | BISAC: PSYCHOLOGY /
    Psychotherapy / Counseling | PSYCHOLOGY / Psychotherapy / General
Classification: LCC RC489.S676 H36 2023 (print) | LCC RC489.S676 (ebook)
    | DDC 616.89/14--dc23/eng/20221114
LC record available at https://lccn.loc.gov/2022044287
LC ebook record available at https://lccn.loc.gov/2022044288

https://doi.org/10.1037/0000338-000

Printed in the United States of America

10 9 8 7 6 5 4 3 2 1

Dedicated to
Allen E. Bergin
mentor, friend, and international pioneer
of the integration of religious values and spirituality into psychotherapy
and
Nicholas J. S. Gibson
present-day champion for the scientific study of psychology, religion,
and spirituality

CONTENTS

Contributors	xi
Acknowledgments	xvii

1. Introduction: Bringing Spiritually Integrated Psychotherapies Into the Health Care Mainstream   **3**
P. Scott Richards, Kenneth I. Pargament, Julie J. Exline, and G. E. Kawika Allen

I. GENERAL APPROACHES FOR SPIRITUALLY INTEGRATED PSYCHOTHERAPY   31

2. Culturally Informed Therapy: An Intervention That Addresses the Psychological Needs of Religious Individuals of Diverse Identities   **33**
Amy Weisman de Mamani, Olivia Altamirano, Daisy Lopez, Merranda Marie McLaughlin, Jessica Maura, Ana Martinez de Andino, Salman Shaheen Ahmad, Laurinda Hafner, and Sarah Griffith Lund

3. Providing a Secure Base: Facilitating a Secure Attachment to God in Psychotherapy   **57**
Suzanne Nortier Hollman and Cheri Marmarosh

4. Relational Spirituality Model in Psychotherapy: Overview and Case Application   **77**
Steven J. Sandage and George S. Stavros

5. Postsecular, Spiritually Integrated Gestalt Therapy   **99**
Philip Brownell and Jelena Zeleskov Doric

vii

viii *Contents*

6. **Shaken to the Core: Understanding and Addressing Spiritual Struggles in Psychotherapy** 119

Kenneth I. Pargament and Julie J. Exline

7. **A Spiritually Inclusive Theistic Approach to Psychotherapy in Inpatient, Residential, and Outpatient Settings** 135

Michael E. Berrett, Randy K. Hardman, and P. Scott Richards

8. **SPIRIT: Spiritual Psychotherapy for Inpatient, Residential, and Intensive Treatment** 157

Sarah Salcone and David H. Rosmarin

9. **Religiously Accommodative and Integrative Rational Emotive Behavior Therapy** 173

Stevan Lars Nielsen, Dane D. B. Abegg, Brodrick T. Brown, David M. Erekson, Rachel A. Hamilton, and Sarah E. Lindsey

II. INTEGRATION OF SPECIFIC SPIRITUAL TRADITIONS INTO PSYCHOTHERAPY 191

10. **Theoretical Foundations and Clinical Applications of Traditional Islamically Integrated Psychotherapy** 193

Fahad Khan and Hooman Keshavarzi

11. **Gospel-Centered Integrated Framework for Therapy: Foundation, Description, Research Findings, and Application** 213

Elena E. Kim, Judy Cha, and Timothy Keller

12. **Gestalt Pastoral Care: An Opening to Grace** 231

Tilda Norberg, David L. Janvier, Wanda Craner, Lyn Barrett, Michael Crabtree, Michelle Zechner, and Mark Thomas

13. **Spiritually Integrated Psychotherapy Among Catholics: A Practice-Based International Investigation** 249

Jeong Yeon Hwang and Wonjin Sim

14. **Jewish Forms of Spiritually Integrated Psychotherapy in Israel** 267

Ofra Mayseless, Marianna Ruah-Midbar Shapiro, Aya Rice, and Liat Zucker

15. **Sufi Psychology: A Heart-Centered Paradigm** 285

Saloumeh DeGood

16. **Christian-Based Spiritually Integrated Psychotherapy for East Asian Canadians and Findings From the CSPEARIT Study** 301

Wai Lun Alan Fung, Purple Yip, Sheila Stevens, Tat-Ying Wong, Yeun-Hee Natalie Yoo, Nancy Ross, Helen K. Noh, and Taryn Tang

17. **A Polynesian Perspective for Navigating the Spiritual Connections in Psychotherapy Practice** 325

Alayne Mikahere-Hall, Hoku Conklin, and G. E. Kawika Allen

III. SPIRITUALLY INTEGRATED PSYCHOTHERAPY FOR SPECIFIC PATIENT POPULATIONS — 345

18. Spiritually Integrated Couple Therapy — 347
Everett L. Worthington, Jr., Jennifer S. Ripley, Zhuo Job Chen, Vanessa M. Kent, and Elizabeth Loewer

19. REACH Forgiveness in Couple, Group, and Individual Psychotherapy — 365
Everett L. Worthington, Jr.

20. Search for Meaning: A Spiritually Integrated Approach for Treating Veterans With Posttraumatic Stress Disorder — 381
Clyde T. Angel, John E. Sullivan, and Vincent R. Starnino

21. Spiritually Focused, Multiculturally Oriented Psychotherapy in the Criminal Justice Detention System — 403
Jennifer Gafford, Courtney Agorsor, Don Davis, Joshua Hook, Cirleen DeBlaere, Sree Sinha, Jeremy Coleman, Emma Porter, and Jesse Owen

IV. MAINSTREAMING SPIRITUALLY INTEGRATED PSYCHOTHERAPIES — 421

22. Training Opportunities and Resources for Spiritually Integrated Psychotherapists and Researchers — 423
P. Scott Richards, Joseph M. Currier, Russell Siler Jones, Michelle Pearce, and Douglas Stephens

Index — 449

About the Editors — 473

CONTRIBUTORS

Dane D. B. Abegg, MS, Counseling Psychology and Special Education, Brigham Young University, Provo, UT, United States

Courtney Agorsor, MA, Department of Counseling Psychology, University of Denver, Denver, CO, United States

Salman Shaheen Ahmad, MS, Department of Psychology, Clinical Division, University of Miami, Coral Gables, FL, United States

G. E. Kawika Allen, PhD, David O. McKay School of Education, Brigham Young University, Provo, UT, United States

Olivia Altamirano, MS, Department of Psychology, Clinical Division, University of Miami, Coral Gables, FL, United States

Clyde T. Angel, DMin, BCC, LPC, Richard L. Roudebush VA Medical Center, Indianapolis, IN, United States

Lyn Barrett, MEd, MDiv, United Church of Christ, Cleveland, OH; Gestalt Pastoral Care Associates, Las Cruces, NM; and Safe Communities, Lancaster, PA, United States

Michael E. Berrett, PhD, LP, Berrett and Company, LLC, Orem, UT, United States

Brodrick T. Brown, PhD, Counseling and Psychological Services, Brigham Young University, Provo, UT, United States

Philip Brownell, MDiv, PsyD, Family Health Services, Twin Falls, ID, United States

Judy Cha, PhD, Redeemer Counseling Services, New York, NY, United States

Zhuo Job Chen, PhD, School of Nursing, University of North Carolina at Charlotte, Charlotte, NC, United States

Jeremy Coleman, PhD, Department of Psychology, Augusta University, Augusta, GA, United States

Hoku Conklin, PhD, Counseling and Psychological Services, Brigham Young University, Provo, UT, United States

Michael Crabtree, PhD, Psychology Department, Washington & Jefferson College, Washington, PA, United States

Wanda Craner, MDiv, GPCM/T, United Church of Christ Ordained Covenant Ministry, Pennsylvania Southeast Conference, Pottstown, PA, and Gestalt Pastoral Care Associates, Boyertown, PA, United States

Joseph M. Currier, PhD, Psychology Department, University of South Alabama, Mobile, AL, United States

Don Davis, PhD, Department of Counseling and Psychological Services, Georgia State University, Atlanta, GA, United States

Cirleen DeBlaere, PhD, Department of Counseling and Psychological Services, Georgia State University, Atlanta, GA, United States

Saloumeh DeGood, PsyD, Sufi Psychology Association, Davis, CA, United States

Jelena Zeleskov Doric, PhD, Faculty of Arts and Humanities, American University of Cyprus, Larnaka, Cyprus; and Dr Jelena Zeleskov Doric Psychology Practice, Wollongong, Australia

David M. Erekson, PhD, Counseling and Psychological Services, Brigham Young University, Provo, UT, United States

Julie J. Exline, PhD, Department of Psychological Sciences, Case Western Reserve University, Cleveland, OH, United States

Wai Lun Alan Fung, MD, ScD, FRCPC, Wycliffe College and Department of Psychiatry, University of Toronto, and Psychology Department, Tyndale University, Toronto, Ontario, Canada

Jennifer Gafford, PhD, Department of Counseling Psychology, University of Denver, Denver, CO, United States

Laurinda Hafner, DMin, Coral Gables United Church of Christ, Coral Gables, FL, United States

Rachel A. Hamilton, BS, Statistics, Brigham Young University, Provo, UT, United States

Randy K. Hardman, PhD, LP, Rexburg, ID, United States

Suzanne Nortier Hollman, PsyD, PhD, Professional Psychology Program, The George Washington University, Washington, DC, and Institute for the Psychological Sciences, Divine Mercy University, Sterling, VA, United States

Joshua Hook, PhD, Department of Psychology, University of North Texas, Denton, TX, United States

Jeong Yeon Hwang, PhD, Institute of Psychology, Pontifical Gregorian University, Rome, Italy

David L. Janvier, MA, LPC, CST, CCTP, GPCM, Janvier Counseling and Associates, Pittsburgh, PA, United States

Russell Siler Jones, ThD, LCMHCS, Residency in Psychotherapy and Spirituality Program, CareNet Counseling (An Affiliate of Wake Forest Baptist Health), Winston-Salem, NC, United States

Daniel K Judd, PhD, Religious Education, Brigham Young University, Provo, UT, United States

Timothy Keller, DMin, Redeemer Presbyterian Church, New York, NY, United States

Vanessa M. Kent, PhD, Counseling Department, Regent University, Virginia Beach, VA, United States

Hooman Keshavarzi, PsyD, Department of Research, Khalil Center, Lombard, IL, United States, and Clinical Psychology Department, Ibn Haldun University, Başakşehir, Turkey

Fahad Khan, PsyD, Department of Research, Khalil Center, Lombard, IL, United States

Elena E. Kim, PhD, Research Institute for Spirituality and Eudaimonia, New York, NY, United States

Sarah E. Lindsey, BS, Psychology, Brigham Young University, Provo, UT, United States

Elizabeth Loewer, MA, Psychology Department, Regent University, Virginia Beach, VA, United States

Daisy Lopez, MS, Department of Psychology, Clinical Division, University of Miami, Coral Gables, FL, United States

Sarah Griffith Lund, MDiv, DMin, MSW, First Congregational United Church of Christ Indianapolis, Indianapolis, IN, United States

Cheri Marmarosh, PhD, Professional Psychology Program, The George Washington University, Washington, DC, United States

Ana Martinez de Andino, PhD, Department of Psychology, Clinical Division, University of Miami, Coral Gables, FL, United States

Jessica Maura, PhD, Department of Psychology, Clinical Division, University of Miami, Coral Gables, FL, United States

Ofra Mayseless, PhD, Faculty of Education, University of Haifa, Mount Carmel, Haifa, Israel

Merranda Marie McLaughlin, MS, Department of Psychology, Clinical Division, University of Miami, Coral Gables, FL, United States

Alayne Mikahere-Hall, PhD, Taupua Waiora Maori Research Centre, National Institute for Public Health and Mental Health Research, Auckland University of Technology, Auckland, New Zealand

Stevan Lars Nielsen, PhD, Counseling and Psychological Services and Counseling Psychology and Special Education, Brigham Young University, Provo, UT, United States

Helen K. Noh, PhD, RP, Counselling Department, Tyndale University, Toronto, Ontario, Canada

Tilda Norberg, MDiv, GPCM/T, Gestalt Pastoral Care Associates, Staten Island, NY, and The New York Conference of The United Methodist Church, White Plains, NY, United States

Jesse Owen, PhD, Department of Counseling Psychology, University of Denver, Denver, CO, United States

Kenneth I. Pargament, PhD, Department of Psychology, Bowling Green State University, Bowling Green, OH, United States

xiv *Contributors*

Michelle Pearce, PhD, Graduate School, University of Maryland, Baltimore, MD, and Department of Psychiatry and Behavioral Sciences, Duke University Medical Center, Durham, NC, United States

Emma Porter, PhD, New York City Health + Hospitals, New York, NY, United States

Aya Rice, MA, Department of Counseling and Human Development, University of Haifa, Mount Carmel, Haifa, Israel

P. Scott Richards, PhD, Bridges Institute for Spiritually Integrated Psychotherapies, St. George, UT, United States

Jennifer S. Ripley, PhD, Psychology Department, Regent University, Virginia Beach, VA, United States

David H. Rosmarin, PhD, ABPP, Spirituality and Mental Health Program, McLean Hospital, Belmont, MA, and Department of Psychiatry, Harvard Medical School, Boston, MA, United States

Nancy Ross, PhD, Psychology Department, Tyndale University, Toronto, Ontario, Canada

Sarah Salcone, MS, Psychology Department, University of South Alabama, Mobile, AL, United States

Steven J. Sandage, PhD, LP, School of Theology and Department of Psychological and Brain Sciences, Boston University, Boston, MA, United States; The Albert & Jessie Danielsen Institute, Boston, MA, United States; and Psychology of Religion, MF Norwegian School of Theology, Religion, and Society, Oslo, Norway

Marianna Ruah-Midbar Shapiro, PhD, Department of Mysticism and Spirituality, Zefat Academic College, Zefat, Israel

Wonjin Sim, PhD, Department of Psychology, Towson University, Towson, MD, United States

Sree Sinha, MA, Department of Counseling Psychology, University of Denver, Denver, CO, United States

Vincent R. Starnino, PhD, LCSW, Richard L. Roudebush VA Medical Center, and School of Social Work, Indiana University, Indianapolis, IN, United States

George S. Stavros, PhD, MDiv, School of Theology, Boston University, and The Albert & Jessie Danielsen Institute, Boston, MA, United States

Douglas Stephens, EdD, LICSW, LMFT, Solihten Institute, Elkhart, IN, United States

Sheila Stevens, MDiv, RP, Tyndale Counselling Services, Tyndale University, Toronto, Ontario, Canada

John E. Sullivan, MSW, LCSW, Richard L. Roudebush VA Medical Center, and IUPUI Conscience Project, Indiana University–Purdue University Indianapolis, Indianapolis, IN, United States

Taryn Tang, PhD, Department of Psychiatry, University of Toronto, Toronto, Ontario, Canada

Mark Thomas, MS, Department of Psychology, University of Pittsburgh, Pittsburgh, PA, United States

Amy Weisman de Mamani, PhD, Department of Psychology, Clinical Division, University of Miami, Coral Gables, FL, United States

Tat-Ying Wong, MD, Grace Health Centre, Toronto, Ontario, Canada

Everett L. Worthington, Jr., PhD, Department of Psychology, Virginia Commonwealth University, Richmond, VA, United States

Purple Yip, MDiv, RP, Purple Yip Counselling, Toronto, Ontario, Canada

Yeun-Hee Natalie Yoo, MDiv, RP, Tyndale Wellness Centre (formerly Family Life Centre), Tyndale University, Toronto, Ontario, Canada

Michelle Zechner, PhD, Department of Psychiatric Rehabilitation and Counseling Professions, Rutgers, The State University of New Jersey, New Brunswick, NJ, United States

Liat Zucker, MA, Department of Counseling and Human Development, University of Haifa, Mount Carmel, Haifa, Israel

ACKNOWLEDGMENTS

We are grateful to Susan B. Reynolds, senior consulting editor for American Psychological Association (APA) Books, for her encouragement and patience. Her support and guidance were crucial. We are also grateful to Beth Hatch, development editor at APA Books, whose feedback greatly enhanced the clarity and quality of the final manuscript.

The research and collaborative efforts between the editors and chapter authors that ultimately led to the production of this handbook were supported in part by the John Templeton Foundation Grant #60877, Enhancing Practice-Based Evidence for Spiritually Integrated Psychotherapy: An Interdisciplinary Big Data Project. We are grateful to the Templeton Foundation for their generous funding. We are also grateful to Nicholas J. S. Gibson, the director of human sciences at the Templeton Foundation, whose scientific, conceptual, and practical support during the grant project was essential to our success.

We are also thankful to our friends and colleagues from around the world who contributed chapters to this handbook. It has been an honor for us to collaborate with this professionally and religiously diverse group of mental health and pastoral practitioners, scholars, and educators. We have learned much from their experience and wisdom.

Finally, we are grateful to our wives, Marcia Tolman Richards, Carolina Sagebin Allen, and Kaye Seegmiller Judd. We treasure their love and support.

HANDBOOK OF
Spiritually Integrated Psychotherapies

1

Introduction

Bringing Spiritually Integrated Psychotherapies Into the Health Care Mainstream

P. Scott Richards, Kenneth I. Pargament, Julie J. Exline, and
G. E. Kawika Allen

Polls and demographic statistics show that there is enormous religious and spiritual diversity in the United States and throughout the world. This diversity is rapidly increasing and spreading due in part to global communication, travel, and immigration (Pew Research Center, 2015).

Significant numbers of adherents to the five major Western, theistic religions (i.e., Christianity, Islam, Judaism, Sikhism, Zoroastrianism) and six major Eastern world religions (i.e., Buddhism, Confucianism, Hinduism, Jainism, Shintoism, Taoism) now live in the United States and Canada (Pew Research Center, 2015). Growing numbers of people, however, are not affiliated with one of the major world religions (Pew Research Center, 2015) but embrace spirituality from within some other spiritual and philosophical perspective, such as transpersonal, humanistic, existential, and Indigenous traditions (e.g., Pew Research Center, 2015; Richards & Bergin, 2014). Others are unaffiliated with a religious tradition but nevertheless consider themselves spiritual (Pew Research Center, 2015). In addition, many people are atheistic or nonreligious. They also face universal human questions about the purpose of life, morality, love, suffering, anxiety, evil, and death (Pew Research Center, 2015; Sedlar et al., 2018).

The breathtaking variety in religious and spiritual beliefs in the world makes it challenging for psychotherapists to effectively address spiritual issues during treatment (American Psychological Association [APA], 2017;

---

https://doi.org/10.1037/0000338-001
Handbook of Spiritually Integrated Psychotherapies, P. S. Richards, G. E. K. Allen, and
D. K. Judd (Editors)
Copyright © 2023 by the American Psychological Association. All rights reserved.

4   *Richards et al.*

Richards & Bergin, 2014). Most practitioners receive little or no training in spiritual aspects of diversity and treatment (Pargament et al., 2013). This lack of training can create problems for psychotherapists and their patients. Consider the following case vignette written by a psychotherapy patient whom we'll call "Katherine;"[1] she has granted us permission to include the story in this chapter:

> When I was 33 years old, and after 14 years of marriage, I was forced into a terrible, painful divorce when my husband committed adultery and left me and my four small children for another woman. My husband and I divorced quickly, and within a month, he had remarried. Then he and his new wife started attending my church. Due to circumstances beyond my control, I was unable to attend a different church, so I continued to attend the same church despite how painful it was to see my former husband and his new wife in the pews. The people in our Christian church community were torn between conflicting loyalties. Most of them chose to stay neutral rather than siding with one or the other of us, thus leaving me feeling very alone and unsupported. I felt like I lost most of my friends and the social support system I had previously enjoyed in my religious community.
>
> The stress I lived under during this time took a tremendous toll on my emotional health. I realized that I needed professional help as I was suffering from anxiety and what later turned out to be trauma-related issues. One day I looked up "psychologists" on the internet and randomly picked one.
>
> The psychologist I chose turned out to be a nice man and seemed very knowledgeable and good at what he did. He had been raised in the Christian tradition but had left it as an adult and no longer believed in God. He was a strong supporter of cognitive therapy, and we worked on that for a while, but we soon ran into difficulties. He saw organized religion as restrictive and suffocating and encouraged me to question my beliefs. I saw my religion as my lifeline to God, who, in my mind, was a real person with whom I had an intimate relationship, even though, at the moment, I was struggling. I still loved God but felt like He had let me down, and I wanted to work through these feelings. However, my psychologist couldn't suspend his disbelief even though this would have benefited me greatly. He was convinced that religion damaged people.
>
> The last time I saw him, I told my psychologist that I had recently gone out on several dates with a divorced man who wanted to have a sexual relationship with me, which I had refused to do. My psychologist asked me why I was unwilling to have a sexual relationship with the man. I told him that I believed sexual relations should be reserved for marriage. My psychologist shook his head and said, "Katherine, I think you'd be happier if you would let yourself enjoy a new sexual relationship." I told him it would violate my religious beliefs. He said, "Maybe you should consider leaving your church." That was the end of therapy for me. I felt like my psychologist should have been more understanding and respectful of my faith and spiritual values and that he shouldn't have tried to push his own beliefs on me.

---

[1]Details of case examples and patient names presented in this chapter have been altered to protect patient confidentiality.

A few weeks after that experience, I started with a new psychologist to whom my pastor had referred me. This psychologist had his own private practice, and his informed consent document said that he had received specialized training in religion and spirituality. He said he was willing to include discussions about faith and spirituality during treatment if that was my desire. He also had 20 years of counseling experience behind him.

It didn't take me long to discover that, when it came to religion, we were completely in sync. My new psychologist believed in God and wasn't ashamed of sharing that with me when I asked him about it. He understood why I felt God had betrayed me and why I wanted so badly to work out my relationship with God. He also understood why I was so devoted and committed to the teachings of my church. We spent hours digging deeply into spiritual issues that my other psychologist had ignored or shown little interest in. My new psychologist never preached or caused me to feel like I was unrighteous or lacking in faith because of the struggles I was going through. I could tell him when I received answers to my prayers, and he believed those answers—he didn't subtly question my sanity. He was competent as a psychologist about my emotional struggles and sensitive and insightful about my religious and spiritual questions and struggles. He was exactly what I needed.

I have simplified my story for the sake of brevity, for there were other, more complicated psychological issues going on, which my psychologist also helped me work through. I know that my religious belief system and spirituality played an important, even vital, role in the process of my recovery. In my view, to ignore the spiritual part of a person is to ignore something essential that ultimately can help make him or her healthy and whole.

As can be seen in this case example, Katherine had religious and spiritual issues that were intertwined with her presenting problems, but her first psychologist struggled to effectively address them, perhaps because of lack of training and perhaps because he may not have worked through his own biases and negative feelings about religion. Fortunately, Katherine persisted in her efforts to get professional help and was able to find a psychologist who was competent in religious and spiritual aspects of diversity and treatment. Katherine's treatment was much more successful when her new psychologist addressed her spiritual beliefs and issues in a more sensitive and competent manner.

The purpose of this *Handbook of Spiritually Integrated Psychotherapies* is to help mental health professionals more fully understand how they can integrate spiritual perspectives and interventions into their practices in an ethical and competent manner so that they can work effectively with patients from a diversity of religious, spiritual, and racial and cultural backgrounds. The book provides helpful clinical insights into an impressive variety of empirically supported, spiritually integrated treatment approaches that have been used with many psychological issues and in many different treatment settings. We anticipate that this book will be helpful for licensed mental health practitioners, graduate students, educators, and researchers in clinical and counseling psychology, psychiatry, clinical social work, marriage and family therapy, and pastoral counseling.

DEFINING SPIRITUALLY INTEGRATED PSYCHOTHERAPIES

Many spiritually sensitive mental health treatment approaches have been developed during the past 40 years (Richards & Bergin, 2005, 2014; Sperry & Shafranske, 2005). Buddhist, Hindu, Christian, Jewish, Muslim, African, African American, Native American, and Pacific Islander psychotherapy approaches have been described (Epstein, 1995; McMinn, 1996; W. R. Miller & Delaney, 2005; Miovic, 2004; Rabinowitz, 1999; Richards & Bergin, 2014). Spiritual approaches have been integrated with many mainstream psychotherapy traditions, and they have been applied in practice with a wide variety of clinical issues and populations (Fukuyama & Sevig, 1999; L. Miller, 2011; W. R. Miller, 1999; Pargament et al., 2013; Smith & Richards, 2005; Sperry, 2001).

In the *APA Handbook of Psychology, Religion, and Spirituality*, Sperry (2013) provided a helpful definition of *spiritually integrated* mental health treatment:

> Spiritually integrated psychotherapy is a term that broadly characterizes a variety of psychotherapeutic approaches that are sensitive to the spiritual dimension. These approaches range from non-Christian approaches and transpersonal psychotherapies . . . to theistic . . . and various Christian approaches . . . and evidence-based religious accommodative forms of psychotherapy. . . . Individuals seeking explicitly spiritually integrated psychotherapy range from relatively healthy spiritual seekers to disordered clients presenting with symptomatic distress or impairment in one or more areas of life functioning . . . spiritually integrated psychotherapy is distinct from pastoral counseling and spiritual direction in its emphasis and treatment focus. It draws on spiritual resources in addressing spiritual issues and struggles to resolve psychological and relational problems. Although it can also foster spiritual change and growth, spiritually integrated psychotherapy accomplishes this as a by-product that accompanies psychological change. (p. 227)

We like *spiritually integrated psychotherapy* as a catchall term that refers to approaches delivered by mental health professionals that draw on spiritual resources to address psychological and relational problems and that are distinct from pastoral counseling and spiritual direction. Consistent with Sperry (2013) and other leaders in the field (e.g., Pargament, 2007), we use the term *spiritually integrated psychotherapy* in this manner in this book.

It may also be helpful to briefly discuss what the integration of spirituality into psychotherapy does *not* mean. For one, it does not mean proselytizing patients toward or away from any particular set of religious or spiritual beliefs, practices, or affiliations. Simply put, this would be unethical. Spiritual integrated psychotherapy rests instead on a respect for the patient's orientation to spirituality, whatever that orientation may be, and values the patient's right to make informed decisions about spiritual issues as in all dimensions of human functioning. This is not to say that the therapist will not have their own orientation to spirituality but, rather, that the therapist guards against overt or covert efforts to impose a particular spiritual worldview on the patient.

In addition, spiritually integrated psychotherapy does not mean a new alternative to other therapeutic orientations. Instead, it could be relevant to any therapeutic approach, including cognitive behavior therapy, dialectical behavior therapy, rational emotive behavior therapy, acceptance and commitment therapy, emotion-focused therapy, existential therapy, or psychodynamic therapy.

Spiritually integrated therapy rests on the assumption that we are spiritual as well as psychological, social, and physical beings. *Spirituality*—the relationship we take to whatever we hold sacred—is a part of our beliefs, practices, emotions, values, and relationships (Pargament et al., 2013). It is intertwined with the problems we experience and the solutions to those problems. Psychotherapy that neglects this dimension is then incomplete. Spiritually integrated therapy simply means the bringing of attention, sensitivity, and evidence-based knowledge about the spiritual dimension into the process of psychotherapy—specifically, the way the patient is understood and the way the patient's problems are addressed in treatment.

WHY DOES SPIRITUALLY INTEGRATED PSYCHOTHERAPY MAKE GOOD SENSE?

With the increasing demands on mental health providers, it is not unreasonable to ask why additional time and energy should be spent on the spiritual dimension of patients' lives. There are some very good empirically based reasons, highlighted briefly here:

- *Religion and spirituality are significant parts of the lives of a majority of people in the United States.* Consider a few indications. According to the 2014 Pew Research Center religious landscape study of a national sample of Americans, 63% reported that they are "absolutely certain" of God's existence, with only 9% indicating that they do not believe in God (Pew Research Center, n.d.). Furthermore, 53% felt that religion is very important to them; only 11% said it is not at all important. In addition, 55% reported that they pray once or more a day, whereas only 23% indicated that they never pray.

- *Spirituality is a resource for many people.* In times of adversity, religion and spirituality are among the first places many individuals look to for support, meaning, comfort, and guidance (Pargament, 2011). For example, following the September 11, 2001, terrorist attacks, 90% of Americans reported that they turned to God for solace and support (Schuster et al., 2001). Spirituality offers a distinctive set of coping resources (e.g., spiritual support, confession and forgiveness, transcendent experience, benevolent reframing of pain and suffering) that are particularly well designed to help people come to terms with human frailty and finitude. Moreover, spirituality is especially concerned about cultivating a life of wholeness (Pargament et al., 2016). Greater use of religious and spiritual resources has been linked to mental health benefits, including recovery among people dealing with psychological problems (Koenig et al., 2012).

- *Spirituality can also contribute to psychological problems.* There is a darker, seamy side (see Pruyser, 1977) to religion and spirituality. Religion and spirituality can be sources of denial, prejudice, avoidance, rigidity, and extremism. The growing research literature on spiritual struggles provides an apt illustration. *Spiritual struggles* are defined as tensions, strains, and conflicts about sacred matters within oneself, with others, and/or with God (Exline, 2013). Spiritual struggles are not uncommon, and they have been robustly associated with psychological distress and problems (Pargament & Exline, 2022).

- *Many people want spiritually integrated help.* Surveys indicate that most patients view religion and spirituality as relevant to their mental health and would welcome the chance to discuss religious and spiritual issues in therapy, including their spiritual struggles (Exline et al., 2000; Harris et al., 2016; Rose et al., 2001). For example, in one survey of patients from six mental health centers, 55% said they would like to be able to talk about religious or spiritual concerns in their therapy (Rose et al., 2001).

- *Integrating spirituality into psychotherapy may enhance the effectiveness of treatment.* According to a recent meta-analysis, spiritually integrated forms of treatment were more effective than nonreligious/spiritually integrated treatments in fostering improved psychological and spiritual functioning (Captari et al., 2018). In analyses that focused on the most rigorous evaluations, spiritually integrated therapies were as effective as nonreligious/spiritual treatments in reducing psychological distress and more effective in facilitating greater spiritual well-being. We say more about the treatment outcome research in this domain later in this chapter and in other chapters throughout the book.

HOW DO WE INTEGRATE SPIRITUALITY INTO PSYCHOTHERAPY?

Integrating spirituality into psychotherapy begins with a recognition that doing so is in the best interests of many of our patients. Having a desire to respond in sensitive and competent ways to our patients' religious and spiritual beliefs is another foundational motivation. With such recognition and motivation, psychotherapists can prepare themselves to be competent in this domain of psychotherapy by gaining competency, staying true to their beliefs, helping patients access spiritual resources, and helping patients address spiritual problems. We say more about each in the following sections.

Gaining Competency

For psychotherapists to work effectively and ethically with spiritual patients and issues, it is essential for them to develop competency in religious and spiritual aspects of diversity. The foundational skills of spiritually sensitive psychotherapists are similar to those required of effective multicultural counselors (Sue & Sue, 1990). Spiritually sensitive psychotherapists also acquire specialized knowledge and training about religious and spiritual aspects of diversity and about religious and spiritual treatment competencies (Richards & Bergin, 2005,

2014). In many diverse groups in the United States, spirituality is deeply entrenched in the framework of their cultures. The unification of culture and spirituality is not only prominent but also inherently permeated in their way of being (Allen et al., 2017).

Psychotherapists can increase their competency to work with patients from diverse religious, spiritual, and cultural backgrounds by seeking (a) general knowledge about the world religions; (b) specific expertise about religious and cultural traditions they frequently encounter in psychotherapy; and (c) knowledge about theories and research in the multicultural, psychology of religion, and sociology of religion fields. They can also read books or take workshops, classes, and online webinars about clinical competencies required for working effectively with cultural, religious, and spiritual issues in psycho-therapy (e.g., Pearce et al., 2019). We also recommend that they seek to stay current with scholarly literature about religion and spirituality in mental health and psychotherapy, seek supervision or consultation from colleagues who have expertise in religious and spiritual aspects of diversity and treatment, and engage in personal spiritual exploration and growth practices (L. Miller, 2011; Richards & Bergin, 2005, 2014; Shafranske & Malony, 1996).

Staying True to One's Own Beliefs

It is also important for psychotherapists to select a spiritually integrative treat-ment approach that is consistent with their personal and professional beliefs. Fear and Woolfe (1999) suggested that "therapists need to operate within a theoretical orientation which encompasses the same underlying metatheo-retical assumptions as their personal philosophy" (p. 253). They suggested that congruence between a practitioner's personal values and theoretical orientation is necessary for treatment effectiveness and to prevent burnout.

Because the mainstream mental health professions are dominated by the naturalist-atheistic worldview that assumes that spiritual realities do not exist (Bergin, 1980; Richards & Bergin, 2005), psychotherapists may feel pressured to abandon or ignore their spiritual beliefs in their work. This seems counter-productive given that most people are religious and believe in spiritual realities (Bergin, 1980).

We recommend that psychotherapists learn about various spiritually integra-tive psychotherapy approaches and integrate one that is most consistent with their own spiritual beliefs into their work. This handbook provides many spir-itually integrative treatment options that psychotherapists can consider as they seek to develop competency in spirituality and psychotherapy.

Helping Patients Access Spiritual Resources in Treatment

When people experience psychological problems, they can lose touch with the resources that, up to that point, helped orient and stabilize their lives. Under emotional stress, many patients "lose their rhythm," eating and sleeping irreg-ularly, losing touch with friends, missing work, and giving up on exercise.

The same point can apply to religious and spiritual resources. In difficult times, patients may become disengaged from the religious activities, spiritual practices, and sources of ultimate purpose that had given meaning to their lives. Encouraging patients to reengage in their religious and spiritual practices can be one part of the larger therapeutic goal of helping patients get back into the normal rhythm of their lives. We see this in the following example, which is a more detailed description of a case initially presented in Pargament (1997, p. 380).

Bob, a 60-year-old truck driver, came to therapy with symptoms of post-traumatic stress disorder. Several months ago, he had pulled over on the side of the road to assist someone whose car was stuck in the middle of the highway. While helping the motorist, another car came around a curve in the road and hit the disabled car head on, instantly killing the young driver. Bob witnessed the horrible accident and over the next weeks experienced nightmares, panic attacks, and flashbacks.

Before the accident, Bob had been content with his life; he had a good job, a solid marriage of 35 years, and children who were prospering. Since the accident, however, Bob had become moody, irritable, and increasingly isolated, symptoms that were not alleviated by medication.

As the therapist got to know Bob, he learned that Bob had been an active member of his church and was good friends with the pastor. All of that had come to an end though with the tragic accident. When asked why he had disconnected from his church, Bob said, "Well, I don't want to burden other people with what I'm going through. It's pretty awful stuff." The therapist pointed out that Bob had been there for others in his church when they were going through hard times. Perhaps he could give them a chance to help him out in return. As a homework assignment, the therapist asked Bob to share something of his experience with one member of his church. Bob agreed, but reluctantly.

Asked how the week had gone in the next session, Bob shook his head ruefully and said,

> I've been love-bombed. I told the minister about what I've been going through and the next thing I know, everyone from the church is calling, stopping over, and bringing me cakes and pies. I swear I've already gained 10 pounds.

Bob's complaints were only half-hearted. He was clearly buoyed by the support from his church, and he began to reinvolve himself in its activities. The solace and comfort he received from members and the clergy played an important role in his recovery.

In some cases, patients may be unaware of resources from within their own religious traditions that could be of help to them. For example, individuals struggling with unrelenting guilt could explore rituals of confession and forgiveness within their faith tradition. Patients unable to give voice to their grief and suffering could look to prayers of lamentation and solace for the words they cannot find themselves. Religious literature could also provide patients with stories of inspirational models of figures who faced and came to terms with the full range of problems in living.

Therapists can also help patients explore, identify, and access untapped spiritual resources within themselves. Consider the following clinical example of "Barbara," a composite character representing bits and pieces of numerous patients from our practice.

Barbara, a 52-year-old single woman, came to therapy complaining of long-standing depression. She felt like she was just going through the motions in her life: wake up, go to work as an accountant, come home, check in on her mother in assisted living, and go to bed by 8 p.m. Barbara had a few friends from work but no hobbies or other outside interests. She had tried antidepressant medication with little effect and had sought out psychotherapy a few times in the past but hadn't found it helpful.

In therapy, Barbara presented as listless and dysphoric, speaking in a dull monotone and showing little affect. Although she denied suicidal thoughts or prior attempts, she was unable to describe anything she looked forward to in her life. She felt as if she were walking in a vast empty desert toward a distant, featureless horizon.

Barbara's depression did not appear to be rooted in childhood abuse or in trauma. She had grown up as the only child of a conservative farming couple who had had Barbara late in life, and Barbara spent a lot of time doing chores by herself on the farm. Although she had no great love for accounting, she went into the field to provide herself with a secure job and income.

Barbara's therapist had a difficult time trying to motivate and energize her patient. Initially, Barbara would follow her therapist's suggestions, such as starting to exercise, getting more regular sleep, and spending more time with friends. However, she would soon lose interest. Frustrated with the lack of progress in treatment, the therapist decided to take a more spiritually integrated approach.

The therapist asked Barbara to think about a time in her life when she felt more energy and enthusiasm, when she felt just plain glad to be alive:

BARBARA: [*Takes a long pause*] Sometimes I would get that feeling on the farm when I was growing up.

THERAPIST: What was that feeling like for you?

BARBARA: I remember one time I was walking in the woods. I was only 10 or 11, but I came across a deer. I stopped, and the deer stopped. I was surprised the deer didn't run away, but it didn't. It just stood there looking right at me. I felt like it was really seeing me, or seeing into me. And I looked back, right into the deer. I felt like we truly saw each other. I know this must sound crazy.

THERAPIST: No, not at all. It sounds like it was a very special moment.

BARBARA: Yes, it was. [*Takes a long pause*] You know, I've never had God speak to me the way other people in church have talked about. But that deer spoke to me, and when it did, it felt like time stood still. It was like we saw into each other's souls. And that's when I knew there was a God. No other way to explain it. I can still see that deer now.

THERAPIST: Have you had any similar experiences since that one?

BARBARA: That's the one that's stayed the most with me. But after that, I started to carry my little camera with me when I took walks on the farm. And sometimes I'd see something that touched me deep inside, and I'd take a picture [*eyes become moist, voice becomes shaky*].

THERAPIST: By your voice and your expression, I can tell that those moments were very important to you and continue to speak to you. Do you still have any of those pictures you took as a child?

BARBARA: [*Nods*] I've kept them in the back of my closet, though it's been years since I've looked at them.

THERAPIST: Could you bring some in for our next session? [*Barbara agrees.*]

The next session was spent looking at the pictures Barbara had taken as a child on her farm. As she described the photos of animals, trees, creeks, and weather, Barbara became more animated than she had ever been in therapy, laughing at some pictures, catching her breath at others, and staring in rapt attention at still others.

THERAPIST: These are lovely pictures. I'm struck how they continue to move you, even 40 years later. They do seem to touch something deep inside you, maybe something sacred.

BARBARA: They are sacred to me, though I had never thought about them that way.

THERAPIST: I'd like you to try something for me, if you're willing. I'd like you to take a walk outdoors sometime this week, take some pictures, and bring them to our next session. Okay? [*With a somewhat puzzled look, Barbara agrees.*]

In the next session, Barbara shared a series of close-up shots of leaves from different trees: oaks, maples, poplars, birches, and sycamores. She spoke in a hushed, reverent voice about the leaves: "Each leaf has its own personality. Each one tells a story. Each one has something to say if you just listen."

Over the next few months, Barbara continued to pursue her nature photography and, as she did, much of the depression that had come to define her life lifted. Even after therapy ended, Barbara continued to send her therapist copies of her photographs. She even began to enter her pictures into art festivals and had received some prizes.

As Barbara's case illustrates, therapists can help patients access internal spiritual resources as well as external religious assets. Barbara's therapist recognized that Barbara had experienced a sacred moment as a child when she encountered the deer in the woods. For Barbara, the moment was transcendent.

It was timeless. It revealed a divine force in the universe. And it elicited awe, wonder, and a deep sense of connectedness. The sacred moment pointed to a "sacred spark" within Barbara. The therapist was able to help her identify that spark and fan it into a small flame that added energy, warmth, and purpose to her life. The significant change in Barbara's mood was consistent with empirical literature showing that people who experience sacred moments more regularly report more positive outcomes in psychotherapy (Pargament et al., 2014) and better mental health more generally (Magyar-Russell et al., 2020).

Helping Patients Address Spiritual Problems in Treatment

Although spirituality can be a potent resource for many people who are experiencing psychological problems, it can also be a source of distress and problems in and of itself. As noted earlier, it is not uncommon for people to experience tensions, strains, and conflicts around spiritual matters focused on oneself, other people, or the supernatural domain (Exline, 2013; Pargament & Exline, 2022). Empirical studies have focused on six specific types of spiritual struggles: (a) divine, (b) demonic, (c) moral, (d) ultimate meaning, (e) doubt-related, and (f) ultimate meaning struggles (Exline et al., 2014). As reviewed in detail elsewhere (see Pargament & Exline, 2022; see also Chapter 6 in this book), these spiritual struggles, individually and as a group, have been associated with distress and decline among people facing a full range of psychological problems and stressors as well as among people from diverse religious orientations (including atheists) and demographic groups. However, some studies also suggest that spiritual struggles may be a source of growth and transformation (e.g., Gall et al., 2011; Hart et al., 2020; for a review, see Pargament & Exline, 2022).

Pargament and Exline (2022) presented the illustration of the case of "Joe," a 62-year-old Jewish man suffering from depression. He had recently lost his job as a vice president in an airplane parts manufacturing company and had become irritable, moody, and isolated from his family. The roots of his depression, however, went further back in time. As a child, he had been a musical prodigy on the piano and had been told by his grandfather that "God has given him a gift." As an adolescent, though, Joe developed a benign tumor on his hand that required surgery, and as a result, his hand suffered irreparable damage. His dreams of a career as a concert pianist were shattered, and he blamed God for his misfortune. "God had turned his back on me," he said, "and I was on my own" (p. 196). Joe was unable to find another source of higher meaning in his life and worked in a job that simply "put food on the table" (p. 196). Losing his position in later life brought back his struggles with God and ultimate meaning. Joe's progress in treatment rested on his therapist's willingness to address his spiritual struggles and discover a new source of meaning later in life: teaching piano to his musically gifted young grandson. "Maybe my real purpose now is to make sure that God's gift of music gets passed on to someone else," he concluded (p. 211). More is shared about working with patients' spiritual problems in psychotherapy later in this handbook (e.g., Chapter 6).

CHALLENGES TO THE MAINSTREAM IMPLEMENTATION OF SPIRITUAL APPROACHES

Meta-analytic and narrative reviews of the outcome research to date have shown that spiritually integrated approaches are most often as effective as secular ones—and sometimes more effective, especially with religiously devout patients (Captari et al., 2018; Hook et al., 2010; Smith et al., 2007; Worthington et al., 2011). The reviews have consistently shown that spiritually integrated psychotherapies are effective. There is also evidence that spiritually integrated psychotherapies result in greater spiritual improvement than do standard secular treatments (Captari et al., 2018).

Although the outcome research to date is encouraging, we think at least three major challenges need to be addressed before spiritually integrated psychotherapies will be more fully implemented in mainstream mental health care. The first challenge is that despite the growth in the evidence base, it is still the case that most spiritually integrative treatment approaches have not been empirically evaluated. Given the growing importance of evidence-based practice (APA, Presidential Task Force on Evidence-Based Practice, 2006), we think it is essential for those who develop spiritually integrated approaches to conduct and publish treatment outcome and process studies (Richards et al., 2015).

A second major challenge for the field of spiritually integrated psychotherapies is that more information is needed about how practitioners incorporate spirituality into their clinical practices. What spiritual interventions do psychotherapists use during treatment, and how often do they use them? What spiritual interventions and approaches are most effective for different types of patients, clinical issues, and treatment settings? We need more clinical descriptions from practitioners about how they integrate spiritual perspectives and interventions into treatment, and we need more practice-based evidence research that links treatment outcomes and processes (Richards et al., 2015). We need more insight into what the best practices are for the integration of spirituality into psychotherapy.

The third challenge that must be overcome is that more training opportunities in religious and spiritual treatment competencies are needed (Richards & Bergin, 2014). Relatively few graduate mental health programs provide training in religious and spiritual aspects of diversity and treatment competence (Oxhandler et al., 2015; Schafer et al., 2011; Vogel et al., 2013). Continuing education offerings for licensed practitioners are also scarce (Pearce et al., 2019). Graduate students and mental health practitioners need more opportunities for education, supervision, and consultation to develop their religious and spiritual treatment competencies.

PLAN FOR THE HANDBOOK

This handbook seeks to respond to these three challenges by providing theoretical, clinical, and empirical information about a wide variety of contemporary spiritually integrative treatment approaches. In 2016, the John Templeton

Foundation awarded Professor P. Scott Richards a $3.57 million grant to conduct a large research project about the processes and outcomes of spiritually integrated psychotherapy with 19 different collaborating research teams in North America, Israel, and several additional countries (see https://bridgescapstoneconference.wordpress.com/bridges-capstone-conference-proceedings/). Many of the authors of the chapters in this book were participants in this large research grant project, and the treatment approaches they describe in their chapters were empirically evaluated as part of the grant project. Several additional scholars and practitioners who have developed and conducted research about spiritually integrated psychotherapy approaches have also contributed chapters to the book.

The chapters in this handbook describe a wide variety of spiritually integrated mental health treatment approaches. Table 1.1 summarizes some important characteristics of the spiritually integrated treatment approach described in each chapter, including what spiritual tradition(s) the approach is grounded in and intended for, what clinical issues or types of patients the approach has been and can be used with, what treatment settings and modalities it has been used in, what types of spiritual interventions are used with the approach, what mainstream theoretical approaches has it been integrated with, and what research evidence has been conducted to date on the approach. Table 1.1 reveals the great variety of spiritually integrated treatment approaches that have been developed and included in this handbook. The approaches included here are appropriate for patients from diverse religious and spiritual traditions, including Christianity, Islam, Judaism, and many other traditions. Nearly all of the approaches are used in an ecumenical and spiritually inclusive manner that is reflective of the need for sensitivity and competence in the great cultural, racial-ethnic, sexual orientation and identity, and religious and spiritual diversity that psychotherapists encounter in our modern world.

The approaches included in the handbook have been used in clinical practice with a wide variety of psychological, relationship, and spiritual issues and problems. They have been used in multiple treatment settings, including outpatient, inpatient, hospitals, community mental health clinics, university counseling centers, private practices, and churches. The approaches have been used in several treatment modalities, including individual, couples, family, and group therapy. Many different types of spiritual practices and interventions have been integrated into these approaches, such as prayer, collaboration with clergy, teaching and modeling spiritual principles and virtues, forgiveness, guided meditation, discussion of sacred texts and religious parables, spiritual assessments, correction of unhealthy images of God, encouragement of reconciliation, and contemplation of grace. These spiritual approaches have been integrated with many traditional mainstream psychotherapy traditions and theories, including psychodynamic, cognitive behavior, emotion-focused, gestalt, relational development theory, family systems, and object relations and attachment theory. Unfortunately, we were unable to include chapters on all spiritually integrated psychotherapy approaches that have been developed. Noticeably absent is a chapter devoted to meditative and mindfulness approaches

TABLE 1.1. Characteristics of Spiritually Integrated Psychotherapy Approaches in This Handbook

Chapter no.	Chapter author(s)	Spiritual tradition(s)	Clinical issues	Settings and modalities	Spiritual interventions	Theoretical integration	Research[a]
2	Weisman de Mamani et al.	• Christian • Ecumenical • Spiritually inclusive	Serious mental illness (e.g., schizophrenia)	• Religious institutions • Family therapy	• Prayer • Collaboration with clergy • Spiritual assessment • Discussions of religious teachings (e.g., forgiveness, gratitude, view of God, empathy) • Guided meditation • Volunteering and service • Spiritual methods of coping • Sharing of religious parables and writings	• Cognitive behavior • Psychoeducation	• Brown & Weisman de Mamani (2018) • Maura & Weisman de Mamani (2018) • Weisman de Mamani et al. (2014) • Weisman de Mamani & Suro (2016)
3	Hollman and Marmarosh	• Theistic • Spiritually inclusive	Religious and psychological attachment struggles	• Outpatient • Individual therapy	Exploration of God image and attachment style issues (e.g., correspondence pathway and compensation pathway)	Attachment theory	• Mohammadi et al. (2017) • Thomas et al. (2011) • Tisdale et al. (1997)

4	Sandage and Stavros	• Ecumenical • Spiritually inclusive	• Variety of psychological issues • Spiritual, religious, and existential concerns	• Outpatient • Individual, couples, group, and family therapy	• Spiritual assessment • Rupture and repair alliance work • Facilitation of emotion regulation practices • Detriangling • Exploration of spiritual and existential meaning • Processing of grief and loss	• Relational development theory • Relational spirituality • Attachment theory • Family systems • Relational psychoanalytic • Cognitive behavior	• Jankowski et al. (2019, 2021) • Paine et al. (2018) • Sandage, Jankowski, et al. (2020)
5	Brownell and Doric	• Christian • Ecumenical	• Variety of relationship issues • Spiritual struggles • Psychological disorders	• Outpatient • Individual, group therapy • Integrated health care centers, couples and families, religious organizations, retreat centers	• Religious and spiritual discussions • Prayer • Field perspective • Spontaneity • Presence (both divine and personal) • Awareness • Contact • Dialogue	• Postsecular • Gestalt therapy • Contemporary gestalt therapy	• Currier et al. (2018) • Duggal & Sriram (2021) • Rothman & Coyle (2020) • Shafranske & Cummings (2013)

(continues)

TABLE 1.1. Characteristics of Spiritually Integrated Psychotherapy Approaches in This Handbook (*Continued*)

Chapter no.	Chapter author(s)	Spiritual tradition(s)	Clinical issues	Settings and modalities	Spiritual interventions	Theoretical integration	Research[a]
6	Pargament and Exline	• Ecumenical • Spiritually inclusive	• Spiritual struggles • Depression • Anxiety • Stress • Sexual abuse • Veterans • HIV/AIDS patients	• Outpatient • Individual, couples, group, and family therapy	• Assessment for spiritual struggles • Naming and normalizing of spiritual struggles • Facilitation of acceptance and reflection	• Integration with variety of therapy traditions	• Dworsky et al. (2013) • Murray-Swank & Pargament (2005) • Pargament & Exline (2022) • Reist Gibbel et al. (2019) • Starnino et al. (2019) • Tarakeshwar et al. (2005)
7	Berrett, Hardman, and Richards	• Theistic • Spiritually inclusive	• Eating disorders • Marital conflict • Mood disorders • Sexual abuse	• Inpatient • Residential • Outpatient • College counseling centers • Individual, couples, and group therapy	• Prayer • Reading sacred writings • Teaching spiritual principles • Spiritual pathways • Contemplation and meditation • Listening to the heart	• Person-centered • Cognitive behavior • Psychodynamic • Family systems • Emotionally focused	• Lea et al. (2015) • Richards et al. (2017)[b] • Sanders et al. (2015, 2019) • Simon et al. (2013)

| 8 | Salcone and Rosmarin | Spiritually inclusive | Variety of psychiatric disorders (e.g., mood/anxiety disorders, psychotic disorders, substance use disorders, PTSD and dissociative disorders, eating and feeding disorders) | • Inpatient and residential medical settings
• Group psychotherapy | • S/R beliefs and reframes
• S/R coping in treatment
• S/R struggles
• Meditation on the Psalms, sacred verses, the power of prayer, forgiveness | • Cognitive behavioral
• Psychospiritual education | Rosmarin et al. (2011, 2019, 2021) |
| 9 | Nielsen et al. | • Theistic
• Spiritually inclusive | Variety of psychological and relationship issues (e.g., depression, anxiety, spiritual struggles, academic difficulties, relationship conflicts) | • Outpatient
• Individual and group therapy
• College counseling centers | • Discussion of scriptures
• Scriptural rationales and disputations of irrational beliefs | REBT | Nielsen et al. (2019)[b] |

(continues)

TABLE 1.1. Characteristics of Spiritually Integrated Psychotherapy Approaches in This Handbook (*Continued*)

Chapter no.	Chapter author(s)	Spiritual tradition(s)	Clinical issues	Settings and modalities	Spiritual interventions	Theoretical integration	Research[a]
10	Khan and Keshavarzi	Islamic (Sunni)	• Depression, anxiety, trauma- and stressor-related disorders • Spiritual and interpersonal-related issues • Acculturation • Religious struggles • Family and marital conflict	• Outpatient • Individual, couples, and family therapy	• Psychospiritual education and relationship • Virtue development (e.g., humility, hope, patience, mercy) • Prayer	• Emotionally focused • Behavioral • Psychodynamic • Humanistic • Cognitive behavior • Other approaches	• Awaad et al. (2020) • Keshavarzi et al. (2020) • Keshavarzi et al. (2020)
11	Kim, Cha, and Keller	Protestant Christian	• Anxiety, depression, eating *disorders, mild* personality disorders, spiritual struggles • Individuals with limited affective abilities (e.g., schizoid personality disorder, catatonic conditions, dysthymia) may not be suitable	• Outpatient • Individual therapy	• R/S assessment • Imaginative reenactments • Meditations over biblical scripture • Prayer • Involvement in spiritual communities • God image exploration • Repentance • Rejoicing • Reflection about Christ	• Object relations theory • Attachment theory • Emotionally focused	• Kim et al. (2019) • Kim & Chen (2021)

| 12 | Norberg et al. | Christian, ecumenical, spiritually inclusive | Wide variety of clinical issues (e.g., depression, anxiety, suicidality, spiritual crisis, facing death, grief/mourning, trauma, sexual trauma, PTSD, addictions, relational conflict, marital issues) | • Outpatient
• Individual counseling
• Small group retreats | • Spiritual companioning
• Spiritual discernment
• Healing prayer
• Gestalt experiments
• Faith imagination
• Personalized healing liturgies
• Collaboration with clergy | • Gestalt theory
• Pastoral care | Thomas et al., 2022 |
| 13 | Hwang and Sim | Catholic Christian | • Struggles in relationships with authority figures and members of religious communities
• Psychosexual and affective development
• Self-esteem and identity, personality disorders
• PTSD
• Childhood trauma
• Spiritual discernment and growth | Individual therapy with patients in Asia, Africa, Latin America, and Europe | • Prayer
• Encouragement of participation in the sacraments of Eucharist (i.e., Mass) and Penance (i.e., Sacrament of Reconciliation or Confession)
• Exploration and discernment images of God
• Confirmation of divine self-worth | • Psychoanalysis
• Cognitive behavior therapy
• Interpersonal psychotherapy | Sim et al. (2021) |

(continues)

TABLE 1.1. Characteristics of Spiritually Integrated Psychotherapy Approaches in This Handbook *(Continued)*

Chapter no.	Chapter author(s)	Spiritual tradition(s)	Clinical Issues	Settings and modalities	Spiritual Interventions	Theoretical Integration	Research[a]
14	Mayseless et al.	• Judaism • Spiritually inclusive	• Variety of psychological and relationship issues • Spiritual struggles	• Outpatient • Individual and couples therapy	• Attending to the heart • Exploration of patients' spiritual soul • Discussion of choice from spiritual perspective • Hope • Listening to spiritual issues • Recognition of inner spiritual goodness • Prayer • Use of Jewish texts • Gratitude to God	Integrate with a variety of traditional therapy approaches (e.g., psychodynamic, cognitive behavior)	• Mayseless et al. (2021; unpublished study)[b]
15	Saloumeh DeGood	Islamic (Sufi)	• Variety of psychological and relationship issues (e.g., depression, anxiety) • Spiritual struggles	• Outpatient • Individual therapy	Wide variety of spiritual interventions (e.g., Sufi spiritual practices, deep breathing, heart concentration, meditation, visualization, spiritual artwork, exploration of heart values, prayer)	• Cognitive behavior • Motivational interviewing • Other traditional approaches	• Bahadorani et al. (2021) • Bozorgzadeh & Grasser (2021) • Crumpler (2002)

16	Fung et al.	• Christian • Ecumenical • Spiritually inclusive	Variety of psychological and relationship issues with East Asian Canadians (e.g., abuse and trauma, academic challenges, grief and loss with immigration, parenting, sexuality, marriage and family issues, spiritual issues, work stress)	• Outpatient • Individual, couples, and family therapy • Group therapy	Wide variety of spiritual interventions (e.g., prayer, meditation, scripture, finding meaning and purpose, attendance at worship services, practicing of spiritual disciplines, gratitude, kindness, seeking of social justice)	Variety of traditional therapy approaches (e.g., psychodynamic, family systems, cognitive behavior, narrative therapies)	• Fung et al. (2021; unpublished JTF study) • Wong et al. (2018)
17	Mikahere-Hall, Conklin, and Allen	Pacific Islanders Indigenous spirituality	Variety of psychological and relationship issues (e.g., family and relationship conflicts, abuse, spiritual struggles, acculturation conflicts, depression, suicide)	• Outpatient • Individual, couples, and family therapy	Culturally accepted spiritual practices (e.g., prayer, discussion of spiritual experiences, discussions of family and deceased ancestors)	• Multicultural • Trauma therapy • Indigenous strengths-based approaches	None cited

(continues)

Introduction 23

TABLE 1.1. Characteristics of Spiritually Integrated Psychotherapy Approaches in This Handbook (*Continued*)

Chapter no.	Chapter author(s)	Spiritual tradition(s)	Clinical issues	Settings and modalities	Spiritual Interventions	Theoretical Integration	Research[a]
18	Worthington et al.	Christian	• Marital conflict, communication skills • Intimacy • Marital enrichment, depression, anxiety	• Outpatient • Couples counseling	• Religious assessment • Religious perspectives about relationship problems • Promotion of hope and faith • Forgiveness • Prayer • Contemplation of grace • Reconciliation	Christian-oriented, hope-focused couple approach; emotionally focused couple therapy; others	• Hook et al. (2014) • Ripley, Solfelt, et al. (2021) • Ripley, Worthington, et al. (2021)
19	Everett L. Worthington, Jr.	• Christian • Theistic • Spiritually inclusive	• Marital conflict • Offenses, hurt, transgressions • Injustice • Difficulties in forgiving • Self-forgiveness	• Outpatient • Individual, couples, group, and family therapy • Hospitals • Criminal justice • Christian churches	Learn and apply the forgiveness model to promote emotional and decisional forgiveness	Eclectic (emphasizing emotional and motivational change); stress and coping theory; psychoeducational	• Toussaint et al. (2020) • Wade et al., (2014, 2018)

20	Angel, Sullivan, and Starnino	Spiritually inclusive	Military veterans • PTSD • Spiritual wounding	• Outpatient • Inpatient (VA hospitals) • Group therapy • Psycho-education	• Spiritual exploration and formation • Working through anger, moral injury, guilt, shame • Forgiveness • Trust and connectedness	• Trauma theory • Exposure therapy • Cognitive processing therapy	Starnino et al. (2019a, 2019b, 2020)
21	Gafford et al.	Spiritually inclusive	Wide variety of psychological and relationship issues (e.g., depression, anxiety, anger, trauma, PTSD, abuse, addictions)	Inpatient; correctional facilities (e.g., jails)	• Attending to cultural humility, cultural opportunities, and cultural comfort • R/S assessment, discussions about religious and spiritual issues, collaboration with clergy • Devotional journaling and readings	Multicultural counseling	Coleman et al. (2022)

Note. S/R = spiritual/religious; REBT = rational emotive behavior therapy; JTF = John Templeton Foundation; R/S = religion/spirituality; PTSD = posttraumatic stress disorder; VA = Veterans Administration.
[a]For the references corresponding to the research citations listed in this column, please refer to the specific chapter in this *Handbook*, unless otherwise noted. [b]See the corresponding reference in the References list for this chapter (i.e., Chapter 1).

to psychotherapy, but fortunately there are many other excellent clinical and theoretical sources about these approaches (e.g., Hendlin, 2016).

Practitioners and researchers who have developed these spiritually integrated psychotherapies have also begun empirically evaluating the effectiveness of their approaches and have reported relevant studies in their chapters. Much work remains to be done in this regard to help spiritually integrated treatment approaches gain greater acceptance in the mainstream mental health and medical professions (Richards et al., 2015; Richards & Worthington, 2010), but the approaches described in the handbook show how much progress has been made in this regard.

In the concluding chapter, we describe training and research opportunities and resources in the field of spiritually integrated psychotherapy that are available for graduate students, mental health practitioners, and researchers. We also offer recommendations for hastening the inclusion of spiritually integrated treatment approaches into the mainstream mental health and medical professions.

REFERENCES

Allen, G. E. K., Richards, P. S., & Lea, T. (2017). Spiritually oriented psychotherapy for trauma and meaning-making among ethnically diverse individuals in the United States. In E. M. Altmaier (Ed.), *Reconstructing meaning after trauma: Theory, research, and practice* (pp. 83–100). Elsevier. https://doi.org/10.1016/B978-0-12-803015-8.00006-1

American Psychological Association. (2017). *Ethical principles of psychologists and code of conduct* (2002, amended effective June 1, 2010, and January 1, 2017). https://www.apa.org/ethics/code

American Psychological Association, Presidential Task Force on Evidence-Based Practice. (2006). Evidence-based practice in psychology. *American Psychologist, 61*(4), 271–285. https://doi.org/10.1037/0003-066X.61.4.271

Bergin, A. E. (1980). Psychotherapy and religious values. *Journal of Consulting and Clinical Psychology, 48*(1), 95–105. https://doi.org/10.1037/0022-006X.48.1.95

Captari, L. E., Hook, J. N., Hoyt, W., Davis, D. E., McElroy-Heltzel, S. E., & Worthington, E. L., Jr. (2018). Integrating clients' religion and spirituality within psychotherapy: A comprehensive meta-analysis. *Journal of Clinical Psychology, 74*(11), 1938–1951. https://doi.org/10.1002/jclp.22681

Epstein, M. (1995). *Thoughts without a thinker: Psychotherapy from a Buddhist perspective*. Basic Books.

Exline, J. J. (Ed.). (2013). Religious and spiritual struggles. In K. I. Pargament, J. J. Exline, & J. W. Jones (Eds.), *APA handbook of psychology, religion, and spirituality: Vol. 1. Context, theory, and research* (pp. 459–476). American Psychological Association. https://doi.org/10.1037/14045-025

Exline, J. J., Pargament, K. I., Grubbs, J. B., & Yali, A. M. (2014). The Religious and Spiritual Struggles Scale: Development and initial validation. *Psychology of Religion and Spirituality, 6*(3), 208–222. https://doi.org/10.1037/a0036465

Exline, J. J., Yali, A. M., & Sanderson, W. C. (2000). Guilt, discord, and alienation: The role of religious strain in depression and suicidality. *Journal of Clinical Psychology, 56*(12), 1481–1496. https://doi.org/10.1002/1097-4679(200012)56:12<1481::AID-1>3.0.CO;2-A

Fear, R., & Woolfe, R. (1999). The personal and professional development of the counselor: The relationship between personal philosophy and theoretical orientation. *Counselling Psychology Quarterly, 12*(3), 253–262. https://doi.org/10.1080/09515079908254095

Fukuyama, M. A., & Sevig, T. D. (1999). *Integrating spirituality into multicultural counseling.* SAGE Publications.

Gall, T. L., Charbonneau, C., & Florack, P. (2011). The relationship between religious/spiritual factors and perceived growth following a diagnosis of breast cancer. *Psychology & Health, 26*(3), 287–305. https://doi.org/10.1080/08870440903411013

Harris, K. A., Randolph, B. E., & Gordon, T. D. (2016). What do clients want? Assessing spiritual needs in counseling: A literature review. *Spirituality in Clinical Practice, 3*(4), 250–275. https://doi.org/10.1037/scp0000108

Hart, A. C., Pargament, K. I., Grubbs, J. B., Exline, J. J., & Wilt, J. A. (2020). Predictors of growth and decline following religious and spiritual struggles: Exploring the role of wholeness. *Religions, 11*(9), Article 445. https://doi.org/10.3390/rel11090445

Hendlin, S. J. (2016). Meditation and the mindfulness trend in psychotherapy: Reflections through the prism of a 50-year meditator. *Psychotherapy Bulletin, 51*(3), 34–43.

Hook, J. N., Worthington, E. L., Jr., Davis, D. E., Jennings, D. J., II, Gartner, A. L., & Hook, J. P. (2010). Empirically supported religious and spiritual therapies. *Journal of Clinical Psychology, 66*(1), 46–72. https://doi.org/10.1002/jclp.20626

Koenig, H. G., King, D. E., & Carson, V. B. (2012). *Handbook of religion and health* (2nd ed.). Oxford University Press.

Magyar-Russell, G., Pargament, K. I., Grubbs, J. B., Wilt, J. A., & Exline, J. J. (2020). The experience of sacred moments and mental health benefits over time. *Psychology of Religion and Spirituality.* Advance online publication. https://doi.org/10.1037/rel0000394

Mayseless, O., Ruah-Midbar Shapiro, M., Rice, A., & Zucker, L. (2021). *Jewish spiritually integrated psychotherapy in Israel* [Unpublished manuscript, in Hebrew]. Faculty of Education, University of Haifa, Israel. https://spirit.haifa.ac.il/פסיכותרפיה-יהודית/

McMinn, M. R. (1996). *Psychology, theology, and spirituality in Christian counseling.* Tyndale House Publishers.

Miller, L. (2011). An experiential approach for exploring spirituality. In J. D. Aten, M. R. McMinn, & E. L. Worthington, Jr. (Eds.), *Spiritually oriented interventions for counseling and psychotherapy* (pp. 325–343). American Psychological Association. https://doi.org/10.1037/12313-013

Miller, W. R. (Ed.). (1999). *Integrating spirituality into treatment: Resources for practitioners.* American Psychological Association. https://doi.org/10.1037/10327-000

Miller, W. R., & Delaney, H. D. (Eds.). (2005). *Judeo-Christian perspectives on psychology: Human nature, motivation, and change.* American Psychological Association. https://doi.org/10.1037/10859-000

Miovic, M. (2004). An introduction to spiritual psychology: Overview of the literature, east and west. *Harvard Review of Psychiatry, 12*(2), 105–115. https://doi.org/10.1080/10673220490447209

Nielsen, S. L., Abett, D. B., Brown, B., & Erekson, D. M. (2019, November 21–24). *Overview of religious commitment and psychotherapy outcomes, focusing on the effects of including scripture in psychotherapy with religious clients* [Paper presentation]. Association for Behavioral and Cognitive Therapy 53rd Annual Convention, Atlanta, GA, United States.

Oxhandler, H. K., Parrish, D. E., Torres, L. R., & Achenbaum, W. A. (2015). The integration of clients' religion/spirituality in social work practice: A national survey. *Social Work, 60*(3), 228–237. https://doi.org/10.1093/sw/swv018

Pargament, K. I. (1997). *The psychology of religion and coping: Theory, research, practice.* Guilford Press.

Pargament, K. I. (2007). *Spiritually integrated psychotherapy: Understanding and addressing the sacred.* Guilford Press.

Pargament, K. I. (2011). Religion and coping: The current state of knowledge. In S. Folkman (Ed.), *The Oxford handbook of stress, health, and coping* (pp. 269–288). Oxford University Press.

Pargament, K. I., & Exline, J. J. (2022). *Shaken to the core: Spiritual struggles in research and clinical practice*. Guilford Press.

Pargament, K. I., Lomax, J. W., McGee, J. S., & Fang, Q. (2014). Sacred moments in psychotherapy from the perspectives of mental health providers and clients: Prevalence, predictors, and consequences. *Spirituality in Clinical Practice, 1*(4), 248–262. https://doi.org/10.1037/scp0000043

Pargament, K. I., Mahoney, A., & Shafranske, E. P. (Eds.). (2013). *APA handbook of psychology, religion, and spirituality: Vol. 2. An applied psychology of religion and spirituality*. American Psychological Association. https://doi.org/10.1037/14046-000

Pargament, K. I., Wong, S., & Exline, J. J. (2016). Wholeness and holiness: The spiritual dimension of eudaimonics. In J. Vittersø (Ed.), *Handbook of eudaimonic well-being* (pp. 379–394). Springer. https://doi.org/10.1007/978-3-319-42445-3_25

Pearce, M. J., Pargament, K. I., Oxhandler, H. K., Vieten, C., & Wong, S. (2019). A novel training program for mental health providers in religious and spiritual competencies. *Spirituality in Clinical Practice, 6*(2), 73–82. https://doi.org/10.1037/scp0000195

Pew Research Center. (n.d.). *Religious landscape study*. https://www.pewforum.org/religious-landscape-study/belief-in-god/

Pew Research Center. (2015, May 12). *America's changing religious landscape* [Report]. https://www.pewforum.org/2015/05/12/americas-changing-religious-landscape/

Pruyser, P. W. (1977). The seamy side of current religious beliefs. *Bulletin of the Menninger Clinic, 41*(4), 329–348.

Rabinowitz, A. (1999). *Judaism and psychology: Meeting points*. Jason Aronson.

Richards, P. S., & Bergin, A. E. (2005). *A spiritual strategy for counseling and psychotherapy* (2nd ed.). American Psychological Association. https://doi.org/10.1037/11214-000

Richards, P. S., & Bergin, A. E. (Eds.). (2014). *Handbook of psychotherapy and religious diversity* (2nd ed.). American Psychological Association. https://doi.org/10.1037/14371-000

Richards, P. S., Crowton, S., Berrett, M. E., Smith, M. H., & Passmore, K. (2017). Can patients with eating disorders learn to eat intuitively? A 2-year pilot study. *Eating Disorders, 25*(2), 99–113. https://doi.org/10.1080/10640266.2017.1279907

Richards, P. S., Sanders, P. W., Lea, T., McBride, J. A., & Allen, G. E. K. (2015). Bringing spiritually oriented psychotherapies into the health care mainstream: A call for worldwide collaboration. *Spirituality in Clinical Practice, 2*(3), 169–179. https://doi.org/10.1037/scp0000082

Richards, P. S., & Worthington, E. L., Jr. (2010). The need for evidence-based, spiritually oriented psychotherapies. *Professional Psychology, Research and Practice, 41*(5), 363–370. https://doi.org/10.1037/a0019469

Rose, E. M., Westefeld, J. S., & Ansley, T. N. (2001). Spiritual issues in counseling: Clients' beliefs and preferences. *Journal of Counseling Psychology, 48*(1), 61–71. https://doi.org/10.1037/0022-0167.48.1.61

Schafer, R. M., Handal, P. J., Brawer, P. A., & Ubinger, M. (2011). Training and education in religion/spirituality within APA-accredited clinical psychology programs: 8 years later. *Journal of Religion and Health, 50*(2), 232–239. https://doi.org/10.1007/s10943-009-9272-8

Schuster, M. A., Stein, B. D., Jaycox, L. H., Collins, R. L., Marshall, G. N., Elliott, M. N., Zhou, A. J., Kanouse, D. E., Morrison, J. L, & Berry, M. A. (2001). A national survey of stress reactions after the September 11, 2001, terrorist attacks. *New England Journal of Medicine, 345*, 1507–1512. https://doi.org/10.1056/NEJM200111153452024

Sedlar, A. E., Stauner, N., Pargament, K. I., Exline, J. J., Grubbs, J. B., & Bradley, D. F. (2018). Spiritual struggles among atheists: Links to psychological distress and well-being. *Religions, 9*(8), Article 242. https://doi.org/10.3390/rel9080242

Shafranske, E. P., & Malony, H. N. (1996). Religion and the clinical practice of psychology: A case for inclusion. In E. P. Shafranske (Ed.), *Religion and the clinical practice of psychology* (pp. 561–586). American Psychological Association. https://doi.org/10.1037/10199-041

Smith, T. B., Bartz, J., & Richards, P. S. (2007). Outcomes of religious and spiritual adaptations to psychotherapy: A meta-analytic review. *Psychotherapy Research, 17*(6), 643–655. https://doi.org/10.1080/10503300701250347

Smith, T. B., & Richards, P. S. (2005). The integration of spiritual and religious issues in racial-cultural psychology and counseling. In R. T. Carter (Ed.), *Handbook of racial-cultural psychology and counseling: Theory and research* (Vol. 1, pp. 132–160). John Wiley & Sons.

Sperry, L. (2001). *Spirituality in clinical practice: Incorporating the spiritual dimension in psychotherapy and counseling*. Brunner-Routledge.

Sperry, L. (2013). Distinctive approaches to religion and spirituality: Pastoral counseling, spiritual direction, and spiritually integrated psychotherapy. In K. I. Pargament, A. Mahoney, & E. P. Shafranske (Eds.), *APA handbook of psychology, religion, and spirituality: Vol. 2. An applied psychology of religion and spirituality* (pp. 223–238). American Psychological Association. https://doi.org/10.1037/14046-011

Sperry, L., & Shafranske, E. P. (Eds.). (2005). *Spiritually integrated psychotherapy*. American Psychological Association. https://doi.org/10.1037/10886-000

Sue, D. W., & Sue, D. (1990). *Counseling the culturally different: Theory and practice* (2nd ed.). John Wiley & Sons.

Vogel, M. J., McMinn, M. R., Peterson, M. A., & Gathercoal, K. A. (2013). Examining religion and spirituality as diversity training: A multidimensional look at training in the American Psychological Association. *Professional Psychology: Research and Practice, 44*(3), 158–167. https://doi.org/10.1037/a0032472

Worthington, E. L., Jr., Hook, J. N., Davis, D. E., & McDaniel, M. A. (2011). Religion and spirituality. In J. C. Norcross (Ed.), *Psychotherapy relationships that work: Evidence-based responsiveness* (2nd ed., pp. 402–419). Oxford University Press. https://doi.org/10.1093/acprof:oso/9780199737208.003.0020

GENERAL APPROACHES FOR SPIRITUALLY INTEGRATED PSYCHOTHERAPY

2

Culturally Informed Therapy

An Intervention That Addresses the Psychological Needs of Religious Individuals of Diverse Identities

Amy Weisman de Mamani, Olivia Altamirano, Daisy Lopez, Merranda Marie McLaughlin, Jessica Maura, Ana Martinez de Andino, Salman Shaheen Ahmad, Laurinda Hafner, and Sarah Griffith Lund

Religious and spiritual beliefs are integral to the identity of many people in the United States; they provide a framework around which people order and make sense of their lives (Hopwood & Witten, 2017; Koenig, 2009; Vahia et al., 2011). In this chapter, we discuss *culturally informed therapy* (CIT), an intervention that addresses the psychological needs of religious individuals of diverse identities. Following Weisman de Mamani et al. (2010), the terms "religion" and "spirituality" are integrated in this chapter, and the abbreviation "R/S" is substituted for these terms and their derivatives (e.g., religion, spiritual, religiousness).

It is important to note that the term "religion" is frequently used to refer to the teachings and rituals associated with R/S, whereas "spirituality" is more often used to refer to one's quest for meaning and belonging as well as to the core values that influence one's behavior (Sperry, 2001). However, in this chapter, we make no distinctions in terms, mainly because, until recently, these constructs were measured by global indices (e.g., frequency of prayer, self-report of strength of faith), and most of the research reviewed in this chapter did not formally distinguish among constructs. Thus, it would be beyond the scope of this chapter to tease apart one from the other when making sense of the findings.

Illustrations of the positive associations between R/S and mental and physical health abound in the literature. For example, the *Handbook of Religion and Health* (Koenig et al., 2012) reviewed around 3,000 studies and found strong

---

https://doi.org/10.1037/0000338-002
Handbook of Spiritually Integrated Psychotherapies, P. S. Richards, G. E. K. Allen, and D. K. Judd (Editors)
Copyright © 2023 by the American Psychological Association. All rights reserved.

associations between increasing R/S and better health in social (e.g., social support, marital stability), emotional (e.g., depression, self-esteem), behavioral (e.g., substance use, altruism), and physical (e.g., cardiovascular health, mortality) domains.

As the literature demonstrating beneficial associations between R/S and mental health expands, several investigators have begun integrating religious components into psychological interventions, with mostly positive results. For example, Gonçalves et al. (2015) conducted a systematic review and meta-analysis of psychological interventions that focus on R/S. The authors identified 23 studies that met their criteria, which were that the study investigated a clear mental health outcome without restrictions regarding the type of disease or population and had a design consistent with randomized clinical trials. Overall, study results strongly indicated that R/S interventions decreased stress, depression, and alcoholism in a variety of conditions and across a range of disorders (Gonçalves et al., 2015).

The intervention described later in this chapter, CIT, is an example of an early R/S integrated treatment that was specific to people living with schizophrenia and their family members. This treatment had one of five therapy modules explicitly dedicated to addressing R/S as a core piece of the intervention. The findings were that the treatment was effective in reducing patient symptom severity in both single family (Weisman de Mamani et al., 2014) and group (Maura & Weisman de Mamani, 2018) formats. This intervention was also found to reduce caregiver burden (Weisman de Mamani & Suro, 2016) and depression, anxiety, and stress among family members of individuals diagnosed with schizophrenia (Brown & Weisman de Mamani, 2018). The team of one of this chapter's authors (Weisman de Mamani) recently published a treatment manual for how to deliver culturally informed therapy for schizophrenia (CIT-S) to individuals with schizophrenia in a single-family format (Weisman de Mamani, McLaughlin, et al., 2021). The intervention has since been modified to make it accessible to people with other disorders, including general mental health concerns, such as stress and bereavement, and the religious emphasis has been greatly expanded. These modifications, including the processes underlying them, are addressed later in this current chapter.

Also in this chapter, we describe the need to increase collaboration between clergy and mental health providers. We then describe the processes that guide CIT's delivery at religious institutions, including how we have worked alongside clergy to better implement the intervention and to increase buy-in and attendance among religious congregants. A discussion of CIT for the general population follows and includes a detailed description of the modules and topics that constitute the treatment. We present a case example that reflects a composite of experiences of several different participants (identifiers have been changed sufficiently to protect clients' identities). We end the chapter by briefly describing our preliminary findings and providing future directions that arise from this work.

R/S INTERVENTIONS: THE NEED FOR COLLABORATION

Despite research that indicates how important religion can be to mental health and how effective religious interventions can be, one shortcoming of the majority of existing religiously based psychological treatments is that they are often offered by mental health practitioners in mental health settings, with little to no guidance or involvement from clergy or other religious personnel (Keith, 2008). Thus, these interventions may not adequately tap important spiritual elements relevant to many people's lives or may do so ineffectively. These interventions may therefore seem threatening, irrelevant, or lacking in substance to R/S mental health consumers, which may reduce treatment effectiveness or, more importantly, lead clients to leave treatment prematurely or shun psychotherapy altogether (Gurak et al., 2017; Yamada & Brekke, 2008).

The help-seeking process for mental illness often begins with an individual's understanding and conceptualization of the problem (Cheung, 1987; Suka et al., 2016). Interpretations of psychological distress are greatly influenced by a person's cultural experience, including one's religious beliefs and practices (Ayvaci, 2016). Many religious people conceptualize mental health symptoms through a religious framework (e.g., punishment from God, spiritual possession; Hwang et al., 2008). Thus, when these individuals experience psychological distress, they may be more likely to turn to religion and religious leaders for help rather than seek professional help from within the mental health system. Indeed, Ayvaci (2016) reported that a quarter of religious people seek help from clergy as the first contact for mental health problems.

Even when R/S individuals do seek professional mental health services, they may drop out prematurely (Maura & Weisman de Mamani, 2017). In a study examining this phenomenon, Gurak et al. (2017) found that greater adaptive and maladaptive religious coping were both associated with an increased likelihood of prematurely dropping out of a family-focused therapy for schizophrenia. The authors interpreted their findings as support for a *religiosity gap* in which R/S individuals may perceive a disconnect between their beliefs and the beliefs of their providers. This disconnect may prompt premature dropout from treatment. This study highlights the importance of systematically including R/S components in traditional mental health interventions.

Recognition of the need for collaboration between religious and mental health care providers is not new. Thomas (2012) indicated that pastors often spend as much time in pastoral counseling as marriage and family therapists do in private practice. The same study showed that pastors are encountering greater mental health or addiction challenges in their congregants than ever before (Thomas, 2012). Despite these calls for collaboration, a review of the research suggests that, with few exceptions, collaboration remains marginal. Specifically, this research suggests that the majority of clergy provide mental health care services directly to their congregants with minimal referrals to mental health care professionals, and in cases in which clergy do refer clients out to mental health professionals, further guidance or consultation between providers is rare (Moran et al., 2005; Wood et al., 2011). Furthermore, as one of this chapter's authors (Lund) illustrated in her book *Blessed Are the Crazy*, religious leaders often see mental illness as either a spirituality problem that should be completely addressed through an individual's relationship with their deity or as a medical problem not fit for discussion within a spiritual setting (Lund, 2014). She noted through her experiences serving as a pastor and speaking within her community that this binary opinion leads to individuals' fearing rejection from their congregation, which may lead to their silence on the topic of mental illness entirely.

Because clergy often serve as frontline mental health workers and face congregants with a wide range of issues, recent work has suggested that clergy themselves may struggle with feeling overwhelmed and unsure of how to guide congregants suffering from mental illness (Percy, 2012). Farrell and Goebert (2008) surveyed 98 clergy members regarding their training in mental health. The majority of clergy members reported feeling that they were inadequately trained to recognize and address mental illness. In addition, the authors reported that clergy largely attributed the etiology of mental illness to be medical rather than psychological in nature, a finding suggesting that many clergy members recognize that comprehensive treatment for mental health difficulties may require medical (as well as spiritual) care. In a similar vein, the large majority of practicing psychologists receive no training in R/S considerations during their graduate education (Vieten et al., 2013) and report generally feeling unprepared to address R/S issues in therapy (Crook-Lyon et al., 2012). Thus, it appears that strengthening relationships between religious and mental health providers could provide numerous benefits to clergy, their congregants facing psychological distress, and mental health professionals alike.

R/S individuals may be more prone to taking a passive stance when they experience mental illness, believing that God will intervene to solve their problems, without seeking further professional advice or guidance (Pargament et al., 1988; Weisman de Mamani et al., 2010). Hence, targeting religion in psychotherapy will require special care because therapists must not only foster adaptive religious beliefs and coping mechanisms but also guard against maladaptive ones. For example, although Krumrei et al. (2013) found that trust in God and positive religious coping (e.g., seeking religious passages that motivate and offer comfort during times of distress) were associated with lower levels of depressive symptoms, they also found that mistrust in God and negative religious coping (e.g., not seeking mental health treatment because of the view that "God will handle things") were associated with greater depressive symptoms. It is our view that having mental health professionals and clergy work together will help psychologists to better identify and reframe maladaptive uses of R/S in a manner that is helpful and bolsters adaptive uses of R/S in a manner that will aid in recovery.

CULTURALLY INFORMED THERAPY

The research just reviewed illustrates the need for psychologists and other mental health practitioners to collaborate more directly with clergy in a systematic and organized fashion. This synergy could break down barriers to treatment for R/S individuals who are struggling with mental illness and in need of help. In this section, we discuss the processes and ethical guidelines underlying our approach to CIT, including how we have recently modified the treatment to better serve religious clients dealing with a range of mental health issues. We use the example of a collaboration that is currently underway at the University of Miami and the Coral Gables United Church of Christ (UCC) that aims to adapt CIT to better incorporate R/S. We then describe the content of the treatment in detail, highlighting the modules and topics that guide its delivery.

CIT-S and the Framework for CIT

The first iteration of CIT was offered as a family-focused therapy for individuals with schizophrenia and their families (called "CIT-S" when specific to those dealing with schizophrenia), with later studies finding it efficacious in group formats as well. CIT-S is a 15-week, religiously integrated, cognitive behavior psychotherapy. CIT has multiple aims that are addressed via five modules: (a) increasing a sense of collectivism; (b) educating about mental illness; (c) fostering adaptive cultural and religious beliefs drawn from participants' own cultural, R/S, and ethnic backgrounds; (d) increasing adaptive communication; and (e) increasing problem-solving skills. Like all cognitive behavior therapies, CIT-S sessions are structured and follow evidence-based practices, they involve active discussions between therapists and clients, worksheets and handouts are a mainstay of treatment, and home learning assignments are provided at the termination of sessions and discussed at the initiation of sessions. Client outcomes are assessed at regular intervals, and therapist adherence to the treatment is also regularly monitored. Because CIT-S was successful not only for individuals with schizophrenia but also for their caregivers, we began to consider developing CIT for general mental health concerns given that the adaptability and religiously integrated nature of the treatment seemed to resonate with many individuals.

By design, CIT is adaptable enough to be offered to individuals of various cultural, R/S, and nonreligious backgrounds. It is offered on a rolling basis, whereby new participants may enter at any stage, and participants who complete one round of the treatment may stay on as long as they feel like they are benefiting. This way, incoming clients can be eased into the group, can see ongoing progress, and may learn from other group members. While CIT was designed to be delivered by a single therapist, it has been successfully delivered by up to three therapists working in collaboration.

Many experts have highlighted the importance of culturally adapting psychological interventions (Forehand & Kotchick, 1996; Lau, 2006). Indeed, one meta-analysis of 78 studies revealed that culturally tailored interventions were more effective than the original versions of the same interventions (Hall et al., 2016). CIT attempts to modify maladaptive beliefs and behaviors throughout treatment while shaping and encouraging adaptive ones. The therapy also examines participants' cultural conceptualizations of mental illness and their own symptoms. Therapy works to shape these conceptualizations in a manner that helps participants cope with their symptoms more effectively. For example, therapists cite literature as they reinforce the efforts of participants who pursue cultural or spiritual forms of healing from various mental health difficulties (e.g., prayers, meditations, seances). At the same time, therapists ask participants about scripture that encourages active self-work alongside (and at times before) asking for God's help.

CIT is culturally informed in that it accesses beliefs, behaviors, practices, and traditions drawn from participants' own cultural backgrounds that may be adaptive or, in some cases, maladaptive in coping with psychological distress. Therapists do not assume to know about the cultural nuances espoused by participants; a core component of CIT involves using open-ended questions to elicit clients' own descriptions of their cultural values, beliefs, and practices. Likewise, therapists do not assume to know about the practices that clients from specific religious backgrounds may engage in as a result of their association with that group. The treatment is intended to be adaptable enough to be delivered even to those who are nonreligious; in the spirituality module (discussed later in the Treatment section), handouts that address existentialism/philosophy can replace those that address R/S. It is our belief that, irrespective of a client's background and belief system, therapists should be able to facilitate meaning making and healing through as many healthy outlets as possible, and doing so will entail learning as much as possible about the culture of the clients served. While therapists are not expected to know everything about a specific culture, they should aim to increase their knowledge base to the extent possible both by asking their clients directed questions and by researching on their own.

Although CIT-S has been shown to be efficacious in improving a variety of psychiatric symptoms for individuals with schizophrenia and their families, several adaptations to this intervention serve to improve treatment engagement and retention in R/S populations. What helped inform these adaptations was an initially disheartening finding by Gurak and colleagues (2017) that participants high in religiosity were more likely to drop out of CIT-S prematurely. This finding was counterintuitive, given that one segment of CIT-S (Module 3: Spirituality) explicitly targets religion and religious forms of coping. On closer examination of these data, however, it became apparent that nearly all participants who left treatment prematurely did so before the religiosity segment of CIT-S began (the religiosity module does not begin until Session 7). Indeed, survival analyses indicated that therapy attrition dropped to zero for participants who completed the religiosity segment of treatment even though another six sessions of treatment followed (Gurak et al., 2017). It was speculated that the premature exit from treatment occurred because the religiosity segment happened too late and was not well enough integrated into the full treatment approach. Thus, early on, many religious individuals may have perceived a disconnect between their beliefs and the beliefs of their mental health providers, therefore prompting them to withdraw from treatment prematurely.

Modifications for CIT

CIT's original goals were to address the R/S gap and determine its efficacy among individuals with general mental health concerns. To address the issue of premature dropout among religious clients and to expand CIT to serve clients with a range of common psychological problems, one of this chapter's authors, Weisman de Mamani, and her team joined forces with chapter coauthor, Laurinda "Laurie" Hafner, who is the senior pastor at the Coral Gables UCC (and who is referred to as "Pastor Laurie" in this chapter).

This project was funded by the John Templeton Foundation's Big Data project on spiritually integrated therapies. The two main aims were (a) to examine whether CIT would be effective in treating a wide range of individuals with commonly existing mental health problems and (b) to assess whether it would be practical to deliver this treatment within religious institutions in collaboration with clergy as well as whether doing so would impact treatment efficacy, satisfaction, and retention.

The Coral Gables UCC is located in South Florida and serves a diverse congregation. Following the initiation of the Weisman de Mamani's team collaboration with Pastor Laurie, the first adaptation made to CIT was to begin providing therapy at the UCC. The UCC is housed in most of the congregants' home community, making it easier to attend and being more familiar than a community clinic. Weekly therapy sessions last an hour to 75 minutes and are held in the church's conference room, similar to other groups an individual may attend at the church. To maintain privacy, sessions are scheduled on a day and time (e.g., Wednesday evening) when fewer congregants are present at the church. The church keepers and employees are aware that therapy sessions are taking place and make sure that stationery and coffee—usually available to congregants—are also available to attendees. The support of Pastor Laurie was instrumental in acquiring the space, privacy, and assistance needed to provide CIT at a religious institution.

To incorporate R/S earlier and into the foundations of CIT, each session begins and ends with a prayer, and themes from the opening prayer (e.g., unity, recovery) are integrated into the session. A short discussion usually follows prayers and revolves around the content of the prayer, particularly if clients comment on the prayer after it is delivered. Therapist(s) are prepared with relevant nondenominational prayers to open and close sessions; however, group members are consistently encouraged to bring in and start sessions with prayers, readings, or mantras that they align with to facilitate R/S conversations that are particularly salient to them. The religious environment promotes the integration of spiritual and mental health wellness, which may break down barriers and reduce resistance to attempting unfamiliar treatment strategies. In addition, because active engagement is a common aspect of church culture at UCC, individuals may feel more inclined to participate fully in answering their worksheet questions or communicating their experiences.

To facilitate communication between religious and mental health providers, it is important to recognize that religious leaders may be more likely to endorse and recommend services to their congregants if they are made aware of mental health services that are offered. Therapists who are interested in treating religious clients may want to approach clergy and share with them the services that are available, as was the case with our team and Pastor Laurie. Attending open houses, giving lectures at church functions to discuss psychotherapy treatment approaches, or providing this information to congregants through church bulletins or pamphlets are also a start, and these activities were a regular component of our own recruitment strategy.

Further, religious leaders may be inclined to share mental health recommendations with congregants if they are reassured that providers will accept and incorporate R/S views into treatment. For many R/S individuals, the church and its religious leaders represent a trusted and important source of support and care. These individuals may, therefore, be more likely to seek out professional mental health services (or a particular provider) if that person or facility is endorsed by a reliable clergy member. Religious institutions could also be excellent platforms for dissemination of important mental health information because churches have regularly scheduled programs that draw large audiences comprising diverse individuals of all ages (Asamoah et al., 2014). Offering these services in R/S settings may also provide clergy opportunities to offer suggestions and to weigh in regarding how to make psychological interventions appealing and relevant to religious clients.

Our collaboration with the UCC has changed how Pastor Laurie goes about making individuals aware of mental health resources and, to some degree, how we go about delivering the treatment. Within a traditional model, pastors generally refer congregants to mental health specialists if they suspect psychopathology that goes beyond their perceived area of expertise. While this is an ethical approach (one should not practice beyond their credentials), if a congregant conceptualizes their distress within a religious context, being referred outside of the church may invalidate that experience and work against a more holistic view of oneself and one's religion. We believe that our earlier finding that religious clients are more likely to drop out of CIT-S than nonreligious clients, with nearly all doing so before the religiosity segment began (Gurak et al., 2017), supports this view. Currently, Pastor Laurie provides information about CIT through interest groups, postservice announcements, the church's social media accounts, and the church newsletter. The majority of congregants who call the Weisman de Mamani team to receive CIT do so after hearing about it at service or seeing the social media posts or newsletter, often over a sustained period, before eventually deciding to try it out when they feel ready. We believe that Pastor Laurie's endorsement and the church's willingness to openly advertise CIT have reduced the stigma associated with mental health within the community.

Pastor Laurie also periodically attends CIT sessions to provide feedback to the mental health therapists. Her knowledge is a useful resource to the therapists, who may be unfamiliar with the different ways in which individuals within the congregation understand and integrate their spiritual experiences into their daily lives. Her presence is also reassuring to clients because she is a trusted member of the church, and the therapists ask her to deliver the opening and closing prayers if attendees did not bring any to share with the group. Aside from this involvement, Pastor Laurie generally does not speak in sessions unless she is asked by attendees to address a question or concern. Later on, she writes to the team to discuss her reflections from the session and any feedback she has for the therapists.

Adaptations to how the team delivers CIT were also made after receiving feedback from Pastor Laurie—for example, about the culture of this particular congregation. Pastor Laurie noted that the team should be careful about the terms we use to refer to "God" (e.g., "God" vs. "higher power" vs. "Lord") because these different terms can hold different meanings for clients. She also advised us not to assume the gender of God and to be flexible in how we refer to God because that is the norm among the attendants of her congregation. As the description of the treatment and composite case example in this chapter show, therapists tend to focus on the application of religious teachings, such as using forgiveness and gratitude, and attempt to use terminology of the client when referencing specific religious beliefs. Despite these neutral intentions, referring to God in the masculine came automatically for the therapists, most likely because of their own cultural backgrounds. Pastor Laurie's sensitivity and expertise allowed her to provide precise feedback to the therapy sessions, and her feedback has improved the quality of CIT being delivered at the UCC beyond what could have been done without her.

Another vastly rewarding strategy that has been part of the process of incorporating R/S into CIT is client feedback. At the end of each session, clients are provided surveys in which they are asked to (among other things) state what they thought was good about the session and what may be improved moving forward. This practice has enabled the therapists to better understand strengths and weaknesses of their approach as well as to ensure that clients are being served in accordance with their own needs. As a result of this feedback, the therapists have been able to attend to client needs that weren't explicitly stated in session, that may be more discreet, or that clients are uncomfortable sharing with the group at large. For example, conversations about a topic that was discretely requested may be facilitated by an opening prayer that touches on the topic, followed by the therapists' asking clients whether they resonated with the prayer, and so on. In another example, after a particularly stressful CIT session was ended with a guided meditation, feedback from multiple attendees resulted in therapists' ending this group more frequently with a guided meditation, as time would allow.

Spending time at the church has also made the therapists more aware of how to use the resources that are available at the church to help clients tackle their issues from psychotherapeutic strategies as well as from a religious perspective. This awareness also allowed therapists to address client concerns regarding religious and clergy involvement within therapy sessions. For example, knowing about and encouraging a depressed client to volunteer at an upcoming church function can be used to treat depression through behavioral activation, a widely used psychotherapeutic technique (Dimidjian et al., 2011). Moreover, mounting evidence indicates that volunteering is associated with improved well-being outcomes, including decreased depression and lower mortality rates (Jenkinson et al., 2013). Volunteerism and service to others are also at the heart of most religious perspectives across denominations and faiths (Cnaan et al., 1993), and at UCC, this was no exception. If requested, CIT therapists may reach out to clergy to help facilitate the client's involvement in volunteering or other activities, such as helping to organize social or religious events at the church.

In CIT, therapists use cognitive behavior strategies to collaboratively and informedly treat psychological symptoms in a way that is in line with clients' beliefs and values as well as their religious standpoints. Adaptations to the treatment should be guided by research and clinician judgment, clients' needs and cultural nuances, and information and feedback gathered from religious leaders or clergy. In addition, incorporating R/S into treatment can be accomplished by offering CIT close to or within places of worship, starting and ending sessions with prayers that are relevant to the topics being discussed, soliciting endorsement of mental health treatment from religious leaders, guiding spiritual practice and growth via meditations, and promoting spiritual avenues of healing through collaboration with religious leaders and engagement in rewarding opportunities. In this way, facilitating harmony between R/S, culture, and mental health work is at the heart of CIT.

Treatment

CIT is organized into five modules to facilitate each of the goals described previously: (a) collectivism, (b) psychoeducation, (c) spirituality, (d) communication, and (e) problem solving. Each of these five modules is delivered over the course of three sessions for a total of 15 weeks of CIT. The various handouts and much greater detail surrounding the treatment can be accessed in *Culturally Informed Therapy for Schizophrenia: A Family-Focused Cognitive Behavioral Therapy Approach—Clinician Guide* (Weisman de Mamani, McLaughlin, et al., 2021). The following sections describe how the treatment is applied to individuals struggling with general mental health concerns.

Collectivism

Collectivism is the first module of CIT. It follows research suggesting that many cultural groups emphasize interdependence and connectedness within families and their inner circles (Sedikides et al., 2003; Singelis, 1994), which is contrary to mainstream American culture, which emphasizes independence and uniqueness. Findings that individuals from developing countries (e.g., India, Nigeria) have better outcomes from serious mental illnesses, such as schizophrenia, when compared with individuals from developed countries (e.g., United States, United Kingdom) are speculated to be driven by these countries' collectivistic beliefs (Lefley, 1990; Weisman, 1997). Despite cultural differences in individualism and collectivism, those from individualistic groups can have collectivistic tendencies (and vice versa), and the family or other important social unit can be a valuable source of healing for all individuals. As a result, the purpose of this module is to identify clients' cultural identities and familial or social resources, and to encourage them to improve the quality, quantity, and benefit acquired from them.

Over the course of collectivism, guided by handouts, therapists ask clients about their cultural, familial, and social systems (religious communities are also a system that is discussed in this module) as well as the culture of these systems. Therapists ask clients what family (or another relevant group) means to them, including its structure, values, cultural customs, and means of expressing support to and connection with each other. Clients are asked about their role in the group, including whether they are satisfied with this role, how they contribute, and whether they believe they should be contributing more or differently. Clients' group goals are addressed, including what their ideal group situation would look like and what steps they believe they can take to bring their group closer to each other.

Throughout the module, therapists encourage and reinforce client efforts to foster collectivism within their inner circles, and they use research to support their arguments. For example, in two home learning assignments, clients are asked to (a) engage in activities that will foster collectivism that is relevant to them, such as reaching out to family members, making new friends in their religious congregation, or signing up for virtual social networking events for artists; and (b) think about what role they would like to play in their inner circle moving forward so that how to accomplish this goal can be discussed in group.

Psychoeducation
Psychoeducation is the second module of CIT. The primary objective of this module is to impart information and techniques related to clients' emotional difficulties and how to manage them. This module is also an opportunity to learn about clients' own conceptualizations of their difficulties, including the strategies they have in place to address them. This module was heavily influenced by earlier work showing that individuals living with serious mental illnesses and their family members greatly benefit from receiving psychoeducation related to their difficulties (Goldstein & Miklowitz, 1994) so that these individuals may then be able to communicate their difficulties more clearly with their family members and other providers. Although the module may appear to be didactic from a distance, collaboration between clients and therapists is necessary for understanding clients' cultural beliefs and is key to the successful delivery of this module.

In psychoeducation, therapists discuss common mental health concerns and their symptoms, such as depression, anxiety, and stress. Clients are asked about their own difficulties with these symptoms, including how they perceive these difficulties and what they generally do about them. Discussions about medication and psychotherapy are facilitated by therapists, who also take time to answer clients' questions and validate their efforts to cope with their mental health difficulties. Using concepts, such as the diathesis–stress model, therapists discuss how mental health difficulties develop; they also discuss the varying courses of mental illnesses. The importance of events, such as the passing of a loved one or a global pandemic, and how different people can react differently to these challenges are often central to these dialogues. This module also addresses ways in which an individual's family (or other important social networks) can help them identify changes in their mental health and how to cope with the difficulties. Psychoeducation home learning assignments, such as these two examples, ask clients to (a) look at the list of depression, anxiety, and stress symptoms and write down which symptoms apply to them as well as how they cope with those difficulties; and (b) think about and write down what it means to have their specific mental health difficulties in their culture, including both positive and negative conceptualizations, if applicable.

Spirituality

Spirituality is the third module of CIT. As discussed at length, the importance of R/S is too often overlooked in mainstream therapies, and a lack of union between these forms of healing is likely contributing to the lack of service being delivered to these groups. As a result of the salience that R/S would hold for many who attend CIT at a religious institution, having a module dedicated to R/S has been especially helpful for those who wish to address this part of their identity within treatment. This module also presents therapists with an opportunity to better understand the community that they are serving and the individuals who are part of the treatment group. The purpose of spirituality, therefore, is to understand clients' R/S belief systems, values, practices, and conflicts, and to guide them toward adaptively using R/S to cope with mental health difficulties or improve overall well-being.

In spirituality, therapists first assess clients' religious or spiritual backgrounds, including the traditions they were raised in, whether R/S is important to them, and what R/S means to them. Those who describe themselves as "nonreligious" are provided handouts with existential or philosophical questions at this point. Clients' current R/S (or existential or philosophical) views are then discussed. The various topics touched on include the following: their concept or view of God (or a higher power); their main identity and the values of this identity that are important to them; the effect of R/S in their daily lives; the rituals and practices they engage in; whether R/S colors the way they see the world; what R/S issues they have struggled with; and if resolved, how those issues were overcome. Sessions involve conversations about R/S notions of forgiveness, empathy, community, and appreciation, concepts that are relevant to individuals of most faiths and are known to be beneficial at individual and collective levels. Using research, therapists discuss and reinforce spiritual methods of coping and their benefits with the goals of helping clients develop emotional awareness and a calm mind. In the following two examples of home learning tasks, clients are asked to (a) engage in a spiritual activity that is important to them but has not been practiced lately so that clients can discuss how engaging in that practice again feels for them; and (b) bring in R/S texts, parables, or materials that are relevant to coping with their mental health difficulties so that others may learn or benefit from their experiences.

Communication

Communication is the fourth module of CIT. Communication patterns vary across individuals of various cultural and ethnic backgrounds. Our cultural beliefs and values shape every aspect of the way we implicitly and explicitly communicate (Chesley & Fox, 2012; Dillon & McKenzie, 1998). In addition, research suggests that successful communication and self-assertiveness are associated with better mental health (Berman, 2010; Speed et al., 2018). On the other hand, difficulties with communication are associated with greater stress in a number of environments, including the family (Kymalainen & Weisman de Mamani, 2008). Kymalainen et al. (2006) also suggested that family members may have particular difficulty communicating about mental health symptoms when those symptoms negatively impact their ability to engage with cultural values and behaviors. Thus, the goal of communication is to help clients learn how to effectively communicate with others in a clear, concise, and assertive yet civil manner. Another aim of communication is to teach clients how to make requests for change from one another in a way that focuses on specific behaviors and steers away from personality traits.

In communication, like in other modules, therapists begin by assessing communication styles that are normative of clients' cultures and families. Norms of communication in other groups that clients are a part of, such as those related to their gender, age, and type of relationship (e.g., parent), are also discussed. Examples of areas touched on include whether participants place a greater emphasis on direct versus indirect communication, whether they defer to authority and do not speak during specific times, and whether certain topics are off limits. Therapists then discuss various communication techniques (inspired by Falloon et al., 1984, and Goldstein & Miklowitz, 1994) that can be used to facilitate harmony within important relationships, such as expressing positive feelings, listening attentively, making a positive request, and expressing specific negative feelings and suggesting a behavioral change. The use of role play is prevalent in this module, and feedback is provided to clients from therapists as well as other group members to workshop communication skills. Two example home learning tasks are to (a) think about areas of communication within their families or social circles that are causing them particular distress and (b) practice the acquired communication techniques at home and report results of these exercises so that the group may engage in troubleshooting and the therapists may scaffold clients' ability to effectively communicate.

Problem Solving

Problem solving is the fifth module of CIT. In general, studies of cultural variations in problem solving have been rare, with one review of the topic identifying only 16 peer-reviewed articles from 1984 to 2008 (Güss & Tuason, 2009). However, it is widely accepted that cultural paradigms, such as individualism versus collectivism, influence how a group perceives difficulties and goes about solving them (Triandis, 2001, 2018). The likelihood of attempting to solve a problem has been found to vary depending on how congruent a problem is with an individual's orientation as individualistic versus collectivistic (Arieli &

Sagiv, 2018). Moreover, whether an individual may benefit from a specific problem-solving style may also vary as a result of their ethnocultural background. One study found that Black individuals who engaged in avoidance-focused coping were less likely to struggle with marijuana use disorder when compared with White individuals for whom problem-focused coping was a better strategy (Van Gundy et al., 2015). The aim of the problem-solving module, therefore, is to teach clients techniques that may enhance their problem-solving abilities in ways that are aligned with their cultural beliefs and values and that support their goals.

As is the norm in CIT, problem solving begins with an examination of the various ways in which clients engage in problem solving in the cultures that they are a part of. Whether faith-based problem solving is a priority, whether certain rules guide if a problem should be discussed openly, and whether client values dictate if something is a major problem versus a minor one are all important questions to ask clients. In addition, how clients decide whether a problem is worth solving, what successful outcomes look like, and whether clients typically follow up on issues can be telling about what works for some and not for others. Therapists then train clients on how to use a five-step problem-solving strategy (inspired by Goldstein & Miklowitz, 1994) that may be tailored to them and their individual situations. The therapists help clients to practice the steps in session using smaller day-to-day difficulties that they face, and they encourage clients to work their way up to more salient problems. For home learning, clients are typically asked to do these two assignments: (a) identify one simple and one complex problem that they would like to work through in the module and (b) engage in problem-solving steps at home, depending on where they are at with their difficulty (e.g., agreeing with family or in-group members on what the exact problem is versus coming up with as many solutions as possible).

CASE EXAMPLE

In this section, we provide a case example illustrating what CIT, offered in a religious setting, may look like in practice. The descriptions presented are a composite of several cases.

Rebecca and her husband, Martin, regularly attended a local church. One Sunday, Rebecca noticed an advertisement in the church bulletin regarding therapy for individuals experiencing depression, anxiety, life changes, or stress. This sparked curiosity, and she approached her church's senior reverend, someone whom Rebecca deeply respects, to inquire about the therapy. The reverend informed Rebecca that she worked with the mental health practitioners who conducted the group therapy and that she frequently provided input to the therapists on how to make the treatment more religiously informed. Although Rebecca had not previously considered therapy, her reverend's reassurance led her to give it a try, especially because she had been feeling unlike herself for a while.

At intake, Mara, the therapist, learned that Rebecca was a 65-year-old retiree who had been married to Martin for 36 years. Both had emigrated from Cuba approximately 30 years ago. Rebecca retired about 5 years ago and began experiencing symptoms of depression and anxiety soon after, such as persistent feelings of sadness and excessive worry. While she was happy and relieved to retire, she found herself with "too much" free time. Before retiring, she attended frequent work-related social gatherings and after-work happy hours. On retirement, it became difficult for her to continue to see her work friends because they were busy during the work week and had other priorities on the weekends. This left her feeling disconnected from her social groups, and she found herself less willing to seek new friendships out of fear that other people would also be too busy for her. Because Martin volunteered most days and they did not have any children, Rebecca was frequently home alone. She reported feeling consistently on edge and never content or relaxed at home, and she often found herself doing things like watching television and rearranging furniture "just to pass time."

Mara used the information from her initial meeting with Rebecca to develop potential focus areas within the treatment. Although Rebecca had full support from Martin, Mara thought this limited network could be straining the relationship in that Martin had become Rebecca's go-to person for everything. As such, she decided that within the collectivism module, an important topic might be discovering ways of boosting Rebecca's current social support network. Within R/S, Mara considered discussing concepts surrounding the meaning of life because Rebecca had noted that the best days of her life—those involving purposeful work—were behind her. In addition, Mara prepared to discuss symptoms of depression within the psychoeducation module as well as stress management, a topic that was relevant to many group members. Mara was excited for the communication module as well and planned to ask whether Rebecca would be willing to take part in a role play in which they pretended she was having a conversation with Martin. For problem solving, initial ideas that Mara generated included how to respond to a friend when plans were canceled and what to do if Rebecca had "too much free time." While these were Mara's initial CIT plans based on Rebecca's case, she maintained a flexible approach and tried to incorporate Rebecca's areas for growth with topics that were relevant to the rest of the group members as well.

At Rebecca's first session, Mara began by reminding group members of the limits of confidentiality and then read a prayer for acceptance and change, both of which Rebecca appreciated. The prayer's focus on accommodating to changing circumstances helped Rebecca to put her retirement in perspective and encouraged her to share this experience with other members. Keeping the prayer in mind, Rebecca shared with the group her dislike of retirement. She also disclosed some resentment toward Martin, whom she felt was still thriving after his change to retirement. She also expressed concern that she was "wasting away" and that she had nothing fun or exciting left to look forward to. Rebecca reluctantly acknowledged that, at times, she felt lost and confused about her role in life. Referencing the earlier prayer, she noted that it was difficult for her to "let go of old ideas that no longer fit" and to "embrace change" as the prayer encouraged. She stated that she began doubting her faith because she felt that life had no real purpose. This doubt, in turn, made her feel guilty because she had always valued her spirituality and her relationship with God while growing up in a religious Cuban family. Rebecca's confession resonated with other members in the group, who reported similar difficulties adapting to changes in roles and managing feelings of emptiness, loss, and shame. Mara highlighted that these were common experiences not only for Rebecca but also for other group members, and this helped set the stage for a supportive and accepting atmosphere.

After hearing Rebecca's perspective, Gabe, a fellow member, said he felt similarly when he retired. Unlike Rebecca, Gabe turned to God in those moments and described that connecting with God helped him make sense of the world and instilled a "new purpose in life." As such, Mara focused the discussion on strategies to encourage better connecting with existing support systems and seeking new ones when warranted. One member highlighted to Rebecca that Martin's volunteer job may be facilitating his transition to help him engage with others and to gain a sense of purpose. A discussion of culture ensued, and Rebecca shared that she may be missing the familial support prominent in Cuban households as a result of not having had children with Martin.

Rebecca reported that hearing other group members' perspectives provided her with greater insights and encouragement to seek out what she needed. Throughout this discussion, members provided support to one another, and many noted an appreciation because this group had become a sort of nonbiological family that made them feel less isolated and more connected and grounded in the world. During one of these sessions, Mara invited the reverend to visit, and at the closing of the session, the reverend offered a prayer in which she expressed gratitude for a culturally and religiously informed therapy as well as prayed that the members continued to learn about healthy ways of managing stressors. This prayer gave Rebecca comfort. She not only felt more at ease with the group but also felt a stronger connection to her church community for supporting this program.

These themes followed along as they transitioned into other therapy modules. In the psychoeducation module (Module 2), it was a relief for Rebecca to learn that her depressive and anxious symptoms are quite common and that several empirically supported techniques used in CIT would help her conceptualize her problems and cope with them in a more adaptive manner. She was particularly pleased that spiritual means of coping were also being given attention throughout.

Although Rebecca had been nervous to talk about her religious views directly because she had previously felt disconnected and a bit disappointed by her faith, within the spirituality module (Module 3), she was able to openly discuss the positive and negative experiences of her past. She realized that certain rituals she had stopped performing (e.g., praying the rosary) had formerly given her great comfort. She cited reasons for ceasing her regular practice in the past, such as the lack of a church that practiced the same way that she did in Cuba, and periods of difficulty in her life that had shaken her belief in God. While she felt abandoned by God at times, other members identified the blessings she had and noted that, with change, God also brought new opportunities that were up to her to receive. Mara recognized this was a great opportunity to discuss how one might foster a "new" purpose—something that had been brought up by Gabe previously. In doing so, she would accomplish both helping Rebecca with concrete ideas as well as commending Gabe for his resilient attitude in the face of significant life changes. Gabe described that one of the things he did was join the community's walking group, and Rebecca decided a good course of action for her might be to increase her engagement with members of her congregation and to increase her religious coping strategies. After receiving the idea from other group members, Rebecca also began to keep a gratitude journal in which she could reflect on her daily blessings.

Communication (Module 4) was especially relevant to Rebecca, who wanted to improve her relationship with her husband. Their recent conversations had often been tense and unsatisfying. Rebecca used a prayer she brought into session ("Our Father") and emphasized how it modeled God's forgiveness and asked her to also "forgive those who trespassed against [her]." With this mindset, within the communication module, she learned to focus on more active forms of listening behaviors (e.g., asking clarifying questions, making eye contact), which assisted in seeing her husband's perspective. Throughout the module, Mara facilitated discussions regarding how Rebecca and Martin's cultural background influenced their communication patterns, and other group members compared and contrasted their own styles with each other. Mara asked Rebecca to role play a conversation with another group member, which they agreed to do. Based on that role-play, Mara and other group members commented on helpful and unhelpful communication they observed, based on the session content.

As part of homework, Rebecca chose to express positive feelings to her husband and to make requests for changes in his behavior in a new format that the therapists suggested might be less likely to backfire and irritate her husband. In her interactions with Martin, she used strategies offered in the problem-solving module (Module 5) to help them deal with some of the couple's specific struggles, such as deciding on where to spend vacations, how often to eat out, and how to respond if Martin canceled plans. In subsequent sessions, Rebecca reported that her conversations with Martin had become much more productive and pleasant and that they were working together more as a team. She reported that these changes have been making them feel closer, much like they had in the beginning of their marriage.

By the end of the group intervention, Rebecca had reconnected with a few of her old work friends, had built a new community of friends whom she met as a volunteer at her church, and reported a closer relationship with Martin. While she acknowledged that it had been difficult to identify and cultivate new relationships, the experience had allowed her to strengthen her faith and to be more open with others to receive the support she felt she needed. Rebecca prayed every evening and found that this purposeful engagement with faith gave her strength. She began viewing her retirement as an opportunity from

God for a new and exciting stage in her life. Through CIT, Rebecca came to expect and accept that life will always present challenges. However, equipped with new communication and problem-solving techniques as well as a community of support behind her, Rebecca felt more confident in her abilities to tackle any new challenge that she might face; with this, her depression and anxiety subsided significantly.

In the preceding case illustration, we offered CIT as one example of a religiously integrated cognitive behavior treatment that we believe has three strengths: (a) it is cost-effective and gives participants an opportunity to provide peer support, learning from others with related issues; (b) it provides a sense of community and offers an opportunity to help participants realize that their challenges are not unique and they are not alone; and (c) it allows consistent communication between therapists and clergy to promote more effective treatment. Within the group setting, participants may form lifelong friends because many are members of the same church or hold similar values and religious beliefs. This is important because a strong social support network is related to better mental health outcomes in individuals with mental illness (Corrigan & Phelan, 2004; Hendryx et al., 2009).

FINDINGS

Although we are currently working on an empirical paper in which we will describe the study findings in detail (Weisman de Mamani, Lopez, et al., 2021), we are encouraged that preliminary data already indicate a significant improvement in participants' reported satisfaction with the quality of their lives after engaging in CIT. As expected, we also found that, from beginning therapy to therapy termination, clients engaged in greater collectivistic activities outside of therapy (engaging and working with family, friends, and others as a team). From a qualitative perspective, we have also received very favorable feedback from clients in the group and from the senior pastor. A few sample comments include:

> Therapists are extremely knowledgeable, patient, and professional. The program provided me with the tools and the learning opportunities to handle my depression.

> I appreciated the opportunity to listen to how other people dealt with unsatisfactory situations in their life. I appreciated the therapists' summaries of what they said. They seemed to be able to capture what that person was saying and summarize it in a way that provided more clarity.

> Having the CIT program has helped me greatly with my illness. It has helped me with my sleeping patterns, my impulsiveness, and my thought process. . . . I also learned valuable coping skills.

Clients also rated their satisfaction with the approaches used in session each week using a 7-point Likert scale (1 = *unsatisfied* to 7 = *total satisfaction*). Ratings were averaged across sessions, and participants indicated very high satisfaction ($M = 6.42$; $SD = 0.69$; mode = 7) with CIT.

We believe that increasing the availability of religiously oriented programs, such as CIT, within religious institutions will not only enhance the quality of existing psychotherapy programs but will also make R/S individuals more likely to seek psychological services for their mental health needs and to remain in treatment long enough to tackle their issues. We eventually hope to see CIT and other psychotherapeutic interventions expanded to additional churches and other religious settings (e.g., synagogues, mosques) across the United States.

CONCLUSION AND FUTURE DIRECTIONS

The research reviewed in this chapter underscores a need for more organized and consistent collaborations between clergy and mental health practitioners. It also provides examples of how one such collaboration is taking place and the ways in which R/S has been incorporated into a culturally informed treatment to increase attendance, retention, and buy-in among members of a religious congregation in South Florida. Mental health professionals working in hospitals and clinics should make a concerted effort to consult or collaborate with religious personnel when treating religious clients. Educators and training supervisors should also aim to teach the notion that religion is salient to many clients and is likely to influence their mental health concerns. Teaching trainees to consult with clergy, when necessary, could help change the culture for the next crop of psychotherapists and improve the mental health of their clients. However, these efforts may still lead to experts in both psychology and spirituality who approach an individual's mental health without fully integrating both concepts for the individual.

This chapter offered an integrative model for a religiously based, cognitive behavior intervention that can be delivered in religious institutions in collaboration with clergy. This project could serve as a model for other religious institutions around the country that wish to offer similar resources to their congregants and community. We are finding that the regular and integrated guidance that we are receiving from pastors and other religious members have enhanced our treatment. Further, offering a psychologically based intervention in a community-based place of worship will not only appeal to religious individuals but may also keep them in treatment longer. With slight variations, this model should be useful in a multitude of settings, and ideally it would be disseminated to other Christian churches, with the approach extended also to synagogues, mosques, and other religious institutions and settings by collaborating with rabbis, imams, and other religious personnel.

REFERENCES

Arieli, S., & Sagiv, L. (2018). Culture and problem-solving: Congruency between the cultural mindset of individualism versus collectivism and problem type. *Journal of Experimental Psychology: General, 147*(6), 789–814. https://doi.org/10.1037/xge0000444

Asamoah, M. K., Osafo, J., & Agyapong, I. (2014). The role of Pentecostal clergy in mental health-care delivery in Ghana. *Mental Health, Religion & Culture, 17*(6), 601–614. https://doi.org/10.1080/13674676.2013.871628

Ayvaci, E. R. (2016). Religious barriers to mental healthcare. *The American Journal of Psychiatry Residents' Journal, 11*(7), 11–13. https://doi.org/10.1176/appi.ajp-rj.2016.110706

Berman, T. (2010). The ability to verbalize one's needs clearly in a geriatric population. In S. S. Fehr (Ed.), *101 interventions in group therapy* (Rev. ed., pp. 233–241). Routledge.

Brown, C. A., & Weisman de Mamani, A. (2018). The mediating effect of family cohesion in reducing patient symptoms and family distress in a culturally informed family therapy for schizophrenia: A parallel-process latent-growth model. *Journal of Consulting and Clinical Psychology, 86*(1), 1–14. https://doi.org/10.1037/ccp0000257

Chesley, N., & Fox, B. (2012). E-mail's use and perceived effect on family relationship quality: Variations by gender and race/ethnicity. *Sociological Focus, 45*(1), 63–84. https://doi.org/10.1080/00380237.2012.630906

Cheung, F. M. (1987). Conceptualization of psychiatric illness and help-seeking behavior among Chinese. *Culture, Medicine and Psychiatry, 11*(1), 97–106. https://doi.org/10.1007/BF00055011

Cnaan, R. A., Kasternakis, A., & Wineburg, R. J. (1993). Religious people, religious congregations, and volunteerism in human services: Is there a link? *Nonprofit and Voluntary Sector Quarterly, 22*(1), 33–51. https://doi.org/10.1177/089976409302200104

Corrigan, P. W., & Phelan, S. M. (2004). Social support and recovery in people with serious mental illnesses. *Community Mental Health Journal, 40*(6), 513–523. https://doi.org/10.1007/s10597-004-6125-5

Crook-Lyon, R. E., O'Grady, K. A., Smith, T. B., Jensen, D. R., Golightly, T., & Potkar, K. A. (2012). Addressing religious and spiritual diversity in graduate training and multicultural education for professional psychologists. *Journal of Psychology and Theology, 41*(1), 94–95.

Dillon, R. K., & McKenzie, N. J. (1998). The influence of ethnicity on listening, communication competence, approach, and avoidance. *International Journal of Listening, 12*(1), 106–121. https://doi.org/10.1080/10904018.1998.10499021

Dimidjian, S., Barrera, M., Jr., Martell, C., Muñoz, R. F., & Lewinsohn, P. M. (2011). The origins and current status of behavioral activation treatments for depression. *Annual Review of Clinical Psychology, 7*(1), 1–38. https://doi.org/10.1146/annurev-clinpsy-032210-104535

Falloon, I. R., Boyd, J. L., & McGill, C. W. (1984). *Family care of schizophrenia: A problem-solving approach to the treatment of mental illness.* Guilford Press.

Farrell, J. L., & Goebert, D. A. (2008). Collaboration between psychiatrists and clergy in recognizing and treating serious mental illness. *Psychiatric Services, 59*(4), 437–440. https://doi.org/10.1176/ps.2008.59.4.437

Forehand, R., & Kotchick, B. A. (1996). Cultural diversity: A wake-up call for parent training. *Behavior Therapy, 27*(2), 187–206. https://doi.org/10.1016/S0005-7894(96)80014-1

Goldstein, M. J., & Miklowitz, D. J. (1994). Family intervention for persons with bipolar disorder. *New Directions for Mental Health Services, 1994*(62), 23–35. https://doi.org/10.1002/yd.23319946205

Gonçalves, J. P., Lucchetti, G., Menezes, P. R., & Vallada, H. (2015). Religious and spiritual interventions in mental health care: A systematic review and meta-analysis of randomized controlled clinical trials. *Psychological Medicine, 45*(14), 2937–2949. https://doi.org/10.1017/S0033291715001166

Gurak, K. K., Weisman de Mamani, A., & Ironson, G. (2017). Does religiosity predict attrition from a culturally-informed family treatment for schizophrenia that targets religious coping? *Journal of Consulting and Clinical Psychology, 85*(10), 937–949. https://doi.org/10.1037/ccp0000234

Güss, C. D., & Tuason, M. T. (2009). Fire and ice: Cultural influences on complex problem solving. *Proceedings of the Annual Meeting of the Cognitive Science Society, 31*, 1942–1947. https://escholarship.org/uc/item/194595pw

Hall, G. C. N., Ibaraki, A. Y., Huang, E. R., Marti, C. N., & Stice, E. (2016). A meta-analysis of cultural adaptations of psychological interventions. *Behavior Therapy, 47*(6), 993–1014. https://doi.org/10.1016/j.beth.2016.09.005

Hendryx, M., Green, C. A., & Perrin, N. A. (2009). Social support, activities, and recovery from serious mental illness: STARS study findings. *The Journal of Behavioral Health Services & Research, 36*(3), 320–329. https://doi.org/10.1007/s11414-008-9151-1

Hopwood, R. A., & Witten, T. M. (2017). Spirituality, Faith, and Religion: The TGNC Experience. In A. Singh & l. m. dickey (Eds.), *Affirmative counseling and psychological practice with transgender and gender nonconforming clients* (pp. 213–230). American Psychological Association. https://doi.org/10.1037/14957-011

Hwang, W.-C., Myers, H. F., Abe-Kim, J., & Ting, J. Y. (2008). A conceptual paradigm for understanding culture's impact on mental health: The cultural influences on mental health (CIMH) model. *Clinical Psychology Review, 28*(2), 211–227. https://doi.org/10.1016/j.cpr.2007.05.001

Jenkinson, C. E., Dickens, A. P., Jones, K., Thompson-Coon, J., Taylor, R. S., Rogers, M., Bambra, C. L., Lang, I., & Richards, S. H. (2013). Is volunteering a public health intervention? A systematic review and meta-analysis of the health and survival of volunteers. *BMC Public Health, 13*(1), Article 773. https://doi.org/10.1186/1471-2458-13-773

Keith, K. (2008). Cross-cultural psychology and research. In S. F. Davis & W. Buskist (Eds.), *21st century psychology: A reference handbook* (Vol. 2, pp. 483–490). SAGE Publications. https://doi.org/10.4135/9781412956321.n103

Koenig, H. G. (2009). Research on religion, spirituality, and mental health: A review. *Canadian Journal of Psychiatry, 54*(5), 283–291. https://doi.org/10.1177/070674370905400502

Koenig, H. G., King, D. E., & Carson, V. B. (2012). *Handbook of religion and health* (2nd ed.). Oxford University Press.

Krumrei, E. J., Pirutinsky, S., & Rosmarin, D. H. (2013). Jewish spirituality, depression, and health: An empirical test of a conceptual framework. *International Journal of Behavioral Medicine, 20*(3), 327–336. https://doi.org/10.1007/s12529-012-9248-z

Kymalainen, J. A., & Weisman de Mamani, A. G. (2008). Expressed emotion, communication deviance, and culture in families of patients with schizophrenia: A review of the literature. *Cultural Diversity & Ethnic Minority Psychology, 14*(2), 85–91. https://doi.org/10.1037/1099-9809.14.2.85

Kymalainen, J. A., Weisman, A. G., Rosales, G. A., & Armesto, J. C. (2006). Ethnicity, expressed emotion, and communication deviance in family members of patients with schizophrenia. *The Journal of Nervous and Mental Disease, 194*(6), 391–396. https://doi.org/10.1097/01.nmd.0000221171.42027.5a

Lau, A. S. (2006). Making the case for selective and directed cultural adaptations of evidence-based treatments: Examples from parent training. *Clinical Psychology: Science and Practice, 13*(4), 295–310. https://doi.org/10.1111/j.1468-2850.2006.00042.x

Lefley, H. P. (1990). Culture and chronic mental illness. *Psychiatric Services, 41*(3), 277–286. https://doi.org/10.1176/ps.41.3.277

Lund, S. G. (2014). *Blessed are the crazy: Breaking the silence about mental illness, family and church*. Chalice Press.

Maura, J., & Weisman de Mamani, A. (2017). Mental health disparities, treatment engagement, and attrition among racial/ethnic minorities with severe mental illness:

A review. *Journal of Clinical Psychology in Medical Settings, 24*(3-4), 187–210. https://doi.org/10.1007/s10880-017-9510-2

Maura, J., & Weisman de Mamani, A. (2018). The feasibility of a culturally informed group therapy for patients with schizophrenia and their family members. *Psychotherapy, 55*(1), 27–38. https://doi.org/10.1037/pst0000109

Moran, M., Flannelly, K. J., Weaver, A. J., Overvold, J. A., Hess, W., & Wilson, J. C. (2005). A study of pastoral care, referral, and consultation practices among clergy in four settings in the New York City area. *Pastoral Psychology, 53*(3), 255–266. https://doi.org/10.1007/s11089-004-0556-3

Pargament, K. I., Kennell, J., Hathaway, W., Grevengoad, N., Newman, J., & Jones, W. (1988). Religion and problem-solving: Three styles of coping. *Journal for the Scientific Study of Religion, 27*(1), 90–104. https://doi.org/10.2307/1387404

Percy, M. S. (2012). *Exploring the attitudes of Episcopal clergy regarding collaboration with clinical psychologists* (Publication No. 3505938) [Doctoral dissertation, Massachusetts School of Professional Psychology]. ProQuest Dissertations and Theses Global.

Sedikides, C., Gaertner, L., & Toguchi, Y. (2003). Pancultural self-enhancement. *Journal of Personality and Social Psychology, 84*(1), 60–79. https://doi.org/10.1037/0022-3514.84.1.60

Singelis, T. M. (1994). The measurement of independent and interdependent self-construals. *Personality and Social Psychology Bulletin, 20*(5), 580–591. https://doi.org/10.1177/0146167294205014

Speed, B. C., Goldstein, B. L., & Goldfried, M. R. (2018). Assertiveness training: A forgotten evidence-based treatment. *Clinical Psychology: Science and Practice, 25*(1), Article e12216. https://doi.org/10.1111/cpsp.12216

Sperry, L. (2001). *Spirituality in clinical practice: Incorporating the spiritual dimension in psychotherapy and counseling*. Brunner-Routledge.

Suka, M., Yamauchi, T., & Sugimori, H. (2016). Help-seeking intentions for early signs of mental illness and their associated factors: Comparison across four kinds of health problems. *BMC Public Health*. Advance online publication. https://doi.org/10.1186/s12889-016-2998-9

Thomas, M. L. (2012). The interprofessional collaborative practice: Clergypersons and mental health professionals. *Pastoral Psychology, 61*(1), 99–112. https://doi.org/10.1007/s11089-011-0408-x

Triandis, H. C. (2001). Individualism and collectivism: Past, present, and future. In D. Matsumoto (Ed.), *The handbook of culture and psychology* (pp. 35–50). Oxford University Press.

Triandis, H. C. (2018). *Individualism and collectivism*. Routledge. https://doi.org/10.4324/9780429499845 (Original work published 1995).

Vahia, I. V., Chattillion, E., Kavirajan, H., & Depp, C. A. (2011). Psychological protective factors across the lifespan: Implications for psychiatry. *The Psychiatric Clinics of North America, 34*(1), 231–248. https://doi.org/10.1016/j.psc.2010.11.011

Van Gundy, K. T., Howerton-Orcutt, A., & Mills, M. L. (2015). Race, coping style, and substance use disorder among non-Hispanic African American and White young adults in South Florida. *Substance Use & Misuse, 50*(11), 1459–1469. https://doi.org/10.3109/10826084.2015.1018544

Vieten, C., Scammell, S., Pilato, R., Ammondson, I., Pargament, K. I., & Lukoff, D. (2013). Spiritual and religious competencies for psychologists. *Psychology of Religion and Spirituality, 5*(3), 129–144. https://doi.org/10.1037/a0032699

Weisman, A. G. (1997). Understanding cross-cultural prognostic variability for schizophrenia. *Cultural Diversity and Mental Health, 3*(1), 23–35. https://doi.org/10.1037/1099-9809.3.1.23

Weisman de Mamani, A., Lopez, D., McLaughlin, M., Ahmad, S. S., & Altamirano, O. (2021). *A pilot study to assess the feasibility and efficacy of a religiously-based, culturally informed therapy* [Manuscript submitted for publication]. Psychology Department, University of Miami.

Weisman de Mamani, A., McLaughlin, M., Altamirano, O., Lopez, D., & Ahmad, S. S. (2021). *Culturally informed therapy for schizophrenia: A family-focused cognitive behavioral approach—Clinician guide*. Oxford University Press. https://doi.org/10.1093/med-psych/9780197500644.001.0001

Weisman de Mamani, A., & Suro, G. (2016). The effect of a culturally informed therapy on self-conscious emotions and burden in caregivers of patients with schizophrenia: A randomized clinical trial. *Psychotherapy, 53*(1), 57–67. https://doi.org/10.1037/pst0000038

Weisman de Mamani, A., Weintraub, M. J., Gurak, K., & Maura, J. (2014). A randomized clinical trial to test the efficacy of a family-focused, culturally informed therapy for schizophrenia. *Journal of Family Psychology, 28*(6), 800–810. https://doi.org/10.1037/fam0000021

Weisman de Mamani, A., G., Tuchman, N., & Duarte, E. A. (2010). Incorporating religion/spirituality into treatment for serious mental illness. *Cognitive and Behavioral Practice, 17*(4), 348–357. https://doi.org/10.1016/j.cbpra.2009.05.003

Wood, E., Watson, R., & Hayter, M. (2011). To what extent are the Christian clergy acting as frontline mental health workers? A study from the North of England. *Mental Health, Religion & Culture, 14*(8), 769–783. https://doi.org/10.1080/13674676.2010.522565

Yamada, A. M., & Brekke, J. S. (2008). Addressing mental health disparities through clinical competence not just cultural competence: The need for assessment of sociocultural issues in the delivery of evidence-based psychosocial rehabilitation services. *Clinical Psychology Review, 28*(8), 1386–1399. https://doi.org/10.1016/j.cpr.2008.07.006

3

Providing a Secure Base
Facilitating a Secure Attachment to God in Psychotherapy

Suzanne Nortier Hollman and Cheri Marmarosh

Bernadette started her first therapy session describing her painful childhood, which was filled with rejection and loss. She endured years of emotional abuse and isolation. When asked how she survived, she recalled both spending time at church and her relationship to God. She said that she often imagined that "God was her father" and that he was the one looking after her when she felt alone. "He was always there protecting me," she said. During the sessions, Bernadette revealed multiple bouts with depression, and over the years, a gradual realization that God, like everyone else, most especially her parents, who were emotionally absent during her childhood, had let her down. She now experienced God as having abandoned her. The sessions were filled with her feelings of betrayal and anger at God, feelings she denied having toward her parents. The therapist spent a significant amount of time exploring an important relationship that is often ignored in psychotherapy: the relationship Bernadette had with God.

In this chapter, we present this composite case of Bernadette ("Ms. B") that synthesizes disguised information derived from real-life psychotherapy sessions with patients. We describe how mental health care providers can support patients who, like Bernadette, struggle to experience a secure and benevolent attachment to God (ATG) that can support them during times of adversity. This approach, based on attachment theory, can be applied to any type of clinical practice ranging from supportive counseling to more structured cognitive behavior psychotherapy. Attachment theory is helpful because it facilitates an

---

https://doi.org/10.1037/0000338-003
Handbook of Spiritually Integrated Psychotherapies, P. S. Richards, G. E. K. Allen, and D. K. Judd (Editors)
Copyright © 2023 by the American Psychological Association. All rights reserved.

understanding of clients' internal working models that influence all relationships, including their relationships with God, and it has implications for distress tolerance and coping with adverse life events.

ATTACHMENT THEORY: A SECURE BASE

According to Bowlby (1988), the attachment system begins primarily as a way of promoting the infant's survival via the provision of a secure base. During distress, the infant seeks out the security-providing attachment figure and then experiences a sense of safety when in close proximity. The ability of the infant to experience felt security during times of distress facilitates emotion regulation and the ability to successfully separate from the caregiver and explore the surrounding environment. In a healthy dyadic relationship, the securely attached infant can both seek the reliable caregiver when needed and separate from the caregiver when curious or ready to explore.

Not all caregivers are able to foster this sense of felt security, and infants are forced to develop alternate strategies to cope with distress. For example, infants who interact with inconsistent or unreliable caregivers must adapt to frequent abandonments. This often makes them extremely vigilant in maintaining their attachment figures' attention. They may cling to the caregiver or engage in behaviors that continue to maintain contact with the caregiver to manage their distress. During the *Strange Situation* (Ainsworth et al., 1978), an assessment tool designed to determine how well infants rely on attachment figures during a time of distress, infants demonstrate a preoccupation with the caregiver, an inability to regain emotion regulation, and intense longings for closeness alternating with intense feelings of anger at the caregiver. Ainsworth et al. (1978) described them as having a preoccupied attachment given their overemphasis on maintaining contact with attachment figures at the expense of exploration.

Adults with this attachment style have the capacity to feel emotions intensely but struggle to cope with their feelings (Fosha, 2000). Like the infants, they rely on hyperactivating strategies that are designed to provoke others into taking care of them, but despite these efforts, they often continue to feel frustrated in their relationships, fearful of being alone or abandoned, and overwhelmed with feelings of inadequacy.

Whereas preoccupied infants cling to their caregivers and struggle with emotion regulation, dismissing infants appear detached and reveal little to no emotional distress when separated (Ainsworth et al., 1978). Although they appear outwardly calm, they have elevated cortisol and heart rates. In essence, they have learned to self-soothe via immersion in exploration, minimize displays of distress, and avoid asking for help during times of distress. They have learned to rely on themselves to regulate emotions (Main & Weston, 1982). As adults, these individuals are extremely successful at avoiding emotional pain, but they often struggle with needs for support or dependency. They have learned from an early age that relying on others fails to elicit an attuned attachment response or to ameliorate distress (Main, 1995; Schore, 1994). As children, they learn to turn off their bids for comfort, and they split off vulnerable emotions that are too painful to manage alone (Dozier et al., 1999; Main, 1995). The repeated experience of longing for comfort only to experience continued disappointment leads to the adaptive, yet defensive, practice of turning off the proximity-seeking behaviors. The deactivation process during childhood shifts the attention away from the caregiver during distress and reduces the emotional shame and despair that follow. As adults, more avoidant individuals continue to suppress their connection to others and deny any needs for caregiving from them (Wallin, 2007).

Perhaps the most damaging style of attachment, one that was identified later by researchers and has the greatest relationship to difficulties in later life, is the disorganized attachment. *Traumatized infants*, those infants who have experienced physical, emotional, or sexual abuse or profound neglect at the hands of their caregivers, appear to have the greatest likelihood of developing a disorganized attachment (Sroufe, 2005). As infants, their desperate needs for safety contradict the life-threatening danger they also experience when they rely on their attachment figures. Instead of feeling safe and secure when in close proximity to attachment figures, they feel overwhelming terror along with the implicit desire to seek out the caregiver during distress. These infants are often described as having a disorganized attachment given their alternations between deactivating strategies—for example, withdrawing out of fear—and hyperactivating strategies—such as seeking reassurance out of fear of abandonment (Main, 2000). Researchers also have demonstrated that these children have an increased likelihood of using dissociation to manage traumatic experience (Carlson, 1998), and as adults, they have more interpersonal and emotion regulating difficulties compared with those with other attachment styles (Mikulincer & Shaver, 2007).

ATTACHMENT TO GOD

Kirkpatrick (1998; Kirkpatrick et al., 1999), Granqvist (2020), and others (Kirkpatrick & Shaver, 1990; Noller, 1992; Pargament, 1997) have argued convincingly that the relationship with God can also function as an attachment relationship. Using Ainsworth's (1985) and Bowlby's (1973, 1980) models of what constitutes attachment, these authors argued that the same conditions that designate a mother–child relationship as an attachment bond can be extended to include God as an attachment figure. Perhaps the most immediately obvious distinguishing characteristic between traditional conceptualizations of what constitutes an attachment figure and ATG is that God is a noncorporeal attachment figure (Granqvist, 2020; Kirkpatrick et al., 1999). Kirkpatrick (1998; Kirkpatrick et al., 1999) and Noller (1992) also referenced the concept of symbolic attachment as relevant to the relationship with a noncorporeal attachment figure. They argued that symbolic attachment is characterized by the capacity to maintain cognitive and affective proximity even when the attachment figure cannot be directly observed. In the same way that the child is able to keep the mother in mind during her absence, the individual is able to maintain an attachment relationship with a noncorporeal deity (Kirkpatrick, 1998; Kirkpatrick et al., 1999; Noller, 1992). While Granqvist (2020) argued that ATG meets the criteria in much the same way that more traditional attachment relationships function, he simultaneously made the point that this attachment relationship falls within "a special subclass of 'noncorporeal' attachments" (p. 43). The main characteristics of this noncorporeal attachment include relationality, love, and parental representations (Granqvist, 2020). Human beings are primed to form affective relational bonds, and accordingly, in monotheistic religions, such as Christianity, Islam, and Judaism, the relationship with God among believers has the potential to become intensely personal, interactive, loving, and psychological. God representations in this context also become parental, and Granqvist (2020) argued that "an exalted attachment figure" (p. 48) is a more useful way to conceive of this relationship.

Proximity seeking and maintenance within this context occur principally through the mechanism of prayer. Prayer to a noncorporeal entity shares many of the attributes of attachment relationships more broadly. The "upward" forms of prayer involve a connection between a human and a higher power (Granqvist, 2020), and contain within them an implicit power differential wherein the deity has the capability of functioning as an attachment figure. This ATG relationship includes the same conditions denoting attachment bonds in human relationships, namely, being a secure base from which to explore the world and functioning as a source of safety. In other words, this relationship therefore functions as a safe haven and secure base, and it is characterized by separation anxiety when the attachment figure is not present and the maintenance of proximity to the attachment figure (Ainsworth, 1985; Bowlby, 1973, 1980; Granqvist, 2020; Kirkpatrick et al., 1999).

God as a Safe Haven

Mary Ainsworth et al. (1978) observed that when children were presented with perceived threats in the Strange Situation, they retreated to their mother for comfort and safety. The argument here is that for many people, God serves as an attachment figure in a similar way. Kirkpatrick et al. (1999) demonstrated that in theistic religions, God, or another supernatural figure, when perceived to be available and responsive, functions as a safe haven. Bowlby's (1969) conception of the attachment figure as safe haven is pertinent here. Bowlby (1982) identified three conditions under which the attachment system may become activated: (a) fear-provoking events that occur in the external environment; (b) adversity through illness, bodily or psychological trauma, or exhaustion (or a combination of each); and (c) the threat or actual loss of an attachment figure through, for example, death or another type of separation. Granqvist (2020) argued that the significant body of research findings demonstrating that people turn toward religion during times of adversity, including

Pargament's (1997) work on religious coping during stressful times, provide evidence for ATG as having the function of a safe haven to which one can return (Granqvist, 2020).

Argyle and Beit-Hallahmi (1975) found prayer to be a religious coping mechanism that most individuals turn to during times of acute distress, and research by Kirkpatrick (2005) and O'Brien (1982) provided further support for prayer as a principal way to cope with serious illness and injury. The argument that turning to God during times of distress denotes ATG as a safe haven appears to be supported by these research findings. Moreover, research studies investigating unconscious processing and threat appraisal have similarly demonstrated an increase in thoughts related to God under stressful circumstances (Birgegard & Granqvist, 2004). Granqvist and Kirkpatrick (2013), for example, found that when Israeli college students were subliminally exposed to the words "failure" and "death," they demonstrated an increased ability to access the concept of God. Kirkpatrick (2005) found that after the death of a loved one, turning to prayer and religion increased; moreover, doing so was correlated with increased coping. Birgegard and Granqvist's (2004) attachment study provided further support for the idea of ATG as being imbued with a safe haven function. In that research study, theistic believers were presented with a subliminal separation threat. After presenting subjects with the threat of "mother is gone," they found an increased wish to draw closer to God (Birgegard & Granqvist, 2004).

God as a Secure Base

Kirkpatrick (2005) argued that when God functions as a secure base, it is the "antidote to fear and anxiety" (p. 66). Bowlby (1973) posited that the attachment figure who functions as a secure base is viewed as stronger and wiser by the child, and in the case of ATG, this translates to a perception of God as imbued with these same characteristics. In addition, God is perceived as omnipotent, all powerful, sturdy, and omnipresent (Granqvist et al., 2010). Granqvist (2020) pointed out that research around God as secure base has placed less emphasis on the relationship between religious beliefs and experiences as well as the effects of these beliefs and experiences related to behavioral and cognitive outcomes when there are no clearly identifiable stressors. Research in this area has focused on so-called indirect effects—for example, the benefits of intrinsic religiosity, that is, religion as a central tenet in living and a felt experience of God as it relates to positive effects for mental and physical health (Batson et al., 1993).

Several studies have found that positive associations between well-being and religious conversion (Ullman, 1982), prayer and well-being (Poloma & Gallup, 1991), and the perception of a personal relationship with God correlated with lower levels of reported loneliness (Kirkpatrick et al., 1999). The overall argument is that this type of proximity seeking manifested in prayer—placing religion and God front and center in one's life, viewing God as omnipotent, having conversion experiences, and perceiving a felt personal relationship—is indicative of God functioning as a secure base that meets an important condition within the attachment theory framework.

Granqvist et al. (2012) argued that the secure base characteristic of God as an attachment figure is also supported by more direct research findings. They cited studies with a sample of Jews in Israel as pertinent to the secure base hypothesis. Granqvist and colleagues primed subjects with the word "God" and introduced a neutral control word. In addition, they included secure base target words—for example, "loving," "responsive," and "accepting," and negative target words, such as "controlling," "harsh," and "strict." The authors concluded that the outcomes showed definitively that subliminal exposure to the "God" prime was associated with the positive secure based target words, not the neutral or negative primes (Granqvist et al., 2012). Other experiments focusing on God as a secure base asked subjects to consider activities that carry risk—for example, scuba diving. Kupor et al. (2015) found that when reminders of God were introduced, research subjects perceived risk at a lower level.

Proximity Seeking and Separation Distress

Proximity seeking, the desire that the infant experiences to remain physically close and the felt security that older children may develop to maintain proximity (Bowlby, 1969, 1982), seems relevant to the relationship that the believer has with a deity. The distress that the infant or child experiences when the attachment figure is absent or unavailable—when proximity maintenance fails—is also mirrored in the attachment relationship with a deity. While God is incorporeal and attachment in this category is characterized by a symbolic quality, the theistic religious conception of God as omnipresent, as eternally watching over believers, and as providing a personal relationship manifests in behaviors that aim to maintain proximity. Believers draw near to God through religious practices, such as prayer, supplication, religious observance, fasting, confession, adoration, and the use of religious symbols and artifacts. Prayer, in particular, has been shown to have the function of proximity seeking and maintenance (Granqvist, 2020; Granqvist & Kirkpatrick, 2008), and Trier and Shupe (1991) have shown that prayer is the most common form of engaging in one's spirituality.

The antithesis of proximity seeking in attachment theory is the threat of separation. Birgegard and Granqvist (2004) examined whether the desire to be close to God increased from pre- to postpriming using either a separation prime—for example, "God has abandoned me"—or a neutral prime, such as "God has many names." Results indicated modest support for the desire to draw close to God, but individual differences were a moderating factor in the effects of separation (Birgegard & Granqvist, 2004). The idea that separation from God leads to distress has been referenced in religious texts for millennia. The "dark night of the soul" experienced by Mother Teresa (2007) and St. John of the Cross (1577/1990) are two well-known examples of the distress of perceived abandonment by, and separation from, God. These experiences are often described as deeply distressing and painful, and they persist for long periods. Pargament (1997) similarly provided examples of Holocaust survivors and soldiers who had experienced or witnessed atrocities; they concluded that their sense of abandonment by God was so complete that God was dead.

Overall, research in this area has not unequivocally demonstrated a pattern of protest, anxiety, and despair seen in infant attachment, but there are correspondences that indicate that these potential responses to loss and separation should be explored further. Kirkpatrick (2005) provided a good argument for this line in inquiry when he contended that "if God functions psychologically as an attachment figure, then separation from or loss of God should engender these same kinds of responses" (p. 71). The moderating effects related to how an individual might experience God in terms of proximity, separation, safe haven and safe base are located within individual differences—more specifically, in an individual's attachment style and in how this, in turn, relates to whether the correspondence or the compensation pathway (defined in a later section) is a part of an individual's developmental path to engagement with God (Granqvist et al., 2010).

ATTACHMENT TO GOD AND ATTACHMENT STYLE

Kirkpatrick (1992; Kirkpatrick et al., 1999) conceptualized ATG as including secure, avoidant, and anxious attachment styles. Individuals who have a secure ATG and who view God as a secure base experience God as present and available when needed. The securely attached person does not, however, routinely rely on their ATG to regulate affective and relational distress. Not only is God a benevolent and stable presence, the securely attached individual experiences fewer instances of activation and deactivation in close relationships that would necessitate the mobilization of this attachment (Granqvist et al., 2010). Kirkpatrick (2005) argued that for those who are religious and securely attached, the God figure is furthermore perceived as comforting, protective, and accessible. This perception enables the person to approach the problems and challenges of everyday living with the belief that a return to the secure base is always an option, especially amid adversity.

Avoidant ATG is characterized by many of the same features that avoidantly attached individuals experience in their other close relationships. The need for self-sufficiency and self-reliance, reluctance to depend on or trust God as a benevolent presence, and withdrawal characterize this attachment style (Beck & McDonald, 2004). Individuals who are anxiously attached experience God as predominantly unreliable, inconsistent, and intermittently available (Kirkpatrick & Shaver, 1992; Rowatt & Kirkpatrick, 2002). Beck and McDonald's (2004) research showed that anxious and avoidant ATG were negatively correlated with feeling satisfied with one's relationship to God and a sense of spiritual well-being. Kirkpatrick's research showed that individuals who are avoidant or anxiously attached to God are more likely to endorse feeling lonely, depressed, and anxious as well as report lower health and life satisfaction than those who view God as a secure attachment figure in their lives (Kirkpatrick & Shaver, 1992).

A number of research studies have established a relationship among child–primary caregiver attachment (Cassibba et al., 2008; Granqvist, 1998; Kirkpatrick & Shaver, 1990; McDonald et al., 2005) adult romantic attachment (Kirkpatrick et al., 1999; Rowatt & Kirkpatrick, 2002), and ATG. These findings have been replicated in cross-cultural research, although studies were predominantly with European samples (Eurelings-Bontekoe et al., 2005; Proctor et al., 2009). Individual differences in ATG are further elucidated by the correspondence and the compensation hypotheses.

CORRESPONDENCE AND COMPENSATION

Kirkpatrick (1998; Kirkpatrick et al., 1999) hypothesized that ATG is a developmental process that can occur through two pathways. The *correspondence pathway* posits that an individual who experiences sensitive, attuned caregiving from a religious caregiver will transfer this secure attachment style onto a corresponding secure ATG. The *compensation pathway* is related to affect regulation specific to the distress experienced in the context of insensitive and misattuned caregivers (Granqvist & Kirkpatrick, 2008).

Attachment to God and the Correspondence Pathway

The correspondence hypothesis draws on the attachment concept of internal working models. It holds that individual religious beliefs and experiences are related to attachment style—that is, an individual relates to God as an attachment figure in a way that corresponds to the individual's attachment to others. Following this line of thought, the correspondence hypothesis posits that the relationship with God, alongside other adult relationships, is formed and maintained in accordance with early childhood attachment experiences. Dickie's (1997) research provided indirect support for the correspondence hypothesis by demonstrating that children between the ages of 4 years and 11 years identified mental images of parents as closely related to images of God. Internal working models of God were found to bear similarity to the perception of the primary caregivers. For example, a child who viewed the father as nurturing and powerful or the mother as compassionate and gentle would transfer these perceptions to their internal depiction of God. Conversely, Jubis (1991, cited in Kirkpatrick, 2005) found that children who had experienced rupture or loss in significant relationships through death or divorce, for example, were less likely to view God as an important attachment figure.

With regard to correspondence with attachment styles specifically, Granqvist et al. (2010) made the case that those with secure internal working models of self and others are more likely to view God and associated religious representations positively and as sources of support. Empirical support for the correspondence pathway as a developmental process is also supported in terms of viewing

God as available when needed. This perception of God as stable and accessible under all circumstances has been tied empirically to caregiving from early attachment figures who were both sensitive and religious, and who, in turn, aided the developmental process inherent in ATG. Three studies by Birgegard and Granqvist (2004) also demonstrated that adults who endorsed both sensitive early caregiving and belief in God increased their use of God to regulate affective distress following subliminal separation primes. This impact and role of early attachment figures on ATG is known as the *social correspondence hypothesis* and has been confirmed by a number of research studies (Cassibba et al., 2008; Granqvist, 2002; Granqvist & Hagekull, 1999). The correspondence hypothesis related to insecure attachment suggests that those who are avoidantly attached will be more likely to perceive God as unavailable and unreachable, whereas the anxious or preoccupied attachment style of relating to God and religion is likely to manifest in a fraught and clingy, emotionally dysregulated attachment relationship (Granqvist, 2020).

Kirkpatrick and Shaver's (1992) research on romantic attachment lends support to the correspondence hypothesis. Their findings indicated that those with a secure attachment in adult romantic relationships were more likely to perceive God as loving and to endorse higher levels of a personal relationship with God. Conversely, those with an avoidant relationship style were more likely to endorse agnosticism and atheism. These findings were replicated in other studies (Granqvist & Kirkpatrick, 2008; Kirkpatrick, 2005). The perception of others as unavailable and attempts at proximity seeking as unlikely to be successful lead to the question of whether God may function as a substitute attachment figure to compensate for the absence of a stable and reliable caregiver. This is known as the compensation hypothesis.

Attachment to God and the Compensation Pathway

Bowlby (1982) theorized that when attempts to engage with the primary attachment figure are unsuccessful, the child may direct behavior toward a substitute object. This effort to locate a substitute attachment figure is most likely to occur during times of adversity—for example, illness, fatigue, or distress. The compensation hypothesis posits that when the relationship with the primary attachment figure is fraught with disappointment, the individual may turn toward God as a substitute attachment figure—that is, as a compensatory attachment figure (Granqvist, 2020; Kirkpatrick & Shaver, 1990). Research by Kirkpatrick and Shaver (1990), Granqvist and Kirkpatrick (2004), and a large study based on the Adult Attachment Interview (AAI; Main et al., 2003) provide support for the premise that perceived deficiencies in love and caregiving from the primary attachment figure can translate into increases in religiosity and a view of God as an important and available attachment figure.

Results from two longitudinal studies conducted by Kirkpatrick (1997, 1998) found that for individuals on the insecure spectrum of attachment, God may function as a compensatory attachment figure. In their research on the breakup of romantic relationships, Granqvist and Hagekull (2003) found that when individuals predicted parental insensitivity in response to this adverse relational event, the relationship with God following the actual breakup was perceived as more important. Abrupt religious conversion experiences have also been found to be associated with parental insensitivity (Kirkpatrick & Shaver, 1990). In a comprehensive review of the current body of literature and research findings, Granqvist (2020) concluded that the compensation pathway has strong empirical support across both cross-sectional and longitudinal research designs. Although ATG as substitute may arguably be seen as a deficiency approach (Noller, 1992), the therapeutic utility of recognizing the compensation pathway may lie in altering this developmental conduit so that the ATG relationship becomes one in which the patient may become earned secure. Granqvist and colleagues (2010) argued that this represents a shift from a "deficiency approach" to a "growth approach" (p. 54). Through this alteration, the hyperactivation cycle that characterizes insecure ATG may be interrupted and replaced with a more regulated and less distress-bearing way of being in relationships.

APPLYING ATTACHMENT THEORY TO PSYCHOTHERAPY

While the initial attachment style of an individual can be located in childhood and remains consistent into adulthood, research studies have shown that attachment style can be modified from insecure to earned secure and that one of the mechanisms that mediate such a change is through the process of psychotherapy. Mikulincer et al. (2013), Taylor et al. (2015), and Kirchmann et al. (2012) have shown that attachment style can change through psychotherapy across presenting problems and diagnoses. A meta-analysis of 36 studies conducted by Levy et al. (2018) examined the relationship between changes in attachment style related to psychotherapy. Findings indicated that anxious and avoidant attachment styles generally improve during the course of psychotherapy, although results for the avoidant style were more mixed. The type of treatment—that is, interpersonal as opposed to noninterpersonal—psychotherapy interventions were not found to be significant.

Even though research specific to the role of psychotherapy in mediating ATG is evolving, a number of studies have shown that positive changes in God representations can occur in psychotherapy. Mohammadi et al. (2017) found that the avoidant ATG score decreased after a structured group therapy program with a small sample of adolescents, and Thomas et al. (2011) reported significant positive changes in ATG following a psychotherapy intervention in 26 Christian adults who experienced difficulties in their relationship with God related to negative God images. Jacques (1998) suggested that therapy could impact negative or maladaptive thinking occurring in one's relationship with God. Tisdale et al. (1997) also found improved internal representations of God and a more positive view of the self following an inpatient treatment program that incorporated a religious and object relations therapeutic approach. In that sample of 99 religious patients diagnosed with depressive disorders, God was viewed as closer, loving, and more present than at admission. These effects persisted a year after treatment ended.

Research that has examined attachment style change across theoretical modalities found that the therapist as secure base and safe haven remains central to the therapeutic process (e.g., Degnan et al., 2016; Diener et al., 2011; Levy et al., 2018). This is in line with Bowlby's (1988) original emphasis on how the therapy relationship can function as a secure base that facilitates increased security in all relationships, including the relationship with God. We posit that Bowlby's five therapeutic tasks, which follow, can be applied to psychotherapy in which the patient's ATG is a focus of therapy:

- First, the therapist needs to serve as a secure base to the patient to start exploring painful and difficult aspects of relationships and life circumstances.

- Second, the patient is tasked with exploring significant current relationships, including affective and behavioral expectations of self and other.

- Third, the therapist explores how past internal working models function in the present relationship with the therapist as the attachment figure.

- Fourth, the patient revisits how long-held perceptions and expectations in relationships are connected to present relationships as well as considers the role of early caregiver attachment figures in shaping these internal working models, which may no longer be applicable.

- Fifth, the patient is encouraged to question current and often long-held internal working models as well as reevaluate these ways of relating and attaching.

Bowlby (1988) concluded his outline of these therapeutic tasks by stating that "by these means the therapist hopes to enable his patient to cease being a slave to old and unconscious stereotypes and to feel, to think, and act in new ways" (p. 140).

Alongside these tasks, in the case example of Ms. B that follows, we demonstrate how the main concepts related to ATG, namely, safe haven, secure base, proximity seeking, and separation distress, become manifest in the treatment. We explore how these concepts are related to the patient's insecure attachment style—characterized by a predominantly anxious preoccupied ATG and to the therapist—and we show the utility of both the correspondence and the compensation pathways in conceptualizing this case. We demonstrate that the patient's internal working model of God changes through attachment-based psychotherapy as the patient moves from an anxious-preoccupied ATG to an earned-secure ATG. This shift has important implications for other important attachment relationships in her life and for an increased capacity to regulate intensely self-critical affective states.

CLINICAL EXAMPLE: THE CASE OF MS. B

Ms. B's ATG emerged as a clinical focus during the middle phase of treatment after she expressed her profound disappointment and anger at what she perceived as an abandonment by God. Born in Central America to a poor, devout Catholic family, she was named after St. Bernadette, the patron saint of illness and poverty. When Ms. B secured a scholarship to an American university, her mother credited the intercession of St. Bernadette for this accomplishment.

Ms. B presented as a 28-year-old, cisgender, heterosexual, Latinx female graduate student who immigrated to the United States from Bolivia 3 years before starting therapy. She requested that she be seen by a female Catholic therapist—"someone who might get how messed up the Church is." Based on this request, she was referred by her college counseling center to a cisgender, female, Catholic therapist—practicing but not devout—in a private practice setting for longer term treatment. The reason for referral included the marginal improvement in symptoms following the breakdown of a romantic relationship as well as Ms. B's anger at feeling abandoned by her university-based therapist when she reached her session limit.

She presented to the new therapist with long-standing relationship concerns, including what she described as a hostile relationship with God. This hostility and feeling of being abandoned also extended toward her parents for what she perceived as their being emotionally unavailable and constantly critical of her. She described herself as an "angry and reluctant Catholic" who worried that God "knows that I hate him, that I hate my parents, and he'll be coming for me." During these times, she engaged in a self-critical monologue, which was followed by episodes of depressive symptoms.

During the early phase of treatment, Ms. B frequently tested the therapist's commitment to her and to the treatment process. She often canceled sessions, or arrived late, and typically prefaced sessions by checking in to see whether the therapist still wanted to work with her. She questioned the therapist's motivations for remaining present to her and expressed surprise and suspicion when the therapist remained nonreactive and available to her when she expressed fear and anger at the prospect that she would be abandoned again. Her internal working model was that of an unavailable, emotionally distant attachment figure who only valued her for her obvious intellect and academic potential.

Ms. B. expressed feeling burdened as the first person in her family to attend college in the United States, and she felt conflicted about feeling gratitude for the opportunity—but also burdened by the responsibility—and devalued because she felt she was commodity to her mother. It was only during the middle phase of treatment that the therapist received confirmation that the first task outlined by Bowlby (1988)—namely, the therapist as a secure base—had been attained. Ms. B had come to the session uncharacteristically early and had broken her usual pattern of either silence or questioning the therapist's commitment to her at the beginning of sessions by spontaneously offering the following:

MS. B: I realize that I failed. I was named after St. Bernadette. I was supposed to do good in the world. Instead, I've done nothing except complain about everything all the time. I've been thinking a lot about God now that I'm single again. And I really don't know if God is there for me. I hope he is. But I think he is mad. Because I haven't been paying attention to him over the past year.

THERAPIST:	There are a lot of feelings and worries here—about being loved.
MS. B:	Yeah, well, I've often wondered if you even want to be here.
THERAPIST:	And yet here I am.
MS. B:	[*Laughs*] Well, yes, here you are, you're still here. So at least there's that.
THERAPIST:	Yes, I am here. And it seems as though God is here with us today also. But not necessarily loving you?
MS. B:	God is always there, but I worry that it's not in a good way.
THERAPIST:	Say more about that.
MS. B:	God is scary. He knows that I've been neglectful of him—that I've been ungrateful.
THERAPIST:	It's very real for you. This fear of God. Can you tell me what God looks like for you as you say that?
MS. B:	God is a giant. Dressed in a black cloak, towering over me, watching over me, seeing and knowing everything I do and think. And I have a lot of bad thoughts. I can't see God's face, and I'm not sure he likes me. He's disappointed in me. And yet I love God. I've always felt that.
THERAPIST:	What is it like to tell me this?
MS. B:	I've never told anyone this. I can't exactly tell a priest that I think this [*starts crying*]. To be honest, I feel so relieved.
THERAPIST:	Relieved to be able to tell someone. To say how complicated this all has been for you. God is scary. But this same God has been there for you sometimes. This is such a confusing relationship.
MS. B:	Yes, and for the longest time I was afraid that you wouldn't understand. That you would judge me, too. Because it is confusing. There was a time when God was there for me when no one else was. Even right after I came here to the U.S., and I was all alone. But then when I got into that horrible relationship, I started to feel really distant from God.

This vignette illustrates that Ms. B's attachment style is insecure and most likely anxious preoccupied. In terms of her relationship with the therapist, she holds a predominantly negative view of herself and an increasingly positive view of the therapist. Her ATG seems to be located in correspondence with her general attachment style—that is, anxious preoccupied, characterized by questioning the degree to which God is available to her, and marked by intense fears about being abandoned by God. This vignette also illustrates how both the correspondence pathway and the compensation pathway may be relevant in Ms. B's case. In the case of the correspondence pathway, Ms. B's anxious preoccupied attachment style mirrors her ATG; in the case of the compensation pathway, she turns to God as an attachment figure during times of relational distress as is evidenced throughout her childhood, after her migration to the United States, and after the breakup of her most recent relationship.

In terms of Bowlby's (1988) therapeutic tasks, Ms. B's most recent breakup and her fraught relationship with her parents, most specifically with her primary attachment figure, her mother, were explored during treatment. What set this treatment apart, however, was using Bowlby's therapeutic task in relation to ATG as a way to revisit, question, and reevaluate her internal working model of self and other. By reconstituting God as a secure base and a safe haven, Ms. B was able to modulate her strong affective reactions more effectively. The therapist pointed out to Ms. B that although she had a pattern of turning to God when other relationships became painful and unavailable to her, she did not have to relinquish God during those times. God as an attachment figure could always be available to her. Ms. B found this thought soothing—the idea of God as safe haven and secure base who was open to her attempts at seeking proximity and of God as an attachment figure who was able to tolerate her fears of abandonment under any circumstance.

The following vignette illustrates the way in which this attachment work occurred toward the end of the middle phase of treatment with the development of the therapeutic relationship as central to shift in the internal working model of how God is represented:

MS. B: How are you? I hope you enjoyed your time away. I've been okay while you were gone. Kind of surprising, I guess.

THERAPIST: You were surprised that you were alright while I was away. Could you say more about that?

MS. B: Well, it wasn't always that way. Remember how, a few months ago, I would get really worried that you'd forget about me—or worse, how I was sure you wouldn't come back at all? Well, it's not like that at all anymore. I have so much to tell you.

THERAPIST: You can trust that I'll be here, that I want to be here.

MS. B: Yes, I mean, sometimes I still have some doubts, but overall, I'm pretty sure it'll be okay even when I'm anxious and that you'll be back, and that you might even look forward to seeing me [*laughs*].

THERAPIST: That is very different from how it was in here. I'm wondering if you're feeling more comfortable in other relationships also.

MS. B: Well, it's interesting that you ask that. I went to Mass the other day, and I suddenly realized that I wasn't that anxious anymore. It was weird because I realized that God looked different to me.

THERAPIST: Different . . .

MS. B: Yes, very different. I realized that God wasn't so overwhelming and scary. Not towering over me anymore. Just a presence. Not like a looming giant ready to berate me.

THERAPIST: It felt different from before.

MS. B: Yes, very different. It felt almost comforting knowing that I wasn't alone and I wouldn't be judged for the not-so-good thoughts I have—I guess the thoughts we all have. And I wondered if that was because you were away, that I was finding a substitute, but then I told myself, "So what if I'm doing that a little?" It's okay because maybe I get to keep both of you with me.

Granqvist (2020) argued that the representations that believers hold of God are anchored in "relational development" (p. 176). The psychotherapy relationship in the case of Ms. B may be seen to have functioned as a substitute attachment figure while the patient was working through her relational trauma, past and present. Theories underlying ATG posit that earned secure attachment can occur through religious compensation, especially if the individual's attachment style is characterized by a high degree of attachment anxiety (Granqvist, 2020). The question of whether Ms. B's attachment style in romantic relationships will mirror what appears to be an earned-secure ATG cannot yet been answered based on the case material. At this time, she remains in treatment. Granqvist pointed out that the compensation pathway in ATG does not necessarily yield earned attachment security more broadly on the AAI (Main et al., 2003). In the case of Ms. B, perhaps an emphasis on the correspondence pathway is therefore a worthy therapeutic goal. If Ms. B can continue to work with her therapist to become earned secure in relation to the therapist, the goal of treatment will include shifts in her internal working model of self and other in which "other" also includes God.

CONCLUSION

In this chapter, we provided an overview of attachment theory and, more specifically, how ATG can inform the theory and practice of psychotherapy. We described how mental health care providers can support patients who, like Bernadette, struggle to experience a secure and benevolent ATG that can support them during times of adversity and in the face of relational trauma. Through a case study, we attempted to illustrate how the theory is helpful because it facilitates an understanding of a patient's internal working models that influence all relationships, including the patient's relationship with the therapist and the relationship with God. When the relationship with God is central to a patient and when that relationship inhibits a patient in finding and maintaining close bonds with others, the theory and research surrounding ATG provides an essential framework for treatment.

The ways in which ATG can be linked to these close relationships will manifest differently for every patient–therapist dyad. We hope that this chapter provides a starting point for therapists willing to explore this link among religion, spirituality, and attachment in close relationships.

REFERENCES

Ainsworth, M. D. (1985). Attachments across the life span. *Bulletin of the New York Academy of Medicine*, *61*(9), 792–812.

Ainsworth, M. D. S., Blehar, M. C., Waters, E., & Wall, S. (1978). *Patterns of attachment: A psychological study of the strange situation*. Lawrence Erlbaum Associates.

Argyle, M., & Beit-Hallahmi, B. (1975). *The social psychology of religion*. Routledge.

Batson, C. D., Schoenrade, P., & Ventis, W. L. (1993). *Religion and the individual: A social-psychological perspective*. Oxford University Press.

Beck, R., & McDonald, A. (2004). Attachment to God: The Attachment to God Inventory, tests of working model correspondence, and an exploration of faith group differences. *Journal of Psychology and Theology*, *32*(2), 92–103. https://doi.org/10.1177/009164710403200202

Birgegard, A., & Granqvist, P. (2004). The correspondence between attachment to parents and God: Three experiments using subliminal separation cues. *Personality and Social Psychology Bulletin*, *30*(9), 1122–1135. https://doi.org/10.1177/0146167204264266

Bowlby, J. (1969). *Attachment*. Basic Books.

Bowlby, J. (1973). *Attachment and loss: Vol. 2. Separation*. Hogarth Press.

Bowlby, J. (1980). *Attachment and loss: Vol. 3. Loss*. Basic Books.

Bowlby, J. (1982). Attachment and loss: Retrospect and prospect. *American Journal of Orthopsychiatry*, *52*(4), 664–678. https://doi.org/10.1111/j.1939-0025.1982.tb01456.x

Bowlby, J. (1988). *A secure base: Parent–child attachment and healthy human development*. Routledge.

Carlson, E. A. (1998). A prospective longitudinal study of attachment disorganization/disorientation. *Child Development*, *69*(4), 1107–1128. https://doi.org/10.1111/j.1467-8624.1998.tb06163.x

Cassibba, R., Granqvist, P., Costantini, A., & Gatto, S. (2008). Attachment and God representations among lay Catholics, priests, and religious: A matched comparison study based on the Adult Attachment Interview. *Developmental Psychology*, *44*(6), 1753–1763. https://doi.org/10.1037/a0013772

Degnan, A., Seymour-Hyde, A., Harris, A., & Berry, K. (2016). The role of therapist attachment in alliance and outcome: A systematic literature review. *Clinical Psychology & Psychotherapy*, *23*(1), 47–65. https://doi.org/10.1002/cpp.1937

Dickie, G. (1997). *Introduction to aesthetics*. Oxford University Press.

Diener, M. J., & Monroe, J. M. (2011). The relationship between adult attachment style and therapeutic alliance in individual psychotherapy: A meta-analytic review. *Psychotherapy*, *48*(3), 237–248. https://doi.org/10.1037/a0022425

Dozier, M., Stovall, K. C., & Albus, K. E. (1999). Attachment and psychopathology in adulthood. In J. Cassidy & P. R. Shaver (Eds.), *Handbook of attachment: Theory, research, and clinical applications* (pp. 497–519). Guilford Press.

Eurelings-Bontekoe, E. H. M., Van Steeg, J. H., & Verschuur, M. J. (2005). The association between personality, attachment, psychological distress, church denomination and the God concept among a non-clinical sample. *Mental Health, Religion & Culture*, *8*(2), 141–154. https://doi.org/10.1080/13674670412331304320

Fosha, D. (2000). *The transforming power of affect: A model for accelerated change*. Basic Books.

Granqvist, P. (1998). Religiousness and perceived childhood attachment: On the question of compensation or correspondence. *Journal for the Scientific Study of Religion*, *37*(2), 350–367. https://doi.org/10.2307/1387533

Granqvist, P. (2002). Attachment and religiosity in adolescence: Cross-sectional and longitudinal evaluations. *Personality and Social Psychology Bulletin*, *28*(2), 260–270. https://doi.org/10.1177/0146167202282011

Granqvist, P. (2020). *Attachment in religion and spirituality: A wider view*. Guilford Press.

Granqvist, P., & Hagekull, B. (1999). Religiousness and perceived childhood attachment: Profiling socialized correspondence and emotional compensation. *Journal for the Scientific Study of Religion, 38*(2), 254–273. https://doi.org/10.2307/1387793

Granqvist, P., & Hagekull, B. (2003). Longitudinal predictions of religious change in adolescence: Contributions from the interaction of attachment and relationship status. *Journal of Social and Personal Relationships, 20*(6), 793–817. https://doi.org/10.1177/0265407503206005

Granqvist, P., & Kirkpatrick, L. A. (2004). Religious conversion and perceived childhood attachment: A meta-analysis. *The International Journal for the Psychology of Religion, 14*(4), 223–250. https://doi.org/10.1207/s15327582ijpr1404_1

Granqvist, P., & Kirkpatrick, L. A. (2008). Attachment and religious representations and behavior. In J. Cassidy & P. R. Shaver (Eds.), *Handbook of attachment: Theory, research, and clinical applications* (2nd ed., pp. 906–933). Guilford Press.

Granqvist, P., & Kirkpatrick, L. A. (2013). Religion, spirituality, and attachment. In K. I. Pargament, J. J. Exline, & J. W. Jones (Eds.), *APA handbook of psychology, religion, and spirituality: Vol. 1. Context, theory, and research* (pp. 139–155). American Psychological Association. https://doi.org/10.1037/14045-007

Granqvist, P., Mikulincer, M., Gewirtz, V., & Shaver, P. R. (2012). Experimental findings on God as an attachment figure: Normative processes and moderating effects of internal working models. *Journal of Personality and Social Psychology, 103*(5), 804–818. https://doi.org/10.1037/a0029344

Granqvist, P., Mikulincer, M., & Shaver, P. R. (2010). Religion as attachment: Normative processes and individual differences. *Personality and Social Psychology Review, 14*(1), 49–59. https://doi.org/10.1177/1088868309348618

Jacques, J. R. (1998). Working with spiritual and religious themes in group therapy. *International Journal of Group Psychotherapy, 48*(1), 69–83. https://doi.org/10.1080/00207284.1998.11491522

Jubis, R. (1991). *An attachment-theoretical approach to understanding children's conceptions of God* [Unpublished doctoral dissertation]. University of Denver.

Kirchmann, H., Steyer, R., Mayer, A., Joraschky, P., Schreiber-Willnow, K., & Strauss, B. (2012). Effects of adult inpatient group psychotherapy on attachment characteristics: An observational study comparing routine care to an untreated comparison group. *Psychotherapy Research, 22*(1), 95–114. https://doi.org/10.1080/10503307.2011.626807

Kirkpatrick, L. A. (1992). An attachment-theory approach psychology of religion. *The International Journal for the Psychology of Religion, 2*(1), 3–28. https://doi.org/10.1207/s15327582ijpr0201_2

Kirkpatrick, L. A. (1997). A longitudinal study of changes in religious belief and behavior as a function of individual differences in adult attachment style. *Journal for the Scientific Study of Religion, 36*(2), 207–217. https://doi.org/10.2307/1387553

Kirkpatrick, L. A. (1998). God as a substitute attachment figure: A longitudinal study of adult attachment style and religious change in college students. *Personality and Social Psychology Bulletin, 24*(9), 961–973. https://doi.org/10.1177/0146167298249004

Kirkpatrick, L. A. (2005). *Attachment, evolution, and the psychology of religion*. Guilford Press.

Kirkpatrick, L. A., & Shaver, P. R. (1990). Attachment theory and religion: Childhood attachments, religious beliefs, and conversion. *Journal for the Scientific Study of Religion, 29*(3), 315–334. https://doi.org/10.2307/1386461

Kirkpatrick, L. A., & Shaver, P. R. (1992). An attachment theoretical approach to romantic love and religious belief. *Personality and Social Psychology Bulletin, 18*(3), 266–275. https://doi.org/10.1177/0146167292183002

Kirkpatrick, L. A., Shillito, D. J., & Kellas, S. L. (1999). Loneliness, social support, and perceived relationships with God. *Journal of Social and Personal Relationships, 16*(4), 513–522. https://doi.org/10.1177/0265407599164006

Kupor, D. M., Laurin, K., & Levav, J. (2015). Anticipating divine protection? Reminders of God can increase nonmoral risk taking. *Psychological Science, 26*(4), 374–384. https://doi.org/10.1177/0956797614563108

Levy, K. N., Kivity, Y., Johnson, B. N., Gooch, C. V. (2018). Adult attachment as a predictor and moderator of psychotherapy outcome: A meta-analysis. *Journal of Clinical Psychology, 74*(11), 1996–2013. https://doi.org/10.1002/jclp.22685

Main, M. (1995). Recent studies in attachment: Overview, with selected implications for clinical work. In S. Goldberg, R. Muir, & J. Kerr (Eds.), *Attachment theory: Social, developmental, and clinical perspectives* (pp. 407–474). Analytic Press.

Main, M. (2000). The organized categories of infant, child, and adult attachment: Flexible vs. inflexible attention under attachment-related stress. *Journal of the American Psychoanalytic Association, 48*(4), 1055–1096. https://doi.org/10.1177/00030651000480041801

Main, M., Goldwyn, R., & Hesse, E. (2003). *Adult attachment scoring and classification systems* [Unpublished manuscript]. Department of Psychology, University of California, Berkeley.

Main, M., & Weston, D. R. (1982). Avoidance of the attachment figure in infancy: Descriptions and interpretations. In C. M. Parkes & J. Stevenson-Hinde (Eds.), *The place of attachment in human behavior* (pp. 31–59). Basic Books.

McDonald, A., Beck, R., Allison, S., & Norsworthy, L. (2005). Attachment to God and parents: Testing the correspondence vs. compensation hypotheses. *Journal of Psychology and Christianity, 24*(1), 21–28.

Mikulincer, M., Shaver, P. R., & Berant, E. (2013). Attachment and therapeutic processes. *Journal of Personality, 81*(6), 606–616. https://doi.org/10.1111/j.1467-6494.2012.00806.x

Mohammadi, M. R., Salmanian, M., Ghobari-Bonab, B., & Bolhari, J. (2017). Spiritual psychotherapy for adolescents with conduct disorder: Designing and piloting a therapeutic package. *Iranian Journal of Psychiatry, 12*(4), 258–264.

Mother Teresa. (2007). *Mother Teresa: Come be my light—The private writings of the "Saint of Calcutta"* (B. Kolodiejchuk, Ed.). Doubleday.

Noller, P. (1992). Religion conceptualized as an attachment process: Another deficiency approach to the psychology of religion? *The International Journal for the Psychology of Religion, 2*(1), 29–36. https://doi.org/10.1207/s15327582ijpr0201_3

O'Brien, M. E. (1982). Religious faith and adjustment to long-term hemodialysis. *Journal of Religion and Health, 21*(1), 68–80. https://doi.org/10.1007/BF02273896

Pargament, K. I. (1997). *The psychology of religion and coping: Theory, research, practice.* Guilford Press.

Poloma, M. M., & Gallup, G. H., Jr. (1991). *Varieties of prayer: A survey report.* Trinity Press International.

Proctor, M.-T., Miner, M., McLean, L., Devenish, S., & Bonab, B. G. (2009). Exploring Christians' explicit attachment to God representations: The development of a template for assessing attachment to God experiences. *Journal of Psychology and Theology, 37*(4), 245–264. https://doi.org/10.1177/009164710903700402

Rowatt, W. C., & Kirkpatrick, L. A. (2002). Two dimensions of ATG and their relation to affect, religiosity, and personality constructs. *Journal for the Scientific Study of Religion, 41*(4), 637–651. https://doi.org/10.1111/1468-5906.00143

Schore, A. N. (1994). *Affect regulation and the origin of the self: The neurobiology of emotional development.* Routledge.

Shaver, P. R., & Mikulincer, M. (2007). Adult attachment strategies and the regulation of emotion. In J. J. Gross (Ed.), *Handbook of emotion regulation* (pp. 446–462). Guilford Press.

Sroufe, L. A. (2005). Attachment and development: A prospective, longitudinal study from birth to adulthood. *Attachment & Human Development, 7*(4), 349–367. https://doi.org/10.1080/14616730500365928

St. John of the Cross. (1990). *Dark night of the soul* (E. A. Peers, Ed. & Trans.). Doubleday. (Original work published 1577)

Taylor, P., Rietzschel, J., Danquah, A., & Berry, K. (2015). Changes in attachment representations during psychological therapy. *Psychotherapy Research, 25*(2), 222–238. https://doi.org/10.1080/10503307.2014.886791

Thomas, M. J., Moriarty, G. L., Davis, E. B., & Anderson, E. L. (2011). The effects of a manualized group-psychotherapy intervention on client God images and attachment to God: A pilot study. *Journal of Psychology and Theology, 39, 39*(1), 44–58. https://doi.org/10.1177/009164711103900104

Tisdale, T. C., Key, T. L., Edwards, K. J., Brokaw, B. F., Kemperman, S. R., Cloud, H., Townsend, J., & Okamoto, T. (1997). Impact of treatment on God image and personal adjustment, and correlations of God image to personal adjustment and object relations development. *Journal of Psychology and Theology, 25*(2), 227–239. https://doi.org/10.1177/009164719702500207

Trier, K. K., & Shupe, A. (1991). Prayer, religiosity, and healing in the heartland, USA: A research note. *Review of Religious Research, 32*(4), 351–358. https://doi.org/10.2307/3511681

Ullman, C. (1982). Change of mind, change of heart: Some cognitive and emotional antecedents of religious conversion. *Journal of Personality and Social Psychology, 43*(1), 183–192. https://doi.org/10.1037/0022-3514.43.1.183

Wallin, D. J. (2007). *Attachment in psychotherapy*. Guilford Press.

4

Relational Spirituality Model in Psychotherapy

Overview and Case Application

Steven J. Sandage and George S. Stavros

Although they don't always realize it, people visit my office to be with my settled, regulated nervous system. . . . Over time, their repeated contact with my nervous system helps their nervous systems settle. . . . But I didn't wrestle or mold or manage an unsettled nervous system into a settled one. Over time, I learned to access a settledness that is always and already present. I usually call it the Infinite Source, but it doesn't require a name, or an explanation, or even a belief. This settling of nervous systems, and this connection to a larger Source, is vital to healing.
—RESMAA MENAKEM (2016), *MY GRANDMOTHER'S HANDS* (p. 152)

This chapter summarizes the contours of our relational spirituality model (RSM) of psychotherapy (Sandage, Rupert, et al., 2020) and offers a case application. The RSM emphasizes a relational development approach to spiritually integrated psychotherapy (SIP). We open this chapter with the reflection by Menakem (2016) because this quote and his overall therapeutic approach to racialized trauma speaks to several core values within the RSM:

- the intersecting influences of embodiment and relational dynamics as well as deep sources of wisdom and healing (which are often, but not always, associated with sacred or ultimate meaning)

This project was supported by a grant (No. 61603) from the John Templeton Foundation on "Mental Healthcare, Virtue, and Human Flourishing."

https://doi.org/10.1037/0000338-004
Handbook of Spiritually Integrated Psychotherapies, P. S. Richards, G. E. K. Allen, and D. K. Judd (Editors)
Copyright © 2023 by the American Psychological Association. All rights reserved.

- the need for clinicians to authentically respect human diversity and to develop the capacities to enter into experiences of suffering, trauma, and existential pain with clients, including intergenerational and collective sources of trauma, such as racism, sexism, homophobia, religious bigotry, transphobia, and other systemic forms of evil

- the importance of self of the therapist (Aponte & Kissil, 2016) or what Menakem (2016) called the "settledness" to be able to cultivate relational dynamics of psychological and spiritual healing and growth

We start by briefly describing some background on the RSM. We then outline key concepts and clinical strategies, illustrate the model in a psychotherapy case, and discuss relevant research findings and future research directions.

BACKGROUND OF THE RSM

The attention to religion and spirituality (R/S) in mental health has greatly expanded in recent decades, and there is now a significant body of research on SIP approaches (Captari et al., 2018) and many different SIP models (as evidenced in this handbook). One gap in the SIP field has been relatively limited attention to models focused on relational development theories and relational and systemic models of therapeutic change. The RSM is intended to contribute to this gap. While numerous volumes are now integrating various R/S practices and coping strategies into psychotherapy, we have also seen the need for more theoretically grounded interdisciplinary approaches that bring together psychotherapy theories and the rich resources of religious studies and theology (Sandage & Strawn, 2022). Interdisciplinary approaches to SIP have often (although not exclusively) been grounded in a particular R/S tradition (e.g., Christianity, Islam, Buddhism) and aimed at clients from that same tradition.

The RSM emphasizes the need for clinician self-awareness of our own particular traditions, beliefs, and values, but it is also intended as an inclusive clinical approach that can be tailored to the diverse, intersectional dynamics within various therapy relationships. Thus, the clinical goal of the RSM is not to offer an R/S generic approach or a therapy from a singular R/S tradition but a differentiated approach led by the humility, openness, and respectful curiosity of relationally attuned clinicians. The RSM offers a way of conceptualizing complex dynamics of relational spirituality within both individual and relational modalities of treatment (couple, family, group), and this offers a counterbalance to the heavy focus on individual therapy within the SIP literature.

One of this chapter's authors (Sandage) initially developed the RSM through conceptual and empirical research on spiritual development with colleagues at Bethel University (in St. Paul, Minnesota) in the context of seeking to integrate clinical training in marriage and family therapy with relational models of spiritual formation and theology (Sandage & Jensen, 2013). Certain relational and spiritual parallels emerged between the challenging and potentially formative processes of graduate training and the systemic dynamics within psychotherapy that frequently involve destabilization of prior developmental structures as a prelude to growth. A program of psychological research on the spiritual development and intercultural competence of graduate students surfaced the core RSM dialectical themes of spiritual dwelling and seeking (defined shortly in the Theoretical Framework section) and related constructs, and this research was brought into interdisciplinary and clinical conversation with relational perspectives in philosophy and theology (Shults & Sandage, 2006). In 2013, Sandage moved to Boston University and The Albert & Jessie Danielsen Institute, where the RSM has been further elaborated and investigated as a relational and diversity-sensitive approach to the integration of clinical practice, training, and research (Sandage, Rupert, et al., 2020; Stavros & Sandage, 2014).

The systemic orientation of the RSM calls for attention to the role of sociocultural contexts, so it is important to note that the primary clinical contexts for the development of the RSM have been outpatient community mental health and private practice settings in the United States. The RSM is a flexible, transdiagnostic framework for integrating spiritual and existential dynamics into relational psychotherapy for a variety of clients' presenting concerns. The majority of clients in our clinical context desire engagement with spiritual, religious, or existential issues (or a combination of the three) in treatment (Sandage, Jankowski, et al., 2020), which is consistent with the wider literature on client preferences for R/S issues in treatment (Harris et al., 2016). However, the RSM underscores responsiveness to the full range of client R/S preferences, including a desire for boundaries from explicit R/S integration in treatment.

Our own theoretical orientation draws heavily on a synthesis of attachment theory, family systems theories, and relational psychoanalytic approaches to psychotherapy; however, our relational spirituality clinical framework can be used with a variety of clinical strategies, including cognitive behavior therapy models (e.g., Boettscher et al., 2019; Correa & Sandage, 2018). The RSM is consistent with the growing dual-factor or positive mental health emphasis in the psychotherapy literature focused on both alleviating symptoms of distress and also facilitating enhanced well-being of clients (Jankowski et al., 2020). Our embrace of postcolonial perspectives in both psychology and religion led us to the recognition that R/S can be both helpful and harmful to individuals and communities depending on the dynamics involved. Indeed, we work with many clients who desire help with spiritual and religious trauma, which requires sensitivity to the complex intersections of R/S dynamics with other aspects of identity and experience.

OVERVIEW OF THE RSM

In this section, we offer a brief overview of key definitions, constructs, and theoretical contours of the RSM as a clinical model. Then we summarize some central ethical, diversity, and justice considerations before outlining RSM clinical strategies for assessment, alliance development, and intervention.

Theoretical Framework

The RSM utilizes a relational definition of *spirituality* as "ways of relating to the sacred" (Sandage, Rupert, et al., 2020, p. 24) with *sacred* referencing whatever a person considers of ultimate importance in their life (for theory and research on the sacred, see Pargament, 2011). Forms of relational spirituality are diverse and can include relational styles ranging from salutary to impairing for mental health functioning. For example, some clients have securely attached styles of relational spirituality that facilitate affect regulation, forming healthy and reciprocal relationships, and prosocial behaviors (Granqvist, 2020). In contrast, clients with disorganized attachment styles of relational spirituality may have significant fear and mistrust of the sacred that contributes to chronic dysregulation and interpersonal conflict. This relational approach to spirituality emphasizes the pivotal roles of implicit limbic-based relational templates for interpreting and shaping experiences of the sacred and systemic sociocultural dynamics that shape experiences of relational spirituality.

We also draw on a multidimensional spiritual, existential, religious, theological (SERT; Rupert et al., 2019) heuristic within the RSM as part of our inclusive and pluralistic framework. We view spirituality broadly as relating to whatever a person considers ultimate, but we also recognize some clients do not consider themselves spiritual. The existential dimension can apply to deep human predicaments of suffering, loss, and meaning-making. Religion can include communities and traditions that offer rituals and practices for relating to the sacred. Theology involves reflective processes around questions of ultimate concern. A client might come to treatment with questions, struggles, or clinically relevant interests in any combination of these SERT dimensions, and some will have highly pragmatic goals that may not initially require explicit engagement with any of these dimensions (Sandage, Jankowski, et al., 2020).

Three core RSM constructs include (a) spiritual dwelling, (b) spiritual seeking, and (c) spiritual struggles. *Spiritual dwelling* involves aspects of relational spirituality that can provide orientation, grounding, communal connections, and affect regulation. Healthy forms of dwelling serve the safe haven function of the attachment system. *Spiritual seeking* involves aspects of relational spirituality engaged through exploring, wrestling with ambiguity and complexity, and opening oneself to new experiences of difference and diversity. Seeking maps onto the secure base function of the attachment system. *Spiritual struggles* are common and include various forms of distress or conflict in relation to the sacred (e.g., doubt, guilt, anger, despair, spiritual warfare). Spiritual struggles often prompt spiritual seeking that can lead to growth, but some clients find themselves stuck in patterns of struggle that impair both spiritual development and mental health.

The RSM also focuses on three relational development systems: (a) attachment, (b) differentiation, and (c) intersubjectivity. The *attachment system* develops in response to human needs for security, trust, relational regulation, and community. The *differentiation system* has evolved in response to needs for cooperation amid human differences that necessitate a balance of self-identity and interpersonal and sociocultural flexibility. The *intersubjectivity system* involves the challenges of human subjectivity and alterity that can range from subjugating and estranging power relations to more highly developed capacities for intimacy, mutual recognition, and the repair of ruptures. These relational development systems are partially overlapping, and yet theory and research on each system contributes unique features to our RSM clinical strategies for relational and spiritual development. A given clinical case might necessitate an initial focus on one or more of these development systems.

Our RSM commitment is to work with the SERT traditions and perspectives of our clients, and yet we also consider it important to remain self-aware of our own SERT beliefs and values as clinicians. We each embrace differentiated relational ontology perspectives within philosophy and theology that view ultimate reality as a differentiated web of benevolent relations. This means we tend to value relational views of well-being and flourishing as well as human diversity and social justice efforts toward more equitable relations. The RSM promotes respectful study of the particularities of various SERT traditions and appreciation for virtues, such as humility, compassion, forgiveness, courage, gratitude, justice, and others, that are markers of healthy relational spirituality across many traditions.

Process and Ethical Guidelines

Our intake process provides clients with informed consent information on our general orientation to treatment, specific policies and practices (e.g., confidentiality, payment, communication, crisis coverage), and ways our clinical values fit the overall mission of The Albert & Jessie Danielsen Institute (n.d.): "alleviating suffering and promoting healing and growth through clinical services, training, and research" ("About" para.). The written materials for clients explain we are committed to providing treatment that attends to the many dimensions of human experience (e.g., psychological, biological, social, spiritual) and that we have expertise in attending to spiritual, religious, and existential issues if clients desire. This packet also explains that our relational spirituality orientation leads us to interpret the term "spirituality" to broadly include ways people engage with whatever is ultimately sacred or important to them, find connection in the world, explore their deepest values, and address questions of purpose and meaning. Clients are invited to indicate whether they see ways spiritual, religious, and existential issues are relevant to their treatment, and we are committed to respecting client preferences in this regard.

Diversity and Justice Considerations

We consider diversity sensitivity and social justice commitment to be core healing dynamics in psychotherapy rather than as add-on considerations, an approach that is still too common in mental health care in the United States. More specifically, the RSM is informed by diversity and justice frameworks from intercultural competence, spiritual and religious competence, postcolonial and feminist theories, and the multicultural orientation model (Comas-Díaz & Torres Rivera, 2020; Davis et al., 2018; Owen et al., 2016; Vieten & Scammell, 2015). We are each qualified administrators of the Intercultural Development Inventory (Hammer et al., 2003) and have described ways that the developmental model integrates with our overall understanding of healthy forms of relational spirituality (see Chapter 6 in Sandage, Rupert, et al., 2020).

Increasing attention to intersectionality in our mental fields invites us to explore with our clients the complex interconnections between various aspects of identity and experience (e.g., culture, race, gender orientation, sexual orientation, spirituality, religion). This clinical work rests on our ongoing formation as clinicians in intercultural/diversity competence and social justice commitment, and this is particularly true for those of us embodying privilege within the White supremacist system in the United States. Research from our lab is consistent with wider findings suggesting that capacities for diversity competence among helping professionals are associated with relational qualities, such as humility, differentiation of self, spiritual seeking, and gratitude (Crabtree et al., 2020; Sandage, Rupert, et al., 2020). From a systemic perspective, we believe it is important to also recognize these diversity and justice dynamics within the organizational contexts and "relational ecologies" in which we practice as clinicians. Too often, an unjust burden falls on therapists from nondominant groups when the clinic or organization as a whole is not committed to growth (Moon & Sandage, 2019).

Relationship Establishment Guidelines

Clinical strategies within the RSM build on the vast empirical literature showing that the therapist–client working alliance is one of the strongest predictors of psychotherapy outcomes (Horvath, 2018). There is an important parallel in many spiritual and religious traditions suggesting the relational dynamics between "patient" and "healer" are central to the healing or transformation process. We draw on frameworks and assessment tools that use Bordin's (1983) three-fold model of the working alliance comprising bond, goals, and task. This helps us attend to the ongoing process of cultivating a collaborative working alliance through authentic connection and attachment, negotiation of key treatment goals, and dialogue about the specific therapeutic strategies intended to achieve those goals. Each of these working alliance dimensions offers a pathway toward spiritual integration in therapy; however, our relational approach also foregrounds the need for sensitive interpersonal attunement and communication in each of these areas to achieve and maintain a collaborative alliance.

Relational dynamics in therapy can also be viewed differently across cultures, so this is another key area for diversity competence (Comas-Díaz, 2006). Much of the literature on the working alliance focuses on positive collaboration; however, we also use the work of Safran and colleagues (2000) on rupture and repair processes that highlights effective ways to negotiate differences and conflicts within the alliance (e.g., Eubanks et al., 2018, 2019; Miller-Bottome et al., 2019). Healthy negotiation of diversity, difference, and conflict represents ways of facilitating the relational development systems of attachment, differentiation, and intersubjectivity. At our clinic, found clients' ratings of the diversity sensitivity of their therapists were positively related to treatment progress beyond the positive effects of the working alliance (which was also positively related to outcome), so this highlights the unique importance of therapists' diversity competence (Sandage, Jankowski, et al., 2020).

The RSM also highlights the value of systemic attention to the wider relational ecology of psychotherapy that, depending on the context of treatment, could include relational dynamics between clients and multiple providers and between clients and administrative staff (Kehoe et al., 2016). This fits with the communal orientation within many R/S and virtue traditions. We found cross-sectional evidence that clients' alliance dynamics with administrative staff at our clinic were related to ratings of treatment progress over and above their working alliance with their therapists. This evidence supports the understanding that the qualities of multiple relationships within some clinic environments may contribute to a kind of holding environment for the treatment process (Sandage et al., 2017).

Assessment Guidelines and Recommendations

We do a comprehensive mental health assessment process at intake, but here we focus on assessment of key RSM theoretical constructs described earlier. First, we use assessment tools for spiritual dwelling, spiritual seeking, and spiritual struggles both at intake and as repeated measures during treatment (Sandage, Jankowski, et al., 2020).[1] We also typically ask clients during intake if they have R/S commitments or interests because that information could be helpful for us to know; if they do, we ask that they describe ways those might be relevant to treatment (see Tan, 1996). Our intake questionnaires also ask open-ended questions about clients' sources of meaning and hope that offer an inclusive assessment in those areas that can tap into R/S or secular orientations.

Second, we both formally and informally assess clients' relational development in the areas of attachment and differentiation.[2] For the attachment system, this means attending to safe haven and secure base functions and differing attachment styles (Wallin, 2007). For the differentiation system,

---

[1] To assess spiritual dwelling, seeking, and struggles, we have used the Spiritual Well-Being Questionnaire (Gomez & Fisher, 2003), the Exploration subscale from the Multidimensional Quest Orientation Scale (Beck & Jessup, 2004), and the short form version of the Religious and Spiritual Struggles Scale (Exline et al., in press; based on Exline et al., 2014; see Sandage, Jankowski, et al., 2020, for clinical validation research), respectively.
[2] To assess attachment and differentiation, we use the Experiences in Close Relationship Scale–Short Form (Wei et al., 2007) and the Differentiation of Self Inventory–Short Form (Drake et al., 2015), respectively.

we assess capacities for self-regulation and coregulation, boundary management, self-identity, and interpersonal flexibility, among other areas.

The third relational development system in focus in the RSM, intersubjectivity, is more difficult to formally assess, but we also seek to informally assess clients' capacities for interpersonal intimacy, mutual recognition, and repair of conflicts. Each of these relational development constructs needs to be assessed with sensitivity to diverse sociocultural backgrounds and contexts. The RSM suggests it is particularly important to assess the ways these relational development systems impact clients' capacities to cope with stress and suffering as well as navigate life transitions, and how these systems construct spiritual, religious, or existential meaning in ways that promote well-being and growth (Sandage, Rupert, et al., 2020).

This last point highlights our RSM orientation toward assessing both mental health symptoms and holistic forms of well-being. We are particularly interested in eudaemonic forms of well-being that include healthy relational development, meaning and purpose in life, and concern for both self and community in combination with positive affect and subjective well-being (Jankowski et al., 2020). Systemic injustice works against the well-being of persons from nondominant groups, and a rigid clinical focus solely on symptoms without attention to well-being can reinforce a colonizing framework and neglects the spiritual values of liberation and social justice. We also assess clients' strengths that provide resources for healing and growth, and we are presently working on clinical validation of several measures that assess relational virtues (e.g., forgiveness, gratitude, humility) that have been associated with mental health and well-being in prior research. The constructs well-being and virtue, among others, are clearly culture laden and can be understood differently across various backgrounds and traditions. Thus, the informal therapy dialogue needs to involve clinicians' recognizing opportunities to explore those personal and social differences in meaning and practice (Owen et al., 2016). Research at our clinic has also identified different trajectories of client change (Jankowski et al., 2019). We know, for example, that some clients may be coping with suicidal ideation and trying to find reasons to live, whereas other clients may be working on enhancing well-being. This requires therapist attunement and flexibility across a range of client profiles in terms of both suffering and growth, and our RSM emphasis on relational development highlights the need for an ongoing assessment of how clients' relational experiences and templates surface within the treatment process.

Intervention Strategies and Techniques

A variety of intervention strategies and techniques can be used within the RSM framework (e.g., rupture and repair alliance work; facilitation of emotion regulation practices, detriangling, exploration of spiritual and existential meaning, the processing of grief and loss; see Sandage, Rupert, et al., 2020), and we have illustrated many of these in previous publications (Sandage, 2022; Sandage et al., 2019; Sandage, Rupert, et al., 2020; Worthington & Sandage, 2016) and also in the case application that appears later. The overall RSM clinic strategy can be summarized as using the therapeutic relationship to facilitate constructive changes in clients' relational development dynamics with self, others, and the sacred. We also integrate the metaphor of pacing and leading from many therapeutic models (Maddock & Larson, 2004) with our RSM emphasis on dialectical balancing of dwelling and seeking to frame our overarching clinical strategy of moving between support/connection and challenge/exploration.

A key strategy is to help clients develop new and adaptive strategies for both self-regulation of affect and coregulation with others, and this can involve exploring the use of spiritual, religious, or existential practices and resources that fit for particular clients. However, we view this process of exploring the use of affect regulation practices as highly relational and one that activates the relational development systems. For some clients with relatively secure attachment histories, this can be rather straightforward. But for other clients with more complicated self–other templates, this process can involve shame, mistrust, dissociation, hyperautonomy, idealization of the therapist or the sacred, and other complicated dynamics that require therapists to remain highly attuned to the relational process in therapy, including efforts to repair ruptures when they occur.

Like many depth-oriented psychodynamic and systemic approaches and many R/S traditions, the RSM also suggests that a nonlinear process of change is common in psychotherapy (Sandage, Rupert, et al., 2020). New and constructive experiences (seeking) for clients can frequently be followed by mild to moderate increases in symptoms of anxiety, confusion, or sadness, and this rise in symptoms of distress can be counterintuitive for many clients. We view these kinds of temporary distress as typically a natural part of exercising the seeking system for developmental change, which can be destabilizing to a client's prior meaning system and coping repertoire (dwelling), but it may also represent homeostatic forces within a clients' relational network and community that are resistant to change. Many R/S traditions include teachings about the ways spiritual growth might lead to opposition from others; this requires wisdom to accurately assess and navigate. In other cases, anxiety, sadness, or other painful emotions might reference a sense of loss that needs to be grieved even as positive changes are also celebrated and enjoyed. The therapy relationship can serve as a holding environment for the spiritual and existential complexities process in ways that balance dwelling and seeking to help clients interpret and manage difficult emotions and relational dilemmas that follow constructive steps of change.

The existential orientation of the RSM also highlights distinctions between surface and depth anxieties (Sandage, Rupert, et al., 2020). Surface anxieties reflect day-to-day concerns related to stressors, goals, and relationships, and improved affect regulation of surface anxieties can be a key goal for many clients. From an RSM perspective, however, the regulation of surface anxieties sometimes brings "online" deeper anxieties and questions about existential predicaments, such as meaning in life, death, loss, control, choices, identity, oppression, and many other existential themes for which there are no simple coping strategies. Indeed, establishing a safe therapeutic relationship with a client will actually create the developmental conditions to allow some clients to explore, reflection on, and construct a sense of ultimate meaning (sacred or secular) and identity for the first time in life. This is not a process that can be rushed, and we view the therapist's role as one of seeking to cultivate healthy relational dynamics for change while also trying to regain the self-differentiation to accept our human limitations in controlling the process of change.

Another core RSM clinical strategy involves assessing and intervening within the relational spirituality triangle of clients, which emerges at the intersections of clients' relational dynamics with other people, the sacred, and the therapist. This strategy involves noting both parallels and differences within the relational spirituality triangle. For example, an ambivalently attached client who consistently denies their own needs, criticizes self, and idealizes others might show this relational pattern in all three domains. With sensitive pacing, we might notice such a parallel with a client and invite their reflections less as an authoritative interpretation and more in a posture of mentalizing and dialogue. Conversely, certain differences might emerge for a client within the relational spirituality triangle; for example, they might be experiencing tremendous security in relation to the sacred and considerable angst or conflict in their primary interpersonal relationships. In some cases, this form of relational spirituality might represent the spiritual bypass described by Welwood (2000) and others as a kind of spiritual defense mechanism against emotional pain and anxiety. Or, a client's relationship with the sacred might be a relational strength within their emerging development that can help them deal with interpersonal disappointments. Again, these differing possibilities necessitate an open and differentiated curiosity among therapists to relate effectively with clients and offer what Benjamin (2018) called a third space for the coconstruction of healing experiences and understandings. Given that the intersections of R/S dynamics and suffering often evoke strong personal reactions means that clinicians will need generous self-awareness and regular relational resources for metabolizing countertransference to be able to cultivate this third space.

RECOMMENDATIONS FOR COLLABORATING WITH CLERGY AND OTHER PROVIDERS

We both were theologically trained before becoming psychologists, and this is also the case for some other staff at our clinic. As described earlier, we value attending to the particularities of clients' R/S and cultural traditions as well as other sources of meaning that shape clients' worldviews, values, and practices. In some cases, this attention to client R/S dynamics leads to seeking consent from clients to communicate with clergy or other R/S leaders involved in clients' healing process to promote collaboration, but more commonly it means inviting clients to relay the impact of those connections. Our clinic also operates a Clergy in Crisis program that offers specialized intensive outpatient services to clergy with mental health and interpersonal struggles, which can involve negotiating boundaries and communication with the referring religious bodies. Each of these situations can include dynamics of relational spirituality with opportunities to negotiate important sensitivities and the balancing of boundaries and respectful accountability.

More broadly, we also find intentional collaboration among helping professionals to be an underrated aspect of mental health treatment and, therefore, give it focus in the RSM. From a systemic perspective, we consider it often important that new therapy inputs into a client system (individual, couple, family) from different providers have some coordination for coherence. In medicine, it is common to have concerns about potential drug interaction effects. While there can be room for divergence among different treatment providers with the same client, we have also seen cases in which providers were working at cross-purposes, or the differing approaches were confusing to a client. With the RSM, we also value healthy and effective interdisciplinary collaboration among providers because this often rests on and further develops humility and other relational virtues that can ultimately benefit both clients and the providers involved.

RSM CASE APPLICATION

Using RSM in the following clinical vignette, we offer clinical considerations as we enter into alliance building, formulation, and active intervention. (Identifying features in this vignette have been changed to protect client privacy.)

Mary is a 25-year-old, single, biracial (Malaysian, Caucasian), cisgender, bisexual woman with no identified religious identity or community. She is employed as an information technology (IT) specialist at a local university and has a reputation as a quiet, reliable, effective employee. She lives with her older sister, Sophia, in a two-bedroom apartment and has a small group of friends, no one whom she considers a best friend. She has never been in a committed intimate relationship, rarely dates, and when she does, it is for no more than two or three encounters with the same person.

With regard to her family of origin, Mary is the younger of two daughters whose parents divorced when she was 9 years old. Her father, Daniel, is Malaysian and identifies as Hindu. He came to the United States for graduate school in 1990 and returned to Malaysia after the divorce in 2005. Other than providing some financial support for his daughters through high school, he has had little contact with the family since the divorce and works for a large petrochemical company in Kuala Lumpur as a chemical engineer. Mary's mother, Kelly, was born and raised in Greater Boston. She is of Irish and French ancestry and is a nonpracticing Roman Catholic. She has worked as an emergency room nurse practitioner at a large teaching hospital for the past 15 years. She raised Mary and Sophia as a single mother after the divorce.

Attachment System Dynamics

Attachment theory provides a clinical lens for appreciating the impact of clients' early development relational experiences on their adult relational functioning and the implicit and explicit expectations clients have for present and future relationships. Mary's adult relational landscape is characterized by a limited amount of interpersonal connection, intensity, or intimacy, whereas her early development is notable for her parents' divorce and a lack of contact with her father since the divorce.

A clinical assessment suggests Mary has developed an avoidant attachment style as her predominant orientation to promote autonomy and protect her from the pain and suffering of loss, shame and rage of abandonment, and despair of unmet relational longing. While an avoidant attachment style is sometimes paired with positive or even grandiose self-appraisals, in Mary's case, her struggles with self-esteem have been managed by distancing from others. The therapist working with Mary would want to attend to ways her attachment style and dynamics might emerge in the therapy relationship and in her relational dynamics with the sacred.

Diversity and Social Justice Considerations

The RSM emphasizes the importance of an intersectional perspective in assessing the multiple diversity and justice considerations in any clinical case. In this case, Mary is contending with several systemic sources of minority stress as a biracial and bisexual woman in the United States and in the male-dominated IT field. She considers herself agnostic rather than "religious," and she has said she finds it "annoying the way Christianity gets privileged" in the United States. She explains this view with examples that reference her mother's Catholic relatives' voicing homophobic sentiments and commenting negatively on her father's Hindu background.

In the beginning of treatment, Mary seemed reluctant to discuss cultural or sexual identity issues, but she gradually began to disclose concerns about racism and sexism in her workplace and neighborhood after her therapist (White, cisgender male) demonstrated openness and capacity for engaging such issues. The RSM also suggests existential and spiritual development are optimally cultivated in compassionate relational and systemic contexts that cultivate healthy selfhood, reflexivity, and mutual recognition. In contrast, Mary had experienced numerous forms of relational trauma and subjugating social contexts that required her to deny her sense of self and her deepest desires for authentic flourishing. She had managed to land a stable but unfulfilling job as a reliable, hardworking employee in a university context where she assumed she would never be recognized or promoted. Her father had experienced many conflicts and frustrations during his time working as an engineer at a university in the United States, and his general absence from her family life seemed to convey a lesson about the virtue of trying to blend in.

Differentiation System

The differentiation developmental system aims to balance capacities for thinking and feeling, intimacy and autonomy, and self-regulation and relational regulation. This initial portion of the vignette begins to shed some light on how difficult it is for Mary find balance in these ways. When she feels something, she feels too much. When she "depends" on another, she suffers a backlash of fear, anger, and regret. When she accesses relational coregulation of her distress, she cannot allow herself to trust it and is afraid she will eventually be abandoned.

Mary began individual psychotherapy 6 months before the session—that is described shortly—in the context of increasing hopelessness, intense loneliness, low energy and motivation, and intensifying suicidal thoughts and impulses. While she never made a suicide attempt, the tenuousness of her safety and the depth of her emotional suffering had been recurring themes in psychotherapy. She and her therapist made an agreement that Mary would contact the therapist during off-hours if her suicidal feelings felt unmanageable. In 9 months of treatment, she did not make use of this resource.

The night before the session, the therapist received a call at 11:45 p.m. from the on-call service stating that Mary was requesting a callback. Mary and the therapist spoke for 15 minutes, and the therapist believed Mary when she told him on the phone that she felt better and that she agreed to meet the next day. The therapist did not fall asleep until 2:30 a.m. and waited anxiously in his office the next day. Mary arrived for their session, 5 minutes late. This vignette comes from that session:

THERAPIST: How did the rest of the night go last night?

MARY: Okay. I watched a little TV and then got to sleep pretty quickly.

THERAPIST: Good [*takes a long pause while Mary looks down silently*]. You decided to call when you were in trouble last night.

MARY: I didn't want to.

THERAPIST: You didn't. Can I ask why?

MARY: I don't want to start depending on anyone.

THERAPIST: Did calling me last night feel like you were depending on me?

MARY: [*Is silent*]

THERAPIST: What do you risk in reaching out when you're hurting like that?

MARY: The risk is that eventually there will come a time when you ask, when you really need help, and there will be no one there.

THERAPIST: Why did you risk it last night?

MARY: It was probably a mistake.

THERAPIST: Oh.

MARY: I did what I was supposed to, not what I wanted.

THERAPIST: You wanted to do something else?

MARY: [*Begins to cry*] I don't know.

THERAPIST: What is it?

MARY: [*Cries*] I don't want to depend on you, or anybody. I can't. I make my life work by taking care of myself. By not counting on anything from anyone. Not at work. Not with my sister. Not with my friends.

THERAPIST: Not from me.

Mary's struggle to balance intimacy with autonomy reflects long-standing ways in which Mary has been attempting to navigate the tenuous and conflictual dynamics within her family of origin. It was here where she learned the "skills" of staying small, quiet, plain, efficient, and self-sufficient as protections against family and social systems that were not attuned to her inner life, her hopes and fears, her desires and creativity. She appears to be trapped within an underdifferentiated survival response to emotional and relational deprivation that is leading her to existential despair about her life.

And yet, we believe it is important to return to the therapist's simple question: "Why did you risk it last night?" While Mary initially pushes back—"It was probably a mistake"—her phone call to the therapist represents a different, perhaps even exploratory, venture into a new, more differentiated way of relating. We might ask ourselves whether there is some initial, delicate movement here between Mary and her therapist that is in the service of Mary's rebalancing her sense of self and other, particularly around issues of closeness, trust, and vulnerability.

SERT Dynamics

Mary and her therapist have arrived at a place in their work that includes powerful existential themes: anxiety about life and death, despair and hope, self-sufficiency and interdependence, trust and abandonment. While there was no explicitly religious or spiritual language in their exchange, the therapist is still listening for and responding to these deep, human, relational movements in Mary and in the therapy related to her sense of self-worth and need for help.

Over time, we have found these kinds of themes often circle around personal beliefs about what is ultimately important to a client and how they relate to their deepest values and desires (i.e., relational spirituality). In addition, we believe it is incumbent on the therapist to be aware of and accountable for one's own SERT history, practices, beliefs, and biases. These points of self-awareness are needed among therapists for three key reasons: (a) to protect the client from value or SERT imposition; (b) as sources of resilience, meaning, and grounding for the therapist; and (c) to provide clarity for considering potential SERT resources for the therapy, when clinically appropriate. We believe that psychotherapeutic engagement with trauma and deep suffering, such as Mary's, requires therapists who are themselves resilient and grounded, who belong to communities and networks of other healing professionals who can support healthy forms of dwelling and seeking, and who have access to SERT resources and practices that actively restore and heal them as persons and as clinicians.

The session continues:

MARY: No. And when I get so depressed and feel so alone....

THERAPIST: Like last night?

MARY: Yes. I feel like it's up to me to solve the problem.

THERAPIST: The problem?

MARY: Yes. [*Takes a long pause*] I didn't like when you talked about "parts" of me last time.

THERAPIST: You didn't?

MARY: No. I'm sick and tired of having parts—part this, part that. Why can't I just be one thing. Things would be better if I was just one thing. I would know who I'm supposed to be, and I could just take care of things myself. No one is ever going to want to be close to me, anyway. I'm a mess.

THERAPIST: So, if you could just get rid of the messy parts, you think that would help . . . that it would make you more lovable?

MARY: That sounds so pathetic.

THERAPIST: Sorry. Let me see if I can say it another way. There is a part of you that wishes it could make life work without any help from anyone—strong, smart, clear, decisive, independent? [*Mary nods.*] But you also wish for connection, to be loved for who you are? [*Mary stares.*] And it's like you're saying, "If I can just get rid of these unlovable, messy parts, maybe then I'll have a chance."

MARY: I hadn't really thought of it that way. Maybe.

Intersubjectivity System

The intersubjectivity system is connected with relational processes of mutuality and power that are dynamically in motion between persons as they interact with one another, including between client and therapist. These processes carry the potential for powerful, contrasting experiences of objectification and mutual recognition, relational rupture and repair, clarity and misunderstanding, and enactments that can evoke dissociative dynamics and self-experiences in the relating persons.

In the earlier vignette, in an attempt to more fully "see" Mary and to have Mary feel like she "is seen," the therapist uses language suggesting Mary's experiences, wishes, and needs for connection are not singular—that different "parts" of her may think, feel and desire different things at different times, and maybe even at the same time. Mary challenges the therapist's "parts" language, culminating in her bitterly stating, "That sounds so pathetic." The therapist must now decide how to respond and begins with an apology, something Shaw (2008) referred to as a "shame diminishing, 'subjectifying' [process]" (p. 56). In the collision between Mary's shamed, defensive subjectivity and the therapist's interpretive subjectivity, a relational rupture occurs that requires acknowledgment and repair. The therapist then tentatively moves forward into continued exploration with Mary. This kind of close attention to process, power, enactment, rupture, and repair is a crucial aspect of how RSM can be used in treating the deep relational suffering and trauma. The session continues:

THERAPIST: Okay. Well, I'd like to share something pretty directly with you.

MARY: That makes me nervous [*pauses*]. But, go ahead.

THERAPIST: I'm not very high on the idea of trying to do a "part-ectomy" in order to solve this dilemma. I appreciate how awful it feels when you're sure you are going to be rejected and that it will be because there is something about you that is unacceptable, unlovable. But there is something about your proposed solution that feels too extreme. Killing off the messy parts of yourself risks inflicting so much damage. I think you might have other options, but it will mean some work.

MARY: Like what?

THERAPIST: Maybe we can help you develop a more compassionate relationship with the messy parts of yourself, the ones that feel unlovable.

MARY: That sounds too hard. I don't know if I have the energy or the motivation to do more.

THERAPIST: Can I make a provisional recommendation?

MARY: Provisional?

THERAPIST: Yes. We agree together to try it, to work together to appreciate both your strength and your vulnerability. I think we can learn more about why the messy parts feel so unlovable—and how you've had to survive painful times in your life when you really were unseen and left alone. We can begin to figure out where there are ways to make your life worth living.

MARY: I'm not sure I believe that's possible.

THERAPIST: I'm not sure either. But I believe that your strength will work in your favor. The strong and messy parts may even decide to join forces at some point. I'm hopeful. And if you want to take a chance on this, I'm in it with you.

MARY: [*Takes deep breath*] I don't know.

THERAPIST: Why don't we both take the time between our sessions to think about it, and we can talk some more when we're back together.

MARY: Okay.

Dialectical Balancing

The RSM approach to psychotherapy balances a number of dialectical tensions: dwelling and seeking, stability and change, support and challenge, containment and intensity (crucible dynamics), security and exploration. We believe these dialectical tensions are deeply relational, existential, and spiritual. When these tensions are held in careful and flexible relational balance, the process can provide necessary developmental conditions and nutrients for healing and growth. In the preceding vignette, the therapist attempts to invite Mary into a relational process, a conversation, and a space that will provide her with opportunities to become increasingly open to life and love. We consider this to be sacred work—and also difficult work—that requires courage on the part of clients and therapists alike.

Over the ensuing 12 months in treatment, Mary was able, at times haltingly, to accept the invitation to tolerate this process of dialectical balancing, of developing a capacity for compassion and hospitality toward parts of herself that she experienced as messy and unlovable. As we suggested, this kind of therapeutic work to transform internalized shame and the effects of relational trauma is anxiety provoking and necessitates the relational regulation of affect to aid clients developing capacities for self-regulation. Much of this work was focused on Mary's identifying and grieving her early experiences of loss, misattunement, and emotional deprivation in her family of origin. After 18 months, Mary's symptoms of depression and anxiety were significantly reduced, and she was experiencing more secure attachment dynamics with herself and others.

This opened space over the following year for another vital aspect of the work involving a complicated process of differentiating from implicit and explicit racist, homophobic, and antiaffirming attitudes and experiences she encountered, particularly through the religious lens of her extended family. The initial part of this journey looked more like a wholesale rejection of religion and spirituality by Mary. However, over time and with the attuned accompaniment of her therapist, Mary was able to reclaim some of the comforting and life-giving teachings, embodied experiences, and rituals of both Hinduism (e.g., meditative yoga practice, occasionally attendance at sacred festivals) and Catholicism (e.g., social justice for the oppressed, community).

In doing so, she began to see within and around herself possibilities for connection, goodness, and flourishing, which involved a more accepting and secure way of relating with herself, her spiritual life, her family, and her friends through the corrective relational experience with her therapist.

RESEARCH FINDINGS AND SUPPORT

The RSM is influenced by interdisciplinary research across numerous areas, including psychotherapy, psychology of religion, couple and family systems, relational and existential branches of philosophy and theology, positive psychology, cultural anthropology, and human development, among others (Sandage, Rupert, et al., 2020). Within psychotherapy research, our current program of clinical research fits within the practice-based research movement that has influenced many contributions in this handbook with the goal of integrating naturalistic research on spirituality into mental health treatment contexts (Currier et al., 2021; Richards et al., 2015).

In addition to the aforementioned research findings, practice-based clinical research in our treatment context has generated support for several key sets of RSM ideas. First, we have found empirical support for a parallel growth model based on relational psychotherapy at our clinic showing that client improvements in well-being tend to follow from improved capacities for relational functioning, and these effects are mediated by improved affect regulation (Jankowski et al., 2019).

Second, we found cross-sectional evidence that clients' spiritual well-being positively predicted their psychosocial functioning over and above the effects from their mental health symptoms, and clients' spiritual struggles negatively predicted the same (Sandage, Jankowski, et al., 2020). We are currently testing these effects over the course of treatment, but this offered some preliminary incremental validity evidence for the clinical relevance of key RSM constructs within a pluralistic treatment context.

Third, we are also investigating character strengths and relational and virtues in psychotherapy. For example, we found humility moderated the relationship between religious commitment and psychosocial functioning and well-being among clients such that a moderate or higher level of humility was necessary for a positive relationship between religion and these outcomes (Paine et al., 2018). This study suggested it might be difficult for religiously committed clients low in humility (and high in narcissism) to find ways to effectively integrate their relational spirituality with healthy functioning. In addition, clients with this profile might require relationally sensitive and spiritually integrated intervention strategies aimed at increasing capacities for humility in the domains of accurate self-awareness and open receptivity to feedback from others.

We have also found preliminary evidence for our virtue ethics model (Jankowski et al., 2020) showing that increased humility among clients during treatment predicted improvements in both well-being and symptoms with changes mediated by improved affect regulation (Jankowski et al., 2021). This set of findings invites many more research questions to explore but suggests the need to further understand clinical connections among relational spirituality, virtue, affect regulation, and positive mental health.

REFERENCES

The Albert & Jessie Danielsen Institute. (n.d.). *Home* [Facebook page]. Retrieved March 8, 2022, from https://www.facebook.com/DanielsenInstitute/

Aponte, H. J., & Kissil, K. (Eds.). (2016). *The person of the therapist training model: Mastering the use of self*. Routledge. https://doi.org/10.4324/9781315719030

Beck, R., & Jessup, R. K. (2004). The multidimensional nature of quest motivation. *Journal of Psychology and Theology*, 32(4), 283–294. https://doi.org/10.1177/009164710403200401

Benjamin, J. (2018). *Beyond doer and done to: Recognition theory, intersubjectivity, and the Third*. Routledge.

Boettscher, H. T., Sandage, S. J., Latin, H. M., & Barlow, D. H. (2019). Transdiagnostic treatment for enhancing positive affect and well-being. In J. Gruber (Ed.), *Positive emotion and psychopathology* (pp. 525–538). Oxford University Press.

Bordin, E. S. (1983). A working alliance based model of supervision. *The Counseling Psychologist*, 11(1), 35–42. https://doi.org/10.1177/0011000083111007

Captari, L. E., Hook, J. N., Hoyt, W., Davis, D. E., McElroy-Heltzel, S. E., & Worthington, E. L., Jr. (2018). Integrating clients' religion and spirituality within psychotherapy: A comprehensive meta-analysis. *Journal of Clinical Psychology*, 74(11), 1938–1951. https://doi.org/10.1002/jclp.22681

Comas-Díaz, L. (2006). Cultural variation in the therapeutic relationship. In C. D. Goodheart, A. E. Kazdin, & R. J. Sternberg (Eds.), *Evidence-based psychotherapy: Where practice and research meet* (pp. 81–105). American Psychological Association. https://doi.org/10.1037/11423-004

Comas-Díaz, L., & Torres Rivera, E. (Eds.). (2020). *Liberation psychology: Theory, method, practice, and social justice*. American Psychological Association. https://doi.org/10.1037/0000198-000

Correa, J. K., & Sandage, S. J. (2018). Relational spirituality as scaffolding for cognitive-behavioral therapy: A case study of spirituality in clinical practice. *Spirituality in Clinical Practice*, 5(1), 54–63. https://doi.org/10.1037/scp0000155

Crabtree, S. A., Bell, C. A., Rupert, D. A., Sandage, S. J., Devor, N. G., & Stavros, G. (2020). Humility, differentiation of self, and clinical training in spiritual and religious competence. *Journal of Spirituality in Mental Health*. Advance online publication. https://doi.org/10.1080/19349637.2020.1737627

Currier, J. M., McDermott, R. C., Stevens, L. T., Isaak, S. L., Davis, E. B., Hollingsworth, W. L., Archer, G. D., & Stefurak, T. (2021). A practice-based evidence investigation of God representations in spiritually integrated psychotherapies. *Journal of Clinical Psychology*, 77(4), 1018–1033. https://doi.org/10.1002/jclp.23075

Davis, D. E., DeBlaere, C., Owen, J., Hook, J. N., Rivera, D. P., Choe, E., Van Tongeren, D. R., Worthington, E. L., Jr., & Placeres, V. (2018). The multicultural orientation framework: A narrative review. *Psychotherapy*, 55(1), 89–100. https://doi.org/10.1037/pst0000160

Drake, J. R., Murdock, N. L., Marszalek, J. M., & Barber, C. E. (2015). Differentiation of Self Inventory–Short Form: Development and preliminary validation. *Contemporary Family Therapy*, 37(2), 101–112. https://doi.org/10.1007/s10591-015-9329-7

Eubanks, C. F., Lubitz, J., Muran, J. C., & Safran, J. D. (2019). Rupture Resolution Rating System (3RS): Development and validation. *Psychotherapy Research*, 29(3), 306–319. https://doi.org/10.1080/10503307.2018.1552034

Eubanks, C. F., Muran, J. C., & Safran, J. D. (2018). Alliance rupture repair: A meta-analysis. *Psychotherapy*, 55(4), 508–519. https://doi.org/10.1037/pst0000185.supp

Exline, J. J., Pargament, K. I., Grubbs, J. B., & Yali, A. M. (2014). The Religious and Spiritual Struggles Scale: Development and initial validation. *Psychology of Religion and Spirituality*, 6(3), 208–222. https://doi.org/10.1037/a0036465

Exline, J. J., Pargament, K. I., Wilt, J. A., Grubbs, J. G., & Yali, A. M. (in press). The RSS-14: Development and preliminary validation of a 14-item form of the Religious and Spiritual Struggles Scale. *Psychology of Religion and Spirituality*.

Gomez, R., & Fisher, J. W. (2003). Domains of spiritual well-being and development and validation of the Spiritual Well-Being Questionnaire. *Personality and Individual Differences*, 35(8), 1975–1991. https://doi.org/10.1016/S0191-8869(03)00045-X

Granqvist, P. (2020). *Attachment in religion and spirituality: A wider view*. Guilford Press.

Hammer, M. R., Bennett, M. J., & Wiseman, R. (2003). Measuring intercultural sensitivity: The Intercultural Development Inventory. *International Journal of Intercultural Relations*, 27(4), 421–443. https://doi.org/10.1016/S0147-1767(03)00032-4

Harris, K. A., Randolph, B. E., & Gordon, T. D. (2016). What do clients want? Assessing spiritual needs in counseling: A literature review. *Spirituality in Clinical Practice*, 3(4), 250–275. https://doi.org/10.1037/scp0000108

Horvath, A. O. (2018). Research on the alliance: Knowledge in search of a theory. *Psychotherapy Research*, 28(4), 499–516. https://doi.org/10.1080/10503307.2017.1373204

Jankowski, P. J., Captari, L. E., & Sandage, S. J. (2021). Exploring virtue ethics in psychodynamic psychotherapy: Latent changes in humility, affect regulation, symptoms, and well-being. *Counselling & Psychotherapy Research*, 21(4), 983–991. https://doi.org/10.1002/capr.12389

Jankowski, P. J., Sandage, S. J., Bell, C. A., Davis, D. E., Porter, E., Jessen, M., Motzny, C. L., Ross, K. V., & Owen, J. (2020). Virtue, flourishing, and positive psychology in psychotherapy: An overview and research prospectus. *Psychotherapy*, 57(3), 291–309. https://doi.org/10.1037/pst0000285

Jankowski, P. J., Sandage, S. J., Bell, C. A., Rupert, D., Bronstein, M., & Stavros, G. S. (2019). Latent trajectories of change for clients at a psychodynamic training clinic. *Journal of Clinical Psychology*, 75(7), 1147–1168. https://doi.org/10.1002/jclp.22769

Kehoe, L. E., Hassen, S. C., & Sandage, S. J. (2016). Relational ecologies of psychotherapy: Administrative attachment in liminal office space. *Psychodynamic Practice*, 22(1), 6–21. https://doi.org/10.1080/14753634.2015.1124596

Maddock, J. W., & Larson, N. R. (2004). The ecological approach to incestuous families. In D. R. Catherall (Ed.), *Handbook of stress, trauma, and the family* (pp. 367–392). Brunner-Routledge.

Menakem, R. (2016). *My grandmother's hands: Racialized trauma and the pathway to mending our hearts and bodies*. Central Recovery Press.

Miller-Bottome, M., Talia, A., Eubanks, C. F., Safran, J. D., & Muran, J. C. (2019). Secure in-session attachment predicts rupture resolution: Negotiating a secure base. *Psychoanalytic Psychology*, 36(2), 132–138. https://doi.org/10.1037/pap0000232

Moon, S. H., & Sandage, S. J. (2019). Cultural humility for Persons of Color: Critique of current theory and practice. *Journal of Psychology and Theology*, 47(2), 76–86. https://doi.org/10.1177/0091647119842407

Owen, J., Tao, K. W., Drinane, J. M., Hook, J., Davis, D. E., & Kune, N. F. (2016). Client perceptions of therapists' multicultural orientation: Cultural (missed) opportunities and cultural humility. *Professional Psychology, Research and Practice*, 47(1), 30–37. https://doi.org/10.1037/pro0000046

Paine, D. R., Sandage, S. J., Ruffing, E. G., & Hill, P. C. (2018). Religious and spiritual salience, well-being, and psychosocial functioning among psychotherapy clients: Moderator effects for humility. *Journal of Religion and Health*, 57, 2398–2415. https://doi.org/10.1007/s10943-018-0612-4

Pargament, K. I. (2011). *Spiritually integrated psychotherapy: Understanding and addressing the sacred*. Guilford Press.

Richards, P. S., Sanders, P. W., Lea, T., McBride, J. A., & Allen, G. E. K. (2015). Bringing spiritually oriented psychotherapies into the health care mainstream: A call for worldwide collaboration. *Spirituality in Clinical Practice, 2*(3), 169–179. https://doi.org/10.1037/scp0000082

Rupert, D., Moon, S. H., & Sandage, S. J. (2019). Clinical training groups for spirituality and religion in psychotherapy. *Journal of Spirituality in Mental Health, 21*(3), 163–177. https://doi.org/10.1080/19349637.2018.1465879

Safran, J. D. (2000). *Negotiating the therapeutic alliance: A relational treatment guide*. Guilford Press.

Sandage, S. J. (2022). Religious differences in spiritually integrated couple therapy. In S. J. Sandage & B. D. Strawn (Eds.), *Spiritual diversity and psychotherapy: Engaging the sacred in clinical practice* (pp. 271–296). American Psychological Association.

Sandage, S. J., Bell, C. A., Moon, S. H., & Ruffing, E. G. (2019). Religious and spiritual problems in couples. In L. Sperry, K. Helm, & J. Carlson (Eds.), *The disordered couple* (2nd ed., pp. 305–321). Routledge. https://doi.org/10.4324/9781351264044-19

Sandage, S. J., Jankowski, P. J., Paine, D. R., Exline, J. J., Ruffing, E. G., Rupert, D., Stavros, G. S., & Bronstein, M. (2020). Testing a relational spirituality model of psychotherapy clients' preferences and functioning. *Journal of Spirituality in Mental Health*. Advance online publication. https://doi.org/10.1080/19349637.2020.1791781

Sandage, S. J., & Jensen, M. L. (2013). Relational spiritual formation: Reflective practice and research on spiritual formation in a seminary context. *Reflective Practice: Formation and Supervision in Ministry, 33*, 95–109.

Sandage, S. J., Moon, S. H., Glenn, E. S., Paine, D. R., Kehoe, L. E., Rupert, D., Bronstein, M., & Hassen, S. C. (2017). Relational dynamics between psychotherapy clients and clinic administrative staff: A pilot study. *Psychodynamic Practice, 23*(3), 249–268. https://doi.org/10.1080/14753634.2017.1335226

Sandage, S. J., Rupert, D., Stavros, G. S., & Devor, N. G. (2020). *Relational spirituality in psychotherapy: Healing suffering and promoting growth*. American Psychological Association. https://doi.org/10.1037/0000174-000

Sandage, S. J., & Strawn, B. D. (Eds.). (2022). *Spiritual diversity and psychotherapy: Engaging the sacred in clinical practice*. American Psychological Association.

Shaw, D. (2008). Enter ghosts: The loss of intersubjectivity in clinical work with adult children of pathological narcissists. *Psychoanalytic Dialogues, 20*(1), 46–59. https://doi.org/10.1080/10481880903559120

Shults, F. L., & Sandage, S. J. (2006). *Transforming spirituality: Integrating theology and psychology*. Baker Academic.

Stavros, G. S., & Sandage, S. J. (Eds.). (2014). *The skillful soul of the psychotherapist: The link between spirituality and clinical excellence*. Rowman & Littlefield.

Tan, S.-Y. (1996). Religion in clinical practice: Implicit and explicit integration. In E. P. Shafranske (Ed.), *Religion and the clinical practice of psychology* (pp. 365–387). American Psychological Association. https://doi.org/10.1037/10199-013

Vieten, C., & Scammell, S. (2015). *Spiritual & religious competencies in clinical practice: Guidelines for psychotherapists & mental health professionals*. New Harbinger Publications.

Wallin, D. J. (2007). *Attachment in psychotherapy*. Guilford Press.

Wei, M., Russell, D. W., Mallinckrodt, B., & Vogel, D. L. (2007). The Experiences in Close Relationship Scale (ECR)–Short Form: Reliability, validity, and factor structure. *Journal of Personality Assessment, 88*(2), 187–204. https://doi.org/10.1080/00223890701268041

Welwood, J. (2000). *Toward a psychology of awakening: Buddhism, psychotherapy, and the path of personal and spiritual transformation*. Shambhala Publications.

Worthington, E. L., Jr., & Sandage, S. J. (2016). *Forgiveness and spirituality in psychotherapy: A relational approach*. American Psychological Association. https://doi.org/10.1037/14712-000

5

Postsecular, Spiritually Integrated Gestalt Therapy

Philip Brownell and Jelena Zeleskov Doric

Gestalt therapy was developed by Frederick ("Fritz") and Laura Perls with the help of numerous others associated with the New York Institute for Gestalt Therapy, including Isadore From, and then other institutes that developed among that first generation of gestalt therapists (Bowman & Brownell, 2015; Bowman & Nevis, 2005; Brownell, 2010). In its formation, gestalt therapy was one of the first instances of a theoretical integration in psychotherapy (Brownell, 2013). That is partially what makes it both assimilative and challenging. In this chapter, we assume the reader has a working knowledge of contemporary gestalt therapy, which would make understanding the concepts presented here more possible. For the reader unfamiliar with contemporary gestalt therapy, we recommend Bar-Yoseph Levine (2012), Francesetti et al. (2014), Brownell (2019a), and the various resources listed in the References section at the end of this chapter as supportive scaffolding.

Here is also the place to say something about the ground of an integration of spirituality with gestalt therapy. Gestalt therapy is not necessarily a concrete, step-by-step process. It requires emotional and spiritual maturity as well as advanced levels of therapeutic experience and skill (P. Scott Richards, personal communication, November 10, 2021). For those interested in such an integration, however, we recommend Brownell (2020) in reference to Christianity (a theocentric perspective) or Gold and Zahm (2018) in reference to Buddhism (a nontheocentric perspective).

Many people point to an early affinity for Eastern spiritual thought in the thinking of some founders (Crocker & Philippson, 2005; Wolfert, 2015). That

---

https://doi.org/10.1037/0000338-005
Handbook of Spiritually Integrated Psychotherapies, P. S. Richards, G. E. K. Allen, and D. K. Judd (Editors)
Copyright © 2023 by the American Psychological Association. All rights reserved.

is debated. Laura Perls was anecdotally also reported to have studied with Christian theologian Paul Tillich. Regardless of the veracity of those stories, the founders themselves made an early choice against the atheistic form of existentialism in Sartre in favor of the more theologically friendly version in Kierkegaard. Subsequently, many individual gestalt therapists have used Buddhist thinking and other spiritual and religious practices with gestalt therapy. This chapter describes the normal practice of contemporary gestalt therapy, now carefully developed from its nascent theoretical structures, as a postsecular perspective (described in the next section) still in keeping with its revolutionary nature.

By popular consent, gestalt therapy is a humanistic, experiential approach. Gestalt therapists know the admonition attributed to Fritz Perls to "lose your mind and come to your senses." It was always an awareness of subjective experience informed by what one could hear, taste, smell, and see: sensory experience. Gestalt therapists value such experience, but that kind of experience cannot be the starting point because experience is not pure:

> If anything extraordinary seems to have happened, we can always say that we have been the victims of an illusion. If we hold a philosophy which excludes the supernatural, this is what we always shall say. What we learn from experience depends on the kind of philosophy we bring to experience. It is therefore useless to appeal to experience before we have settled, as well as we can, the philosophical question. (Lewis, 1947/2002, p. 303)

It is the philosophical that will tell a person to pay attention to what can be observed in the physical world or to measure those observations. It is the philosophical that advocates attention to the quantification of objective observations as correlates to truth. It is the philosophical that tells a person there has to be more than numbers when it comes to life—to pay attention to subjective experience. It is the philosophical that separates the supernatural from the natural. It is the philosophical that limits concern to an immanent frame, a this-world-only perspective, rejecting the possibility that something meaningful transcends it. Thus, when the Vienna Circle attempted to wed philosophy to science, their philosophical dedication to empiricism compelled them to eliminate all traces of the metaphysical (Edmonds, 2020). Some forms of psychology still approach the profession accordingly (Slife et al., 2019).

Today, tension stretches across current gestalt therapy between modernism and postmodernism, between the philosophies of positivism and postpositivism, the methodologies of quantitative and qualitative, the challenges of objectivity and subjectivity, ontology and epistemology, the nomothetic and the idiographic, and all the various ways we think and act, moving further and further from the Enlightenment. The tensions are felt in gestalt therapy's evolving research movement, in the questions of how metaphysics now fits in its conversations, and just how much spirituality or religion ought to be considered integral to the practice of gestalt therapy. It is related to the tension that is now being felt, predominantly in Western societies but also elsewhere, between the secular and the postsecular, and it is pushed by the publishing of such books as *Christianity and Gestalt Therapy* (Brownell, 2020) or *Buddhist*

Psychology & Gestalt Therapy Integrated (Gold & Zahm, 2018) and *Consenting to Grace: An Introduction to Gestalt Pastoral Care* (Norberg, 2005).

Spiritually integrated psychotherapy, in general, is a postsecular concept. Spiritually integrated gestalt therapy resides within that larger consideration.

THE POSTSECULAR: A GROUNDING CONSIDERATION

What is the *postsecular*? It is the realization that Enlightenment science, modernism, and secularism did not work the way people thought they would. It is the recalibration of some of their basic assumptions.

The Enlightenment emphasized the sovereignty of reason and the evidence of the senses (mostly against the authority of the church and so above all else). It advocated liberty, progress, toleration, fraternity, constitutional government, and the separation of church and state. The secular hypothesis asserted that religion would wane and gradually disappear, but more importantly, it included "the secularization of Western *culture*" and "the development of modern societies from the viewpoint of rationalization" (Habermas, 1998, p. 2).

In contrast, contemporary gestalt therapy in a postsecular perspective widens gestalt therapy to include what cannot be seen directly and cannot be held in one's hand and measured physically but can be experienced outside of sensory data or objective studies of material reality. Further, it does so without having to add to gestalt therapy theory. It includes what has effect but cannot be reduced. It includes spirituality and religion not only as abstract constructs or social considerations but also as reflective of human experience that cannot be appreciated with a secular commitment that functions entirely within an immanent frame. Thus, it challenges the secular and materialistic assumptions of a clinical theory that developed as a revision of Freud, as revolutionary thought (Kuhn, 1962/2012), but that was caught between modernism and postmodernism, between its own version of a naturalistic attitude (Husserl, 1970) and a phenomenology set free to investigate spiritual experience (Buber, 1952; Henry, 2003; Horner, 2000; Levinas, 1998; Rivera, 2015).

CONTEMPORARY GESTALT THERAPY THEORY

Brownell and Roubal (2019) pointed to an outline of contemporary gestalt therapy in a descriptive treatment manual. That manual described gestalt therapy's large tenets, such as phenomenology, relationality, a field perspective, and an experimental approach. That manual is a useful tool for conducting not only practice but also the evaluation of practice. As Roubal (2019) stated,

> I see psychotherapy as a mixture of art, craft, and science. Manuals can cultivate the craft aspect of our work, so they can serve us as a way of supporting the artistic creativity on one side, and also, through research, as a way of developing the scientific aspect of Gestalt therapy on the other side. (p. 221)

As such, it is also a unified theory leading to a unified practice and has been operationalized in a gestalt therapy validity scale (Fogarty et al., 2019). We briefly describe the large categories and then proceed to show how they can be understood from a postsecular, spiritually integrated perspective. Then we briefly indicate what types of clients might benefit from this approach and point to research that might support it.

A Hermeneutic Phenomenology

Dan Bloom (2019) stated that gestalt therapists "pay attention to what develops and appears from within the therapy process, and indeed our attention is itself intrinsic in the process itself" (p. 183). He claimed that gestalt therapy is a form of clinical phenomenology that investigates the life world of the client, which is a universal "scene" of one's life; a world of common experience; a "world apperceived, [perceived and assimilated] apprehended, and interpreted in a specific way" (Gurwitsch, 1970, p. 52).

That is what makes gestalt therapy also a hermeneutic approach. It is not just concerned with raw experience. It is concerned with the significance in what people experience, including the enduring life themes that steer a course through living.

Hermeneutics is a class of principles for interpretation, of meaning making, and in therapy, one could say it helps formulate the meaning-for-other and the meaning-for-self (Brownell, 2010). Two hermeneutic principles that are particularly important in gestalt therapy are the hermeneutic circle and the fusion of horizons.

Hermeneutic Circle

The concept of a circle can be understood as the shifts that take place in comprehending an appearing (a phenomenon) as either a whole or as a grouping of parts. As one circumnavigates such a circle, the significance—the meaning—shifts. Von Zweck et al. (2008) described that as follows:

> When the phenomenon is viewed as a whole, the integration of individual parts to create and define the entire experience is recognized. Conversely, when the phenomenon is considered in terms of individual parts, the importance of the whole in contextualizing or illuminating each piece is recognized. (p. 119)

Thus, the *hermeneutic circle* can also be understood as a gestalt exercise in foreground–background figure formation. When attempting to consider a complex situation, the kind often encountered in therapy, both therapist and client will experience shifts as they move around the circle. Some of the considerations they will typically encounter will be the level of complexity with which people see their worlds, the ground on which each person stands, and the strength of the sense of self by which one supports the process of contacting (Brownell, 2018). Sometimes they will seem like separate parts, and sometimes they will only be meaningful as elements of a larger situation.

Fusion of Horizons

The horizon in phenomenology is everything that can be imagined, all that is possible for and to a person in their life world. "If something is not in a person's horizon, it never comes to mind. The horizon is the extent of the life world" (Brownell, 2019b, p. 178) When a person's horizon is closed to various subjects—impoverished—not much is believed to be possible, and one's possibilities seem slim. It's as if there is an unfolding scroll with everything possible listed on it, and if something is not there, the person simply never thinks of it. A person in such a condition also experiences a dearth of creativity. On the flip side, a person whose horizon is open and expansive enjoys vivid, spontaneous, and wide-ranging creativity; the horizon is constantly expanding; and that person's possibilities seem almost limitless (Brownell, 2012).

Thus, the *fusion of horizons* is like the collision of life worlds. "To a gestalt therapist versed in field theory, it is the way contact between the person and whatever is considered to be 'other' generates a field of experience—a phenomenal field" (Brownell, 2012, p. 113). It is a field not only of raw experience but also of intentionality, of meaning, in which the fusion in question is not the loss of self through confluence but of enrichment and expansion through contacting.

A Relational Process

Lynne Jacobs asserted that people are always emergent from a context, always related to the fabric of such contexts, having been born into a world always already there. "We have no experience that is prior to relatedness. . . . We are always reacting and responding to each other. This is inescapable, unavoidable. Every act we initiate is always also a response or reaction to our situation" (Jacobs, 2019, pp. 205–206). This addresses a fundamental relatedness that underlies the typical components of a clinical relationship (i.e., presence, inclusion, and commitment to dialogue). This basic orientation is a starting point for understanding the dynamics of contacting in a therapeutic process.

We are always *of the situation*, but when we act, we extend ourselves into that situation as visitor in the worlds of others. Although embodied, we are not in the prison of our physicality, minds encased in the bones of our skulls or selves limited to the sinews and skin that cover us. We have influence with other people. We manifest a *spirituality*, understood as the oscillating set of values, emotions, convictions, desires, determinations, and beliefs that inhabit our internal dialogues (Brownell, 2015):

> Spirit is the immaterial aspect of a whole person, which is the capacity to contemplate, be fascinated by, engage with, tremble before yet yearn to be with that which significantly transcends the self. . . . Spirit is the medium for contact with God. In nontheistic religious systems, spirit or spirituality is a capacity to appreciate beauty or mystery. (Brownell, 2015, p. 38)

This is the realm of the lived body, the immaterial landscape of one's experience. It is the residence of the Ich, the I, the εγω (ego), the owner and organizer of one's life. It is also extended into the world in such a way as to encounter others at the primordial level of existence (Brownell, 2020). Our minds, if you would, are situated in the world, and our mental processes extend into that world, making mental activities at once aspects of the organism and the environment. That is what makes human beings organism–environment by nature. We are *of the situation* by virtue of transcending the limits of our corporeality.

An example of such extended self is the game of Scrabble in which the moving around of the tiles enables a player to think of new words (Clark & Chalmers, 1998). The player does not simply think of new words and then move the tiles. It is the moving of the tiles that suggests to the person various possibilities. The person plays a better game of Scrabble by virtue of using the movement of tiles to think. Another example is the placement of fingers on the keyboard of this computer, which ignites creativity of thought. I (Brownell) think through my fingers touching the keyboard. I experience myself in a new way as a function of such extension; in such moments, I manifest a keyboarding-self.

In the same way, we are fundamentally extended in our life worlds through relationship with others. We live through them, not enmeshed or confluent but extended. Thus, our clinical dialogues are not limited to two separate bodies—the meeting and exchanging of body heat and words; they are the revealing of ourselves in and through engagement in the affectively laden spaces in which such contacting occurs.

A Field Perspective

Theories about the field and theories *of* field abound in gestalt therapy and outside of it in other clinical perspectives. The *field* has been defined as all things having effect, reflecting the works of Kurt Lewin and Kurt Goldstein, and it has been refined in gestalt therapy literature for several decades, going back to Wheeler's (1991) work titled *Gestalt Reconsidered*. Parlett and Lee (2005) described the field as "the entire situation of the therapist, the client, and all that goes on between them. . . . When we talk of the 'atmosphere changing,' we are talking about the field" (p. 43).

Gianni Francesetti (2019) described two aspects of current field theory in gestalt therapy when he wrote about phenomenal and phenomenological fields:

> *Wonder about the world* is the best definition of the phenomenological attitude. The *phenomenal* field is suffered, in the sense that it seizes us and we are *subject-to* what emerges. It is *pathos* (i.e., suffered) and hence it is the actualisation of what comes into play. The *phenomenological* field is the result of a shift, implying the movement from being *subject-to* to being *subject-of*. It is an enhancement of freedom. It is not a meta-position as it is not above or outside the phenomenal field, but at the same time it is a position from which we can take notice, with curiosity and wonder, of what is happening to us, between us and around us. (p. 277)

The difference between phenomenal and phenomenological fields can also be likened to the difference between sensing sensation versus making sense of sensation. But, of course, neither takes place in a vacuum. They occur in the actual context of life ongoing and unfolding. So, there is also an *ontical field*: It is the actual context, the world in which we live, and it does what it does regardless of what we think about it.

Here, Francesetti offered observations about the phenomenal field that introduced a realm that is quite relevant to the postsecular perspective. He stated that the phenomenal field is not an object, such as a chair, but that it also cannot be reduced to "mere subjective, internal experience" (Francesetti, 2019, p. 273). It is a halfway or quasithing like an atmosphere. "Thus, we find ourselves dealing with a region of existence that defies a Cartesian and positivistic description of the world based on its reduction to subjects and objects. . . ." (p. 273).

Although Francesetti (2019) made a case for the phenomenal field in a clinical context being cocreated, not all quasithings are that way. Some, like atmospheres, are not cocreated; they are caught. And they are aspects of the ontical field encountered by both therapist and client and so not "we" experiences as such. There is not space to explain this fully here as was done in a previous place (Brownell, 2020). It is sufficient to say that atmospheres are basic to phenomenal fields, and both are sensed at the level of the lived body, where the sense of being a living organism in a context of this world transcends the binary of subject and object. The lived body is itself a quasithing that extends beyond the confines of the physical body, becoming a field factor in and of itself.

An Experimental Collaboration

Jan Roubal (2019) wrote an excellent chapter in the descriptive treatment manual for gestalt therapy on one of the most misunderstood aspects of contemporary gestalt therapy: the experiment. He said, "An experiment in Gestalt therapy is an active intervention that furthers the collaborative exploration of a client's experience" (p. 223). While experiment in behavioral therapy is often more of a technique for challenging faulty hypotheses that constrain the client, *the experiment* in gestalt therapy is a creative and unique movement to action that catalyzes new experience from which both therapist and client might learn: "Let's try this and see what happens." However, it is not just a wild leap into the darkness.

Roubal (2019) clearly described what the experiment is and how to use it. He claimed that the therapeutic relationship establishes a laboratory in which experiments form organically; they are discovered together. Starting with a shift from the dialogical attitude to a mindset clearly focused on experiment, the therapist readies themself. The therapist holds that readiness for the duration of the experiment. There ensues a process of grounding in the here and now, active suggesting, openness to discoveries, courage for creativity, and strategic leadership in which one leads by following.

The process of creating and developing an experiment is a relational interaction in which the client takes an active part. The therapist suggests tasks and leads the process during an experiment, but this leadership is of a paradoxical nature, a humble one, the least visible as possible. The therapist is sensitive to the resources and risks and needs of the situation, always ready to give space to the naturally, maybe even surprisingly, evolving process. They continuously monitor that they are pacing together through the adventurous journey of the experiment (Roubal, 2019).

Experiments in gestalt therapy differ from techniques in that *techniques* are set interventions one uses to bring about predetermined results, whereas *experiments* are explorations of the unknown to learn from novel experience. The well-known chair work that is often identified with gestalt therapy may have once been the creative exploration of novel experience, but it has long since become a fixed form and a technique for resolving splits and breaking up fixed gestalts and introjects, especially in hybrid forms of gestalt therapy, such as emotion-focused therapy and schema therapy. Techniques are more associated with a medical model in which an intervention is prescribed in some measure or dosage to bring about a known result. Experiments, however, are more akin to the philosophy of existentialism, used by skilled craftsmen, creating unique pieces of risk. While the starting point is to be process oriented, the procedure is to learn through doing (Roubal, 2009).

CONTEMPORARY GESTALT THERAPY AS A POSTSECULAR APPROACH

What sets gestalt therapy off from the naturalism and secularism that came out of the Enlightenment, and the logic of Enlightenment science taken to extremes in radical empiricism, is its keen interest in subjective experience and the realization that people live beyond their skins in relational networks that rely on extended cognition, the emergent sense of self, and the influence of social and cultural spheres of influence called "fields." Another way to see this is to realize that gestalt therapy, because of its reliance on phenomenology, relationality, and field dynamics, resides between the naturalistic attitude of Enlightenment science that gave rise to modernity and the deconstructivist perspective of postmodernity.

To assert the life world, the lived body, the self, and atmospheres would not simply be a metaphysical claim. They are paraphysical, personalistic, and yet still phenomenological. The field of the patient–therapist is real, but it is immaterial. You cannot smell it. You cannot touch it, but it can touch you. The life world is the matrix of both material and immaterial factors, both biological and social, both natural and frankly supernatural that have effect. The lived body is a quasithing that is at once real and yet not measurable. It is the residence of the self, but the self cannot be reduced to simple neuropsychological processes as if a certain region of the brain would be its home. And, of course, postsecular gestalt therapy accepts the value of spirituality and religion as elements that affect and are important to a majority of people in the world. They are even relevant many times when their rejection becomes a significant enduring theme. They are also relevant as important factors in social life, geopolitical processes, and economics. So, postsecular gestalt therapy is the realization that spirituality and religion are in play as belonging to the basic theory of gestalt therapy and not just the relative experiences of various clients.

To come at this from a different direction, consider these words: "The wind blows where it wishes and you hear the sound of it, but do not know where it comes from and where it is going; so is everyone who is born of the Spirit" (the words of Jesus; *New American Standard Bible*, 1995, John 3:8). No one questions the reality of the wind; yet, we cannot see it. We understand that it is the movement of air, but is "air" real? We do not question that air is real, but simply analyzing the amounts of oxygen and other components does not really exhaust the reality of air. We rely on the ability to breathe air even though we cannot see it. We can see what the wind moves, the effect of wind, and we can sense it as it sweeps against our skin, but we cannot see wind itself. That is the way it is with spiritual things. We live because we have the breath of life, and that life—the values, the emotions, the convictions, the beliefs, not just the actions, of people—moves us. We cannot touch, smell, weigh, or see what moves them, but what moves them often ends up moving us as well.

To determine who would benefit most from postsecular, spiritually integrated gestalt therapy, it must be recognized that we are not talking about some basically different form of gestalt therapy. So, anyone who would have responded well to contemporary gestalt therapy outside of the postsecular and spiritually integrated perspective would do so within it. Beyond that, people who have a spiritual tradition or religious home base would benefit from an approach such as this that is at once relational, phenomenological, field theoretical, and experimental and that includes the ability to process how meaningful it is for such people to worship, spend time in contemplation, or reach out to God in prayer. For that matter, they might benefit from the exploration of a felt "stuckness" with God or a disappointment with their religious experience so that these things seem to fail them at a time when their faith seems most to call for them.

Dallas Willard (1988) wrote a book on the spiritual disciplines that Jesus used to organize his life, and they broke down into disciplines of engagement and those of disengagement. These disciplines provide a ready resource for conducting experiments, or talking about self-regulation, but that kind of resource falls into the postsecular perspective. Patients whose enduring themes involve a history of legalistic, rule-bound expectations might not need just to deal with the issue of introjects, as would be the custom in traditional gestalt therapy, but also to deal with the theology of grace, something a gestalt therapist might have been tempted to refer the patient to clergy to untangle. The patient might also benefit from prayer when the moment seems especially critical.

CASE VIGNETTE

The following case describes one example of working in a postsecular, spiritually integrated fashion in gestalt therapy. (The client's identifying information has been changed and obscured.)

"James" was a young adult. He was living on his own but not doing well. He was socially awkward and had trouble in relationships. Further, he condemned himself and felt guilty. It was part of his cycle of depression. He could not provide specific examples of trespasses, moral failures, or legal transgressions, but he had an abiding sense of guilt. James told the story of growing up in a Christian family in which his father had aspired to be a pastor and that his father had finally risen to that level in a nondenominational church. James felt as if he could never please his father. The feeling of failure, of not measuring up, was like the proverbial dark cloud that hung over his head. Actually, it did more than that; it was the fragrance of his person, and he carried it with him wherever he went.

As therapist, I (Brownell) asked how much he would like to make religious practices, such as prayer, a part of our work together. He did not want that. He had not thrown his faith out the window, but the practice of organized Christianity had been too frustrating and painful for him. He was not sure if God accepted him, but he was sure his father did not and that he had been a disappointment to his father.

Working with James there arose in me—repeatedly—the issue of grace. It was not just a concept like associating to a tenet of theology, an idea. It was a yearning on his behalf. It kept coming up, kept being "in the room" with us. This was not simple forgiveness but the erasing of the measuring rod that identified failure. It was the move from a performance-based economy in relationship to one of acceptance and favor—favor that is not earned but simply given.

So, one day in session, I prayed under my breath, a silent prayer on my own behalf as a way of dealing with what kept coming up—that if there might be something I needed to say about grace, that the way would be given. That door with James opened, and I went through it:

THERAPIST: What do you know about grace?

JAMES: [*Stops himself; does nothing but look at the therapist*]

THERAPIST: What is happening?

JAMES: This sounds like church.

THERAPIST: I'm sorry. [*The word "grace" kept coming to me as we talked, and I needed to get it out so that it was something I wasn't carrying all by myself.*]

JAMES: People keep telling me about that. What am I supposed to do?! How do I do grace? I can't do it.

THERAPIST:	Well, exactly. Or rather what I know about this is that I can't do it either.
JAMES:	Then why did you bring it up?
THERAPIST:	What does that word bring to mind for you?
JAMES:	My father drilled it into us, and he made us memorize that verse with it . . . "by grace you are saved and that not of yourselves. It is the gift of God . . ." but I never got that. I don't know what those words mean.

There ensued a phenomenological exploration of his repeated experience of failing to please his father because he not only did not seem to do what his father wanted but he could not even understand what his father meant. Such a phenomenological exploration makes explicit to awareness the subjective experience of the client, and then, within a relational frame, the impact of that awareness on the relationship between therapist and client.

The postsecular approach does not require that a person do religious things. It simply allows that the supernatural might be a viable ground in the therapeutic relationship. From where, really, did the impulse to talk about grace come? The postsecular allows religious and spiritual process to enter rather than adhering to a materialistic and naturalistic bias reflective of a secular horizon that keeps them out.

ETHICS, DIVERSITY, AND GUIDELINES FOR RESEARCH AND PRACTICE

Gestalt therapists value difference; it's one way to grasp what contacting actually is. Difference is also another way of comprehending diversity. When people really meet, there is excitement in the presence of another who is not the same. Navigating that difference, however, can be difficult, problematic. Being present to another who is at once same in the sense of being human but not the same in the sense of having diverse experiences, values, beliefs, goals, emotions, ways of making sense, biases, and commitments can challenge one's security and throw a person off balance. It leads to both attraction and repulsion, to acceptance and rejection, to affection and loathing.

This is something understood beyond the bounds of gestalt therapy and the reason professional organizations create principles for conduct and ethics codes governing practice. General Principle E: Respect for People's Rights and Dignity of the *Ethical Principles of Psychologists and Code of Conduct* for the American Psychological Association (2017) states, for instance, that

> Psychologists are aware of and respect cultural, individual, and role differences, including those based on age, gender, gender identity, race, ethnicity, culture, national origin, religion, sexual orientation, disability, language, and socioeconomic status, and consider these factors when working with members of such groups.

The third point in the code of ethics for the European Association for Gestalt Therapy (2017) appreciates "the differences of race, extraction, ethnicity, gender, sexual identity or preference, handicap, age, religion, language, social or economic status and of the need for spirituality" (A. Code of Ethics, 3). As part of a keynote panel for the 2010 conference of the Association for the Advancement of Gestalt Therapy, Lynne Jacobs referred to Charles Taylor, saying,

> As human beings we are inescapably ethically situated in relation to each other. He considers that "one of the most basic aspirations of human beings [is] the need to be connected to, or in contact with, what they see as good, or of crucial importance, or of fundamental value." (Jacobs, 2010, p. 1)

These are postsecular assertions. To appreciate differences with regard to religion and the need for spirituality is to operate with an open frame. To realize that religion and the need for spirituality can also be expressions of the need to be connected to, or in contact with, what is seen as good, of crucial importance and of fundamental value, is to fully embrace a postsecular perspective—one's allowing for spiritually integrated practice.

Postsecular guidelines for research in gestalt therapy include these:

- Acknowledge and account for researcher bias with regard to results in general but more specifically in regard to religion and spirituality, the privileging of positivistic/naturalistic perspectives, the possibility of human error.

- Account for the limits of observation and measurement; although systematic observation is crucial, observation itself influences outcome; operational definitions miss part of the situation through reduction of complexity; all measures are partial and suggestive rather than final or absolute; matters pertaining to God are often ineffable.

- Accept that value in a life world often exceeds statistical significance.

- Recognize that phenomenological (qualitative) kinds of designs are crucial to understanding spiritual dynamics.

- Understand that research into the social factors resident in field dynamics often includes religious or spiritual experiences and values; they are pertinent.

Postsecular guidelines for practice in gestalt therapy include these:

- Gestalt therapists examine themselves for secular blind spots with regard to religion and spirituality and attempt to open themselves to possibilities beyond their personal belief systems.

- Gestalt therapists inquire with clients about religious or spiritual influences in their lives and self-disclose regarding the same in their own.

- Competence with regard to religious experience and spiritual belief systems (theologies) is part of being culturally competent in the practice of gestalt therapy.

- Gestalt therapists seek to resolve inherent conflicts and secular biases within gestalt therapy theory itself.

RESEARCH AND POSTSECULAR, SPIRITUALLY INTEGRATED GESTALT THERAPY

Although not much research has been conducted on spirituality in gestalt therapy, it helps to keep in mind the levels of research relevant to gestalt therapy in general. They also apply to research focused on spirituality in gestalt therapy. There is gestalt-specific research, gestalt-hybrid research, and gestalt-consilient research. *Gestalt-specific research* focuses on the theory and practice—directly—of contemporary gestalt therapy. *Gestalt-hybrid research* is research into an approach that blends gestalt techniques with something else (e.g., emotion-focused therapy, schema therapy). *Gestalt-consilient research* is research on some corollary that overlaps in a significant way with some aspect of gestalt therapy (e.g., mindfulness, therapeutic presence, kinesthetics). Also of significance are the subjective interests, values, and beliefs of psychotherapists who have openly pondered spirituality as an appropriate consideration because they would be consilient with those in gestalt therapy who have done the same.

The spiritual dimension was thought to lie outside the realm of science and was distant from psychotherapy for decades despite clients' bringing existential questions into psychotherapy more often than what was assumed. We are still in the process of understanding how psychotherapy is related to spirituality (Barnett, 2016; Vandenberghe et al., 2012). According to Bugeja (2008), our soul is vital to heal our emotional wounds, and integration of spirituality and psychotherapy is more than necessary. Some researchers connect gestalt therapy with pastoral counseling (Hamilton, 1997), Christian ministry (Richardson, 1976), or helping clients to relate to their religious values (Zamborsky, 1982, as cited in Williams, 2006).

In the context of gestalt therapy, spirituality can be observed, and research can be conducted in relation to processes of field theory, awareness, fertile void, and I–Thou relationship and dialogue (Bugeja, 2008), among others. Field theory, with its principles of relevance and organization, has strong roots in a spiritual ground and could be investigated as the pneumenal field. Also, awareness is spiritually embedded, and the client who aims to be self-aware can achieve this through the experience of the fertile void (Naranjo, 1993). Acceptance of the fertile void as a zero point, the center of possibility where everything can emerge and also everything can fade away, constitutes the ground experienced only in the current moment, the now (Wolfert, 2015).

Kennedy (1997) stated that three principles facilitate spirituality in gestalt therapy: (a) cocreative dialogue, (b) temporality, and (c) horizontalism. In addition, Crocker (1999) defined "spirituality" as the ability of a person to be present, accepting, and interacting with a significant mystery while being aware of body processes.

Campos and Ribeiro (2017) confirmed that the prevalence and importance of working on themes of spirituality can facilitate efficacy of treatment. According to Pargament et al. (2014), when spiritual moments in therapy are perceived as "sacred moments" by therapists and clients, that perception promotes resilience, mental health, and well-being of clients. Henning-Geronasso and Moré (2015) suggested that integration of spirituality with psychotherapeutic process, and reconnection with the sacred, supports clients to get in contact with themselves and the world. Hycner (1993) indicated that therapist's abilities and attitudes, such as presence and nonjudgment with the ability to respect clients' beliefs, respectfully contribute to the healing process.

Another important concept in gestalt therapy that relates to spiritual practice is the concept of forgiveness (E. S. Harris, 2007). Many research studies have confirmed that forgiving can be related to decreased stress, less anxiety, and more loving feelings toward oneself and others (Enright & Fitzgibbons, 2000). It also contributes to positive changes in subjective well-being, sense of empowerment, and psychological healing (Richards & Bergin, 1997).

Encouraging forgiveness can be perceived as a spiritual intervention in psychotherapy that brings about completion of incomplete figures and "unfinished business," but direct references to forgiveness are infrequent in gestalt therapy literature, except in writings of particular authors (Kepner, 1995; Polster & Polster, 1973). Because gestalt therapy emphasizes finishing or completing experience (Perls et al., 1951), exploring forgiveness and its relationship to spiritual outcomes in therapy might be an interesting area for future gestalt research studies.

Numerous research studies have aimed to understand the relationship between spirituality and psychotherapy. For example, a research study conducted to investigate the lack of seeking psychotherapy services in Muslim populations, even when needed, revealed that Muslim people will not seek psychotherapy services because of the assumption that their religious values, commitments, and orientations will not be adequately recognized by therapists. This necessitated the need to assimilate the Islamic construct of "soul" into a psychotherapeutic approach (Rothman & Coyle, 2020).

Another study focused interest on effectiveness of spiritual psychotherapy when working with adolescents suffering from conduct disorder. According to Salmanian et al. (2020), insecure attachment can produce symptoms of conduct disorder, but modification of attachments to God can consequently improve this disorder through developing God-as-attachment-figure. In the randomized controlled trial conducted with adolescents suffering from conduct disorder, a spiritually integrated psychotherapy package of 14 sessions focused on self-awareness and attachment, satisfaction and prayer, spiritual awareness and belief in unity, and belief in the sacred as well as the possibility of transformation was used. Results confirmed that developing God-as-attachment-figure can improve the avoidance attachment patterns common among adolescents with conduct disorder. In another study, it was found that when working with a youth population, it was beneficial in terms of spirituality to engage in a self-reflection process and reflexivity (Arczynski et al., 2016).

In a study of spiritual struggles among people with mental illness, Gibbel et al. (2019) used an intervention entitled "Winding Road" (group therapy treatment) that targeted negative religious coping. The authors found that participants reported significantly less spiritual struggle and greater forgiveness, less stigma related to their spiritual struggle, and a decrease in addictive behaviors.

The consilient, mindfulness-based stress reduction and meditation approach came from the Buddhist tradition of incorporating spiritually and religiously based strategies into secular psychotherapy (Plante, 2020). Similarly, yoga practice that has been secularized to apply to diverse populations worldwide, even to those not interested in Hinduism, confirmed that spiritually based strategies are widely useful in clinical practice (Horovitz & Elgelid, 2015). As emotional and spiritual dimensions of life are intertwined, psychotherapists need to collaborate with spiritual directors and be attentive if patients have spiritual concerns (Saadeh et al., 2018).

Prout et al. (2021) examined individuals who sought Christian counseling to address their psychological and interpersonal distress and spiritual beliefs. Results confirm that psychological distress is associated with less adaptive religious and spiritual health, whereas negative religious coping is inversely correlated with forgiveness and daily spiritual practices.

Effects of accommodating mindfulness to the Christian spirituality of evangelical Christian patients in regard to shame, depression, anxiety, stress and spiritually related resiliency factors confirm that mindfulness strategies can be adapted for these clients. Growth in a client's belief in God's grace can impact treatment conceptually and in terms of outcomes (Jones et al., 2021).

Spiritual beliefs and practices have been seen to promote therapist resilience and self-care (Duggal & Sriram, 2021). Furthermore, incorporating spirituality into treatment of trauma survivors is very significant because survivors often enter therapy struggling with global spiritual meaning systems that cannot accommodate their experiences of trauma. Spiritual struggles relate to clients abandoning their faith or having difficulties forgiving themselves. Spiritual struggles are associated with more severe symptoms of posttraumatic stress disorder, whereas resolving spiritual concerns can promote well-being in a client. Attending to spiritual concerns in psychotherapy is seen as an essential aspect of ethical and culturally sensitive treatment (Saunders et al., 2010; Sperry, 2012; Sperry & Shafranske, 2005; Vieten et al., 2013, as cited in Park et al., 2017). Current research studies support spiritually integrated care in trauma survivors in which the client's own spiritual meaning systems represent an important tool to meet treatment goals as opposed to imposing other belief systems that may not resonate with the client (Shafranske & Cummings, 2013; Walker et al., 2015, as cited in Park et al., 2017).

Specific treatment approaches that integrate spirituality and that have gained empirical support are Re-Creating Your Life programs for patients with cancer (Cole, 2005; Cole & Pargament, 1999, as citied in Park et al., 2017), Solace for the Soul programs for women who have survived sexual abuse (Murray-Swank & Pargament, 2005, 2008, as cited in Park et al., 2017), and Building Spiritual Strength programs for survivors of combat trauma (J. I. Harris et al., 2011, as cited in Park at el., 2017). Empirical research has also confirmed that during treatment, veterans' preferences toward spirituality or religious interventions should be considered (Currier et al., 2018).

CONCLUSION

Approaches to psychotherapy that facilitate clients' spirituality have been often found to be more effective than other types of intervention (Smith et al., 2007). Empirical research of spirituality in psychotherapeutic practice supports the need to consider, evaluate, and select treatment interventions according to the spiritual beliefs, values, and practices of clients while maintaining therapist self-awareness related to the biases, values, beliefs, and preferences of therapists.

In the light of current research studies related to spirituality and psychotherapy, gestalt therapy would benefit by expanding its research base and developing explorations of spiritually related themes, such as forgiveness, spiritual sensitivity, spontaneity, trust, and other clinical dynamics, that are consistent with contemporary gestalt therapy theory. Postsecular, spiritually integrated gestalt therapy could be a useful and important approach in the treatment of various clinical presentations, and the general field suggests gestalt therapy, like other approaches, stands to benefit by enlarging its scope to assimilate the postsecular, spiritually integrated perspective.

REFERENCES

American Psychological Association. (2017). *Ethical principles of psychologists and code of conduct* (2002, amended effective June 1, 2010, and January 1, 2017). https://www.apa.org/ethics/code/

Arczynski, A. V., Morrow, S. L., & Englar-Carlson, M. (2016). Cultivating a spiritually integrative psychotherapy approach with youth: An exploratory qualitative study. *Spirituality in Clinical Practice, 3*(3), 196–207. https://doi.org/10.1037/scp0000086

Barnett, J. E. (2016). Are religion and spirituality of relevance in psychotherapy? *Spirituality in Clinical Practice, 3*(1), 5–9. https://doi.org/10.1037/scp0000093

Bar-Yoseph Levine, T. (Ed.). (2012). *Gestalt therapy: Advances in theory and practice.* Routledge. https://doi.org/10.4324/9780203157763

Bloom, D. (2019). Gestalt therapy and phenomenology: The intersecting of parallel lines. In P. Brownell (Ed.), *Handbook for theory, research, and practice in gestalt therapy* (2nd ed., pp. 183–202). Cambridge Scholars Publishing.

Bowman, C., & Brownell, P. (2015). Prelude to contemporary gestalt therapy. In B. Mistler & P. Brownell (Eds.), *Global perspectives on research, theory and practice: A decade of gestalt!* (pp. 190–196). Cambridge Scholars Publishing.

Bowman, C. E., & Nevis, E. C. (2005). The history and development of gestalt therapy. In A. L. Woldt & S. M. Toman (Eds.), *Gestalt therapy history, theory, and practice* (pp. 3–20). SAGE Publications. https://doi.org/10.4135/9781452225661.n1

Brownell, P. (2010). *Gestalt therapy: A guide to contemporary practice.* Springer Publishing.

Brownell, P. (2012). *Gestalt therapy for addictive and self-medicating behaviors.* Springer Publishing.

Brownell, P. (2013) Assimilating/integrative: The case of contemporary gestalt therapy. In T. G. Plante (Ed.), *Abnormal psychology across the ages: Vol. 2. Disorders and treatments* (pp. 221–234). Praeger/ABC-CLIO.

Brownell, P. (2015). *Spiritual competency in psychotherapy.* Springer Publishing.

Brownell, P. (2018). *Gestalt psychotherapy and coaching for relationships.* Routledge.

Brownell, P. (Ed.). (2019a). *Handbook for theory, research, and practice in gestalt therapy* (2nd ed.). Cambridge Scholars Publishing.

Brownell, P. (2019b). Hermeneutic coaching. In S. English, J. M. Sabatine, & P. Brownell (Eds.), *Professional coaching principles and practices* (pp. 175–184). Springer Publishing Company.

Brownell, P. (2020). *Christianity and gestalt therapy: The presence of God in human relationships*. Routledge. https://doi.org/10.4324/9781351014076

Brownell, P., & Roubal, J. (2019). Two "takes" on treatment manuals in gestalt therapy. In P. Brownell (Ed.), *Handbook for theory, research, and practice in gestalt therapy* (2nd ed., pp. 150–156). Cambridge Scholars Publishing.

Buber, M. (1952). *Eclipse of God: Studies in the relation between religion and philosophy*. Humanity Books.

Bugeja, T. (2008). The spiritual dimension of gestalt psychotherapy. In D. Baldacchino & L. Ross (Eds.), *Spirituality: The human dimension in care* (pp. 95–114). Institute of Health Care.

Campos, A. F., & Ribeiro, J. P. (2017). Psicoterapia e espiritualidade: Da Gestalt-terapia a pesquisa contemporanea [Psychotherapy and spirituality: From gestalt therapy to contemporary research]. *Phenomenological Studies—Revista da Abordagem Gestáltica, 23*(2), 211–218.

Clark, A., & Chalmers, D. (1998). The extended mind. *Analysis, 58*(1), 7–19. https://doi.org/10.1093/analys/58.1.7

Cole, B., & Pargament, K. (1999). Re-creating your life: A spiritual/psychotherapeutic intervention for people diagnosed with cancer. *Psycho-Oncology, 8*(5), 395–407. https://doi.org/10.1002/(SICI)1099-1611(199909/10)8:5<395::AID-PON408>3.0.CO;2-B

Cole, B. S. (2005). Spiritually-focused psychotherapy for people diagnosed with cancer: A pilot outcome study. *Mental Health, Religion & Culture, 8*(3), 217–226. https://doi.org/10.1080/13694670500138916

Crocker, S. F. (1999). *A well-lived life: Essays in gestalt therapy*. GIC Press.

Crocker, S. F., & Philippson, P. (2005). Phenomenology, existentialism, and Eastern thought in gestalt therapy. In A. L. Woldt & S. M. Toman (Eds.), *Gestalt therapy history, theory, and practice* (pp. 65–80). SAGE Publications. https://doi.org/10.4135/9781452225661.n4

Currier, J. M., Pearce, M., Carroll, T. D., & Koenig, H. G. (2018). Military veterans' preferences for incorporating spirituality in psychotherapy or counseling. *Professional Psychology, Research and Practice, 49*(1), 39–47. https://doi.org/10.1037/pro0000178

Duggal, C., & Sriram, S. (2021). Locating the sacred within the therapeutic landscape: Influence of therapists' religious and spiritual beliefs on psychotherapeutic practice. *Spirituality in Clinical Practice*. Advance online publication. https://doi.org/10.1037/scp0000250

Edmonds, D. (2020). *The murder of Professor Schlick*. Princeton University Press.

Enright, R. D., & Fitzgibbons, R. P. (2000). *Helping clients forgive: An empirical guide for resolving anger and restoring hope*. American Psychological Association. https://doi.org/10.1037/10381-000

European Association for Gestalt Therapy. (2017). *Code of ethics and professional practice*. https://www.eagt.org/joomla/images/Downloads/EAGTDocs/Ethical_Code_&_Complaints_Procedure_09-2017_OK.pdf

Fogarty, M., Bhar, S., & Theiler, S. (2019). The gestalt therapy fidelity scale. In P. Brownell (Ed.), *Handbook for theory, research, and practice in gestalt therapy* (2nd ed., pp. 341–354). Cambridge Scholars Publishing.

Francesetti, G. (2019). The field perspective in clinical practice: Towards a theory of therapeutic phronesis. In P. Brownell (Ed.), *Handbook for theory, research, and practice in gestalt therapy* (2nd ed., pp. 268–302). Cambridge Scholars Publishing.

Francesetti, G., Gecele, M., & Roubal, J. (Eds.). (2014). *Gestalt therapy in clinical practice: From psychopathology to the aesthetics of contact*. Istituto di Gestalt HCC.

Gibbel, M. R., Regueiro, V., & Pargament, K. I. (2019). A spiritually integrated intervention for spiritual struggles among adults with mental illness: Results of an initial evaluation. *Spirituality in Clinical Practice, 6*(4), 240–255. https://doi.org/10.1037/scp0000207

Gold, E., & Zahm, S. (2018). *Buddhist psychology & gestalt therapy integrated: Psychotherapy for the 21st century.* Metta Press.

Gurwitsch, A. (1970) Problems of the life-world. In A. Schutz & M. A. Natanson (Eds.), *Phenomenology and social reality: Essays in memory of Alfred Schutz* (pp. 35–61). M. Nijhoff.

Habermas, J. (1998). *The philosophical discourse of modernity* (F. G. Lawrence, Trans.). The MIT Press.

Hamilton, J. D. (1997). *Gestalt in pastoral care and counseling: A holistic approach.* Routledge.

Harris, E. S. (2007). Working with forgiveness in gestalt therapy. *Gestalt Review, 11*(2), 108–119. https://doi.org/10.5325/gestaltreview.11.2.0108

Harris, J. I., Erbes, C. R., Engdahl, B. E., Thuras, P., Murray-Swank, N., Grace, D., Ogden, H., Olson, R. H. A., Winskowski, A. M., Bacon, R., Malec, C., Campion, K., & Le, T. (2011). The effectiveness of a trauma focused spiritually integrated intervention for veterans exposed to trauma. *Journal of Clinical Psychology, 67*(4), 425–438. https://doi.org/10.1002/jclp.20777

Henning-Geronasso, M. C., & Moré, C. L. O. O. (2015). Influência da Religiosidade/Espiritualidade no Contexto Psicoterapêutico [The influence of religiousness/spirituality in the psychotherapeutic context]. *Psicologia: Ciência e Profissão, 35*(3), 711–725. https://doi.org/10.1590/1982-3703000942014

Henry, M. (2003). *I am the truth: Toward a philosophy of Christianity.* Stanford University Press.

Horner, R. (2000). Emmanuel Levinas on God and philosophy. *Philosophy in the Contemporary World, 7*(1), 41–46. https://doi.org/10.5840/pcw2000717

Horovitz, E. G., & Elgelid, S. (Eds.). (2015). *Yoga therapy: Theory and practice.* Routledge/Taylor & Francis Group. https://doi.org/10.4324/9781315746296

Husserl, E. (1970). *The crisis of European sciences and transcendental phenomenology: An introduction to phenomenological philosophy* (D. Carr, Trans.). Northwestern University Press.

Hycner, R. (1993). *Between person and person: Toward a dialogical psychotherapy.* The Gestalt Journal Press.

Jacobs, L. (2010, June 1–6). *Ethical inspiration and complex experiencing* [Keynote panel presentation]. Association for the Advancement of Gestalt Therapy 10th International Conference on Continuity and Change in Gestalt Therapy, Philadelphia, PA, United States. https://www.academia.edu/28078032/Ethical_inspiration_and_Complex_Experiencing_AAGT_Conference_on_Continuity_and_Change_in_Gestalt_Therapy_Keynote_Panel

Jacobs, L. (2019). Relationality and relational process in gestalt therapy. In P. Brownell (Ed.), *Handbook for theory, research, and practice in gestalt therapy* (2nd ed., pp. 203–219). Cambridge Scholars Publishing.

Jones, T. L., Garzon, F. L., & Ford, K. M. (2021). Christian accommodative mindfulness in the clinical treatment of shame, depression, and anxiety: Results of an *N*-of-1 time-series study. *Spirituality in Clinical Practice.* Advance online publication. https://doi.org/10.1037/scp0000221

Kennedy, D. (1997). Presence of mind: Literary, and philosophical roots of a wise psychotherapy [Book review]. *British Gestalt Journal, 6*(2), 121–127.

Kepner, J. I. (1995). *Healing tasks: Psychotherapy with adult survivors of childhood abuse.* Jossey-Bass Publishers.

Kuhn, T. (2012). *The structure of scientific revolutions.* University of Chicago Press. (Original work published 1962)

Levinas, E. (1998). *Of God who comes to mind.* Stanford University Press.

Lewis, C. S. (2002) Miracles. In *The complete C. S. Lewis* (pp. 301–462). Harper One, Harper Collins. (Original work published 1947)

Murray-Swank, N. A., & Pargament, K. I. (2005). God, where are you?: Evaluating a spiritually-integrated intervention for sexual abuse. *Mental Health, Religion & Culture, 8*(3), 191–203. https://doi.org/10.1080/13694670500138866

Murray-Swank, N. A., & Pargament, K. I. (2008). Solace for the soul: Evaluating a spiritually-integrated counselling intervention for sexual abuse. *Counselling and Spirituality, 27*(2), 157–174.

Naranjo, C. (1993). *Gestalt therapy: The attitude & practice of an atheoretical experientialism*. Crown House Publishing.

New American Standard Bible. (1995). Lockman Foundation. https://www.bible.com/bible/100/JHN.3.NASB1995

Norberg, T. (2005). *Consenting to grace: An introduction to gestalt pastoral care*. Gestalt Pastoral Care.

Pargament, K. I., Lomax, J. W., McGee, J. S., & Fang, Q. (2014). Sacred moments in psychotherapy from the perspectives of mental health providers and clients: Prevalence, predictors, and consequences. *Spirituality in Clinical Practice, 1*(4), 248–262. https://doi.org/10.1037/scp0000043

Park, C. L., Currier, J. M., Harris, J. I., & Slattery, J. M. (2017). *Trauma, meaning, and spirituality: Translating research into clinical practice*. American Psychological Association. https://doi.org/10.1037/15961-000

Parlett, M., & Lee, R. G. (2005). Contemporary gestalt therapy: Field theory. In A. L. Woldt & S. M. Toman (Eds.), *Gestalt therapy history, theory, and practice* (pp. 41–64). SAGE Publications. https://doi.org/10.4135/9781452225661.n3

Perls, F., Hefferline, R. F., & Goodman, P. (1951). *Gestalt therapy: Excitement and growth in the human personality*. The Julian Press.

Plante, T. G. (2020). St. Ignatius as psychotherapist? How Jesuit spirituality and wisdom can enhance psychotherapy. *Spirituality in Clinical Practice, 7*(1), 65–71. https://doi.org/10.1037/scp0000214

Polster, E., & Polster, M. (1973). *Gestalt therapy integrated*. Brunner/Mazel.

Prout, T. A., Magaldi, D., Kim, E. E., & Cha, J. (2021). Christian therapists and their clients. *Spirituality in Clinical Practice, 8*(1), 1–15. https://doi.org/10.1037/scp0000238

Richards, P. S., & Bergin, A. E. (1997). *A spiritual strategy for counseling and psychotherapy*. American Psychological Association. https://doi.org/10.1037/10241-000

Richardson, R. W. (1976). *The implications of gestalt therapy for Christian ministry*. Colgate Rochester Divinity School, Bexley Hall, Crozer Theological Seminary.

Rivera, J. (2015). *The contemplative self after Michel Henry: A phenomenological theology*. University of Notre Dame Press.

Rothman, A., & Coyle, A. (2020). Conceptualizing an Islamic psychotherapy: A grounded theory study. *Spirituality in Clinical Practice, 7*(3), 197–213. https://doi.org/10.1037/scp0000219

Roubal, J. (2009). Experiment: A creative phenomenon of the field. *Gestalt Review, 13*(3), 263–276. https://doi.org/10.5325/gestaltreview.13.3.0263

Roubal, J. (2019). An experimental approach: Follow by leading. In P. Brownell (Ed.), *Handbook for theory, research, and practice in gestalt therapy* (pp. 220–267). Cambridge Scholars Publishing.

Saadeh, M. G., North, K., Hansen, K. L., Steele, P., & Peteet, J. R. (2018). Spiritual direction and psychotherapy. *Spirituality in Clinical Practice, 5*(4), 273–282. https://doi.org/10.1037/scp0000172

Salmanian, M., Ghobari-Bonab, B., Hooshyari, Z., & Mohammadi, M.-R. (2020). Effectiveness of spiritual psychotherapy on attachment to God among adolescents with conduct disorder: A randomized controlled trial. *Psychology of Religion and Spirituality, 12*(3), 269–275. https://doi.org/10.1037/rel0000241

Saunders, S. M., Miller, M. L., & Bright, M. M. (2010). Spiritually conscious psychological care. *Professional Psychology: Research and Practice, 41*(5), 355–362. https://doi.org/10.1037/a0020953

Shafranske, E. P., & Cummings, J. P. (2013). Religious and spiritual beliefs, affiliations, and practices of psychologists. In K. I. Pargament, A. Mahoney, & E. P. Shafranske (Eds.), *APA handbook of psychology, religion, and spirituality: Vol. 2. An applied psychology of religion and spirituality* (pp. 23–41). American Psychological Association. https://doi.org/10.1037/14046-002

Slife, B., Möller, E., & Chun, S. (2019). The excluded other in psychological research: Diary of a probing theist. In P. Brownell (Ed.), *Handbook for theory, research, and practice in gestalt therapy* (2nd ed., pp. 65–87). Cambridge Scholars Publishing.

Smith, T. B., Bartz, J., & Richards, P. S. (2007). Outcomes of religious and spiritual adaptations to psychotherapy: A meta-analytic review. *Psychotherapy Research, 17*(6), 643–655. https://doi.org/10.1080/10503300701250347

Sperry, L. (2012). *Spirituality in clinical practice: Theory and practice of spiritually oriented psychotherapy* (2nd ed.). Routledge.

Sperry, L., & Shafranske, E. P. (Eds.). (2005). *Spiritually integrated psychotherapy.* American Psychological Association. https://doi.org/10.1037/10886-000

Vandenberghe, L., Costa Prado, P., & de Camargo, E. A. (2012). Spirituality and religion in psychotherapy: Views of Brazilian psychotherapists. *International Perspectives in Psychology: Research, Practice, Consultation, 1*(2), 79–93. https://doi.org/10.1037/a0028656

Vieten, C., Scammell, S., Pilato, R., Ammondson, I., Pargament, K. I., & Lukoff, D. (2013). Spiritual and religious competencies for psychologists. *Psychology of Religion and Spirituality, 5*(3), 129–144. https://doi.org/10.1037/a0032699

Von Zweck, C., Paterson, M., & Pentland, W. (2008). The use of hermeneutics in a mixed-methods design. *The Qualitative Report, 13*(1), 116–134.

Walker, D. F., Courtois, C. A., & Aten, J. D. (2015). *Spiritually oriented psychotherapy for trauma.* American Psychological Association.

Wheeler, G. (1991). *Gestalt reconsidered: A new approach to contact and resistance.* Gardner Press.

Willard, D. (1988). *The spirit of the disciplines.* HarperCollins Publishers.

Williams, L. (2006). Spirituality and gestalt: A gestalt-transpersonal perspective. *Gestalt Review, 10*(1), 6–21. https://doi.org/10.5325/gestaltreview.10.1.0006

Wolfert, R. (2015). The spiritual dimensions of gestalt therapy. In B. Mistler & P. Brownell (Eds.), *Global perspectives on research, theory and practice: A decade of Gestalt!* (pp. 197–202). Cambridge Scholars Publishing.

Zamborsky, L. (1982). *The use of gestalt therapy with clients expressing religious values issues* [Unpublished doctoral dissertation]. Kent State University.

6

Shaken to the Core

Understanding and Addressing Spiritual Struggles in Psychotherapy

Kenneth I. Pargament and Julie J. Exline

Mr. W, a 55-year-old married father with a history of major depressive and alcohol use disorders, was seen in a medical hospital following a self-inflicted gunshot wound (Kao et al., 2019).[1] Plagued with guilt over his drinking and extramarital affairs, the patient had found himself dwelling on the question of whether God could forgive him for his sins. In an effort to find the answer, he decided to "gamble with God" by playing Russian roulette with a gun loaded with one live bullet and five blanks. He reasoned that if God loved him, he would be spared. Mr. W pulled the trigger and was hit with the live bullet. He survived, although he required several weeks of hospitalization for severe facial injuries. How should Mr. W be approached in psychotherapy?

As many of the chapters in this handbook have shown, spirituality can be a resource in treatment for people who are experiencing psychological problems. However, spirituality also has the potential to create or exacerbate mental health concerns, as we see in the story of Mr. W. Spirituality can be a source of problems that range from avoidance and denial to prejudice and aggression, to rigidity and extremism. There is, in short, a darker, seamy side to spiritual and religious life (see Pruyser, 1977). A growing body of research

---

[1]The name of Mr. W was altered to protect his confidentiality. Case descriptions in this chapter that come from Pargament and Exline (2022) are composites assembled from different clinical cases seen by the authors.

Our thanks to the John Templeton Foundation for their support of our research on spiritual struggles (JTF No. 36094 and No. 55916).

https://doi.org/10.1037/0000338-006
Handbook of Spiritually Integrated Psychotherapies, P. S. Richards, G. E. K. Allen, and D. K. Judd (Editors)
Copyright © 2023 by the American Psychological Association. All rights reserved.

points to the importance of addressing spiritual problems in the context of psychotherapy. For instance, it would be difficult to imagine how Mr. W could be treated effectively without attending to the spiritual dimension of his problems. One form of spirituality that can be problematic at times (although it may also be a source of growth) has received perhaps the most attention in the literature: spiritual struggles. *Spiritual struggles* are defined as tensions, strains, and conflicts about sacred matters (Exline, 2013; Pargament, 2007). In this chapter, we first briefly review what we are learning about spiritual struggles and then we discuss how practitioners can address spiritual struggles in treatment (for a more extensive discussion, see Pargament & Exline, 2022).

WHAT WE ARE LEARNING ABOUT SPIRITUAL STRUGGLES

Spiritual struggles can be grouped conceptually into three general dimensions. *Supernatural struggles* involve tensions centered on beliefs about higher powers (i.e., God or gods) or demonic or evil entities. *Intrapsychic struggles* take the form of conflicts and strains about moral issues, ultimate meaning, and the truths of religious or spiritual beliefs. *Interpersonal struggles* manifest as conflicts with other people or institutions about spiritual matters. Embedded in spiritual struggles are questions that are often existential in nature (Pargament & Exline, 2022): Who am I? Why am I here? How should I live my life? Is the world safe and trustworthy? Am I alone in the universe? Am I loved? What is true? How can I make sense of and deal with suffering? Although these questions may not be explicitly linked to spiritual matters, life's most fundamental existential concerns often do become fraught with sacred power and significance. And when they do, struggles become spiritual struggles.

Several years ago, our team developed a measure of six specific types of spiritual struggles (Religious and Spiritual Struggles Scale [RSS]; Exline et al., 2014):

- *divine struggles*: anger or disappointment with God; feeling punished, abandoned, or unloved by God
  sample item: felt angry at God

- *demonic struggles*: worries that problems are caused by the devil or evil spirits; feelings of being attacked or tormented by the devil
  sample item: felt attacked by the devil or by evil spirits

- *doubt-related struggles*: feeling confused about religious or spiritual beliefs; feeling troubled by doubts or questions about religion or spirituality
  sample item: felt troubled by doubts or questions about religion or spirituality

- *moral struggles*: tensions and guilt about not living up to one's higher standards; wrestling with attempts to follow moral principles
  sample item: felt guilt for not living up to my moral standards

- *struggles of ultimate meaning*: concerns that life may not really matter; questions about whether one's own life has deeper meaning
    sample item: questioned whether my life will really make any difference in the world

- *interpersonal struggles*: conflicts about religious matters involving other people and institutions; anger at organized religion; feeling hurt, mistreated, or offended by others in relation to religion or spirituality
    sample item: had conflicts with other people about religious or spiritual matters

Factor analysis indicated that spiritual struggles can be studied in terms of both specific types of struggle and total struggles.

Spiritual struggles are not unusual. They are an integral part of the life stories of many people, including exemplary religious figures from the world's major religious traditions, such as Moses, Jesus, Muhammad, and the Buddha. Contemporary accounts of struggle are not hard to find, either; they appear among people of diverse ages, gender, ethnicity, socioeconomic backgrounds, and religious affiliation, including those who label themselves "nones" and atheists (see Pargament & Exline, 2022). For example, in large-scale surveys of community and college student samples, 33% reported that they had experienced a spiritual struggle in the past few months (Wilt, Grubbs, et al., 2016). Similarly, one third of a sample of military veterans indicated that they had been dealing with at least one spiritual struggle (Currier et al., 2018). The prevalence of spiritual struggles appears to be even higher among people facing medical and mental health problems. Among patients with advanced cancer, 58% reported some kind of spiritual struggle (Winkelman et al., 2011). Approximately 50% of outpatients being treated for a mood disorder (Rosmarin et al., 2014) and older adults with depression (Murphy et al., 2016) reported that they were experiencing a spiritual struggle.

Pargament and Exline (2022) have developed a framework for understanding the roots of spiritual struggles and their consequences for health and well-being. Figure 6.1 does not present a formal testable model of spiritual struggles; instead, it offers a pictorial way of thinking about spiritual struggles as part of the larger human search for significance.

Roots of Spiritual Struggles

According to this perspective, people are intentional beings, motivated to find purpose and meaning in their lives. Spirituality becomes involved in the human search for significance when the destinations people seek in life and the pathways they follow to reach these destinations take on a sacred character. People are guided in their search for significance by an orienting system of beliefs, practices, experiences, coping skills, and personality characteristics, as well as a network of social relationships that provide a sense of direction and stability. At times, however, the search for meaning is less than smooth

FIGURE 6.1. A Framework for Understanding Spiritual Struggles

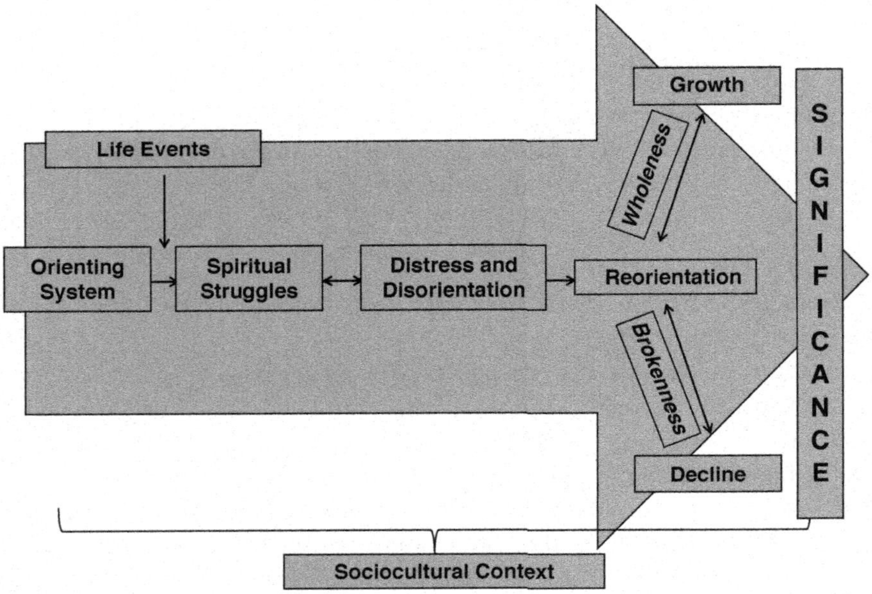

Note. Adapted from *Working With Spiritual Struggles in Psychotherapy: From Research to Practice* (p. 26), by K. I. Pargament and J. J. Exline, 2022, Guilford Press. Copyright 2022 by Guilford Press. Adapted with permission.

and straightforward, and the individual's sense of purpose and orientation to life are shaken, including their fundamental spiritual beliefs, values, and practices. These are times of spiritual struggle.

From the outset, it is important to stress that spiritual struggles are not a form of psychopathology or spiritual immaturity. Rather, they are a natural part of development. Just as people struggle at times cognitively, emotionally, and physically, they also experience periods of spiritual struggle. And as with the development of other human dimensions, struggles in the spiritual domain are shaped by personal, social, and situational factors. More specifically, spiritual struggles are rooted in the purposes individuals seek out of life, their orienting systems, and life events and transitions. People can direct their lives to purposes that are limited or problematic and experience spiritual struggles as a result. For instance, spiritual struggles are more likely when individuals pursue inauthentic dreams (Wilt et al., 2021), addictive goals (Grubbs et al., 2017), and avoidant spiritual strivings (e.g., avoiding God's displeasure; Emmons & Schnitker, 2013).

Limitations in the orienting system can also increase the person's vulnerability to spiritual struggles. For example, people who report more neuroticism, psychiatric disability, and difficulty tolerating negative emotions are more likely to experience spiritual struggles (e.g., McConnell et al., 2006; Wilt et al., 2017). Narrow representations of God, such as the "God of Absolute Perfection" who insists on flawless performance and the "Heavenly Bosom" who offers unconditional love and protection while asking nothing of the individual in return (see Phillips, 1997), can also set the stage for spiritual struggles because these representations do not help people face the full range of life challenges.

People are more likely to encounter spiritual struggles during times of major transition and life stress. Emerging adulthood, for example, is a period when struggles are especially commonplace (Krause et al., 2017). Trauma and major life events, such as combat exposure (Park et al., 2017), child abuse (Janů et al., 2022), and the accumulation of life stressors (Pomerleau et al., 2020), have also been linked to higher levels of spiritual struggle. People are especially vulnerable to struggle when they experience events that threaten, damage, or violate their most sacred values, as in the case of clergy sexual abuse (Rossetti, 1995).

Consequences of Spiritual Struggles

Even though spiritual struggles are a natural part of life, they are generally disorienting and distressing, and they can be associated with psychological problems in some instances. In this vein, empirical studies have consistently linked spiritual struggles to poorer mental health status (for a review, see Pargament & Exline, 2022). In one study of a nationally representative sample, higher levels of spiritual struggle were associated with more depressive symptoms and generalized anxiety (Abu-Raiya et al., 2015). Among veterans returning from the Iraq and/or Afghanistan wars, spiritual struggles were tied to increased risk of suicidality (Currier et al., 2017). Spiritual struggles were also correlated with greater depression, anxiety, and stress among people in Saudi Arabia dealing with the COVID-19 pandemic (Yıldırım et al., 2021). Of note, spiritual struggles may account in part for the negative impact of trauma on psychological adjustment. For example, in one study of a national sample, spiritual struggles partially mediated the link between major life events and poorer mental health (Pomerleau et al., 2020). Similar findings have been reported in research with people experiencing psychological problems. To name a few, spiritual struggles have been associated with depression and anxiety among psychiatric inpatients (Rosmarin et al., 2013); suicidality among veterans with posttraumatic stress disorder (PTSD; Kopacz et al., 2016); and anxiety, depression, shame, and hopelessness among male sex offenders (Robertson et al., 2020).

Overall, the research points to robust associations between spiritual struggles and poorer mental health. Much of this research, however, has been cross-sectional and does not speak to the question of causation. Pargament and Lomax (2013) noted three possible models of causal linkage: (a) spiritual struggles could conceivably lead to poorer mental health (primary struggles), (b) psychological problems could trigger spiritual struggles (secondary struggles), or (c) spiritual struggles could both lead to and result from psychological maladjustment (complex struggles). How best to understand the causal relationship between struggles and mental health has important practical implications. If, for example, spiritual struggles are a by-product of psychological distress, then the struggles might be resolved by simply helping people find relief from their distress. If, however, spiritual struggles play a primary role in the development of poorer mental health, then they would need to be addressed directly. And if there is a reciprocal relationship between spiritual struggles and mental health, then effective treatment would call for attention to both the spiritual and psychological dimension of the client's concerns.

A growing number of longitudinal studies have begun to shed light on these cause-and-effect questions. The primary spiritual struggles model has received the strongest and most consistent support. In a recent meta-analysis of 32 longitudinal studies, Bockrath et al. (2021) found that spiritual struggles were significant predictors of increases in negative psychological adjustment (e.g., depression, anxiety, stress, addiction, PTSD, suicidal ideation) over time. A small number of studies have offered some support for a secondary struggles model. For example, in a 6-month follow-up study of African Americans who had lost a loved one to homicide, those who manifested more complicated grief were more likely to develop spiritual struggles over time (Neimeyer & Burke, 2011). As yet, few studies have tested a complex model and the possibility that spiritual struggles could be both a cause and effect of mental health problems.

Much of the empirical literature paints a rather dark portrait of spiritual struggles. But are the links between struggles and mental health problems the full story? Is there the possibility of growth following spiritual struggles? Certainly, we can find stories of personal transformation in the sacred texts from the world's religions. Indeed, it could be argued that the narrative of growth and transformation through spiritual struggles is perhaps the most central theme in the lives of the greatest religious figures, from Moses and Jesus to the Buddha and Muhammad. More contemporary accounts of growth emerging from spiritual struggles can also be found. For example, in her book, *Scarred by Struggle, Transformed by Hope*, Chittister (2003) described the dramatic change she experienced as the result of her own spiritual struggle:

> [Spiritual struggle] gives life depth and vision, insight and understanding. It not only transforms us, it makes us transforming as well. . . . It teaches us our place in the universe. It teaches us how little we really need in life to be happy. It teaches us that every day life starts over again. (pp. 82, 85)

Although these accounts of growth are noteworthy, more systematic research has yielded more mixed findings at best. Spiritual struggles have been associated with reports of positive change in some research. For example, in a study of college students experiencing struggles with the divine or doubt-related struggles, students were to select whether they felt they had grown and/or declined as a result of their struggles. Almost half of the participants (49%) reported that they had grown through their struggle, 29% indicated they had experienced both growth and decline, and 21% reported that they had neither grown nor declined. Strikingly, only 3% felt they had simply declined as a result of their struggle (Desai & Pargament, 2015). Similarly, in a very different culture and context—drought survivors in Botswana—spiritual struggles were predictive of posttraumatic growth (Zeligman et al., 2020). In contrast, however, other studies have tied spiritual struggles to reports of personal and spiritual decline (e.g., Park et al., 2017; Wilt et al., 2019).

What do we conclude from these mixed findings? At the very least, it appears that growth following spiritual struggles is not inevitable. More often than not, these studies suggest, spiritual struggles may be a source of distress and decline rather than growth and transformation. Thus, practitioners should be careful not to sentimentalize spiritual struggles; pain in the spiritual realm does not always lead to gain. And yet, we should also be careful not to discount the personal accounts and studies that speak to the possibility of transformation through spiritual struggles.

This leads to a key question: What determines whether spiritual struggles lead to growth and/or decline? A small but growing body of research has begun to examine this question, and several factors have been identified that may shape the trajectory of spiritual struggles at this vital fork in the road toward greater wholeness and growth rather than brokenness and decline. These include the willingness to face rather than avoid spiritual struggles (Dworsky et al., 2016), support rather than stigmatize in the midst of struggles (Exline & Grubbs, 2011), the ability to reframe spiritual struggles in a larger benevolent spiritual perspective (Saritoprak et al., 2017), the experience of sacred moments that offset the effects of spiritual struggles (Magyar-Russell et al., 2020), openness to change rather than inflexibility (Hart et al., 2020), and the capacity to make meaning out of the struggle (Wilt, Exline, et al., 2016).

In short, a growing body of study points to the important implications spiritual struggles have for mental health. It follows that spiritual struggles should not be overlooked in the clinical context. How clients understand and deal with their spiritual struggles may affect their progress in treatment and their mental health outcomes. Practitioners can play a valuable role in helping struggling clients reorient themselves and regain their equilibrium. Therapists can also support and guide clients through their times of struggle toward wholeness and growth rather than decline. We turn our attention now to a few recommendations for approaching spiritual struggles in clinical work (for a more extensive discussion, see Pargament, 2007; Pargament & Exline, 2022).

HOW PRACTITIONERS CAN ADDRESS SPIRITUAL STRUGGLES IN CLINICAL WORK

In this section, we briefly describe several of the ways practitioners can work with clients in psychotherapy who may be experiencing spiritual struggles. A more complete description can be found in Pargament and Exline (2022).

Assess for Spiritual Struggles

Many therapists may feel reluctant to broach the topic of spirituality, and spiritual struggles in particular, for fear of overstepping their bounds and offending their clients. Yet, surveys of clients indicate that a majority are interested in talking about religious and spiritual issues in treatment (Rosmarin, 2018). An even larger percentage of clients experiencing spiritual struggles voice interest in discussing this topic (Exline et al., 2000). Thus, we recommend that therapists assess for spiritual struggles as a routine part of the initial interview. In the process of inquiring into the ways the client's problems have been impacting them psychologically, socially, and physically, a similar question can be raised about the possibility of spiritual struggles: "How have your problems affected you religiously or spiritually?"

This question may not necessarily lead to a positive response. Clients may hesitate to talk about their spiritual struggles for a variety of reasons, such as fear of the therapist's reaction, guilt about their struggles, or simply a lack of awareness. Nevertheless, practitioners should remain alert to indications of struggle as psychotherapy unfolds. Clients may make use of "psychospiritual" language that steers clear of explicit religious references (e.g., God, prayer) yet hints at a deeper transcendent dimension to the questions and concerns they are grappling with: "When will my suffering end?" "What have I done to deserve this punishment?" "I feel so contaminated." "Life is so unfair." Therapists can raise psychospiritual questions themselves that open the door to possible discussions of spiritual struggles, such as "How has this experience changed you at your deepest levels?" and "What parts of your life are causing you the greatest suffering or despair?"

When it becomes clear that the client may be experiencing spiritual struggles, the therapist can broach the topic explicitly by asking, "Have you been experiencing tensions, conflicts, or struggles about religion or spirituality? Can you tell me more?" This may spark a more in-depth conversation in which the therapist and client explore the roots of the client's spiritual struggles, the ways they have impacted the client, and how the client has tried to understand and deal with their struggles. The information gleaned from this process of assessment can help shape the course of treatment. It is important to add that the process of assessing spiritual struggles through questions and dialogue in therapy can be buttressed by more systematic assessment through validated measures. To this end, we recommend the use of the longer or shorter forms of the RSS (Exline et al., in press, 2014).

Name and Normalize Spiritual Struggles

As we have stressed, even though spiritual struggles have been linked with distress and declines in psychological functioning, they should not be equated with pathology. Struggles can be a normative part of development, experienced by even the most devout individuals, not only the world's great religious exemplars but also contemporary figures, such as Gandhi, Mother Teresa, and Elie Wiesel. In addition, while spiritual struggles can be a source of distress and disorientation, they also offer the potential for growth and transformation.

Clients going through periods of spiritual tension and conflict may feel that they are "losing their minds" or lacking a strong faith. Research suggests that they may also feel shame and guilt, as well as fears of critical, even condemning, reactions from others (Exline & Grubbs, 2011). This makes it particularly important for therapists to reassure clients that they are not losing their minds, give a name to their experience, and note that spiritual struggles are, for many people, a normal part of their spiritual development and may lead ultimately to growth and transformation. In this vein, therapists can preface conversations about spiritual struggles by saying, "Many people in a situation like yours would have some struggles around religion or spirituality, negative feelings in relationship to God, or doubts about their faith. I wonder if you've had any experiences like that?"

Facilitate Acceptance and Reflection

As with other painful emotions and experiences, some clients may try to suppress their spiritual struggles—often with detrimental effects. Therapists can help clients accept their spiritual struggles by encouraging them to simply notice and observe the thoughts and feelings that accompany these conflicts. Mindfulness exercises, such as one developed by Kornfield (2009), can be of value in this regard:

> If you have been fighting inner wars with your feelings . . . sense the struggle you have been waging. Notice the struggles in your thoughts as well. Be aware of how you have carried on the inner battles. Notice the inner armies, the inner dictators, the inner fortifications. Be aware of all that you have fought within yourself. . . . Gently, with openness, allow each of these experiences to be present. . . . In each area of struggle, let your body, heart, and soul be soft. Open to whatever you experience without fighting. Let it be present just as it is. Let go of the battle. Breathe quietly and let yourself be at rest. Invite all parts of yourself to join you at the peace table in your heart. (p. 30)

CASE EXAMPLE: JAMAL

With greater acceptance of spiritual struggles, clients are in a better position to reflect on their experiences with the help of their therapists and explore ways they might come to terms with their spiritual tensions, questions, and conflicts. Consider the following case of Jamal, a 20-year-old college sophomore and physics major, who was experiencing troubling doubts about the truths of some of the claims of his religious tradition:

> Jamal came to therapy complaining of insomnia, anxiety, and ruminations. Raised in a close-knit Muslim family and community, his academic prowess had won him a university scholarship and the great pride of his family. His courses in the hard sciences, though, were raising questions for him that were difficult to reconcile with his religious beliefs: "With all that I'm learning," he said, "I have a hard time seeing a God above pulling all of the strings." Jamal had broached some of his concerns with his imam and family, but their response was to "pray harder to make his doubts go away." Jamal's inability to pray his doubts away left him feeling only worse for being a bad Muslim.
>
> Initially, Jamal had hoped his therapist might eliminate his doubts and distress by providing direct answers to his religious questions. His therapist, however,

suggested a different approach to treatment: "I can't and wouldn't want to try to give you answers to your questions. Even if I had them, those would be my answers, not yours. Instead, I want you to try to make sense out of your questions for yourself. In here, my role is to serve as a guide who can help you find your own way through this thicket."

Over the course of therapy, Jamal explored what Islam meant to him. He talked about the power of the mystical feelings he occasionally experienced through prayer. He spoke of the values of Islam that he held dear, such as charity, modesty, hospitality, and forgiveness. He was able to describe the sense of closeness and warmth he felt in his family and community. What became clear to Jamal through this reflective process was that he did not want to turn away from his faith.

This recognition did not eliminate Jamal's struggles with religious doubt. He continued to question some core Islamic beliefs. But he became more open to exploring his struggles. Along the way, he found other Muslims on campus who were willing to share spiritual struggles of their own. Through this process, Jamal's orientation to his doubts broadened and deepened, and he started to consider the possibility that he might be able to live as a Muslim with some doubts, at least for now. As Jamal engaged his struggles in therapy, his symptoms of anxiety and sleeplessness began to diminish, though he continued to be preoccupied with religious and spiritual issues. (Pargament & Exline, 2022, pp. 227–239)

Practitioners have begun to develop and evaluate treatment programs to assist a variety of groups experiencing spiritual struggles, with some promising results. These include programs for military veterans (Starnino et al., 2019), adult survivors of sexual abuse (Murray-Swank & Pargament, 2005), patients with HIV/AIDS (Tarakeshwar et al., 2005), college students (Dworsky et al., 2013), and people with psychiatric problems (Reist Gibbel et al., 2019).

For example, Dworsky et al. (2013) developed Winding Road, a 9-week, group-based intervention for college students from diverse religious and spiritual backgrounds who are struggling spiritually. The program was designed to reduce stigma around spiritual struggles; facilitate acceptance of struggles; foster understanding of struggles; and enhance emotional, behavioral, and spiritual well-being. Over the course of the program, participants made significant improvements in relation to their spiritual struggles, including more positive affect, greater ability to regulate their emotions, lower levels of shame and stigma, and reductions in psychological distress. Some described not only less distress but also a new perspective on their struggles and personal growth. As one student noted,

> I had a lot of rash emotions coming into this experience . . . [Now] I look at my struggles as more of a positive. . . . I've matured in my view of the struggle—it doesn't have to be resolved right now. . . . Now it's not so much of a struggle as an evolution. (Dworsky et al., 2013, p. 328)

CONCLUSION

In this chapter, we have underscored the importance of understanding and addressing spiritual struggles in psychotherapy. This process does not have to be intimidating or overwhelming. By attending to spiritual struggles in therapy, we are not recommending a new form of treatment. In addition, this work does not call for a degree in theology or religion. Assessment of spiritual struggles, along with helping clients name, normalize, accept, and reflect on their struggles, build on the basic clinical skills that account for a great deal of the effectiveness of treatment: listening, empathy, trust, genuineness, and valuing.

Clinical work with spiritual struggles does call for a deep appreciation of the sensitive character of the spiritual dimension of clients' lives. Because conflicts involving faith touch on matters of deepest belief, commitment, values, and purpose in life, they are delicate issues that must be addressed with special sensitivity. This may be a challenge for some therapists who, as a group, tend to be considerably less religious than the clients they serve (Shafranske & Cummings, 2013). As a result, some practitioners may underestimate the prevalence and power of religion and spirituality in the lives of their clients. And yet, by minimizing or expressing disinterest or discomfort around the topic of spiritual struggles, practitioners close off potentially valuable dialogue and directions in the therapy room. Thus, it is important for therapists to be aware of their own orientation to spirituality and guard against biases that might interfere with successful treatment. At times, it will also be important for therapists to work collaboratively with pastoral counselors, clergy, chaplains, and spiritual directors. These religious professionals can provide religious and spiritual counsel and rituals that lie beyond the therapist's professional boundaries and competence.

We believe that therapists can enhance their effectiveness by further education about the diverse ways people experience and express spirituality in their lives; by understanding how spirituality can be helpful or harmful at times; by becoming more skillful in bringing spirituality into the therapeutic conversation; by helping clients access their spiritual resources; and by assisting clients when their spirituality is a source of struggle, distress, and disorientation. These are important spiritual competencies that represent a vital part of culturally sensitive care (Vieten & Scammell, 2015).

Because most therapists have not received training in spiritually integrated care, additional education and supervision may prove helpful. In this regard, Pearce and her colleagues developed an eight-module online educational program to foster spiritual competencies in mental health care that proved successful in improving the knowledge, skills, and attitudes of practitioners (Pearce et al., 2019, 2020). Addressing spiritual struggles was one important part of this training program.

We are only beginning to understand spiritual struggles and how they may be best approached in treatment. Further research is needed on the roots and consequences of spiritual struggles and, in particular, how the causal models of struggles—primary, secondary, or complex—apply to different clinical cases. More study is also called for that focuses on the implications of specific forms of spiritual struggle—divine, demonic, moral, ultimate meaning, doubt-related, and interpersonal—for mental health and psychological treatment. Because much of the research on spiritual struggles comes out of Western, Christian contexts, additional studies are needed that consider how to understand and address spiritual struggles among people from other cultures and religious affiliations and orientations, including agnostics, atheists, and the "nones." Finally, spiritual struggles should be brought more into the mainstream of psychological theorizing and research. For example, researchers might conduct evaluative studies of the impact of established psychotherapies and psychotropic medication on spiritual struggles and psychological functioning.

We are spiritual as well as emotional, social, and physical beings. Spirituality is an integral part of all human experience. This point holds true for psychotherapy as well. Spirituality cannot be fully separated from the problems people bring to treatment, the possible solutions to those problems, or the process of change more generally. The question then is not whether spirituality will have a role in therapy but whether the therapist will integrate the spiritual dimension into treatment in a thoughtful way. By integrating spirituality more explicitly into therapy, practitioners can enrich and deepen the process of change and foster greater wholeness and growth.

REFERENCES

Abu-Raiya, H., Pargament, K. I., Krause, N., & Ironson, G. (2015). Robust links between religious/spiritual struggles, psychological distress, and well-being in a national sample of American adults. *American Journal of Orthopsychiatry, 85*(6), 565–575. https://doi.org/10.1037/ort0000084

Bockrath, M. F., Pargament, K. I., Wong, S., Harriott, V. A., Pomerleau, J. M., Homolka, S. J., Chaudhary, Z. B., & Exline, J. J. (2021). Religious and spiritual struggles and their links with psychological adjustment: A meta-analysis of longitudinal studies. *Psychology of Religion and Spirituality*. Advance online publication. https://doi.org/10.1037/rel0000400

Chittister, J. D. (2003). *Scarred by struggle, transformed by hope*. William B. Eerdmans.

Currier, J. M., McDermott, R. C., McCormick, W. H., Churchwell, M. C., & Milkeris, L. (2018). Exploring cross-lagged associations between spiritual struggles and risk for suicidal behavior in a community sample of military veterans. *Journal of Affective Disorders, 230*(1), 93–100. https://doi.org/10.1016/j.jad.2018.01.009

Currier, J. M., Smith, P. N., & Kuhlman, S. (2017). Assessing the unique role of religious coping in suicidal behavior among U.S. Iraq and Afghanistan veterans. *Psychology of Religion and Spirituality, 9*(1), 118–123. https://doi.org/10.1037/rel0000055

Desai, K. M., & Pargament, K. I. (2015). Predictors of growth and decline following spiritual struggles. *International Journal for the Psychology of Religion, 25*(1), 42–56. https://doi.org/10.1080/10508619.2013.847697

Dworsky, C. K. O., Pargament, K. I., Gibbel, M. R., Krumrei, E. J., Faigin, C. A., Haugan, M. R. G., Desai, K. M., Lauricella, S. K., Lynn, Q., & Warner, H. L. (2013). Winding Road: Preliminary support for a spiritually integrated intervention addressing college students' spiritual struggles. *Research in the Social Scientific Study of Religion, 24*, 309–340. https://doi.org/10.1163/9789004252073_013

Dworsky, C. K. O., Pargament, K. I., Wong, S., & Exline, J. J. (2016). Suppressing spiritual struggles: The role of experiential avoidance in mental health. *Journal of Contextual Behavioral Science, 5*(4), 258–265. https://doi.org/10.1016/j.jcbs.2016.10.002

Emmons, R. A., & Schnitker, S. A. (2013). Gods and goals: Religion and purposeful action. In R. F. Paloutzian & C. L. Park (Eds.), *Handbook of the psychology of religion and spirituality* (2nd ed., pp. 256–273). Guilford Press.

Exline, J. J. (2013). Religious and spiritual struggles. In K. I. Pargament, J. J. Exline, & J. W. Jones (Eds.), *APA handbook of psychology, religion, and spirituality: Vol. 1. Context, theory, and research* (pp. 459–475). American Psychological Association. https://doi.org/10.1037/14045-025

Exline, J. J., & Grubbs, J. B. (2011). "If I tell others about my anger toward God, how will they respond?" Predictors, associated behaviors, and outcomes in an adult sample. *Journal of Psychology and Theology, 39*(4), 304–315. https://doi.org/10.1177/009164711103900402

Exline, J. J., Pargament, K. I., Grubbs, J. B., & Yali, A. M. (2014). The Religious and Spiritual Struggles Scale: Development and initial validation. *Psychology of Religion and Spirituality, 6*(3), 208–222. https://doi.org/10.1037/a0036465

Exline, J. J., Pargament, K. I., Wilt, J. A., Grubbs, J. G., & Yali, A. M. (in press). The RSS-14: Development and preliminary validation of a 14-item form of the Religious and Spiritual Struggles Scale. *Psychology of Religion and Spirituality.*

Exline, J. J., Yali, A. M., & Sanderson, W. C. (2000). Guilt, discord, and alienation: The role of religious strain in depression and suicidality. *Journal of Clinical Psychology, 56*(12), 1481–1496. https://doi.org/10.1002/1097-4679(200012)56:12<1481::AID-1>3.0.CO;2-A

Grubbs, J. B., Exline, J. J., Pargament, K. I., Volk, F., & Lindberg, M. J. (2017). Internet pornography use, perceived addiction, and religious/spiritual struggles. *Archives of Sexual Behavior, 46*(6), 1733–1745. https://doi.org/10.1007/s10508-016-0772-9

Hart, A. C., Pargament, K. I., Grubbs, J. B., Exline, J. J., & Wilt, J. A. (2020). Predictors of growth and decline following religious and spiritual struggles: Exploring the role of wholeness. *Religions, 11*(9), Article 445. https://doi.org/10.3390/rel11090445

Janů, A., Malinkakova, K., Kosarkova, A., & Tavel, P. (2022). Associations of childhood trauma experiences with religious and spiritual struggles. *Journal of Health Psychology, 27*(2), 292–304. https://doi.org/10.1177/1359105320950793

Kao, L. E., Shah, S. B., Pargament, K. I., Griffith, J. L., & Peteet, J. R. (2019). "Gambling with God": A self-inflicted gunshot wound with religious motivation in the context of a mixed-mood episode. *Harvard Review of Psychiatry, 27*(1), 65–72. https://doi.org/10.1097/HRP.0000000000000218

Kopacz, M. S., Currier, J. M., Drescher, K. D., & Pigeon, W. R. (2016). Suicidal behavior and spiritual functioning in a sample of Veterans diagnosed with PTSD. *Journal of Injury and Violence Research, 8*(1), 6–14. https://doi.org/10.5249/jivr.v8i1.728

Kornfield, J. (2009). *A path with heart: A guide through the perils and promises of spiritual life.* Bantam Books.

Krause, N., Pargament, K. I., Hill, P., Wong, S., & Ironson, G. (2017). Exploring the relationships among age, spiritual struggles, and health. *Journal of Religion, Spirituality and Aging, 29*(4), 266–285. https://doi.org/10.1080/15528030.2017.1285844

Magyar-Russell, G., Pargament, K. I., Grubbs, J. B., Wilt, J. A., & Exline, J. J. (2020). The experience of sacred moments and mental health benefits over time. *Psychology of Religion and Spirituality.* Advance online publication. https://doi.org/10.1037/rel0000394

McConnell, K. M., Pargament, K. I., Ellison, C. G., & Flannelly, K. J. (2006). Examining the links between spiritual struggles and symptoms of psychopathology in a national sample. *Journal of Clinical Psychology, 62*(12), 1469–1484. https://doi.org/10.1002/jclp.20325

Murphy, P. E., Fitchett, G., & Emery-Tiburcio, E. (2016). Religious and spiritual struggle: Prevalence and correlates among older adults with depression in the BRIGHTEN program. *Mental Health, Religion & Culture, 19*(7), 713–721. https://doi.org/10.1080/13674676.2016.1244178

Murray-Swank, N. A., & Pargament, K. I. (2005). God, where are you? Evaluating a spiritually-integrated intervention for sexual abuse. *Mental Health, Religion & Culture, 8*(3), 191–203. https://doi.org/10.1080/13694670500138866

Neimeyer, R. A., & Burke, L. A. (2011). Complicated grief in the aftermath of homicide: Spiritual crisis and distress in an African American sample. *Religions, 2*(2), 145–164. https://doi.org/10.3390/rel2020145

Pargament, K. I. (2007). *Spiritually integrated psychotherapy: Understanding and addressing the sacred*. Guilford Press.

Pargament, K. I., & Exline, J. J. (2022). *Working with spiritual struggles in psychotherapy: From research to practice*. Guilford Press.

Pargament, K. I., & Lomax, J. W. (2013). Understanding and addressing religion among people with mental illness. *World Psychiatry, 12*(1), 26–32. https://doi.org/10.1002/wps.20005

Park, C. L., Smith, P. H., Lee, S. Y., Mazure, C. M., McKee, S. A., & Hoff, R. (2017). Positive and negative religious/spiritual coping and combat exposure as predictors of post-traumatic stress and perceived growth in Iraq and Afghanistan veterans. *Psychology of Religion and Spirituality, 9*(1), 13–20. https://doi.org/10.1037/rel0000086

Pearce, M. J., Pargament, K. I., Oxhandler, H. K., Vieten, C., & Wong, S. (2019). A novel training program for mental health providers in religious and spiritual competencies. *Spirituality in Clinical Practice, 6*(2), 73–82. https://doi.org/10.1037/scp0000195

Pearce, M. J., Pargament, K. I., Oxhandler, H. K., Vieten, C., & Wong, S. (2020). Novel online training program improves spiritual competencies in mental health care. *Spirituality in Clinical Practice, 7*(3), 145–161. https://doi.org/10.1037/scp0000208

Phillips, J. B. (1997). *Your God is too small*. Touchstone Books.

Pomerleau, J. M., Pargament, K. I., Krause, N., Ironson, G., & Hill, P. (2020). Religious and spiritual struggles as a mediator of the link between stressful life events and psychological adjustment. *Psychology of Religion and Spirituality, 12*(4), 451–459. https://doi.org/10.1037/rel0000268

Pruyser, P. W. (1977). The seamy side of current religious beliefs. *Bulletin of the Menninger Clinic, 41*(4), 329–348.

Reist Gibbel, M., Regueiro, V., & Pargament, K. I. (2019). A spiritually integrated intervention for spiritual struggles among adults with mental illness: Results of an initial evaluation. *Spirituality in Clinical Practice, 6*(4), 240–255. https://doi.org/10.1037/scp0000207

Robertson, T. M., Magyar-Russell, G. M., & Piedmont, R. L. (2020). Let him who is without sin cast the first stone: Religious struggle among persons convicted of sexually offending. *Religions, 11*(11), Article 546. https://doi.org/10.3390/rel11110546

Rosmarin, D. H. (2018). *Spirituality, religion, and cognitive-behavioral therapy: A guide for clinicians*. Guilford Press.

Rosmarin, D. H., Bigda-Peyton, J. S., Öngur, D., Pargament, K. I., & Björgvinsson, T. (2013). Religious coping among psychotic patients: Relevance to suicidality and treatment outcomes. *Psychiatry Research, 210*(1), 182–187. https://doi.org/10.1016/j.psychres.2013.03.023

Rosmarin, D. H., Malloy, M. C., & Forester, B. P. (2014). Spiritual struggle and affective symptoms among geriatric mood disordered patients. *International Journal of Geriatric Psychiatry, 29*(6), 653–660. https://doi.org/10.1002/gps.4052

Rossetti, S. J. (1995). The impact of child sexual abuse on attitudes toward God and the Catholic Church. *Child Abuse & Neglect, 19*(12), 1469–1481. https://doi.org/10.1016/0145-2134(95)00100-1

Saritoprak, S. N., Exline, J. J., Hall, T. W., & Pargament, K. I. (2017, April 7–8). *Does God use struggles to transform us?: Both Christians and Muslims can approach struggles with a transformational mindset* [Paper presentation]. American Psychological Association, Division 36, Society for the Psychology of Religion and Spirituality, Annual Mid-Year Conference on Religion and Spirituality, Chattanooga, TN, United States.

Shafranske, E. P., & Cummings, J. P. (2013). Religious and spiritual beliefs, affiliations, and practices of psychologists. In K. I. Pargament, A. Mahoney, & E. Shafranske (Eds.), *APA handbook of psychology, religion, and spirituality: Vol. 2. An applied psychology of religion and spirituality* (pp. 23–42). American Psychological Association. https://doi.org/10.1037/14046-002

Starnino, V. R., Angel, C. T., Sullivan, J. E., Lazarick, D. L., Jaimes, L. D., Cocco, J. P., & Davis, L. W. (2019). Preliminary report on a spiritually-based PTSD intervention for military veterans. *Community Mental Health Journal, 55*(7), 1114–1119. https://doi.org/10.1007/s10597-019-00414-8

Tarakeshwar, N., Pearce, M. J., & Sikkema, K. J. (2005). Development and implementation of a spiritual coping group intervention for adults living with HIV/AIDS: A pilot study. *Mental Health, Religion & Culture, 8*(3), 179–190. https://doi.org/10.1080/13694670500138908

Vieten, C., & Scammell, S. (2015). *Spiritual and religious competencies in clinical practice: Guidelines for psychotherapists and mental health professionals*. New Harbinger Publications.

Wilt, J. A., Exline, J. J., Grubbs, J. B., Park, C. L., & Pargament, K. I. (2016). God's role in suffering: Theodicies, divine struggle, and mental health. *Psychology of Religion and Spirituality, 8*(4), 352–362. https://doi.org/10.1037/rel0000058

Wilt, J. A., Grubbs, J. B., Exline, J. J., & Pargament, K. I. (2021). Authenticity, presence of meaning, and struggle with ultimate meaning: Nuanced between- and within-person associations. *Journal of Research in Personality, 93*, Article 104104. https://doi.org/10.1016/j.jrp.2021.104104

Wilt, J. A., Grubbs, J. B., Pargament, K. I., & Exline, J. J. (2016). Personality, religious and spiritual struggles, and well-being. *Psychology of Religion and Spirituality, 8*(4), 341–351. https://doi.org/10.1037/rel0000054

Wilt, J. A., Grubbs, J. B., Pargament, K. I., & Exline, J. J. (2017). Religious and spiritual struggles, past and present: Relations to the Big Five and well-being. *The International Journal for the Psychology of Religion, 27*(1), 51–64. https://doi.org/10.1080/10508619.2016.1183251

Wilt, J. A., Pargament, K. I., Exline, J. J., Barrera, T. L., Stanley, M. A., & Teng, E. J. (2019). Spiritual transformation among veterans in response to a religious/spiritual struggle. *Psychology of Religion and Spirituality, 11*(3), 266–277. https://doi.org/10.1037/rel0000208

Winkelman, W. D., Lauderdale, K., Balboni, M. J., Phelps, A. C., Peteet, J. R., Block, S. D., Kachnic, L. A., VanderWeele, T. J., & Balboni, T. A. (2011). The relationship of spiritual concerns to the quality of life of advanced cancer patients: Preliminary findings. *Journal of Palliative Medicine, 14*(9), 1022–1028. https://doi.org/10.1089/jpm.2010.0536

Yıldırım, M., Arslan, G., & Alkahtani, A. M. (2021). Do fear of COVID-19 and religious coping predict depression, anxiety, and stress among the Arab population during health crisis? *Death Studies*. Advance online publication. https://doi.org/10.1080/07481187.2021.1882617

Zeligman, M., Majuta, A. R., & Shannonhouse, L. R. (2020). Posttraumatic growth in prolonged drought survivors in Botswana: The role of social support and religious coping. *Traumatology, 26*(3), 308–316. https://doi.org/10.1037/trm0000237

7

A Spiritually Inclusive Theistic Approach to Psychotherapy in Inpatient, Residential, and Outpatient Settings

Michael E. Berrett, Randy K. Hardman, and P. Scott Richards

Spirituality is universal. It is available to every human being.
—DAVID N. ELKINS (1998, p. 32)

Helping patients renew spiritual connections that facilitate psychosocial healing and recovery is challenging and requires both spiritual and clinical competence (Berrett et al., 2010; Pargament, 2007; Richards & Bergin, 2005). The foundational attitudes of a spiritually inclusive approach are humility and a willingness to explore a patient's religious, spiritual, and cultural beliefs and resources during treatment, if the patient wishes. Spiritually inclusive psychotherapists must generalize multicultural attitudes and skills to the religious and spiritual domains, which requires knowledge about religious and spiritual aspects of human diversity and specialized treatment competencies (Richards & Bergin, 2005, 2014).

In this chapter, we describe our spiritually inclusive theistic framework and approach for psychotherapy. We hope that it will help mental health professionals more fully embrace and honor the healing potential of their patients' beliefs and resources, regardless of the patient's religious orientation, race, ethnicity, culture, beliefs, and values.

The authors contributed equally to the content of this chapter, so order of authorship is listed alphabetically. We have been colleagues for 30 years in clinical practice, research, and writing. This chapter is a culmination and synthesis of ideas that have emerged from our collaboration.

https://doi.org/10.1037/0000338-007
Handbook of Spiritually Integrated Psychotherapies, P. S. Richards, G. E. K. Allen, and D. K. Judd (Editors)
Copyright © 2023 by the American Psychological Association. All rights reserved.

WHAT IS SPIRITUALLY INCLUSIVE PSYCHOTHERAPY?

In our spiritually inclusive theistic psychotherapy approach, we seek to treat the whole individual—physical, mental, emotional, relational, and spiritual—and thus include their spiritual questions, concerns, wounds, struggles, strengths, faith, beliefs, and potential in the healing process. We assume that each member of the human race has a spiritual nature and that by attending to that spirituality in the clinical process of treatment and healing, they can not only find their spiritual essence but can nurture it to the benefit of themselves, their families, and even to influence their community and world in positive ways.

We seek to be sensitive, respectful, and inclusive of everyone's spiritual or religious beliefs. We seek to honor the diversity of humanity and the uniqueness and agency of everyone. We respect patients' spiritual beliefs rather than dismiss or disparage them. In our approach, each person's spiritual beliefs and practices are used to their benefit toward the goals of healing, recovery, and growth. We work inclusively with patients from a wide range of spiritual beliefs and worldviews from atheistic to religiously orthodox: New Age, Eastern, spiritual but not religious, Jewish, Christian, Muslim, Indigenous, humanistic and existential, nature- or Mother Earth–centered, traditionally religious. All are welcome. We seek to live in harmony with principles and values that are essential for psychological and spiritual healing and growth, including compassion, kindness, charity, service, and engagement in worthy causes that bless individuals and make our world better. Our approach focuses on and strives for inclusivity.

Our spiritually inclusive approach does not replace traditional evidence-based psychological and medical approaches. It is woven into existing therapy models. Our willingness to include spirituality and give patients permission to openly talk about their spirituality or religious life is affirming and helpful to them. It helps patients explore, expand, and enlarge their spiritual resources and influences to assist in their journeys of healing and change. The amount of time we focus on and discuss spirituality depends on the patient and their desire, receptivity, and need, ranging from minimal, brief, and infrequent discussions to regular, significant, and frequent discussions and follow-through during therapy sessions. We start wherever patients are in their spirituality and build on their spiritual strengths and resources according to their preferences and desire.

WHY IS A SPIRITUALLY INCLUSIVE APPROACH NEEDED?

To ignore the spirituality of our patients is to ignore an important part of them—and arguably, the most important part. This may be the very essence and core of who they are. On the other hand, to attend to their spirituality honors our patients. It tells them that "what is important to you is important to me." Honoring the importance of the spiritual pushes no specific spiritual belief, doctrine, or template on them, but it does invite them to recognize, clarify, and use their own spirituality toward healing and recovery from illness as well as toward personal growth and development. Nurturing the spiritual nurtures resiliency; hopefulness; and, for many, a fulfilling life.

A spiritually inclusive approach is important because all spiritual approaches are rooted, in some fashion, in lofty and universally accepted spiritual principles, such as love, kindness, compassion, forgiveness, responsibility, belonging, honesty, congruence, and integrity. Striving to live such principles in the process of recovery can lift individuals, deepen relationships, improve communities, and change the world for good. Psychotherapy must honor diversity and promote acceptance, respect, and inclusion. Including the spiritual does honor patients, helps them feel safer, nurtures trust in the relationship, and strengthens the therapeutic alliance. Including discussions about our patients' spirituality during treatment increases our understanding of them, helps them understand themselves better, and allows therapists to identify and use their spiritual strengths and resources during the healing process.

Spiritual beliefs are often some of the most important beliefs individuals have. Therefore, honoring and using them in treatment can enhance reasons and motives to work hard in treatment and recovery. Spiritual beliefs and values are often tied to patients' sense of purpose, mission, and vision—their deepest desires and dreams—to the very core of their identity. Helping patients remember, connect with, and honor their spiritual beliefs and values can increase motivation and consistency in self-care, improving their lives and the lives of those within their circle of influence. Many of patients, because of mental and emotional illness—especially in cases of addiction, abuse, trauma, and eating disorders—begin to believe that their identity is the same as the illness, and they can lose track of their sense of self. Helping patients reconnect with their spiritual identity can bring them back to a clearer sense of identity and worth, including their purpose, potential, goodness, and value.

A spiritually inclusive approach is important because during treatment we are seeking health and wellness for our patients beyond symptom cessation; beyond behavioral change; and even beyond resolution, healing, or management of mental and emotional struggles or illness. We seek to help them grow, develop, actualize, fulfill, and become everything they could and can become.

During psychotherapy sessions, spiritually inclusive psychotherapists are careful not to push their own spiritual or religious views and beliefs onto their patients by rigidly ignoring or degrading the spiritual beliefs and concerns of the patient, nor do they impose any specific spiritual views or practices. They ask patients if they have spiritual or religious issues that are impacting their lives or exacerbating mental, emotional, and relational struggles for which they have sought treatment. They ask patients if they feel that their spirituality or religious beliefs or practices would be important in their healing process from the illness or struggles they are facing, and if so, how those spiritual beliefs and practices may be important or helpful. They ask patients if they would like to include spiritual or religious concerns and issues in their mental health treatment—or not.

Using informal or formal assessment tools and questions, spiritually inclusive psychotherapists take the time necessary to learn about and understand their patients' spiritual and religious beliefs as a part of an overall assessment. Such an assessment helps the clinician best honor their patients' diversity, be respectful about their beliefs, and use those beliefs in the benefit of their recovery and wellness.

Spiritually inclusive psychotherapists use general and universally accepted spiritual principles as an ongoing part of the psychotherapeutic process. They create and include interventions that address specific spiritual wounds, dilemmas, or issues of concern to their patients that may be negatively affecting their functioning and wellness. They implement spiritual approaches and interventions that do not replace but, rather, strengthen and add to evidence-based medical and clinical best practice modalities of treatment.

CONCEPTUAL MODEL FOR SPIRITUALLY INCLUSIVE THEISTIC PSYCHOTHERAPY

Figure 7.1 presents a conceptual model for our spiritually inclusive theistic treatment approach. We have adapted and expanded on the model from previous publications (Richards et al., 2018, 2020).

The left side of Figure 7.1 illustrates that spiritual disconnection may adversely affect a person's psychological and relationship functioning, and vice versa (Pargament, 2007). We define *spiritual connection* as patients' felt sense of the quality of their relationship with God, Higher Power, the sacred, or spiritual source.

In our clinical work, we have noticed that the loss of spiritual connection in patients' lives is manifested in numerous ways, including a loss of spiritual identity and worth; disconnection from spiritual beliefs and practices; a shift to extrinsic rather than intrinsic religious motivations; negative God image; loss of spiritual intuitions; loss of passion, purpose, and meaning; withdrawal from religious community; and loss of social support. These spiritual struggles may contribute to the development of an external locus of identity and worth as well as an orientation to life that focuses on the past or future, not the present.

Spiritual disconnection and struggles may exacerbate, cause, or be caused by psychosocial struggles and problems, including unresolved trauma, behavioral disorders, mood disorders, perfectionism, obsessions, compulsions, addiction, negative body image, poor self-esteem, relationship conflict, and poor life functioning and unhappiness. Of course, not all spiritual struggles cause psychological and relationship problems, or vice versa. In our clinical work, we have observed that spiritual connections may remain strong during psychosocial struggles and help patients cope and heal (Richards et al., 2018). Emotionally healthy people are not immune to spiritual struggles, nor are spiritually minded people immune to psychological problems. But our clinical experience suggests that spiritual and psychosocial functioning may be intertwined,

FIGURE 7.1. Role of Religion and Spirituality in Treatment and Recovery

SPIRITUAL DISCONNECTION

Loss of spiritual identity and worth
Extrinsic religious orientation
Negative God image
Loss of spiritual intuitions
Disconnection from passion and purpose
Difficulty receiving and giving love
Alienation from spiritual community

External locus of identity; past or future focus of life

PSYCHOSOCIAL PROBLEMS

Unresolved trauma
Mood disorders
Behavioral disorders
Perfectionism
Obsessions and compulsions
Addictions
Low self-esteem
Negative self-image
Relationship conflict and dysfunction
Poor functioning and unhappiness

Unhealthy life cycle

SPIRITUALLY INCLUSIVE THEISTIC TREATMENT

Conceptual Foundations
Theistic worldview; multidisciplinary, treatment-tailored, best practices; evidence-based care

SPIRITUAL PATHWAYS FOR TREATMENT AND HEALING

Basic Competencies
- Create spiritually safe environment
- Conduct spiritual assessment
- Learn client's spiritual language
- Support setting of spiritual treatment goals
- Give attention to spiritual struggles and resources
- Evaluate spiritual outcomes

Advanced Competencies
(See Figure 7.2)
- Focus on primary spiritual processes
- Integrate universal spiritual principles
- Support use of spiritual practices

Treatment

SPIRITUAL CONNECTION

Reclamation of spiritual identity and worth
Reconnection to spiritual beliefs and practices
Religious motivations internalized and intrinsic
Positive image of God
Regaining of spiritual intuitions
Ability to receive and give love
Connection to passion and purpose
Reclamation of social support
Acceptance in spiritual community

Internal locus of identity; living in present is focus

PSYCHOSOCIAL HEALING

Healing from trauma
Positive emotions
Respectful and uplifting behaviors
Self-acceptance and compassion
Freedom from judging self and others
Goodwill toward self and others
Fulfilling, close relationships
Living one's passion and purpose
Spiritual peace and well-being

Healthy life cycle

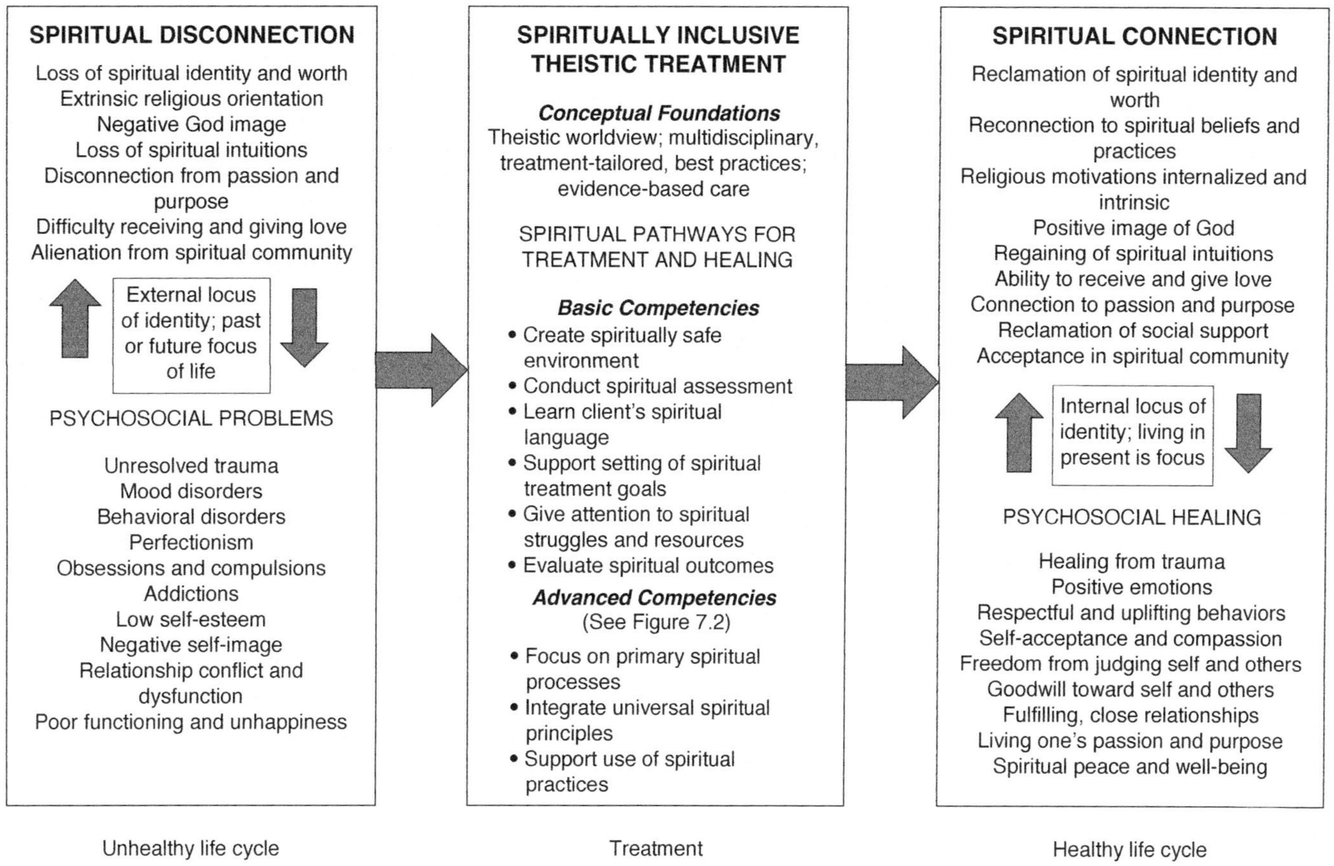

Note. Adapted from "An Exploration of the Role of Religion and Spirituality in the Treatment and Recovery of Patients With Eating Disorders," by P. S. Richards, C. C. Caoili, S. A. Crowton, M. E. Berrett, R. K. Hardman, R. N. Jackson, and P. W. Sanders, 2018, *Spirituality in Clinical Practice, 5*(2), pp. 88–103 (https://doi.org/10.1037/scp0000159). Copyright 2018 by the American Psychological Association.

and that problems in one can contribute to difficulties in the other (Pargament, 2007; Richards & Bergin, 2005, 2014).

The middle of Figure 7.1 is intended to illustrate that spiritually inclusive theistic treatment can break unhealthy reciprocal influences between spiritual struggles and psychosocial functioning by helping patients reconnect with spirituality (Richards & Bergin, 2005; Richards et al., 2007). This can help patients begin a healthy cycle of recovery in which spiritual and psychosocial resources and functioning influence each other in mutually healing ways.

The middle of Figure 7.1 also shows that our approach is grounded theologically, philosophically, and theoretically in the theistic worldview, which assumes that God exists, that human beings are the creation of God, and that there are spiritual influences and resources available that can help people cope, heal, and recover (Bergin, 1980; Richards & Bergin, 2005; Richards et al., 2007). The figure also indicates that we integrate spiritual perspectives and interventions in a treatment-tailoring fashion with mainstream, evidence-based, medical, and psychological treatment practices (Richards et al., 2007). The figure lists some basic competencies for spiritually inclusive psychotherapy, including establishing a spiritually safe environment, conducting a spiritual assessment, learning our patients' spiritual language, setting spiritual treatment goals, giving attention to spiritual struggles and resources, and evaluating spiritual outcomes. The figure also lists three advanced competencies and therapeutic strategies—we call them "spiritual pathways for treatment and healing"—including focusing on primary spiritual processes, integrating universal spiritual principles, and supporting the use of spiritual practices. We provide more details about the three spiritual pathways in the next section.

The right side of Figure 7.1 illustrates that psychosocial healing and recovery is enhanced by renewed spiritual connections, and vice versa. As patients renew connections with their spiritual source, their spiritual identity is affirmed and renewed; they shift from an extrinsic to intrinsic spiritual orientation; their image of God becomes more loving and benevolent; they learn to again experience and trust spiritual intuitions; they relearn how to give and receive love; they experience a renewed sense of purpose, meaning, and passion for life; and they reclaim social support and acceptance in their spiritual community. Patients' locus of identity and self-worth may shift over time from external, materialistic criteria to valuing and living in harmony with internal spiritual principles and values (Berrett et al., 2010, 2018; Dahlsgaard et al., 2005; Richards & Bergin, 2005; Richards et al., 2007; Seligman et al., 2005).

THREE SPIRITUAL PATHWAYS TO RECOVERY AND HEALING IN PSYCHOTHERAPY

Figure 7.2 illustrates that our approach has three primary spiritual pathways for helping patients use their spiritual nature and beliefs in the process of psychotherapy and in recovery and healing from mental, emotional, relational,

FIGURE 7.2. Three Spiritual Pathways in Treatment and Healing

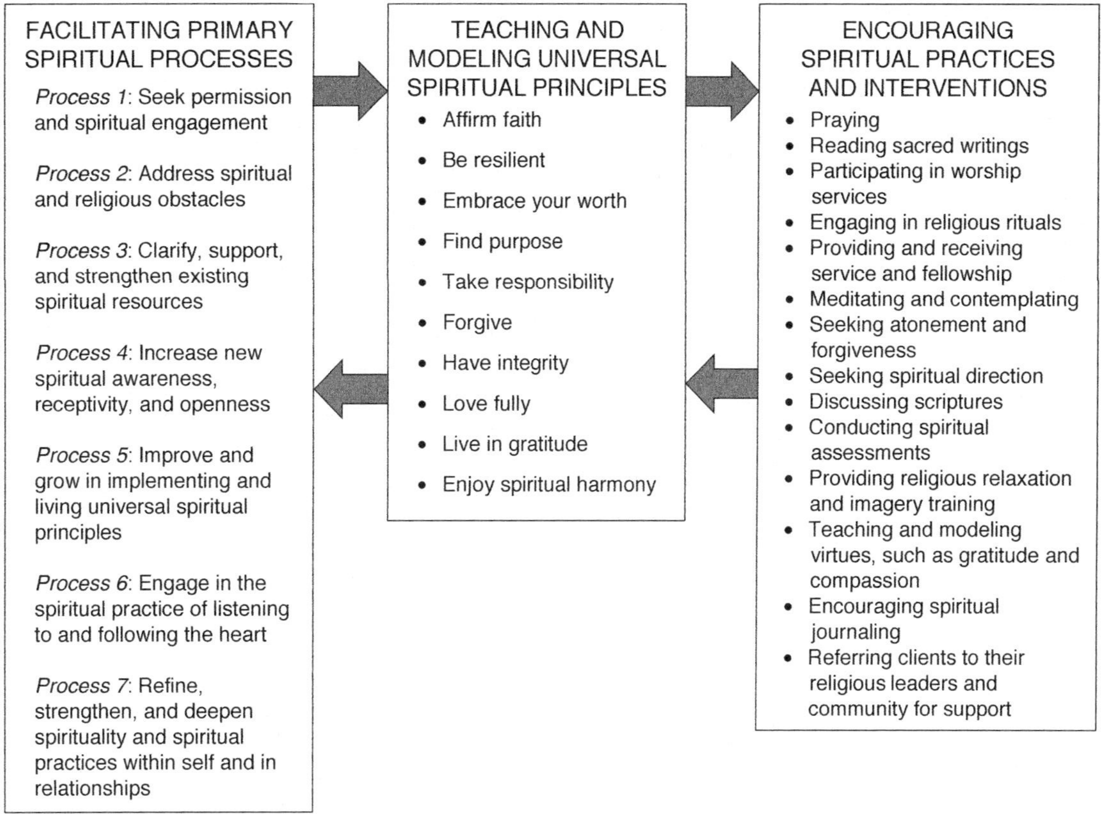

FACILITATING PRIMARY SPIRITUAL PROCESSES

Process 1: Seek permission and spiritual engagement

Process 2: Address spiritual and religious obstacles

Process 3: Clarify, support, and strengthen existing spiritual resources

Process 4: Increase new spiritual awareness, receptivity, and openness

Process 5: Improve and grow in implementing and living universal spiritual principles

Process 6: Engage in the spiritual practice of listening to and following the heart

Process 7: Refine, strengthen, and deepen spirituality and spiritual practices within self and in relationships

TEACHING AND MODELING UNIVERSAL SPIRITUAL PRINCIPLES

- Affirm faith
- Be resilient
- Embrace your worth
- Find purpose
- Take responsibility
- Forgive
- Have integrity
- Love fully
- Live in gratitude
- Enjoy spiritual harmony

ENCOURAGING SPIRITUAL PRACTICES AND INTERVENTIONS

- Praying
- Reading sacred writings
- Participating in worship services
- Engaging in religious rituals
- Providing and receiving service and fellowship
- Meditating and contemplating
- Seeking atonement and forgiveness
- Seeking spiritual direction
- Discussing scriptures
- Conducting spiritual assessments
- Providing religious relaxation and imagery training
- Teaching and modeling virtues, such as gratitude and compassion
- Encouraging spiritual journaling
- Referring clients to their religious leaders and community for support

and spiritual illness or struggle. These global pathways are (a) facilitating primary spiritual processes during treatment; (b) teaching and modeling universal spiritual principles relevant to healing and recovery; and (c) helping patients engage in personal spiritual practices and spiritual interventions that are consistent with their spiritual beliefs—all toward recovery, healing, and wellness. As suggested by Covey (1991), "Principles are the core of the matter—the 'why of doing' therapeutic and spiritual work. Practices are the 'what to do' in therapeutic work, and the processes are the 'how to do it.'" (p. 25). Within these three primary spiritual pathways are many specific spiritual principles, practices, and processes that can become spiritual pathways to healing as well.

Spiritual processes, principles, and practices all overlap greatly. For example, there are psychotherapeutic processes that therapists can use to facilitate the growth of loving relationships for their patients. For example, therapists can focus on and bring up the topic of love in the patient's life to bring this principle into the patient's awareness and into the therapeutic work. Therapists can label patients' efforts and actions as love if patients don't see their ability to love. They can challenge patients to express love more fully. The principle of loving others also has practices that invite, promote, and increase the giving, receiving, and deepening of love in relationships. For example, practices therapists might recommend to help patients grow in their ability to give and receive love might include encouraging patients to thank others directly for the love they have been given or performing charitable acts of service and kindness to family members and friends. We now highlight some of the spiritual processes that we use with patients during the course of treatment.

Pathway 1: Facilitating Primary Spiritual Processes During Treatment

In each session, we primarily focus on psychological, emotional, and relationship concerns and issues with patients but spend some time focused on spiritual processes. If spiritual growth is a primary goal for the patient, we focus on that, too. Otherwise, we generally encourage patients to include and use their spirituality and religious beliefs and practices to help them with their emotional and relationship issues. As therapy progresses and the therapeutic relationship and trust are stronger, we more actively focus on and use the patient's spiritual and religious strengths, experiences, and capacities to help them in the change process. We see the psychological and spiritual areas of therapy work as two complementary focuses that often interact and interconnect with each other during treatment.

The spiritual processes discussed shortly can take place at any time during therapy, depending on the readiness and spiritual needs of the patient. We allow the patient to decide on the timing of a particular spiritual focus, discussion, and intervention. We have observed that there is a typical pattern in the spiritual processes of therapy consistent with seven processes.

Process 1: Seek Permission and Spiritual Engagement

We gather background information about spirituality and religion in the patient's life and obtain patients' permission to include and use spiritual strengths and resources to help them with their psychological, relationship, and spiritual needs and goals. Sometimes we ask what religious or spiritual goals patients have for themselves and want to include as part of therapy discussions. We ask explicitly for their permission to include and use their spirituality as well as their own spiritual and religious resources, connections, and practices as a part of the therapy. Patients hear and know early in the therapy process that we value, respect, and support the spiritual and religious aspects of their lives because we know it can be a valuable and helpful resource for them. We find it is often important to develop and build a deep level of trust in the therapeutic relationship before spending much time on spiritual and religious matters. Each week, we check in and ask patients about what is happening for them in the spiritual area of their lives to see if we can use their spiritual experiences and insights in our therapy work. It is important for the therapist to take an active (not passive) approach in bringing up and inviting spiritual focuses and discussions early in therapy. We also encourage patients to initiate and bring up important and relevant spiritual information on their own to discuss in sessions.

Process 2: Address Spiritual and Religious Obstacles

It is important to clarify and address obstacles and impediments to patients' spirituality and to work on spiritual struggles, wounds, and challenges that interfere with their spirituality. We find it is important to engage in that spiritual resolution process early in therapy, especially with religious patients. We have learned over the years that for some patients, we cannot ignore or gloss over their spiritual obstacles if we are going to fully help them to be successful in the deep spiritually integrated aspects of therapy. If spiritual obstacles are present, they need to be the first spiritual focus and work in therapy. We use spiritual discussions, understandings, and interventions to help patients address and resolve their spiritual obstacles. Resolving spiritual obstacles often opens up new spiritual insights and experiences for patients. This early spiritual problem solving is essential to help patients deepen their spiritual awareness and gain understandings that can help them work on their challenges.

Process 3: Clarify, Support, and Strengthen Existing Spiritual Practices

To clarify and use patients' existing spiritual strengths and practices can be a helpful and powerful process in therapy. In addition to recognizing and talking with patients about how their current spiritual practices can help them reach their therapy goals, it is also important to find new ways to strengthen and enlarge patients' spiritual skills and practices. We have found it helpful with religious patients to talk with them about prayer and their prayer practices as well as to strengthen and sometimes improve their prayer patterns to help them personally and in their therapy work. Other examples of spiritual practices that may already be present in patients' lives could be meditation, yoga, spiritual self-reflection, service and charitable behaviors, empathy and compassion for others, generosity, a spiritual connection to nature, honesty and integrity, kind and loving interactions with other people, spiritual study and contemplation, gratitude, quiet alone times to nurture spiritual connections, church attendance, religious activities and observances, faith, and devotions. Identifying, discussing, supporting, and strengthening patients existing spiritual practices can be helpful in healing and growth.

Process 4: Increase New Spiritual Awareness, Receptivity, and Openness
The next spiritual process is increasing and enlarging patients' receptivity to and trust in spiritual influences and experiences. We talk with patients about ways to look, listen, and recognize and respond to the spiritual influences and manifestations they experience. For some patients, this new spiritual awareness and openness may be quiet, reflective, intuitive, and subtle. It may occur during meditation, when enjoying nature, listening to music, reading enlightening literature, writing in their journal, or participating in supportive groups and social communities. For religious patients, this may include looking for and noticing experiences and connections with God or the Higher Power in their lives. We ask and encourage religious patients to look for the hand of God, Providence, divine intervention, spiritual manifestations, small miracles, spiritual intuitions, answers to prayers, and sudden or unexpected moments of spiritual inspiration and enlightenment that occur in their lives. During sessions, we may ask patients to share and talk about their spiritual experiences and help them explore what these spiritual moments mean for them. Having therapy conversations about the meanings, purpose, and significance of spiritual moments and experiences can be important and validating for patients.

Process 5: Improve and Grow in Implementing and Living Universal Spiritual Principles
A natural extension and implementation of patients' growing spiritual awareness and receptivity is to help them change or improve their efforts to live congruently with important spiritual principles. Universal spiritual principles can include forgiveness, honesty, charitable acts, gratitude and thankfulness, integrity, and so forth. We help patients identify and select which spiritual principles are important to them. We work on helping them choose one or two universal principles they wish to work on. As they do, patients often come to know that there is a spiritual power and influence beyond themselves that is helping them make needed life changes and improvements.

Process 6: Engage in the Spiritual Practice of Listening to and Following the Heart
When trust in the therapy relationship is high, it is possible to help patients engage in the spiritual practice of listening to their hearts. We encourage patients to learn to follow and act in courageous ways on their heartfelt, intuitive

impressions and inspiration. The heart is a powerful and symbolic resource for patients' spirituality and wisdom (McCraty et al., 2004a, 2004b; McCraty, Bradley, & Tomasino, 2004). Based on the expressed needs and experiences of the patient, over the course of therapy, we identify and focus on different aspects of listening to the heart work. Because the impressions of the heart occur in the present moments of patients' lives, we work with them to improve their ability to live in the present and to make new, positive, and courageous choices in the here and now by being more in tune with and following the impressions of their hearts. We help patients ask "heart questions" such as, "What do I know in my heart?" "What is my heart telling me right now?" Spiritual impressions of the heart are uplifting, edifying, affirming, encouraging, hopeful, empowering, and kind. We teach patients that spiritual self-kindness is an expression of the heart that will help open up their hearts to more spiritual light and insights in their daily lives.

We help patients recognize and separate the "matters of the mind" from the "matters of the heart" so their spiritual sense of self-identity comes from the trusted impressions of their hearts. When patients do this, they are no longer tied to their old false, judgmental, and negative beliefs about themselves (negative self-talk coming from their minds). A positive and affirming spiritual sense of self that comes from, or through, patients' spiritual hearts can be life changing.

Process 7: Refine, Strengthen, and Deepen Spirituality and Spiritual Practices Within Self and in Relationships

As therapy progresses, we keep supporting patients in the process of refining, strengthening, and deepening spiritual connections, influences, and practices. We seek to strengthen their spiritual sense of self, their spiritual attunement, and their spiritual resources. We help them internalize, deepen, and live congruently with their spiritual natures, including their hopes and desires. We support patients' growing sense of self-trust and spiritual trust in how they approach and solve unexpected challenges. We encourage them to use their improved spiritual awareness to be loving and congruent, to give and receive love in more courageous ways, and to heal and strengthen their relationships.

Pathway 2: Teaching and Modeling Universal Spiritual Principles

The use of universally accepted spiritual principles in psychotherapy has solid grounding in the field of spiritual approaches in psychotherapy. Nearly all frameworks of spirituality have some version of promoting or nurturing basic spiritual principles that lift individuals and promote a better community and society for the good of all.

Striving to live lofty and internalized principles lifts individuals and those around them as well as makes our world a better place. Doing so helps individuals grow and develop in ways that are important to them. It changes hearts and builds character.

The acceptance and popularity of the use of universal spiritual principles or principled living in human growth, leadership, and relationships are manifested in the popularity of best-selling books that promote universal principles, including *The Four Agreements*, by Don Miguel Ruiz (1997), and *Principle-Centered Leadership*, by Stephen R. Covey (1991). Most people have spiritual principles that they strive to live by, and many of these are held in common (universality) by people throughout the world, although there are differences and individual diversity in how such principles are interpreted and applied, which therapists must recognize and respect.

In clinical practice, we have used two ways to approach universal spiritual principles in treatment with patients. In one approach, therapists identify specific spiritual principles that are related to their patients' issues and that they believe may be potentially helpful in their patients' treatment. The therapist gives these spiritual principles attention during treatment by discussing them, engaging in reflective and experiential activities, and encouraging patients to consider their degree of congruence with the principles. In another approach, we ask direct questions to ascertain which spiritual principles matter the most to our patients. For example, we might ask the patient, "What spiritual principle of life do you believe in and strive to practice on a daily basis?" When patients reveal which principles are important to them, therapists can then teach concepts, ask questions, and help patients consider how they are doing in living that principle in their life.

One of the more powerful processes of principle-based psychotherapy is to encourage patients to seek to live congruently with the principles they believe in. Many patients care about having integrity, so we can use their integrity to help them improve their lives. For example, when we ask patients to make commitments, they will strive to keep those commitments because of their desire to not disappoint the clinician and their desire to live with integrity. Integrity with self-embraced spiritual principles is important; it is difficult to have self-respect and internal peace without at least a measure of striving and congruence.

Specific principles for living are for the patient to choose—not for the clinician to push—and the depth of integrity to chosen principles are also the patient's choice. The therapist's job is to ask the right questions to help the patient understand and embrace the real consequences of their choices and thereby examine, affirm, or refine those choices.

Most people believe in universal spiritual principles they live by that they could recommend to others. Many of these principles look similar despite some differences in philosophies and spiritual beliefs. Many mental health professionals, religious leaders, and researchers have written about spiritual principles and virtues—for example, M. Scott Peck (psychiatrist), the 14th Dalai Lama (Gyalwa Rinpoche; spiritual leader), and Martin Seligman (researcher and founder of the positive psychology movement). Some of these principles and virtues include kindness, compassion, generosity, integrity, faith, courage, humility, self-control, and forgiveness. Principles can be used to empower, motivate, and strengthen psychotherapy patients. They can help patients pursue and achieve goals that are meaningful and make changes that transcend behavioral and symptom change.

Tables 7.1, 7.2, and 7.3 provide examples of three spiritual principles we teach and model during treatment: Principle 1: Affirm Faith, Principle 7: Have Integrity; and Principle 8: Love Fully. We describe core themes, clinical guidelines, interventions, and activities that we use when teaching these principles. Because of space limitations, we cannot provide detailed information all of the spiritual principles that we incorporate into treatment; however, we have provided this information in other publications (Berrett et al., 2010, 2019; Richards et al., 2007).

TABLE 7.1. Principle 1: Affirm Faith

Core themes	• Faith is real, and it is a strength and a power that transforms and blesses individuals.
	• Faith is a motivator: It leads to action and activity.
	• Faith is not just for a religious principle; it can be religious, spiritual, emotional, or psychological. It depends on the beliefs of the individual.
	• Faith is a choice. We all get to decide where, in what, and in whom we will put our faith.
	• Treatment does not even begin without faith on the part of the provider and the patient.
	• We can misplace our faith in illness, addiction, doubts, shame, our weaknesses, and our limitations. We can also put our faith in ourselves, our strengths, and our beliefs as well as in others, God, treatment providers, and in recovery.
	• Hope comes from having success, noticing progress, and believing in positive power within us and positive power beyond us.
	• Hope comes from finding positive meaning, beliefs, or learnings from difficulties and struggles. One example is: "Things happen for a reason."
Clinical guidelines, interventions, and activities	• Let your patients know often of your faith in them, in the process of treatment and healing, and in their capacity to transcend and overcome difficulties.
	• Ask the patient to write on a piece of paper and then share in what they have placed their faith in the past, and in what they would like to place their faith now.
	• Point out to the patient evidence of their faith.
	• Ask patients to find, notice, accept, write, declare, share, and celebrate their steps of progress.
	• Ask patients, "What have you learned from your struggle?"
	• Ask patients, "What have you learned about how strong you are in your struggles?"
	• Discuss with patients the meaning of this quote (George Eliot): "It's never too late to become who you might have been."

TABLE 7.2. Principle 7: Have Integrity

Core themes	• The process of valuing helps us find and maintain priorities in our lives, which keep our focus, time, and energy on track with what is most important to us.
	• Not all values and principles are of equal value. Some are more important than others (e.g., protecting individuals from harm is more important than being on time).
	• Principled living helps individuals grow, develop, recover, heal, and make a positive difference in the lives of others and the world at large.
	• When individuals live in accordance with principles they have internalized as their own, they have integrity, internal peace of mind and heart, and a greater sense of self-respect.
	• Congruence is alignment, a type of self-honesty, and a prerequisite to realness or genuineness. Congruence is more of a psychological construct, whereas integrity is more of a spiritual one. With integrity, there is an alignment to one's spiritual self, to one's own heart, and to one's spiritual source.
	• Explain to patients the concept of "listening to the heart." Delineate the difference between thoughts, feelings, and messages of heart and discuss the role of "the heart" in integrity, self-care, self-honesty, and internal spiritual guidance.
Clinical guidelines, interventions, and activities	• When helping patients consider their own principles for living and their integrity with them, focus more energy on helping them see "what is" rather than "what is missing." Help them see the good they cannot see.
	• Ask patients to write and share two main principles that they care about deeply, that they have internalized as their own, and that guide their lives. Ask how these principles show up in their lives each day and how these principles can help them in the recovery process.
	• For activity in dyads, have patients share when they have taken the "high road" with honesty and integrity and what the impact of that decision was on themselves and others.
	• Have patients write in their journals messages, impressions, understandings, and truths of the heart. Suggest that they go back to those messages often and honor them.

TABLE 7.3. Principle 8: Love Fully

Core themes	• Love may not be enough to stand alone for healing, but it is still the most powerful force of healing in the world.
	• Love is a spiritual experience.
	• Love is unconditional. If love is conditional, then it is not love.
	• Although love is unconditional, healthy relationships must always have boundaries.
	• Holding back on expressing our love—fearing our love—prevents us from giving the gift of love.
	• Resisting or rejecting love out of fear or feelings of undeserving prevents us from accepting the gift of love.
	• Deepening love requires vulnerability.

TABLE 7.3. Principle 8: Love Fully (*Continued*)

Clinical guidelines, interventions, and activities	• Ask the patient to discuss how they resist or reject love (e.g., by refusing to ask for help).
	• Assign patients to ask for help and to accept and receive it.
	• Assign patients to give altruistic and compassionate service to someone in need.
	• Ask patients to practice verbally expressing their love more fully, completely, genuinely, and vulnerably than they usually do.
	• Make giving and receiving love—and any obstacles to these— a frequent topic in psychotherapy.
	• Do imagery with patients with someone whose life they have influenced. Help the patient "see" that individual; get in touch with their own influence; recognize their impact on that person; and hear expressions of gratitude to them (the patient) for their interest, help, support, love, and impact on that individual's life.
	• For theistic patients, consider helping them notice God's love in their life, which may increase their openness to notice, feel, and embrace self-kindness.

Pathway 3: Encouraging Spiritual Practices and Interventions

Many spiritual practices and interventions can facilitate the process of spiritual reconnection, healing, and growth for patients (Berrett et al., 2010, 2018; Richards & Bergin, 2005). These include spiritual practices, such as praying, reading sacred writings, participating in worship services, engaging in religious rituals, providing and receiving service and fellowship, meditating and contemplating, seeking atonement and forgiveness, and seeking spiritual direction (Plante, 2009; Richards & Bergin, 2005). Psychotherapists have also creatively adapted many spiritual practices as interventions for psychotherapy treatment, such as discussing scriptures; providing religious relaxation and imagery training; teaching patients how to meditate; helping patients understand the process of forgiveness; teaching and modeling virtues, such as gratitude and compassion; encouraging spiritual journaling; and referring patients to their religious leaders and community for spiritual direction and support (Richards & Bergin, 2005).

Spiritual practices and interventions for psychotherapy that are grounded in theistic religious traditions, such as Christianity, Islam, and Judaism, have not been embraced in the mainstream mental health professions because of ideological biases (Bergin, 1980; Plante, 2016; Richards & Bergin, 2005; Slife et al., 2012). We think this is unfortunate because research confirms that theistic spiritual practices have much healing potential (Richards & Bergin, 2005). We hope that psychotherapists will more fully support and encourage theistic patients who wish to draw on the spiritual practices in their traditions to enhance healing and recovery. We refer readers who want more information about such spiritual practices and interventions to other publications (e.g., Plante, 2009; Richards & Bergin, 2005; Richards et al., 2007).

CASE REPORT OF SPIRITUALLY INCLUSIVE THEISTIC PSYCHOTHERAPY

We now share a brief case report of a patient to illustrate how a spiritually inclusive theistic psychotherapy approach might be applied in outpatient psychotherapy practice. The details and identifying information about this patient and therapist have been altered to protect their confidentiality.

Description of the Psychotherapist

The psychotherapist, we will call him "Dr. M," is a licensed psychologist, White man, about 50 years-old, and a Christian. Dr. M has practiced psychotherapy for about 20 years and integrates spiritual perspectives and interventions with several mainstream therapeutic traditions, including person-centered, cognitive behavior, psychodynamic, emotionally-focused, and family systems. Dr. M worked with the patient in outpatient psychotherapy in a practice in Utah.

Description of the Patient

The patient, Jane (not her real name), is a married, 39-year-old White woman, and a mother of 4 children (ages 7 years to 14 years). Jane is a religiously devout Christian. She is intelligent, creative, spiritually minded, and a loving and capable mother. She is also a talented singer and performs professionally in a choir and in theater productions. Jane loves singing sacred, religious music and says she "feels God's pleasure and approval" when singing and performing.

History and Presenting Problems

Jane reported that while she was in college, and before her marriage, she began to feel extremely preoccupied about her body image weight. To maintain what she believed was an ideal thin body weight, she began binging and purging. She reported that her preoccupation with thinness and body image actually started during her childhood because father and mother both considered it a moral failure to be overweight. When Jane presented for treatment with Dr. M, she was dieting, binging and purging, and engaging in excessive exercise on a daily basis. She also reported that she was struggling with anxiety and depression, although she was continuing to function quite well with her responsibilities as a mother and homemaker. She acknowledged that her marriage relationship "was not great."

Assessment and Diagnosis

Dr. M asked Jane to complete several psychological and eating disorder assessment measures. Jane scored in the clinical range on all of these measures, which indicated that she was experiencing clinically significant levels of psychological, relationship, spiritual, eating/body image, physical health concerns and distress, low self-esteem, and moderately severe depression. Jane's scores were comparable to those obtained by patients who need inpatient and residential eating disorder treatment.

Dr. M diagnosed Jane with bulimia nervosa, major depression (moderate), obsessive thoughts about body image and thinness, perfectionism, anxiety, and marital dissatisfaction. When Jane refused inpatient treatment, Dr. M agreed to provide weekly psychotherapy to Jane on the condition that Jane would agree to (a) getting a physical examination from a medical doctor to rule out serious physical problems from the eating disorder; and (b) meeting with a dietitian for periodic dietary assessment, monitoring, and counseling. Jane agreed, and after the medical checkup ruled out life-threatening medical conditions, Dr. M began outpatient psychotherapy with her.

Relationship Establishment and Therapy Goals

During the first few psychotherapy sessions, Dr. M listened as Jane shared her story and explored her feelings about her eating disorder, marriage, religious and spiritual beliefs, love of music and singing, and the challenges of motherhood. During these sessions, Dr. M established a trusting therapy relationship with Jane, which was facilitated when he let Jane know that he respected and felt interested in her religious and spiritual beliefs and that she could talk about her spiritual beliefs and concerns during treatment whenever she desired.

As Dr. M worked with Jane during the next 2 years. By mutual agreement, they worked on the following issues and goals: (a) help Jane quit binging and purging and exercising compulsively and excessively; (b) help Jane become more accepting of her body image; (c) help Jane develop a healthy relationship with food; (d) help Jane resolve her marital problems and if necessary, help her leave the marriage; (e) help Jane develop more self-compassion; (f) help Jane learn to protect herself and children from her husband's emotional and physical abuse; (g) help Jane turn to God and her spirituality instead of eating disorder behaviors when experiencing stress.

Treatment Processes and Therapeutic Interventions

During the course of treatment, Dr. M spent much of the time in therapy session with Jane, allowing her to share and explore her thoughts, concerns, and feelings about the issues she was struggling with and working on—including the importance of spirituality in her life and the ways that her eating disorder and marriage problems challenged her spiritually with feelings of shame and inadequacy. Jane reported that she found it extremely helpful to have the opportunity to process her thoughts and feelings several times each month. Dr. M used several spiritual interventions during treatment that have been recommended as helpful with eating disorder patients, including teaching Jane to listen to and trust the impressions of her heart; holding up the therapeutic mirror of spiritual identity and worth; using guided spiritual imagery during sessions; suggesting readings for Jane about self-compassion, self-forgiveness, and intuitive eating; and encouraging Jane to engage in spiritual practices (e.g., singing) that are renewing to her (e.g., Richards et al., 2007). Dr. M also provided much support to Jane to help her confront her husband's emotional, verbal, and physical abuse and to help her set boundaries to prevent continued abuse of her and her children.

At the core of Dr. M's treatment approach was his belief that Jane is a creation of God of inherent worth and goodness who has great capability and unlimited potential for growth. Dr. M communicated his belief in Jane's worth, goodness, and capability on many occasions and in many different ways during the course of treatment. As treatment progressed, Jane came to believe in her worth, goodness, and capabilities, and she realized that she wanted to treat herself consistently with this belief. She also realized that she deserved to be treated in more loving, kind, and respectful ways by her husband—and that if he would not stop his emotional abuse and neglect of her and her children, she would divorce him. This possibility was frightening to her because of her religious beliefs about the sanctity of marriage and that divorce should be a last resort, but she explored her fears and found peace in her heart that God did not expect her to stay in an abusive, neglectful marriage.

Treatment Outcomes

Jane has been in remission with her binging and purging for about 1 year, and she is no longer compulsively engaging in excessive exercise. She is much better at challenging her "eating disorder mind"—or unhealthy beliefs and thoughts about food, dieting, and body image—and she is eating intuitively. She has become more accepting of her body and the changes in her body that are occurring as she moves into her "fabulous forties." Jane is less perfectionistic and more compassionate and accepting of herself. She is more assertive and has established much healthier boundaries with her husband, standing up to him when he starts "acting like a jerk."

Jane is still receiving psychotherapy with Dr. M a couple of times per month. Dr. M recently referred Jane and her husband for couples counseling because Jane wants to give her marriage relationship "one last chance" before she ends the marriage. Jane is still prone to taking on too much (e.g., work, music, children, marriage), which elevates her stress and anxiety and increases the risk she will relapse into her eating disorder, but she recognizes this risk now and is better able to self-correct when she starts down this path. Jane's emotional and marital struggles have, at times, challenged her faith and spiritual beliefs, but she continues to return to her core belief and faith that God loves her and approves of her efforts to heal and grow. Jane continues to express and affirm her deep feelings of faith, spirituality, and love of God during treatment sessions and through her singing and performing.

TREATMENT OUTCOME FINDINGS FOR SPIRITUALLY INCLUSIVE THEISTIC TREATMENT

We designed, implemented, and researched a spiritually inclusive theistic psychotherapy treatment approach in an inpatient and residential treatment program for women and adolescent girls with eating disorders and coexisting mental and emotional illnesses and concerns. This treatment was given at Center for Change, a nationally known and respected specialty hospital in Orem, Utah.

Patients admitted to Center for Change receive multimodal and comprehensive evidence-based treatment, including medical, psychiatric, nutritional, psychotherapeutic, family and relational therapy, and group therapy. The spiritually inclusive treatment in the program was thus a small part of an overall eclectic and comprehensive approach. The treatment program used pre- and postassessment of clinical treatment outcomes as well as ongoing and continuous assessment for the purpose of giving feedback to providers and improving and adjusting treatment for each individual patient, and for making ongoing improvements to the clinical program.

The spiritual components of treatment included spiritual assessments during the initial intake assessment process, therapist and staff training in cultural diversity and sensitivity, yoga, meditation and mindfulness, use of nature or the outdoors in intervention and solitude, experiential therapies, a 12-step group, individual therapist permission and invitation to patients to use their own spiritual beliefs as a part of treatment, and a weekly spirituality group as one of many different therapeutic groups in the program. The spirituality group was theme based and focused on 10 universally accepted spiritual principles (Berrett et al., 2019): (a) affirm faith, (b) be resilient, (c) embrace your worth, (d) find purpose, (e) take responsibility, (f) forgive, (g) have integrity, (h) love fully, (i) live in gratitude, and (j) enjoy spiritual harmony.

Research findings from an experimental outcome study we conducted showed that the spiritually inclusive treatment approach and the principle-based spirituality group produced positive treatment outcomes in the inpatient and residential eating disorder treatment units (Richards et al., 2006). The spirituality group was found on multiple indicators to have stronger clinical outcomes compared with two other treatment groups, which offered emotional support or cognitive therapy psychoeducation. In another study, Richards et al. (2017) found that eating disorders patients can learn to effectively and healthily eat intuitively by listening to their bodies and the impressions of their heart.

In another controlled and randomized study conducted by researchers not affiliated with Center for Change (Simon et al., 2013), a standardized measure of psychological and relationship symptoms was used for continuous assessment throughout treatment. Therapists received feedback about their patients' progress during the course of treatment, which improved therapeutic outcomes. The finding also showed that the inpatient and residential units were effective, which provided support for the value of the spiritually inclusive treatment approach and the other spiritual components of the treatment program, including the spirituality group.

We have also conducted two practice-based evidence research studies and one intensive case study in a college counseling center at Brigham Young University in Rexburg, Idaho (BYU-Idaho). We used practice-based evidence research designs in these studies in which the psychotherapists provided their spiritually inclusive theistic treatment as usual, except they engaged in routine monitoring of their treatment processes and patient outcomes with process and outcome measures developed by our team (Sanders et al., 2015). These studies provided additional empirical support for the effectiveness of our spiritually inclusive theistic psychotherapy approach for a wide variety of clinical issues (Lea et al., 2015; Sanders et al., 2015, 2019). On average, the patients at BYU-Idaho reported moderate to large reductions in psychological distress (ES = .85), spiritual distress (ES = .68), and relationship distress (ES = .64). The studies also provided much insight into how and when the psychotherapists integrated spiritual perspectives and interventions into psychological treatment.

CONCLUSION

We live in world that has no shortage of rejection, judgment, exclusion, and division. This extends through the field of psychotherapy and the helping professions. The principles of inclusion, finding common ground, noticing and illuminating similarities, and actively seeking unity and harmony have never been needed more. It is our belief and stance that if spirituality does not include tolerance, acceptance, kindness, and love, then it lacks the core and basic foundations of what spirituality is.

Our spiritually inclusive theistic approach is one model and example of bringing in the spiritual—the sacred—into the therapy room, the psychotherapy process, and the journey of recovery and healing. Our intent is not to sell our particular ideas and approaches on the integration of the spiritual into psychotherapy but, rather, to give an example of what is possible and what has been found effective and meaningful to many patients.

In our approach, we truly seek to emphasize *spiritually inclusive*. We recognize and value spiritual traditions and treatment approaches that are different from our own, and we believe they deserve to be honored and respected. We view ourselves as theistic *and* inclusive. We respect the spiritual beliefs that each patient brings to treatment, and we help them use their own sense of spirituality in treatment and recovery. We feel honored to learn about and join our patients in their beliefs and their chosen pathways as they do the work for healing and growth in their lives.

REFERENCES

Bergin, A. E. (1980). Psychotherapy and religious values. *Journal of Consulting and Clinical Psychology, 48*(1), 95–105. https://doi.org/10.1037/0022-006X.48.1.95

Berrett, M. E., Crowton, S. A., & Richards, P. S. (2018). Finding self again: The dismantling of eating disorder and trauma identity. In A. J. Seubert (Ed.), *Trauma and eating disorders* (pp. 337–350). Springer Publishing Company. https://doi.org/10.1891/9780826172655.0026

Berrett, M. E., Hardman, R. K., & Richards, P. S. (2010). The role of spirituality in eating disorder treatment and recovery. In M. Maine, B. H. McGilley, & D. W. Bunnell (Eds.), *Treatment of eating disorders: Bridging the research–practice gap* (pp. 367–385). Academic Press. https://doi.org/10.1016/B978-0-12-375668-8.10022-1

Berrett, M. E., Hardman, R. K., & Richards, P. S. (2019). *Spiritual renewal: A principle-based approach to recovery, growth, and inner peace* [Unpublished manuscript]. Center for Change, Orem, Utah.

Covey, S. R. (1991). *Principle-centered leadership*. Free Press.

Dahlsgaard, K., Peterson, C., & Seligman, M. E. P. (2005). Shared virtue: The convergence of valued human strengths across culture and history. *Review of General Psychology, 9*(3), 203–213. https://doi.org/10.1037/1089-2680.9.3.203

Elkins, D. N. (1998). *Beyond religion: A personal program for building a spiritual life outside the walls of traditional religion*. Quest Books.

Lea, T., Richards, P. S., Sanders, P. W., McBride, J. A., & Allen, G. E. K. (2015). Spiritual pathways to healing and recovery: An intensive single-N study of an eating disorder patient. *Spirituality in Clinical Practice, 2*(3), 191–201. https://doi.org/10.1037/scp0000085

McCraty, R., Atkinson, M., & Bradley, R. T. (2004a). Electrophysiological evidence of intuition: Part 1. The surprising role of the heart. *Journal of Alternative and Complementary Medicine, 10*(1), 133–143. https://doi.org/10.1089/107555304322849057

McCraty, R., Atkinson, M., & Bradley, R. T. (2004b). Electrophysiological evidence of intuition: Part 2. A system-wide process? *Journal of Alternative and Complementary Medicine, 10*(2), 325–336. https://doi.org/10.1089/107555304323062310

McCraty, R., Bradley, R. T., & Tomasino, D. (2004). The resonant heart. *Shift: At the Frontiers of Consciousness, 5*, 15–19.

Pargament, K. I. (2007). *Spiritually integrated psychotherapy: Understanding and addressing the sacred*. Guilford Press.

Plante, T. G. (2009). *Spiritual practices in psychotherapy: Thirteen tools for enhancing psychological health*. American Psychological Association. https://doi.org/10.1037/11872-000

Plante, T. G. (2016). Beyond mindfulness: Expanding integration of spirituality and religion into psychotherapy. *Open Theology, 2*(1), 135–144. https://doi.org/10.1515/opth-2016-0011

Richards, P. S., & Bergin, A. E. (2005). *A spiritual strategy for counseling and psychotherapy* (2nd ed.). American Psychological Association. https://doi.org/10.1037/11214-000

Richards, P. S., & Bergin, A. E. (Eds.). (2014). *Handbook of psychotherapy and religious diversity* (2nd ed.). American Psychological Association. https://doi.org/10.1037/14371-000

Richards, P. S., Berrett, M. E., Hardman, R. K., & Eggett, D. L. (2006). Comparative efficacy of spirituality, cognitive, and emotional support groups for treating eating disorder inpatients. *Eating Disorders, 14*(5), 401–415. https://doi.org/10.1080/10640260600952548

Richards, P. S., Caoili, C. C., Crowton, S. A., Berrett, M. E., Hardman, R. K., Jackson, R. N., & Sanders, P. W. (2018). An exploration of the role of religion and spirituality in the treatment and recovery of patients with eating disorders. *Spirituality in Clinical Practice, 5*(2), 88–103. https://doi.org/10.1037/scp0000159

Richards, P. S., Crowton, S., Berrett, M. E., Smith, M. H., & Passmore, K. (2017). Can patients with eating disorders learn to eat intuitively? A 2-year pilot study. *Eating Disorders, 25*(2), 99–113. https://doi.org/10.1080/10640266.2017.1279907

Richards, P. S., Hardman, R. K., & Berrett, M. E. (2007). *Spiritual approaches in the treatment of women with eating disorders*. American Psychological Association. https://doi.org/10.1037/11489-000

Richards, P. S., Weinberger-Litman, S., Berrett, M. E., & Hardman, R. K. (2020). Spirituality, religion, and eating disorders. In D. H. Rosmarin & H. G. Koenig (Eds.), *Handbook of spirituality, religion, and mental health* (2nd ed., pp. 99–118). Elsevier. https://doi.org/10.1016/B978-0-12-816766-3.00006-9

Ruiz, D. M. (1997). *The four agreements: A practical guide to personal freedom.* Amber-Allen Publishing.

Sanders, P. W., Richards, P. S., McBride, J. A., Hardman, R. K., & Barnes, D. (2019, September 12). *Spiritually integrated psychotherapy in a college counseling center: Preliminary findings* [Paper presentation]. Brigham Young University-Idaho Counseling Center, Rexburg, ID, United States.

Sanders, P. W., Richards, P. S., McBride, J. A., Lea, T., Hardman, R. K., & Barnes, D. V. (2015). Processes and outcomes of theistic spiritually oriented psychotherapy: A practice-based evidence investigation. *Spirituality in Clinical Practice, 2*(3), 180–190. https://doi.org/10.1037/scp0000083

Seligman, M. E. P., Steen, T. A., Park, N., & Peterson, C. (2005). Positive psychology progress: Empirical validation of interventions. *American Psychologist, 60*(5), 410–421. https://doi.org/10.1037/0003-066X.60.5.410

Simon, W., Lambert, M. J., Busath, G., Vazquez, A., Berkeljon, A., Hyer, K., Granley, M., & Berrett, M. (2013). Effects of providing patient progress feedback and clinical support tools to psychotherapists in an inpatient eating disorders treatment program: A randomized controlled study. *Psychotherapy Research, 23*(3), 287–300. https://doi.org/10.1080/10503307.2013.787497

Slife, B. D., Reber, J. S., & Lefevor, G. T. (2012). When God truly matters: A theistic approach to psychology. In E. L. Piedmont (Ed.), *Research in the social scientific study of religion* (Vol. 23, pp. 213–237). Brill. https://doi.org/10.1163/9789004229549_014

8

SPIRIT

Spiritual Psychotherapy for Inpatient, Residential, and Intensive Treatment

Sarah Salcone and David H. Rosmarin

Spiritual psychotherapy for inpatient, residential, and intensive treatment (SPIRIT) is a flexible group protocol for providing spiritually integrated psychotherapy within a variety of acute psychiatric settings. The flexible, clinician-led, cognitive behavior therapy (CBT)–informed approach is unique in that it can be used for a range of both spiritually and clinically diverse patient populations. In this chapter, we describe the development of this protocol, the treatment approach, and considerations in implementation. We also discuss our prior research on the feasibility of the SPIRIT protocol.

THE STORY OF SPIRIT

The development of the SPIRIT protocol began with a couple different story pathways. One of the authors of this chapter (Salcone) first became interested in the topic of spirituality and mental health in 2015 as a postbaccalaureate nursing assistant. The inpatient unit specialized in psychotic disorders, and, unsurprisingly, it was common to see patients admitted with symptoms of hyperreligiosity and religious delusions.

For example, a 40-year-old woman was hospitalized with psychotic symptoms for the first time in her life.[1] She was a devout Christian who was also

---

[1] Details in all case examples in this chapter have been altered to protect patient confidentiality.

https://doi.org/10.1037/0000338-008
Handbook of Spiritually Integrated Psychotherapies, P. S. Richards, G. E. K. Allen, and D. K. Judd (Editors)
Copyright © 2023 by the American Psychological Association. All rights reserved.

ethnically Jewish. She presented with a specific delusion that she had "Schindler's list"—similar to the plot of the popular World War II movie, *Schindler's List* (Spielberg, 1993)—in her body, so she needed an x-ray to get the list out to save the people on the list. I (Salcone) recall a time I was sitting with her in the milieu, and she asked if I was religious. I skirted the question as I was trained and redirected the question toward her religious beliefs. This felt like a lucid conversation with her in the midst of her acute illness. She spoke about being Jewish and growing up Christian, but as soon as the conversation switched to her present experience, it was back to topics that she would ruminate on—needing to get out of the hospital to get an x-ray and going back to the delusions that were part of her illness. This moment really struck me because I noticed that the staff would avoid talking to her about anything religious. Instead, they would tiptoe around conversations involving anything religious or spiritual, most likely out of concern that discussing religion could be a trigger for her delusional thinking. Even as she improved clinically, she continued to listen to Christian music, pray before eating meals and before going to sleep, and read her Bible daily, all of which, in the context of her faith, were normal behaviors.

This case is a prime example of the experiences I encountered that made me curious about the association between spiritual/religious symptoms, patients' baseline beliefs, and treatment approaches. For the patients in particular who were so fixated on spiritual/religious topics, I wondered if we could use spirituality as an intervention for them as well. These questions led me to work with David Rosmarin (one of this chapter's authors) in the Spirituality and Mental Health Program (SMHP), who had similar experiences at Massachusetts-based McLean Hospital regarding spiritual topics in treatment.

One of Rosmarin's most memorable cases was within his first week as a predoctoral intern at an intensive CBT-based treatment program at McLean Hospital. A female patient in her mid-20s, who was not a patient on his caseload, approached him during the lunch break and asked if she could speak to him about God. He was not so surprised that she approached him because he is a practicing Orthodox Jew who wears a yarmulke, but he did not have his supervisor's permission to speak to patients about their spiritual lives or have the clinical tools to do so. He responded by suggesting she ask for a chaplaincy visit, even though he knew the hospital did not employ an on-site chaplain. Within the first 6 months of his fellowship, 10 additional patients approached him, and each asked for essentially the same thing: They wanted to address their spirituality in the context of their psychiatric treatment (Rosmarin, 2018).

So, Rosmarin approached his mentor, the director of the hospital's psychology training program, and told him about the trends he was observing in a relatively nonreligious region of the United States (Pew Research Center, n.d.). The director agreed that it appeared many of their patients have spiritual needs; however, there was no formal program to address those needs. With the support of his mentors (Thröstur Björgvinsson, the director, and Kenneth Pargament, Rosmarin's graduate school mentor) and a thorough review of the literature,

Rosmarin teamed up with a fellow intern and developed materials for a therapy group because, at that time, he could not find any clinical protocols for spiritually integrated psychotherapy for psychiatric patients. The therapy group, called "Spirituality & CBT," was presented to the clinical team.

Even before reading the protocol, the clinical team vocalized a lot of concerns, including what to do if a patient decompensated during the group, or if patients fought over different religious views, or if the clinician offended a patient. They had other questions, too: Who would be appropriate to have participate? Are you going to allow patients presenting with psychosis to participate? Is this going to be a mandatory group? The clinical team was assured that this would be a voluntary group, and to answer the remaining questions, the researchers would consult with more colleagues and check the literature before officially running the first group. The researchers also planned to ask patients to complete a survey to provide feedback at the end of the group.

With approval from the clinical team, the Spirituality & CBT group was placed on the weekly schedule. After a few months, the pilot data and protocol were reported for publication (Rosmarin et al., 2011). These are the highlights of the study: Of the patients who participated, 42.2% did not identify as Catholic, Jewish, or Protestant, and 15.5% reported no religious affiliation at all. In addition, patients' reported levels of religion/spirituality did not correlate with the extent to which they reported perceived benefit of the group, and the majority of patients reported gaining a lot from the group and that the group was respectful of various religious and spiritual affiliations. There were no decompensations or adverse events reported from the Spirituality & CBT group (Rosmarin et al., 2011).

After an additional fellowship year, Rosmarin was able to launch a study to assess the extent to which patients had an interest in spiritually integrated psychotherapy within the intensive treatment program at McLean Hospital. Before completing data collection, the study coauthors tried to anticipate what the percentage of patients in the program would be. The director of the program anticipated that 10% of patients would want spiritually integrated treatment. Another coauthor guessed it would be 15%, whereas Rosmarin predicted the highest guess of 25%.

The results were much larger than expected, with 58.2% of patients reporting interest in discussing spiritual aspects to a "fairly," "moderately," or "very much" extent in treatment. Even more surprising: Further data analyses indicated that patients with psychosis, obsessive-compulsive disorder (OCD), or mania were as likely as others to want spiritually integrated care. The only significant clinical predictor was a diagnosis of current depression (Rosmarin et al., 2015). The study summarized that more than half of patients in the intensive program were interested in addressing spiritual issues in treatment, and this interest did not waver by diagnosis (except for patients with current depression).

In addition, while religious affiliation predicted increased interest in spiritually integrated therapy, 42% of religious patients did not report interest in spiritually integrated treatment, and conversely, 37% of unaffiliated/ nonreligious patients reported a high interest in addressing spirituality in their care. These data suggest that clinicians should not assume on the basis of religious affiliation alone that patients want to integrate spirituality into their mental health treatment (Rosmarin et al., 2015).

A few years after this study, through an accumulation of interest and generous donor funding, the SMHP at McLean Hospital was established to provide clinical protocols for spiritually integrated psychotherapy throughout the hospital programs as well as consultation services for individual patients. Quickly, SMHP became inundated with work and realized that applying for funding would be complicated. To evaluate protocol-driven psychotherapy in a psychiatric hospital, it is not possible to isolate the efficacy of groups with psychopharmacology, electroconvulsive therapy (ECT), case management, individual psychotherapy sessions, and family meetings simultaneously happening within the treatment that patients receive. However, the Bridges Consortium was a perfect fit.

The Bridges Consortium was a grant-funded interdisciplinary project funded by the John Templeton Foundation to advance research, practice, and training about spiritually integrated psychotherapies, with the goal of innovating new methods of delivering spiritually integrated care and examining feasibility in clinical practice. Rosmarin proposed revising and expanding the Spirituality & CBT group protocol to a more flexible model to deliver to patients across the hospital. We are thankful that the SPIRIT study was funded, resulting in the SPIRIT group protocol: a flexible, spiritually integrated group psychotherapy protocol for use in various levels of care and multiple diagnostic profiles.

DESCRIPTION OF THE SPIRIT TREATMENT APPROACH

The SPIRIT group protocol is a flexible protocol with a CBT-informed approach for clinically and spiritually or religiously diverse patient populations. While there are a few clinician-led spiritually integrated interventions for clinical mental health populations (Harris et al., 2011; Huguelet et al., 2011; Richards et al., 2009; Weisman de Mamani et al., 2010), we are unaware of any interfaith group interventions for use with various treatment levels of care and a range of clinical diagnostic profiles (Rosmarin et al., 2019). In addition, the SPIRIT protocol, including the development and description, has been published with online supplemental materials for clinicians to review and implement in their own psychiatric treatment settings (Rosmarin et al., 2019).

SPIRIT groups typically are delivered on a weekly basis and are appropriate for three levels of care: (a) inpatient, (b) residential, and (c) intensive outpatient or partial hospitalization. The SPIRIT protocol could potentially be used in an outpatient setting; however, this has not yet been explored. Depending on the patient population and setting, group length ranges between 30 minutes and 55 minutes. The overall group structure is in two parts: The first begins with disclaimers and a question to create dialogue, and the second half is dedicated to psychoeducation by providing concrete strategies for patients to implement spiritual content into mental health treatment.

The group protocol begins with a brief introduction and some disclaimers. The group is not meant to proselytize or allow space for others to do so, and group participants are asked to be respectful of others who may have different views. Group introduction also includes goals of the group, which are to help participants identify how spirituality/religion may be relevant to their mental health symptomology as well as identify methods to integrate spirituality into treatment.

With the goals in mind, clinicians begin the first half of the session by asking group members how they believe spirituality or religion is relevant to their mental health. Clinicians are encouraged to ask participants to vocalize their answers, redirect where needed, and guide the conversation toward themes. Typically, there are four response themes regarding how spirituality/religion is relevant to psychiatric symptoms. Spiritual/religious themes can manifest within symptoms (e.g., scrupulosity, hyperreligiosity). In addition, spirituality/religion can be a positive coping mechanism by providing meaning, hope, or connection. Conversely, spirituality/religion can be a source of strain and exacerbate current psychiatric struggles (also called "spiritual struggles" or "negative spiritual coping"). Some participants may find that spirituality/religion is not directly relevant to their mental health; however, they may be curious about the topic and may still benefit from strategies and resources presented during the group. All of these typical responses are important for the clinician to address and to provide psychoeducation, even if no participants in the group endorsed spiritually themed symptoms, positive spiritual coping, or negative spiritual coping. It is important to highlight that the goal of this dialogue is to focus on the functional role of spirituality/religion in a psychological context rather than on a spiritual history.

The flexible menu approach after this opening question allows the clinician the freedom to choose from seven handouts: (a) Spiritual/Religious Beliefs and Reframes, (b) Spiritual/Religious Coping in Treatment, (c) Spiritual/Religious Struggles, (d) Meditating on the Psalms, (e) Sacred Verses, (f) The Power of Prayer, or (g) Forgiveness. These handouts can be used one at a time to introduce a method of spiritual integration or can be used over multiple sessions. Further, multiple handouts can be discussed in a single group session. It is up to the clinician to determine what is appropriate for the group members at any given time. Because these handouts have previously been described in detail (Rosmarin et al., 2019), the descriptions that follow are brief. Each of these handouts should facilitate further dialogue within the group.

Handout 1: Spiritual/Religious Beliefs and Reframes

The Spiritual/Religious Beliefs and Reframes handout focuses on cognitive restructuring within the CBT approach. It "contains a list of statements categorized into six spiritual themes: we are never alone; nothing is impossible; life is a test; we can only control the process, not the outcome; everything happens for a reason; and nothing is permanent" (Rosmarin et al., 2019, p. 78). These statements are meant to add meaning to ongoing challenges and aid in coping with distress. It is important for the clinician to recognize that there will be patients who focus on statements they dislike, and the clinician may need to guide patients to reframe those statements to be helpful to them. By the end of the session, clinicians should help patients identify at least one phrase that they can use as a coping statement.

Handout 2: Spiritual/Religious Coping in Treatment

The Spiritual/Religious Coping in Treatment handout emphasizes spiritual practices as a form of behavioral activation in CBT. This handout introduces "a list of common spiritual activities that can be used to reduce emotional distress, including prayer, meditation on a spiritual statement, seeking religious support, reading religious texts, forgiving, performing good deeds, using religious framing, counting blessings, and finding meaning" (Rosmarin et al., 2019, p. 78). Clinicians can use this list of activities to prompt patients to reflect on spiritual activities they may have used in the past and how these activities could impact their mood. Similar to the previous handout, clinicians should encourage patients to identify at least one spiritual/religious activity they will incorporate within treatment.

Handout 3: Spiritual/Religious Struggles

The Spiritual/Religious Struggles handout provides examples of how spirituality can negatively impact mental health via spiritual struggles or negative religious coping. It encompasses three main categories: (a) interpersonal, (b) intrapersonal, and (c) divine spiritual struggles (Ano & Vasconcelles, 2005). The category *intrapersonal struggles* refers to inner spiritual tension, whereas *interpersonal struggles* involves conflicts between people containing spiritual themes. The category *divine spiritual struggles* involves tension with issues of faith. Because this handout uses more advanced language, the clinician may need to provide simplified definitions for the group. In addition, spiritual struggles tend to be a more emotionally salient topic for those who are experiencing this type of distress, and the goal of the group is to not to resolve spiritual struggles during the group session but to simply help patients identify struggles and explore how these struggles may impact their treatment. Clinicians may want to challenge patients' struggles or provide an alternative reframe to a patient's distress; however, they should refrain from doing so and simply validate patients' emotions and experience. We expand on spiritual struggles later in the section on treatment implementation.

Handout 4: Meditating on the Psalms

The Meditating on the Psalms handout provides a behavioral activation and cognitive reframing perspective—using the selective texts from the Psalms—in that the Psalms are often recited in meditative or prayerful behavior or to provide hope or encouragement. The Psalms are relevant for Judeo–Christian faiths, so clinicians may want to use other handouts when working with patients who do not affiliate with a Judeo–Christian faith. Clinicians should encourage patients to identify verses that resonate with them so that they can implement those verses as a behavioral activation activity or as a coping statement.

Handout 5: Sacred Verses

The Sacred Verses handout uses the same concepts as the Meditating on the Psalms handout using an interfaith perspective. This handout contains a collection of passages from various faith traditions; the passages are organized by themes that are common across different spiritual practices, including faith, self-compassion, peace, courage, and hope. Similar to the previous handout, clinicians should facilitate a discussion regarding which passages or themes resonate most with patients and help them identify how they can connect these statements to treatment.

Handout 6: The Power of Prayer

The Power of Prayer handout focuses on prayer within both a cognitive and behavioral framework. This handout contains two parts: opening questions and discussion questions. The opening questions serve to prompt patients to consider different reasons people may engage in prayer as well as reflect on the different forms of prayer and various functions prayers may serve to impact mood. The discussion questions are to help patients identify how prayer functions in their personal lives and to recognize common barriers and struggles related to prayer. When struggles arise, it is important for clinicians to validate those emotions and encourage patients to discuss those topics with their individual psychotherapists in treatment.

Handout 7: Forgiveness

The Forgiveness handout takes a behavioral approach in breaking down the steps to forgiveness. The handout acknowledges that forgiveness is a challenging, complex topic and covers various steps to forgiveness, whether those steps include forgiving yourself, others, or your Higher Power. Clinicians can use this handout to facilitate a dialogue about the difficulties in extending forgiveness and where individuals are at in the steps to forgive.

TREATMENT IMPLEMENTATION

In regard to facilitating the SPIRIT group protocol, we describe in this section the processes that we provided to clinicians at McLean Hospital as part of the SPIRIT study (see the Description of the SPIRIT Study section later in this chapter). While we highlight that clinical training for SPIRIT group implementation is fairly straightforward, we have a few recommendations pertaining to training, clinician expectations regarding group goals and facilitation, and guidelines in identifying and addressing spiritual struggles in a group setting. We also offer recommendations for follow-up for patients who express spiritual struggles, including involving spiritual care providers, such as chaplains, if available.

Clinicians who facilitated SPIRIT groups at McLean Hospital were first trained in how to administer the group protocol. Training was flexible and comparable with training for other psychotherapy treatment interventions. Clinicians first met with study staff before familiarizing themselves with the written protocol. Those who were comfortable with the materials were observed facilitating a SPIRIT group for research continuity purposes and encouraged to contact staff if questions arose. For clinicians who requested more support, staff provided additional meetings, observation, and feedback. Throughout the SPIRIT study, clinicians were invited to a quarterly luncheon to foster dialogue and support among clinicians, receive feedback regarding the group, and facilitate a sense of community among the staff. This approach is not necessary to successfully integrate spiritually integrated therapy into a hospital setting, but it was a useful strategy during the SPIRIT study to ensure that clinicians felt supported and adhered to the SPIRIT protocol as well as to keep lines of communication open between clinicians and study staff.

When administering the SPIRIT protocol in various levels of care and diagnostic profiles, there will be differences in insight and cognitive abilities to engage with the material. For those receiving treatment on an inpatient level of care, clinicians may want to use the Spiritual/Religious Coping in Treatment handout or the Spiritual/Religious Beliefs and Reframes handout, both of which are less conceptually challenging materials compared with the Spiritual/Religious Struggles handout. Conversely, some participants may be participating in SPIRIT groups toward the end of treatment and may be better equipped to engage with the more advanced material. The SPIRIT protocol is flexible to accommodate these differences, but clinicians may need to adjust language at times to account for individual differences within a group intervention.

Clinicians who provided SPIRIT groups varied in educational and career backgrounds, ranging from postbaccalaureate mental health specialists to master's-level social workers, art therapists, nurses, chaplains, and doctoral-level psychologists. Most notably, these clinicians provided SPIRIT groups within the specialized programs where they were already employed. Therefore, these clinicians were part of the clinical care for the patients in the SPIRIT groups they facilitated. We found this to be an advantage of our group implementation because clinicians were already trained in the diagnostic profile they served, and having those clinicians facilitating the groups for their patients bolstered therapeutic alliance and rapport with patients who were interested in discussing spiritual issues in their care. We highly recommend that clinicians facilitating SPIRIT groups be clinically competent for the patients whom they serve.

We want to emphasize that SPIRIT is not simply an opportunity to discuss spiritual topics in a group but is a clinical approach to psychological change. Specifically, the group intervention is not for proselytizing or to facilitate religious change; rather, it is to foster positive aspects of spirituality when appropriate and psychologically relevant as well as to ameliorate negative aspects of spirituality that contribute to distress. The role of the clinician within SPIRIT groups is to focus on how spiritual issues function within the person and demonstrate how SPIRIT can be implemented into care to be functionally adaptive for the individual. Clinicians must be able to identify functioning in a spiritual domain to adequately and successfully facilitate SPIRIT. Those who struggle with identifying how aspects of their patients' spiritual lives impact their mental health should seek supervision and consultation.

Along those same lines, clinicians also need to be able to identify the difference between spiritual symptoms and spiritual struggles. *Spiritual symptoms* are manifestations of spiritual content into psychiatric symptoms—for example, religious delusions, hyperreligiosity in mania, or scrupulosity. Patients who experience spiritual symptoms tend to confuse their spiritual life with their spiritual symptomatology, and it is important for clinicians to help patients distinguish between these domains. In a group setting, this can be especially challenging depending on patients' level of insight, mood, and emotional stability in the session. If appropriate, clinicians can attempt to engage patients in reality testing or psychoeducation, explaining that for some individuals with religious or spiritual backgrounds, symptoms can present within this domain of their lives. It is important to clarify that it is very rare for spirituality or religion to cause psychiatric symptoms; however, spiritual or religious issues may exacerbate mental health distress (i.e., spiritual struggles). This clarification is valuable for patients because it can prevent or alleviate spiritual struggles in which patients blame their spiritual or religious practice for their mental health symptomatology.

Further, clinician acuity for delineating between spiritual symptoms and spiritual struggles is especially vital among severe psychiatric illnesses, such as OCD and psychosis. It is not uncommon to have spiritual symptoms within these disorders, and religious or spiritual patients with these diagnostic profiles may be especially hesitant to discuss spirituality for fear that their beliefs will be pathologized. Providing psychoeducation regarding the relationship between spiritual issues and symptoms can additionally bolster rapport among patients with spiritual/religious beliefs.

When spiritual struggles arise within a SPIRIT session, it can be overwhelming at first for clinicians to address significant distress in a group setting. Naturally, clinicians may be tempted to challenge negative thoughts, voice an alternative viewpoint, or refocus patients toward more positive and hopeful aspects of spirituality. However, these responses risk invalidating patient emotions. The goal of SPIRIT is not to solve spiritual issues or to foster positive emotions but to facilitate understanding for patients on the function of spirituality and religion in their lives. Thus, when patients voice spiritual struggles, clinicians should simply validate the painful emotions being expressed and encourage patients to continue vocalizing their experience as well as communicate this spiritual distress in treatment with their individual psychotherapist. We acknowledge that this is challenging to balance in a group setting because negative emotions have the potential to compound among group members in a session.

Clinicians should reframe the conversation if the topic skews too far from voicing spiritual struggles and drifts into vilifying spirituality or religion as a whole; the focus should always be on the function of spiritual content within mental health. If available, it may be beneficial to initiate follow-up after a SPIRIT session with a chaplain or spiritual care provider as a consultant during treatment. The following case example highlights the role of SPIRIT groups within an individual's treatment progression and integration into mental health care.

CASE EXAMPLE: MS. SMITH

Ms. Smith is a 79-year-old Caucasian woman who was brought to McLean Hospital for inpatient treatment following the death of her husband. Her adult children encouraged her to seek care because of prolonged apathy, sadness, and odd behavioral changes in the context of her religious practice. Twelve months before admission, her husband of more than 50 years died after a long battle with cancer. Ms. Smith was his primary caretaker, with only one of her four adult children living in state to assist. Three months before admission, her children noticed sudden changes in Ms. Smith's mood and behavior. In addition to low mood, apathy, and diminished frequency of caring for herself, Ms. Smith also showed a sudden increase in time spent in religious practice.

While Ms. Smith is a devout Catholic who has attended weekly services, prayed, and read her Bible daily, in the 3 months before admission, her religious behavior increased to daily church attendance, hours of daily prayer, and extensive time reading the Bible to the extent of skipping meals or sleep. Her children discovered she had stopped taking her prescribed antidepressant medication, and when they confronted her, Ms. Smith stated that she no longer needed her antidepressants and that her faith was more effective than her prescriptions. Her children also noticed that although Ms. Smith was attending daily services, she was not spending time in social activities—within the church or in the local community—that she participated in before her husband's death.

According to Ms. Smith's children, they became concerned for her because she has a history of depression, and this increase in spiritual practice was very unusual for her. Ms. Smith had been hospitalized three times in her lifetime related to depression, with the most recent being 10 years prior. On admission, she did endorse that she would rather be with her husband in Heaven than still alive but had no active plans or suicidal intent.

Ms. Smith attended a SPIRIT group session in her second week of hospitalization. During discussion with the behavioral activation handout, Ms. Smith expressed hesitancy with engaging in religious practice, stating that her religion made her sick. With more discussion, the group clinician discovered that she was a devout Catholic who, before her acute illness, received the majority of her social support via her church community before her husband's death. With this information, the clinician discussed a chaplaincy consult with

Ms. Smith, and the chaplain was brought onto the treatment team to facilitate psychoeducation and spiritual guidance throughout treatment. In bringing chaplaincy consultation into Ms. Smith's individual treatment, she was able to receive psychoeducation regarding how her psychiatric symptoms manifested in aspects of her spiritual life.

Ms. Smith continued to attend SPIRIT groups during her hospitalization, and through the use of handouts and materials, learned adaptive ways to use her spirituality to cope during treatment. Ms. Smith also discovered within the SPIRIT groups that she was experiencing spiritual struggles; while she was hesitant to disclose which struggles resonated with her during the group, she spoke with the chaplain and her treatment team about her struggles because she recognized that they contributed to her depressive symptoms. With Ms. Smith's permission, her priest was invited to visit during inpatient treatment as a trusted source of social and spiritual support for her.

On discharge, Ms. Smith returned to her religious and spiritual practices and reported that she believed her hospitalization improved her faith as well as helped her to both rediscover her purpose in life and process the grief related to her husband's death. She found the addition of SPIRIT groups in treatment to be a "vital" component of her care because it was a place to process her faith without judgment and understand how it played a role in her mental health.

DESCRIPTION OF THE SPIRIT STUDY

The SPIRIT study, as previously mentioned, was funded via the Bridges Consortium and, more largely, by the John Templeton Foundation. The goal of the study was to demonstrate feasibility of SPIRIT to provide spiritually integrated group psychotherapy that can accommodate various acute psychiatric diagnostic profiles and treatment level of care. The results of the study are presented briefly in this section, but a more thorough description of the results are awaiting publication (see Rosmarin et al., 2021).

Setting

For those who may be unfamiliar, McLean Hospital is a freestanding psychiatric hospital affiliated with Harvard Medical School. The treatment approach is similar to other psychiatric hospitals in that it uses medication management alongside case management, neurotherapeutics, milieu therapy, and psychotherapy groups. The hospital also separates treatment acuity into inpatient, residential, and intensive (partial hospital) levels of care. Treatment programs are also specialized by diagnostic profile. Thirteen programs at McLean Hospital implemented SPIRIT groups during the SPIRIT study. Inpatient units included the treatment of mood/anxiety disorders, psychotic disorders, substance use disorders, posttraumatic stress and dissociative disorders, and mood disorders in older adults. Residential level of care included specialized treatment for eating and feeding disorders, co-occurring substance use with other disorders, and psychotic disorders/other chronic disorders. The two intensive/partial hospitalization programs specialized in posttraumatic stress and dissociative disorders as well as various psychiatric disorders. The intensive/partial programs are often prescribed as a step-down program after inpatient hospitalization.

This setting was useful in that we could assess SPIRIT groups' ability to integrate the intervention into a multidisciplinary setting. This treatment approach is applicable to various hospital treatment settings and can be seamlessly integrated into similar facilities. At the same time, the specialized programs allowed us to examine the feasibility of SPIRIT groups across diagnostic profiles as well as levels of care. In addition, all programs participating in the SPIRIT study also had access to and used spiritual care services, including clinical consultation and chaplaincy services, which clinicians found useful to address spiritual struggles that patients recognized in SPIRIT groups and to integrate those services into individual patient treatment. This model of integrating spiritual services in medical care is also common practice among many hospitals and treatment centers.

Participants and Procedures

Clinicians were recruited to provide weekly SPIRIT groups for their respective treatment programs for a 15-month period. Clinicians provided their degree; training experience regarding spiritual care; spiritual/religious affiliation; and demographics, including age, gender, race, and ethnicity. In total, 22 clinicians participated, and clinician diversity was comparable with the patient demographics. The majority of clinicians had master's degrees (41%), followed by bachelor-level clinicians (41%) and doctoral-level psychologists (18%). In addition, most clinicians reported a personal religious affiliation (Protestant, 36%; Buddhist, 14%; Catholic, 14%; Jewish, 9%; Muslim, 5%); however, several reported no affiliation (23%, $n = 5$). When asked if they had taken graduate-level coursework in spirituality before SPIRIT group training, more than half of the participating clinicians reported having minimal prior coursework in the subject.

Patients voluntarily participated in SPIRIT groups on specialized psychiatric units for mood, anxiety, psychotic, alcohol/substance-related, traumatic, eating/feeding, personality, and other disorders. At the end of each group, patients completed survey items from the Clinically Adaptive Multidimensional Outcome Survey (Sanders et al., 2018), which assesses for spiritual/religious affiliation, importance of spirituality and religion, and belief in God as well as spiritual distress items (including concerns about spiritual life, loss of spiritual direction, spiritual guilt, and feeling distant from God). Patients also completed two items rating the extent to which the group carried out the goals: (a) helping to identify spiritual/religious resources that can be used to reduce distress and (b) helping to identify spiritual struggles that contribute to clinical distress. In addition, research staff accessed patient medical records to obtain additional demographic and clinical data (e.g., age, gender, race, employment status, psychiatric diagnoses, medications, ECT, suicidality, self-harm, recent hospitalization within the past 6 months). No adverse events were reported with any patients during the course of the study.

Demographically, patients ($N = 1,443$) were diverse. In terms of primary diagnosis, 433 (30%) presented with depression, 335 (23%) had a primary substance use disorder, 300 (20%) had a diagnosis of bipolar disorder, 174 (12%) patients had a psychotic disorder, and 68 (4.7%) patients were diagnosed with a trauma-related disorder. The remaining patients had a primary diagnosis of anxiety, obsessive-compulsive–spectrum, impulse-control, developmental, or a personality disorder. Many of these patients were clinically complex with multiple psychiatric diagnoses, and only 36.4% of patients participating in the SPIRIT groups had one psychiatric diagnosis.

Regarding spiritual characteristics, patients were also fairly diverse. The largest religious affiliation reported was Catholic (28.6%), followed by Protestant (15%) and Jewish (6.4%), with other major world religions present at less than 3% of the sample (Buddhist, 2%; Muslim, 0.6%; Hindu, 0.4%). Surprisingly, 21.8% of patients reported being "Spiritual but Not Religious," and 17.4% reported no spiritual or religious affiliation. Although Massachusetts is a fairly nonreligious part of the United States (Pew Research Center, n.d.), it was surprising to have so many nonreligious patients voluntarily attend a spiritually based treatment group. It speaks to the importance of not assuming that spiritual resources are for religious patients alone because some individuals who may not have a faith community still have spiritual needs they wish to address in treatment (Rosmarin et al., 2015).

Results

In general, patients appeared to like the SPIRIT groups. Nearly 70% of participants reported that SPIRIT helped them identify spiritual/religious resources to use in treatment to a "fair," "moderate," or "very much" extent. In addition, patients were equally likely to identify spiritual resources from SPIRIT groups regardless of age, gender, race, and socioeconomic status. We did find that college students were slightly less likely to identify spiritual resources ($p = .05$), and we considered that perhaps college students have concentration difficulties because of psychopathology, so it may not be a finding specific to SPIRIT groups but an indicator of their acute state. Regarding clinical characteristics, there were no significant differences in response to SPIRIT groups based on clinical factors, including primary diagnosis, number of diagnoses, number of medications, antipsychotic medications, receipt of ECT treatment, or recent hospitalization in the past 6 months.

In terms of spiritual characteristics, patients with a religious affiliation were more likely to report perceived benefit from the group to a higher degree than those who were spiritual but not religious and those without a spiritual/religious affiliation. In the same vein, those with any belief in God or a Higher Power also reported a higher perceived benefit from SPIRIT groups compared with those who reported no belief in a Higher Power.

To determine whether patients who reported spiritual struggles could identify their spiritual struggles in the SPIRIT group, we performed analyses only on patients who reported at least a minimum level of spiritual struggles, a cutoff score of 2 on the Clinically Adaptive Multidimensional Outcome Survey spiritual distress subscale. In our sample, 958 patients reported experiencing spiritual struggles. Of this patient subset, 76.7% of them reported that the SPIRIT group helped them identify struggles contributing to distress to a "fair," "moderate," or "very much" extent. In addition, religious affiliation was not associated with patients' identification of struggles.

Interestingly, patients who attended groups facilitated by younger clinicians (compared with older clinicians) reported more benefit from SPIRIT groups. Similarly, patients who attended groups run by nonreligious clinicians also reported that they got more benefit from SPIRIT groups compared with groups facilitated by religiously affiliated clinicians. Initially, we considered an interaction between these factors; however, clinicians' religious affiliation remained a significant predictor of lower patient identification of spiritual resources (and benefit), even after controlling for clinician age. Age also remained a significant predictor when controlling for affiliation. There was also no interaction between clinician religious affiliation and patient religion, and therefore religious clinicians were less effective in helping patients identify spiritual resources during SPIRIT groups, regardless of patient religious affiliation. Clinician factors—demographic and spiritual—were not related to patients' identification of struggles.

These clinician differences present a conundrum because many clinicians who are interested in providing spiritually integrated care are religious themselves. Based on our results, the individuals who are interested in spiritually integrated care are less effective at providing the treatment. A potential reason may be that religious clinicians have a harder time stepping back from their personal biases to provide true interfaith treatment. This highlights the importance of disseminating clinical training on spiritually integrated treatment regardless of clinician religious affiliation.

NEXT STEPS

Why should spirituality be integrated into psychiatric care? To highlight the core aspects of the SPIRIT study and protocol, it is feasible to integrate interfaith psychotherapy interventions into existing, multidisciplinary treatment facilities, even with various acute psychiatric conditions and without adverse events. In addition, the SPIRIT protocol can be administered by any type of mental health clinician; it is not limited to certain educational background trainings. Ultimately, spiritually integrated care is relevant because many patients—whether they are religious, spiritual, both, or neither—are interested in incorporating spirituality into their mental health treatment.

In our experience, spiritually integrated care is most successfully implemented with clinicians who do not have a strong religious practice themselves or are able to step back from their biases and foster interfaith dialogue. For clinicians who may be religious but are invested in providing spiritually integrated care for their patients, we recommend being mindful of one's own biases and resisting the urge to encourage a spiritual practice within one's own faith tradition without acknowledging other practices equally in group. Patients need to feel safe to share their experiences in a group setting, which begins with clinicians' setting the tone of the group. If clinicians feel they are struggling to promote interfaith dialogue in group, we recommend they seek counsel from a fellow clinician or supervisor for guidance and feedback.

One limitation of the SPIRIT study is that patient participants voluntarily attended SPIRIT groups. Because patients self-presented in this setting, it is difficult to determine the extent to which SPIRIT promotes recovery in a multipronged approach to treatment in acute care. It would also be challenging to parse apart various factors of treatment or design a randomized controlled trial in an interdisciplinary hospital setting. We hope to examine clinically relevant spiritual change in the future in gathering hospitalwide data on intake regarding patients' spiritual histories and interest in spiritually integrated care. Even in a self-selected sample, demonstrating an increase in positive spiritual coping and amelioration of spiritual struggles at patient discharge would exhibit efficacy of SPIRIT and spiritually integrated care as a whole for contributing to reducing spiritual distress during psychiatric treatment.

Spirituality and religion should be regarded as an aspect of cultural competency in treatment. When clinicians understand the patient population they are serving, they can use a culturally informed lens for clinical guidance. As a therapist would continue to ask questions to understand a cultural facet of their patient's life experience, so it is appropriate to ask clarifying questions regarding spiritual life when assessing how this domain fits within the context of one's mental health. Clinician knowledge and skillset regarding psychiatric care is more relevant in providing quality spiritually integrated care than knowledge in the domain of spirituality or religion in general. To this end, clinicians should always fall back on their clinical training to resolve issues that may arise in SPIRIT group sessions.

We are hopeful that SPIRIT may be disseminated to other acute psychiatric facilities to meet the needs of many patients in the intersection of spirituality and treatment. Since the beginning of psychology as a field of study, there have been tensions between science and faith. It is time to bridge this gap to meet the needs of our patients. Most of all, if patients desire to incorporate their spiritual lives into mental health, to neglect this domain of life is to fail to provide the best care.

REFERENCES

Ano, G. G., & Vasconcelles, E. B. (2005). Religious coping and psychological adjustment to stress: A meta-analysis. *Journal of Clinical Psychology, 61*(4), 461–480. https://doi.org/10.1002/jclp.20049

Harris, J. I., Erbes, C. R., Engdahl, B. E., Thuras, P., Murray-Swank, N., Grace, D., Ogden, H., Olson, R. H. A., Winskowski, A. M., Bacon, R., Malec, C., Campion, K., & Le, T. (2011). The effectiveness of a trauma focused spiritually integrated intervention for veterans exposed to trauma. *Journal of Clinical Psychology, 67*(4), 425–438. https://doi.org/10.1002/jclp.20777

Huguelet, P., Mohr, S., Betrisey, C., Borras, L., Gillieron, C., Marie, A. M., Rieben, I., Perroud, N., & Brandt, P.-Y. (2011). A randomized trial of spiritual assessment of outpatients with schizophrenia: Patients' and clinicians' experience. *Psychiatric Services, 62*(1), 79–86. https://doi.org/10.1176/ps.62.1.pss6201_0079

Pew Research Center. (n.d.). *Religious landscape study.* https://www.pewforum.org/religious-landscape-study/

Richards, P. S., Smith, M. H., Berrett, M. E., O'Grady, K. A., & Bartz, J. D. (2009). A theistic spiritual treatment for women with eating disorders. *Journal of Clinical Psychology, 65*(2), 172–184. https://doi.org/10.1002/jclp.20564

Rosmarin, D. H. (2018). *Spirituality, religion, cognitive-behavioral therapy: A guide for clinicians.* Guilford Press.

Rosmarin, D. H., Auerbach, R. P., Bigda-Peyton, J. S., Björgvinsson, T., & Levendusky, P. G. (2011). Integrating spirituality into cognitive behavioral therapy in an acute psychiatric setting: A pilot study. *Journal of Cognitive Psychotherapy, 25*(4), 287–303. https://doi.org/10.1891/0889-8391.25.4.287

Rosmarin, D. H., Forester, B. P., Shassian, D. M., Webb, C. A., & Björgvinsson, T. (2015). Interest in spiritually integrated psychotherapy among acute psychiatric patients. *Journal of Consulting and Clinical Psychology, 83*(6), 1149–1153. https://doi.org/10.1037/ccp0000046

Rosmarin, D. H., Salcone, S., Harper, D., & Forester, B. P. (2019). Spiritual Psychotherapy for Inpatient, Residential, and Intensive Treatment. *American Journal of Psychotherapy, 72*(3), 75–83. https://doi.org/10.1176/appi.psychotherapy.20180046

Rosmarin, D. H., Salcone, S., Harper, D. G., & Forester, B. (2021). Predictors of patients' responses to Spiritual Psychotherapy for Inpatient, Residential, and Intensive Treatment (SPIRIT). *Psychiatric Services, 72*(5), 507–513. https://doi.org/10.1176/appi.ps.202000331

Sanders, P. W., Richards, P. S., & McBride, J. A. (2018). Development of the Clinically Adaptive Multidimensional Outcome Survey. *Psychotherapy Research, 28*(6), 925–939. https://doi.org/10.1080/10503307.2016.1277039

Spielberg, S. (Director and Producer). (1993). *Schindler's list* [Film]. Amblin Entertainment and Universal Pictures.

Weisman de Mamani, A. G., Tuchman, N., & Duarte, E. A. (2010). Incorporating religion/spirituality into treatment for serious mental illness. *Cognitive and Behavioral Practice, 17*(4), 348–357. https://doi.org/10.1016/j.cbpra.2009.05.003

Religiously Accommodative and Integrative Rational Emotive Behavior Therapy

Stevan Lars Nielsen, Dane D. B. Abegg, Brodrick T. Brown, David M. Erekson, Rachel A. Hamilton, and Sarah E. Lindsey

Rational emotive behavior therapy (REBT), the first cognitive behavior therapy (CBT), focuses on changing maladaptive irrational beliefs (iBs) to adaptive rational beliefs (rBs). REBT was developed by Albert Ellis—whom I (Nielsen) refer to hereafter as "Al" because that is what I called him when he was alive and we were friends—after a 6-year dive into psychoanalysis. First, Al struggled to find a training analyst. At the time, only physicians were allowed to do such training. Al was one of the first psychologists to cross this physicians-only barrier (Ellis, 1962; Still & Dryden, 1998). Al then practiced psychoanalysis until he found that his clients did better with philosophically oriented, persuasive, emotionally evocative discussion and advice mixed with the behavior modification techniques he used with himself (Ellis, 1956, 1957, 1958, 1962).

Until his 90th year, Al advanced REBT through extensive practice, teaching, training, and collaboration. Ray DiGiuseppe, Albert Ellis Institute training director, once told trainees, "Al has likely done more therapy than anyone else ever has or ever will" (R. DiGiuseppe, personal communication, July 18, 2000). Indeed, institute appointment books show that Al conducted at least 250,000 individual sessions (Matweychuk et al., 2019).

A staunch atheist, Al initially maintained that religion opposed the goals of mental health. He came to see the value of accommodating and integrating clients' religion during therapy. For several years, the authors of this chapter have successfully integrated religious principles into their REBT work with religious clients. This chapter provides a brief overview of REBT and explains

---

https://doi.org/10.1037/0000338-009
Handbook of Spiritually Integrated Psychotherapies, P. S. Richards, G. E. K. Allen, and D. K. Judd (Editors)
Copyright © 2023 by the American Psychological Association. All rights reserved.

173

how clinicians can integrate religion into REBT. It examines common REBT techniques and provides an illustrative case study. The chapter ends with a summary of the research findings on accommodating and integrating religion in REBT, followed by proposed next steps for the field.

BRIEF OVERVIEW OF REBT

Al developed the ABC model to help clients understand the origins of emotions and the ABCDE method for treating unhealthy emotions (Ellis, 1962, 1994). The ABC model posits that it is not Activating events (As) that create emotional Consequences (Cs) but, rather, A + B (Beliefs about A) that create Cs (Ellis, 1962, 1994). Further, iBs cause and sustain self-defeating and unhealthy emotional Consequences (Cs), whereas rBs create and sustain helpful and healthy Cs.

In the ABCDE method, therapists show clients how to change their unhealthy emotions by Disputing (D) iBs, yielding effective Emotional experiences (Es). In other words, disputing iBs changes iBs to rBs. Although simple, the ABC model and ABCDE method fit contemporary, scientific models of cognition and emotional experience (see Barrett, 2017; Kahneman, 2011).

Al cited Stoicism as a philosophical foundation of REBT: "Men are disturbed not by things, but by the views which they take of things" (Epictetus, ca. 125/1948, Chapter V). Rational-emotive philosophy is, however, more a mixture of Stoic, Epicurean, pragmatic, and existential ideas that focus on the value of immediate and long-term meaning, productivity, and fun. REBT's ultimate goal is helping clients adopt a rational-emotive philosophy of life with automatic rBs.

Absolutism

At first, Al described iBs as 12 distinct, absolutistic self-statements (Ellis, 1962). Factor analyses revealed that iBs fit into four general groupings of absolutism: (a) demanding, (b) awfulizing, (c) frustration intolerance, and (d) human rating (DiGiuseppe, 1996). The personally arbitrary, absolutistic appraisals in demands, awfulizing, frustration intolerance, and human rating are the primary cause of self-defeating emotional experiences. Self-defeating qualities in emotional experience can be distinct from unpleasantness. An unpleasant emotional experience can be helpful and healthy; a pleasant emotional experience can be self-defeating and unhealthy.

Applying the ABC model in the following thought experiment shows how absolutism in iBs creates self-defeating emotion: Identical twins win Olympic gold medals in a tandem event. Winning is A, the Activating event. One twin B, Believes, "My skills are good, and I was on my game." The other twin B, Believes, "Of course we won; I'm a superior person." The human rating Belief, *I'm a superior person*, yields C, the emotional Consequence of arrogance. A skill and performance rating Belief yields the emotional Consequence of confidence.

Rating a human is absolutistic because it overgeneralizes from human characteristics to an indefinably complex, whole human. Demands, awfulizing, and frustration intolerance are similarly absolutistic in their appraisal of the immeasurable complexity of life.

Emotional experiences are unique constructions. The pleasant versus unpleasant valence we assign to events will vary from person to person and from situation to situation. Absolutism in iBs is simpler and more general. Rational-emotive theory predicts that self-defeating emotional experience almost always includes absolutism evident as demanding, awfulizing, frustration intolerance, and human rating. Figure 9.1 presents the related emotions from the twin thought experiment just presented with several other, related pairs of healthy and unhealthy emotions. The figure illustrates the role of absolutistic iBs in self-defeating, unhealthy emotional experiences compared with the role of moderate rBs in helpful, healthy emotional experiences.

Belief Change

REBT sessions focus on changing iBs to rBs through D, Disputing of iBs. Disputing is a directive, educational, emotionally evocative—especially humorous!—persuasive, philosophically oriented, consciousness-raising discussion mixed with behavior modification techniques and homework assignments (Ellis, 1962). Forcefulness—humor is forceful!—is tailored to a client's tolerance. Sessions might include imagery tasks, role plays, role reversals, and emotionally evocative gestalt work. Homework tasks include completing worksheets; listening to session recordings; performing habit reversal tasks; self-imposing reinforcement and punishment; performing imagery tasks; doing shame-attacking exercises; proselyting others to rational-emotive ideas; reading self-help books; and even singing, humming, or whistling rational-emotive songs.

Disputing absolutistic iBs can be simple and direct. There can be no consensual logic, no science, no legal principles in the arbitrary absolutism of iBs; iBs are personally arbitrary. The art of REBT is teaching and demonstrating this, showing clients the link between their particular iBs and their problems, and then helping clients adopt rBs and a rational-emotive philosophy of life.

Ellis, Religion, and REBT

Al was famous and infamous for his criticism of religion:

> The conclusion seems inescapable that religion is, on almost every conceivable count, directly opposed to the goals of mental health.... It encourages a fanatic, obsessive-compulsive kind of commitment that is, in its own right, a form of mental illness. (Ellis, 1971, p. 12)

His fame and infamy included criticizing and twice debating Allen Bergin on this topic before standing-room-only American Psychological Association (APA) convention audiences.

Their debates were prompted by Bergin's (1980) paper, "Psychotherapy and Religious Values," in the *Journal of Consulting and Clinical Psychology* and

FIGURE 9.1. REBT Model of Self-Defeating Emotional Experiences

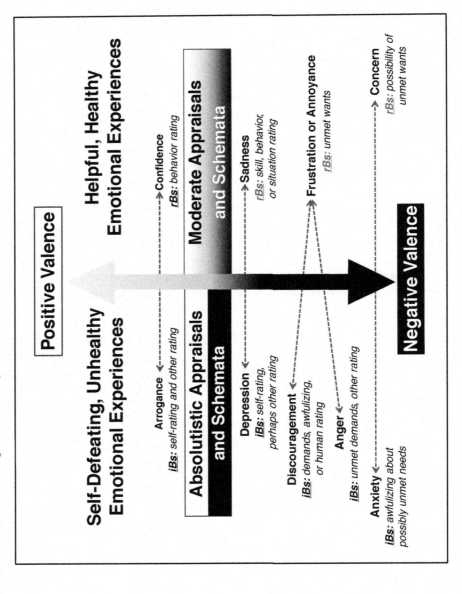

Note. Absolutistic appraisals and organizing schemata are present in irrational beliefs (iBs) that cause and sustain self-defeating and unhealthy emotional experiences. Rational beliefs (rBs) are moderate and create and sustain helpful and healthy emotional experiences.

the response, in the same journal, by Al (Ellis, 1980) in his paper "Psychotherapy and Atheistic Values: A Response to A. E. Bergin's 'Psychotherapy and Religious Values.'" Bergin proposed that clients are harmed by the animus many psychologists have toward religion and that clients would be much better served by systematically including religion in psychological theories and research. Al proposed that devout religion harms people. These are their most frequently cited scholarly papers.

One of this chapter's authors, Stevan Nielsen, met Al on a dare from Bergin. Nielsen asked Bergin when he would again debate Al. Bergin responded, "I'm tired of that. Why don't you debate him?" Nielsen had already concluded that adding scripture to REBT seemed to make REBT a very effective treatment for his devout, Latter-day Saint clients at Brigham Young University (BYU). Instead, Nielsen wrote Al and proposed that at the 1992 APA convention in Washington, DC, they discuss using scripture in REBT. Al agreed, beginning an unlikely friendship and collaboration between Al (an atheist) and Nielsen (a devout Latter-day Saint[1]).

Al later joined with Nielsen and Brad Johnson, an evangelical Christian, in writing a book describing religion-accommodative and religion-integrative REBT (Nielsen et al., 2001). Their view, and our view in writing this chapter, is that accommodating religion during therapy is a matter of multicultural sensitivity and competency (APA, 2017a, 2017b).

Rational Emotive Assessment With Religious Clients

Therapists who specialize in doing REBT (REBTers) accept and accommodate demographics, culturally unique experiences, and religion as A, Activating events, that may activate iBs. It is iBs about Activating events that create self-defeating problems; iBs are the focus. It might be said that REBT accommodates almost everything in a client's life except iBs, and REBTers accommodate iBs until clients agree to work to change. Clients define their problems, but REBT presumes that iBs create the self-defeating elements in client problems. The more a client is upset about religion, the more likely it is that iBs about religion contribute to or create the upset.

It might be said that REBTers check their beliefs about religion at the consulting room door. Like checking one's hat or coat at the coat check room at a nice restaurant, this does not mean giving up beliefs about religion; it means holding these beliefs in abeyance during the therapy session. If a client is atheist, agnostic, conflicted about religion, or devoutly religious, check religious beliefs, agnosticism, or atheism unless or until they became relevant.

---

[1]To avoid confusion about the role of Jesus Christ in its theology, The Church of Jesus Christ of Latter-day Saints discourages the labels "Mormon Church," "Latter-day Saint Church," "LDS Church," "Mormon," and "Mormons." Use of the Church's full name and thereafter "the Church" is preferred. "Member of the Church" or "Latter-day Saint" is a label preferred over "Mormon."

INTEGRATION OF RELIGION IN REBT

When Nielsen et al. (2001) wrote about integrating religion with REBT, they viewed spirituality as too broad, varied, and vaguely defined to allow for clear integration of spirituality in therapy. They explored and demonstrated how specific religious content, especially scripture, could be systematically integrated in REBT. Codified beliefs, including scripture, are more likely to have discrete meaning that can be used systematically to dispute iBs.

Scripture is frequently central to a believer's life, providing aspirational goals, transcendent meaning and values, and instructions for moral living. Scripture often provides ultimate truths by which believers understand themselves, their relationships with others, life, death, and that which follows death. If clients accept the ABC model and the ABCDE method as well as agree that scripture provides truth, scriptural alternatives to iBs can be exceptionally persuasive.

Writing about self-help books, Al proposed that the Bible has had more positive impact on people's lives than all the psychotherapy ever practiced (Ellis, 1993). This doesn't make the Bible true, he wrote; it shows that human wisdom literature can include healthy thinking. The Bible and other religious texts are not usually organized as self-help books, however. Because REBTers are sensitized to iBs, they may be particularly adept at finding rational antidotes to iBs—rBs—in scripture, perhaps more adept than their religious clients. For example, although Hank Robb (1988) is an atheist, his interest in religion and REBT experience helped him find rational antidotes to iBs in the Bible, rational antidotes that he shares with those who believe in the Bible. Nielsen (2004) found that an observant Muslim client was pleased to help him search *The Qur'an* for rBs that disputed her human rating, demanding, and awfulizing. She guided him in searching *The Qur'an*, while he helped her see rBs in what they read in *The Qur'an*.

Absolutism in Religion

Religion is full of absolutism. Creation bespeaks the absolutism of an omnipotent God. Religious commandments often delineate absolute right and wrong. REBT is neutral about such religious absolutism. As noted, self-defeating emotions arise because of absolutistic iBs about A, Activating events. REBT's goal is to help clients see and change their personal, absolutistic iBs about religious verities, not change religious verities.

REBT and Guilt

Religious clients are not alone in feeling guilt, of course, but religion often prohibits or commands behaviors that are not issues for outsiders. As noted earlier, religious rules are best seen as Activating events. It is iBs about Activating events, including iBs about breaking religious rules, that will be the source of self-defeating forms of guilty emotion.

The self-defeating emotion of guilty shame usually arises from self-downing iBs, including self-blame. The self-defeating emotion of guilty anxiety may arise from demanding that one should not have sinned, which is hopeless in the absence of time travel; believing that one must never, ever sin again, which is probably hopeless, given human nature; or believing that one's sins are awful, when sin is inherently human. Furthermore, based on scripture, sins can be forgiven by God. Note that self-defeating guilt is more about the absolutism in iBs than misbehaviors: "*It* is *AWFUL* that I sinned. *I* am *ROTTEN* for sinning." Guilt emotions that arise from such iBs lead to self-defeating emotions rather than to correcting the problems called sins.

Notice that appropriate guilt emotions, such as regret and remorse, arise from viewing the consequences of sin as undesirable and unwanted. Guilty regret and remorse are more likely to lead to restitution, the changing of one's behavior, and other forms of religious repentance.

Scripture as Evidence

Scripture provides organizing meaning in the lives of many religious people. Our experience at Counseling and Psychology Services (CAPS) at BYU is that our observant Latter-day Saint clients welcome discussion of scripture during therapy. Many verses in the Latter-day Saint canon—Old and New Testaments, *Book of Mormon* (*BofM*; The Church of Jesus Christ of Latter-day Saints [The Church], 2013a), *Doctrine and Covenants* (*D&C*; The Church, 2013b), and *The Pearl of Great Price* (*PGP*; The Church, 2013c)—succinctly counter demanding, awfulizing, frustration intolerance, and human rating. However, because iBs are automatic, they usually hide in plain sight. Believers may memorize scriptures that yield rBs but miss the significance of rBs in scriptures because they do not see how iBs hurt them.

A critical step in REBT is teaching the B–C connection, the link between iBs and self-defeating emotional Consequences and between rBs and healthy emotion. When religious clients understand the role of iBs in their problems, rBs in scripture are more likely to impact their problems. Here are four examples of rBs evident in Latter-day Saint scripture.

Demanding

Latter-day Saint theology describes moral agency as a divine gift to humans. If we have moral agency, we are free in many ways, including *free to sin*:

> The Lord said unto Enoch: Behold these thy brethren, they are the workmanship of mine own hands, and I gave unto them their knowledge, in the day I created them; and in the Garden of Eden, gave I unto man his *agency* [emphasis added]. (The Church, 2013c, *PGP*, Moses 7:32)

The religious verity of God-given moral agency counters the iB that people *should* or *must* behave in any particular way.

Awfulizing

Scripture is filled with parables and stories that illustrate rational principles. An emotionally evocative story in the *BofM* (The Church, 2013a) illustrates that how people evaluate events creates both healthy and unhealthy emotion. Calling an event "awful" creates self-defeating *and* religion-defeating emotions. The story also shows that awfulizing is not inevitable.

The prophets Alma and Amulek were commanded to preach repentance to the people of Ammonihah. The city's leaders arrested and tortured Alma and Amulek, then forced them to watch as they killed women and children among their converts by burning them alive. This is among the goriest scenes in all scripture. Amulek implored Alma to use the power of God, the Priesthood, to stop what he called an "awful scene" (The Church, 2013a, *BofM*, Alma 14:10).

With the prophet Alma as mouthpiece, God told Amulek that the situation was not to be stopped. Indeed, it was not even bad enough to stop, although Alma and Amulek, and certainly God, had sufficient divine power to stop what was happening. God told them that the martyrs were going directly to God in glory and the perpetrators would be punished for this gross sin (The Church, 2013a, *BofM*, Alma 14:11). The situation is, thus, worse for the perpetrators than for the martyrs. Amulek is "awfulizing" about the women and children, when the perpetrators' fate is much worse.

Amulek is afraid for himself, providing a useful way to illustrate the effects of awfulizing about things that might happen. "Now Amulek said unto Alma: Behold, perhaps they will burn us also" (The Church, 2013a, *BofM*, Alma 14:12). Some clients actually chuckle at the obviousness of Amulek's statement.

Alma's response shows both that he is upset in a different way and explains why he is less upset in this different way: "And Alma said: Be it according to the will of the Lord" (The Church, 2013a, *BofM*, Alma 14:13). Amulek's iB was that the situation is awful—he says so—and Amulek was more upset. Alma's rB was acceptance of the Lord's will and Alma feels less upset. Clients never think that Alma is happy about the prospect of being burned, but he is not controlled by his upset.

Frustration Intolerance

The *D&C* states, "Wherefore, be not weary in well-doing, for ye are laying the foundation of a great work. And *out of small things proceedeth that which is great* [emphasis added]" (The Church, 2013b, *D&C* 64:33). This verse acknowledges human weariness, then provides a ready-made rB: Consistent, sometimes tedious, detail-oriented work creates "great" outcomes.

Human Rating

Most of our young Latter-day Saint clients at BYU are very familiar with the prophet king Benjamin, having memorized several of his statements. They are often surprised by two things he told his people. First, he explains that he has flaws: "But I am like as yourselves, subject to all manner of infirmities in body *and mind* [emphasis added] . . ." (The Church, 2013a, *BofM*, Mosiah 2:11). Then, he more explicitly challenges human rating: "And I, *even I* [emphasis added], whom ye call your king, am no better than ye yourselves are . . ." (The Church, 2013a, *BofM*, Mosiah 2:26). His rhetoric ("even I") shows that he understood that many of his subjects rated him above them. Better still for REBT, he says that he is no better than his subjects, providing a nearly ready-made rB for disputing self-downing.

TECHNIQUES

There are many ways to dispute iBs: evoking emotions—especially mirth—role playing, homework, reinforcement, and even discussing the past. The focus in discussing the past would be a client's iBs about the past: "What are you telling yourself about your past?" Kopec et al. (1994) and Beal et al. (1996) described five common disputation strategies and styles: logical, empirical, pragmatic, heuristic, and rational-alternative strategies delivered with didactic, Socratic, metaphorical, humorous, or self-disclosing styles. The five strategies and styles yield 25 unique strategy and style combinations. Strategies or styles could also be combined with one another—for example, a Socratic style could be used in a humorous manner. Table 9.1 provides a few examples of disputations from among these combinations.

CASE STUDY

This case demonstrates several religious REBT interventions used with an observant Latter-day Saint college student. Most of the sessions were conducted remotely because of the coronavirus (COVID-19). Scriptures and concepts from this student's religious beliefs helped her get past self-defeating emotions interfering with her life. Her name, "Ruth," the names of the men she dated—"Boaz" and "David"—and identifiable details from her life have been changed. She consented to the use of de-identified details from her case for this chapter. (The same is true for "Rahab," who is mentioned briefly in Table 9.1.)

Ruth, a single, White, 20-year-old, college sophomore, cisgender woman, self-described as a devout Latter-day Saint, wanted help with her anxiety. She completed the 45-item Outcome Questionnaire (OQ; Lambert et al., 2004) before most of her sessions (see Figure 9.2).

On her intake forms, Ruth wrote,

> I feel like I am almost always in a state of anxiety and worry. Perfectionism weighs heavily on me; even the tiniest of things *get me down on myself* [emphasis added] and get my mind whirring down a seemingly endless, anxious path. I would like to not always be in a constant state of worry, so I can act normally instead of stressing.

TABLE 9.1. Techniques for Disputing Irrational Beliefs

Technique	Example
Pragmatic, evidentiary (scriptural) strategy and didactic style, disputing human rating	"You're telling yourself you're a loser. That won't help you. It will almost certainly discourage you. I suggest you tell yourself what God would tell you: You have great worth" (The Church, 2013b, D&C 18:10).
Evidentiary (scriptural) strategy and Socratic, humorous style, disputing human rating	"Scripture says, 'Remember, the worth of souls is great in the sight of God' (The Church, 2013b, D&C 18:10). Could that *possibly* include people who get a C–, or—*heaven forbid!—an F* on a test?"
Rational-alternative, pragmatic strategy and Socratic style, disputing demanding	"Can you feel the difference between saying you *must* do something and saying you *want* to do it?"
Evidentiary (scriptural) strategy and Socratic, humorous style, disputing demanding	"Help me remember: Wasn't it God who gave humans agency? Does His gift of agency mean that you must study for your test? Perhaps agency applies to everything except studying for your test."
Heuristic strategy and Socratic style for several iBs related to perfectionism	"If you were a new missionary and it was your first day learning an unfamiliar language, such as Chinese or Hungarian, what would you tell yourself about your first attempts to speak the new language?"
Pragmatic strategy (implied) and humorous style, disputing human rating	"Let's sing a hymn about human worth and see how you feel. It's to the tune of *Row, Row, Row Your Boat*: Rate, rate, rate your worth, Cultivate your pain! Assuredly, hurriedly, self-inflict misery! Drive yourself insane!" (Nielsen, 1999)
Rational-alternative strategy and didactic, self-disclosing style, disputing human rating	One incisive REBT goal is to abolish much of what we call the ego (Ellis, 1976). Verbs of the form "I am" can be insidiously self-downing. Rahab (a pseudonym), shamed herself, calling herself "a worthless slut." Nielsen (the therapist) replied, "I *never* allow myself to believe '*I am a psychologist.*' No! It's my profession and my hobby, *not* my identity. What might you say to yourself?"

Note. D&C = *Doctrine and Covenants* (The Church of Jesus Christ of Latter-day Saints [The Church], 2013b); REBT = rational emotive behavior therapy.

Ruth was clear in her first session with the therapist, Nielsen:

RUTH: It's a cycle of upset. I want to break the cycle.

NIELSEN: Great. You know, you've done a lot of my work for me.

RUTH: I have?

NIELSEN: Sure. You showed me what's happening in the intake form. I'll show you, using the ABC model of emotion: A, the Activating event, is you feeling anxious about something. Then you B, Believe, degrading things about yourself because of your anxiety. C, the

FIGURE 9.2. Ruth's OQ Scores

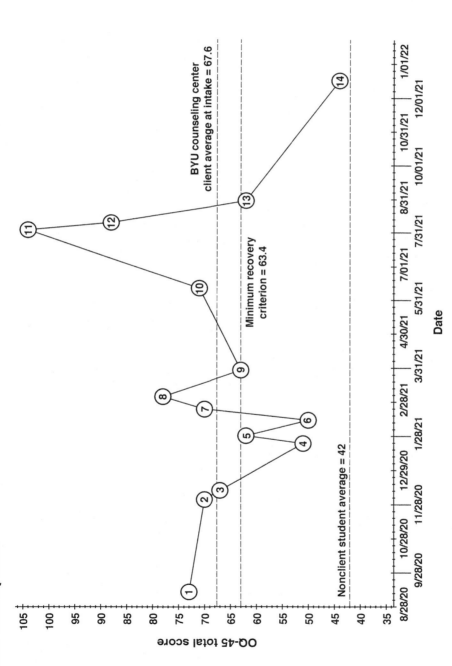

Note. Higher scores come from report of more frequent, more severe symptoms. Ruth's distress dropped gradually as she worked to dispute her self-rating (scores 1, 2, and 3), then decreased dramatically as she did social approach and shame-attacking exercises (4, 5, and 6). When her boyfriend ended the relationship, Ruth felt very upset (11 and 12), then decided "it's not the end of the world" and "his loss as much as mine" (13). By the end of the semester (14), she had begun dating someone new. OQ-45 = 45-item Outcome Questionnaire (Lambert et al., 2004); BYU = Brigham Young University.

	Consequence of B, is that you feel *more* anxious. The added anxiety is a new A, Activating event. You B, Believe, more negative things about yourself because you are more anxious. C, you feel more anxious because of B, and that's a new A, and so on. Your anxiety "whirs!"
RUTH:	That's what happens.
NIELSEN:	Are you a believer? [*Ruth nods*.] Where does the Lord tell you in scripture to degrade yourself? What does He say about your worth?
RUTH:	"Remember, the worth of souls is great in the sight of God" [The Church, 2013b, *D&C* 18:10].
NIELSEN:	I think you quoted that perfectly, except that you left out some punctuation.
RUTH:	[*Laughs*] Oh, come on!
NIELSEN:	Do you have your scriptures? [*Ruth nods*.] Let's see if I can quote it and remember the punctuation. Ready? "Remember, the worth of souls is great in the sight of God"—*semicolon*—meaning the sentence *and idea* continue—"For, behold, the Lord your Redeemer suffered death in the flesh; wherefore he suffered the pain of *all men* [verbal emphasis added], that all men *might* [verbal emphasis added] repent and come unto him" [The Church, 2013b, *D&C* 18:10 and 11]. Did I remember the punctuation?
RUTH:	You remembered one semicolon, forgot another, and forgot the commas [*laughs*].
NIELSEN:	Any evidence that the worth of a soul goes down, even for *willfully* refusing to repent? Is there a footnote that says *you* are of less worth because *you have anxiety attacks*?
RUTH:	No, I guess not. But it sucks that I get so upset.
NIELSEN:	It sucks to be upset, but you tell yourself that *you* suck! *You're not what you do!*

We read Mosiah 23:6 and 7 in the *BofM* (The Church, 2013a) in which the Lord tells the prophet Alma to tell his people not to esteem themselves *lower* than him *or anyone else*. We read Mark 10:18 in which Jesus Christ tells the rich man *there are no good people*. Ruth agreed that if there are *no good people*, there are *no bad people*. She agreed to listen to a recording of the session, to write "U-S-A" for "unconditional self-acceptance" on the palm of her hand, and to read two articles about REBT.

Ruth worked hard to challenge her self-downing, but her distress decreased slowly at first (see Figure 9.2; OQ scores 1, 2, and 3). When in-person Church worship services and BYU classes began, she set social goals. She did shame-attacking exercises by raising her hand in classes, then, when called on, saying she had forgotten her question; she did this twice in every class for a week. Ruth set and met the goal to introduce herself to a new person in every class session and in every Church meeting for 2 weeks. Her homework brought more rapid improvement (see Figure 9.2; scores 4, 5, and 6).

Ruth introduced herself to Boaz (pseudonym), a man in one of her classes whom she found attractive. She accepted the challenge to ask him on a date. Her anxiety increased slightly (see Figure 9.2, score 5), then decreased when he said yes and they spent time together (score 6).

Ruth returned home for the summer, then returned to BYU a month before school started so she could spend time with Boaz. Shortly after her return, he told her he wanted to take some time off from the relationship, then ended the relationship. She felt deeply discouraged (OQ 11):

NIELSEN: What are you telling yourself about Boaz breaking up with you?

RUTH: I'm wondering what's wrong with me?

NIELSEN: That's a rhetorical question, meaning you ask it because you believe there *is* something wrong with you. *And there is something wrong with you!* But it's not something *especially* wrong with *you*. It's the same thing that is wrong with Boaz, me, and *everyone else!* Not the Savior, of course. But we are all fallible human beings—FHBs! We're *all* FHBs!

RUTH: But why doesn't he want to date me?

NIELSEN: It might be nice to know, but you're making it more important than it needs to be. No matter who you are, no matter how you behave, some people will like you, and some people will dislike you. And you know the best example of that, don't you?

RUTH: The Savior?

NIELSEN: Right! He behaved the best of all humans, and it got him crucified. So how people behaved toward Jesus, was it more about Jesus or more about how they responded to him?

RUTH: Both, I guess—the bad things they did are more about them than about Jesus.

NIELSEN: Look, you're telling yourself that there must be something *uniquely wrong* about you because Boaz doesn't want to date you. What might you now begin to tell yourself about his decision?

RUTH: It's more about Boaz than it is about me.

NIELSEN: How can we get you to *believe* that?

We continued this kind of discussion for two sessions. She told herself that it wasn't the end of the world and that it was Boaz's loss as much as hers. Her OQ score dropped to the nonclinical range, at 62 (see Figure 9.2, score 13). She cancelled her next session and did not reschedule.

In a follow-up phone session, Ruth reported that she was quite happy to be dating David (a pseudonym). She had made many new friends in her new Latter-day Saint ward. Her OQ score of 44 (see Figure 9.2, score 14) is statistically indistinguishable from the nonclient, college student average of 42. She said she might reschedule when David leaves to serve a 2-year, Latter-day Saint mission, although she thought she would be okay. Changing what Ruth told herself about dating, making friends, and about her anxiety helped her get more of what she wanted.

RESEARCH FINDINGS

Randomized Clinical Trials

Randomized clinical trials (RCTs) that mixed religious and spiritual interventions (RSIs) with CBT (Propst 1980a, 1980b; Propst et al., 1992) and with REBT (Johnson et al., 1994; Johnson & Ridley, 1992) to treat depressed Christian clients were the first studies showing that RSIs yield therapeutic outcomes as good or better than secular therapy. Two meta-analyses isolated some of these positive RSI effects (Captari et al., 2018; T. B. Smith et al., 2007). T. B. Smith and colleagues (2007) isolated the effectiveness of "Biblical disputation" (p. 647), and both meta-analyses showed that RSIs yield as much symptom improvement among religious clients as secular interventions but do better at improving religious clients' sense of well-being than secular interventions.

Templeton Spiritually Integrative Psychotherapy Research

Our team (the authors of this chapter) recently conducted a practice-based study of religion in psychotherapy, supported by a grant from the John Templeton Foundation. We looked for and found evidence for the positive effects of using scripture as an RSI. Templeton spiritually integrative psychotherapy (TSIP) therapists coded sessions for topics discussed (e.g., anxiety, depression, family, guilt), therapeutic orientation (e.g., CBT, client-centered therapy, REBT), and interventions used (e.g., defusion, disputation, reflective listening), including use of scripture. TSIP therapists treated 1,311 CAPS clients; 759 clients completed OQs before treatment and at follow-up. The 61 TSIP therapists coded 5,865 elements of therapy sessions, including 542 uses of scripture (9.24% of coded events).

We estimated the therapeutic effects of using scripture with linear regression. We first regressed follow-up OQs on pretreatment OQs, then on total number of scriptures coded. Pretreatment OQ score was, of course, a strong predictor of follow-up OQ: $B_{OQpretreatment} = 0.50$, $p = .002$. OQ scores decreased or improved by about 50%. Scriptures also predicted a reduction in symptoms, $B_{scriptures} = -1.11$, $p < .01$. Each scripture discussed during therapy predicted a 1.11 point decrease in OQ at follow-up. The full regression equation was: $OQ_{follow-up} = 33.9 + (0.50 \times OQ_{pretreatment}) - (1.11 \times \text{number of scriptures used})$; $F(2, 747) = 129.4$, $p < .001$.

Approximately one point of improvement for each scripture discussed is a nice, concise effect. Nielsen used scriptures more often than any other TSIP therapist, approximately 5 times per client, but the effect could not be isolated to him or to REBT. The effect was unchanged when gender, age, and numbers of sessions attended were added to the regression equation. Randomly controlled use of scripture might be necessary to establish and isolate effects from using scripture during REBT.

CAPS REBTers

The team compared client change among CAPS clients treated by nine CAPS therapists who, over the past 25 years, have expressed allegiance to REBT compared with change among the 260 CAPS therapists who have never expressed allegiance to REBT. Among the nine, we included doctoral students treating clients under the supervision of REBTers. Assignment of clients to therapist is quasirandom. Most clients are assigned to the next available therapist; some women ask for a woman therapist. Three of the nine REBTers are women; slightly more than 35% of the 260 non-REBT therapists are women. REBTers used scripture at least sometimes when treating religious clients, and at least 90% of our clients described themselves as devout Latter-day Saints.

Figure 9.3 presents first and last OQ scores among the nine REBTers' 3,378 clients, compared with first and last OQ scores among the 26,834 clients treated by the other 260 therapists. Both the REBT and non-REBT therapist groups included licensed professionals and therapists in training. We applied repeated measures analysis of variance (ANOVA) to these OQ scores. The overall ANOVA effect for change from first to last OQ was significant, $F(1, 30,210) = 1,010.06$, $p < .001$, Cohen's $d = 0.35$. The overall effect for being a client treated by an REBTer or a non-REBTer was also significant, $F(1, 30,210) = 4.13$, $p = .044$. The most important comparison, evident in the change by therapist interaction effect, was significant, $F(1, 30,210) = 36.87$, $p < .001$, Cohen's $d = 0.07$. This significant F value fits the pattern evident in Figure 9.3: Clients treated by REBTers improved more than clients treated by the non-REBT therapists.

The statistical midpoint between OQ scores among clients and nonclients in the OQ standardization samples is 63.44; a score greater than 63.44 is statistically closer to scores of clients in treatment; a score lower than 63.44 is closer to scores of nonclients. A reference line for this minimum recovery criterion is depicted in Figure 9.3. On average, clients treated by REBTers crossed the line. Clients treated by other therapists did not, on average, cross the line, but the 95% confidence interval for their clients does just cross the criterion line.

This comparison provides rough evidence that religion integrative REBT yielded better outcomes. The comparison is not well controlled because we cannot document exactly which clients received scriptural RSIs mixed with REBT, and assignment to therapists was not fully random.

FIGURE 9.3. Change From Pretreatment to Final Outcome Questionnaire Score, REBT Versus Other Therapy

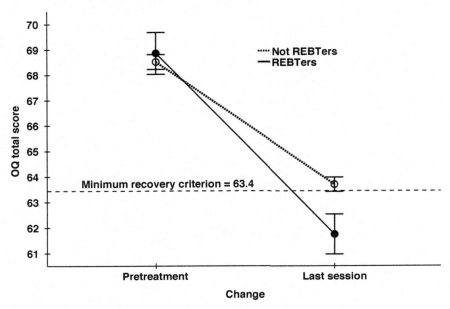

Note. See Lambert et al. (2004) for the Outcome Questionnaire (OQ). Change among 3,378 clients treated by nine Counseling and Psychology Services (CAPS) therapists who describe themselves as frequently using rational emotive behavior therapy (REBTers) was compared with change among the 26,838 clients treated by 260 other CAPS therapists who have never described themselves as REBTers. A significant change by therapists' interaction effect is evident, showing that clients treated by the REBTers improved significantly more than clients treated by the other CAPS therapists, $F(1, 30,210) = 36.87$, $p < .001$, Cohen's $d = 0.07$.

NEXT STEPS

When interviewed by Nielsen, Al proposed that it's important to study the effects of a wide range of ideas on emotional experience and therapy outcome (Nielsen & Ellis, 1994). He included religious ideas, rational-emotive ideas, and any other ideas that influence people. The authors of this chapter have found evidence that using scripture as an RSI was associated with our clients improving. We are convinced that using scripture during REBT with observant Latter-day Saint clients helps them accept and benefit more from REBT. These are, however, still correlational relationships between scripture use and improvement. Our team will now attempt to design an RCT to experimentally test the effects of using scripture during REBT.

REFERENCES

American Psychological Association. (2017a). *Ethical principles of psychologists and code of conduct* (2002, amended effective June 1, 2010, and January 1, 2017). https://www.apa.org/ethics/code/index.aspx

American Psychological Association. (2017b). *Multicultural guidelines: An ecological approach to context, identity, and intersectionality.* https://www.apa.org/about/policy/multicultural-guidelines.pdf

Barrett, L. F. (2017). *How emotions are made: The secret life of the brain.* Mariner Books.

Beal, D., Kopec, A. M., & DiGiuseppe, R. (1996). Disputing clients' irrational beliefs. *Journal of Rational-Emotive and Cognitive Behavior Therapy, 14,* 215–229. https://doi.org/10.1007/BF02238137

Bergin, A. E. (1980). Psychotherapy and religious values. *Journal of Consulting and Clinical Psychology, 48*(1), 95–105. https://doi.org/10.1037/0022-006X.48.1.95

Captari, L. E., Hook, J. N., Hoyt, W., Davis, D. E., McElroy-Heltzel, S. E., & Worthington, E. L., Jr. (2018). Integrating clients' religion and spirituality within psychotherapy: A comprehensive meta-analysis. *Journal of Clinical Psychology, 74*(11), 1938–1951. https://doi.org/10.1002/jclp.22681

The Church of Jesus Christ of Latter-day Saints. (2013a). *The Book of Mormon: Another testament of Jesus Christ.*

The Church of Jesus Christ of Latter-day Saints. (2013b). *The doctrine and covenants of the Church of Jesus Christ of Latter-day Saints.*

The Church of Jesus Christ of Latter-day Saints. (2013c). *The pearl of great price.*

DiGiuseppe, R. (1996). The nature of irrational and rational beliefs: Progress in rational emotive behavior theory. *Journal of Rational-Emotive & Cognitive-Behavior Therapy, 14*(1), 5–28. https://doi.org/10.1007/BF02238091

Ellis, A. (1956, August 30–September 5). *Recent innovations in psychotherapeutic strategy* [Paper presentation]. Sixty-Fourth Annual Convention of the American Psychological Association, Chicago, IL, United States.

Ellis, A. (1957). Outcome of employing three techniques of psychotherapy. *Journal of Clinical Psychology, 13*(4), 344–350. https://doi.org/10.1002/1097-4679(195710)13:4<344::AID-JCLP2270130407>3.0.CO;2-9

Ellis, A. (1958). Rational psychotherapy. *The Journal of General Psychology, 59*(1), 35–49. https://doi.org/10.1080/00221309.1958.9710170

Ellis, A. (1962). *Reason and emotion in psychotherapy.* Lyle Stuart.

Ellis, A. (1971). *The case against religion: A psychotherapist's view.* Albert Ellis Institute.

Ellis, A. (1976). RET abolishes most of the human ego. *Psychotherapy: Theory, Research & Practice, 13*(4), 343–348. https://doi.org/10.1037/h0086502

Ellis, A. (1980). Psychotherapy and atheistic values: A response to A. E. Bergin's "Psychotherapy and religious values." *Journal of Consulting and Clinical Psychology, 48*(5), 635–639. https://doi.org/10.1037/0022-006X.48.5.635

Ellis, A. (1993). The advantages and disadvantages of self-help therapy materials. *Professional Psychology: Research and Practice, 24*(3), 335–339. https://doi.org/10.1037/0735-7028.24.3.335

Ellis, A. (1994). *Reason and emotion in psychotherapy* (Rev. & updated). Carol Publishing Group.

Epictetus. (1948). *The enchiridion* (T. W. Higginson, Trans.). The Liberal Arts Press. (Original work published ca. 125)

Johnson, W. B., Devries, R., Ridley, C. R., Pettorini, D., & Peterson, D. R. (1994). The comparative efficacy of Christian and secular rational emotive therapy with Christian clients. *Journal of Psychology and Theology, 22*(2), 130–140. https://doi.org/10.1177/009164719402200206

Johnson, W. B., & Ridley, C. R. (1992). Brief Christian and non-Christian rational-emotive therapy with depressed Christian clients: An exploratory study. *Counseling and Values, 36*(3), 220–229. https://doi.org/10.1002/j.2161-007X.1992.tb00790.x

Kahneman, D. (2011). *Thinking: Fast and slow.* Farrar, Straus and Giroux.

Kopec, A. M., Beal, D., & DiGiuseppe, R. (1994). Training in RET: Disputational strategies. *Journal of Rational-Emotive and Cognitive Behavior Therapy, 12,* 47–60. https://doi.org/10.1007/BF02354489

Lambert, M. J., Morton, J. J., Hatfield, D., Harmon, C., Hamilton, S., Reid, R. C., Shimokowa, K., Christopherson. C., & Burlingame, G. M. (2004). *Administration and scoring manual for the Outcome Questionnaire-45*. American Professional Credentialing Services.

Matweychuk, W., DiGiuseppe, R., & Gulyayeva, O. (2019). A comparison of REBT with other cognitive behavior therapies. In M. E. Bernard & W. Dryden (Eds.), *Advances in REBT: Theory, practice, research, measurement, prevention and promotion* (pp. 47–77). Springer. https://doi.org/10.1007/978-3-319-93118-0_3

Nielsen, S. L. (1999). *Rational-emotive hymns—Music and the broken word*. Counseling and Psychological Services, Brigham Young University.

Nielsen, S. L. (2004). A Mormon rational emotive behavior therapist attempts Qur'anic rational emotive behavior therapy. In P. S. Richards & A. E. Bergin (Eds.), *Casebook for a spiritual strategy in counseling and psychotherapy* (pp. 213–230). American Psychological Association. https://doi.org/10.1037/10652-013

Nielsen, S. L., & Ellis, A. (1994). A discussion with Albert Ellis: Reason, emotion and religion. *Journal of Psychology and Christianity*, *13*(4), 327–341.

Nielsen, S. L., Johnson, W. B., & Ellis, A. (2001). *Counseling and psychotherapy with religious persons: The rational emotive behavior therapy approach*. Lawrence Erlbaum.

Propst, L. R. (1980a). The comparative efficacy of religious and nonreligious imagery for the treatment of mild depression in religious individuals. *Cognitive Therapy and Research*, *4*(2), 167–178. https://doi.org/10.1007/BF01173648

Propst, L. R. (1980b). A comparison of the cognitive restructuring psychotherapy paradigm and several spiritual approaches to mental health. *Journal of Psychology and Theology*, *8*(2), 107–114. https://doi.org/10.1177/009164718000800202

Propst, L. R., Ostrom, R., Watkins, P., Dean, T., & Mashburn, D. (1992). Comparative efficacy of religious and nonreligious cognitive-behavioral therapy for the treatment of clinical depression in religious individuals. *Journal of Consulting and Clinical Psychology*, *60*(1), 94–103. https://doi.org/10.1037/0022-006X.60.1.94

Robb, H. B. (1988). *How to stop driving yourself crazy with help from the Bible*. Albert Ellis Institute.

Smith, T. B., Bartz, J., & Richards, P. S. (2007). Outcomes of religious and spiritual adaptations to psychotherapy: A meta-analytic review. *Psychotherapy Research*, *17*(6), 643–655. https://doi.org/10.1080/10503300701250347

Still, A., & Dryden, W. (1998). The intellectual origins of rational therapy. *History of the Human Sciences*, *11*(3), 63–86. https://doi.org/10.1177/095269519801100304

II

INTEGRATION OF SPECIFIC SPIRITUAL TRADITIONS INTO PSYCHOTHERAPY

10

Theoretical Foundations and Clinical Applications of Traditional Islamically Integrated Psychotherapy

Fahad Khan and Hooman Keshavarzi

Early Muslim scholars translated the works of Greek philosophers and elaborated on them to advance the understanding of conditions related to the human psyche in an Islamic context (Awaad & Ali, 2016). Because Islam encourages the pursuit of knowledge and accepts reason and empirical evidence as admissible sources of information alongside scripture, there has never been a dichotomy between sacred and secular knowledge (Awaad et al., 2020). Early Muslim scholars were able to comfortably advance mental health practice (*tibb al-ruhānī*) as a subdiscipline of medicine and even established one of the earliest documented hospitals in Baghdad in the 9th century (Tbakhi & Amr, 2008). This chapter sheds light on Islamic epistemology and its methodological understanding in the formation of the traditional Islamically integrated psychotherapy (TIIP) model (Keshavarzi & Khan, 2018). TIIP's approach, underlying assumptions, and ontological model are discussed, and a brief case study is presented to demonstrate TIIP concepts and interventions.

ISLAMIC EPISTEMOLOGY

The term "psychology" originates from the Greek language and means the study of the spirit or soul. The field was named to reflect the study of mental activities, cognition, and emotions as by-products of a metaphysical soul or "mind." At the center of this field was a relational perception of the human mind (Rotman,

2021). Historically, Muslim scholars cited religious motivations for their contributions to the work of earlier Greek and Hellenistic philosophers and thinkers (Awaad et al., 2020), and Islamic tradition (i.e., Qur'an and prophetic traditions) encouraged and cultivated this thought process (Awaad et al., 2020).

The fundamental ontological and epistemological assumptions regarding human psychology have often been influenced by social histories, worldviews, values, and culture. Such assumptions are not generalizable to all cultures. Kincheloe et al. (2011) identified some basic processes of theory formation. Their criticalist approach highlighted factors with implications for the entrenchment and advancement of dominant theories that inform psychological best practices, policies, and guidelines (Collins & Stockton, 2018). Knowledge and theory development in the Muslim world occurred in a different manner than in early Europe. Although various sociohistorical currents led to the production of diverse Islamic literature on the topic of psychology, a common epistemological framework guided dominant Islamic Sunni scholarship and was the source of evaluating knowledge production (Ragab, 2015).

For Muslims, there are three sources of knowledge (*asbab al-'ilm*): (a) empirical or sensory knowledge acquired through observation or empirical study; (b) rational knowledge—a priori (*badīhī*) or acquired (*istidlālī*) knowledge gained through human reason that is capable of realizing certain necessary truths; and (c) verified reports of truth, which include divine revelation in the form of Qur'an (recited revelation) and prophetic traditions (*Sunnah*) and large numbers of converging eyewitness reports of some objective reality. It is important to recognize that Muslims consider all three sources legitimate, harmonious, and equally valuable (Keshavarzi & Ali, 2020). As for the development of an understanding of human ontology, it is important to take into consideration the hierarchic arrangement of knowledge across all three domains into (a) the definitive/certain (*qaṭ'ī*) and (b) the probabilistic/inferential (*ẓannī*). Definitive proofs provide certain knowledge and cannot be dismissed, while probable truths are graded and admissible according to their associated strength and scope of usage (Keshavarzi & Ali, 2020). This grading of knowledge provides a reconciliatory approach to the construction of the psychological sciences as it provides a mechanism for the appropriate placement of information, irrespective of whether it is Western or Eastern in origin. This grading scheme identifies the degree of potential truth in a piece of information and provides the basis for a framework of the human psyche. The TIIP model adopted this epistemological framework, drawing from empirical truths, scholarly literature (both Islamic and contemporary), and Islamic scripture.

THE TRADITIONAL ISLAMICALLY INTEGRATED PSYCHOTHERAPY APPROACH

An Islamically integrated approach was initiated by Keshavarzi and Haque (2013), who outlined an approach to care based on Muslim contributions that provided an integrative framework for psychological practice. They developed a practical model and described it as "traditional" in reference to its grounding in the Sunni Islamic teachings (Keshavarzi & Khan, 2018). This qualification was for the express purpose of outlining the stream of Islamic sources, assumptions, and methodology employed in the construction of the model given the various interpretations of Islam (Keshavarzi & Ali, 2020). Islamically integrated psychotherapy also encompasses diverse approaches and models of Islamic psychotherapy (York Al-Karam, 2018). The model has been further refined by Khan, Ali, and others working in the research department at the Khalil Center in New York, where TIIP is taught and practiced (Keshavarzi, Khan, Ali, & Awaad, 2020).

One of the underlying assumptions of the TIIP model is that health and wellness exist on a continuum, and this model has been used to treat a variety of psychological disorders and their associated spiritual illnesses. Most of the individuals seeking care at the Khalil Center suffer from family- or social-related issues (41%), followed by anxiety-related (20%) or mood-related (19%) issues, trauma or stressor (10%), schizophrenia or psychosis (2%), and neurodevelopmental (1%) issues. TIIP has been used to successfully treat most of these conditions as well as spiritual illnesses. Conceptualization and treatment of specific problems, such as marital issues and obsessive–compulsive disorder, have also been formulated (Keshavarzi, Khan, & Syed, 2020). It is important to note that spiritual illnesses are not treated by TIIP for their own sake but rather within the context of psychological functioning or development of psychospiritual resilience. The work of the TIIP practitioner takes a holistic approach to mental health, in contrast to the support provided by a spiritual or pastoral counselor. Clear boundaries have been developed to avoid conflict between mental health practitioners and pastoral clergy and to avoid infringement on each other's respective domains of practice.

Underlying Assumptions and Framework of TIIP

The following are some of the underlying assumptions of the TIIP model:

- Empirical, rational, and scriptural sources of knowledge are all equally valid and admissible for use in the science of human psychology, while hierarchically graded according to the strength of their evidence.

- All humans are born with a predisposed inclination for universal good and connection with the divine (*fitrah*), although there is a state of inner intrapsychic tension between animalistic and angelic drives (see the section titled TIIP Ontological Model of the Human Psyche).

- Health and wellness are seen on a continuum rather than the presence or absence of disorders or decrease or increase in functioning.

- Assessment, evaluation, and treatment occur in the context of primordial assumptions regarding the origins of humans and include postmortem/afterlife considerations.

- Practitioners' internal factors are just as important as those of patients in the facilitation of the process of change.

- Since TIIP operates from a multiplex ontological view, the human psyche is considered a multidimensional ontological property containing various elements. The body and the metaphysical psyche are interwoven and operate through a continuous feedback loop. Treatment must address each level in an appropriate manner. No single therapeutic approach can be equally applied to all human beings, and treatment goals must be constructed bearing the variability of clinical expressions in mind.

- Treatment cannot be focused on a single dimension to the exclusion of the others because all dimensions are interconnected and a change in one element of the psyche will result in a residual change in others.

The TIIP model, much like the Islamic spiritual tradition, does not consider the presence or absence of disorder to represent the whole human range of psychospiritual health and well-being; that is, someone who is not diagnosed with a disorder may still be unhealthy. Recent research trends and psychological theoretical movements have also shifted toward the importance of character reformation as well as viewing mental health and well-being on a continuum (Peterson & Seligman, 2004). For example, the dual continuum model of mental health asserts that health and well-being do not depend solely on the presence or absence of mental illness and that an individual may be on two continua: one continuum indicates the presence or absence of mental health and the other the presence or absence of mental illness (Westerhof & Keyes, 2010). In fact, the TIIP model goes a step further in that it takes into consideration the presence of spiritual illnesses that secular models often ignore. For instance, Islamic spirituality views jealousy or envy (*hasad*) as a spiritual illness that, if left untreated, can lead to significant issues in this world and in the next. Research has shown that jealousy, especially within the context of a relationship, can become "morbid" and lead to symptoms of anxiety, paranoia, anger, hate, and bitterness (Maggini et al., 2006), and even homicidal thoughts and behaviors (Campbell et al., 2003). Another example is what the Prophet Muhammad (peace and blessings be upon him) categorized as one of the three spiritual destroyers: avarice (shuḥḥ). Avarice, or greed, which is not treated by modern-day clinicians, has been shown to cause an individual to focus inward and ignore others (Zhu et al., 2019), which can lead to a variety of unethical and illegal behaviors, such as fraud, theft, deception, and corruption (Cohen et al., 2009; Gilliland & Anders, 2011; Seuntjens et al., 2019).

The TIIP Ontological Model of the Human Psyche

The ontological model of the human psyche as conceptualized through the TIIP lens consists of several layers (see Figure 10.1). Perhaps the most important aspect of the human ontology, *fitrah*, or primordial human essence, is on the topmost tier. This concept stems from a prophet tradition that relates that "every child is born upon the *fitrah*," as well as the verse of the Qur'an that says "this is the natural disposition given to you by God, upon which He

FIGURE 10.1. An Overview of Human Ontology From Traditional Islamically Integrated Psychotherapy Model

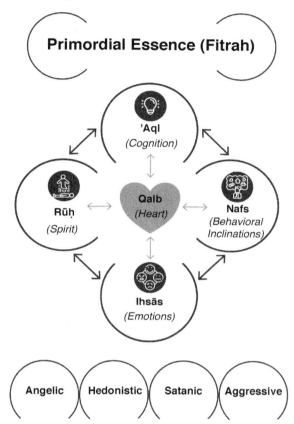

originated all humankind" (Qur'an, 30:30). *Fitrah* (the divine) in the TIIP model is translated as primordial essence because it stems from the primordially endowed human faculty to recognize good and evil and distinguish truth from falsehood. Research findings have suggested that children as young as 2 years old can learn to recognize and practice prosocial behaviors and that these behaviors increase in frequency and sophistication as they age (Svetlova et al., 2010). At the Yale Baby Lab, Hamlin et al. (2007) reported preverbal infants as young as 6 to 10 months being able to socially evaluate the actions of others and preferring individuals who were helpful to those who were hindering.

Although human beings possess the inherent ability to recognize good and possess a natural inclination toward it, the TIIP model recognizes that the "human" component of this blend leads to formation of drives composed of four types: (a) angelic, (b) hedonistic, (c) satanic, and (d) aggressive. Imām al-Ghazālī posited that the hedonistic/appetitive (*shahwah*) and aggressive (*ghadab*) drives are not inherently bad or evil, and satanic drives emerge if the appetitive and aggressive drives are not kept in check (Al-Ghazali, 1990, p. 137).

There is a constant struggle between the forces of the divine/angelic drives and appetitive/aggressive drives. Imam al-Suhrawardi (d. 632) referred to the tension between the metaphysical divine essence (*rūḥ 'ulwī samāwī*) and the metaphysical life force (*rūḥ ḥayawānī*; Al-Suhrawardi, 1993, p. 247).

In regard to the composition of the human being, Islamic scholastic theologians generally view them as containing two parts: the (a) physical and (b) metaphysical or the body and soul (Al-Bajuri, 2002b). Imām al-Ghazālā (d. 1111) and Imam al-Bajuri (d. 1860) referred to the overall metaphysical entity as the *latīfah rabānniyah,* or the human divine subtle essence (Al-Bājuri, 2002b; Al-Ghazali, 1990). This essence has several expressions (*i'tibārāt*): *'aql* (cognition), *nafs* (behavioral inclinations), and *rūḥ/qalb* (spirit/heart). Drawing from this classical division of the human being, the psyche is metaphysical in nature but also interacts with and controls the body. For example, the dominant position of the discursive theologians is that the 'aql is the central cognitive or reasoning governing source of the brain, where the brain is necessary in order to fully express its cognitive faculties (Al-Bajuri, 2002b). It is the "mind" behind the brain that explains the spontaneity, will, intent, and nonrandom movement of the brain. If the brain is damaged, then the 'aql is unable to execute its rational functions.

The TIIP model draws from the classic conceptualization and adds a secondary element of emotion (*iḥsās*). While emotion is not seen as an independent entity but simply as an expression of other aspects of the human psyche, it was adopted and enlisted as another entity in the model for the purposes of psychological conceptualization and facilitation of treatment. The centrality of emotions and emotion-based research in modern psychology warrants their inclusion.

The TIIP model divides the elements of the psyche into (a) *'aql* (cognition), (b) *nafs* (behavioral inclination), (c) *iḥsā*s (basic emotions), (d) *rūḥ* (spirit), and (e) *qalb* (metaphysical heart). As noted previously, the "heart" refers to the spiritual/metaphysical heart, which serves as a homeostatic receptacle of health and pathology. Changes in other components will positively or negatively affect the heart (Keshavarzi & Ali, 2020).

'Aql (Cognition)
'Aql is the human rational faculty that, if developed, is capable of sound reasoning and attainment of knowledge. It is able to achieve realizations and intuition if human senses and perception are functioning at optimal capacity (Al-Taftazani, 2000). In fact, according to Islamic spiritual conceptualization, a fully developed 'aql provides rationality, knowledge attainment, appreciation of consequences, ability to distinguish right from wrong, and even regulation of emotions (Al-Bajuri, 2002a; Al-Ghazali, 1990).

Nafs (Behavioral Inclination)
The nafs, often compared with the Freudian model of Id, Ego, and Superego (Abu Raiya, 2014), is not inherently bad (Rothman & Coyle, 2020). Rather, the two main drives embedded within the nafs are the appetitive/hedonistic

(*shahwah*) and aggressive/survival (*ghadab*). The overindulgence or primitive expression of these two drives leads to a state of *ammarah bi al-su* (Qur'an, 12:53), or commanding toward evil. Training, regulation, and denial of desires for overconsumption lead to elevation and growth, and the nafs enters the stage of *nafs lawwāmah* (Qur'an, 75:2), or the reprimanding self. Finally, once it is successfully trained and the desire for overconsumption is extinguished, the nafs enters a stage of calm and serenity known as *nafs mutma'innah* (Qur'an, 89:27; Hammad, 2007). It is no longer shackled by the dictates and drives of carnal desires, and the inner tension is relieved. Note that the *nafs* has been translated here as "behavioral inclination" to reflect the underlying automaticity to act based on instincts or training.

Ihsās (Basic Emotions)

Islamic scholars consider emotions to be beyond the biosocial processes and to possess spiritually inherent motivational drives. They have described emotions as both top-down/cognitively influenced responses and bottom-up biologically primitive motivational reactions (Ortony & Turner, 1990). Sufi poets, such as Rumi, have even considered positive and negative emotions as "guests" from the divine (Helminski, 2005). In the TIIP model, ihsas is considered a secondary aspect of the human experience that is a byproduct of the interactions among other facets of the psyche. Thus, emotions may arise out of hidden or overt thinking ('aql) or from the primitive drives of the nafs. Islam recognizes that emotional manifestation is on a spectrum, and either too little or too much is considered unhealthy. For instance, Ashraf Ali Thanwi (d. 1943) noted that "without anger man may not survive. Suppose an enemy attacks you or a wild beast targets you and you do not show anger, then you will be devoured" (Uthmani, 2007, Vol. 3, p. 39). However, too much anger may lead to acting impulsively and can be destructive (Al-Ghazali, 1990).

Rūḥ (Spirit)

The rūḥ consists of two mechanisms: (a) the *rūḥ 'ulwī samāwī*, which is an inherent inclination toward the sacred and a longing for reconnection and remembrance of the divine; and (b) the life force (*rūḥ ḥayawānī*), which gives life to the body and contains animalistic tendencies and survival inclinations (Keshavarzi & Ali, 2020). The former yearns to connect with the divine through mystical experiences. The 19th-century American philosopher William James categorized mystical experiences as those that contain characteristics of ineffability, noetic quality, transiency, and passivity. These experiences are discrete and temporary, either abruptly occurring or resulting from mystical experiences, such as meditation (Ireland, 1903). Spiritual, transcendental, or ecstatic experiences have been shown to affect neurobiology. For example, meditation reduces metabolism of glucose in the caudate nucleus, which improves outcomes in obsessive–compulsive disorder (Baxter et al., 1992), up-regulates activation in the ventro-lateral prefrontal cortex, and improves emotional regulation (Schaefer et al., 2002). From variant psychotherapeutic approaches acting on emotions and cognitions to direct action on the spiritual reality of the human, spiritual techniques are essential to any Islamic psychology approach (Keshavarzi, Yusuf, et al., 2020).

In the TIIP model, development of the spiritual connection is conducted through righteous actions (e.g., prayer, fasting, charity, intimate contemplation); however, the most essential of these is the divine remembrance, or *dhikr*. Often, Muslims practice dhikr through verbal incantations of verses, prayers, or attributes of God. However, the most beneficial form of divine remembrance is one in which an individual is fully engaged in an ideal mind–body–soul connected state evoking a state of divine proximity. Intensive concentration on a ritual symbol has been shown to produce a transformative state of consciousness similar to a mystical state of being (Laughlin, 1996). These mind–body synchronizations can lead to alignment of the frontal cortex and the limbic system, resulting in the activation of the parasympathetic nervous system and a heightened state of calmness relaxation (Saniotis, 2018). Dhikr has also been effective in reducing anxiety in patients with cancer (Sulistyawati et al., 2019) and chronic kidney failure (Nugraha Kusuma et al., 2020), as well as women in labor (Nurbaeti, 2015) and preoperative patients (Octary et al., 2020).

Qalb (Metaphysical Heart)

Muslim theologians, such as Imams al-Ghazali and al-Suhrawardi, have posited that there are two types of hearts, the physical heart, which may contain gas-like life forces, and the metaphysical heart, which is separate yet interacts with the physical heart (Al-Ghazali, 2008). This metaphysical heart is the locus of human being and is the container of health and dysfunction (Al-Suhrawardi, 1993). Its condition (sick or healthy) depends on the actions of other elements of the psyche. The ultimate goal is balance across all components of the human psyche and an integrative whole or unity of being (*ittiḥād*) that consequently results in a healthy heart (*qalb salīm*; Keshavarzi & Ali, 2020).

TIIP Process of Change

The TIIP model considers the relationship between the practitioner and the patient as one that is best described by al-Ghazālī's relational term *Rafīq*, which can be loosely translated as "intimate friend." *Rafīq* comes from the root word *rifq*, which means companionship and denotes a relationship that is collaborative and authoritative rather than hierarchical (Khan et al., 2020). TIIP extends this concept of Rafīq into the therapeutic context, positing that it not only draws from psychological education and training but also considers the metaphysical dimensions of healing. A TIIP practitioner readily draws from the Islamic spiritual tradition in an attempt to foster holistic psycho-spiritual equilibrium. Furthermore, it is understood that both the patient and the practitioner are on similar journeys of personal development. Therefore, a Rafiq must also be aware of their own deficiencies, particularly if they enter into the psychotherapeutic relationship, and consider their own internal biases and work toward their own well-being. Clinicians are continually aware of their own issues and actively work on them so they do not infringe on their work with their patients.

Given this collaborative authoritative approach, the TIIP model outlines four hierarchical stages in the process of change (see Figure 10.2). In each of these four stages, the clinician employs the mechanisms of change (bottom half of the diagram) in an attempt to induce the principles of change (top half of the diagram) within the patient.

Stage 1

This stage lays the groundwork for the therapy process by building a strong therapeutic bond (*murābaṭah*). The psychospiritual assessment and initial case formulation has six major goals: (a) building a therapeutic alliance; (b) assessment of motivation to change; (c) assessment of religiosity; (d) psychospiritual diagnosis and conceptualization; (e) assessment of internal and external psychospiritual functioning; and (f) orienting the patient to the psychotherapy process through psychoeducation, discussing the prognosis, and setting therapeutic goals (Khan, 2020). During this stage it is also critical to determine which elements of the psyche are the primary source of dysfunction. For example, the problem might originate in over- or underregulation of emotions, the presence of cognitive distortions, existential or spiritual struggles, or unrestrained behavioral impulses. Identifying the source will help direct treatment during Stage 3, as directive interventions target the primary elements first and treat the others as resultant effects.

Assessment and initial alliance building typically consist of the employment of empathic following and attunement techniques that lower anxieties and defensiveness. The practitioner provides psychoeducation in which the patient responds to questions to address ambivalence and gauge the level of commitment, motivation, and potential compliance with the treatment goals. This commitment is important because the patient will be required to engage in some difficult therapeutic tasks over the course of therapy, such as facing uncomfortable intrapsychic tensions and opposing unhealthy behavioral inclinations. Once an alliance (*murābaṭah*) is formed, the patient is more likely to embrace the demands of the process, which enhances the overall treatment

FIGURE 10.2. The Process of Change in TIIP

outcomes (Keshavarzi & Ali, 2020). Preparing the patient for the therapeutic process is critical to aligning therapist and patient expectations. Also, many patients may be new to therapy or may be transferring from modalities of psychotherapy that differ drastically from the TIIP process.

Stage 2
In this stage, the aim is for the patient to experience introspective self-awareness (*inkishāf*). The clinician facilitates this through guided self-examination (*mukāshafah*). Experiential unraveling of the patient's internal psychological worlds increases their self-awareness. During this stage, the therapist explains the internal ontological model of the human psyche, and coconceptualization of the patient's psychological issues are formulated accordingly. In this stage, the goal is for the patient to further understand how, when, where, and which part of the psyche is activated moment to moment as the individual is engaged emotionally, cognitively, spiritually, and behaviorally. This understanding allows the patient to appreciate the multiple layers of the psyche, how one level affects another, and how they combine to create an overall experience of distress. According to many Islamic scholars, such as Imam al-Ghazali, Abu Zayd al-Balkhi (d. 322), and Abu Bakr al-Razi (d. 313), *inkishāf* requires a psychospiritual relationship with a spiritual mentor because it can be difficult for an individual to fully uncover their own deficiencies (Al-Ghazali, 1990). Therefore, the TIIP Rafiq serves as a psychospiritual mirror that can help the patient uncover the workings of their internal world (Khan et al., 2020). This is critical because human behavior is the product of inner mechanisms, and research has shown that many aspects of action occur without awareness (Blakemore & Frith, 2003).

This self-awareness, similar to what is emphasized in the mindfulness literature (Brown & Ryan, 2003), must encapsulate all aspects of the internal psyche, including its ontological aspects. This awareness includes

- open, receptive awareness of the surroundings and its experiences (Martin, 1997) as encouraged by the Qur'an (3:191);
- increased emotional intelligence through perceptual clarity about internal emotional states as well as external manifestations (Salovey et al., 2004);
- active wakefulness to cognitive tasks in an open and assimilative manner (Bodner & Langer, 2001);
- internal state awareness and self-reflectiveness leading to private self-consciousness (Cramer, 2000; Fenigstein et al., 1975; Trapnell & Campbell, 1999); and
- self-monitoring and the ability to self-reflect (Snyder, 1974; Trapnell & Campbell, 1999).

Stage 3
The primary goal of the third stage is to facilitate a state of psychospiritual equilibrium or a state of balance across all composite parts of the psyche (i.e.,

'aql, rūh, nafs, iḥsās, and qalb). This is perhaps where more directive intervention begins. By this stage, patients have become oriented to the process, treatment goals are set, and an increased self-awareness has been facilitated. Thus, treatment naturally transitions into some more directive and even emotionally taxing interventions. This entails focusing on one or more of the elements based on a determination of where the primary sources of dysfunction originate (as described in Stage 1). This phase strives for a restoration of balance across all elements. For instance, if the individual presents with under-regulated destructive emotions, one of the goals would be to regulate such emotions and strive for a healthy balance (Keshavarzi & Keshavarzi, 2020). If the patient struggles with overindulgence and fulfilling his desires, such as sexual or lifestyle issues, he would be challenged to engage in the practice of positive opposition of the self (mukhalafat al-nafs) to control such self-destructive desires and tendencies (Keshavarzi & Nsour, 2020).

Research has established that the notion of psychospiritual balance is important to nurturing health (Seligman et al., 2004), whether it is in our thoughts (Krueger & Funder, 2004; Tsai, 2013), emotions (Gross, 2014; Gross & Muñoz, 1995), resistance to behavioral inclinations of desires and temptations (Hofmann et al., 2012; Vohs & Baumeister, 2011), or spirituality (Lukoff, 2019; Waaijman & Carm, 2004). The TIIP model aims to engender that balance through the process of directive interventions (mu'ālajah), which vary depending on which domain of the psyche is being addressed. For cognition, the goal is to engender an actively contemplative mind through reflection and psycho-education; for emotional health, the goal is to facilitate the expression of maladaptive emotions and transform to more balanced, adaptive expressions; for behavioral inclinations (nafs), it is to confront and resist discomfort, which is often characterized by avoidance behaviors that enable a pathological vicious cycle; and for the spirit, the focus is on ridding the patient of spiritual diseases and filling the void and emptiness with the remembrance of God and virtuous characteristics. Furthermore, Islamic spirituality emphasizes the importance of clearing out that which is unhealthy before attempting to implant praiseworthy traits because doing so requires the preparation of fertile psychic ground. For example, if a Muslim has an implanted su al-zan or a negative interpretative lens of others, then this must be cleansed before the implantation of positive actions so the overall negative filter does not undermine the positive actions.

Stage 4
This stage arises at the successful completion of the previous three stages. Once an individual develops a strong bond with the practitioner, increases self-awareness, and instills psychospiritual balance in all areas of their psyche, they move on to instilling an inner integrative unity (ittiḥād) that focuses on the acquisition of virtues and development of resilience. Furthermore, an individual who has surpassed the range of functioning and progressed from having psychospiritual maladies has prepared the ground for further psychospiritual development. At this stage, the goal is to align all of the elements of

the psyche so no dissonance remains between them. Once psychospiritual equilibrium is attained, all parts serve the same purpose, the experience of fragmentation is removed, and the patient experiences an integrative holistic experience. At this stage, the individual is able to take on higher-level spiritual practices to elevate and further protect themselves by instilling psychological and spiritual resilience.

Ijtima'i Focus

Islam places a great deal of emphasis on community. Ibn Khaldun (d. 1406) posited that compassion for one's relatives is not only part of human nature but also a "divine gift put into the hearts of men" (Khaldun & Rosenthal, 1967, p. 98). Islam emphasizes the rights of family members, neighbors, and community members. Imām al-Ghazalī claimed that society exerts influence on intrinsic human inclinations, and these communally influenced inclinations are constantly interacting with human feelings, thoughts, and behaviors (al-Ghazali, 2008). Therefore, the TIIP model also emphasizes the importance of the nature of the human within the context of their surroundings when considering treatment. A feature of psychotherapy that is often neglected is the importance of family, community, and environmental surroundings.

CASE ILLUSTRATION, TREATMENT PROCESS, AND INTERVENTION

This section describes the implementation of the TIIP model. The case is discussed primarily from the point of view of the individual therapy approach with some illustrations of the processes and interventions used in marital therapy. All identifiable information has been modified to protect the identity of the patient.

Patient

Harris is a 30-year-old, married, Indian man. He sought therapy services initially for marital issues. He was further referred for individual therapy for problems related to underlying anxiety and depression that sometimes manifested in outbursts of anger.

Harris was born in Pakistan and moved to the United States when he was a teenager. He reported being emotionally dependent on his parents, continuously seeking his mother's approval. He reported few instances of trauma in his earlier life. He did not come from a religious family; however, this changed over time as his family became more observant. Although his college degree was STEM-related, he and his brothers decided to pursue religious studies. After college, he decided to marry someone from another culture. His family did not approve of this decision.

After marrying the person of his choice, the family cut off all ties with Harris and his wife. Separately, he reported having significant relationship issues with his wife. He exhibited an excessive amount of emotional dependence on her, often seeking reassurance. His wife also experienced emotional volatility, resulting in instability within the relationship. Harris often mentioned an overarching feeling of being overwhelmed, a sense of isolation, and emotional pain.

Harris did not have any medical or other health-related issues. He was prescribed a beta-blocker to help him alleviate his anger outbursts, especially since these episodes were accompanied by panic-like symptoms. He reported a lot of work-related stress, but he enjoyed his religious education, which was intellectually stimulating.

TIIP Case Conceptualization

As evidenced in his presentation and concerns, Harris's primary issue was related to his iḥsās, or emotions. He suffered from symptoms of depression and anxiety, and experienced bouts of intermittent explosive anger. His depression and anxiety were manifestations of maladaptive primary emotions of sadness due to unmet needs for connection. However, his anxiety was also related to a lack of predictability and control over his environment. Thus, his anxiety was triggered when his wife became angry with him or he was overwhelmed by his wife or work and school responsibilities. His anger manifested in expressions of frustration as a secondary emotion that served to cover his underlying sadness and feelings of helplessness. His overindulgence in utilization of anger led to further neglect of his needs, resulting in a vicious cycle. Some of these emotional vulnerabilities arose developmentally. An inability to form a healthy relationship with his parents extended to his marital relationship, which was characterized by instability, replete with extreme expressions of love or threats of rejection and turmoil. His lack of emotional awareness and inability to regulate his emotional needs or self-soothe led to a very low level of overall frustration tolerance with his wife.

These unmet needs not only manifested as emotional (iḥsāsi) concerns as an adult but also were driven by repressed behavioral (nafsāni) drives. All children have primitive needs for attention and are naturally egocentric. At a young age, children learn through the process of reward and punishment and are naturally driven by a need for social attention. If these needs are not met, the self does not fully develop, and an overreliance on punishment leads to an underlying low self-worth that carries into adulthood. In Harris's case, these attentional needs were expressed in the form of "childlike" behaviors at the stage of the *nafs al-ammarah* (commanding toward evil) state, responding with yelling or screaming. Furthermore, when overwhelmed, he was unable to face the discomfort of even normal relationship distress, an indication of very low levels of frustration tolerance that often led him to leave the house or threaten divorce.

Harris's cognition ('aql) played an important role in his psychospiritual functioning. When these emotions were triggered or needs were unmet, his thoughts became negative. This was especially evident in the bouts of anger and a tendency to catastrophize his environmental circumstances. However, he did possess some capacity for religious reframing and positive self-talk. Despite his difficulty in accessing these resources when emotionally activated, he was able to recall these positive thoughts and demonstrate insight, and these beliefs motivated his willingness to acknowledge his errors and work on repair. His theological studies had a lot to do with this, with Islamic references encouraging the positive.

By stimulating his spirit (rūḥ) through religious exercises, Harris reduced his psychological distress. In paticular, he went to the mosque to pray, asked God for assistance and relief, and learned to accept His will and let go of control. However, when he was not able to maintain connection with such religious rituals, his rūḥ was impacted by the inability to maintain patience combined with low levels of God consciousness during such episodes. The ability to maintain God consciousness can have a powerful effect on regulating behavioral extremes. Additionally, Harris had a weak sense of *ridā bi al-qaḍā*, or contentment with the decree of God, as he displayed regrets and disgruntlement with his circumstances during difficult times.

Ultimately, all of these extreme states in the four aspects of his psyche had an overall negative effect on his heart (qalb), which could be balanced through the process of change.

Intervention and the Process of Change

Since Harris sought therapy services himself, he was highly motivated to change. His religiosity was assessed using the Muslim Experiential Religiousness scale (Ghorbani et al., 2014) and the Islamic Positive Religious Coping subscale from the Psychological Measure of Islamic Religiousness scale (Abu Raiya et al., 2008). His scores on both scales indicated a high level of overall religiosity. His score on the Brief Symptom Inventory indicated symptoms of anxiety and depression. He was diagnosed with adjustment disorder with mixed anxiety and depressed mood. He also met the criteria for intermittent explosive disorder. Treatment included individual as well as family work. Only spiritually integrated interventions are discussed in this section.

A strong therapeutic relationship was attained through empathic interventions. Due to Harris's high level of religiosity, as well as his formal Islamic education, the TIIP model was explained as part of the psychoeducational process. This further helped build rapport. The patient reported relying on Islamic concepts and rituals as his main coping tools, so he enthusiastically embraced the TIIP model.

Harris was instructed to increase awareness of his emotional functioning, beginning with day-to-day emotional changes and narrowing down to moment-to-moment changes. A key approach to increasing his emotional awareness was to evoke his emotions during sessions. This was followed by reflection by the therapist and facilitation of emotion transformation and regulation. Aside from the impact of attachment-related concerns leading to childhood unmet needs, the individual therapist helped focus on the behavioral inclinations (nafs) that these experiences generated in the present day. For example, Harris still sought approval and support from his parents (mainly his mother) despite being an adult and knowing that she would not provide him with this support and approval. Harris was then asked to specifically identify how his *nafsāni* desires manifested in the form of behaviors on a day-to-day basis. Common daily behaviors that would be considered *nafsāni* based included the following:

- avoiding confrontation, such as leaving the house when upset and stonewalling his wife
- acting out with fits of rage and becoming verbally abusive
- sleeping beyond what's needed and healthy (e.g., 6–7 hours)
- eating beyond what's needed to satisfy hunger
- eating out frequently
- socializing too frequently
- seeking approval and attention of others
- putting others down as a way of elevating himself intrapsychically
- praising himself instead of being humble

During the awareness-building process, Harris was encouraged to reflect on how his emotions affected the other elements of his psyche.

The marital therapist attempted to help the couple see each other's experience more clearly by focusing on helping them understand that it was the process of communication that led to dysfunction while the "content" of what they were actually fighting over was less important. The marital therapist also helped them observe how their marital interactions perpetuated the deprivation of need fulfillment. Instead of offering criticisms and using secondary anger, which evoked underlying emotional triggers and accompanying defensiveness, they were shown how to "see" each other's experiences.

In an attempt to create an overall state of psychospiritual equilibrium, many emotional (*ihsāsi*) interventions were used with Harris, including a two-chair dialogue from a spiritual lens of compassion. This helped Harris soften his view of himself and his parents and work toward better closure. It resulted in engendering a sense of forgiveness and greater understanding of the limitations of his parents, breaking the all good/all bad perspective he held regarding them.

The marital therapist helped Harris and his wife to sidestep over usage of the secondary emotion of anger and encouraged them to discuss their underlying vulnerable feelings of pain. Islamic notions of humility, viewing the other positively (*husn al-dhan*), and selflessness were employed to engender greater commitment and motivation to engage in the therapeutic process. This helped lead them to the emergence of needs and how to communicate them, which took the focus off of who was at fault or the problem itself, and transitioned them to talking more about their core experiences and need fulfillment (i.e., talking about the solution instead of dissecting the problem).

After balancing the core elements of his psyche, Harris focused on how each of the elements could serve the others through complementarity. This entailed looking at how he may be able to engender greater positive thinking that contained themes of hope and positive views of his wife, parents, and self, which could be complemented by behaviors to demonstrate this positivity.

Virtue development was part of the focus of this stage. Additionally, spiritual exercises in the form of prayers were encouraged, with a focus on asking God for assistance against his regressive instincts, praying for his wife and parents and expressing patience and mercy. After prayers, he was encouraged to contemplate seeing the "hidden" blessings in his distress. How could he interpret his situation from a negative one to learned optimism that would help him to frame his life in spiritually positive terms? These features would allow him to attain congruence between his professed beliefs of good character and his ability to translate those beliefs into his thinking, behaviors, and spiritual exercises.

Harris's symptoms improved as evidenced by a decrease in his Brief Symptom Inventory score. He reported having better control over his emotional functioning, including the anger outbursts. His relationship with his wife continued to be challenging; however, he was able to draw boundaries and not get emotionally pulled into any extremes.

CONCLUSION AND FUTURE IMPLICATIONS

The TIIP model is rooted in an Islamic epistemological and ontological approach. It attempts to conceptualize and treat the human mind, body, and soul in a holistic manner to avoid a reductionistic approach that may overlook important factors. TIIP values the role of the practitioner (Rafiq) as a facilitator who accompanies the patient on the journey toward not only psychological but also spiritual perfection. Although much research is still needed to understand its application in other disorders and settings, TIIP has been effective with patients suffering from depression, anxiety, and certain trauma- and stressor-related disorders, as well as spiritual and interpersonal issues. We understand the primary limitation that although this model cannot be completely implemented with every client, its foundational epistemological and ontological approach as well as the underlying principles may benefit the practice of psychotherapy at large. The goal of reviving and re-presenting Islamic psychological understanding is to put forth an approach that challenges the current reductionistic postmodern one in understanding the most complicated creatures: human beings.

REFERENCES

Abu-Raiya, H. (2014). Western psychology and Muslim psychology in dialogue: Comparisons between a Qura'nic theory of personality and Freud's and Jung's ideas. *Journal of Religion and Health, 53*(2), 326–338. https://doi.org/10.1007/s10943-012-9630-9

Abu Raiya, H., Pargament, K., Mahoney, A., & Stein, C. (2008). A psychological measure of Islamic religiousness: Development and evidence for reliability and validity. *The International Journal for the Psychology of Religion, 18*(4), 291–315. https://doi.org/10.1080/10508610802229270

Al-Bajuri, I. (2002a). *Ḥāshiyat al- Imām al- Bayjūrī 'alā Jawharat al- Tawḥīd*. Dar al-Salam.

Al-Bajuri, I. (2002b). *Tuḥfat al- Murīd 'alā Jawharat al- Tawḥīd* [A gift for the aspirant or "the aspirant's gift": "Being a marginalia" on "The Essential Creed"]. Dar al-Bayruti.

Al-Ghazali, A. H. (1990). *Mukhtaṣar: Iḥyā' 'Ulūm al- Dīn.* Mua'ssas al-Kutub al-Thaqafiyyah.

Al-Ghazali, A. H. (2008). *Revival of religion's sciences: Ihya Ulum Ad-Din.* Dar Al Kotob Al Ilmiyah.

Al-Suhrawardi, S. (1993). *'Awārif al- Ma'ārif.* Dar al-Ma'arif.

Al-Taftazani, A. H. (2000). *Sharḥ al- 'Aqā'id al- Nasafiyyah.* Maktabat al-Bushra.

Awaad, R., & Ali, S. (2016). A modern conceptualization of phobia in al-Balkhi's 9th century treatise: Sustenance of the body and soul. *Journal of Anxiety Disorders, 37,* 89–93. https://doi.org/10.1016/j.janxdis.2015.11.003

Awaad, R., Elsayed, D., Ali, S., & Abid, A. (2020). Islamic psychology. In H. Keshavarzi, F. Khan, B. Ali, & R. Awaad (Eds.), *Applying Islamic principles to clinical mental health care: Introducing traditional Islamically integrated psychotherapy.* Routledge. https://doi.org/10.4324/9781003043331-6

Baxter, L. R., Jr., Schwartz, J. M., Bergman, K. S., Szuba, M. P., Guze, B. H., Mazziotta, J. C., Alazraki, A., Selin, C. E., Ferng, H. K., Munford, P., & Phelps, M. E. (1992). Caudate glucose metabolic rate changes with both drug and behavior therapy for obsessive-compulsive disorder. *Archives of General Psychiatry, 49*(9), 681–689. https://doi.org/10.1001/archpsyc.1992.01820090009002

Blakemore, S.-J., & Frith, C. (2003). Self-awareness and action. *Current Opinion in Neurobiology, 13*(2), 219–224. https://doi.org/10.1016/S0959-4388(03)00043-6

Bodner, T., & Langer, E. (2001, June 14–17). Individual differences in mindfulness: The mindfulness/mindlessness scale [Paper presentation]. 13th Annual Meeting of the American Psychological Society [now Association for Psychological Science], Toronto, ON, Canada.

Brown, K. W., & Ryan, R. M. (2003). The benefits of being present: Mindfulness and its role in psychological well-being. *Journal of Personality and Social Psychology, 84*(4), 822–848. https://doi.org/10.1037/0022-3514.84.4.822

Campbell, J. C., Webster, D., Koziol-McLain, J., Block, C., Campbell, D., Curry, M. A., Gary, F., Glass, N., McFarlane, J., Sachs, C., Sharps, P., Ulrich, Y., Wilt, S. A., Manganello, J., Xu, X., Schollenberger, J., Frye, V., & Laughon, K. (2003). Risk factors for femicide in abusive relationships: Results from a multisite case control study. *American Journal of Public Health, 93*(7), 1089–1097. https://doi.org/10.2105/AJPH.93.7.1089

Cohen, T. R., Gunia, B. C., Kim-Jun, S. Y., & Murnighan, J. K. (2009). Do groups lie more than individuals? Honesty and deception as a function of strategic self-interest. *Journal of Experimental Social Psychology, 45*(6), 1321–1324. https://doi.org/10.1016/j.jesp.2009.08.007

Collins, C., & Stockton, C. (2018). The central role of theory in qualitative research. *International Journal of Qualitative Methods, 17,* 1–10.

Cramer, K. M. (2000). Comparing the relative fit of various factor models of the self-consciousness scale in two independent samples. *Journal of Personality Assessment, 75*(2), 295–307. https://doi.org/10.1207/S15327752JPA7502_9

Fenigstein, A., Scheier, M. F., & Buss, A. H. (1975). Public and private self-consciousness: Assessment and theory. *Journal of Consulting and Clinical Psychology, 43*(4), 522–527. https://doi.org/10.1037/h0076760

Ghorbani, N., Watson, P. J., Geranmayepour, S., & Chen, Z. (2014). Measuring Muslim spirituality: Relationships of Muslim experiential religiousness with religious and psychological adjustment in Iran. *The Journal of Muslim Mental Health, 8*(1), 77–94. https://doi.org/10.3998/jmmh.10381607.0008.105

Gilliland, S. W., & Anders, J. (2011). Perceptions of greed: A distributive injustice model. In S. W. Gilliland, D. D. Steiner, & D. P. Skarlicki (Eds.), *Emerging perspectives on organizational justice and ethics* (pp. 137–166). Information Age.

Gross, J. J. (2014). Emotion regulation: Conceptual and empirical foundations. In J. J. Gross (Ed.), *Handbook of emotion regulation* (2nd ed., pp. 3–20). Guilford Press.

Gross, J. J., & Muñoz, R. F. (1995). Emotion regulation and mental health. *Clinical Psychology: Science and Practice, 2*(2), 151–164. https://doi.org/10.1111/j.1468-2850.1995.tb00036.x

Hamlin, J. K., Wynn, K., & Bloom, P. (2007). Social evaluation by preverbal infants. *Nature, 450*(7169), 557–559. https://doi.org/10.1038/nature06288

Hammad, A. Z. (2007). *The gracious Quran: A modern-phrased interpretation in English*. Lucent Interpretations.

Helminski, K. (2005). *The Rumi collection*. Shambhala Publications.

Hofmann, W., Baumeister, R. F., Förster, G., & Vohs, K. D. (2012). Everyday temptations: An experience sampling study of desire, conflict, and self-control. *Journal of Personality and Social Psychology, 102*(6), 1318–1335. https://doi.org/10.1037/a0026545

Ireland, W. W. (1903). The varieties of religious experience: A study in human nature. Being the Gifford lectures on natural religion, delivered at Edinburgh in 1901–2 by William James, LL.D., etc. London, 1902: Longmans. Royal octavo, pp. 534. *The Journal of Mental Science, 49*(204), 146–150. https://doi.org/10.1192/bjp.49.204.146

Keshavarzi, H., & Ali, B. (2020). Foundations of traditional Islamically integrated psychotherapy (TIIP). In H. Keshavarzi, F. Khan, B. Ali, & R. Awaad (Eds.), *Applying Islamic principles to clinical mental health care: Introducing traditional Islamically integrated psychotherapy* (pp. 13–37). Routledge. https://doi.org/10.4324/9781003043331-3

Keshavarzi, H., & Haque, A. (2013). Outlining a psychotherapy model for enhancing Muslim mental health within an Islamic context. *The International Journal for the Psychology of Religion, 23*(3), 230–249. https://doi.org/10.1080/10508619.2012.712000

Keshavarzi, H., & Keshavarzi, S. (2020). Emotionally oriented psychotherapy. In H. Keshavarzi, F. Khan, B. Ali, & R. Awaad (Eds.), *Applying Islamic principles to clinical mental health care: Introducing traditional Islamically integrated psychotherapy* (pp. 171–208). Routledge. https://doi.org/10.4324/9781003043331-12

Keshavarzi, H., & Khan, F. (2018). Outlining a case illustration of traditional Islamically integrated psychotherapy. In C. Y. Al-Karam (Ed.), *Islamically integrated psychotherapy: Processes and outcomes with Muslim clinicians* (pp. 175–207). Templeton Press.

Keshavarzi, H., Khan, F., Ali, B., & Awaad, R. (Eds.). (2020). *Applying Islamic principles to clinical mental health care: Introducing traditional Islamically integrated psychotherapy*. Routledge.

Keshavarzi, H., Khan, F., & Syed, B. (2020). Islamically integrated treatment of obsessive-compulsive disorder scrupulosity (Waswasa) in Muslim patients. In N. Tinaz, A. Ayten, M. Zengin, & H. Ekşi (Eds.), *Spiritual counselling and care in health and prison services: Diverse experiences and practices* (pp. 229–251). Ensar Publishing.

Keshavarzi, H., & Nsour, R. (2020). Behavioral (Nafsānī) psychotherapy. In H. Keshavarzi, F. Khan, B. Ali, & R. Awaad (Eds.), *Applying Islamic principles to clinical mental health care: Introducing traditional Islamically integrated psychotherapy* (pp. 236–265). Routledge. https://doi.org/10.4324/9781003043331-14

Keshavarzi, H., Yusuf, A., Kaplick, P., Ahmadi, T., & Loucif, A. (2020). Spiritually (Rūḥanī) focused psychotherapy. In H. Keshavarzi, F. Khan, B. Ali, & R. Awaad (Eds.), *Applying Islamic principles to clinical mental health care: Introducing traditional Islamically integrated psychotherapy* (pp. 266–290). Routledge. https://doi.org/10.4324/9781003043331-15

Khaldun, I., & Rosenthal, F. (1967). *The Muqaddimah: An introduction to history*. Princeton University Press.

Khan, F. (2020). Quantitative and qualitative assessment of the ontological domains of the psyche in TIIP. In H. Keshavarzi, F. Khan, B. Ali, & R. Awaad (Eds.), *Applying Islamic principles to clinical mental health care: Introducing traditional Islamically integrated psychotherapy* (pp. 117–140). Routledge. https://doi.org/10.4324/9781003043331-9

Khan, F., Keshavarzi, H., & Rothman, A. (2020). The role of the TIIP therapist. In H. Keshavarzi, F. Khan, B. Ali, & R. Awaad (Eds.), *Applying Islamic principles to clinical mental health care: Introducing traditional Islamically integrated psychotherapy* (pp. 38–66). Routledge. https://doi.org/10.4324/9781003043331-4

Kincheloe, J. L., McLaren, P., & Steinberg, S. R. (2011). Critical pedagogy and qualitative research: Moving to the bricolage. In N. K. Denzin & Y. S. Lincoln (Eds.), *The Sage handbook of qualitative research* (pp. 163–178). Sage.

Krueger, J. I., & Funder, D. C. (2004). Towards a balanced social psychology: Causes, consequences, and cures for the problem-seeking approach to social behavior and cognition. *Behavioral and Brain Sciences, 27*(3), 313–327. https://doi.org/10.1017/S0140525X04000081

Laughlin, C. D. (1996). *The mystical brain: Biogenetic structural studies in the anthropology of religion.* https://www.biogeneticstructuralism.com/articles.htm

Lukoff, D. (2019). Spirituality and extreme states. *Journal of Humanistic Psychology, 59*(5), 754–761. https://doi.org/10.1177/0022167818767511

Maggini, C., Lundgren, E., & Leuci, E. (2006). Jealous love and morbid jealousy. *Acta Biomedica, 77*(3), 137–146.

Martin, J. R. (1997). Mindfulness: A proposed common factor. *Journal of Psychotherapy Integration, 7*(4), 291–312. https://doi.org/10.1023/B:JOPI.0000010885.18025.bc

Nugraha Kusuma, A., Rahmawati, D., Lusiani, M., & Dede, R. (2020). The effect of Dhikr therapy on anxiety levels in chronic kidney failure patients that have done hemodialysis therapy in Indonesia. *Enfermeria Clinica, 30,* 175–178. https://doi.org/10.1016/j.enfcli.2019.11.048

Nurbaeti, I. (2015). The effectiveness of dhikr toward decreasing anxiety and labor pain during active phase of first stage among primigravida. *Journal NERS, 10*(1), 30–37. https://doi.org/10.20473/jn.V10I12015.30-37

Octary, T., Akhmad, A. N., & Susito, S. (2020). The effect of dhikr therapy on anxiety in preoperative patients at surgical room in Pemangkat General Hospital in 2020. *Tanjungpura Journal of Nursing Practice and Education, 2*(2).

Ortony, A., & Turner, T. J. (1990). What's basic about basic emotions? *Psychological Review, 97*(3), 315–331. https://doi.org/10.1037/0033-295X.97.3.315

Peterson, C., & Seligman, M. E. P. (2004). *Character strengths and virtues: A handbook and classification.* Oxford University Press.

Ragab, A. (2015). The medieval Islamic hospital: Medicine, religion, and charity. In *The medieval Islamic hospital: Medicine, religion, and charity* (pp. i–ii). Cambridge University Press. https://doi.org/10.1017/CBO9781316271797

Rothman, A., & Coyle, A. (2020). Conceptualizing an Islamic psychotherapy: A grounded theory study. *Spirituality in Clinical Practice, 7*(3), 197–213. https://doi.org/10.1037/scp0000219

Rotman, Y. (2021). The relational mind: In between history, psychology and anthropology. *History of Psychology, 24*(2), 142–163. https://doi.org/10.1037/hop0000175

Salovey, P., Mayer, J. D., Goldman, S. L., Turvey, C., & Palfai, T. P. (2004). Emotional attention, clarity, and repair: Exploring emotional intelligence using the Trait Meta-Mood Scale. In J. W. Pennebaker (Ed.), *Emotion, disclosure, & health* (pp. 125–154). https://doi.org/10.1037/10182-006

Saniotis, A. (2018). Understanding mind/body medicine from Muslim religious practices of salat and dhikr. *Journal of Religion and Health, 57*(3), 849–857. https://doi.org/10.1007/s10943-014-9992-2

Schaefer, S. M., Jackson, D. C., Davidson, R. J., Aguirre, G. K., Kimberg, D. Y., & Thompson-Schill, S. L. (2002). Modulation of amygdalar activity by the conscious regulation of negative emotion. *Journal of Cognitive Neuroscience, 14*(6), 913–921. https://doi.org/10.1162/089892902760191135

Seligman, M. E. P., Parks, A. C., & Steen, T. (2004). A balanced psychology and a full life. *Philosophical Transactions of the Royal Society of London: Series B. Biological Sciences, 359*(1449), 1379–1381. https://doi.org/10.1098/rstb.2004.1513

Seuntjens, T. G., Zeelenberg, M., van de Ven, N., & Breugelmans, S. M. (2019). Greedy bastards: Testing the relationship between wanting more and unethical behavior. *Personality and Individual Differences, 138,* 147–156. https://doi.org/10.1016/j.paid.2018.09.027

Snyder, M. (1974). Self-monitoring of expressive behavior. *Journal of Personality and Social Psychology, 30*(4), 526–537. https://doi.org/10.1037/h0037039

Sulistyawati, R. A., Probosuseno, & Setiyarini, S. (2019). Dhikr therapy for reducing anxiety in cancer patients. *Asia-Pacific Journal of Oncology Nursing, 6*(4), 411–416. https://doi.org/10.4103/apjon.apjon_33_19

Svetlova, M., Nichols, S. R., & Brownell, C. A. (2010). Toddlers' prosocial behavior: From instrumental to empathic to altruistic helping. *Child Development, 81*(6), 1814–1827. https://doi.org/10.1111/j.1467-8624.2010.01512.x

Tbakhi, A., & Amr, S. S. (2008). Ibn Rushd (Averroës): Prince of science. *Annals of Saudi Medicine, 28*(2), 145–147. https://doi.org/10.4103/0256-4947.51736

Trapnell, P. D., & Campbell, J. D. (1999). Private self-consciousness and the five-factor model of personality: Distinguishing rumination from reflection. *Journal of Personality and Social Psychology, 76*(2), 284–304. https://doi.org/10.1037/0022-3514.76.2.284

Tsai, K. C. (2013). Being a critical and creative thinker: A balanced thinking mode. *Asian Journal of Humanities and Social Sciences, 1*(2), 1–9.

Uthmani, T. (2007). *Spiritual discourses* (Vols. 1–4). Darul Ishaat.

Vohs, K. D., & Baumeister, R. F. (Eds.). (2011). *Handbook of self-regulation: Research, theory, and applications* (2nd ed.). Guilford Press.

Waaijman, K., & Carm, O. (2004). Challenges of spirituality in contemporary times. In *Context and expressions of Filipino spirituality* (pp. 91–113). Center for Spirituality, Manila. https://hdl.handle.net/2066/59845

Westerhof, G. J., & Keyes, C. L. M. (2010). Mental illness and mental health: The two continua model across the lifespan. *Journal of Adult Development, 17*(2), 110–119. https://doi.org/10.1007/s10804-009-9082-y

York Al-Karam, C. (2018). *Islamically integrated psychotherapy: Uniting faith and professional practice*. Templeton Press.

Zhu, Y., Sun, X., Liu, S., & Xue, G. (2019). Is greed a double-edged sword? The roles of the need for social status and perceived distributive justice in the relationship between greed and job performance. *Frontiers in Psychology, 10*, 2021. https://doi.org/10.3389/fpsyg.2019.02021

11

Gospel-Centered Integrated Framework for Therapy

Foundation, Description, Research Findings, and Application

Elena E. Kim, Judy Cha, and Timothy Keller

The field of psychology has recognized that the integration of religion and psychotherapy can provide valuable mental health benefits to clients (Koenig et al., 2012). As distressing worldwide and local events continue—a worldwide pandemic, terrorism, financial collapses, and social injustices—the need for individuals to develop meaning in order to endure stressful and traumatic life experiences has become increasingly important. In fact, successful meaning making has been known to help individuals adjust better to painful and upsetting events (Park, 2013). Religion and spirituality (R/S) have been widely used to assist individuals in meaning making (Lysne & Wachholtz, 2011), and studies have linked the use of R/S to mental health outcomes (Koenig et al., 2012). Research has also discovered an inverse relationship between R/S and a host of mental health illnesses, such as depression, anxiety, substance use, and suicidality (Koenig et al., 2012), and a positive correlation with psychological functioning, such as enhanced self-esteem (Maton, 1989), purpose in life (Carroll, 1993), a focus on virtues (Hill & Butter, 1995), and positive affect (Galea et al., 2007). In fact, enhanced changes to clients' God images or reliance on R/S strategies have also been linked to outcomes in secular psychotherapy, suggesting that positive therapeutic outcomes may already be attributable to R/S factors (Kim et al., 2019; Rye & Pargament, 2002; Tisdale et al., 1997). The substantiated relationship between R/S and mental health has led to a growing need to integrate R/S into therapy in a meaningful, effective, and safe manner.

https://doi.org/10.1037/0000338-011
Handbook of Spiritually Integrated Psychotherapies, P. S. Richards, G. E. K. Allen, and D. K. Judd (Editors)
Copyright © 2023 by the American Psychological Association. All rights reserved.

Redeemer Counseling Services (RCS), a Christian counseling clinic, became aware of this need and in 1990 started integrating Protestant Christian doctrine into therapeutic practices. RCS initially served as an outpatient clinic for the members of a large Protestant church located in New York City. However, in 2001, clinicians received an upsurge in Christian clients across denominations in the aftermath of the 9/11 terrorist attacks. RCS has grown into a clinic serving approximately 2,000 clients annually. Although the majority of clients are White (54%) and Asian American/Pacific Islander/Southeast Asian (26%), there is a small representation of other groups, such as Black (11%), Hispanic (5%), and multiracial (5%). The most common mental health issues treated include anxiety, depression, eating disorders, and mild personality disorders.

RCS therapists began developing a therapeutic milieu by sharing successful therapist–client experiences and adapting interventions to complement their clients' religious worldviews. They used their knowledge as clinicians to identify meaningful patterns, describe processes using functional psychological terms, and provide conceptualizations appropriate for their clients' religious identities. Through this practice, RCS clinicians developed a Gospel-centered integrative framework for therapy (GIFT). They adapted their psychological interventions to include Christian beliefs while contextualizing therapy for those who wanted Christianity to be an important aspect of their mental health, overall wellness, and purpose in life (RCS, 2016).

In this chapter, we describe the theological and psychological foundations that served as the basis for the GIFT, therapeutic techniques and interventions clinicians typically use when guiding clients through this framework, and a case study. We also provide details on training and empirical research results related to the therapeutic processes of the framework. The conclusion presents ethical considerations, limitations, and future steps.

THEOLOGICAL AND PSYCHOLOGICAL FOUNDATIONS

Protestant Christian beliefs served as the foundation for the GIFT. In the 1830s, Alexis de Tocqueville (1988), observing the American citizenry, said that there was a "strange melancholy that haunts the inhabitants of democratic countries in the midst of their abundance," and he observed that "the incomplete joys of this world will never satisfy [the human] heart" (p. 296). In a similar vein, Keller (2011) suggested that the despair individuals experience stems from the adoption of modern-day idols, which are objects, persons, or pursuits that people use to feel significant, secure, and worthy. In pursuit of these goals, individuals worship "counterfeit gods" by placing their trust in objects and pursuits that provide them with a sense of self-worth or identity, as opposed to receiving this through an intimate relationship with the Christian God. These counterfeit gods are deemed so central to an individual's life that losing them can make them feel that life is not worth living.

Protestant Christian doctrine has maintained the belief that validation and a sense of self-worth can only be obtained by worshiping the actual, living, and real Christian God. The founders of the Christian faith believed that divine provisions, such as narratives, truths, laws, and a living example, Jesus Christ, were all bestowed on humanity by an actual God (Westminster Assembly, 1992). The Protestant Christian Church studied these provisions to define their God concept, or mental representation of God within the context of a faith tradition (Davis et al., 2013). Specifically, the Protestant Church believes in a God concept with three characteristics: (a) God is personal, (b) God loves freely (i.e., receiving love is not dependent on an individual's performance), and (c) God's love is costly (i.e., God made great sacrifices to give his love freely to all; Keller, 2009). For the purposes of this chapter, Christian God, Christ, and God will be used to refer to this Protestant Christian God concept.

Within this faith tradition, a sense of self-worth is obtained when individuals have an intimate relationship whereby God serves as the entity that validates them (Keller, 2011). Christianity believes in the doctrine of Original Sin, or that every person is born with a built-in urge to resist dependence on God or to worship objects and idols. This act of rebellion severs the relationship between humanity and God, which is believed to cause an unavoidable experience of deep and inner shame (Augustine, 1876). The Protestant Christian church believes that the only resolution is to receive grace, which is an undeserved love and mercy given to individuals as a result of God's desire (Packer, 2011). As such, it is believed that idols cannot be removed with just a general belief in God; they must be progressively replaced through a living encounter with the Christian God. Building a close and authentic relationship with God is a difficult challenge that requires consistent focus, meditation, and immersion in the Bible, where God reveals himself. "Set your minds on things above" where "your life is now hidden with Christ in God" (*New International Version* [*NIV*], 1978/2011, Colossians 3:3). Until an individual moves from technically believing that they are loved by God to having their hearts and imaginations enraptured by God, modern-day idols are believed to be impossible to remove. Freedom from idols occurs when individuals know the difference between obeying rules of outward conduct and trusting in Christ for their peace and life (Keller, 2011). An authentic relationship with God entails not just following a set of rules but engaging in an emotional exchange of affections with God (RCS, 2016).

This Protestant perspective is in accord with a few theoretical foundations of the psychology of religion that highlight the importance of the relationship between children and caregivers. Rizzuto (2011) used object relations theory and D. W. Winnicott's (1953) transitional phenomena to develop a theory for the psychology of religion. Rizzuto posited that an individual's mental health is connected to their God image, or a God construct that is tied to an individual's internal attachment system. Object relations theory posited that children's relationships with their caregivers develop patterns of expectations for how they experience other individuals (Fairbairn, 1943). It has been theorized that as children grow older they often use transitional objects, or entities that are hybrid-illusions, to understand the outside world. Rizzuto expanded these theories by suggesting a child's God image could also serve as a transitional object. It is believed that they could carry these representations throughout their lives as they crafted a God image to fit their evolving experiences and needs, which would then have an impact on the child's psychological well-being.

Bowlby's (1969) attachment theory has also served as a theoretical foundation for the psychology of religion. According to Bowlby, infants that perceive their caregivers as a reliable source of protection and security (securely attached) are more likely to explore their environment confidently and to seek their caregivers during moments of distress (Ainsworth, 1985). However, infants who do not perceive caregivers as reliable and safe are likely to have difficulty managing distressing emotions (Ainsworth et al., 1978). Kirkpatrick (1992, 1995) furthered this theory to R/S relationships. If individuals' God images possess traits that symbolize secure havens (e.g., benevolent, omnipresent), they could develop safe attachments and obtain security from their God images (Granqvist & Kirkpatrick, 2013; Kirkpatrick, 1995). However, individuals who have God images that are untrustworthy (e.g., unforgiving, judgmental) are likely to form insecure attachments, which could elicit anxiety and distress. Similar to these theories, the GIFT highlights the significance of developing an authentic and safe relationship with the Christian God (RCS, 2016).

INTERVENTION STRATEGIES AND TECHNIQUES

Therapists using the GIFT conceptualize their clients' pain and healing process with a lens that is consistent with Protestant beliefs. Clinicians make a concerted effort to understand their clients' core sufferings and how they are linked to clients' modern-day idols, and healing is viewed through the Christian growth process of repentance, faith, and obedience.

Assessment

The first step in GIFT is to conduct an intake interview to determine whether the client is a viable candidate. Individuals with clinical, diagnostic, and therapeutic issues that pertain to limited affective abilities may not be suitable for treatment. Specifically, clients who struggle with schizoid personality disorder, catatonic conditions, or dysthymia may not be an appropriate fit because emotional reactions are integral to the process and outcome of this treatment. In these cases, therapists may decide to focus on assisting clients in becoming more attuned to their internal affective experiences. Additionally, clients who exhibit symptoms that are likely to interfere with treatment may not be good candidates. An integral step within the GIFT is to uncover clients' core hurts, which may be a difficult process. If clients engage in therapy-interfering behaviors, such as experiencing psychosis, exhibiting high risk of suicide or homicide, crying uncontrollably, shutting down, or threatening to quit therapy

(Chapman & Rosenthal, 2016), therapists may choose to focus on treatments that mitigate these intrusions prior to starting treatment.

Another integral aspect of the intake assessment interview is to gather information regarding clients' spiritual and religious histories and their current religious and spiritual practices. A few questions during this section of the intake may include, "Did you grow up going to church?" "Has your faith in Christ been a source of strength in your life?" "Do you attend church?" and "Do you practice your faith in your daily life?" Answers to these questions help therapists understand clients' spiritual and religious upbringings, current intrinsic and extrinsic religious coping mechanisms, attachment to their God image, and daily spiritual experiences.

As part of the assessment, clinicians ask questions about clients' internal and intrapsychic spiritual experiences. Therapists aim to understand clients' spiritual struggles and level of religious orthodoxy. For instance, "What thoughts or feelings come up for you when you think about a significant event or experience?" "What is your greatest fear about this situation?" "How do you feel when you think about yourself?" "How do you make sense of God in light of what you are going through?" and "What do you feel toward God?" Answers to these questions help clinicians gain an understanding of the client's view of themselves, how the client interprets meaning from life events, their affective experiences related to these views and events, and how they perceive God in the midst of their internal feelings of despair.

Once candidacy and an understanding of the client's spiritual experiences and identity are assessed, the next focus of treatment is to identify how the client's shame has developed into a system of unconscious and conscious beliefs, behaviors, and emotions, or what is called the system of self-redemption (SOSR). This is a complex system that includes five components: reactive emotions, behavioral reactions, core hurts, view of self, and idolatrous strategies. SOSRs are unique to each client because they are formed within the context of individual life stories and experiences (RCS, 2016).

The most easily identified components of the SOSR are reactive emotions and behavioral reactions. When clients experience an event, such as a loss, a fight with a friend, or a relapse to addiction, they are often aware of the conscious components. In fact, clients often seek therapy to manage difficult affective experiences or maladaptive behavioral reactions that are complicating their interpersonal relationships. By processing and exploring clients' explicit reactive emotions and behavioral reactions, they can become more aware of their underlying unconscious and unmet desires. For instance, examining their anxiety may assist clients in identifying their desire for control, or processing sadness could lead clients to realizing their desire for unconditional acceptance (RCS, 2016).

As clients acknowledge unmet desires, they can begin identifying the unconscious components of the SOSR, or their core hurts, view of self, and idolatrous strategies. *Core hurts* are usually repeated wounds from the client's past that are reinforced through current experiences. Although the initial understanding of the client's core hurt is addressed during the intake assessment, more details are discovered throughout the course of treatment. Specifically, clients may be asked to observe their inner thoughts and feelings as they process significant life events. Both the therapist and client aim to observe consistent themes, narratives, and self-evaluations that the client may hold. As they begin to listen to the client's inner dialogue, they come to realize that the client is carrying a pathogenic view of self. This is a subjective interpretation wherein clients identify with an internal belief that informs their shame. This complex combination of conscious and subconscious components contributes to what the GIFT has labeled *idolatrous strategies* (RCS, 2016).

Idolatrous strategies are a complex, unconscious network of dynamic relationships wherein clients develop a chosen lifestyle to avoid their core hurts or becoming aware of their view of self. When clients are unable to implement their idolatrous strategies, awareness of their core hurts and view of self are expected to trigger their reactive emotions and behavioral reactions. No matter how much clients strive to redeem themselves through these strategies, it is believed that they will end up becoming enslaved by their own systems. Ultimately, the GIFT requires clinicians to assess the five components to uncover the clients' SOSRs, or quests they have created to redeem themselves (RCS, 2016).

In essence, SOSRs reveal how clients use modern-day idols to save themselves instead of having a relationship with God. Although objects used as idols are often beneficial, within the context of the SOSR, their usage is characterized as an act of "worship." Specifically, instead of depending on God, clients are relying on their strategies or idols to derive their sense of worth, purpose, and meaning. Worship involves not only elevating objects, persons, or pursuits to the place of God but also trusting in them to satisfy innate desires. At the core of this act, clients are determining how to save themselves by taking over the role that God desires to have in their lives. As long as clients remain at the center of their own lives and rely on their own strategies, lasting change is expected to be difficult. Although this act of worship is considered misplaced, developers of the framework believe it highlights clients' longings for a relationship with God that can repair their core hurts and view of self and a desire to free themselves from relying on their idolatrous strategies (RCS, 2016).

Spiritual Heart Change Process

The process of psychotherapeutic change within the GIFT was modeled after the Christian tenets of repentance, faith, and obedience. Jesus Christ's crucifixion and resurrection narratives are used to transform individuals who desire to have an experience with Christ as a fellow sufferer, savior, and shepherd. During this process, the therapist may encourage the client to have experiential moments with their God image by using therapeutic interventions specific to that client, such as imaginative reenactments, meditations over biblical scripture, prayer, and involvement in spiritual communities. The aim is to encourage clients to have an authentic, lived experience with their God image. The overall GIFT change process is theorized through the Five R's: receive, remember, repent, rejoice, and reflect (RCS, 2016).

Spiritual heart change begins when the client is able to receive comfort and compassion from their God image by realizing that they are not alone. Clients recognize that Christ relates to them because he also experienced the pain of rejection. "He was despised and rejected by mankind, a man of suffering, and familiar with pain" (*NIV*, 1978/2011, Isaiah 53:3). In the midst of the client's despair, therapists may encourage them to use their imagination to experience their God image, receiving empathy and compassion instead of judgment and rejection.

Clients remember God's sacrificial act of love as they recall that Christ willingly accepted an unjust punishment on the clients' behalf: "But he was pierced for our transgressions, he was crushed for our iniquities; the punishment that brought us peace was on him, and by his wounds we are healed" (*NIV*, 1978/2011, Isaiah 53:5). Clients are encouraged to meditate on various biblical narratives and scriptures as they come to a deeper understanding of God's sacrificial compassion. Through this, they become more aware of the destructive nature of their idols and the harm caused by their pursuits to satisfy their sense of self-worth.

They repent by grieving their brokenness; however, this awareness is not expected to emotionally dysregulate or reinforce their sense of shame. Instead, clients are likely to gain a sense of ownership and responsibility as their sense of self-worth is strengthened through Christ's compassion. During this process, clients consider replacing their modern-day idols as they begin trusting that their God image can satisfy their sense of self-worth. A distinct clinical behavior has been observed in which clients exhibit ownership for their attitudes, thoughts, and behaviors. They also understand that these desires evolve from life experiences, that their patterns of behaviors are unable to satisfy their inner desire for self-worth, and that an incomplete understanding of the Christian God contributes to their desire to pursue idols. During this process, therapists not only help clients become aware of how their core hurts shape their God images but also encourage them to be open to changing their God images. Clients may ponder over narratives in which God is portrayed as an unconditionally loving caregiver or begin to observe and receive love from their spiritual communities. As their God images begin to alter, clients are more likely to let go of their idols in personally relevant ways. Through this, they develop a desire to engage in a meaningful relationship with their new Christian God image and commit to embracing a Spirit-led life (RCS, 2016).

Clients are then expected to rejoice in Christ's resurrection and the new identity they form through their spiritual relationship with him: "And he died for all, that those who live should no longer live for themselves but for him who died for them and was raised again" (*NIV*, 1978/2011, 2 Corinthians 5:15). Through this renewed relationship, clients reorient their faith and begin to trust that a reunion with Christ provides them a sense of self-worth and purpose in life. During this process, clients often expand their God image to incorporate qualities that allow for a deeper sense of safety and intimacy, such as loving, empathic, powerful, and compassionate. They also explore the implications of their new identity within the context of this relationship as their self-acceptance, self-esteem, and self-confidence increase (RCS, 2016). The aim of this process is not to focus on duty but to emphasize genuine obedience where clients are reacting as a result of their authentic connection and spiritual experiences with their God image.

Obedience entails clients reflecting the qualities of the Christian God image to others. As a reaction to the joy and positive affective experiences clients have with their Christian God image, they are expected to mirror the qualities that Christ exhibits to them. Continually receiving grace, love, and understanding in their relationship with God allows clients to better relate to others in a manner that mirrors their interactions with Christ. Behavioral changes are often described as clients becoming new beings with new adaptive responses to situations that once burdened them with emotional hurt. For instance, past interactions that may have caused them to experience a deep sense of hurt or invalidation may no longer hold the same interpretive meaning. Through their relationship with Christ, clients receive continuous validation, which helps them to avoid maladaptive responses to existing realities. Instead, clients respond to preexisting triggers with more adaptive emotional reactions and, in turn, more effective interpersonal skills. Therapists have observed changes such as extending forgiveness, becoming more accepting of others' shortcomings, establishing supportive communities that assist in ending addictive behaviors, and developing a new purpose in life. For example, the purpose of being a medical doctor may become more about serving those who are in pain rather than pursuing financial security or status. During this process, clients explore how their faith can be reflected in various aspects of their lives (RCS, 2016).

The intent of the GIFT is to help clients become motivated by the compassion, love, and unconditional sense of self-worth they receive through their relationship and intimate experiences with their Christian God image: "We love because he first loved us" (*NIV*, 1978/2011, 1 John 4:19). Developers of the GIFT have underscored the importance of Christ's love as the resource that guides clients through repentance, faith, and obedience (RCS, 2016).

TRAINING CLERGY

Given that theological beliefs are the foundation of clergy's knowledge and work, it is imperative that clinicians demonstrate common ground when collaborating with pastors. From the beginning, the developers of the GIFT have shared the theological belief that all individuals suffer from Original Sin and that the solution is to receive Grace from God. By aligning with these core Christian doctrines, clinicians and clergy at Redeemer Presbyterian Church were able to develop a mutually trusting and synergistic relationship and integrate the clergy's knowledge of Christianity with the clinicians' experience of change processes (RCS, 2016).

As a result of this trusting partnership, clinicians at RCS were able to highlight the importance of declarative knowledge and procedural skills when training clergy on how to engage in a counseling relationship with their church members (Bennett-Levy, 2006). Specifically, when teaching declarative knowledge (knowledge that individuals can write, talk, or read about; Bennett-Levy, 2006), clinicians focused on the tenets of psychotherapy: psychological safety and therapeutic alliance. A key role of clergy is to assist congregational members during times of distress and crisis. However, pastors may unintentionally overlook the necessity of connection and experiential processes with theological solutions and perspectives. Therefore, clinicians emphasized the importance of building psychological safety, its integral role in developing therapeutic alliance, and the relationship between alliance and lasting therapeutic change. Clinicians connected these counseling practices to Biblical scripture: "Instead, speaking the truth in love, we will grow to become in every respect the mature body of him who is the head, that is, Christ" (*NIV*, 1978/2011, Ephesians 4:15).

Once declarative knowledge was taught, training then focused on procedural skills (implicit skills that are the manifestation of declarative knowledge) in practice through experiential learning (Bennett-Levy, 2006). To help pastors understand the importance of safety and alliance during vulnerable moments, they observed a role-playing exercise in which one pair of clinicians exhibited safety and alliance while discussing a difficult crisis and another did not. Then pastors engaged in a similar exercise by sharing their core hurts with another clergy member in the training program. At the completion of the exercise, trainees shared their experiences of receiving care from other pastors, whether they felt a sense of safety and connection, and what this experience would have been like if they had not felt a strong alliance. By undergoing these process-focused concepts and by developing experientially focused training modules, local clergy became better equipped to counsel members of their congregations (RCS, 2016).

EMPIRICAL SUPPORT FOR THE GIFT

To examine and clarify the spiritual heart change process within the GIFT, Kim and Chen (2021) conducted a detailed task analysis study. *Task analysis* is a research methodology that maps out distinct and sequential clinical process steps in psychotherapy after closely analyzing in vivo therapy sessions (Greenberg, 1984, 2007). Kim and Chen studied 28 client–therapist dyad participants and selected three in which the client had successfully experienced the Five R's of the GIFT. External and valid process measures were then used to support the selection of the three cases. The researchers closely observed the clinical interactions and compared them with two client–therapist dyads that did not successfully complete the spiritual heart change process. A 10-step process model emerged from the results of this study (see Figure 11.1; Kim & Chen, 2021).

At the beginning of the model, clients felt a sense of shame, brokenness, and guilt that was often linked to negative self-criticisms (Step 1). However, during treatment, clients started to connect their negative emotions and self-appraisals to other areas of their lives (Step 2), which caused them to exhibit heightened levels of guilt, shame, fear, and sadness. They feared that their patterns of behavior were innate traits that could not be changed (Step 3). This sense of despair drove clients to plead for a solution (Step 4). As clients became more attuned to their pain and hopelessness, they became more aware of their need for love, empathy, and understanding, and began desiring an intercession from God that was intertwined with implicit messages of compassion and acceptance (Step 5; Kim & Chen, 2021).

In conjunction with these early steps, clients also experienced an ambivalence between their current God image and beliefs they held about the Christian God. Initially, clients doubted that their God image would be empathic or be able to provide an adequate solution (Step 5a). During treatment, clients began to express hope that the Christian God could provide an adequate and empathic intervention (Step 5b). As clients became more in touch with their despair (Step 4), their desire for Christ to become their God image developed into a strong need, and the intensity of their affective experiences increased (Kim & Chen, 2021).

Clients then had a corrective emotional spiritual experience with their in vivo God image. In the midst of their despair and spiritual ambivalence, clients suddenly received compassion from an in vivo God image, or a new God construct that was dynamic, alive, intimate, and authentic (Kim & Chen, 2021). This corrective emotional experience, which is an affective event that disconfirms past events clients had with earlier significant figures (Castonguay & Hill, 2012), became a spiritual experience, or a *corrective emotional spiritual experience*. Through this, they received messages embedded with empathy, forgiveness, love, and validation (Step 6). Immediately following the receipt of Christ's compassion, clients often had strong emotional reactions of joy and love (Step 7; Kim & Chen, 2021).

In the final steps, clients engaged in a direct dialogue with their in vivo God image (Kim & Chen, 2021). After receiving compassion, clients immediately confronted their in vivo God images with questions about their core hurts, view of self, and strategies (Step 8; Kim & Chen, 2021; RCS, 2016), and they received responses that directly countered their negative self-evaluations (Step 9). Specifically, negative views of self that clients had previously believed to be true were no longer accepted as wholly accurate. Instead, messages of love and validation received from their in vivo God image were accepted as new internal truths (Kim & Chen, 2021). Receiving these validations and empathic messages was also a dialectical experience whereby feelings of hopelessness still resonated with them, but they were simultaneously able to accept messages of love and acceptance. By the end of the model, positive

FIGURE 11.1. Empirical Model of the Gospel-Centered Integrative Framework for Therapy

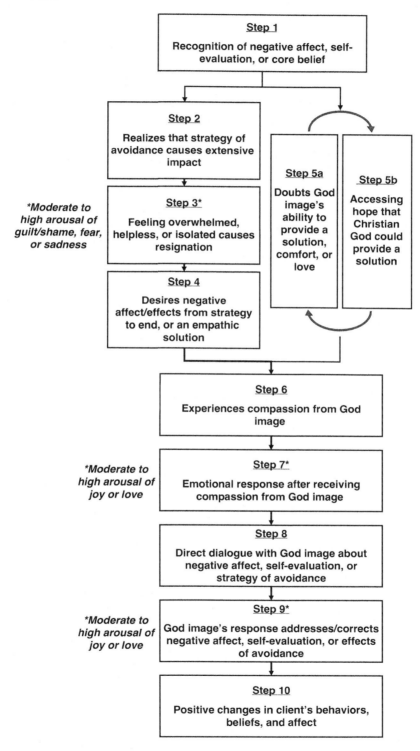

Note. From "Task Analysis of a Christian-Integrated Psychotherapy Framework," by E. E. Kim and E. C. Chen, 2021, *Psychotherapy*, advance online publication (https://doi.org/10.1037/pst0000406). Copyright 2021 by the American Psychological Association.

changes in the clients' behaviors, beliefs, and affects were observable. They reported feeling more self-acceptance, self-confidence, and joy in their daily lives (Step 10; Kim & Chen, 2021).

A separate qualitative study examining clients' experiences of the GIFT associated treatment to therapeutic outcomes (Kim et al., 2019). A grounded theory study (Charmaz, 2000; Glaser & Strauss, 1967) explored the experiences of nine clients who were identified by RCS therapists as having a significant spiritual experience while undergoing the GIFT. All clients stated that their Christian identity was an important aspect they desired to access during treatment, and the study's results indicated that all clients attributed their positive therapeutic change to their religious and spiritual experiences. Specifically, all clients reported that developing a new God image, experiencing a safer and more intimate relationship with God, and developing new existential/religious beliefs were vital to their change processes. These three change catalysts were found to influence a host of positive outcomes in the clients' lives. Eight participants stated that they gained the ability to identify and relinquish control, hurt, or sadness by increasing their trust in God. Many others reported an improvement in their symptoms, self-esteem, self-worth, and self-confidence. These changes were also followed by more positive affect, enhanced purpose in life, gratitude, and altruism (Kim et al., 2019).

CASE STUDY

The Client

Rajan[1] was a 38-year-old, cisgender, South Asian, heterosexual man who identified as a conservative Protestant Christian and began psychotherapy due to the onset of panic attacks. He reported that his faith was an important aspect of his identity and desired to integrate Christianity into the psychotherapeutic process. He was born and raised in the United States and grew up in an upper-middle-class immigrant family. He was a corporate lawyer during the time he was in treatment.

Rajan was paired with a licensed marriage and family therapist, Paul, who was a 53-year-old, cisgender, heterosexual, Korean American man who also identified as Protestant Christian. Paul specialized in internal family systems and held a master's degree in divinity. He had been practicing at RCS for 25 years, 10 years of which he also served as a supervisor. During his time as a clinician, Paul specialized in the integration of Christian doctrine and internal family systems therapeutic techniques.

RCS is a Christian mental health clinic located in New York City that is run by a Protestant Christian Church. Most counselors at RCS received their

---

[1]Names and identifying details have been changed to protect client confidentiality.

counseling degrees from Christian universities, and all underwent training to learn how to use the GIFT.

Rajan entered counseling after experiencing mild to moderate panic attacks at work. He reported an accelerated heart rate, chest pains, sweating, and shortness of breath about three to four times a week. He also had mood-related symptoms, such as uncontrollable crying, depressed mood for most of the day, diminished interest in pleasurable activities, and insomnia. His first panic attack occurred after discovering an error at work, and subsequent panic attacks were easily triggered by thoughts related to his work and impending deadlines. After the initial intake, he was diagnosed with major depressive disorder and panic disorder.

The client grew up as the youngest child in a relationally fragmented family. His father was emotionally distant and avoided closeness with his children and wife by spending most of his time working. Rajan's mother cared for four children and felt overextended. She was filled with resentment toward her husband due to his lack of involvement. When together, his parents spent most of their time in bitter arguments or hostile silence. Rajan's attempts to gain his father's attention were often ignored, leaving the client feeling rejected and reinforcing his feelings of inadequacy. His interactions with his mother were monopolized by criticisms of not performing well enough in his chores or schoolwork. His father's dismissal of him, along with his mother's criticism, formed the basis of his attachment and relationships.

Rajan carried these messages of unworthiness into adulthood. When a long-term romantic relationship ended in college and he failed to land his first-choice job after graduation, Rajan became depressed and anxious. He had assumed that it was natural to feel sad when he experienced disappointment, but by the time he reached his late 20s, Rajan reported having difficulty with sleep and experiencing prolonged periods of depressed mood. He married in his early 30s, but marital problems and stressors at work started to exacerbate Rajan's underlying symptoms. He finally sought treatment after experiencing repeated panic attacks at work.

Treatment Process

Rajan began therapy by examining his emotions and behavioral reactions. Although symptoms stemming from anxiety and depression were initially examined, additional therapy helped Rajan realize feelings of sadness and fear (emotions) as he overextended himself in his career and relationships (behavioral reactions). He realized an internal unmet desire for acceptance by performing in his career and intimate relationships, which appeared to be a reaction to the numerous wounds Rajan encountered in his relationship with his dismissive and critical parents, or his core hurt. These past and current experiences solidified Rajan's view of self, the internal belief that he was unlovable.

Rajan discovered that his strategies involved working hard and pleasing others to feel a sense of validation, acceptance, and worth. These were learned in childhood when he sought his parents' approval, and it became his nature to protect himself from rejection by working hard at school and at home. He applied these self-protective strategies as an adult to ward off the pain of his core hurt and to redeem his view of self. He spent countless hours trying to impress his boss and overextended himself as he tried to please his wife and family.

When Rajan's strategies failed, his core hurts resurfaced and his view of self was reinforced, evoking powerful emotions of panic and despair. As Rajan relied on his efforts to construct a sense of worthiness, he perceived himself as more unlovable, inadequate, and unacceptable. Realizing the ubiquitous effects of his negative view of self, Rajan felt a deep sense of despair and resignation. His lack of validation at work and in relationships drove Rajan deeper into feeling hopeless as his panic attacks began to emerge. Unveiling Rajan's SOSR helped him realize that he had developed an idol of self, or an overreliance on his own abilities to justify his sense of worth as opposed to receiving it from God. By becoming attuned to his despair, Rajan was able to discern his need for an empathic and unconditionally accepting God.

A distinctive aspect of the GIFT was to encourage Rajan to look for a solution from the Christian God. Rajan oscillated between desiring a relationship with God that could get him through his despair and doubting whether this was possible. During therapy, Rajan stated, "God is too busy for me" or "God feels distant." However, gentle interventions instilled Rajan with spiritual hope as he started believing that God was capable of providing for his needs. Specifically, Rajan talked about a passage in the Bible that increased his hope that Christ could be compassionate toward him, "Jesus saw the crowd and had compassion. This doesn't solve my problems, but it feels like an immediate need that was met." As Rajan's hope and belief in Christ increased, so did his desire to turn away from his strategies. His tendency to redeem his view of self abated, and his hope that God could be his ultimate solution intensified.

The therapist encouraged Rajan to have a corrective emotional spiritual experience with his in vivo God image. When Rajan talked about his feelings of isolation, the counselor encouraged him to bring God into his pain by asking, "How does Christ feel toward you?" Through this request, Rajan engaged in an imaginative reenactment in which he experienced God's compassion, "I felt humiliated, but I heard Christ saying, 'Oh, I get that.'" Rajan became flooded with feelings of love and joy as he received acceptance and love from Christ.

The therapist then encouraged Rajan to have a direct conversation with the in vivo God image regarding his view of self and his strategies: "Share more about your feelings of loneliness to God." Rajan sought an answer to his deeply rooted core hurt. He asked, "Is there something wrong with me that I feel this weak? When I was 8 years old, I used to feign illness because I couldn't even face the school day." By engaging in this dialogue, Rajan received an answer from God, "I made you purposely the way you are. It's not a mistake. I also know what it's like to not want to face something difficult." Rajan was able to accept an answer that had the power to overthrow his negative view of self and absolve him from his core hurt.

One vital foundation of the GIFT is to not only question God directly but also receive powerful answers capable of changing the client's view of self. By accepting an answer from an in vivo God image that Rajan believed to be unconditionally loving and omnipotent, he was able to replace negative self-evaluations with positive affirmations of love and acceptance. Through this spiritual transformation, Rajan felt less shame and exhibited more self-confidence, "There seems to be less of a reason to feel ashamed of being weak. I still feel weak, but I don't feel as ashamed for being weak." Rajan also began feeling less anxious at work, experienced fewer panic attacks over time, and felt less crushed when receiving feedback from his wife. Through treatment, Rajan developed an authentic and intimate experience of God's love. Rather than experiencing God as rejecting or critical, like he had in the past, God was revealed as gracious, empathic, and welcoming. Rajan stopped looking for validation from work and intimate relationships and instead found his self-worth and freedom through his relationship with God.

DISCUSSION

Ethical Considerations in Using the GIFT

The GIFT originated within the context of an outpatient community clinic under the guidance of Protestant Christian doctrine. Given this specific milieu, it is imperative to define appropriate client populations and ethical issues therapists should consider when using the GIFT for psychotherapeutic treatment.

One significant aspect of the GIFT is encouraging clients to have corrective emotional spiritual experiences with an in vivo God image. Individuals holding monotheistic religious beliefs, generally, could be appropriate clients. However, those who adopt beliefs and practices in line with Protestant Christian doctrine, specifically, are more appropriate candidates. Particularly, the GIFT would be appropriate for clients who desire to incorporate Christianity into their psychotherapy, have God images that reflect the Protestant Christian God concept, or are open to developing this religious belief system. With clients who do not fit these criteria, it is important not to engage in explicit conversations about the Christian God concept, instead, practitioners should build a strong therapeutic alliance by encompassing the implicit qualities of the Protestant Christian God.

Limitations

Research results and developers of the GIFT have also highlighted a few limitations to the generalizability of this framework. First, research results indicated that clients who underwent the GIFT had significant emotional responses when interacting with their in vivo God image. As such, this framework may be best suited for individuals who have the capacity to be attuned to their affective experiences. Second, although RCS is located in a diverse urban area, there are some limitations due to the lack of diversity within their clientele. As mentioned earlier, clients are mostly White (54%) or Asian American/Pacific Islander/Southeast Asian (26%), and the vast majority have a socioeconomic standing of middle class or higher (75%). As such, the GIFT may not be an appropriate framework when treating clients who are significantly different from this racial and socioeconomic profile. Third, as mentioned previously, clients who engage in therapy-interfering behaviors may need to first focus on mitigating these interferences before starting the GIFT.

CONCLUSION

Literature connecting R/S factors and mechanisms to positive psychological functioning and well-being has continued to grow since the mid-20th century (Koenig et al., 2012; Weber & Pargament, 2014). Perhaps as a result of this growing knowledge and desire among clients to incorporate R/S into psychotherapy, there has been an increased need to analyze safe and effective methods when integrating R/S into practice (American Psychological Association, 2002). Although there is still meaningful work ahead to further the field's understanding of how to effectively integrate Christianity into psychotherapy, continued collaboration among clergy, practitioners, and researchers can further the ability to provide healing and wholeness to clients who seek this type of treatment.

REFERENCES

Ainsworth, M. D. (1985). Attachments across the life span. *Bulletin of the New York Academy of Medicine, 61*(9), 792–812. https://www.ncbi.nlm.nih.gov/pmc/articles/PMC1911889/pdf/bullnyacadmed00065-0026.pdf

Ainsworth, M. D., Blehar, M. C., Waters, E., & Walls, S. (1978). *Patterns of attachment: Assessed in the strange situation and at home.* Erlbaum.

American Psychological Association. (2002). Ethical principles of psychologists and code of conduct. *American Psychologist, 57*(12), 1060–1073. https://doi.org/10.1037/0003-066X.57.12.1060

Augustine, S. (1876). *The confessions.* Clark.

Bennett-Levy, J. (2006). Therapist skills: A cognitive model of their acquisition and refinement. *Behavioural and Cognitive Psychotherapy, 34*(1), 57–78. https://doi.org/10.1017/S1352465805002420

Bowlby, J. (1969). *Attachment and loss: Vol. 1. Attachment.* Basic Books.

Carroll, S. (1993). Spirituality and purpose in life in alcoholism recovery. *Journal of Studies on Alcohol, 54*(3), 297–301. https://doi.org/10.15288/jsa.1993.54.297

Castonguay, L. G., & Hill, C. E. (2012). Corrective experiences in psychotherapy: An introduction. In L. G. Castonguay & C. E. Hill (Eds.), *Transformation in psychotherapy: Corrective experiences across cognitive behavioral, humanistic, and psychodynamic approaches* (pp. 3–9). American Psychological Association. https://doi.org/10.1037/13747-001

Chapman, A. L., & Rosenthal, M. Z. (2016). *Managing therapy-interfering behavior: Strategies from dialectical behavior therapy.* American Psychological Association.

Charmaz, K. (2000). Grounded theory: Objectivist and constructivist methods. In N. K. Denzin & Y. S. Lincoln (Eds.), *Handbook of qualitative research* (pp. 509–535). Sage Publications.

Davis, E. B., Moriarty, G. L., & Mauch, J. C. (2013). God images and god concepts: Definitions, development, and dynamics. *Psychology of Religion and Spirituality, 5*(1), 51–60. https://doi.org/10.1037/a0029289

De Tocqueville, A. (1988). *Democracy in America*. Harper Perennial.

Fairbairn, W. R. D. (1943). The repression and the return of bad objects (with special reference to the "war neuroses"). *Psychology and Psychotherapy: Theory, Research and Practice, 19*, 327–341. https://doi.org/10.1111/j.2044-8341.1943.tb00328.x

Galea, M., Ciarrocchi, J. W., Piedmont, R. L., & Wicks, R. J. (2007). Child abuse, personality, and spirituality as predictors of happiness in Maltese college students. *Research in the Social Scientific Study of Religion, 18*, 141–154.

Glaser, B. G., & Strauss, A. L. (1967). *The discovery of grounded theory: Strategies for qualitative research*. Aldine.

Granqvist, P., & Kirkpatrick, L. A. (2013). Religion, spirituality, and attachment. In K. I. Pargament, J. J. Exline, & J. W. Jones (Eds.), *APA handbook of psychology, religion, and spirituality: Vol. 1. Context, theory, and research* (pp. 139–155). American Psychological Association. https://doi.org/10.1037/14045-007

Greenberg, L. S. (1984). A task analysis of intrapersonal conflict resolution. In L. Rice & L. Greenberg (Eds.), *Patterns of change: Intensive analysis of psychotherapy process* (pp. 67–123). Guilford Press.

Greenberg, L. S. (2007). A guide to conducting a task analysis of psychotherapeutic change. *Psychotherapy Research, 17*(1), 15–30. https://doi.org/10.1080/10503300600720390

Hill, P. C., & Butter, E. M. (1995). The role of religion in promoting physical health. *Journal of Psychology and Christianity, 14*(2), 141–155.

Keller, T. (2009). *The reason for God: Belief in an age of skepticism*. Penguin.

Keller, T. (2011). *Counterfeit gods: The empty promises of money, sex, and power, and the only hope that matters*. Penguin.

Kim, E. E., & Chen, E. C. (2021). Task analysis of a Christian-integrated psychotherapy framework. *Psychotherapy*. Advance online publication. https://doi.org/10.1037/pst0000406

Kim, E. E., Chen, E. C., & Brachfeld, C. (2019). Patients' experience of spirituality and change in individual psychotherapy at a Christian counseling clinic: A grounded theory analysis. *Spirituality in Clinical Practice, 6*(2), 110–123. https://doi.org/10.1037/scp0000176

Kirkpatrick, L. A. (1992). An attachment-theory approach to the psychology of religion. *The International Journal for the Psychology of Religion, 2*(1), 3–28. https://doi.org/10.1207/s15327582ijpr0201_2

Kirkpatrick, L. A. (1995). Attachment theory and religious experience. In R. W. Hood (Ed.), *Handbook of religious experience* (pp. 446–475). Religious Education Press.

Koenig, H. G., King, D., & Carson, V. B. (2012). *Handbook of religion and health*. Oxford University Press.

Lysne, C. J., & Wachholtz, A. B. (2011). Pain, spirituality, and meaning making: What can we learn from the literature? *Religions, 2*(1), 1–16. https://doi.org/10.3390/rel2010001

Maton, K. I. (1989). The stress-buffering role of spiritual support: Cross-sectional and prospective investigations. *Journal for the Scientific Study of Religion, 28*, 310–323.

New International Version Bible. (2011). Zondervan. (Original work published 1978)

Packer, J. I. (2011). *Knowing God*. InterVarsity Press.

Park, C. L. (2013). Trauma and meaning making: Converging conceptualizations and emerging evidence. In J. A. Hicks & C. Routledge (Eds.), *The experience of meaning in life: Classical perspectives, emerging themes, and controversies* (pp. 61–76). Springer. https://doi.org/10.1007/978-94-007-6527-6_5

Redeemer Counseling Services. (2016). *Redeemer Counseling Services psychotherapeutic approach* [White paper].

Rizzuto, A. M. (2011). *The birth of the living God: A psychoanalytic study*. University of Chicago Press.

Rye, M. S., & Pargament, K. I. (2002). Forgiveness and romantic relationships in college: Can it heal the wounded heart? *Journal of Clinical Psychology, 58*(4), 419–441. https://doi.org/10.1002/jclp.1153

Tisdale, T. C., Key, T. L., Edwards, K. J., Brokaw, B. F., Kemperman, S. R., Cloud, H., Townsend, J., & Okamoto, T. (1997). Impact of treatment on God image and personal adjustment, and correlations of God image to personal adjustment and object relations development. *Journal of Psychology and Theology, 25*(2), 227–239. https://doi.org/10.1177/009164719702500207

Weber, S. R., & Pargament, K. I. (2014). The role of religion and spirituality in mental health. *Current Opinion in Psychiatry, 27*(5), 358–363. https://doi.org/10.1097/YCO.0000000000000080

Westminster Assembly. (1992). *The Westminster confession of faith*. Jazzybee Verlag.

Winnicott, D. W. (1953). Transitional objects and transitional phenomena; a study of the first not-me possession. *The International Journal of Psycho-Analysis, 34*(2), 89–97.

12

Gestalt Pastoral Care
An Opening to Grace

Tilda Norberg, David L. Janvier, Wanda Craner, Lyn Barrett, Michael Crabtree, Michelle Zechner, and Mark Thomas

Historically, spirituality has been absent from the mental health field. Those engaged in therapy are seen through a disease lens in which faith or belief in God is excluded from the therapeutic milieu and, at times, even pathologized (O'Rourke, 1996). Concurrently, psychological modalities were viewed as antithetical to many faith traditions. Both of these positions view people seeking treatment or healing as fragmented individuals, denying the inherent complexities of human beings and leaving them with significantly split components of self. However, a growing interest in integrating spirituality into treatment and understanding how faith plays a role in the healing process has changed the therapeutic landscape. Recent literature reflects the integration of Christianity into practice that strives to move toward a more authentic "bio-psycho-social-spiritual" model of treatment (Gingrich & Gingrich, 2017; Saad et al., 2017).

Spirituality continues to be an important and significant factor in a mentally healthy lifestyle (Harris et al., 2016; Richards & Bergin, 2000). According to Harris et al. (2016), many who seek therapy for reasons other than spirituality still desire a practitioner who addresses spirituality. Gestalt Pastoral Care (GPC) is one such approach. GPC's foundational premise, that God is always working to bring each individual to wholeness, sets it apart from the many psychological approaches rooted in Freud's psychoanalytic theory and the prominent cognitive behavioral therapy. The majority of attempts to integrate spirituality into psychotherapy began with a basis in psychology, and attempts have been made to fit spirituality into these existing psychological constructs.

---

https://doi.org/10.1037/0000338-012
Handbook of Spiritually Integrated Psychotherapies, P. S. Richards, G. E. K. Allen, and D. K. Judd (Editors)
Copyright © 2023 by the American Psychological Association. All rights reserved.

Conversely, GPC's integrative foundation begins with spirituality and blends the basic tenets of gestalt theory and practice with pastoral care rooted in the healing ministry of Jesus (Norberg, 2006). GPC is not easily categorized. The Reverend Tilda Norberg, who founded GPC, explained the approach as neither a spiritual approach that employs a little gestalt nor a therapy modality that incorporates a little prayer. It is a "both and" approach that has been caring for people holistically for 4 decades (Norberg, 2017).

The aim of this chapter is to provide an introductory understanding of the theory and practice of GPC. The beginning section provides a brief history of GPC; the treatment settings; and aspects of the theoretical and theological underpinnings of the approach, including treatment strategies and interventions. This is followed by a case study that showcases application of the GPC model and an overview of research on the effectiveness of GPC.

HISTORY OF GESTALT PASTORAL CARE

GPC started to evolve in the early 1970s, when Rev. Tilda Norberg began integrating her pastoral role as an ordained United Methodist minister with her training as a gestaltist. Norberg used healing prayer as a modality and observed intense psychological issues emerging in her clients, which led her to develop a unified model of faith and therapeutic healing. At first, Norberg was resistant to integration; however, she was convinced that God was leading her to create this new way of blending the spiritual and psychological. During the process of developing this new model, the amalgamation of the theory and approach became more finely tuned. In time, Norberg conducted healing sessions with this approach and observed her clients growing rapidly and holistically, integrating the spiritual, physical, psychological, and emotional parts of self. Moreover, she observed that many individuals desired to integrate all these aspects of self within the context of growth.

Norberg offered individual sessions in her private practice and eventually developed weekend retreats called Opening to Grace. After a group of clergy and therapists experienced the healing benefits of this new synthesis in 1984, Norberg was asked to provide training to others who were interested in learning her approach. As she developed this foundational course, Gestalt Pastoral Care was born. In 1990, a group of practitioners who used GPC expanded on the training and established Gestalt Pastoral Care Associates (GPC, 2020). Subsequently, as the organization grew and training expanded, Norberg published several books on this approach, including the seminal work *Consenting to Grace* (Norberg, 2006).

TREATMENT SETTINGS

GPC practitioners achieve a wide range of skills through professional training in areas of ministry and clinical practice. Regardless of their credentials—whether ordained as clergy or licensed as a clinician—all GPC Ministers work with individuals one on one and in the group setting of an Opening to Grace retreat.

A wide range of licensed mental health professionals (psychologists, professional counselors, social workers, and marriage and family counselors) have successfully implemented the GPC approach within their respective clinical settings; however, it requires a paradigm shift. Therapists are usually trained in traditional approaches that are rooted in the idea that a set of techniques is applied to particular diagnoses, symptoms, or circumstances. When a specific symptom presents, the therapist reaches into the proverbial therapeutic toolbox and applies the designated technique. Conversely, gestalt theory is philosophical in nature. Instead of focusing on technique it centers on a way of being, stressing the importance of the practitioner's personhood and how they show up to meet the client (Joyce & Sills, 2018; Mann, 2010).

GPC training emphasizes this personal development by requiring all participants to learn the approach by experientially engaging in their own personal growth work grounded in spiritual development and expansion. (GPC reflects this approach by referring to the individuals receiving healing as "workers" rather than "clients.") Personal growth work and deepening spirituality allow the GPC Minister to be grounded in the moment, possess the capacity to hold space for whatever material the worker presents, and discern how God is guiding the process. What happens in a GPC session is rooted in a discernment process that holistically utilizes all aspects of a person rather than simply applying a technique. The challenge for traditionally trained therapists is the tendency to engage in analysis and interpretation in an attempt to problem solve or seek solutions. This keeps the client in a cognitive mode of processing rather than in their body, focusing on their experience in the present moment. Additionally, clinicians should be aware that the ability to be present in the body can be a challenge for certain people. Because GPC explores and works with parts of self, the approach would be contraindicated for people who are highly dissociative, are unable to emotionally self-regulate, or have elaborate defenses that block self-awareness (Dolliver, 1981).

TYPES OF CLIENTS AND CLINICAL ISSUES

The demographics of people receiving ministry from GPC is shifting. The original founding members of the organization were White, middle-class women. For the most part, this was the population that was drawn to the approach. However, in the late 1980s, Tilda Norberg taught GPC principles to the men incarcerated at Arthur Kill Correctional Facility on Staten Island in New York, where the main demographic was African American men. In 2018, the GPC group recognized that the population in which it served had become homogenous and intentionally created a Diversity Task Force to inform policy and provide access to services across the demographic spectrum. The Diversity Statement was affirmed by a special meeting of the GPC Board of Trustees on June 26, 2020 (GPC, 2020). Subsequently, a fund was developed to provide financial access to those with mental health needs and to provide training for people of color, nonbinary individuals, and other marginalized groups (see the section titled Diversity Considerations for details).

GPC has been used to reduce or ameliorate a variety of clinical symptoms and facilitates deep internal shifts within clients. Symptoms that have been addressed using GPC concepts include depression, anxiety, suicidality, spiritual crisis, facing death, grief/mourning, trauma, sexual abuse, sexual trauma, posttraumatic stress disorder (PTSD), sexual dysfunction, sexual addiction, drug and alcohol addictions, relational conflict, marital issues, attachment ruptures, and family-of-origin wounds (Thomas et al., 2022).

THEORETICAL AND THEOLOGICAL FOUNDATIONS

Defining GPC is not an easy task, and it cannot be simply placed in the established categories of "clinical" or "spiritual." The model does not superimpose prayer onto the therapeutic process, nor does it apply particular gestalt techniques to spiritual practices. The GPC model is a hybrid of both. It integrates gestalt growth work, spiritual companioning, and healing prayer, which is rooted in the healing ministry of Jesus (Norberg, 2017).

Gestalt Growth Work

The "ability to form and close gestalts" summarizes the process of gestalt growth work (Perls, 1976, p. 9). Unprocessed gestalts are what Perls referred to as "unfinished business"; that is, traumas or unhealed parts of self that remain from the past and any yearning that emerges in the present (Norberg, 2006, p. 21; Perls, 1969, pp. 134–139). Perls (1969) asserted that unfinished business is constantly presenting itself for healing, and if the worker is coached to become more aware, the client will begin to notice somatic impulses, such as clenched fists or jiggly knees (Norberg, 2006; Perls, 1969, pp. 25–26). Working with these somatic impulses through gestalt experiments can lead to discoveries and changes that are not only somatic but also emotional and spiritual. Increasing workers' awareness of their present circumstances and suggesting ways to engage experientially with whatever is surfacing at the moment undergirds the GPC process, which is why it is called "working" (Norberg, 2006).

The German word *Gestalt* means wholeness. Therefore, the gestalt approach is radically holistic in its acknowledgment that emotions and body are intricately connected (Perls, 1969). Gestalt work fosters moment-by-moment awareness by simply noticing and calling attention to physical sensations, gestures, or tone of voice (Norberg, 2006). Whatever awareness emerges for the worker is viewed as health pushing forth. For example, if a worker becomes aware of her stiff neck or achy shoulders, she might be invited to playfully "be" her neck and shoulders; that is, to describe herself as if her neck and shoulders could speak. A typical response may not only be somatic but might also have emotional and spiritual meaning. The "message" may even come as a surprise to the worker. For example, "I'm stiff and I hurt and I can't bend very much. I have such a weight on my shoulders, and I'm stuck with it! I just have to bear up." Workers are guided to trust their own internal process

(Norberg, 2006; Perls, 1969). Perls (1976) believed that each person is responsible for their own growth and has the ability to choose health. GPC borrows this tenet from gestalt theory; therefore, it is not appropriate for a GPC Minister to provide analysis or interpretations.

The reason analysis and interpretations are avoided is rooted in gestalt therapy's philosophy of phenomenology, which focuses on how the client organizes self in present moment experience. Health is present when an individual is able to successfully adjust to their environment. Gestalt theory refers to this as a "creative adjustment" (Joyce & Sills, 2018; Mann, 2010). Clients who are stuck or unable to adjust experience a fixed gestalt that requires support from the environment. Other approaches label a fixed gestalt as a disorder or condition. However, GPC views this phenomenon like a stream that has been blocked by sticks or debris and is in need of clearing (Norberg, 2006). The GPC Minister serves as a spiritual companion who is willing to pay attention to the flow of emotions revealed through body awareness.

Spiritual Companioning

A practitioner who guides others in the healing process of GPC is called a Gestalt Pastoral Care Minister and is considered a spiritual companion. The essential premise is that the Holy Spirit is directing both the GPC Minister and the worker. The ability of the GPC Minister to discern the Holy Spirit's movement is paramount to the work. Therefore, the intensive training program of ministers requires the development of discernment skills, which are grounded in contemplative spiritual practices. All GPC Ministers are mandated to pursue continual personal growth by actively engaging in therapy or spiritual direction (Norberg, 2006).

Comprehensive spiritual formation training anchors the GPC Minister in the present moment, allowing access to personal intuition, discernment, and God's gentle movement, which incarnates the supportive, hospitable, transforming, and accepting ways of God. Being grounded in spiritual practices allows the GPC Minister to create a safe environment by offering a stable, contemplative presence for the worker to discover God's vision for their wholeness. The GPC Minister's ability to listen deeply and discern is integral to the worker's healing and growth process. Gestalt theory references "inner tugs," but GPC views these experiences as gifts from God disguised as inner nudges. The encounter between the GPC Minister and the worker is considered holy ground and is characterized by a sense of reverence and holiness as God directs the process (*New Revised Standard Version* [*NRSV*], 1989,[1] Phil. 2:1–11; Norberg, 2006). This means that the GPC Minister may need to stretch their own ideas of how God may be working in a particular person and be willing to surrender their own ideas of how a particular person might be invited to grow.

---

[1] Parenthetical citations of Scripture all refer to the *New Revised Standard Version of the Bible,* published in 1989.

Healing Prayer

Humans innately hunger for God, and God deeply desires to find a home within us. Prayer is the primary communication instrument between God and people. Various forms of prayer are inherent to GPC (Norberg, 2006). According to Norberg and Webber (1998), *healing prayer* invites a person's total being into the presence of God: "whenever we are truly open to God, some kind of healing takes place, because God yearns to bring us to wholeness. Through prayer and the laying on of hands, Jesus meets us in our brokenness and pain, and there loves, transforms, redeems, resurrects, and heals" (p. 26).

Prayer creates a spaciousness inside the worker that facilitates tangible emotional growth. Healing prayer moves a worker from a thought about God to an experience of God that is often felt in the body. This is especially the case when healing prayer includes faith imagination (see the section titled Intervention Strategies and Techniques).

The Healing Ministry of Jesus

Even in a modern scientific era, it is difficult to truly quantify the results of Jesus's healing through research. There is no neat systematization of how Jesus implemented specific healing interactions. Scripture informs us that Jesus used a variety of avenues for healing, which depended on the unique circumstances of individuals. The healing ministry of Jesus incorporated a lively sense of the person's physical, emotional, and spiritual needs, and was always rooted in God's love. For example, there are passages of Scripture that directly cite faith as a critical component of healing (Mark 10:52). In other cases, the faith of others (friends or family) is a factor in Jesus's healing of an individual (Mark 2:1–12) or there is no direct mention of faith as a factor in Jesus's healing (Mark 1:29–31). The New Testament provides multiple illustrations of how Jesus used various means for healing. There are times when Jesus only whispers a word and others where He uses a combination of words and touch. He also uses conventional healing means of the time, such as mud and spit (Beckman & Nerheim, 1985; John 9:1–41; Mark 8:22–25).

Furthermore, Jesus's healing ministry pushed the bounds of his culture and faith community to reach those in need. This is observed in his ministry to the Samaritan woman (John 4:4–26), the woman with an issue of blood (Mark 5:25–34), and the lepers (Luke 17:11–19; Mark 1:40–45). Jesus's healing ministry was rooted in and motivated by God's unconditional love (1 John 4:16). GPC seeks to embody this love and to reach anyone who seeks healing, including people of other faiths or those with no faith at all. It is this love that informs GPC training, shapes the personhood of GPC Ministers, and guides the healing work.

ETHICAL GUIDELINES

Gestalt Pastoral Care Associates operates on the standards detailed in the official policy, *Standards of Ethical Practice for Gestalt Pastoral Care* (GPC, 2020). These guidelines are rooted in the sacred nature inherent in the GPC model and designed to protect both providers and consumers. The document requires adherence to high standards of professionalism and ethical behavior in the following areas: competence, supervision, continuing education, self-evaluation, confidentiality, sexual harassment, and professional boundaries. The policy clearly states:

> Harassment of any kind is not productive and shall not be tolerated. . . . Any individual bound by these By-Laws who is subject to verbally abusive language relating to race, color, religion (creed), gender, gender expression age, national origin (ancestry), disability, marital status, sexual orientation, pregnancy, political affiliation or military status in any of its activities or operation or who experiences inappropriate physical touching or suggestive language is encouraged to report it immediately to the President. Any individual bound by these By-Laws who is aware of such verbally or physically abusive conditions should report such activity immediately. (GPC, 2020)

Annually, GPC Ministers and trainers are required to meet professional compliances. These include anti–sexual harassment training, background checks, continuing education requirements, professional liability coverage, and ongoing therapy or spiritual direction. In addition, regular meetings are held with the GPC Ministers and trainers to explore any concerns or ethical dilemmas.

DIVERSITY CONSIDERATIONS

Diversity considerations are written into GPCA's bylaws:

> GPCA, Inc., does not and shall not discriminate on the basis of race, color, religion (creed), gender, gender expression, age, national origin (ancestry), disability, marital status, sexual orientation, pregnancy, political affiliation or military status in any of its activities or operation, except as allowed by law. We are committed to providing an inclusive and welcoming environment for program participants, staff, volunteers, subcontractors, and vendors. (GPC, 2020)

Additionally, the organization's Diversity Task Force continually strives to implement policies that address diversity and social justice issues in order to bring God's gift of healing to all people. Recently the Diversity Task Force created a document to address the depth and breadth of institutional racism (GPC, 2020).

RELATIONSHIP ESTABLISHMENT GUIDELINES

Relationship and rapport building start before a worker participates in an individual session or retreat. GPC Ministers are trained to cultivate a contemplative ministry of presence that enables practitioners to hold space nonjudgmentally for whomever is seeking help, regardless of the presenting issue, denomination, or faith (Norberg, 2006). Those who seek help from GPC Ministers are provided with a disclosure detailing guidelines on what to expect. Preaching, coercing, persuading, analyzing, and advice giving are not strategies that are used in GPC sessions (Norberg, 2006). GPC strives to provide an authentic, person-centered experience. The worker is invited to co-create the process empowered with the choice to stop, say "no," or change course at any time. The worker experientially senses the GPC Minister's calm and safe presence, which opens the pathway to risk the kind of vulnerability that leads to the revelation and healing of deep wounds.

ASSESSMENT GUIDELINES

Traditionally, gestalt theory and practice is a nonpathologizing modality (Joyce & Sills, 2018; Mann, 2010; Perls et al., 1951). The mental health field deems pathology as a problem, whereas gestalt theory views it as a creative adjustment. Roubal et al. (2017) explained that "from a Gestalt perspective, symptoms are products of a creative self and display human uniqueness. Psychopathology thus represents a unique creative adjustment in a difficult situation" (p. 3). GPC maintains a similar perspective. Norberg (2006) further explained that

> Gestalt growth work embraces a health model, calling forth the health that already exists in even the most fragmented person. Gestalt work is not so much turned toward what is wrong with a person, but toward what's blocking the health that is surely present. Diagnosis of illness is much less important than becoming aware of where new life is just wanting to break out. (p. 15)

Therefore, GPC Ministers are not evaluating criteria for a clinical diagnosis. They are engaging in a discernment process that pays attention to cues that are openings to avenues for healing or resolution, such as experimenting with a new way of acting, expressing, or verbalizing (Norberg, 2006). Perls (1976) described this process as the ability to close an open gestalt or change a fixed gestalt.

While GPC Ministers do not conduct formal assessments, they are continually assessing how the worker is engaging in the here and now by paying attention moment by moment to the dynamic field conditions, relational patterns, and internal processing (Norberg, 2006). Since the process is holistic and embodied, physical observations are noted, such as body movements, voice, facial expressions, feelings. Ministers also note what is absent (Norberg, 2006). This continual assessment process is paramount for supporting the central intervention of creating and implementing experiments.

INTERVENTION STRATEGIES AND TECHNIQUES

The terms *intervention* and *technique* are not commonly used in the GPC nomenclature; *practice* and *invitation* are the preferred terms. The concern is that a "technique" will be used formulaically and not in the context of discerning God's leading in the dynamic relationship between the worker and GPC Minister. Norberg (2006) viewed the healing process as resting in the GPC Minister's ability to trust and discern God's leading in guiding a worker through the process of addressing an unresolved or fixed gestalt. This is the process that leads to health and wholeness. The GPC Minister is trained in the areas of gestalt growth work, spiritual companioning, and healing prayer. However, it is the discernment process of God's leading that determines which interventions are used as well as when and how to implement them. This section briefly highlights some of the main practices employed in a GPC session or retreat setting, including gestalt experiments, faith imagination, and personalized healing liturgies.

Gestalt Experiments

As mentioned previously, God continually prompts unfinished business to be healed; therefore, becoming aware of this process is necessary and is accomplished through creating experiments. Experiments are the hallmark intervention of gestalt therapy and the main method for fostering awareness and cultivating change in GPC. The purpose of experiments is to create a "safe emergency," allowing the worker to experience a corrective experience in a secure environment (Polster & Polster, 1974). Norberg (2006) explained that "experiments are powerful because they can offer access to inner worlds and facilitate work with the material found there" (p. 142). The material that presents is from the past. However, the worker is experiencing the material in the present moment. The GPC process enhances awareness and shifts bodily sensations that equip the worker to be empowered to choose a new path and experience a different outcome. Moreover, Norberg (2006) expressed that "experiments teach how to maintain awareness and how to live in it" (p. 145); thus, closing a gestalt or changing a fixed one.

The practice of creating and implementing experiments is rooted in what the GPC Minister observes or senses in interactions with the worker in the present moment. For instance, the worker may be tapping their foot, constricting their breath, avoiding eye contact, crying, or using a particular tone of voice. Experiments are designed "to enable the person to move from remembering to re-experiencing, from talking to doing, from explaining to discovering" (Norberg, 2006, p. 149). The following examples demonstrate how these experiments are implemented by the GPC Minister while spiritually companioning the worker:

- Perhaps [a worker is] invited to make a figure of speech explicit: *Let yourself be a pain in the neck, would you? Speak as if your painful neck has a separate voice.*

- Maybe [a worker] would allow her past to be part of the present moment: *Would you let yourself be eight years old for a few minutes instead of just remembering and talking about that time? What do you experience?*

- [The worker] might be invited to let an action flow from an interior place: *Would you let your sadness have a physical motion? How about a sound as well? . . . What are you aware of now that you've done it?*

- Almost certainly [the worker] will be asked simply to broaden her awareness of the present: *Are you willing to be aware of your chest? What's happening there right now?* (Norberg, 2006, p. 143)

Additional simple experiments bring awareness to a worker's breath, bodily movements, gestures, and tone of voice. The GPC Minister may invite the worker to notice a part of the body that is moving or ask the worker to exaggerate subtle movements in order to evoke awareness. A minister may invite the worker to allow a body part to speak in order to broaden awareness. For instance, a worker's foot rapidly shakes, and the minister asks, "Would you allow your foot to have a voice?" Or the worker makes a statement that evokes emotion, and the minister may ask, "Would you be willing to repeat that again and notice what happens inside your body?"

Often, a worker continues to carry the pain and wounding that has been perpetrated by others. A significant and commonly practiced invitation is guiding a worker from talking about to talking to (Norberg, 2006, p. 143). Instead of "talking about" an abuser, parent, or sibling, the GPC Minister invites the worker to speak to the person. Practically, the GPC Minister can place a pillow in proximity to the worker and ask, "Would you be willing to allow this pillow to be your father and speak to him?" Often these simple yet powerful invitations produce new discoveries and elicit change within the worker.

Faith Imagination

While God's Spirit undergirds the entire GPC process, the worker does not always experience God's tangible presence. Norberg (2006) found that integrating gestalt experiments and prayer that used a worker's imagination was a way to have a felt sense experience of the Divine. She "thought of faith imagination as a powerful kind of Gestalt experiment and . . . Gestalt experiments . . . as a kind of prayer" (p. 158).

Norberg (2006) provided an example of faith imagination when she invited Maria, a 53-year-old worker, to explore a childhood trauma. When she was 6 years old, Maria accidentally wet her pants, and as punishment Maria's mother forced her to sit on the ashes in the fireplace. The hot grate burned permanent scars on her body. Norberg recalled noticing Maria reexperiencing the moment. Norberg reached out and held Maria's hands, looked into her eyes and asked, "Would you be willing to invite Jesus in the room with the fireplace with you?" Maria reported, "Immediately, I saw Jesus enter the room and push my mother out of the way." Maria continued, "Jesus said, 'Your daughter does not belong in the ashes!'" Jesus immediately picked up 6-year-old Maria and took her place in the ashes. In the imagery, Maria was in Jesus's lap being embraced. In that moment, "she could feel the searing pain drain from her legs . . . as if Jesus absorbed [my] pain into his body" (p. 58). Maria was able to claim this truth in the experience: "I don't belong in the ashes . . . I belong right here, being held by the Lord." Soon afterward, she noticed the scars had faded (p. 58).

Personalized Healing Liturgies

Healing liturgies in GPC may include confession, forgiveness, communion, prayer, and foot washing, among other traditions. Norberg (2007) viewed all of life as liturgy, and she borrowed from the Church's rich liturgical history to create personalized healing liturgies. She explained, "Personalized healing liturgies serve as a bridge between pastoral care and the worship traditions of the church, and incorporate material from both Christian liturgical traditions and scripture, as well as one person's particular need for healing or growth" (p. 9). The outcome "can be a greatly deepened, grounded, and integrated faith—even in times of greatest despair, God is still with us" (Norberg, 2007, p. 30). What is important is the communal aspect of healing liturgies. Norberg (2007) stressed the "need to share them with a group of people who use the same symbolic language. Sharing a liturgy among friends and family gives authority and substance" (p. 28).

The following is an example of a personalized healing liturgy: Margaret, 80 years old, created a personal healing liturgy at an Opening to Grace retreat she attended. The pain and loss of being forced to abort a pregnancy had persisted within her for more than 60 years. Once the procedure was completed, Margaret was never allowed to speak of it again. Shrouded in shame and guilt, she buried the feelings deep within. The participants at the retreat all agreed to operate as "The Church" and assisted her in participating in her personalized healing liturgy. Margaret developed a beautiful funeral service that included giving the baby a name. Margaret was allowed to express all the feelings that had been bottled up decades. She experienced the support of the Church family surrounding her at the retreat center without shame, guilt, or condemnation. Her feelings were welcomed and encouraged. Margaret expressed spaciousness and lightness inside and felt that she was able to come to an acceptance of what happened.

RECOMMENDATIONS FOR COLLABORATING WITH CLERGY

GPC has a rich history of building rapport with clergy and faith communities. A strength of the GPC model is its inherent spiritual and pastoral nature. Additionally, GPC was founded by a pastor, and many who have completed the training program are clergy, spiritual directors, or other church leaders. These church leaders experience the healing benefits of GPC and, in turn, desire to take the work back to their respective faith communities in various forms. Teaching Sunday school classes, leading group studies, creating workshops, presenting at church conferences, and conducting Opening to Grace retreats are some of the many ways leaders develop the GPC ministry of healing within their congregations or denominations. Several denominations have officially recognized GPC by formally appointing GPC Ministers as a denominational call of specialized ministry and by accepting GPC training in lieu of required clinical pastoral education credits. Several seminaries have invited GPC Ministers to teach courses on spiritual healing, integrating spiritual, psychological, and pastoral care. Additionally, denominations, churches, and seminaries also refer their leaders in need of care to GPC Associates.

CASE STUDY ILLUSTRATING GPC TREATMENT PROCESSES AND INTERVENTIONS

Case History

Jemma (composite worker), is a 66-year-old, White Methodist woman with a history of sexual abuse. In middle school, Jemma's biological father sexually abused her, and, around the same time, she was raped by a boy in her neighborhood. Jemma married at 18, had two children, then divorced after 37 years of marriage. She is a retired mathematics teacher and lives alone.

In her early 30s, Jemma experienced "a crash" while on vacation with her children. She described this as profound sadness, feeling overwhelmed, bouts of uncontrollable tears, a sense of hopelessness, and self-hatred. Jemma checked herself into a psychiatric hospital for 4 weeks and experienced flashbacks of the sexual abuse. Officially, she was diagnosed with PTSD and prescribed medication.

Subsequently, Jemma confronted her parents about the abuse and her father confirmed the details. Her therapy was difficult and stretched over years, working with a total of five different therapists. While she gained insight into the impact of childhood sexual abuse, the cognitive processing of these prior therapies was not effective. She continued to experience weight gain, body dysmorphia, depression, anxiety, panic attacks, sleeplessness, dissociation during sex, and low self-esteem. Existentially, she struggled to understand where God was in the midst of her pain and suffering. Jemma then attended a GPC Opening to Grace retreat, where she met Karen, a GPC Minister, and started individual work.

Karen is a 60-year-old, White woman, who earned a master's of divinity and was a certified spiritual director. She worked as a pastor of a Protestant congregation and a spiritual director. After completing the GPC training program, she opened a private practice as a GPC Minister, where she spiritually companions workers individually and in Opening to Grace retreat settings.

Assessment and Diagnosis

GPC does not formally conduct assessments or diagnose disorders. GPC follows the tenets of gestalt theory and person-centered care that cultivates awareness and allows the worker to be responsible for their own healing process in the moment without labels or categorizing. Material emerging in the present moment guides the process from the worker's spoken words, heard in tone, observed by body language, or nudged by the Holy Spirit. Jemma's experience in the Opening to Grace retreat was significant. While she could not articulate what actually happened, she reported an internal shift and a sense of "relief." Experiential shifts often occur prior to cognitive understanding.

Outline of the Process

Typical GPC sessions often include elements with the GPC Minister responding to the current moment: setting the tone, prayer, exploration, refining the figure, gestalt experiments, inviting the Divine, closing the gestalt. This section explains these elements through Jemma's experience of the GPC process.

Set the Tone
To provide safety and reassurance to Jemma, Karen explained the GPC process and answered Jemma's questions about it. Karen stressed Jemma's element of choice and assured her that she could stop the process at any time or change any experiments.

Prayer
The GPC Minister offers to pray at the beginning of each session, inviting the Divine's presence and to guide the work. Jemma welcomed this offer, and Karen invited the Holy to be present, requested a few moments of silence, and ended with "Amen" to signal the end.

Exploration
This step begins with an open-ended question, such as, "What are you aware of?" Jemma reported feeling intense anger. However, a worker can begin with any feeling, bodily sensation, or image. The worker only needs to be willing and open to work. As Jemma reported feeling angry, Karen observed and listened for verbal and nonverbal cues, bodily movements, and energy. Karen explored by asking, "Where in your body do you feel anger?" Usually, a worker reports a bodily sensation. Jemma's anger was in her chest. Karen prayed internally and sought discernment from the Divine.

Refining the Figure
Karen, through the Holy Spirit's prompting, intuited that Jemma's anger was directed toward a person. However, she did not impose her hunch. Instead, she allowed Jemma to give meaning to what happened in the moment by simply asking, "What's happening?" Jemma replied, "I hate my father!" As Karen discerned the progression of energy up to this point, Jemma's hatred toward her father was the main figure that emerged for healing. Once a figure is identified, the process moves into experimenting.

Experimenting
Often in GPC experiments, pillows or other objects are used for placeholders to represent parts of self, feelings, or people. To provide choice and power to the worker, the invitation to experiment is always prefaced by asking permission. Karen used a pillow to represent Jemma's father and asked, "Would you allow this pillow to represent your father?" Once permission is granted, the worker is invited to speak to the pillow as if the person were really there. This process broadens awareness and evokes parts of self and feelings that have been repressed. As Jemma turned to the pillow representing her father, she expressed her hatred toward her father and articulated that she wanted him to feel the same pain that he caused her. As this process happened, Jemma's breath was rapid and shallow. The GPC Minister continually noticed these bodily changes in each step of the process, which informed the next experiment.

Karen asked Jemma, "Would you be willing to notice your breath?" This question allowed Jemma to take a deep breath to calm her body and opened up space for the next impulse. Jemma reported that she just wanted to hit her father. Karen affirmed this impulse and invited Jemma to use the nearby Wiffle bat to hit the pillow representing her father. The physical process of the experiment unearthed the feelings that Jemma had buried for decades. In order to give language where workers have not had voice, experiments may include making statements of specific injuries along with a physical action. Karen suggested making a statement during each strike of the bat. For instance, "I hate that you violated me!", "I hate that you damaged my ability to trust!", "I hate that you stole my innocence!" This process continued for a period of time, and when done, Jemma dropped the bat and let out a big sigh of relief. This place of the process allows workers to experience a shift. Jemma said she felt "free" and "light as air." Furthermore, Jemma also no longer felt the hatred, anger, or sensations in her chest. However, she still felt distant from God.

Inviting the Divine
It is critically important to avoid imposing a perspective of the Divine onto a worker. Much abuse and trauma has occurred related to religion, church, and images of God. Jemma felt abandoned by God as it seemed God was absent in times of significant need. The notion of "Father God" was extremely difficult for Jemma as her biological father was her abuser. Therefore, Karen explored possible object figures in Jemma's early life when she felt cared for and loved. Jemma identified her grandmother, and from this point forward connected with God as "Gram God," which allowed her to experience God's love profoundly and heal her perceived rejection by God.

Closing the Gestalt
Closing the Gestalt is a circling back to the elements surrounding the figure. Jemma addressed lingering emotions about her father, which reduced her physical pain and led to new sensations of freedom and lightness. The process supported a healed image of God that allowed her to feel loved. To solidify her work, Jemma created a prayer in the form of a personalized healing liturgy and invited Karen and several friends to witness this process as they gathered at church.

RESEARCH FINDINGS AND SUPPORT

This section provides details regarding supports for the GPC approach. The first is a practice-based evidence study that was part of a global big data project. The second used a qualitative method that obtained personal meaning from individuals who experienced the modality.

Practice-Based Evidence

Thomas et al. (2022) conducted the first research study to examine the effectiveness of GPC as a psychological treatment modality. Through a grant awarded by

Brigham Young University's Bridges Consortium and funded by the Templeton Foundation, a sample of 290 participants (mean age = 55.2, 75.2% female, 92.7% Christian) were recruited from outpatient mental health treatment settings. Patients engaged in one of two GPC treatment modalities: individual sessions with a certified GPC Minister ($n = 112$) or an intensified Opening to Grace group retreat where GPC was the primary form of intervention ($n = 178$). Individual sessions were typically conducted with a GPC Minister for a weekly 1-hour session, and the intensified retreat typically involved 4 to 8 hours spread over 1 to 2 days. At the first session (pretreatment) and last session (posttreatment), participants completed four empirically validated instruments that assessed their emotional health and spiritual well-being: Clinically Adaptive Multidimensional Outcome Survey, the Clinical Outcomes in Routine Evaluation, Primary Care PTSD Screen for *DSM-5*, and the Spiritual Index of Well-Being. A series of paired t tests comparing pretreatment and posttreatment differences found that both individual and retreat group types of GPC were associated with statistically significant reductions in depressive, anxiety, and trauma symptoms as well as spiritual issues. Follow-up analyses showed that the group retreat modality was associated with greater reduction in relationship distress and, to a lesser extent, spirituality and physical health concerns when compared to the individual modality.

The data suggest that GPC can be effective at reducing clinical symptomatology. In particular, retreat modality may be even more effective than individual sessions of GPC. The retreat modality has additional social and spiritual elements, such as group members supporting and participating in others' healing, that may contribute to the steeper reduction in clinical symptomatology than in individual sessions. In addition to exploring these differences in GPC modality type, future work should compare the effectiveness of GPC with a standard treatment control group as a means to compare the unique benefits of GPC against those of other available treatments.

Other Research Findings and Support

Participants in the project were requested to complete an optional anonymous feedback survey at the end of the retreat or session with their practitioner to aid in program evaluation and to identify participant experiences of the process, which were separate from the quantitative posttesting. Four open-ended questions were asked: (a) What was most beneficial to you about participating in the Gestalt Pastoral Care? How has GPC helped you? (b) What changes (if any) have you noticed in your emotional/and or spiritual state of mind before and after participating in GPC? (c) How has GPC impacted your life already? and (d) How do you hope or expect it will translate into positive life changes in the future? Participants were provided an electronic survey link or hard copy of the survey. Each participant responded to the three questions with multiple statements, which were each analyzed and coded. To capture the complexity and richness of the feedback statements, multiple codes and observations were utilized within one response.

Preliminary qualitative analysis of a sample of electronic feedback forms ($n = 17$) was conducted by an external researcher unaffiliated with GPC by retrieval with program evaluation experience. Forms were reviewed and recurring themes were identified using content analysis strategies within NVivo 12, with several themes often noted within the same response. The primary theme from the feedback was that healing ($n = 24$) was particularly relevant to their GPC experience. Participants reflected on the power of GPC in helping them achieve emotional balance and spiritual well-being and contrasted the work undertaken during GPC to traditional mental health modalities. The importance of a combined strategy to address emotional and spiritual wellness was reflected, or as one participant noted: "It demonstrated—beautifully—that psychological and spiritual well-being aren't mutually exclusive and can—and should—be addressed together." The next theme noted relationship to the Divine ($n = 19$). The participants noted that the GPC experience helped them feel "cared for" and "feel the presence" of their experience of the Divine (e.g., God, Christ, Spirit, Divine), and they noted that this relationship was helpful in addressing their emotional pain and uncertainty. The third theme identified was GPC process ($n = 12$). Participants reflected on the unique strategies and approaches offered by GPC, including "the difficult work" of sessions, the use of inanimate objects as representations for constructs, and how the experience offered an accepting atmosphere and community. Personal reflection was also identified by participants in their feedback, including self-acceptance ($n = 11$) and self-awareness ($n = 8$). Participants noted that their experiences with GPC led to an improved understanding of who they were, raised awareness of when they were distressed, and provided spiritual strategies that could be employed. Participants reported their feedback within the context of mental health. For example, the theme of coping ($n = 8$) emerged as participants spoke about the challenges in their life and strategies to use spiritual practices to manage these challenges. Additionally, feeling emotions ($n = 8$) was mentioned as a result of participation in GPC, as opposed to an inability to express emotions or be aware of current emotional states. Participant's emotional growth ($n = 8$) was also identified as a theme, representing evolution of a person and a sense of personal accomplishment through the process. The theme of hope ($n = 7$) arose to represent the participant's perception that they had knowledge and skills that could support emotional and spiritual wellness and a sense of positivity for the future. Finally, perspective ($n = 7$) was a theme that emerged. Participants noted that how they experienced life and their challenges had evolved as a result of GPC sessions. Word frequency queries identified "life" ($n = 22$), "work" ($n = 17$), "God" ($n = 16$), and "helped" ($n = 15$) as the most frequently occurring words in the evaluations.

CONCLUSION

GPC is a spiritually guided modality that incorporates gestalt work, healing prayer, and spiritual companioning to promote emotional health, personal growth, and overall well-being. The approach requires practitioner training and certification using standardized teaching techniques and attention to ethical helper practices. The modality has been demonstrated to support and improve emotional wellness through the reduction of depression, anxiety, and posttraumatic symptoms across practitioner, location, and individuals, with larger improvements identified in group settings. Additionally, workers, or people going through the process, identify the modality as more helpful than previous traditional psychotherapy and suggest this may be related to the intersectionality of healing both emotionally and spiritually. GPC offers promise as a modality for emotional and spiritual well-being through the integration of spirituality and mental health, from a foundation of faith and embedded within faith communities.

REFERENCES

Beckman, R. J., & Nerheim, S. J. (1985). *Toward a healing ministry: Exploring and implementing a congregational ministry*. Augsburg Publishing House.

Dolliver, R. H. (1981). Some limitations in Perls' Gestalt therapy. *Psychotherapy: Theory, Research, & Practice, 18*(1), 38–45. https://doi.org/10.1037/h0085959

Gestalt Pastoral Care. (2020). *Welcome to Gestalt Pastoral Care*. https://www.gestaltpastoralcare.org/

Gingrich, H. D., & Gingrich, F. C. (Eds.). (2017). *Treating trauma in Christian counseling*. InterVarsity Press.

Harris, K. A., Randolph, B. E., & Gordon, T. D. (2016). What do clients want? Assessing spiritual needs in counseling: A literature review. *Spirituality in Clinical Practice, 3*(4), 250–275. https://doi.org/10.1037/scp0000108

Joyce, P., & Sills, C. (2018). *Skills in Gestalt counselling and psychotherapy*. Sage.

Mann, D. (2010). *Gestalt therapy: 100 key points and techniques*. Routledge. https://doi.org/10.4324/9780203845912

New Revised Standard Version of the Bible. (1989). National Council of Churches. *NRSV Online*. https://www.biblegateway.com/versions/New-Revised-Standard-Version-NRSV-Bible/

Norberg, T. (2006). *Consenting to grace: An introduction to Gestalt Pastoral Care*. Penn House Press.

Norberg, T. (2007). *Gathered together: Creating personal liturgies for healing and transformation*. Upper Room Books.

Norberg, T. (2017). *Gestalt Pastoral Care: What in the world is it?* [Unpublished manuscript]. Gestalt Pastoral Care.

Norberg, T., & Webber, R. D. (1998). *Stretch out your hand: Exploring healing prayer*. Upper Room Books.

O'Rourke, C. (1996). Listening for the sacred: Addressing spiritual issues in the group treatment of adults with mental illness. *Smith College Studies in Social Work, 66*(2), 177–196. https://doi.org/10.1080/00377319609517453

Perls, F. (1976). *The Gestalt approach and eyewitness to therapy*. Bantam.

Perls, F., Hefferline, R., & Goodman, P. (1951). *Excitement and growth in the human personality*. The Gestalt Journal Press.

Perls, F. S. (1969). *Gestalt therapy verbatim*. Real People Press.

Polster, E., & Polster, M. (1974). *Gestalt therapy integrated: Contours of theory and practice* (Vol. 6). Random House.

Richards, P. S., & Bergin, A. E. (Eds.). (2000). *Handbook of psychotherapy and religious diversity*. American Psychological Association. https://doi.org/10.1037/10347-000

Roubal, J., Francesetti, G., & Gecele, M. (2017). Aesthetic diagnosis in gestalt therapy. *Behavioral Sciences, 7*(4), 70. https://doi.org/10.3390/bs7040070

Saad, M., De Medeiros, R., & Mosini, A. (2017). Are we ready for a true biopsychosocial-spiritual model? The many meanings of "spiritual." *Medicine*, 4(4), 1–6.

Thomas, M., Crabtree, M., Janvier, D., Craner, W., Zechner, M., & Bussian, L. B. (2022). Bridging religion and spirituality with gestalt psychotherapy to improve clinical symptoms: Preliminary findings using Gestalt Pastoral Care. *Psychotherapy*. Advance online publication. https://doi.org/10.1037/pst0000425

13

Spiritually Integrated Psychotherapy Among Catholics
A Practice-Based International Investigation

Jeong Yeon Hwang and Wonjin Sim

In the Catholic Church (hereafter, "the Church"), healing ministries for mental and physical infirmities have a long history. The cure of the sick was an essential part of the apostolate of Jesus and his disciples, whose head—Peter—was the first Pope of the Church. Various spiritual traditions in the Church acknowledge the importance of ensuring the psychological and spiritual wellness of the faithful and providing them with diverse means to do so via, for example, sacraments, prayers, accompaniments, and charitable services. Moreover, the spiritual exercises of St. Ignatius (Ignatius of Loyola, 1548/1991) and other meditative and contemplative practices, which focus on the personal spiritual experience of Christians, have been vibrantly alive in the Church and its healing ministries.

From the end of the 19th century, psychology has influenced Catholics in their knowledge of human beings and works for the care of souls. With the foundation of the Institute of Psychology at Pontifical Gregorian University in 1971, Rulla and his colleagues (Healy et al., 2007; Imoda, 1998; Rulla, 1971, 1986) sought to create a sound theoretical foundation for therapeutic practices based on Christian values. For 50 years since its founding, the Institute of Psychology has educated a significant number of priests, religious sisters and brothers, and laity to become psychologists, formators, and educators.

Spiritually integrated psychotherapy among Catholics (SIP-C) refers to the therapeutic works of the counselors and psychotherapists among the alumni of the Institute of Psychology at Pontifical Gregorian University who participated in the interdisciplinary big data project of Scott Richards and his colleagues

---

https://doi.org/10.1037/0000338-013
Handbook of Spiritually Integrated Psychotherapies, P. S. Richards, G. E. K. Allen, and D. K. Judd (Editors)
Copyright © 2023 by the American Psychological Association. All rights reserved.

regarding enhancing practice-based evidence (PBE) for spiritually integrated psychotherapies in 2017 (see Richards et al., 2015). After they studied the Christian view of the human person, psychology, spirituality, personality assessments, and psychotherapies at the Institute of Psychology, they returned to their mission countries and began working as psychotherapists and counselors according to the regulations of respective states.

SIP-C practitioners are living their vocations in the Church. *Vocation* signifies the calling of God to human persons so that God and those who are called may establish an alliance in love and collaborate for justice and peace, which characterize the kingdom of God (Rulla, 1971). This vocation also indicates a specific status of a believer in the faith community, such as a priest, religious sister, and laity in the Catholic Church. According to Rulla (1986), the divine calling is possible because God has created a human being with the psychological and spiritual potential to understand the divine invitation and respond to it. With this perspective, therapists not only achieve treatment outcomes based on psychotherapy approaches but also facilitate the person's growth and mature interactions with God.

The majority of SIP-C clients consist of priests, religious, and laity who have a desire to integrate psychological and spiritual dimensions in the process of realizing Christian values (see Sebastian, 2014). For them, SIP-C practitioners can be a significant help because they can understand well the particular context of the priesthood and religious life. Typical issues include struggles in human relationships with the authority figures and members of religious communities, psychosexual and affective development, self-esteem and identity, personality disorders, posttraumatic stress disorder, childhood trauma, and spiritual discernment and growth (Sim et al., 2021; see also Shafranske, 2000). They attempt to guide clients to be responsible for the challenges in their personal vocational journey and overcome self-centered tendencies and interests for the commitment to the practice of religious and spiritual virtues (Healy et al., 2007; Rulla, 1986). SIP-C is not linked to any particular psychotherapy approach, but the theoretical orientations which the therapists frequently use are psychoanalysis, cognitive behavior therapy, and interpersonal psychotherapy (Sim & Hwang, 2020).

In this chapter, we describe the theological and psychological rationales as well as treatment process and guidelines of SIP-C, illustrate specific spiritual interventions and effects with a case example, and discuss some of the most important findings from our recent international PBE research (Sim et al., 2021). The strategies and techniques of SIP-C are offered throughout this chapter for current and future counselors and psychotherapists so they may gain insights into effective spiritual interventions and apply those interventions with clients from diverse parts of the world.

DESCRIPTION OF THE TREATMENT APPROACH

In this section, we present a synthetic description of the theoretical foundations, treatment guidelines, assessment methods, and intervention strategies of SIP-C. Particularly, we provide therapeutic insights into a Christian perspective on human beings, cultural diversity issues, and traditional religious practices among SIP-C practitioners.

Theoretical and Theological Foundations of the Approach

The vision of humans in SIP-C can be explained with three theoretical concepts: (a) self-transcendence, (b) the basic dialectic of human life, and (c) attitudes toward values. First, self-transcendence implies that persons go beyond the boundaries of experience, understanding, judgment, and decision to realize moral and religious values and be in love with God (Lonergan, 1973; Rulla, 1986). This operation of self-transcendence is present in all human conscious and intentional endeavors.

Second, the dialectic between the self as transcending and the self as transcended is ontologically inherent in a human being (Healy et al., 2007; Lonergan, 1973). It represents a tension between two motivational forces in the human. Whereas the self as transcended tends to seek the subjective satisfaction of its needs, the self as transcending has conscious intentionality to go beyond the current security or limitations of the self to respond to the call of God and achieve theocentric values, such as faith, hope, and love. Although these two forces can maintain a healthy tension for growth, they may become antagonistic (Healy, 2000). Particularly when the self as transcended resists against the realization of religious ideals, one's own potential for self-transcendence cannot be realized.

Third, the maturity of Christians depends on their attitudes toward varied values (Healy et al., 2007; Rulla, 1986). People seek natural values (e.g., comfort, wealth, power) while also pursuing divine values (e.g., justice, faith, charity). *Natural values* tend to be instrumental and stimulate secular and self-centered desires, whereas *divine values* are morally honorable and promote religious and self-transcendent motivations. In other words, the natural values are important for individuals on a relatively superficial level, whereas the divine values are related to the ultimate purposes of human life. When there is no order between different values, people tend to disguise the pursuit of secular values with the external representation of moral and religious values. For example, one may help the needy to be praised by them, or one may harshly criticize and dominate others in the name of prophetic authenticity (Costello, 2002). The priests and religious may not faithfully live up to their promises of commitment but reveal self-centered attitudes and egoistic behaviors in their relationships and works, particularly when they are not aware of deep-seated ambivalent tendencies toward values (see Rulla, 1986). SIP-C focuses on the inherent, complex tension of human beings with respect to natural and divine values.

Process and Ethical Guidelines for the Approach

By its nature, SIP-C differs from spiritual direction. The primary emphasis of SIP-C remains on the application of psychological and spiritual interventions for the treatment of the cognitive, emotional, motivational, and behavioral issues that impede and challenge the psychological and spiritual growth of clients (see Imoda, 1998; Sebastian, 2014). On the other hand, spiritual direction aims at helping believers develop their personal relationships with the Divine by paying attention to the experience of being in love with God in prayer, liturgy, reflection, mediation, and other moments of religious inspiration (Barry & Connolly, 1982). Therefore, it is necessary for therapists to clearly indicate the nature of SIP-C to clients and not engage in the usual pattern of spiritual direction, even if they are confident in this type of accompaniment as well.

It is essential for Catholic therapists to respect Christian values and Church teachings as well as appreciate the spiritual experiences of clients (Plante, 2008; Shafranske, 2000). This does not mean imposing the values and commandments of the Church on clients but, rather, understanding the positive roles of the values and teachings in the life of the faithful. When clients find it difficult to fulfill the ideals of the Church, therapists—without devaluing these ideals based on personal opinions—can explore the pain of clients, sympathize with them, and help them experience the mercy of God. Moreover, it is crucial to respect and appreciate the devotional practices and mystical experiences of clients as long as they are consistent with Church teachings and traditions. Similarly, clinicians should not pathologize any particular devotions or mystical experiences of clients (Richards & Bergin, 2000) but, instead, help them reflect on the significance of their religious practices in their psychosocial and spiritual life.

Cultural Diversity Considerations Among Catholics

Compared with countries in Europe and North America, people in Asia, Africa, and Latin America are less likely to seek professional psychological help because of an unfamiliarity with psychotherapy, fear of stigmatization, and insufficient mental health services as a result of societal underdevelopment (Kao et al., 2016; Kim & Omizo, 2003; Koç & Kafa, 2019; Nagai, 2015). In this context, the presence of priests and religious people with qualifications for psychotherapy and counseling denotes some important points. In these cultural settings, local people tend to seek help and support from the authority figures of a religious community (Richards & Bergin, 2005). When believers trust in the priests and nuns of their faith communities, they tend to present their psychological and relational issues without fear of stigma and obtain help in both spiritual and psychological dimensions. Moreover, quite a few believers in non-Western cultures attribute psychological difficulties to a spiritual phenomenon and seek traditional religious practices, such as rituals and prayers in the community (Girma et al., 2013; Hechanova et al., 2018; Koschorke et al., 2017; Shibre et al., 2001). Based on people's respect for religious figures and traditions of spiritual healing in their communities, local Catholics may feel relatively free in approaching SIP-C practitioners who are priests and religious.

From interviews with Catholic psychotherapists and counselors, we present some relevant ideas about the characteristics of Catholic clients, by continents (J. F. Nnantamu et al., personal communication, September, 6, 2020). In Latin

America, most clients dedicate themselves to the process of healing and growth via SIP-C. The popular religiosity and Catholic culture in their families and communities tend to help them open toward the spiritual dimension of self-transcendence. However, many individuals frequently stay with the external features of problems without reflecting on the roots of issues. In Africa, quite a few clients seek help from psychologists when they find no other remedies to their problems. In East Africa (e.g., Kenya, Uganda), clients often consider therapists as seniors to be respected and have difficulties with interventions, such as free association, because they expect some instructions from the therapists. They typically follow spiritual interventions willingly but sometimes become stuck with magical beliefs. Among Asian clients, the repression of emotions tends to be strongly present. Many Asians do not express both negative and positive emotions openly with others because they do not wish to burden or provoke others. Although many Asians tend to be submissive to their superiors and leaders of religious communities, their apparent and immediate acceptance of orders from authority figures can create internal conflicts, particularly when they feel that they should not express their contrasting ideas and negative sentiments regarding these orders. Among Europeans, there is a substantial openness toward psychotherapy and counseling. They tend to frankly express their emotions and share their ideas during sessions. In terms of value system, many young European clients show resistance to traditional religious values without having healthy alternatives to them.

Relationship Establishment and Collaboration Guidelines

Plante (2003) suggested that Catholics tend to feel comfortable with Catholic therapists because they share the faith and culture of the Church. This tendency can be even more strong among Catholic priests and religious sisters and brothers. For them, SIP-C practitioners, most of whom are also priests and religious, can serve as good guides and companions for their healing and growth because they can understand the uniqueness of their vocations, including celibacy, and human difficulties in the vow of obedience to their bishops and superiors. In addition, the lay Catholics among the SIP-C therapists are precious resources because some priests, religious sisters and brothers, and also laity prefer lay practitioners to the clergy and religious. In general, SIP-C therapists do not find serious difficulties in rapport-building with clients. These clients tend to be cooperative and open to the suggestions of therapists, including referrals to psychiatrists for psychotropic medications (Richards & Bergin, 2000, p. 478).

The collaboration between practitioners and the superiors and spiritual directors of clients is essential throughout the entire SIP-C process. Quite a few Catholic clients begin the therapy process on the recommendation of spiritual directors (and with the permission and/or invitation of their superiors, especially in the case of clients who are religious sisters and brothers or seminarians). Nevertheless, it is critical that psychotherapists, superiors, and spiritual directors accompany and guide the clients in distinctive manners. Psychologists should perform therapeutic interventions according to their specialties with respect for the unique roles of their collaborators (Breuninger et al., 2014). In the spirit of collaboration, psychotherapists should avoid intentionally criticizing or blaming the superiors or pastors of their clients except in cases in which abuses are clearly to be attributed to those leaders (see Richards & Bergin, 1997). In many cases, clients have ambivalent feelings toward their superiors or pastors and create internal and external tensions with them. The biased attitudes of therapists do not help the clients reflect on their emotional reactions toward their superiors. It is important for SIP-C therapists to collaborate with psychiatrists who understand the importance of spirituality for mental health.

Assessment Guidelines and Recommendations

The personality assessment of SIP-C typically comprises objective and projective tests, interviews, and feedback. The Minnesota Multiphasic Personality Inventory–2 (MMPI-2; Butcher et al., 1989) is most commonly used as an objective tool (see Isacco & Plante, 2020), and the Rorschach Inkblot Test (Rorschach, 1921), Rotter Incomplete Sentences Blank (Rotter, 1950), and Thematic Apperception Test (TAT; Murray, 1943) are generally adopted as projective methods by SIP-C practitioners (see McGlone et al., 2010). During the interviews, SIP-C practitioners explore the client's family background, religious background (sacraments received—e.g., Baptism, Confirmation), educational background, social relationships (e.g., friends, authority figures in school and church), mental and physical health, life history, sexual development, religious activities, spiritual experience, vocation discernment, social services, church ministries, prayer life, psychosocial difficulties, and so forth (see Shafranske, 2000). They frequently provide feedback to clients in the form of a verbal report to explain the main results of the assessment and relate them to the future steps of clients for personal growth.

It is recommended to have three sessions for this assessment. The first session may include an interview with general questions about client's problems and issues plus two projective tests, such as Rotter Incomplete Sentences Blank (Rotter, 1950) and TAT (Murray, 1943). Clients can take the objective tests after the first session. The second session consists of the interview with additional questions and the Rorschach test (Rorschach, 1921). The third session is planned to provide feedback. It is important to explain the process of assessment before or during a formal intake. When clients know that they have an opportunity to hear the psychologist's feedback, they tend to be motivated and focused.

Spiritual Intervention Strategies and Techniques

Most believers in the presence and power of the Divine understand that prayer can help them cope with stress and feel the love of God and the power of healing (Richards & Bergin, 2005). For SIP-C, most therapists offer prayers for their clients and invite them to pray for their healing and growth during sessions (Sim et al., 2021). Quite a few therapists engage in meditation or reflection before or after the session to be aware of the presence of God and the guidance of the Holy Spirit. Above all, prayer is invaluable because of the human need for the grace of God for spiritual growth and healing. Although humans possess a potential for self-transcendence toward divine values, they experience the resistances of the actual self or ego against the realization of religious ideals. They simply cannot actualize their potential without the grace of God (Lonergan, 1973). Both therapists and clients should believe in the power of divine grace and acknowledge that this grace is stronger than any psychological disorders and temptations (May, 1988).

Many researchers have suggested that clients who suffer from depression, anxiety, and other types of emotional problems benefit psychologically and spiritually from prayer practices (Boelens et al., 2012; Johnson, 2018; Richards & Bergin, 2005; South & McDowell, 2018). Studies of people with high levels of stress have reported that prayer reduces the level of emotional exhaustion among Catholic teachers (Chirico et al., 2020) and the danger of burnout among Christian pastors (Chandler, 2010). Prayer tends to have positive effects on psychological and spiritual well-being, particularly when it is less self-centered and more centered on God (Whittington & Scher, 2010).

Catholics believe that God communicates divine grace to a believer through seven sacraments: (a) Baptism, (b) Confirmation, (c) Eucharist, (d) Penance, (e) Anointing of the Sick, (f) Matrimony, and (g) Holy Orders. Particularly, Eucharist (i.e., Mass) and Penance (i.e., the Sacrament of Reconciliation or Confession) are two main practices of the faithful in ordinary life. Regular Mass attendance is associated with a lower level of psychological distress (Ellison et al., 2001). The practice of the Sacrament of Penance tends to diminish aggression, fear, and guilt (Martinez-Pilkington, 2007; Vitz & Mango, 1997). Because SIP-C therapists acknowledge the positive effects of these sacraments for their clients, they try to help them to participate in the sacraments with an appropriate attitude. During the session of SIP-C, therapists can guide clients to examine their intrinsic and extrinsic motivations for frequenting the sacraments and to discern the grace of God that they need for healing and growth. By reflecting on the personal experiences of the sacraments, clients can sense their close connections to the Divine and integrate the spiritual and psychological benefits of sacraments in their life.

Because SIP-C practitioners understand the importance of personal encounters between God and clients in prayer, it is essential for them to identify the images of God in the mind of clients. The image of a loving and merciful God has been known to be related to the positive effects of spiritual interventions (Currier et al., 2021; see Dickie et al., 1997). When therapists examine the influence of the divine image on clients, they can analyze the self-image of clients in connection with the divine image. A negative image of God tends to be associated with a negative image of self (Francis et al., 2001). Thus, the correction of the false divine image, such as a merciless punisher or disinterested father—which are contrary to the faith of the Church—can help the transformation of a negative self-image (e.g., unforgivable sinner, unloved child). In this process, people tend to have multiple images of God as the result of varied psychological and spiritual experiences (Davis et al., 2013). Therapists may help clients discern what divine images are true and authentic, based on the Scriptures and the Church's teachings; analyze how the inauthentic and negative images of God have been formed; and examine whether they are connected to the psychological wounds of clients. This discernment and analysis of the images of God may help clients find a true and positive self-image, confirm divine self-worth, and raise self-esteem (Benson & Spilka, 1973; Lawrence, 1997; see Gallagher, 2005).

CASE STUDY ILLUSTRATING TREATMENT PROCESSES AND INTERVENTIONS

The following case exemplifies the main treatment processes and interventions of SIP-C. To protect privacy, some client and counselor information has been fabricated.

Therapist, Client, and Setting

The counselor, Peter Ngo, a Vietnamese Catholic priest in his mid-50s, abides and works in an international seminary in Manila, the Philippines. He obtained a licentiate (i.e., equivalent to a master's degree) in psychology and completed a 2-year internship at the Institute of Psychology at Pontifical Gregorian University in Rome, Italy. In 2012, he began working as a counselor and spiritual director for the international seminary. Six years later, he joined the SIP-C research project.

The client, Andy, is a 32-year-old Vietnamese priest. He was ordained a priest 4 years earlier, had worked at a parish for 1 year, and then came to the Philippines to take theology courses for a licentiate. He was introduced to Father Ngo for professional help by his former spiritual director. Although it was difficult for the therapist to accept a new client given his tight schedule, he decided to have seven sessions with Andy to help him cope with his immediate stress and prepare him to undertake a long-term SIP-C. The sessions took place at his office at the international seminary.

Client History, Assessment, and Diagnosis

Andy is the first child with a younger sister from a low middle-class family in a small city. When he was 9 years old, his parents physically separated because of financial issues. Thereafter, he was raised by his mother. Because she had to work all day long, he took care of his sister at home and felt lonely and sometimes desperate.

After he entered the seminary, his life and study went well except during vacations. When he stayed in a parish during the vacations, the priest of that parish imposed many regulations on Andy, such as curfew and etiquette. He felt anxiety and inadequacy in front of the priest. After his priestly ordination, he worked as an assistant to another priest and began to enjoy his ministries at a parish. Celebrating sacraments and building friendly relationships with parishioners were the main sources of his joy. Then, he was sent abroad to study theology. Andy began to face general challenges, such as learning a foreign language and adapting himself to a new culture, and the psychological difficulties and spiritual confusion because of unwanted, intrusive thoughts about the evil rituals and messages of a video that he had watched in the past.

Andy was diagnosed with obsessive–compulsive disorder. At the initial interview, the two characteristics of obsessions by the *Diagnostic and Statistical Manual of Mental Disorders* (5th ed. [*DSM-5*]; American Psychiatric Association, 2013)—namely, anxiety-provoking unwanted intrusive thoughts/images and attempts to suppress them—were confirmed. Sometimes his behaviors became compulsive—for example, he often anxiously offered prayers on his knees in his bedroom or chapel late at night for an extended period when he was unable to sleep because of persistent malicious thoughts. Nevertheless, his capacity for studying was not seriously impaired. Along with this initial assessment, Father Ngo referred him to his colleague for a personality assessment of SIP-C with interviews, MMPI-2 (Butcher et al., 1989), TAT (Murray, 1943), and other tools. Eventually, obsessive–compulsive disorder was confirmed.

Treatment Process and Outcomes

At the first session with Father Ngo, Andy evaluated his pain as 8 on a scale ranging from 1 (*not at all anxious*) to 10 (*extremely anxious*). He stated that it had been 10 before he contacted his former spiritual director for help. At the seventh session, the level of pain was indicated as 3. For the reduction of emotional distress, Andy was invited to express the emotions and thoughts that he had repressed for a long time. At the second session, he was able to express his pain, self-pity, and anxiety with tears. In terms of spiritual issues, he initially focused exclusively on his problems, such as sinfulness and helplessness. Thus, Father Ngo invited him to recall some precious events in his vocational journey. Andy shared several spiritual experiences in the past—for example, when he was 17 years old, he was hit by a truck but was not seriously hurt. At that time, he felt the protection of God. Father Ngo intervened with a question: "Do you believe that God who protected you at that incident is still with you?" Andy replied, "Yes." Then, Father Ngo asked how Andy had felt when he sensed the presence of God. Andy reported emotional changes, saying that he felt warm and bright. Moreover, through the examination of the quality of his constant prayers, Andy noticed that he frequently made petitions to God for healing but doubted if God could cure or protect him. He was invited to seek the grace of God to believe firmly in the healing power of God as well.

Guilt and anxiety were two negative feelings that were related to Andy's false beliefs about sins and obsessions. He had guilt feelings not because he committed sins in his words and behaviors but because he had in his mind unwanted intrusive thoughts about the satanic images and messages of a video clip on the internet that he had watched in the past. Andy thought that he committed sins because he had those unwanted thoughts. Father Ngo explained that intrusive thoughts themselves should not be judged as a sin, but the intentional dwelling on the thoughts for pleasure could be problematic (Ignatius of Loyola, 1548/1991). He said that this clarification became a significant relief at the third session.

Andy's anxiety was related to his concerns that he might harm others because of the presence of evil thoughts in his mind. His insight into the nature of the intrusive thoughts was poor because he believed that they could contaminate him as well as others (see American Psychiatric Association, 2013). Initially, he did not want to explain the contents of his obsessions because his sharing might harm his therapist, Father Ngo. In the fourth session, a corrective emotional experience occurred. He was able to share the contents of the video, such as evil rituals and curses, and found that no one was damaged. He was relaxed and pleased, observing that nothing terrible happened. His insight about his obsessions became fairly good.

In addition, Andy worked to understand the roots of these satanic images by reflecting on his relationships in the past throughout the sessions. In his free association at the fourth session, he found that his mother and parish priest during the vacations of seminary education might be related to the horrifying images. He began to share his difficulties in his relationships with them, particularly their harsh treatments. In the following session, he also acknowledged his immature thoughts with respect to his self-image. He proudly considered himself to be a light in front of others in shadow. This belief was in contrast to his negative self-image that the intrusive thoughts provoked. He thought that both of them were not his true self-image. In his endeavor to find his authentic image, he recalled a dream that he had on the feast of the Assumption of the Virgin Mary some years ago. In that dream, he was praying together with Mother Mary. He looked pure without guile. He intuitively felt that that image was his genuine self-image. He believed that there is some part or self in him that cannot be defiled by either sinful ideas or immature attitudes. This insight brought him confidence and strength.

The intrusion of evil thoughts did not disappear completely. Before he fell into sleep, Andy suffered from them. However, he was relatively free from the intrusive thoughts during the period of exams because his obsessions tended to weaken when he focused on his studies. At the seventh session, Andy shared that he had gained insight into his relationship with God in that he came to realize that God might desire his healing more earnestly than he did. With this insight, he expressed his wish to cooperate with God and know the meaning of his suffering in his vocational journey.

Therapist Commentary

Many priests and religious sisters and brothers in the Catholic Church suffer from perfectionism (see Flett et al., 2014). In a way, they are educated to be undefiled and unblemished in their thoughts, words, and actions. The search for this high level of self-discipline can create psychological and spiritual difficulties, including a false sense of guilt, a rigidity of thought and behavior, and social anxiety. Andy, in this case, was a sincere and intelligent priest but suffered seriously from his imperfect and defiled self-image. Thus, personal and spiritual growth should be differentiated from perfectionism and pursued with an acceptance of the dialectic nature of a human person (e.g., holy and secular, altruistic and egoistic) and a need for divine grace (Lonergan, 1973; Rulla, 1986).

The discernment of spirits according to the spiritual exercises of St. Ignatius (Ignatius of Loyola, 1548/1991; Plante, 2017) can be a powerful tool for Christian practitioners. The spiritual discernment signifies that Christians prudently reflect and deliberate on what brings them happiness and serenity versus what brings them discouragement and instability, what makes them come close to God versus what makes them avoid God, and what helps them recognize an authentic divine image and self-image versus what leads them to distort the divine image and self-image (see Barry & Connolly, 1982; Gallagher, 2005; Plante, 2020). By being attentive to varied thoughts, images, and sentiments, clients can determine the positive internal movements that lead them to feel serenity, think clearly, and make good decisions. In the case of Andy, he was able to discern sins from obsessions with the help of Father Ngo. This ability made a difference in his sense of guilt. Similarly, practitioners can learn the discernment of good and evil movements in the human psyche and help their clients to cope with spiritual distress.

RESEARCH FINDINGS AND SUPPORT

The study by the authors of this chapter and colleagues (Sim et al., 2021) examined the process and outcome of SIP-C in Asia, Africa, Latin America, and Europe. Whereas SIP-C therapists and clients are culturally and geographically diverse, they demonstrate a unity as one Church under the Pontificate in that they share traditional values on the care of souls and have interests in integration between theology and psychology (Healy et al., 2007; Kugelmann, 2011; Plante, 2015; Rulla, 1986). In this international context, we investigated the types of spiritual interventions across different continents and the impact of spiritual interventions on therapy outcomes.

Our team used a PBE research design (Barkham et al., 2010; Castonguay et al., 2013) that allows less intrusive investigation and is more similar to real-life practice settings than randomized controlled trials. Consistent with PBE, SIP-C practitioners provided therapy as usual and conducted presession measures by clients—the Clinically Adaptive Multidimensional Outcome Survey (CAMOS; P. W. Sanders et al., 2018; see also Richards et al., 2015) and the Clinical Outcomes in Routine Evaluation (CORE-10; Barkham et al., 2010)—and a postsession measure by therapists, the Clinically Adaptive Therapist Session Checklist (CA-TSC; Richards et al., 2014). Thirty-four therapists

(18, cisgender male; 16, cisgender female; age: $M = 47.63$ years, $SD = 8.28$ years; all were Catholic priests or religious sisters except three laypersons) and 359 clients (181, cisgender male; 145, cisgender female; 1, transgender; 32, unknown; age: $M = 32.42$ years, $SD = 9.90$ years; 355, Christian; 4, Hindu) participated in the study. The treatment sites were located in 13 countries (i.e., Kenya, Uganda, India, Myanmar, South Korea, the Philippines, Vietnam, Columbia, Mexico, Belorussia, Czech Republic, Italy, and Malta).

In terms of types of spiritual interventions, SIP-C therapists most frequently used "encouraging personal prayer," "affirming trusting God," and "encouraging listening to the heart" when we examined them as a whole without distinction of countries. These results are similar to the meta-analytic review of Smith et al. (2007) and empirical studies in the United States (Currier et al., 2021; P. W. Sanders et al., 2015). Considering that our study included participants outside the United States, we suggest that these spiritual interventions tend to be commonly adopted across cultures (i.e., in and outside of the United States).

Regarding cultural differences in spiritual intervention uses, "discussing hope" was one of the most frequently used spiritual interventions in Asia and Africa but not in Europe and Latin America. We may attribute this difference to the theological perspective and demographic changes in Asia and Africa. Many people in Asia and Africa suffer from poverty and violence, and religion has empowered the believers and helped them cope with harsh realities (Agbiji & Swart, 2015; Mackie, 1989). Moreover, the future of the Church is promising because the Catholic population has grown vigorously in many countries in Africa and Asia in recent years (Center for Applied Research in the Apostolate, 2015). Hence, the importance of and ground for hope seem to be present among Catholics in Asia and Africa. In addition, "discussing self-control" was one of the most frequently used spiritual interventions only in Asia, which could be explained by Asian culture's emphasis on self-control and emotional restraint (Ford & Mauss, 2015; Miyamoto et al., 2014).

In contrast to Asia and Africa, "listening to spiritual issues" was one of the frequently used interventions in Latin American and Europe. Given that Christianity has a long history in Europe and Latin America, discussion about spiritual issues seems to have become an integral part of these cultures. Instead, many believers in Asia and Africa are likely to consider spirituality as a value to learn and accept from seniors and teachers in the Church, including SIP-C practitioners (J. F. Nnantamu et al., personal communication, September 6, 2020). In Latin America, however, "spiritual confrontation" and "spiritual self-disclosure" were most frequently used when compared with other continents. In this continent, because of the introduction of Christianity during colonization, some Catholics tend to be passive and subservient in their religious and spiritual practices, and therapists may confront this passive tendency, share their spiritual practice, and encourage clients to develop healthy attitudes (see Gill, 1994; T. G. Sanders, 1970).

In terms of therapeutic effects, the clients who participated in SIP-C showed a significant decrease in spiritual and nonspiritual distress, following a log-linear pattern over the course of therapy (i.e., steeper decrease earlier that became more flattened as sessions went on). Each log-session unit change was associated with .99 point decrease of spiritual distress ($p = .004$) and 4.04 point decrease of nonspiritual distress ($p = .007$) in CAMOS (P. W. Sanders et al., 2018), and 1.73 point decrease in CORE-10 (Barkham et al., 2010; $p = .025$). In addition, a moderate frequency of spiritual interventions in a session (i.e., close to the grand mean, which was 5.85 interventions per session) was associated with a higher decline in nonspiritual distress in both CAMOS and CORE-10 when compared with a lower number of spiritual interventions. However, the two measures revealed contrasting features regarding the relationship between higher and moderate frequencies of spiritual interventions. CAMOS indicated that a moderate number of spiritual interventions was more effective than a higher number, whereas for CORE-10, a higher number was associated with a sharper decline of psychological distress when compared with a moderate number of spiritual interventions.

CONCLUSION

We encourage Catholic practitioners to adopt spiritual interventions in their treatment for Catholic clients with psychological and spiritual difficulties. Ordinary spiritual practices, such as prayer and spiritual conversations, can help them to lower the level of both psychological and spiritual distress.

In our study, we were not able to fully incorporate the particular practices of Catholics, such as devotions to the Immaculate Heart of Mary and novenas (i.e., offering specific prayers with special intentions for 9 successive days or weeks). Future studies need to identify uniquely Catholic devotions to study their effects on psychological and spiritual distress and well-being as well as to create a Catholic version of the CA-TSC (Richards et al., 2014). Moreover, we suggest that qualitative investigations on cultural adaptations of the SIP-C with international samples would help obtain a deeper understanding of the process and effect of a spiritual intervention.

REFERENCES

Agbiji, O. M., & Swart, I. (2015). Religion and social transformation in Africa: A critical and appreciative perspective. *Scriptura, 114,* 1–20. https://www.scielo.org.za/scielo.php?script=sci_arttext&pid=S2305-445X2015000100010&lng=en&tlng=en

American Psychiatric Association. (2013). *Diagnostic and statistical manual of mental disorders* (5th ed.). https://doi.org/10.1176/appi.books.9780890425596

Barkham, M., Mellor-Clark, J., Connell, J., Evans, C., Evans, R., & Margison, F. (2010). Clinical Outcomes in Routine Evaluation (CORE)—The CORE measures and system: Measuring, monitoring and managing quality evaluation in the psychological therapies. In M. Barkham, G. E. Hardy, & J. Mellor-Clark (Eds.), *Developing and delivering practice-based evidence: A guide for the psychological therapies* (pp. 175–219). Wiley-Blackwell. https://doi.org/10.1002/9780470687994.ch8

Barry, W. A., & Connolly, W. J. (1982). *The practice of spiritual direction.* Harper & Row.

Benson, P., & Spilka, B. (1973). God image as a function of self-esteem and locus of control. *Journal for the Scientific Study of Religion, 12*(3), 297–310. https://doi.org/10.2307/1384430

Boelens, P. A., Reeves, R. R., Replogle, W. H., & Koenig, H. G. (2012). The effect of prayer on depression and anxiety: Maintenance of positive influence one year after prayer intervention. *International Journal of Psychiatry in Medicine, 43*(1), 85–98. https://doi.org/10.2190/PM.43.1.f

Breuninger, M., Dolan, S. L., Padilla, J. I., & Stanford, M. S. (2014). Psychologists and clergy working together: A collaborative treatment approach for religious clients. *Journal of Spirituality in Mental Health, 16*(3), 149–170. https://doi.org/10.1080/19349637.2014.925359

Butcher, J. N., Dahlstrom, W. G., Graham, J. R., Tellegen, A., & Kaemmer, B. (1989). *Manual for administration and scoring. Minnesota Multiphasic Personality Inventory–2: MMPI-2.* University of Minnesota Press.

Castonguay, L., Barkham, M., Lutz, W., & McAleavey, A. (2013). Practice oriented research: Approaches and applications. In M. J. Lambert (Ed.), *Bergin and Garfield's handbook of psychotherapy and behavior change* (6th ed., pp. 85–133). John Wiley & Sons.

Center for Applied Research in the Apostolate. (2015, June 4). *Global Catholicism: Trends & forecasts* [Report]. https://cara.georgetown.edu/staff/webpages/Global%20Catholicism%20Release.pdf

Chandler, D. J. (2010). The impact of pastors' spiritual practices on burnout. *Journal of Pastoral Care & Counseling, 64*(2), 1–9. https://doi.org/10.1177/154230501006400206

Chirico, F., Sharma, M., Zaffina, S., & Magnavita, N. (2020). Spirituality and prayer on teacher stress and burnout in an Italian Cohort: A pilot, before–after controlled study. *Frontiers in Psychology, 10*, Article 2933. https://doi.org/10.3389/fpsyg.2019.02933

Costello, T. (2002). *Forming a priestly identity: Anthropology of priestly formation in the documents of the VIII synod of bishops and the apostolic exhortation* Pastores Dabo Vobis. Editrice Pontificia Universita Gregoriana.

Currier, J. M., McDermott, R. C., Stevens, L. T., Isaak, S. L., Davis, E. B., Hollingsworth, W. L., Archer, G. D., & Stefurak, T. (2021). A practice-based evidence investigation of God representations in spiritually integrated psychotherapies. *Journal of Clinical Psychology, 77*(4), 1018–1033. https://doi.org/10.1002/jclp.23075

Davis, E. B., Moriarty, G. L., & Mauch, J. C. (2013). God images and God concepts: Definitions, development, and dynamics. *Psychology of Religion and Spirituality, 5*(1), 51–60. https://doi.org/10.1037/a0029289

Dickie, J. R., Eshleman, A. K., Merasco, D. M., Shepard, A., Wilt, M. V., & Johnson, M. (1997). Parent–child relationships and children's images of God. *Journal for the Scientific Study of Religion, 36*(1), 25–43. https://doi.org/10.2307/1387880

Ellison, C. G., Boardman, J. D., Williams, D. R., & Jackson, J. S. (2001). Religious involvement, stress, and mental health: Findings from the 1995 Detroit Area Study. *Social Forces, 80*(1), 215–249. https://doi.org/10.1353/sof.2001.0063

Flett, G. L., Hewitt, P. L., & Heisel, M. J. (2014). The destructiveness of perfectionism revisited: Implications for the assessment of suicide risk and the prevention of suicide. *Review of General Psychology, 18*(3), 156–172. https://doi.org/10.1037/gpr0000011

Ford, B. Q., & Mauss, I. B. (2015). Culture and emotion regulation. *Current Opinion in Psychology, 3*, 1–5. https://doi.org/10.1016/j.copsyc.2014.12.004

Francis, L. J., Gibson, H. M., & Robbins, M. (2001). God images and self-worth among adolescents in Scotland. *Mental Health, Religion & Culture, 4*(2), 103–108. https://doi.org/10.1080/13674670126955

Gallagher, T. M. (2005). *The discernment of spirits: An Ignatian guide for everyday living*. The Crossroad Publishing Company.

Gill, A. J. (1994). Rendering unto Caesar? Religious competition and Catholic political strategy in Latin America, 1962–79. *American Journal of Political Science, 38*(2), 403–425. https://doi.org/10.2307/2111410

Girma, E., Tesfaye, M., Froeschl, G., Möller-Leimkühler, A. M., Müller, N., & Dehning, S. (2013). Public stigma against people with mental illness in the Gilgel Gibe Field Research Center (GGFRC) in Southwest Ethiopia. *PLOS ONE, 8*(12), Article e82116. https://doi.org/10.1371/journal.pone.0082116

Healy, T. (2000). The challenge of self-transcendence. In F. Imoda (Ed.), *A journey to freedom: An interdisciplinary approach to the anthropology of formation* (pp. 70–115). Peeters.

Healy, T., Kiely, B., & Versaldi, G. (2007). Origins and bases of a study of the human person. In A. Manenti, S. Guarinelli, & H. Zollner (Eds.), *Formation and the person: Essays in theory and practice* (pp. 8–30). Peeters.

Hechanova, M. R. M., Alianan, A. S., Calleja, M. T., Melgar, I. E., Acosta, A., Villasanta, A., Bunagan, K., Yusay, C., Ang, A., Flores, J., Canoy, N., Espina, E., Gomez, G. A., Hinckley, E. S., Tuliao, A. P., & Cue, M. P. (2018). The development of a community-based drug intervention for Filipino drug users. *Journal of Pacific Rim Psychology, 12*, Article e12. https://doi.org/10.1017/prp.2017.23

Ignatius of Loyola. (1991). *The spiritual exercises of Saint Ignatius: A translation and commentary* (G. E. Ganss, Trans.). Loyola University Press. (Original work published 1548)

Imoda, F. (1998). *Human development: Psychology and mystery*. Peeters.

Isacco, A., & Plante, T. G. (2020). Introduction to a special issue on addressing Catholic clergy issues in psychological research and practice. *Spirituality in Clinical Practice, 7*(4), 215–219. https://doi.org/10.1037/scp0000241

Johnson, K. A. (2018). Prayer: A helpful aid in recovery from depression. *Journal of Religion and Health, 57*(6), 2290–2300. https://doi.org/10.1007/s10943-018-0564-8

Kao, Y.-C., Lien, Y.-J., Chang, H.-A., Wang, S.-C., Tzeng, N.-S., & Loh, C.-H. (2016). Evidence for the indirect effects of perceived public stigma on psychosocial outcomes: The mediating role of self-stigma. *Psychiatry Research, 240*, 187–195. https://doi.org/10.1016/j.psychres.2016.04.030

Kim, B. S. K., & Omizo, M. M. (2003). Asian cultural values, attitudes toward seeking professional psychological help, and willingness to see a counselor. *The Counseling Psychologist, 31*(3), 343–361. https://doi.org/10.1177/0011000003031003008

Koç, V., & Kafa, G. (2019). Cross-cultural research on psychotherapy: The need for a change. *Journal of Cross-Cultural Psychology, 50*(1), 100–115. https://doi.org/10.1177/0022022118806577

Koschorke, M., Evans-Lacko, S., Sartorius, N., & Thornicroft, G. (2017). Stigma in different cultures. In W. Gaebel, W. Rössler, & N. Sartorius (Eds.), *The stigma of mental illness—End of the story?* (pp. 67–82). Springer International Publishing. https://doi.org/10.1007/978-3-319-27839-1_4

Kugelmann, R. (2011). *Psychology and Catholicism: Contested boundaries*. Cambridge University Press. https://doi.org/10.1017/CBO9780511975486

Lawrence, R. T. (1997). Measuring the image of God: The God image inventory and the God image scales. *Journal of Psychology and Theology, 25*(2), 214–226. https://doi.org/10.1177/009164719702500206

Lonergan, B. J. F. (1973). *Method in theology*. Darton, Longman & Tood.

Mackie, S. G. (1989). God's people in Asia: A key concept in Asian theology. *Scottish Journal of Theology, 42*(2), 215–240. https://doi.org/10.1017/S0036930600056453

Martinez-Pilkington, A. (2007). Shame and guilt: The psychology of sacramental confession. *The Humanistic Psychologist, 35*(2), 203–218. https://doi.org/10.1080/08873260701274272

May, G. G. (1988). *Addiction and grace*. Harper & Row.

McGlone, G. J., Ortiz, F. A., & Karney, R. J. (2010). A survey study of psychological assessment practices in the screening and admission process of candidates to the priesthood in the U.S. Catholic church. *Professional Psychology: Research and Practice, 41*(6), 526–532. https://doi.org/10.1037/a0021546

Miyamoto, Y., Ma, X., & Petermann, A. G. (2014). Cultural differences in hedonic emotion regulation after a negative event. *Emotion, 14*(4), 804–815. https://doi.org/10.1037/a0036257

Murray, H. A. (1943). *Thematic Apperception Test*. Harvard University Press.

Nagai, C. (2015). Responding to Southeast Asian spirituality in clinical practice. *Spirituality in Clinical Practice, 2*(2), 106–119. https://doi.org/10.1037/scp0000070

Plante, T. G. (2003). Psychological consultation with the Roman Catholic Church: Integrating who we are with what we do. *Journal of Psychology and Christianity, 22*(4), 304–308. https://scholarcommons.scu.edu/psych/44

Plante, T. G. (2008). What do the spiritual and religious traditions offer the practicing psychologist? *Pastoral Psychology, 56*(4), 429–444. https://doi.org/10.1007/s11089-008-0119-0

Plante, T. G. (2015). Six principles to consider when working with Roman Catholic clients. *Spirituality in Clinical Practice, 2*(3), 233–237. https://doi.org/10.1037/scp0000075

Plante, T. G. (2017). The 4 Ds: Using Ignatian spirituality in secular psychotherapy and beyond. *Spirituality in Clinical Practice, 4*(1), 74–79. https://doi.org/10.1037/scp0000122

Plante, T. G. (2020). St. Ignatius as psychotherapist? How Jesuit spirituality and wisdom can enhance psychotherapy. *Spirituality in Clinical Practice, 7*(1), 65–71. https://doi.org/10.1037/scp0000214

Richards, P. S., & Bergin, A. E. (1997). *A spiritual strategy for counseling and psychotherapy*. American Psychological Association. https://doi.org/10.1037/10241-000

Richards, P. S., & Bergin, A. E. (2000). Religious diversity and psychotherapy: Conclusions, recommendations, and future directions. In P. S. Richards & A. E. Bergin (Eds.), *Handbook of psychotherapy and religious diversity* (pp. 469–489). American Psychological Association. https://doi.org/10.1037/10347-019

Richards, P. S., & Bergin, A. E. (2005). *A spiritual strategy for counseling and psychotherapy* (2nd ed.). American Psychological Association. https://doi.org/10.1037/11214-000

Richards, P. S., Sanders, P. W., Lea, T., McBride, J. A., & Allen, G. E. K. (2015). Bringing spiritually oriented psychotherapies into the health care mainstream: A call for worldwide collaboration. *Spirituality in Clinical Practice, 2*(3), 169–179. https://doi.org/10.1037/scp0000082

Richards, P. S., Sanders, P. W., McBride, J. A., & Lea, T. (2014, August 7–10). *Bridging the research–practice gap with a clinically adaptive internet-based outcome system* [Paper presentation]. American Psychological Association's 122nd Annual Convention, Washington, DC, United States.

Rorschach, H. (1921). *Psychodiagnostik: Methodik und ergebnisse eines wahr-nehmungdiagnostischen experiments* [*Psychodiagnostics: Methodology and results of a perception-diagnostic experiment*]. Ernst Bircher Verlag.

Rotter, J. B. (1950). *The Rotter Incomplete Sentences Blank*. Psychological Corporation.

Rulla, L. M. (1971). *Depth psychology and vocation: A psycho-social perspective*. Gregorian University Press.

Rulla, L. M. (1986). *Anthropology of the Christian vocation: Interdisciplinary bases* (Vol. 1). Gregorian University Press.

Sanders, P. W., Richards, P. S., & McBride, J. A. (2018). Development of the Clinically Adaptive Multidimensional Outcome Survey. *Psychotherapy Research, 28*(6), 925–939. https://doi.org/10.1080/10503307.2016.1277039

Sanders, P. W., Richards, P. S., McBride, J. A., Lea, T., Hardman, R. K., & Barnes, D. V. (2015). Processes and outcomes of theistic spiritually oriented psychotherapy: A practice-based evidence investigation. *Spirituality in Clinical Practice, 2*(3), 180–190. https://doi.org/10.1037/scp0000083

Sanders, T. G. (1970). The Church in Latin America. *Foreign Affairs, 48*(2), 285–299. https://doi.org/10.2307/20039441

Sebastian, B. (2014). *From restoration of the self to the recovery of human mystery: An interdisciplinary study on the transformation of narcissism in psychotherapy: Psychoanalytic self psychology and a model based on Christian anthropology in dialogue*. Claretian Publications.

Shafranske, E. P. (2000). Psychotherapy with Roman Catholics. In P. S. Richards & A. E. Bergin (Eds.), *Handbook of psychotherapy and religious diversity* (pp. 59–88). American Psychological Association. https://doi.org/10.1037/10347-003

Shibre, T., Negash, A., Kullgren, G., Kebede, D., Alem, A., Fekadu, A., Fekadu, D., Madhin, G., & Jacobsson, L. (2001). Perception of stigma among family members of individuals with schizophrenia and major affective disorders in rural Ethiopia. *Social Psychiatry and Psychiatric Epidemiology*, 36(6), 299–303. https://doi.org/10.1007/s001270170048

Sim, W., & Hwang, J. Y. (2020, March 19–20). *International process and outcome study of spiritually integrated psychotherapy*. Bridges Capstone Conference [Virtual meeting]. https://bridgescapstoneconference.wordpress.com

Sim, W., Li, X., Hwang, J. Y., Hill, C. E., An, M., & Kim, D. H. (2021). The process and outcome of spiritually integrated psychotherapies: A cross-cultural study in Asia, Africa, Europe, and Latin America. *Psychotherapy*. Advance online publication. https://doi.org/10.1037/pst0000409

Smith, T. B., Bartz, J., & Richards, P. S. (2007). Outcomes of religious and spiritual adaptations to psychotherapy: A meta-analytic review. *Psychotherapy Research*, 17(6), 643–655. https://doi.org/10.1080/10503300701250347

South, R. M., & McDowell, L. (2018). Use of prayer as complementary therapy by Christian adults in the Bible Belt of the United States. *Religions*, 9(11), Article 350. https://doi.org/10.3390/rel9110350

Vitz, P. C., & Mango, P. (1997). Kernbergian psychodynamics and religious aspects of the forgiveness process. *Journal of Psychology and Theology*, 25(1), 72–80. https://doi.org/10.1177/009164719702500107

Whittington, B. L., & Scher, S. J. (2010). Prayer and subjective well-being: An examination of six different types of prayer. *The International Journal for the Psychology of Religion*, 20(1), 59–68. https://doi.org/10.1080/10508610903146316

14

Jewish Forms of Spiritually Integrated Psychotherapy in Israel

Ofra Mayseless, Marianna Ruah-Midbar Shapiro, Aya Rice, and Liat Zucker

The past 3 decades have seen a surge of renewed interest in blending religious traditions and spiritual doctrines and practices into modern psychology for the purpose of understanding and cultivating the human psyche (Miller, 2015; Pargament, 2007; Pargament et al., 2013; Richards, 2009; Richards & Bergin, 2005, 2014; Sperry & Shafranske, 2005). This chapter focuses on some of the innovative ways Judaism and modern psychology are being integrated in psychotherapy praxis in Israel.

The chapter begins with background on Judaism and the Israeli context within which these new "Jewish psychotherapies" have emerged. We then survey the scene of Jewish psychotherapies in Israel. Next, the main qualitative and quantitative findings of the research conducted with Jewish licensed psychotherapists are discussed, and several short case descriptions illustrate

---

The study described in this chapter was conducted at the University of Haifa by Ofra Mayseless and Marianna Ruah-Midbar Shapiro. Liat Zucker was the project coordinator and senior research assistant, and Aya Rice was a senior research assistant. The first two authors contributed equally.

The chapter builds on a research project that investigated psychotherapies integrating Jewish spirituality in Israel as part of a larger multinational research on the integration of spirituality in psychotherapy supported by a grant from the John Templeton Foundation and under the direction of P. Scott Richards and other members of the Bridges Institute for Spiritually Integrated Psychotherapies research lab, who, at the time, were at Brigham Young University. The opinions expressed in this chapter are those of the authors and do not necessarily reflect the views of the John Templeton Foundation or Brigham Young University.

https://doi.org/10.1037/0000338-014
Handbook of Spiritually Integrated Psychotherapies, P. S. Richards, G. E. K. Allen, and D. K. Judd (Editors)
Copyright © 2023 by the American Psychological Association. All rights reserved.

some of the Jewish spiritual therapeutic methods described in the qualitative analysis. We conclude with a discussion of future research directions.

JEWISH RELIGIOUS TRADITION AND CONTEMPORARY JEWISH IDENTITIES IN ISRAEL

Judaism is the religious tradition and culture of the people of Israel and has been a major source of reference for other major monotheistic Abrahamic religions, mainly Christianity and Islam. Today, there are about 14 million Jews worldwide, most of whom live in the United States and Israel. Judaism has always been diverse and dynamic, and has included various contradictory movements and ideas. Such diversity continues to this day in both Israel and the Diaspora. Followers of Judaism believe in the oneness of God who created the cosmos and rules it, delivered the Hebrews from slavery in Egypt, made a covenant with them and gave them the Bible, and revealed himself through ancient prophets.

Traditionally, after the Jerusalem temple was ruined in the 1st century by the Romans, worship was conducted in synagogues, and spiritual leaders became biblical sages called *rabbis*. Alongside the written *Torah* (Old Testament of the Bible), the oral *Torah* flourished as well as esoteric currents, creating an abundance of scriptural literature containing Jewish law, creative commentaries, legends, liturgy, and more. Jewish law, *halakha* (close to the Hebrew words "going" or "walking"), was a significant issue in these scriptures and Jewish life, which then became a central criterion differentiating Jews in modernity. The axis of halakhic adherence includes "secular" Jews who no longer adhere to the halakha, on the one hand, and ultra-Orthodox Jews who are very strict and stringent about it, on the other hand, with many variations in between (Arian & Keissar-Sugarmen, 2012).

Conceptualizations among Jews of the relations between religious and national/ethnic identities, customs and commandments, and the belief in God are quite complex. For example, a person born Jewish who does not practice any of the religious requirements or believe in any of its teachings is still considered Jewish. On the other hand, many stress that being religious in Judaism is contingent on actual behavior and not necessarily belief (Cohen et al., 2013). Thus, secular Jews may adhere to various degrees of traditional belief and practice but perceive themselves as exempt from external religious authority or from total obligation to religion. (For further information on the religion and spirituality of Jews, see Cohen et al., 2013.)

In Israel, the classic division into groups based on religious identity (in the Jewish population, which comprises about 80% of Israeli civilians)—both in the scholarly literature and in the public discourse—is into four main groups: (a) ultra-Orthodox (*Charedi*), (b) Modern/Zionist Orthodox, (c) Traditional, and (d) secular. Only about 20% of Israel's Jewish population consider themselves religious, whether identifying as religious Zionists (10%) or as ultra-Orthodox (9%). About 80% of Israeli Jews identify themselves as Traditional or secular, indicating that they are not committed to a strictly religiously observant lifestyle. About 40% are termed traditional, meaning they are partially committed to Jewish traditional beliefs and halakhic observance. The remaining 42.5% (*Statistical Abstract of Israel*, 2013) identify themselves as secular in the sense of not belonging to a religious community and not observing halakha (Arian & Keissar-Sugarmen, 2012).

However, despite the statistical minority of the "religious" among Jews in Israel, they are considered to hold the hegemony concerning Jewish matters in the State. The Orthodox narrative is often reiterated by the secular and Traditional sectors, according to which Orthodox Judaism reflects the authentic Jewish tradition (Sorotzkin, 2011). At the same time, this secular-religious dichotomy has recently been undermined (Ruah-Midbar, 2012).

Indeed, the classic division between ultra-Orthodox, Modern/Zionist Orthodox, Traditional Jews, and the secular has come under much public and scholarly dispute because it fails to capture the social and cultural complexity in attitudes toward the variations in Jewish identity. For example, the secular population in Israel remains connected to religion and largely maintains Jewish religious symbols and customs (mostly the Jewish holidays and study of the Bible), although they often replace the religious content with modern nationalistic content (Avineri, 1994; Liebman & Don-Yehiya, 1983; Shapira, 1997). It has been found that the sweeping majority of Jews in Israel adhere to at least some aspects of Jewish thought and tradition, such as believing in the existence of God (80%); celebrating Jewish holidays in the traditional manner (85%); and conducting the main Jewish life cycle rituals, such as weddings and mourning practices (more than 90%; Arian & Keissar-Sugarmen, 2012).

The past 2 decades have seen significant changes in the map of religious identities of Israeli Jews with an increased erosion of the dichotomy between religious and secular, a greater presence of postsecular believers, enhanced cultural Jewish practices and rituals among the secular, and the rise of the "spiritual but not religious" identity (Azulay & Tabory, 2008; Lahav, 2017; Ruah-Midbar & Klin-Oron, 2010). In addition, there are also transitions between various groups, such as the complex *teshuvah movement*, whereby penitents create their own style of religion based on an ongoing critical survey of the various options (Sharabi, 2012).

Another confounding issue relates to the intertwining of state and religion in Israel. Religious laws (halakha), customs, and symbols are dominant in Israel, maintaining legal authority over issues, including marriage laws, and often evoking resentment toward religiosity and Jewish orthodoxy (Pelleg & Leichtentritt, 2009). As a result, there is ongoing public protest against these issues of coercion.

New Age phenomena are increasingly present in Israel, forming some "Jew Age" syntheses (Ruah-Midbar, 2012) that are characterized by a wide spectrum of attitudes toward halakha, from indifference or opposition, through various hybrids between tradition and New Age, to preservation of Orthodox practices (Ruah-Midbar & Klin-Oron, 2010). The significance of Jew Age phenomena to the present research is in the way they spiritualize Judaism through the use and incorporation of psychological perspectives, resulting in a new array of psychotherapeutic practices and understandings.

THE FIELD OF JEWISH SPIRITUALLY INTEGRATED PSYCHOTHERAPY IN ISRAEL

During the 20th century, psychological concepts and psychotherapeutic tools became central within modern secular Western society and were frequently hostile to religion. This has often left people in the religious sector without sufficient solutions to their emotional distress. They are frequently referred to a secular psychological resolution that may cause difficulties for them as well as for the authorities in the groups that referred them. This is clearly documented within Jewish circles, especially orthodox ones but also among less orthodox circles (e.g., George et al., 2000; Greenberg & Witztum, 2001; Loewenthal, MacLeod et al., 2000). A religious audience often feels uncomfortable or at a disadvantage in a psychotherapeutic setting of modern secular origins. In addition to their distinct concerns, universal issues, such as sexuality and purpose and meaning in life, are also intertwined with religious practices and beliefs. As a result, Jewish spiritually integrated psychotherapy has emerged to address these important cultural and client needs.

Clinically trained therapists in Israel who hold a religious and/or spiritual worldview, though, must contend with the dilemma of how to reconcile two worldviews, each with its own advantages and shortcomings because each only holds a partial perspective of client needs. Thus, Jewish spiritually integrated psychotherapy also answers the need of therapists who wish to integrate psychology into Judaism. In general, the Israeli scene of Jewish psychotherapies comprises therapists with different levels of affinity to Judaism and adherence to halakha as well as varying interpretations of Judaism and what it means to their life. These therapists serve the various sectors of Israeli Jews.

Given this complex background, the past few decades have witnessed a flourishing of attempts to bridge the gap between Jewish spirituality and Western secular psychotherapy in the form of therapies that incorporate both. The field of Jewish spiritual–religious psychotherapy in Israel is extremely diverse, lively, and ever expanding. The manner in which Jewish spirituality is integrated within psychotherapy varies and reflects a variety of creative perspectives that address this challenge.

BRIEF DESCRIPTION OF THE MIXED-METHODS RESEARCH

In this chapter, we shed further light on this evolving field of Jewish psychotherapy in Israel by presenting findings and case studies[1] from the first mixed-methods research to study Jewish forms of spiritually integrated psychotherapy

---

[1]Details, including names, in all case examples presented in this chapter have been altered to protect client confidentiality and therapist privacy.

in Israel. The quantitative study included 16 certified therapists in Israel who integrated Jewish spirituality into their work with 26 clients. Translation of the questionnaires required cultural adaptations to the Jewish–Israeli context and the addition of specific questions that were culturally relevant. The duration of the data collection process was approximately 10 months. Both practitioners and clients were asked to complete a questionnaire preceding and following each session; included were the questionnaires required by the large-scale Bridges Institute for Spiritually Integrated Psychotherapies research project. The research questions addressed by the quantitative methodology were related to the background and attitudes of the clients and the practitioners: When do practitioners use different types of spiritual interventions, how often, and to what purposes? How effective are these interventions?

The qualitative part of the research aimed to deepen knowledge and understanding of issues such as: What spiritual interventions are used, and how are they conducted? In what way are these interventions spiritual according to the therapists? And in what way are they Jewish? How do therapists perceive the spiritual/Jewish nature of their work? The qualitative study included 15 semi-structured in-depth interviews (around 2 hours in length) with therapists who practice Jewish spiritually integrated psychotherapy. We specifically targeted practitioners from diverse schools of Jewish psychotherapy, and about half of the interviewees were heads or founders or central figures of such known schools. Also, about half were drawn from the group that participated in the quantitative study. Material was also taken from presentations of some therapists who participated in conferences or sessions organized by the research project (e.g., The Center for the Study of Human Spirit's "Gateways to Spirituality in Psychotherapy and Counseling" 2019 conference in Haifa and the World Psychiatric Association's "International Congress in Spirituality and Psychiatry" in Jerusalem, also in 2019).

Thematic analysis (Braun & Clarke, 2012) was implemented to systematically identify, organize, and offer insight into patterns of meanings (themes), allowing the researchers to see and make sense of shared meanings across the interviews. The qualitative analysis also applied investigator triangulation (Denzin, 2006) for analyzing the thematic interpretations of the original texts. Two research assistants conducted parallel analyses of the interviews and discussed them together to interpret them as a whole.

The study focused on methods of Jewish psychotherapy in Israel, which are steeped both in the Jewish tradition as well as in common Western therapeutic methods, by licensed psychotherapists. An additional group not addressed in this chapter includes methods developed by religious/spiritual individuals (e.g., rabbis) who do not have formal training as psychotherapists but created theories and practices they call "Jewish psychotherapy." Here, we do not address methods that offer only Jewish theological answers to personal concerns but disregard insights and tools common in "classic" psychotherapy. We also do not include methods that combine a more liberal perception of Jewish tradition as is common in the alternative spiritual sphere (New Age). These two spheres—one more committed to Jewish tradition and therefore largely ignoring modern secular psychotherapeutic tools and the other that tends toward liberal-universalistic-eclectic approaches characteristic of the New Age spiritualities—are both worthy of study in and of themselves but are not included in this chapter. The focus of this chapter is only on legally qualified psychotherapists, such as social workers, clinical psychologists, art therapists, and counselors.

The research included two main groups: (a) psychotherapists who work on their own and (b) psychotherapists who developed their own method and opened schools to teach their method. The first group included therapists who espouse eclectic practices from various Jewish and/or alternative spiritual methods. Quite a few of these therapists have participated in training programs of the second group. Members of this group sometimes practice conventional psychotherapy without any Jewish characteristics. Thus, these psychotherapists may not expose their clients to any Jewish element, although this aspect impacts the therapist's personal understanding, conceptualizations, and way of being.

The second group included psychotherapists who developed unique methods of integrating Jewish elements (and sometimes also other alternative spiritual methods) with conventional psychotherapeutic work. Some of these therapists have developed quite extensive schools and training programs to teach these methods. The three most prominent methods are presented in the following section.

THE FOUNDERS OF THE MAIN SCHOOLS OF JEWISH PSYCHOTHERAPY IN ISRAEL

In this section, we provide a brief description of three founders of well-known schools in Israel that teach methods that integrate Jewish spirituality in therapy. Each of these methods was developed by the founder of the school, and the schools were established to impart this knowledge to others. We describe the founder and also a few characteristics of the method.

Mordechai Rotenberg

Mordechai Rotenberg is an emeritus professor of social work at the Hebrew University in Jerusalem. His many published books (in English, Hebrew, French, and Japanese), present his creative doctrine, which combines Jewish tradition, sociology, psychology, criminology, and social work (Rotenberg, 1987, 2004, 2005, 2012). In 2009, he was awarded the Israel Prize, the highest prize given by the Israeli authorities, for his contributions in a variety of domains.

Rotenberg's model of Jewish psychology focuses on several unique characteristics that he adapted from the Jewish tradition, especially Lurianic Kabbalah (a type of Jewish mysticism) and Hassidism (a Jewish, modern European, popular spiritual-social movement). These characteristics include dialogue and dialectics; multiple interpretations; the doctrine of "restriction" (*tzimtzum* in kabbalistic terms) whereby the infinity of the divine makes room for creation; the connection between y*etzer* (literally meaning "instinct" but also refers to "libido"); and y*etzira* (literally meaning "creation").

In 2006, Rotenberg founded The Rotenberg Institute—Center for Jewish Psychology in memory of Boaz Rotenberg (his son, who died in military action). The institute offers training programs for certified therapists and educators. Rotenberg grew up in an ultra-Orthodox home, yet he no longer identifies as such; his daughter, Michal Fachler, who currently directs the institute, identifies as Orthodox. Although Rotenberg's theory is not committed to an ultra-Orthodox worldview, many of the students are Traditional or Orthodox Jews.

Yair Caspi

Yair Caspi is a clinical psychologist whose doctoral dissertation (at the Jewish Yeshiva University in New York) on eclecticism in psychotherapy served as the basis for the development of his "Jewish psychology" method, which he began teaching in 1999 as part of a nonacademic program under the auspices of Tel-Aviv University. In 2009, he founded an independent institute that provides courses for therapists and also group psychotherapy.

Caspi comes from an Orthodox background but is no longer affiliated with that sector; he defines himself as a "secular-religious Jew." His students are mostly from the secular and Traditional sectors. Caspi's philosophy addresses questions that draw on the Jewish tradition, such as: What is the hidden false God I worship? What prayer hides within me and must be revealed? His method speaks of five "paths of knowledge" and, accordingly, five routes on the journey towards *tikkun*, a complex term that literally means "to repair." According to Lurianic Kabbalah, during creation, divine light shattered and scattered, which is what needs to be "repaired" through collecting the divine sparks and restoring them to their divine source. The ultimate goal of these paths is to assist the seeker to find themselves and their true God. Caspi has written a number of books, one of which has been translated into English (*Inquiring of God*; Caspi, 2002; see also Caspi, 2017; Caspi & Shalev, 2021).

Michael Binyamin Aboulafia

Michael Binyamin Aboulafia is an Orthodox rabbi as well as a child and adolescent psychiatrist. His "integrative Jewish psychotherapy" method combines traditional psychotherapy together with psychopharmacological treatment, a holistic mind–body approach, and Jewish spirituality (Aboulafia, 2011, 2012, 2017, 2019). Aboulafia's clients and students are often of the Orthodox community. As a religious Orthodox Jew who holds a humanist psychological approach, his method is founded on both trust in humankind and in spiritual faith. Aboulafia's method accepts the common tools of psychology and psychiatry but also incorporates Jewish content and insights into the understanding of the mind, its ailments, and its path toward healing with a firm belief that God takes part in the therapeutic process. In addition to operating three clinics in Israel and writing nearly a dozen books on the topic, he also established the Aboulafia Institute that trains coaches (who receive a certificate from the institute), certified therapists (who receive a certificate in psychotherapy from the University of Haifa), and teachers.

These three major schools of Jewish psychotherapy in Israel that were created by certified psychotherapists are quite eclectic. They have developed diverse and creative ways of incorporating spirituality and especially Judaism in secular psychotherapy. They also have incorporated a large number of notions from New Age spirituality (e.g., mind–body connection, the centrality of the self).

INSIGHTS FROM THE MIXED-METHODS RESEARCH

We present several major findings that shed light on the way certified psychotherapists, who identify themselves as integrating Jewish spirituality into their practice, work. In presenting these findings we combine findings from the quantitative and qualitative studies.

Psychotherapists and Clients Consider the Integration of Jewish Spirituality as Central to Psychotherapy and Have Heterogeneous Religious Identity

Although the therapists and clients who participated in the research were heterogeneous in their religious Jewish identity, both sides perceived the integration of spirituality as central to psychotherapy and welcomed that integration. Psychotherapists came from a variety of religious/spiritual perspectives, ranging from secular to ultra-Orthodox, reflecting a heterogeneous group that integrates Jewish spirituality in their clinical practice. In line with this portrayal that emerged in the answers to the questionnaires, the overarching characteristic arising from the analysis of the interviews with the psychotherapists was a sense of complexity, particularly pertaining to the therapists' spiritual/secular/religious identity. Interviewees showed some objection to the categorization that distinguishes among a "secular," "religious," or "spiritual" identity. They instead offered a dialectical sense of integration and continuation among the three concepts. Perhaps because of this sensitivity, more than half of the interviewees mentioned the incorporation of questions pertaining to clients' spirituality as part of the intake. For example, participants Benny and Jacob both asked during the intake if the client has a relationship with God and about the place of spirituality in the client's life. Miriam shared this: "I ask what do they believe in. Some people immediately respond, while others need some help to understand the question." By introducing questions relating to spirituality, the therapists provided the message that such concerns are legitimate and relevant within the therapeutic framework.

Clients, too, were quite heterogeneous in their religious orientation or identity, and the majority of them were ready to discuss religious and spiritual issues in therapy, reporting that the Jewish tradition is important in their lives. Furthermore, therapists from both the quantitative and qualitative studies reported that even though they did not have any guidance in their formal psychotherapy training about how to incorporate spirituality or Jewish spirituality into therapy, their professional life was in tune with their personal spiritual perspective and development. This finding may be partly explained by the training many of these therapists underwent in one of the aforementioned training programs in Jewish psychotherapy, which accords with their decision to participate in the research. Altogether, from both perspectives, psychotherapists and clients considered the integration of Jewish spirituality as central to psychotherapy and welcomed that integration despite their diverse backgrounds in religious identity.

Therapists Adopt an Attitude of Universalism and Are Open, Flexible, and Cautious

In contrast to the firm identity reported by the participating therapists as fully integrating Jewish spirituality into psychotherapy, the therapists discussed a series of attitudes and practices that presented a more dialectic and nuanced picture of their clinical practice. They advocated universalistic values and evinced openness, flexibility, and caution when introducing spirituality or Jewish elements. For example, based on their responses to the questionnaire, the therapists' approach to integrating spirituality comprised being responsive to clients' need and questions as well as actively initiating integration when they thought it was appropriate but without using a dogmatic and sectarian approach. Indeed, in the quantitative part of the research, there were no significant connections between specific interventions, including spiritual ones and Jewish ones, and outcomes (i.e., increase in positive emotions or attitudes or decrease in negative ones). The clearest association found with the therapists' interventions was one between adopting the therapist's suggestions and an increase in well-being as assessed by calculating a positive-to-negative emotions ratio.

In line with their nonsectarian sense of identity, therapists also expressed an attitude of universalism regarding their therapeutic approach. All interviewees stated that their therapeutic methods suit all Jewish factions. Furthermore, they perceived those methods as also suitable for non-Jewish populations (although they do not actually have non-Jewish clients).

An additional measure used that reflected the therapists' complex identity and universal attitude related to the finding that nearly all mentioned being cautious about explicitly discussing the Jewish spiritual element of treatment with their clients to avoid client antagonism or perceived coercion. This sense of caution was closely related to their concern with and ability to play with language when interacting with clients from different Jewish factions. For example, some of the therapists mentioned adapting their language/metaphors/stories according to a client's background. Sharon shared this:

> I often translate terms. I won't necessarily say, "You are seeking the hidden Divine light," obviously, . . . but I can say, "Wow. I feel that the essence here is that you longed for something positive. . . ." This way, I enable them. Yes, . . . I really don't force it [Jewish spirituality] on them. I hope I don't.

This sense of caution was even more pronounced for some of the religious therapists who wear distinctly Jewish religious signifiers (e.g., a yarmulke for men or a skirt and head covering for women). Shmuel, for example, discussed the negative connotation the yarmulke he wears evoked among a young female patient who suffered sexual abuse from her religious father. It was distressing for her to see her male therapist also wearing this signifier of a religious lifestyle and belief system. Her suspicion of the therapist because of this signifier was relieved when he stated that Judaism would not be a part of therapy. However, for Shmuel, his Jewish faith and belief in the presence of God in any therapeutic encounter are a foundation of his work.

In an interview with Shmuel, he explained what happened at the successful conclusion of this treatment when the patient inquired what type of therapy he used. He then also provided an elaborate explanation of the way he perceived the place of Jewish spirituality in the therapeutic process. Shmuel recounted, "I described the different methods without mentioning the Jewish aspect at all, because, as I said, God is not an object; He just allows the treatment to delve deeper." He then added,

> My ability to endure the pain of her traumatic past together with her comes from my Jewish spiritual faith. Faith gives the therapist the confidence to be brave and approach pain without fear, out of a clear understanding that without lows, there can be no highs. This is the manifestation of the *Sefira of Eternity*.[2] According to *Eternity*, one goes from dependence to independence, from anxiety to self-assurance. And that is what treating trauma is all about, diving deep into the pain while feeling confident that it's possible to be there without being overwhelmed with fear.

Thus, according to Shmuel, God's presence in the therapeutic situation, although not necessarily explicitly mentioned, lies at the center of the healing process. In his words: "As I see it, the whole essence of the therapeutic session is a kind of manifestation of God's work but without talking about Him."

Therapists Use Numerous Jewish-Spiritual Tools

Both in the questionnaires completed following each session with their clients and in their interviews, the psychotherapists reported using numerous spiritual interventions or tools. In the quantitative part of the research, clinicians reported

---

[2] *Sefira of Eternity*: The *Sefirot* (plural in Hebrew of *sefira*), in theosofic Kabbalah, are 10 attributes/emanations/faces/forces through which *Ein Sof* ["the infinite aspect of God"] reveals itself. Each *Sefira* has a quality and a name. *Sefira of Eternity Netzah* ["infinity"] is the seventh *sefira* ["sphere or emanation"].

a high frequency of interventions of a general nature. At least one such general intervention was used in all the sessions (see Table 14.1 for frequently reported interventions). Still, therapists also referred to distinct spiritual and distinct Jewish interventions. Therapists decided what—for them—was a spiritual or a Jewish intervention (see Table 14.1 for the most frequent ones).

This combination of general psychotherapeutic tools and spiritual and distinctive Jewish ones accord with therapists' universalistic, open, nonsecretarial, and cautious attitude. Because therapists particularly mentioned the use of Jewish texts and prayer as specific Jewish spiritual tools and practices, we discuss each of them in the following sections. We also present a case study that makes use of the specific tool.

Use of Jewish Texts

Interviewees described using texts from Jewish sources in therapy, including stories, fables and folktales from the Jewish tradition, and quotes from the

TABLE 14.1. Frequency of Use of Various Interventions by the Clinicians Participating in the Quantitative Study

General category of intervention and type of specific intervention	Percentage of number of therapy sessions in which an intervention was used (out of the total sessions conducted by the therapists)
Interventions of a general nature	100%
Unconditional acceptance	57.1%
Use of metaphors	49.0%
Assigned homework practice	48.0%
Attention to client's emotions	45.9%
Encouragement of awareness of the present moment	41.8%
Emotion identification	41.8%
A focus on a supportive, warm environment	40.8%
Spiritual intervention (defined as spiritual by the therapist)	76%
Telling client to be attentive to their heart	64.3%
Exploration of the client's spiritual soul	39.3%
Discussion of choice from a spiritual perspective	30%
Hope	30%
Listening to spiritual issues	30%
Recognition of spiritual inner goodness	18%
Prayer	17%
Unique Jewish interventions (defined as Jewish by the therapists)	20%
Use of Jewish texts	20%
Gratitude to God	20%

Jewish scriptures. Some said these texts underlay their therapy as a whole, but clients were not necessarily aware of this. These stories, despite their Jewish source, are introduced into the dialogue because of their universal significance and thus may be relevant for both nonreligious Jews as well as non-Jewish clients. One therapist described how she brought in biblical stories that seemed pertinent to a client's situation and then asked the client whether and how the stories resonated with them. Another therapist brought in stories of biblical characters that exemplified their complex nature as a way of broadening the client's perspective and acceptance of her own complexity. Another therapist described how she brought the text into the therapy, and she and the client read it together and meditated on certain words to allow the text to resonate within the client.

One study participant, Nurit, is a secular psychotherapist who developed a method she calls "Bible Therapy" that combines neurolinguistic processing (i.e., NLP) with biblical stories. Her spiritual perspective as well as the biblical stories were not necessarily overtly expressed in the therapy; however, both guided all of her therapeutic interventions. Nurit described how she explicitly brought a biblical story into treatment in one case:

> Jeanne [the client] was 32 and married for 8 years when she came to me for therapy. Six years of unsuccessful fertility treatments left her depleted and distressed. Jeanne told me of her long and difficult process of trying to have a child. I told her of the story of Sarah, the first matriarch in the Bible, who was barren. Jeanne listened and replied that she is like the modern Sarah but has lost faith, and only a miracle can save her. She despairingly concluded: "Sarah had God. What do I have?"
>
> Jeanne longed to have faith and hoped our sessions would help evoke such faith that she could indeed become a mother. Being a practical woman, Sarah suggested to her husband, "Behold now, the LORD hath restrained me from bearing; go in, I pray thee, unto my handmaid; it may be that I shall be builded up through her" (Genesis 16:2). In dialogue with the biblical story and Sarah's practicality, we decided that Jeanne required a division of tasks: Jeanne's husband would be responsible for the technical aspects of the relationship with their doctors, and Jeanne would remain connected solely to her body and inner world. In our sessions, Jeanne and I focused on identifying the fears Jeanne held that were holding back her faith. Through our work, we eventually unraveled her fears and created a positive belief system. We ended therapy when Jeanne was in her 16th week of pregnancy.

Prayer

The interviews revealed that therapists often use prayer in therapy in various ways. Itamar, a religious but not ultra-Orthodox psychologist, emphasized the central importance of prayer in his work and how this reconnection with the Creator can open the way to additional connections in life:

> Prayer is a very important tool because it transforms the will. . . . To my understanding, the original contract of mankind is with the Creator, and once one has that, one discovers many other potential allies. The world is full of potential allies, and each one can provide something.

Hadar, a religious marriage and family therapist, noted how her exposure to Jewish psychology impacted her work with victims of severe abuse. She incorporated an act of prayer into her treatment:

> Before I was exposed to Jewish psychology, I would strengthen the "I deserve" attitude—for example, "I deserve to be seen, I am worthy of love and understanding," particularly among women who were victims of sexual abuse or came from very difficult homes. . . . But today, I will take that very same practice and alter it, when appropriate, to a kind of prayer, or even a demand from the Almighty: 'Do you hear, God? Can you make things better for me?' In this way, I bring in prayer.

This act of prayer is not necessarily explicit. Naor, for example, was one of the therapists who mentioned praying by themselves before or during a session without the client's knowledge:

> The first practice is prayer. I begin every therapy with a small prayer, where I ask the Almighty to help me be His messenger, to help them, for the person to develop, for me to conduct my role in the best possible way, without any bias. And sometimes during the therapy itself, when I feel I don't know what to do, it's unclear to me, I ask for help.

An unconventional inclusion of prayer was shared by one of the therapists in the following story. Hava is a religious drama therapist who incorporates Hasidic elements into her work.[3] For her, the patient's conscious relationship with God is one of the centerpieces of the therapeutic work from which one can grow and create change in one's life. Here, Hava describes how her therapy with a young woman named Esther exemplifies this:

> Esther was 35 and single when she came to me for therapy, saddened by the lack of a romantic relationship in her life. After a year and a half of traditional psychodynamic inquiry, I suggested "Placing God on the chair and asking Him a few questions." Esther came from a religious background but was disconnected from her religious sources; something there had broken. Esther agreed to my suggestion, and she began speaking to God directly, at times together in the session. At some point, we decided to pray at the tomb of a *tzaddik*[4] we both knew. We went together, each with her own prayers. On the way back, we spoke about how strange it is for psychological treatment to include something spiritual, such as conversations with God and prayer at a tzaddik's tomb.

---

[3]*Hasidic Judaism* is a Jewish religious group that arose as a spiritual revival movement in the territory of contemporary Western Ukraine during the 18th century and spread rapidly throughout Eastern Europe. Present-day Hasidism is a subgroup within ultra-Orthodox Judaism, and its members adhere closely both to Orthodox Jewish practice—with the movement's own unique emphases—and the traditions of Eastern European Jews. Hasidic thought draws heavily on kabbalistic teachings that emphasize God's immanence in the universe, the need to be one with him at all times, the devotional aspect of religious practice, and the spiritual dimension of corporeality and mundane acts.

[4]*Tzaddik* [namely, "righteous one"] is a title given in Jewish tradition to people considered righteous, such as biblical figures and later spiritual masters. Visiting and praying at the tombs of such *tzaddikim* ["righteous people"] is a folk custom, whereby asking for aid in matters of matching is one of the common themes.

A short time afterward, she met the man she eventually married and with whom she had three children. What enabled this change to occur? Was there actually a divine intervention? Was it my willingness to transgress the customary boundaries and accompany her to the tzaddik's tomb, showing her how much I truly cared for her and had faith myself? Was it the integration she experienced between her psychological and spiritual selves that the therapy advanced? Perhaps it was a combination of all of these. What is clear is that without the explicit spiritual dimension in therapy, her healing would have remained incomplete.

CONCLUDING REMARKS

The findings of an in-depth research conducted on psychotherapy that integrates Jewish spirituality in Israel revealed a complex and fascinating picture of the characteristics of this field of psychotherapy as well as the attitudes of the therapists engaged in its practice. The perspectives expressed by the therapists uncovered a type of dialectic: They have a sense of integration between their psychotherapeutic training and their connection to spirituality and Judaism, yet they often refrain from overtly sharing this with their clients. They perceive themselves as offering a type of therapy that is universal in nature and suitable for everyone. They adapt their interventions according to their clients' needs and often rely on their spiritual perspective, state of awareness, or personal faith as a central intervention or "tool." In other words, the Jewish spiritual component is integrated within them and is not necessarily explicitly mentioned.

The Jewish spiritual components in psychotherapy were conceptualized by the therapists mostly as universal, and they hesitated to overtly express Jewish elements unless portrayed as touching universal psychological issues. This also manifested in their use of general therapeutic interventions with much higher frequency than spiritual or Jewish spiritual ones. Examples with both religious and nonreligious clients include a religious therapist wearing a yarmulke who does not mention with his client the Jewish spiritual faith central to his work, or a secular therapist who uses biblical texts as if they are neutral and not religious texts.

These dialectics probably relate to the complexity of Jewish identity in Israel and also reflect a postmodernist perspective in that the dialectics coalesce opposites in a way that is experienced as integrated, and thus they do not create internal conflict for the therapists (at least according to their reports). Clients appear to benefit from therapy, and their well-being increases when they report following their therapist's suggestions regardless of which intervention was used. This finding about clients' well-being aligns and resonates with the perspective of the therapists—that what is most important is for the therapist to tune in to the client rather than the specifics of the intervention. Nevertheless, specific Jewish spiritual tools and practices were elucidated, especially the use of Jewish texts and prayer, which were illustrated by the vignettes.

LIMITATIONS OF THE PRESENT STUDY AND DIRECTIONS FOR FUTURE RESEARCH

The research presented shed light on the field of Jewish spiritually integrated psychotherapy in Israel and revealed a number of interesting and important findings that are also pertinent to the integration of spirituality into psychotherapy in general. However, the research does have a number of limitations. The analysis presented here is preliminary and provides only an initial glimpse into the main findings. Furthermore, the research is not based on a representative sample of the field of Jewish spiritually integrated psychotherapy. Although the research did include therapists from the three main approaches in Israel, there are additional approaches because many individual therapists have created their own unique forms of integration.

In addition, the study included only those therapists who were willing to identify as Jewish spiritually integrated therapists and who agreed to participate in the research. Quite a few therapists refused to participate in the study (particularly the quantitative study) because, in Israel, it is uncommon or unacceptable for clients to answer questionnaires pertaining to their therapy held in private clinics. Importantly, the study did not include therapists or methods that are prevalent and yet included therapists who did not undergo traditional psychotherapeutic training. Future research should include these groups as well as larger samples to delve more deeply into these initial and promising findings.

Finally, the focus of the present research was on psychotherapy that integrates Jewish spirituality in Israel. Naturally, the Israeli sociocultural context significantly impacted the understanding of the findings. In other sociocultural contexts, it is likely that Jewish spiritually integrated psychotherapy will manifest and be experienced quite differently. This, too, is worthy of exploration in future research.

REFERENCES

Aboulafia, M. B. (2011). *Thoughts of a therapist about love: A journey among the principles of Jewish psychology [From the room of a Jewish therapist]* [in Hebrew]. Abulafia Institute.

Aboulafia, M. B. (2012). *The art of acceptance and acknowledgment: The guide to education out of love* [in Hebrew]. Miskal.

Aboulafia, M. B. (2017). *The gardener and the fruit: A little guide to a happy life*. Abulafia Institute.

Aboulafia, M. B. (2019). *"Shuvi Nafshi": Textbook of Jewish integrative psychotherapy* [in Hebrew]. Abulafia Institute.

Arian, A., & Keissar-Sugarmen, A. (2012). *A portrait of Israeli Jews: Beliefs, observance, and values of Israeli Jews, 2009*. The Guttman Center for Surveys of the Israel Democracy Institute and AVI CHAI Israel Foundation.

Avineri, S. (1994). Zionism and Jewish religious tradition: The dialectic of disenthrallment and secularisation. In S. Almog, J. Reinhartz, & A. Shapira (Eds.), *Zionism and religion* (pp. 9–18) [in Hebrew]. The Zalman Shazar Center for Jewish History.

Azulay, N., & Tabory, E. (2008). From houses of study to houses of prayer: Religious-cultural developments in the Israeli secular sector [in Hebrew]. *Social Issues in Israel, 6*, 121–156. https://www.jstor.org/stable/23388899

Braun, V., & Clarke, V. (2012). Thematic analysis. In H. Cooper, P. M. Camic, D. L. Long, A. T. Panter, D. Rindskopf, & K. J. Sher (Eds.), *APA handbook of research methods in psychology: Vol. 2. Research designs: Quantitative, qualitative, neuropsychological, and biological* (pp. 57–71). American Psychological Association. https://doi.org/10.1037/13620-004

Caspi, Y. (2002). *Inquiring of God: Foundations of Talmudic & biblical psychology* (M. Kohane & B. Rosenberg, trans.; Hebrew version). Amazon Digital Services LLC.

Caspi, Y. (2017). *The boy who almost saved his mother* [in Hebrew]. Kibbutz Hameuchad.

Caspi, Y., & Shalev, A. (2021). *Book of talents* [in Hebrew]. Miskal, Rishon LeZion.

The Center for the Study of Human Spirit. (2019, March 11). *Gateways to spirituality in psychotherapy and counseling* [Conference]. University of Haifa, Haifa, Israel. https://spirit.haifa.ac.il/conferences-and-events/gateways-to-spirituality-in-psychotherapy-and-counselling/?lang=en

Cohen, A. B., Gorvine, B. J., & Gorvine, H. (2013). The religion, spirituality, and psychology of Jews. In K. I. Pargament, J. J. Exline, & J. W. Jones (Eds.), *APA handbook of psychology, religion, and spirituality: Vol. 1. Context, theory, and research* (pp. 665–679). American Psychological Association. https://doi.org/10.1037/14045-037

Denzin, N. K. (Ed.). (2006). *Sociological methods: A sourcebook* (5th ed.). Aldine Transaction.

George, L. K., Larson, D. B., Koenig, H. G., & McCullough, M. E. (2000). Spirituality and health: What we know, what we need to know. *Journal of Social and Clinical Psychology, 19*(1), 102–116. https://doi.org/10.1521/jscp.2000.19.1.102

Greenberg, D., & Witztum, E. (2001). Treatment of strictly religious patients. In M. T. Pato & J. Zohar (Eds.), *Current treatments of obsessive-compulsive disorder* (2nd ed., pp. 173–191). American Psychiatric Publishing.

Lahav, H. (2017). Jewish secular-believer women in Israel: A complex and ambivalent identity. *Israel Studies Review, 32*(2), 66–88. https://doi.org/10.3167/isr.2017.320205

Liebman, C. S., & Don-Yehiya, E. (1983). The dilemma of reconciling traditional culture and political needs: Civil religion in Israel. *Comparative Politics, 16*(1), 53–66. https://doi.org/10.2307/421595

Loewenthal, K. M., MacLeod, A. K., Goldblatt IV, V., Lubitsh, G., & Valentine, J. D. (2000). Comfort and joy? Religion, cognition, and mood in Protestants and Jews under stress. *Cognition & Emotion, 14*(3), 355-374. https://doi.org/10.1080/026999300378879

Miller, L. J. (Ed.). (2015). *The Oxford handbook of psychology and spirituality*. Oxford University Press.

Pargament, K. I. (2007). *Spiritually integrated psychotherapy: Understanding and addressing the sacred*. Guilford Press.

Pargament, K. I., Mahoney, A., Exline, J. J., Jones, J. W., & Shafranske, E. P. (2013). Envisioning an integrative paradigm for the psychology of religion and spirituality. In K. I. Pargament, J. J. Exline, & J. W. Jones (Eds.), *APA handbook of psychology, religion, and spirituality: Vol. 1. Context, theory, and research* (pp. 3–19). American Psychological Association. https://doi.org/10.1037/14045-001

Pelleg, G., & Leichtentritt, R. D. (2009). Spiritual beliefs among Israeli nurses and social workers: A comparison based on their involvement with the dying. *Omega—Journal of Death and Dying, 59*(3), 239–252. https://doi.org/10.2190/OM.59.3.d

Richards, P. S. (2009). Toward religious and spiritual competence for psychologists: Some reflections and recommendations. *Professional Psychology: Research and Practice, 40*(4), 389–391.

Richards, P. S., & Bergin, A. E. (2005). *A spiritual strategy for counseling and psychotherapy* (2nd ed.). American Psychological Association. https://doi.org/10.1037/11214-000

Richards, P. S., & Bergin, A. E. (Eds.). (2014). *Handbook of psychotherapy and religious diversity* (2nd ed.). American Psychological Association. https://doi.org/10.1037/14371-000

Rotenberg, M. (1987). *Re-biographing and deviance: Psychotherapeutic narrativism and the Midrash*. Praeger Publishers.

Rotenberg, M. (2004). *Hasidic psychology: Making space for others*. Transaction Publishers.

Rotenberg, M. (2005). *Creativity and sexuality: A kabbalistic perspective*. Transaction Publishers.

Rotenberg, M. (2012). *Life as a biblical journey: The secret of desire and desert creation* [in Hebrew]. Miskal.

Ruah-Midbar, M. (2012). Current Jewish spiritualities in Israel: A new age. *Modern Judaism—A Journal of Jewish Ideas and Experience, 32*(1), 102–124. https://doi.org/10.1093/mj/kjr026

Ruah-Midbar, M., & Klin-Oron, A. (2010). Jew age: Jewish praxis in Israeli new age discourse. *Journal of Alternative Spiritualities and New Age Studies, 5*(1), 33–63.

Shapira, A. (1997). *New Jews old Jews* [in Hebrew]. Am Oved Publishers.

Sharabi, A. (2012). "Teshuvah baskets" in the Israeli teshuvah market. *Culture and Religion, 13*(3), 273–293. https://doi.org/10.1080/14755610.2012.706227

Sorotzkin, D. (2011). *Orthodoxy and modern disciplination: The production of the Jewish tradition in Europe in modern times*. Hakibutz Hameuchad Press.

Sperry, L., & Shafranske, E. P. (Eds.). (2005). *Spiritually oriented psychotherapy*. American Psychological Association. https://doi.org/10.1037/10886-000

Statistical Abstract of Israel. (2013, September 16). The Israel Central Bureau of Statistics. https://www.cbs.gov.il/en/publications/Pages/2013/Statistical-Abstract-of-Israel-2013-No64.aspx

World Psychiatric Association Section on Religion, Spirituality and Psychiatry. (2019, December 1–4). International Congress in Spirituality and Psychiatry 4th Global Meeting in Spirituality and Mental Health. Jerusalem, Israel. https://www.emedevents.com/c/medical-conferences-2019/international-congress-in-spirituality-and-psychiatry-jerusalem-dec-2019

15

Sufi Psychology
A Heart-Centered Paradigm

Saloumeh DeGood

As its name suggests, "psychology" was originally intended to be the study of the soul: "Psyche" means "soul," and "ology" means "the study of" (Etymonline, n.d.). Before becoming its own field, psychology included philosophy, anthropology, and religion, all coming together to understand the human being. In the 1800s, Wilhelm Wundt opened the first psychological laboratory, and experimental psychology was born (Boring, 1950). When it became clear that research is productive and yields tangible results, other laboratories were founded, and psychology became its own scientific field (Ben-David & Collins, 1966).

With all the research and data developing, the focus naturally moved to using research as a means to understand the human being. This development has been invaluable for the field; however, it does not take into account either the intangible and ineffable parts of the human being or the aspects that our current scientific instruments do not have the ability to capture, such as the soul or spirit. In addition, by isolating specific experiences of the individual in research, such as researching maladaptive cognitions or anxiety symptoms, the holistic nature of the human being and how the different aspects affect one another and the whole are easy to overlook. The result is a focus on relieving stress on the different "parts" of the individual, which can involve changing cognitions, decreasing emotions, and correcting relationships with useful tools and techniques. The underlying core issue that results in these various manifestations, though, may not be discussed.

---

https://doi.org/10.1037/0000338-015
Handbook of Spiritually Integrated Psychotherapies, P. S. Richards, G. E. K. Allen, and D. K. Judd (Editors)
Copyright © 2023 by the American Psychological Association. All rights reserved.

The M.T.O. Sufi Psychology[1] paradigm returns the inclusion of the soul and the holistic view of the human being into contemporary psychology. Sufism has a 1,400-year-old history, and psychology has been documented in its teachings and writings throughout (Wilcox, 1995). However, M.T.O. Sufi Psychology's current practical form is best described by His Holiness Nader Angha, its founder and Sufi Master of the M.T.O. Shahmaghsoudi School of Islamic Sufism, who has used the following analogy:

> It is as if psychology studies the characteristics of the lamp, such as its height, its weight, and the materials from which it is constructed. Is it a table lamp or a floor lamp? Small or large? A "night light" or reading lamp? How heavy is it? How is the weight distributed? What shape is it? Is it constructed of ceramic, wood, plastic, glass, or metal? The size, color, material, and the shape of the shade might be of concern, and perhaps the condition, length and color of the cord. Psychology would examine the wiring and the maximum allowable bulb voltage. The location and type of the switch, whether it is analog or digital, might all be noted. All these aspects are changeable.
>
> To continue the analogy, psychotherapy would then be concerned with any change that would be necessary to make the lamp appropriate for the position in which we wished to put it. Does the color match the room? Is the lamp attractive? Does the style fit the décor? Does the shade allow enough light? Is the base high enough? Is there enough weight at the bottom so that the lamp is not easily tipped over? Is the wiring frayed? Can you reach the switch easily? The various types of psychotherapy attempt to alter the different aspects of the outer characteristics of the lamp—color, size, shape, weight, type of bulb, shade, cord, or switch. This is useful. We need and want different lamps for different purposes.
>
> However, no matter how much one studies or changes the outer characteristics of the lamp, it will not work unless it is plugged in. To provide light, the lamp must be connected to a source of power. Changes to the lamp are unimportant if there is no connection to the Source. Without connection to a source of power, the lamp cannot provide light.
>
> In this example, Sufism is concerned with the reason for making a lamp in the first place. It is concerned with lighting the lamp, with providing a connection to the Source so that the lamp will fulfill its function. Sufism is concerned with the power that provides the light, not with the shape or color of the lamp. Sufism is concerned with the one stable, unchangeable aspect of the lamp—the connection to the Source. (Wilcox, 1995, p. 3)

This analogy perfectly describes that although managing and balancing the different aspects of the human being are important, the fundamental question must also be answered pertaining to each individual's identity. The lamp needs to be plugged into the outlet and connected to provide light. That light is what actually distinguishes it as a lamp, and lighting up a room is its purpose; otherwise, it is simply a decorative piece of furniture. The M.T.O. Sufi Psychology paradigm focuses on each individual's discovering their true identity and their potential and capabilities as well as connecting to the Source, and that connection to the Source—that purpose—informs all the other "parts."

---

[1] The M.T.O. acronym refers to Maktab Tarighat Oveyssi Shahmaghsoudi, the school of Islamic Sufism from which this approach originates.

Importantly, this approach does not negate current psychological modalities (e.g., cognitive behavior therapy [CBT], developmental psychology, stress-diathesis theory). Instead, it uses those modalities to address the symptomology as has been researched; however, this approach also uses additional methods, described in this chapter, to address the true identity of the human being and the underlying connection to the Source, thus creating a more holistic model.

The search for one's identity and purpose has been well documented to be a natural part of life and development (Erikson, 1980; Frankl, 1988; Maslow, 1999); therefore, the M.T.O. Sufi Psychology modality can be used with all individuals as they all, in varying degrees, are seeking both. The great Sufi Master Sadegh Angha references this inherent search for self-knowledge when he stated that Sufism "is the way that people must ultimately follow, whether they want to or not, because there is no other way" (S. Angha, 1999, p. ii). In other words, because Sufism is the discipline of self-knowledge and human beings are inherently seeking self-knowledge, then they are on the path of Sufism regardless of the label that is placed on it.

Although Sufi Psychology applies to many people on a natural and inherent level, it is especially useful for those who are actively seeking answers to these questions. In addition, this method can be used with a wide variety of clinical issues, except for patients with organic brain disorders, developmental disorders, a primary substance abuse disorder, or active psychosis.

This chapter presents a brief overview of Islamic Sufism and explain how it contributes to the field of psychology through Sufi Psychology. In addition, a case study and research studies are presented to show both the qualitative and quantitative aspects of this growing modality.

ISLAMIC SUFISM

Sufism is known as the inner dimension of Islam, but a more common definition is that Sufism is a path of self-knowledge. It focuses on each individual's discovering their true identity. It is a practice based in experience and discovery that centers on the teachings of the Prophet Mohammad (peace be upon him), who has said, "You be you" and "He who knows himself, knows God." Importantly, what is referred to as "God" some may call "Energy," "Lord," "Universe," "Existence," and so on. Sufism is not concerned with the semantics of words because they are strictly a limited vehicle with which to communicate. Sufism's focus is on the reality of the experience.

An important teaching in Sufism is that to truly know something, one must experience it in the depths of their being. For this reason, less emphasis is placed on theory, not because there is none but because it creates mental representations and a false sense of knowledge. For example, a description of water as a clear liquid with no smell or taste that is used to hydrate and make tea may be repeated and explained to others. However, although one may feel that they know what water is, their thirst is not quenched by the words, and they still may be unable to differentiate it from another clear liquid. So, how true is that knowledge? In Sufism, the goal is for each individual to *truly know*, and that can only be gained from experience. Therefore, instead of starting with God, Existence, and things that are large and difficult for one's limited senses to grasp, Sufi Master Nader Angha takes the bottom-up approach and begins with the one thing that each individual can know and be certain of: "I." At the School of Islamic Sufism, the individual is the researcher, the laboratory, and the subject of study whose goal is to truly know all aspects of oneself.

Individuals on the path of Sufism, or Sufi students, practice the pillars of Islam, but in addition to the physical acts, they ground their practice in spiritual and contemplative methods. The majority of the work that is done through the teachings of M.T.O. Shahmaghsoudi is breaking down the mental representations, labels, fears, gathered ideologies, and other influences of the cultural/social world so that students can bravely explore the depths of their being and truly know this vast Existence and their presence in it. This is how many of the students of M.T.O. may identify with various religious and non-religious groups, such as Jewish, Christian, Agnostic, or Muslim, but also consider themselves a Sufi student on the path of self-knowledge.

M.T.O. SUFI PSYCHOLOGY

With the brief overview of Sufism, it is easy to see how its teachings can lend themselves to psychology and the practice of psychotherapy. Typically, one defines themself by their social and familial roles, cultural and religious standards, physical body, preferences, and temperaments. However, these traits are changeable, so one's identity cannot be based on them because it would be unstable (Bozorgzadeh et al., 2017). These traits are more akin to the shade, wiring, frame, and position of the lamp as described in the earlier analogy by Sufi Master Nadar Angha. Sufism directs one to the essence of their being, which is the source of knowledge within the heart—or the light in the analogy. This source is free from the limitations and fluctuations of the material world and thus is a stable and steady foundation, which is referred to as *I*, the true identity of the individual. "It is the priority of one on the Sufi path . . . to discover who we are and what our purpose is, and to touch the source of infinite knowledge that is embedded with us" (Ayazi, 2010, pp. 23–24).

According to the teachings of Nader Angha, human beings have two dimensions: physical and spiritual. The *physical dimension* is the dimension of "matter and materialism" (N. Angha, 2002, p. 124). Living primarily in this dimension is to focus and identify only with the physical body, senses, emotions, and brain and how they interact with the outside world. In this dimension, the human being seeks tranquility by quenching the desires of the body and mind. However, because the body and mind keep changing, the desires keep fluctuating. Thus, the individual can never achieve serenity in this dimension alone. They are left to chase insatiable desires, engage in transactionary responses, and be consumed by their self-focused impulses. As Nader Angha taught:

> They create imbalance in themselves and in their surroundings and experience stress, greed, insecurity, fear, fatigue, and depression.... If human beings limit themselves to the shackles of desires and meaningless actions, they will never know their true identity and their innermost source of knowledge. (N. Angha, 2002, p. 124)

If one's sense of identity were defined by this dimension, it would be a difficult one to grasp given that aspects of this dimension constantly change. Yet most people would perceive that their sense of identity has remained intact throughout all the changes they have experienced, meaning they did not cease to be at any point. That constant and undisturbed sense is a reminder of the spiritual dimension that in the Sufi paradigm is eternal.

The *spiritual dimension* is the "internal source of balance and tranquility" (N. Angha, 2002, p. 124). It is not bound by race, ethnicity, culture, or gender, and it is "the true value of each individual" (N. Angha, 2002, p. 125). It is ineffable, and it is from this dimension that the more delicate traits of hope, love, forgiveness, strength, creativity, and compassion emerge. These traits, often associated with saints and self-actualization, have been shown to have powerful psychotherapeutic benefits. For example, studies have shown that hope is positively correlated with life satisfaction (Valle et al., 2006) and an increase cognitive flexibility (Breznitz, 1986), love has been shown to reduce anxiety (Acevedo et al., 2012) and increase longevity (Holt-Lunstad et al., 2010), creativity has been associated with higher positive affect (Conner et al., 2018), and compassion has been associated with increased happiness (Shapira & Mongrain, 2010) and higher levels of well-being (Zessin et al., 2015). Although these traits stem from the spiritual dimension, they are impacted by our environment and experiences. For example, one's sense of hope may be diminished by the events in the physical world. In Sufi Psychology, it is recognized that as a single unit of existence, the various aspects of the human being affect one another; it is a dynamic process.

Sufi Psychology uses the Sufi paradigm in the conceptualization of the patient—that is, to see the patient as a complete unit of existence and consider both dimensions. "Sufism re-establishes the lost harmony through proper education and development, and leads each individual to the discovery of himself/herself as a true unit of existence" (N. Angha, 2002, p. 126).

In contrast to the Western psychological viewpoint that the brain is in charge of the human being and is the main agent for change, Sufi Psychology focuses on the heart. In Sufism, the Source of Life is within the heart (S. Angha, 2012), and in M.T.O. Sufi Psychology, the heart and brain work together. The heart, based on its knowledge of the spiritual dimension, directs the brain, which, in turn, directs the body and all its processes (e.g., cognitions, behaviors; N. Angha, 2002). In essence, Sufi Psychology seeks to reorganize the internal hierarchical structure of the human being by directing individuals to lead with their heart—the gateway to the spiritual dimension—and not their brain.

Process

In the practice of Sufi Psychotherapy, the clinician conceptualizes the patient using the Sufi paradigm. Since this paradigm includes both physical and spiritual dimensions, the clinician will also incorporate other psychological modalities to target symptom reduction in the physical dimension. Because Sufi Psychology is about self-knowledge, it includes evidence-based practices that increase one's understanding of themselves, such as CBT, which provides an understanding of the role our cognitions play with respect to our emotions and behaviors.

When working with a patient who is encountering external stressors, a therapist integrating Sufi Psychology may initially use various theoretical modalities to ease the strain on the physical dimension (e.g., CBT to explore cognitive distortions or motivational interviewing to promote behavior change) while simultaneously using Sufi approaches to address the spiritual dimension and remind the patient that there is more to them. By reminding individuals of the spiritual dimension, patients begin to recognize that there is more to their experience than their thoughts and emotions. From a Sufi Psychology perspective, one of the underlying factors of psychological disorders, such as depression and anxiety, is a lack of familiarity with one's true identity, or, as viewed in Sufism, a loss of connection to the spiritual dimension. When one lacks knowledge about the spiritual dimension, they may experience their identity only in terms of the physical dimension; they may mistake their emotions, thoughts, and experiences to be the entirety of who they are and may overidentify with them. In such a case, for example, one may feel overwhelmed with the sadness that they are experiencing and feel they may remain this way forever, or they may feel that they "are depressed." This style of perceiving and thinking may lead to more chronic conditions of depression and other psychological disorders (Burns, 2008).

In addition, by strictly relying on the tools of this dimension, including schemas, comparisons and standards set forth by society, culture, religion, and other groups, the individual has no choice but to define their identity and determine their adequacy in this way. As research has demonstrated, comparisons with others results in diminished self-worth, decreased self-esteem, and a reduction in self-efficacy (Powers et al., 2007; Swallow & Kuiper, 1988). Because Sufism promotes a unique and individual journey for each person to know their true identity, there is no comparison with others. The techniques are unique and experiential, and most are from the nonlinear domain—that is, they are experiential and oftentimes nonverbal.

The following are some of the techniques of Sufi Psychology:

- Examine and discuss spiritual well-being/health.

- Review spiritual needs and ways of meeting them.

- Explore personal spiritual history, including the effects of earlier spiritual or religious teachings/experiences and influences of family and ancestors.

- Encourage spiritual exploration.
- Encourage spiritual reading and activities.
- Use nonlinear approaches, including stories, arts, music, movement, and poetry. The 13th-century Sufi poet Rumi, for example, said, "If you are irritated by every rub, how will your mirror be polished?" (Rumi, 1998, p. 24). During exploration of this quote with the patient, they begin to focus on what it means to be polished, which directs them to their sense of purpose. The calamities and difficulties they experience are simply recognized as "rubs" in their personal journey toward "polish."
- Use M.T.O. Sufi-based practices, such as Tamarkoz, deep breathing, heart concentration, meditation, visualization, and Movazeneh. *Tamarkoz* is a Sufi meditation practice that is unique to the M.T.O. Shahmaghsoudi School of Islamic Sufism (for more information, see http://tamarkoz.org/). *Movazeneh* is a component of Tamarkoz and involves slow movements designed to harmonize and balance the electromagnetic energy fields of the body. The therapist may use the Tamarkoz method, for example, to reduce anxiety. (Tamarkoz is described at length in the Research section later in this chapter.)
- Encourage the discovery of the innermost self, the spiritual dimension.
- Encourage the excavation of purpose and use that as "the North Star"—for example, return to an individual's purpose in all matters when making decisions.
- Engage in spiritual artwork—for example, use paint and color to represent spiritual feelings and experiences.
- Explore heart values versus brain values—for example, help the patient to differentiate the two.
- Take a strengths-based exploration of situations and problems.
- Use Socratic questioning for patient to turn inward.
- Understand the role of the *nafs* (soul) and how to develop it and use it as a motivating agent for change.
- Understand and recognize how the different components of oneself operate (e.g., the brain, emotions, body/cells) and how to navigate them.
- Engage in silent prayer (the therapist).
- Do spiritual journal writing.
- Encourage personal prayer.
- Enable heart-reliant empowerment—for example, learn to listen to one's heart or "inner voice" and trust that.
- Attend to the heart—for example, become more aware of what one needs to feel balanced and to make decisions, such as determining when one needs to spend time in solitude and reflect.

- Shift the worldview from victim stance to student stance.

- Engage in present-focused interventions or practice. Ask, for instance, about the present moment and use the process in the present moment as a learning opportunity.

- Instill hope.

- Promote compassion and forgiveness for oneself and others.

- Encourage self-discipline and gradually develop it.

- Become aware of the impact of electromagnetic forces on one's circumstance—for example, engage in experiential exercises to understand one's electromagnetic field and how people may be affected by others and things around us.

The Teacher and the Clinician

The way of Sufism requires a Teacher—a Spiritual Guide—who has gone down this road before and knows the direction. A Teacher is necessary because on the path of self-knowledge, one's narrative and cognitions may need to be challenged. As is evident from the body of research on schemas, cognitive distortions, and preconceived notions, one's desires, expectations, and experiences color what that person perceives and thus may prevent their recognition of the truth of matters. The great Sufi Master Sadegh Angha (1999) has said that "whatever is distinguished and formed through the senses and thoughts is our own creation and is thus an idol and not the truth" (p. 29).

The Teacher, who is familiar with the spiritual dimension, can help the patient sort through those gathered ideas and experiences and redirect them to what is true as opposed to the physical dimension and what has been created by the limited perception of one's experience. The individual does not choose the Teacher because one does not know more than they have experienced; thus, they cannot determine if someone has the necessary knowledge for a path that they have not been on. In Sufism, one's Teacher is appointed from within. It is an experiential process from the heart and not a decision that the brain processes. That being said, the Sufi Psychology clinician is *not* a Teacher and is not equipped to guide.

In Sufi Psychotherapy, the clinician is a student on the path of Sufism. They are trained in psychology and Sufi Psychology, and their job is to remind the patient that there is more to them than the physical dimension. One of the fundamental teachings of Sufism is that "the urge to know is inherent in each human being" (N. Angha, 2000, p. 3). This teaching guides the clinician's work. The clinician spends time reminding the patient that there is more to them than these biological workings and that they have a source of strength and stability within. They remind the patient of the spiritual dimension, of hope, and of resilience. The clinician trusts that in recognizing this part of themselves, the patient will begin to seek to know their true identity. The Sufi Psychology clinician plants the seed, and the patient, depending on their personal journey, may sow it if and when it is right for them.

Diversity

Sufi Psychology ultimately focuses on individuals being the master of their own experience and reactions. The individual's sense of self is not based strictly on their physical dimension, which changes constantly, as is evidenced by the transient nature of emotions, desires, cognitions, and the natural changes of the physical body and cells. Sufi teachings focus on the soul, the part of the human being that has remained stable and constant throughout life. This stable source is a part of all individuals, and because Islamic Sufism focuses on this source, these teachings are universal and can be applied to all individuals regardless of their religious and cultural backgrounds.

CASE ILLUSTRATION

The case example that follows is of a patient with whom this methodology was used. Details, including names, in the case example have been altered to protect client confidentiality and therapist privacy.

MG is an 11-year-old, bisexual, Caucasian girl with an extensive history of self-injurious behaviors, suicidal thoughts, and depressed mood. She identifies as part of the goth subculture and has seen numerous therapists with no decrease in symptomatology. She and her family report that they have no religious or spiritual beliefs, although MG, at times, discusses interest in the Church of Satan. MG seems older than her age, and her interests and maturity contribute to her lack of social support at school because there are no other goth kids there. Thus, she often eats alone during lunch. She has some online older friends, who live in Europe and also identify with the goth subculture. At the beginning of treatment, MG reports feeling hopeless that things will never change. Per her parents' report, she rarely smiles and isolates in her room.

After building rapport, the Sufi Psychology clinician addresses the immediate concerns of MG's self-injurious behavior using the evidenced-based emotion regulation model, which is used for self-injurious behavior (Levitt et al., 2004). This model helps decrease MG's behavior and gives her an understanding of the importance of increasing her emotional tolerance and capacity. In addition, the clinician uses experiential techniques of Sufi Psychology that emphasize an exploration of MG's identity and source of strength. Because MG is an artist at heart, painting, music, and poetry are also used so she can express herself. Rumi poetry particularly resonates with her.

His poems are teaching stories and provide powerful metaphors to withstand difficulty. One story that MG particularly likes is a Sufi story of the old man, his son, and donkey. This story has been verbally retold for many generations. Here is one variation:

> An old man and his son were walking into town next to their donkey and they encountered some townspeople who laughed at them. They said how ridiculous they were for not riding on a donkey as is intended. The old man did not want his son to be ridiculed, so he placed his son on the donkey and they continued to walk into town.
>
> Another group of townspeople passed by and sneered. They made comments about how selfish the son is that he is forcing his frail father to walk while he, at the pinnacle of health, is riding comfortably. The old man did not want his son to be ridiculed, so he switched places with his son, so he is riding the donkey and his son is walking alongside and they continued to walk into town.
>
> A third group of townspeople passed by and yelled at the old man. They made comments about what a poor father he was to make his son walk while he sat comfortably. The old man did not want to be ridiculed and misunderstood, so he raised his son onto the donkey so they were both riding it and continued to walk into town.
>
> Another group of townspeople pass by and scream about animal rights and what the donkey is enduring. The old man did not want to be ridiculed, so he and his son picked up the donkey and carried it into town.
>
> As they walked through town, people whispered and commented on the strange and ignorant duo who clearly do not know what to do with a donkey (Nouri, 1904).

This story allowed MG to see the challenges with trying to please people. It allowed her to remember that there is no right or wrong answer that will make everyone happy. Frequently during therapy, she discussed ways that she used this story when doubting herself. MG needed to feel stable in her sense of self and identity. The clinician used experiential Sufi Psychology techniques related to exploring and attending to MG's heart and understanding how she operates.

After about 6 months in treatment, MG's school tested students' level of depression as part of mental health awareness week. MG's depression scores were high. She was called to the social worker's office, who expressed concern for MG's well-being. MG replied,

> Yes, my emotions are sad, and my thoughts are trying to match it by focusing on the negatives or suggesting things would be better if I wasn't here. It makes me want to isolate. But I know this will pass so I'm focusing on my art and music in the meanwhile.

This reply demonstrated that although aspects of her body, mind, and emotions may have been stressed, MG was using something else that was beyond the effects of those aspects to identify with. She understood that she is more than these "parts"—more than the physical dimension. From the Sufi Psychology lens, MG recognized and experienced a spiritual part of her being that she could rely on in times when her physical dimension was stressed.

RESEARCH

Research on Sufi Psychology is limited. Because each patient's experience and journey is unique to them, researching and quantifying this approach is difficult. This section discusses the Templeton grant practice-based study and research on the Tamarkoz method, which is an intervention specific to M.T.O. Sufi Psychology.

Templeton Grant/Brigham Young University Bridges Big Data Study

In 2018, the Sufi Psychology Association was awarded a John Templeton Foundation grant through Brigham Young University to conduct a practice-based, bottom-up, study on the effects of Sufi Psychology. This type of research is a less intrusive method to monitor the treatment process as it is naturally occurring. Practice-based evidence has been shown to produce findings that are more valid and generalizable to real-life treatment settings and enables researchers to link naturally occurring therapeutic processes with treatment outcomes (Barkham et al., 2010).

The study followed patients of psychologists and clinicians who used M.T.O. Sufi Psychology in outpatient therapy. Patients receiving Sufi Psychotherapy provided self-report data, and multilevel models were fit to examine within-person variation as well as within- and between-person change over time. Results suggested that patients' self-reported levels of distress—specifically therapeutic, relationship, psychological, spiritual, and critical distress—were significantly reduced over therapeutic sessions. Interestingly enough, the same amount of change was observed regardless of the clinician (Bozorgzadeh & Grasser, 2021). This is the first study of Sufi Psychology, and it lays the groundwork for future considerations.

The Tamarkoz Method

The Tamarkoz method is an experiential practice unique to M.T.O. Shahmaghsoudi. It is defined as the "art of self-knowledge through concentration and meditation" (M.T.O. Tamarkoz, n.d., para. 1). If Sufism is the path of self-knowledge, Tamarkoz practice is the vehicle. It consists of five evidence-based techniques that build on one another to decrease the extraneous activity of the mind and body and bring all aspects of the being into harmony. Through this method, one builds awareness of how their mind and body operate and discovers how to navigate and control their functions. For example, mind relaxation, a meditative technique of the Tamarkoz method that uses directive imagery, allows the practitioner to learn how to quiet the chatter in their mind and focus their attention. With practice, one learns how to do this on their own and gain mastery over their mind (Brewer et al., 2011).

The Tamarkoz method consists of the following techniques: mind relaxation, breathing exercises, meditative movements called Movazeneh, deep relaxation, and visualization. These practices are done in a particular order with the focus on the heart and conclude in a heart concentration. "The heart is the seat of knowledge in the teachings of Sufism. This is why meditation in the heart is so crucial and important" (N. Angha, 2011, p. 121). Further details on the theory and mechanism of this method can be learned in Nader Angha's (2001) book *Dahm: Expansion and Contraction Within Being.*

To date, three preliminary studies have been completed on the Tamarkoz method, and many are still in progress. A pilot study on breast cancer patients focused on the effects of Tamarkoz classes on emotional state and DNA repair (Crumpler, 2002). Results from this study indicated greater amounts of Sufi practices were correlated with lower levels of emotional distress and higher levels of emotional well-being. Participants who practiced Tamarkoz for longer periods were found to maintain highly functional DNA repair systems. Another pilot study conducted on heart patients at Kaiser Permanente Hospital showed a statistically significant decline in depression and a decrease in the use of nursing services among participants of Tamarkoz classes (Crumpler, 2005).

In another study, the Tamarkoz method was shown to significantly decrease perceived stress and heart rate as well as significantly increase positive emotions and daily spiritual experiences in participants at the University of California, Berkeley (Bahadorani et al., 2021). Interestingly enough, half of the participants in the study identified as atheist or agnostic, and they reported significant increases in daily spiritual experiences. This finding suggests that the technique is not limited to those who identify with a particular religious affiliation and that the technique provides "a mechanism by which spirituality and positive emotions are increased even among individuals with no religious ideology" (Bozorgzadeh et al., 2017, p. 215).

Although the number of published studies on the Tamarkoz method is limited, many of its techniques have been shown to improve health, including deep breathing (Allen & Friedman 2012; Evers et al., 2007; Paul et al., 2007; Seaward 2009), guided visualization (Margolin et al., 2011; Newberg & Waldman, 2010), movement balancing or movement meditation (Caldwell et al., 2010; Carmody & Baer 2008; Wolf et al., 1996; Yeh et al., 2004), and spirituality (Alexander et al., 1994; Koenig, 2012; McKinney & McKinney, 1999; Wachholtz & Pargament, 2005).

As can be seen, the field of Sufi Psychology is fairly new. The research conducted is preliminary but has promise. Future considerations involve more specific studies on M.T.O. Sufi Psychology and Tamarkoz using the current findings to inform the research method and hypotheses.

Because M.T.O. Sufi Psychology's approach to psychology is based on self-knowledge and unique experience, it puts the power in the hands of the individual. This method removes comparisons, expectations, and superficial day-to day living. It encourages each individual to search for truth of their being—for the Source—that gives the lamp purpose and its true value. Knowledge of one's abilities and strength brings with it a sense of confidence and balance.

"Each person is a complex and unique masterpiece. . . . You are the measure for everything. . . . You have everything that you need. All you need to do is release the boundaries you have created, then 'reality' will unveil" (N. Angha, 2011, pp. 11–12).

For more information, see

- Sufi Psychology Association (https://www.sufipsychology.org/)
- The Tamarkoz method (http://tamarkoz.org/)
- Maktab Tarighat Oveyssi Shahmaghsoudi School of Islamic Sufism (http://mtoshahmaghsoudi.org/)

REFERENCES

Acevedo, B. P., Aron, A., Fisher, H. E., & Brown, L. L. (2012). Neural correlates of long-term intense romantic love. *Social Cognitive and Affective Neuroscience*, 7(2), 145–159. https://doi.org/10.1093/scan/nsq092

Alexander, C. N., Robinson, P., Orme-Johnson, D. W., & Schneider, R. H. (1994). The effects of transcendental meditation compared to other methods of relaxation and meditation in reducing risk factors, morbidity, and mortality. *Homeostasis in Health and Disease*, 35, 243–264.

Allen, B., & Friedman, B. H. (2012). Positive emotion reduces dyspnea during slow paced breathing. *Psychophysiology*, 49(5), 690–696. https://doi.org/10.1111/j.1469-8986.2011.01344.x

Angha, N. (2000). *Sufism: The reality of religion*. M.T.O. Shahmaghsoudi Publications.

Angha, N. (2001). *Expansion and contraction withing being*. M.T.O. Publications.

Angha, N. (2002). *Theory "I": The unlimited vision of leadership*. M.T.O. Shahmaghsoudi Publications.

Angha, N. (2011). *Sufism Lecture Series*. M.T.O. Publications.

Angha, S. (1999). *Dawn*. M.T.O. Shahmaghsoudi Publications.

Angha, S. (2012). *The hidden angles of life*. MTO Publications.

Ayazi, M. (2010). Islamic Sufism and education for peace. In E. J. Brantmeier, J. Lin, & J. P. Miller (Eds.), *Spirituality, religion, and peace education* (pp. 19–35). Information Age Publishing.

Bahadorani, N., Lee, J. W., & Martin, L. R. (2021). Implications of Tamarkoz on stress, emotion, spirituality and heart rate. *Scientific Reports*. Advance online publication. https://doi.org/10.1038/s41598-021-93470-8

Barkham, M., Hardy, G. E., & Mellor-Clark, J. (Eds.). (2010). *Developing and delivering practice-based evidence: A guide for the psychological therapies*. Wiley-Blackwell. https://doi.org/10.1002/9780470687994

Ben-David, J., & Collins, R. (1966). Social factors in the origins of a new science: The case of psychology. *American Sociological Review*, 31(4), 451–465. https://doi.org/10.2307/2090769

Boring, E. G. (1950). *A history of experimental psychology* (2nd ed.). Appleton-Century-Crofts. (Original work published 1942)

Bozorgzadeh, S., Bahadorani, N., & Sadoghi, M. (2017). Sufism and optimal health. In D. D. VonDras (Ed.), *Better health through spiritual practices* (pp. 205–227). ABC-CLIO.

Bozorgzadeh, S., & Grasser, L. R. (2021). The integration of the heart-centered paradigm of Sufi Psychology in contemporary psychotherapy practice. *Psychotherapy*. Advance online publication. https://doi.org/10.1037/pst0000414

Brewer, J. A., Worhunsky, P. D., Gray, J. R., Tang, Y. Y., Weber, J., & Kober, H. (2011). Meditation experience is associated with differences in default mode network activity and connectivity. *Proceedings of the National Academy of Sciences*, 108(50), 20254–20259. https://doi.org/10.1073/pnas.1112029108

Breznitz, S. (1986). The effect of hope on coping with stress. In M. H. Appley & R. Trumbull (Eds.), *Dynamics of stress: Physiological, psychological, and social perspectives* (pp. 295–306). Plenum Press. https://doi.org/10.1007/978-1-4684-5122-1_15

Burns, D. D. (2008). *Feeling good: The new mood therapy*. Harper.
Caldwell, K., Harrison, M., Adams, M., Quin, R. H., & Greeson, J. (2010). Developing mindfulness in college students through movement-based courses: Effects on self-regulatory self-efficacy, mood, stress, and sleep quality. *Journal of American College Health, 58*(5), 433–442. https://doi.org/10.1080/07448480903540481
Carmody, J., & Baer, R. A. (2008). Relationships between mindfulness practice and levels of mindfulness, medical and psychological symptoms and well-being in a mindfulness-based stress reduction program. *Journal of Behavioral Medicine, 31*(1), 23–33. https://doi.org/10.1007/s10865-007-9130-7
Conner, T. S., DeYoung, C. G., & Silvia, P. J. (2018). Everyday creative activity as a path to flourishing. *The Journal of Positive Psychology, 13*(2), 181–189. https://doi.org/10.1080/17439760.2016.1257049
Crumpler, C. (2005). Tamarkoz (Sufi meditation) for heart patients: A pilot study. *Sufism: Science of the Soul, 7*(1), 9–10.
Crumpler, C. A. (2002). Sufi practices, emotional state, and DNA repair: Implications for breast cancer. *Sufism: Science of the Soul, 4*(1), 25–37.
Erikson, E. (1980). *Identity and the life cycle*. W. W. Norton & Company. (Original work published 1968)
Etymonline. (n.d.). Psychology. In *Online Etymology Dictionary*. Retrieved February 4, 2021 from https://www.etymonline.com/word/psychology
Evers, C., Starr, C., & Starr, L. (2007). *Biology today and tomorrow with physiology* (2nd ed.). Thomson Brooks/Cole.
Frankl, V. E. (1988). *The will to meaning: Foundations and applications of logotherapy*. Penguin Group. (Original work published 1969)
Holt-Lunstad, J., Smith, T. B., & Layton, J. B. (2010). Social relationships and mortality risk: A meta-analytic review. *PLOS Medicine*. Article e1000316. Advance online publication. https://doi.org/10.1371/journal.pmed.1000316
Koenig, H. G. (2012). Religion, spirituality, and health: The research and clinical implications. *ISRN Psychiatry, 2012*, Article 278730. https://doi.org/10.5402/2012/278730
Levitt, J. L., Sansone, R. A., & Cohn, L. (2004). *Self-harm behavior and eating disorders: Dynamics, assessments, and treatment*. Brunner-Routledge.
Margolin, I., Pierce, J., & Wiley, A. (2011). Wellness through a creative lens: Mediation and visualization. *Journal of Religion & Spirituality in Social Work: Social Thought, 30*(3), 234–252. https://doi.org/10.1080/15426432.2011.587385
Maslow, A. H. (1999). *Toward a psychology of being* (3rd ed.). John Wiley & Sons. (Original work published 1968)
McKinney, J. P., & McKinney, K. G. (1999). Prayer in the lives of late adolescents. *Journal of Adolescence, 22*(2), 279–290. https://doi.org/10.1006/jado.1999.0216
M.T.O. Tamarkoz. (n.d.) *Welcome to Tamarkoz*. http://tamarkoz.org/
Newberg, A., & Waldman, M. R. (2010). *How God changes your brain: Breakthrough findings from a leading neuroscientist*. Ballantine Books.
Nouri, A. (1904). *Nasreddin Khodjas Schwänke und Streiche: Türkische Geschichten aus Timurlenks Tagen* [*Nasreddin Khodja's farces and pranks: Turkish stories from Timurlenk's days*]. Breslau, Wroclaw: Schlesische Verlags-Anstalt von S. Schottlaender.
Paul, G., Elam, B., & Verhulst, S. J. (2007). A longitudinal study of students' perceptions of using deep breathing meditation to reduce testing stresses. *Teaching and Learning in Medicine, 19*(3), 287–292. https://doi.org/10.1080/10401330701366754
Powers, T. A., Koestner, R., & Zuroff, D. C. (2007). Self criticism, goal motivation, and goal progress. *Journal of Social and Clinical Psychology, 26*(7), 826–840. https://doi.org/10.1521/jscp.2007.26.7.826
Rumi, J. (1998). *The Rumi collection*. Shambhala Publications.
Seaward, B. L. (2009). *Managing stress: Principles and strategies for health and well-being*. Jones and Bartlett Publishers.

Shapira, L. B., & Mongrain, M. (2010). The benefits of self-compassion and optimism exercises for individuals vulnerable to depression. *The Journal of Positive Psychology, 5*(5), 377–389. https://doi.org/10.1080/17439760.2010.516763

Swallow, S. R., & Kuiper, N. A. (1988). Social comparison and negative self-evaluations: An application to depression. *Clinical Psychology Review, 8*(1), 55–76. https://doi.org/10.1016/0272-7358(88)90049-9

Valle, M. F., Huebner, E. S., & Suldo, S. M. (2006). An analysis of hope as a psychological strength. *Journal of School Psychology, 44*(5), 393–406. https://doi.org/10.1016/j.jsp.2006.03.005

Wachholtz, A. B., & Pargament, K. I. (2005). Is spirituality a critical ingredient of meditation? Comparing the effects of spiritual meditation, secular meditation, and relaxation on spiritual, psychological, cardiac, and pain outcomes. *Journal of Behavioral Medicine, 28*(4), 369–384. https://doi.org/10.1007/s10865-005-9008-5

Wilcox, L. (1995). *Sufism and psychology*. ABJAD.

Wolf, S. L., Barnhart, H. X., Kutner, N. G., McNeely, E., Coogler, C., & Xu, T. (1996). Reducing frailty and falls in older persons: An investigation of Tai Chi and computerized balance training. *Journal of the American Geriatrics Society, 44*(5), 489–497. https://doi.org/10.1111/j.1532-5415.1996.tb01432.x

Yeh, G. Y., Wood, M. J., Lorell, B. H., Stevenson, L. W., Eisenberg, D. M., Wayne, P. M., Goldberger, A. L., Davis, R. B., & Phillips, R. S. (2004). Effects of Tai Chi mind–body movement therapy on functional status and exercise capacity in patients with chronic heart failure: A randomized controlled trial. *The American Journal of Medicine, 117*(8), 541–548. https://doi.org/10.1016/j.amjmed.2004.04.016

Zessin, U., Dickhäuser, O., & Garbade, S. (2015). The relationship between self-compassion and well-being: A meta-analysis. *Applied Psychology. Health and Well-Being, 7*(3), 340–364. https://doi.org/10.1111/aphw.12051

16

Christian-Based Spiritually Integrated Psychotherapy for East Asian Canadians and Findings From the CSPEARIT Study

Wai Lun Alan Fung, Purple Yip, Sheila Stevens, Tat-Ying Wong, Yeun-Hee Natalie Yoo, Nancy Ross, Helen K. Noh, and Taryn Tang

In this chapter, we provide an overview of Christian-based spiritually integrated psychotherapy in Ontario, Canada, focused on East Asian Canadians. Some references are made to findings from the Christian-Based Spiritually Integrated Psychotherapy for East Asians Research Initiative of Toronto (CSPEARIT) project conducted as part of the Bridges Consortium for Spiritually Integrated Psychotherapy. The study had three recruitment sites, all outpatient centers located in Toronto, Canada: (a) Tyndale University, which includes Tyndale Counselling Services, serving the student population, and Tyndale Family Life Centre, serving clients coming from the surrounding communities; (b) Grace Health Centre; and (c) Living Water Counselling Centre.

WHY IS THE APPROACH NEEDED?

Toronto is the largest city in Canada and one of the most culturally diverse cities in the world. Immigrants bring their families, culture, language, traditions, and spiritual faith to the city. According to the 2011 Census, the Chinese are the second largest visible minority group in Canada, comprising 21.1% (numbering

---

The first three authors contributed equally to this chapter. We wish to thank those who participated in our research and the site champions who assisted with the study.

https://doi.org/10.1037/0000338-016
Handbook of Spiritually Integrated Psychotherapies, P. S. Richards, G. E. K. Allen, and D. K. Judd (Editors)
Copyright © 2023 by the American Psychological Association. All rights reserved.

1,324,700) of the visible minority population and 4.0% of the total population; the number of Korean Canadians is around 161,130 (Chui & Flanders, 2011). The province of Ontario has the largest share of immigrants in Canada (53.3%), and the vast majority of them live in Toronto. Indeed, the Chinese and Koreans are the two largest East Asian communities in Toronto, comprising 10.8% and 1.4% of the population, respectively (Lindsay, 2001). The majority of immigrants of Chinese origin arrived in Canada relatively recently. Between 1986 and 1991, the Chinese population in the Greater Toronto Area (GTA) doubled to 240,000 (Lee, 2000). By 2001, 52% of ethnic Chinese immigrants had arrived between 1991 and 2000 and another 25% had arrived between 1981 and 1990 (Lindsay, 2001). In addition, Christianity is well represented in the Chinese and Korean communities in Toronto. For instance, there are more than 200 Chinese Christian churches in the GTA, and the largest of these would have an average weekly attendance of more than 4,500 congregants. The weekly attendance at the largest Korean Christian churches in the GTA would also be well over 2,000 congregants.

Although Toronto has many publicly funded services, there was a lack of immigrant-based, language-specific services for immigrants in the 1980s. Thus, immigrants who settled in the GTA started and provided immigrant-focused counseling services. In Toronto, Living Water Counselling Centre (LWCC) and Grace Health Centre (GHC) were both founded in the 1980s and pioneered language-specific, faith-based treatment for the Chinese community. These services are important as mental health issues in Chinese communities in Western countries have often been underrecognized and undertreated (Ahmad et al., 2018; Ahmad et al., 2022).

In Toronto, many faith communities are considered the "second home" to immigrants. These faith communities provide outreach, social services, counseling, companionship, employment support, shelter, education, and other informal settlement services. Especially for seniors, international students, and single parents, the church community provides the relationships, guidance, and support that eases the difficulties in the immigration and integration process.

We have found that many clients, regardless of their ethnicity, are looking for a therapist who shares their faith and understands their worldview, cultural background, and immigration experience as well as respects their faith traditions. They often ask for a therapist who will work with them to meaningfully integrate faith into their daily lives or help them discern the will of the sacred to inform their decision-making process. Spiritually integrated psychotherapy makes sense to both clients and therapists.

WHO DEVELOPED IT?

The regulatory body for psychotherapy in the province of Ontario, Canada, recently included spiritually integrated psychotherapy as one of the recognized therapeutic modalities of psychotherapy (College of Registered Psychotherapists of Ontario [CRPO], 2021b). However, a long history of integrating faith into psychotherapy existed prior to the recent recognition (Ball & Goodyear, 1991; Worthington et al., 1996). This is particularly the case for the Korean community. In 2001, 51% of the Korean population reported that they belonged to either a mainline Protestant denomination or another Christian group, whereas 25% of the Korean population reported that they were Catholic (Lindsay, 2001). Upon arriving in Canada, one of the first actions toward settlement is to locate a Korean church and a faith community.

Korean Christians are known for their spiritual disciplines. In the GTA, more than 10 Korean retreat centers offer spiritual retreat and spiritual direction. Faith plays an important role in the daily routines of many Koreans. Morning prayer, fasting, and other spiritual disciplines are ingrained into their daily lives. Korean immigrants respect their faith leaders and often seek counseling from them. Naturally, therapists who are considered as leaders in the community are expected to integrate faith into their counseling service.

Faith integration has been an integral part of the counseling services offered at Tyndale Counselling Services (TCS) and Tyndale Family Life Centre (FLC). While more than one method exists, and each therapist has the freedom to practice spiritual integration as they see fit in accordance with the interest and needs of their clients, all therapists identify themselves as Christians. Most therapists at the counseling center are graduates from Tyndale Seminary of Tyndale University and received training both in theology and counseling. On top of their theological training, TCS and FLC host an annual seminar on spiritually integrated psychotherapy for their staff to raise awareness and enhance competence. The annual training emphasizes the need to integrate faith in psychotherapy, incorporates the spiritual concerns of the client in the conceptualization of issues, introduces spiritual techniques with illustrations, educates therapists on seeking supervision and consultation to address challenges, and evaluates the outcome and effectiveness of spiritually integrated psychotherapy.

IN WHICH TREATMENT SETTING(S) HAS IT BEEN USED AND FOUND HELPFUL?

In the CSPEARIT study, all three sites were outpatient counseling centers, and all of the therapists on staff at the three centers identified themselves as practicing Christians. Most clients seen at LWCC and GHC are of Chinese descent, and a significant proportion of clients seen at TCS are of East Asian descent. All three centers have a strong component of providing clinical training to counseling trainees who are doing their practicum in the last year of their graduate school program. Many of the licensed therapists and clinical supervisors of the three centers are graduates from the counseling program at the Tyndale Seminary of Tyndale University.

Almost all TCS clients are Christians, as are most of the FLC clients. A high percentage of FLC clients are referred by clergy or church members. According to the clinical director of TCS (coauthor S. S.), clients prefer therapists who not only understand and respect their faith background but also have a faith background themselves. The therapist's faith background does not necessarily need to be the same faith tradition as the client. Many FLC clients from a Muslim, Catholic, or Jewish background prefer a faith-based counseling center to a secular counseling center.

LWCC is an outpatient counseling center that receives referrals from churches and ministers. LWCC created counseling partnerships with churches for a third-party payment that allows members from the congregation to access counseling services. Spiritually integrated psychotherapy is practiced in group and individual formats.

At GHC, psychotherapy is provided mostly by medical doctors who are family physicians or general practice physicians and who have formal psychotherapy training. They are called "GP psychotherapists" or "medical psychotherapists." As the psychotherapy services they provide are considered medical services, and the fees of physician services in Ontario are covered by the government under the Ontario Health Insurance Plan, the GHC has been able to serve individuals who may not otherwise be able to afford or have private insurance coverage for the fees of psychotherapy services. All the physicians at GHC have identified themselves as practicing evangelical Christians. The treatment approach integrates the medical approach with faith and psychotherapy to provide cross-cultural holistic treatment to individuals, couples, families, and groups. To make services more accessible to churchgoers, some of the treatment groups are run in partnership with churches by using church Sunday school time. Clients who are attending the church service on Sunday can easily attend the group treatment taking place at their church.

FOR WHAT TYPES OF CLIENTS AND CLINICAL ISSUES IS IT HELPFUL?

Clients seeking psychotherapy or counseling are individuals, couples, and families suffering from or dealing with a variety of issues. These include but are not limited to abuse and trauma, addiction and various mental health issues, academic challenges, life transition difficulties, grief and loss in the process of immigrating, parenting challenges, financial issues, gender and sexuality related issues, relationships, marriage and family issues, self-care issues, emotional stress, management of emotions, spiritual issues, time management issues, and work stress.

Koenig (2012) examined the relationships between spirituality and positive and negative mental health outcomes. Koenig concluded that spirituality has been associated with positive outcomes, including well-being, happiness, hope, optimism, and gratefulness; and negative outcomes, including depression, suicide, anxiety, substance abuse, delinquency or crime, marital instability, and personality traits. In our multisite study, we found that therapists—including East Asian therapists—who integrate faith in the counseling process tend to use it across all clinical issues. All three centers provide individual therapy, couple and family therapy, and group treatment. This outcome is consistent with Koenig's (2012) findings.

DESCRIPTION OF THE TREATMENT APPROACH

Theoretical and Theological Foundations

Every counseling theory is based on an understanding of personhood. Spiritually integrated psychotherapy is grounded in theological anthropology. To be a competent spiritually integrated psychotherapist, we encourage therapists to pursue an in-depth understanding of the theology of the human person. An Ontario theologian, Dr. Victor Shepherd (2014), has captured the core elements of theological anthropology in his class, titled The Theology of the Human Person. Many therapists in the CSPEARIT study have taken this course. The following paragraphs aim to highlight his teachings.

A human being is created in the image of God (*imago dei*). Psychiatry focuses on the pathology of an illness, whereas spiritually integrated psychotherapy focuses on the sacred image one bears. Instead of viewing behaviors as willful actions based on calculated choices, faith-integrated therapists are aware of the "helplessness" and "suffering" (Shepherd, 2015) of a fallen creature and the inability of "willing" out of sin. Therefore, redemption, repentance, restoration, and forgiveness—by God, by others, and by oneself—are often integral parts of the healing process.

As a human being created by and bearing the image of God, a person is created as a *relational being* (Anderson, 2010). In other words, you are who you belong to. To be human is to relate and belong to the creating God. To be human is to relate and belong to other fellow humans. In the counseling process, a spiritually integrated therapist cultivates a safe place for this subject-to-subject encounter by creating a trusting, safe therapeutic relationship with clients.

Change happens in a safe, trusting therapeutic relationship. It happens during the experience of grace in the process. Change happens in the intimate subject-to-subject encounter with another human person and with the sacred. Change is "bringing about positive change in the client's thinking, feeling, behavior and social functioning" (CRPO, 2021c, para. 1). A spiritually integrated psychotherapist sees a person as a holistic being who has a soul. Change is about becoming more holistic, listening to one's own heart, and attending to the need of the soul as well.

Change can also mean making choices based on the Word, rather than "fleshly" desires. Discerning the will and the heart of the sacred is an integral part of spiritually integrated psychotherapy. Clients seeking a faith emphasis in psychotherapy often want to clarify if their issues are consequences of their own or someone else's sin. Clients also have a strong need to discern the will of God in the course of change.

In our study, most of the therapists are graduates of Tyndale Seminary and received a master's-level degree with theological and clinical counseling training. Although these therapists are not trained in one identified or specific spiritually integrated counseling model, all of them would have received training in courses such as The Theology of the Human Person, Foundational Perspectives in Christian Counseling, and Spiritual Formation. These courses help students reflect on a biblical understanding of the nature of the human person, the nature of sin, a biblical understanding of marriage and the family system, generational sin and trauma, the tradition of Christian healing, discerning the guidance of the Holy Spirit, and practicing spiritual disciplines, including prayer, fasting, Bible study, and meditation. Some of the therapists have also taken elective courses, including Counseling and the Holy Spirit as well as Spiritual Warfare, which further investigate spiritual understandings of clinical issues, the nature of mental illness, and the interface between psychiatry, psychology, and spirituality (Tan, 2011; Tan & Gregg, 2010).

As part of the clinical counseling training in the seminary, trainees receive counseling themselves. The intention behind this practice is to allow a therapist-to-be an opportunity to be a client so they can understand and appreciate what clients might experience. In addition, they can reflect on how their family of origin has shaped and formed them and how their boundaries, personality, cultural background, and spirituality inform them as a human being, a father, mother, daughter, brother, or spouse, and as a therapist. Most important, it provides therapists in training the chance to reflect on how their faith informs their worldview, consider their faith tradition, locate their own prejudice and bias, and increase their awareness of their subjective context. When therapists in training experience the change brought by reflecting on their subjective context through their own counseling, they are in a better position to extend empathy when journeying with clients without judgment, prejudice, or bias.

Process and Ethical Guidelines for the Approach

As the regulatory body of psychotherapy in Ontario, the College of Registered Psychotherapists of Ontario (CRPO, 2021b) acknowledges spiritually integrated psychotherapy as one of the recognized therapeutic modalities; therefore, there is a need to formalize the training, define the process, identify the tools and intervention strategies, and develop ethical and clinical guidelines for this specific counseling approach.

One of the principles of practicing psychotherapy is safe and effective use of self. According to the CRPO (2021a), safe and effective use of self is defined as

> the psychotherapist's learned capacity to understand his or her own subjective context and patterns of interaction as they inform his or her participation in the therapeutic relationship with the client. It also speaks to the psychotherapist's self-reflective use of his or her personality, insights, perceptions and judgments in order to optimize interactions with clients in the therapeutic process. ("Safe and Effective Use of Self")

Faith is a key element in one's subjective context. Faith informs a person's worldview, decision making, understanding of right and wrong, moral standard, understanding of marriage, the meaning and purpose of life, calling and vocation, eternity and future, and the origin of human beings. While therapists are not supposed to impose their personal value and biases onto clients, it is impossible to avoid being biased unless the therapists reflect on their faith as the subjective context.

As Pargament (2007) pointed out, spiritually integrated psychotherapy has three elements: the spirituality of the client, the spirituality of the therapist, and the process of change. Therapists are bringing their faith and their spiritual beliefs and experience to the counseling process to support clients who are integrating their faith in their recovery through change. While therapists are offering suggestions and guidance, therapists are also embracing new spiritual experience in the process of change. In the context of Christian-based spiritually integrated psychotherapy, unless therapists are open and receptive to the guidance of the Holy Spirit, they may not be able to cocreate change according to their client's wish and the lead of the Holy Spirit but may manipulate or try to force a change according to the therapist's own biases and beliefs.

We would encourage every therapist who is practicing spiritually integrated psychotherapy to reflect on the following questions:

Regarding clients' spirituality

- To what degree do I understand and respect my client's worldview based on their faith background?
- How does my client's faith or spirituality inform the problems they are facing, the meaning of the problem, coping, change, and outcome?

Regarding therapists' spirituality

- How does my faith inform my worldview and my practice?
- How can I join with my client in a meaningful way around our shared areas of faith?
- How does my faith tradition speak to the client's experience and issues? How might it get in the way?
- Does the client or the issues presented trigger my memories or previous experience? How might that help and/or hinder our work together?

Other ethical concerns

- Am I imposing my own faith and beliefs on my client? How will I know if or when this is happening?
- What are my biases, prejudice, or religious beliefs that prohibit me from maintaining my neutrality?
- Am I competent in addressing my client's spiritual concerns?
- Are there any boundary or dual relationship issues, potential manipulation, or misuse of power in the therapeutic relationship?

- Are my conceptualization, intervention, and therapeutic strategies within the scope of practice of psychotherapy?
- Am I offering spiritually integrated psychotherapy, pastoral counseling, spiritual direction, or discipleship? How do I see the similarities and differences?

Diversity Considerations

In Canada, the Human Rights Act prohibits discrimination or declining services to clients based on their religious, cultural, or racial background and gender and sexual orientation. Although all three counseling centers are known for their evangelical Christian background, all three counseling centers provide services to clients from many Christian denominations and other faith traditions, including but not limited to Buddhist, Muslim, Catholic, Jewish, and Indigenous backgrounds, as well as clients who do not have affiliation with any faith or religious tradition.

Since Toronto is one of the most culturally diverse cities in the world, licensed therapists are expected to be culturally sensitive. At TCS, the leadership makes an effort to ensure the staff reflects the diverse cultural background of the student body. In the 2020–2021 academic year, TCS had 48 staff members, and, in order of prevalence, they come from Chinese, White, Korean, Black, South Asian, Middle Eastern, Hispanic, and mixed heritage and are able to provide counseling in English, Mandarin, Cantonese, Korean, Arabic, Spanish, French, and Malayalam. At LWCC and GHC, the majority of the client population identified as Chinese or affiliated with the Chinese culture. There is a strong representation of Chinese on staff. Most of the therapists, medical doctors, and staff are fluent in both Chinese (Cantonese and/or Mandarin) and English.

Relationship Establishment Guidelines or Guiding Principles

In all three counseling centers, therapists and the clinical staff pay special attention to boundaries, confidentiality, privacy, and dual relationships asderly Christian community, particularly in some ethnic communities, is relatively small and tightly knit in Toronto. Therapists and clients may be going to the same church or share mutual friends. Therapists could be the church leaders, Sunday school teachers, deacons, or even ministers. Clients may be referred to a specific Christian therapist as the referring minister is also an acquaintance of the therapist.

On one hand, issues of transference from the clients could take place. For instance, clients may worry that therapists would disclose their spiritual or religious struggles to their ministers or other people from their faith community. On the other hand, clients may assume that their therapists would integrate religious elements in the counseling process, such as expecting therapists to apply religious teaching in counseling their children or assuming therapists will confront divorce, addiction, or certain sexual behaviors based on Christian values.

Many of the therapists in the CSPEARIT study—especially those of East Asian descent—are known in Christian circles and considered as leaders in the faith community. Given that most of the therapists are also graduates of Tyndale Seminary, where they received formal training in theology, a lot of clients consider them as experts both in counseling and the Christian faith. As for therapists, countertransference could be a potential challenge. The challenge becomes even more obvious in the East Asian Christian community as they tend to respect authoritative figures, including ministers and counselors. Trained therapists, especially those who receive formal training in theology, are considered an authority. This religious authority element widens the power differential between the client and the therapist. If the transference and countertransference dynamics are not managed and addressed, the religious authority over clients can create the potential for coercion. Goals and direction of therapy can be skewed based on the therapist's religious bias or unintentional coercion.

As a result, proper training in methods and process of spiritually integrated psychotherapy is essential. The practice of safe and effective use of self should include reflecting on the impact of one's religious and spiritual beliefs in the counseling process (CRPO, 2021a). Spiritually integrated supervision should be developed to support practicing safe and effective spiritually integrated psychotherapy.

Assessment Guidelines and Recommendations

In all three counseling centers, an experienced therapist or the intake coordinator conducts an intake session with the client. In preparation, the client fills out the client intake form, and this information is reviewed in the intake session to assist in the assessment and placement of the client with a therapist. Questions include denominational or religious affiliation, positive assets (clients often list their faith), spiritual health, and any concerns and expectations for therapy, including whether spiritual integration is desired and any specific requests related to that.

In the assessment process, it is sometimes recommended that a client with more severe mental health issues consider having a consultation with one of the Christian medical doctors or psychiatrists on staff. We have noted that individuals and families who are people of faith are more open to this option when the practitioner is also a person of faith.

Another purpose of the intake session is to match the client's needs and preferences with a therapist. The matching decision is based partially on the consultation with the client on their preferences in terms of personality, approach, cultural background, language, availability, and other factors important to the client. In addition, the person conducting the intake considers the complexity of the presenting issues and experience and clinical interests of the therapists on the team. The care and effort given to arranging a good client–therapist match is especially important for centers (like those in our study) that have interns and therapists with more limited experience on the team.

Once therapy has begun, regular feedback from the client about its effectiveness and outcomes of the treatment, including the faith-based aspects, is important. In research conducted on factors accounting for success in therapy, 60% of the success was due to alliance factors, which involve the perception of the client about the therapeutic relationship (Duncan et al., 2004; Hubble et al., 2010). This would include the need for the therapist to be in tune with the client's worldview, values, beliefs, culture, and view of therapy; check in with the client to see if they are on the right track; be in agreement on the goals of therapy; and practice Carl Rogers's core conditions for therapy (unconditional positive regard, genuineness, and congruency). Outcomes improved significantly when therapists had their clients assess the alliance and give outcome feedback (Duncan et al., 2004; Hubble et al., 2010). The therapist creates a culture of feedback so the client feels safe enough to give their opinion and engage as an active participant in their treatment. The therapist must then integrate the feedback from the client into the clinical care and continue to adjust and accommodate to the client's perceptions and preferences to maximize the chances of positive outcomes.

Intervention Strategies and Techniques

The CRPO (2021b) makes a distinction between counseling and psychotherapy. In providing psychotherapy, therapists should be applying intervention strategies based on five broad categories of therapeutic modalities (CRPO, 2021b, para. 1):

- cognitive and behavioral therapies
- experiential and humanistic therapies
- psychodynamic therapies
- somatic therapies
- systemic and collaborative therapies

Spiritually integrated psychotherapy is listed under the category of "experiential and humanistic therapies" together with art therapy, emotion-focused or emotionally focused therapy, gestalt therapy, multicultural therapy, music therapy, play therapy, psychodrama, Rogerian person-centered therapy, Satir transformational systemic therapy, and sex therapy (CRPO, 2021b).

In view of the listed therapeutic modalities in the same category, one can assume spiritually integrated psychotherapy has a strong component of personal experience, brought by both the client and the therapist. The experience of change is also a shared experience between the client and the therapist in the counseling process.

The humanistic therapy tradition emphasizes the importance of being one's true self to live the most fulfilling life. The true self can choose and change one's choices and actions and vice versa. While a therapist is helping a client find and define their true self, the therapist is also bringing their true self (Peteet, 2014) and becomes a channel for grace to flow through the change process. A spiritually integrated psychotherapist believes one's true self can only be found in God.

Most therapists who are practicing spiritually integrated psychotherapy are incorporating prayer, meditation, and scripture in the process. But a much broader range of techniques and tools are available for therapists to use in therapy, such as helping clients find and define the meaning, purpose, and calling in their life; encouraging attendance at community services and rituals; practicing spiritual disciplines, volunteerism, and service to others; living a life based on ethical values; practicing forgiveness, gratitude, and kindness; seeking social justice and acceptance of self and others (even with faults); being part of something larger than oneself; and appreciating the sacredness of life (Plante, 2009; Richards & Bergin, 2014; Sperry & Shafranske, 2005).

Recommendations for Collaborating With Clergy

Over the years at TCS and FLC, we have seen the benefits of clergy who have themselves undergone counseling or psychotherapy. They are more likely to understand what therapy is, what it can and cannot do, when and how to refer, and how to support their congregant who is referred for counseling without crossing the boundary and being intrusive or interfering in the counseling work.

Many clergy members who refer to the services (both student and public divisions) are alumni of Tyndale University and have undergone some counseling sessions during their time at Tyndale. All students have access to TCS for free or very low fees. Approximately 30% of the current students in any given year undergo counseling at Tyndale. Students in one master's-level program for people already in ministry come for self-awareness sessions through TCS. They have the opportunity to explore insights from psychometric instruments such as the Myers-Briggs Type Indicator, understand more about how their family of origin experiences and patterns influence their ministry and personal relationships, and look at how they deal with boundaries and stress in their professional and personal life. In addition, students in this program meet with a spiritual director and mentor to enhance their own personal, spiritual, and professional growth. Students in the master's level counseling program also do some self-awareness sessions as well as spiritual direction sessions to encourage them to deal with their own issues before helping others with theirs.

All three counseling centers involved in our study collaborate with churches and faith leaders on a regular basis. Indeed, collaborations between mental health professionals and faith communities in promoting mental health and addressing mental health issues have been strongly recommended, with various models proposed and utilized (Fung, Mirhom, et al., 2021; Fung, Shepherd, et al., 2021; Okamoto et al., 2021). Examples of the types of collaborations are:

- offering seminars and conferences requested by or relevant to faith communities

- consulting with faith leaders who are dealing with a difficult mental health situation

- providing basic mental health training for leaders

- working with faith communities to reduce stigma around counseling as well as mental illness
- finding creative ways to offer more affordable services to those who need it (e.g., churches offering subsidies or counseling centers, including interning counselors who need experience and supervision)
- providing support, self-care, and counseling for faith leaders and their families
- accepting invitations from faith leaders to speak in the worship service
- teaching students planning to become faith leaders and psychotherapists at seminary about boundaries, dual relationships, transference and countertransference, confidentiality, the use and misuse of the power inherent in their role, and so on
- hosting therapy groups in their faith community
- providing an office in a faith community for a therapist to work from to receive referrals from the church and surrounding community
- talking in therapy, as appropriate, about the possible benefits of involvement of client(s) in their faith community and in spiritual practices
- assisting faith communities to form a mental health committee to provide training and resources to support individuals and families suffering from mental illness

Next, we present two case studies illustrating treatment process and interventions.

CASE STUDY 1: REESTABLISHMENT OF IDENTITY AND CONFIDENCE THROUGH SPIRITUAL INTERVENTIONS

This case study[1] provides an example of the effectiveness of spiritual interventions in addressing anxiety related to low self-esteem, self-doubt, and learned passivity toward life.

The psychotherapist in this case study was a Korean woman in her late 40s. As an evangelical Christian, she enjoys encounters with God through regular Bible reading, prayer, and fellowship with other believers. She has been working in the mental health field since graduation with a counseling-focused master's of divinity degree in 2005. She is currently practicing psychotherapy in a Christian counseling center setting using therapies such as spiritually integrated, psychodynamic, family systems, cognitive behavior (CBT), and narrative. She is also teaching mental health-related courses at a higher education level.

---

[1]This case study was written by Yeun-Hee Natalie Yoo. Details have been changed to protect client confidentiality.

The client was seen over a total of 25 weekly 1-hour sessions at a Christian university counseling center in Toronto, Canada. She was an elite Korean woman in her mid-40s who was married with a child. The client was a devout evangelical Christian who enjoyed serving in a leadership role at her church. She was working full time as a legal professional while taking ministry-related courses on a part-time basis.

The client first came to therapy claiming anxiety and frustration with herself and her overall passivity toward life. She requested support on improving self-awareness and confidence, gaining a sense of direction for the future, and implementing spiritual habits in daily life. Her major complaints included self-doubt, self-loathing, stress, guilt, and helplessness. She claimed feeling "sick and tired" of putting others before herself and wanting to find ways to live "differently." The client rated her level of distress as 10 out of 10 (1 *low*–10 *high*). This was the first time she was seeking psychotherapy, and she denied having taken any psychotropic medications in the past.

In terms of the client's history, she was born in Toronto as the youngest child of four in a high-achieving Korean immigrant family. She identified her father as being traditionally authoritarian, strong-willed, and opinionated. He had given up a successful career to become a missionary when she was in elementary school. He was frequently away on mission projects while her mother, a submissive type, took care of the children. Her mother had dreams of pursuing a career of her own but never acted on them. The client claimed that her parents had been overprotective and overinvolved throughout her life. She depended on their opinion when making important life decisions, thinking they would know better and to avoid disappointing them. For example, she had chosen law school over Bible college to satisfy their hopes for her to have a prestigious career. She did not enjoy the studies and constantly doubted her capacity to become a legal professional. Furthermore, the client remembered experiencing sexism and racism at school and being cautious about identifying herself as a Christian out of fear of further discrimination. Upon graduation, she married a Korean classmate and gave birth to a girl. Her husband was loving but traditional regarding gender roles. She did not question her role as the main caregiver of their child while working full time. The client also depended on her husband to make major decisions for the family.

The therapy process began with a conceptualization of the client's narrative using the psychodynamic and family systems model. We explored the impact of her being born as the youngest child, taking up the role as the one "who makes everyone happy," growing up as a second-generation immigrant to parents who upheld traditional Korean values and strict religious lifestyle, experiencing race and gender-related discrimination as well as a father's frequent absences, and striving to live up to parents' high expectations. On the basis of this preliminary understanding, the client welcomed the idea of using the Great Commandment (Matthew 22:36–40) as the framework for intervention. The focus was on reestablishing her identity and reorganizing life priorities according to this passage: first to love God, second to love ourselves, and last, to love others as we love ourselves. These areas were worked on simultaneously throughout the course of therapy.

To begin with, the client diligently worked on finding ways to "deepen her relationship with God." She initiated carving out time in the morning for Bible reading and prayer and set aside time in the evening for reflection and journaling. These times led her to become more aware of God's work not only in the present but also in the past. In particular, the realization of God's divine intervention in her becoming a legal professional helped her to experience his love at a deeper level and gain confidence in her identity as "his beloved child." This, in turn, led her to become more comfortable in accepting her strengths and weaknesses identified through the Myers-Briggs Type Indicator and working on obtaining balance between each of the four poles.

Our second area of focus was "loving self." We began this process by addressing the simple fact that happy people tend to make others happy. We then spent time identifying and validating her undeniable contributions to the well-being of her family and friends. This process led to a discussion on the need to establish necessary boundaries in accordance to her current life stage and health-related needs. At this stage, CBT was primarily used to revise her outdated ways of thinking, feeling, and behaving. The client particularly appreciated this process as it not only helped her to celebrate her life up to the present, but also freed her from feeling guilty about having and expressing her own needs.

Last, we worked on ways of "loving others," based on the client's love for God and herself. In terms of her relationship with other family members, she began to focus more on offering them her presence instead of constantly pressuring herself to "do" something for them. The client also endeavored to integrate faith with her career based on our discussions on work as a vocation. With encouragement and support, she began taking on opportunities that were in line with her interests and actively involved herself in improving the company's workflow. She also became more comfortable with identifying herself as a Christian and was pleasantly surprised when her Christian colleagues asked her to facilitate a weekly meditation group.

This case study illustrates the effectiveness of spiritual interventions in addressing issues such as anxiety caused by low self-esteem, self-doubt, and learned passivity toward life. A variety of counseling modalities were used—psychodynamic, family systems, CBT, and narrative—along with the spiritual interventions to reestablish the client's sense of identity and life priorities. At the time of closure, the client claimed feeling less anxious (5.5 out of 10) about being herself and having more confidence in relationships, work, and her future. In summary, the therapy progress can be understood as an outcome of the client's love for God, efforts to implement faith to real matters of life, and support from family, friends, and colleagues.

CASE STUDY 2: OVERCOMING DEEP SELF-LOATHING AND SHAME WITH SPIRITUAL INTERVENTIONS IN A GROUP CONTEXT

The following case study[2] illustrates the use of spiritual interventions in a group context for a Christian of Chinese descent.

Description of the Therapist

The therapist was a Chinese evangelical Christian man in his late 50s who has been in practice for over 30 years in a family medicine clinic setting and has been partnering with local Chinese faith communities to facilitate groups based on CBT (Burns, 1993), dialectical behavioral therapy (DBT; Linehan, 1993) and emotionally focused therapy (Johnson, 2019). He has an academic appointment in the Department of Family and Community Medicine at the local medical school and is adjunct faculty at the local Chinese seminary in addition to directing a postgraduate training program in marriage and family therapy in the family medicine clinic. The therapist has a doctorate in medicine, master's of divinity, master's of theological studies, and is a certified international trainer in emotionally focused therapy (Johnson, 2019).

Setting

The client was seen in the context of a CBT and DBT group at a local Chinese faith community in Toronto, Canada. The family medicine clinic with seven physicians has been partnering with local Chinese faith communities to conduct workshops and seminars, train lay carers, and run psychoeducation groups for over 25 years as a way to provide accessible and culturally sensitive groups in this low resource setting.

Client Demographic Characteristics

The client was a middle-class, university-educated Chinese man in his 60s attending an evangelical church where he is involved with ministry to seniors. The client is married with no children and was able to attend the group with his wife.

Presenting Problems, Concerns, and Client History

The client presented with depression with continuing symptoms despite treatment with medication and follow-up by a psychiatrist and mental health team. Prominent symptoms included loss of interest and pleasure, insomnia, lack of energy, stress, anxiety, inability to relax, difficulty concentrating, and

---

[2]This case study was written by Tat-Ying Wong. Details have been changed to protect client confidentiality.

316 *Fung et al.*

immense self-loathing, guilt, and shame over his absence during his mother's illness and death overseas. He has a younger brother overseas, who looked after their mother during her long illness. He has been involved in caring for seniors at his church and has completed some seminary studies.

Assessment and Diagnosis

As part of the group process and outcome evaluation, participants were asked to complete instruments at the beginning and end of the group using the website of the family medicine clinic. Most of the instruments were adapted from *Ten Days to Self-Esteem* (Burns, 1993), a CBT self-help manual. The client's initial scores indicated moderate distress, moderate depression, mild anxiety, slight relationship satisfaction, and moderately low self-esteem (see Table 16.1). The client's diagnosis was major depressive disorder, and he was already taking antidepressants and under the care of a psychiatrist and specialized mental health clinic. The depression started after the death of his mother 1 year ago and was related to unresolved guilt and shame and continued self-loathing over not going overseas to take care of his mother when she was ill and when she passed away. This feeling was in the context of the Chinese cultural value of caring for elderly parents reinforced by his Christian beliefs.

Treatment Process and Outcomes

The large group was based on *Ten Days to Self-Esteem* (Burns, 1993) and *Skills Training Manual for Treating Borderline Personality Disorder* (Linehan, 1993) with the worksheets provided to the participants in both English and Chinese. The large group was held at a medium-sized Chinese faith community during the Christian education time on Sunday with smaller breakout groups facilitated by lay members. Related biblical concepts and principles on managing emotions were added to each CBT/DBT skill. For example, a quote from Isaiah 30:15,

TABLE 16.1. Pre- and Postintervention Scores

Instrument	Preintervention score	Postintervention score	% improvement
Psychosocial Screen (Hudson, 1982)	38	22	42%
Burns Depression Checklist (Burns, 1993)	26	12	54%
Burns Anxiety Inventory (Burns, 1993)	21	14	33%
Relationship Satisfaction Scale (Burns, 1993)	28	38	36%
Index of Self Esteem (Hudson, 1982)	37	26	30%
PHQ-9 (Kroenke et al., 2001)	12	8	33%

"in quietness and trust is your strength," was used to introduce mindfulness. The concept of healthy thoughts and thought distortions was illustrated with Philippians 4:8: "Finally, brothers and sisters, whatever is true, whatever is noble, whatever is right, whatever is pure, whatever is lovely, whatever is admirable—if anything is excellent or praiseworthy—think about such things" (*New International Version*, 1973/2011).

The 90-minute groups continued for three terms with 11 sessions each term, including teaching, skills demonstration, small group sharing, and skills practice. The worksheets from the manuals with guided practice were used to teach mindfulness skills, distress tolerance skills (first term), cognitive skills (second term), and behavioral skills and interpersonal effectiveness skills (third term). Due to the integration with relevant scriptures, the client readily accepted the CBT/DBT concepts and skills. By the end of the CBT/DBT group, the client had improved with scores in the nonclinical range (Table 16.1). He reported that he was no longer feeling stress, anxiety, down, and bad about his childhood and was able to relax and concentrate.

In one particular group session, using a cognitive therapy worksheet (Burns, 1993), the client was helped to face his overwhelming guilt and shame over not being there physically for his mother when she was ill and when she passed away. He was guided to meditate on the image of Christ on the cross delegating the care of his mother to John the disciple when Christ was not in a position to do so himself because of his calling. The client also realized that he supported his brother in his caregiving duties financially and emotionally and was not a bad son. This powerful spiritual intervention dramatically reduced his overwhelming guilt and shame and self-loathing. Once the fuel for his depression was eliminated, he improved clinically and was able to achieve complete remission of his depressive symptoms.

Therapist Commentary

This case showed the importance of spiritual interventions in a client under psychiatric care with only partial improvement of his depression fueled by self-loathing and overwhelming guilt and shame. CBT and DBT integrating spiritual interventions in a group setting helped him achieve complete clinical remission. The faith community setting provided the client and his wife with opportunity for spiritual support through fellowship and prayer. Scriptures related to his distorted thoughts and beliefs helped him to shift from self-loathing and seeing himself as a bad son to self-acceptance and seeing himself as doing his best as a son by delegating the care of his overseas mother to his brother and supporting them financially and emotionally.

Unpublished analysis of the outcome data for the group showed equal efficacy compared with individual therapy, which is consistent with research on the effectiveness of groups (Yalom & Leszcz, 2008). The group format not only reduced accessibility barriers and stigma in a low resource setting but also utilized existing infrastructure and resources within a local faith community to prevent and treat mental health issues. The small groups encouraged experiential learning about acceptance, love, and forgiveness through powerful personal and scriptural narratives. Group therapeutic factors promoting deep experiential learning and change include group cohesion, universality, interpersonal learning, guidance, reenactment, self-understanding, instillation of hope and addressing existential issues (Yalom & Leszcz, 2008).

RESEARCH FINDINGS AND SUPPORT

In this section, we first present an overview of some key findings from the Templeton Foundation-funded CSPEARIT study, the first multisite study to our knowledge that has investigated the use of Christian-based spiritually integrated psychotherapy with East Asian Canadians. We then discuss findings from some other studies on spiritually integrated psychotherapy for East Asians as well as the impact of psychotherapists' religion and spirituality on therapy-related outcomes.

Templeton Foundation Practice-Based Evidence Study Findings

In the Templeton Foundation-funded practice-based CSPEARIT study, 24 therapists participated in the study (20 identified as female and four as male). The median age of therapists was 51 years (range: 33–67). All 24 therapists (100%) identified as Christians, and all had a master's degree or higher, with four having medical degrees. In terms of ethnicity, 13 therapists (54.2%) identified as Chinese, four (16.7%) as Korean, five (20.8%) as White, and two (8.3%) as others. All therapists worked at one of the three treatment sites for this study: Tyndale University, Grace Health Centre, or the Living Water Counselling Centre. Most therapists (31; 88%) were licensed psychotherapists with a median of 4 years (range: 1–33) of independent practice experience, with three therapists (12%) still under supervision by licensed psychotherapists.

The total number of client subjects was 206 (149 females, 56 males, 1 unidentified). The median age of client subjects was 43 years (range: 19–74). In terms of ethnicity, 140 clients (68%) identified as Chinese, 15 (7.3%) as Korean, 33 (16%) as White and 18 (8.7%) as others. The majority of clients (94.9%) identified as Christians although nine opted not to declare a religious affiliation at all. In addition, 185 (89.9%) clients stated that religion was important to them, and 186 (90.3%) clients stated that they would be open to discussing religious or spiritual issues in therapy.

In total, there were 3,252 therapy sessions consisting of individual therapy (117 clients), couple therapy (14 clients), or group therapy (75 clients). The median number of therapy sessions was four (range: 1–36). The three most commonly utilized therapeutic modalities were CBT-based approaches and client-centered and interpersonal psychotherapies. In terms of spiritual interventions, the five most common approaches were "affirmed trusting God," "encouraged personal prayer," "encouraged listening to the heart," "listened to spiritual issues," and "affirmed client's divine worth." The pattern of spiritual interventions utilized also differed by therapist ethnicities. For instance, "encouraged personal prayer" was utilized in 17.9% of therapy sessions by Chinese therapists compared to 5.8% of sessions by White therapists whereas "as therapist engaged in silent prayer" was utilized in 19.7% of sessions by White therapists compared to 2.7% of sessions by Chinese therapists.

The clinical outcomes of the psychotherapy for clients were measured primarily by the Clinically Adaptive Multidimensional Outcome Survey (CAMOS-25; Sanders et al., 2018) and its five subscales (psychological distress, relationship distress, spiritual distress, physical health distress, therapy progress concerns) as well as the Clinical Outcomes in Routine Evaluation (CORE-10; Barkham et al., 2013). Overall, the clinical outcome scores as measured by CAMOS-25 and four of its five subscales (psychological distress, relationship distress, spiritual distress, therapy progress concerns) as well as CORE-10 all decreased over time. As lower scores on these scales would indicate less severity, these scores would demonstrate the general effectiveness of the spiritually integrated psychotherapy under study in this project. There was no change in the CAMOS-25 subscale of "physical health distress," which could be due to the settings of the three treatment centers being outpatient clinics where clients had pursued the psychotherapy primarily for issues not directly related to physical health, thus the psychotherapy did not lead to significant changes in physical health distress.

Given the nested structure of this data set, with multiple sessions per client and multiple clients per therapist, a multilevel modeling (MLM) approach was used to address several study hypotheses regarding the use of spiritual interventions. MLM is used to account for the interdependencies in nested data structures and produce trustworthy results when the assumption of independence is violated. It was found that the effect of the match between clients' and therapists' self-rated importance of spirituality is significantly and positively related to the number of spiritual interventions used (B = 0.09, SE = 0.04, p = .042). In other words, when both the client and the therapist hold similar attitudes about the importance of spirituality, the therapist would tend to use more spiritual approaches during the therapy. On the other hand, two-level MLM models revealed no significant relationships between the number of spiritual interventions used and (a) clients' and therapists' match/similarity in cultural values (as measured by the Asian Value Scale-Revised; B = 0.14, SE = 0.69, p = .842); (b) the client's spiritual distress (as measured by the CAMOS-25 [Sanders et al., 2018] spiritual distress subscale; B = 0.02, SE = 0.06, p = .779). In addition, three-level MLM models revealed no significant relationships between the number of spiritual interventions used and any of the changes in CAMOS-25 subscale scores and CORE-10 scores over time.

Other Research Findings and Supports

Spiritually Integrated Psychotherapy for East Asians
Research studies on how cultural variables influence spiritually integrated psychotherapy have been scarce, especially for East Asian cultures. For instance,

it has been suggested that mindfulness and acceptance-based psychotherapies or contextual therapies—such as acceptance and commitment therapy, DBT, and mindfulness-based cognitive therapy—have promise for application with Asian Americans, for these therapies feature aspects that are congruent with or reflect East Asian cultural values, norms, or worldviews (Hall et al., 2011). Even so, culturally syntonic contextual therapy approaches have yet to be developed or evaluated (Hall et al., 2011).

One of the coauthors of this chapter, Dr. T.-Y. Wong, reported on the efficacy of an emotionally focused therapy (EFT)–based group for couples for Chinese Canadians in Toronto (Wong et al., 2018). This is the first published study of an EFT-based group in the Chinese population. The group took place at a Christian church, but the participants included both Christians and non-Christians. Wong et al. (2018) reported that while EFT or EFT-based interventions might be just as useful for people of Asian origin as they are for people in Western cultures, an educational approach might be more acceptable to Chinese participants since the Chinese collectivist culture values education, learning, and achievement; such an approach also reduces the shame, loss of face, and stigma associated with traditional psychotherapy. Moreover, the Chinese faith community in Toronto is generally conservative and somewhat suspicious of mainstream North American and European psychological concepts. As such, integrating excerpts from the Bible helped foster a theological understanding of attachment and addressed any mistrust that participants might have had about the theory underlying the group interventions. Furthermore, due to the fear of losing face and the focus in the Chinese culture on the group rather than on the individual, the pace of the EFT-based group was deliberately slowed to allow participants to become more comfortable with one another before asking them to engage in the expression of emotions such as fear, loneliness, and sadness. As such, culturally appropriate psychotherapies, including those with spiritual components, would be crucial for the effectiveness of such therapies in the Asian population.

Effects of Therapist Religiousness and Spirituality on Therapy-Related Variables

In a systematic review of 29 original, peer-reviewed journal articles that examined the relations between psychotherapists' religiousness and spirituality (R/S) and therapy attitudes and behaviors, the therapeutic relationships, and treatment outcomes (Cummings et al., 2014), a few important findings are particularly noteworthy.

First, the therapist's R/S had significant effects on their attitudes and behaviors in therapy. Therapists perceived addressing religiosity or spirituality as highly appropriate or important if they were affiliated with a religious tradition (Beatty et al., 2007), rated themselves as religious (Kivley, 1986) or spiritual (Shafranske & Gorsuch, 1984), scored high on scales of religious commitment and spirituality (Cornish et al., 2012; Kellems et al., 2010) and worked at an explicitly Christian counseling agency (Wade et al., 2007). Therapists who worked at Christian agencies were more likely than those working at secular agencies to proactively use R/S interventions, such as praying with or for a client, using religious language, and recommending religious literature or participation (Wade et al., 2007); however, both groups of therapists (those working at a Christian agency or a secular one) were equally likely to agree that they would discuss religion if it came up in a therapy session (Wade et al., 2007).

Second, therapists' R/S may affect their use of R/S interventions. Shafranske and Malony (1990) found that therapists who hold negative attitudes toward R/S reported less use of R/S interventions. Similarly, in a study utilizing multiple regression analysis, religious variables such as therapists' religious behaviors and Christian beliefs significantly predicted use of R/S interventions (Walker et al., 2005). However, two studies found no significant relationship between therapists' R/S and use of R/S interventions (Diblasio & Proctor, 1993; Walker et al., 2008). More research is necessary to understand the relationship between therapists' R/S and the use of R/S interventions.

Third, studies looking at the effects of therapists' R/S on treatment outcome have been mixed and varied. More research is required to understand the complexity of this relationship.

CONCLUDING REMARKS

There is a paucity of literature in the use of spiritually integrated psychotherapy with clients of East Asian descent. However, from our clinical experience and findings from the practice-based CSPEARIT study, we know that Christian-based spiritually integrated psychotherapy is well accepted by East Asian Canadians, and lead to clinically meaningful improvements in various psychosocial outcomes in a sample where most clients and therapists had rated spirituality and religion to be important for them.

A wide variety of spiritual interventions are utilized in Christian-based spiritually integrated psychotherapy with East Asian Canadians, and more types of interventions may not necessarily lead to better outcomes. Instead, therapists appear to be the best judge of which combination of spiritual interventions is optimal for each client in order to enhance their clinical outcomes and treatment adherence.

Match in Asian cultural values between the client and therapist may not be a crucial factor influencing clinical outcomes. Instead, the cultural sensitivity of the therapist may be more important. Additionally, having spirituality integrated into psychotherapy may help enhance the willingness of East Asian Canadians—especially those who have rated spirituality and religion to be important—to accept psychotherapy and mental health treatments overall.

Recently, some mainstream regulatory bodies, such as the College of Registered Psychotherapists of Ontario, have increased their recognition of spiritually integrated psychotherapy; nevertheless, entities such as medical regulatory bodies and insurance companies still significantly resist these approaches. Further research is needed to investigate the effectiveness of different forms of spiritually integrated psychotherapy with clients of East Asian descent, for example, by incorporating other faith traditions into psychotherapy.

REFERENCES

Ahmad, F., Maule, C., Wang, J., & Fung, W. L. A. (2018). Symptoms and experience of depression among Chinese communities in the West: A scoping review. *Harvard Review of Psychiatry, 26*(6), 340–351. https://doi.org/10.1097/hrp.0000000000000202

Ahmad, F., Wang, J., Wong, B., & Fung, W. L. A. (2022). Interactive mental health assessments for Chinese Canadians: A pilot randomized controlled trial in nurse practitioner-led primary care clinic. *Asia-Pacific Psychiatry, 14*(1), e12400. https://doi.org/10.1111/appy.12400

Anderson, R. (2010). *On being human*. Wipf and Stock Publishers.

Ball, R. A., & Goodyear, R. K. (1991). Self-reported professional practices of Christian psychologists. *Journal of Psychology and Christianity, 10*(2), 144–153.

Barkham, M., Bewick, B., Mullin, T., Gilbody, S., Connell, J., Cahill, J., Mellor-Clark, J., Richards, D., Unsworth, G., & Evans, C. (2013). The CORE-10: A short measure of psychological distress for routine use in the psychological therapies. *Counseling & Psychotherapy Research, 13*(1), 3–13. https://doi.org/10.1080/14733145.2012.729069

Beatty, A. E., Hull, M., & Arikawa, H. (2007). Correlates of therapist's religious attitude and conservatism. *Mental Health, Religion & Culture, 10*(5), 527–535. https://doi.org/10.1080/13674670601105982

Burns, D. (1993). *Ten days to self-esteem*. Quill William Morrow.

Chui, T., & Flanders, J. (2011). *Immigration and ethnocultural diversity in Canada* [Analytical document]. Statistics Canada. http://www12.statcan.gc.ca/nhs-enm/2011/as-sa/99-010-x/99-010-x2011001-eng.cfm

College of Registered Psychotherapists of Ontario. (2021a). *Definitions*. https://www.crpo.ca/definitions/

College of Registered Psychotherapists of Ontario. (2021b). *Modalities of psychotherapy*. https://www.crpo.ca/modalities-of-psychotherapy/

College of Registered Psychotherapists of Ontario. (2021c). *What is psychotherapy?* https://www.crpo.ca/find-a-registered-psychotherapist/what-is-psychotherapy/

Cornish, M. A., Wade, N. G., & Post, B. C. (2012). Attending to religion and spirituality in group counseling: Counselors' perceptions and practices. *Group Dynamics: Theory, Research, and Practice, 16*(2), 122–137. https://doi.org/10.1037/a0026663

Cummings, J. P., Ivan, M. C., Carson, C. S., Stanley, M. A., & Pargament, K. I. (2014). A systematic review of relations between psychotherapist religiousness/spirituality and therapy-related variables. *Spirituality in Clinical Practice, 1*(2), 116–132. https://doi.org/10.1037/scp0000014

Diblasio, F. A., & Proctor, J. H. (1993). Therapists and the clinical use of forgiveness. *The American Journal of Family Therapy, 21*(2), 175–184. https://doi.org/10.1080/01926189308250915

Duncan, B. L., Miller, S. D., & Sparks, J. A. (2004). *The heroic client: A revolutionary way to improve effectiveness through client-directed, outcome-informed therapy*. Jossey-Bass.

Fung, W. L. A., Mirhom, M., Okamoto, T., & Shepherd, V. A. (2021). Principles and practice in educating Christians about mental health: A primer. In J. R. Peteet, H. S. Moffic, A. Hankir, & H. G. Koenig (Eds.), *Christianity and psychiatry* (pp. 231–247). Springer. https://doi.org/10.1007/978-3-030-80854-9_16

Fung, W. L. A., Shepherd, V., Chong, K. Y. A., Sharma, S. D., & Sharma, A. (2021). Fruitful collaborations with religious and spiritual communities to foster mental health in general society: An international perspective. In A. Moreira-Almeida, B. P. Mosqueiro, & D. Bhugra (Eds.), *Spirituality and mental health across cultures* (pp. 435–458). Oxford University Press. https://doi.org/10.1093/med/9780198846833.003.0026

Hall, G. C. N., Hong, J. J., Zane, N. W. S., & Meyer, O. L. (2011). Culturally competent treatments for Asian Americans: The relevance of mindfulness and acceptance-based psychotherapies. *Clinical Psychology: Science and Practice, 18*(3), 215–231. https://doi.org/10.1111/j.1468-2850.2011.01253.x

Hubble, M. A., Duncan, B. L., & Miller, S. D. (Eds.). (2010). *The heart and soul of change: What works in therapy*. American Psychological Association.

Hudson, W. W. (1982). *The clinical measurement package: A field manual*. Dorsey Press.

Johnson, S. M. (2019). *Attachment theory in practice: Emotionally Focused Therapy (EFT) with individuals, couples, and families*. Guilford Press.

Kellems, I. S., Hill, C. E., Crook-Lyon, R. E., & Freitas, G. (2010). Working with clients who have religious/spiritual issues: A survey of university counseling center therapists. *Journal of College Student Psychotherapy, 24*(2), 139–155. https://doi.org/10.1080/87568220903558745

Kivley, L. R. (1986). Therapist attitude toward including religious issues in therapy. *Journal of Psychology and Christianity, 5*(3), 37–45.

Koenig, H. G. (2012). Religion, spirituality, and health: The research and clinical implications. *International Scholarly Research Network, 2012*, Article ID 278730. https://doi.org/10.5402/2012/278730

Kroenke, K., Spitzer, R. L., & Williams, J. B. W. (2001). The PHQ-9: Validity of a brief depression severity measure. *Journal of General Internal Medicine, 16*(9), 606–613. https://doi.org/10.1046/j.1525-1497.2001.016009606.x

Lee, F. (2000). Chinese in Ontario. *Polyphony, 15*, 13–31. http://lib-contentdm2.lib.sfu.ca/cdm/ref/collection/mcc/id/5139

Lindsay, C. (2001). *The Chinese community in Canada* [Analytical paper]. Statistics Canada. https://www150.statcan.gc.ca/n1/pub/89-621-x/89-621-x2006001-eng.pdf

Linehan, M. M. (1993). *Skills training manual for treating borderline personality disorder*. Guilford Press.

New International Version Bible. (2011). New International Version Bible Online. https://www.thenivbible.com/ (Original work published 1973)

Okamoto, T., Mirhom, M., Wang, K., & Fung, W. L. A. (2021). Models of delivering Christian psychiatric care. In J. R. Peteet, H. S. Moffic, A. Hankir, & H. G. Koenig (Eds.), *Christianity and psychiatry* (pp.199–215). Springer. https://doi.org/10.1007/978-3-030-80854-9_14

Pargament, K. I. (2007). *Spiritually integrated psychotherapy: Understanding and addressing the sacred*. Guilford Press.

Peteet, J. R. (2014). What is the place of clinicians' religious or spiritual commitments in psychotherapy? A virtues-based perspective. *Journal of Religion and Health, 53*, 1190–1198. https://doi.org/10.1007/s10943-013-9816-9

Plante, T. G. (2009). *Spiritual practice in psychotherapy*. American Psychological Association.

Richards, P. S., & Bergin, A. E. (Eds.). (2014). *Handbook of psychotherapy and religious diversity* (2nd ed.). American Psychological Association. https://doi.org/10.1037/14371-000

Sanders, P. W., Richards, P. S., & McBride, J. A. (2018). Development of the clinically adaptive multidimensional outcome survey. *Psychotherapy Research, 28*(6), 925–939. https://doi.org/10.1080/10503307.2016.1277039

Shafranske, E. P., & Gorsuch, R. L. (1984). Factors associated with the perception of spirituality in psychotherapy. *Journal of Transpersonal Psychology, 16*(2), 231–241.

Shafranske, E. P., & Malony, H. N. (1990). Clinical psychologists' religious and spiritual orientations and their practice of psychotherapy. *Psychotherapy: Theory, Research, Practice, Training, 27*(1), 72–78. https://doi.org/10.1037/0033-3204.27.1.72

Shepherd, V. (2014, May 20). Course notes on the theology of the human person. *Sermons and writings of Victor Shepherd*. http://victorshepherd.ca/category/course-material/theology-of-the-human-person

Shepherd, V. (2015). The story of our life: Written by God who suffers with us and for us: The role of the church in the treatment of mental illness. *Canadian Theological Review, 4*(1), 15–23.

Sperry, L., & Shafranske, E. P. (Eds.). (2005). *Spiritually oriented psychotherapy*. American Psychological Association. https://doi.org/10.1037/10886-000

Tan, S. Y. (2011). *Counselling and psychotherapy: A Christian perspective*. Baker.

Tan, S. Y., & Gregg, D. H. (2010). *Disciplines of the Holy Spirit*. Zondervan.

Wade, N. G., Worthington, E. L., Jr., & Vogel, D. L. (2007). Effectiveness of religiously tailored interventions in Christian therapy. *Psychotherapy Research, 17*(1), 91–105. https://doi.org/10.1080/10503300500497388

Walker, D. F., Gorsuch, R. L., & Tan, S. Y. (2005). Therapists' use of religious and spiritual interventions in Christian counseling: A preliminary report. *Counseling and Values, 49*(2), 107–119. https://doi.org/10.1002/j.2161-007X.2005.tb00257.x

Walker, D. F., Gorsuch, R. L., Tan, S. Y., & Otis, K. E. (2008). Use of religious and spiritual interventions by trainees in APA-accredited Christian clinical psychology programs. *Mental Health, Religion & Culture, 11*(6), 623–633. https://doi.org/10.1080/13674670701867648

Wong, T.-Y., Greenman, P. S., & Beaudoin, V. (2018). "Hold Me Tight": The generalizability of an attachment-based group intervention to Chinese Canadian couples. *Journal of Couple & Relationship Therapy, 17*(1), 42–60. https://doi.org/10.1080/15332691.2017.1302376

Worthington, E. L., Jr., Kurusu, T. A., McCullough, M. E., & Sanders, S. J. (1996). Empirical research on religion and psychotherapeutic processes and outcomes: A 10-year review and research prospectus. *Psychological Bulletin, 119*(3), 448–487. https://doi.org/10.1037/0033-2909.119.3.448

Yalom, I. D., & Leszcz, M. (2008). *The theory and practice of group psychotherapy* (5th ed.). Basic Books.

17

A Polynesian Perspective for Navigating the Spiritual Connections in Psychotherapy Practice

Alayne Mikahere-Hall, Hoku Conklin, and G. E. Kawika Allen

Karakia Tīmata
Ranginui ki runga	Ranginui above
Papatūānuku ki raro	Papatūānuku below
Ka puta	From whence sprung
Te ira tangata	The human element
I te wheiao	Emerging into the world
Ki te ao mārama	Of light and knowledge
Tūturu whakamaua	Let us come together
Kia tina	With purpose
Haumi e hui e	United and ready
Tāiki e	To progress

The ongoing dialogue for a spiritually integrated psychotherapy is deeply relational, spatial, and contextual, shaped by the environments we occupy in the world—specifically, the people and the places we call home. There is increasing Indigenous demand for mental health treatment interventions that are culturally congruent with calls for greater inclusiveness and a broader understanding of Indigenous mental health beyond an individual focus characteristic of psychological approaches (Haitana et al., 2020; Mikahere-Hall, 2017; Reeves & Stewart, 2015; Stewart, 2008). Supporting this demand is the increasing rise of Indigenous ontology, epistemology, and methodologies in research and in practice across a range of mental health disciplines (Henry & Pene, 2001).

---

https://doi.org/10.1037/0000338-017
Handbook of Spiritually Integrated Psychotherapies, P. S. Richards, G. E. K. Allen, and D. K. Judd (Editors)
Copyright © 2023 by the American Psychological Association. All rights reserved.

For the most part, Western sciences have dominated and set the standards for mental health understanding and case formulation, removing spirituality as a key consideration. Scientific thought encourages empirically informed mental health pathology that is objective, less descriptive, and prescriptive, all of which is detailed in succeeding editions of the *Diagnostic and Statistical Manual of Mental Disorders* (*DSM*; American Psychiatric Association, 2013; McWilliams, 1999). Increasingly, Indigenous peoples are reclaiming Indigenous knowledge, engaging with methodologies and methods in the research space to provide solutions across a broad range of disciplines to include mental health research (Lawson-Te Aho, 2013; Mikahere-Hall, 2017; Moewaka Barnes, 2000; L. T. Smith, 2012; Webber, 2019). These efforts are working to find answers at both local and national levels while contributing to a worldwide effort to eliminate psychological and social pain and suffering.

In this chapter, we discuss therapies of the South Pacific region, primarily Aotearoa New Zealand. *Aotearoa* is the Indigenous Māori name for what is more commonly recognized as New Zealand where Auckland is the largest city and also branded as the Polynesian capital of the world (Friesen et al., 2016). We use this Indigenous name to increase the visibility of marginalized groups and to strengthen mental health awareness and practices. This chapter attempts to provide insights and unpack the context in which traditional and contemporary treatment interventions are fashioned drawing on Māori (the Indigenous people of Aotearoa New Zealand) and Pacifica mental health approaches and perspectives informed by Indigenous research methodologies (Waitoki et al., 2018). These approaches are discussed within the context of discounted peoples and as a pushback to colonizing processes that have harmed our hearts and minds, creating consequential structural inequities and health inequalities.

We have chosen to steer away from the usual mental health formulations that seem distant and disconnected from our realities. Instead, we invite you on a journey into our world so that you may experience through words what we see in our work. First, we highlight key concepts from Polynesian history and spirituality; next, we explain how to integrate this spirituality into psychotherapy. We then provide a case study to illustrate our approach.

PACIFIC SEASCAPES AND SPIRITUAL CONNECTIONS

Polynesian identity is premised on a lasting connection with *Wai-* (water) as a life-giving spiritual sustenance and our connections with *Moana-nui-a-kiwa* (the Pacific Ocean). We begin our discussions on a larger regionally based identity to provide an account of the commonality we share with Moana-nui-a-kiwa.

Moana-nui-a-Kiwa: The Pacific Ocean

Moana-nui-a-kiwa is well known throughout Polynesia as the great Oceania or Pacific Ocean. The many islands that have arisen from the depths of Moana-nui-a-kiwa are occupied by the people of the South Pacific. We have our own stories to tell about our histories, our people, and our lives. For centuries, our *tupuna |kupuna* (ancestors) have sailed Moana-nui-a-kiwa on *waka|vaka* (seafaring vessels) as expert explorers, traversing the Pacific Ocean using navigational knowledge and expertise. The tides, the currents, and the prevailing winds provide the pathways to a deep connection across and in between the many island nations that are located in the South Pacific region of the world. Moana-nui-a-kiwa is a living force where Pacific Island peoples have developed their own scientific knowledge and metaphorical language to capture our emotional ties to our geographical region of the world. Epeli Hau'Ofa's (2008) writings provide profound insights concerning the desire Pacific people have for "Our Sea of Islands" (p. 27) speaking with passion about "The Ocean in Us" (p. 41).

The enduring and deep connection with waka|vaka and Moana nui-a-kiwa have been emblemized and symbolically utilized to envision and shape therapy practice in Aotearoa. For example, Figure 17.1 shows the logo of Waka Oranga, National Collective of Māori Psychotherapy Practitioners Aotearoa (Mikahere-Hall et al., 2020), hereinafter referred to as Waka Oranga. Waka Oranga was established in 2007 by a core group of Māori psychotherapists with a shared belief that Western informed psychotherapy did not go far enough to respond effectively to the mental health needs of Māori. Long-standing Māori health disparities were seen as wider systemic and structural inequities (Reid & Robson, 2007) that did little to consider the complexities and attributes ascribed by culture. Since its conception, Waka Oranga has tailored and nuanced psychotherapy according to the collective and shared beliefs of Māori (Reid & Robson, 2007; Turner, 2021). The star constellation symbolizes the Matariki (Pleiades) cluster.

> Stars were—and still are—used by Māori as a way to calculate time and seasons, navigate oceans, preserve knowledge and stories, maintain customary practices, and inspire action and achievement . . . The waka acts both as a container and a transporter. (Mikahere-Hall et al., 2020, p. 26)

Figuratively, the waka contains the body of knowledge from past to present, which is then carried into the future. The paddles represent the people who have taken on the task of paddling the waka and doing the work that drives

FIGURE 17.1. Logo: Waka Oranga-National Collective of Māori Psychotherapy Practitioners

Note. Reprinted with permission from Waka Oranga National Collective of Māori Psychotherapy Practitioners.

and supports the healing agenda. The water represents life sustenance and the moana (sea), the important food pantry of Pacific peoples and people far and wide. Moana and water represent "fluidity between both conscious and subconscious states" (Mikahere-Hall et al., 2012, p. 26). Moana connects with the stars the Mata-Ariki, to mean the all-expansive eyes of Atua (God), where Ranginui sky father above and Papatūānuku earth mother below provide the ecological basket for human existence (Hall et al., 2012; Mikahere-Hall et al., 2020). Waka Oranga's approach is about changing the philosophical lens to tailor interventions to work culturally, to contribute to the healing success of Indigenous people, and to continue to expand the horizons as it relates to a culturally congruent psychotherapy (Mikahere-Hall et al., 2020).

Indigenous Pacific people have existed and populated the numerous islands, parted for prosperity, and returned not as we once were. It is our kin folk our *aiga |whānau* (families) who have remained as keepers of the *ahi kaa* (home fires) thus maintaining the important cultural bonds to the *whenua* (land) and *kainga* (home). Moana-nui-a-kiwa, the Pacific Ocean, serves to bring us together and yet differentiates the nature in which our identities have been shaped.

KŌREROTIA: SPEAKING FROM THE MARGINS

Within the landscape of Aotearoa New Zealand there lies a serious mental health problem. Mental health equity and inequity arise as consequences of organizational structures and their supporting systems. Processes of colonization have led to power structures that have disadvantaged Māori and disadvantaged Pacifica people through the persistent and unequal distribution of power and resources (Robson et al., 2006). Understanding health inequities and their root causes helps to inform psychotherapy practitioners to better the conditions that lead to poorer health outcomes (Reid & Robson, 2007). Economics is an important health determinant that is shown to be the lever of differential health outcomes. Wilkinson and Pickett (2009) described social hierarchies to understand "why health gets worse at every step down the social ladder, so that the poor are less healthy than those in the middle, who in turn are less healthy than those further up" (p. ix). Statistics show disproportionately higher rates of mental health illness, family violence, child abuse, and incarceration rates for Māori, and the world's highest suicide rates are among young Pacific Island and Māori men. A report into youth suicide rates questions why young Māori have higher suicide rates compared with non-Māori and what the nation intends to do about this (Ngā Pou Arawhenua et al., 2020).

Mikahere-Hall et al. (2022) suggested that Indigenous Māori suicide rates reflect the struggle to live and a nationwide tolerance for Māori suffering. Lawson-Te Aho (2017) recommended reframing Māori suicide prevention research to shift the gaze, "reframing Māori (the indigenous people of New Zealand) suicide prevention research away from a strong emphasis on clinical research towards research that is more self-determining and historically and culturally contextualised" (p. 1). Culturally defined concepts such as *whakapapa* (genealogy) and *whānau* (an extended family system) are used to theorize pathways for healing (Hall, 2015; Lawson-Te Aho, 2013). *Kōrerotia*, the practice of speaking from the margins, acknowledges both the voices of those people who persistently live on the borders of society and the tenacity it takes to overcome this lived reality.

USING INDIGENOUS METHODOLOGIES TO HEAL AND LIBERATE

To address Indigenous people's suffering, psychotherapists and mental health practitioners must have a better understanding of it. This understanding must be based on meaningful encounters with other Indigenous people. A growing groundswell of Indigenous scholarship decolonizes methodologies (L.T. Smith, 2006a, 2006b, 2012) and promotes Indigenous epistemology and knowledge systems to develop research theory and methods. Indigenous research methodologies shift the gaze from empirical research, which can be heavily laden with universal assumptions that dismiss and denigrate the importance of spirituality. Historically and today, Indigenous peoples have been on the receiving end of research that has harmed them and frequently positions Indigenous peoples as problematic (Hokowhitu et al., 2020). Meaningful Indigenous research encounters provide the opportunity for Indigenous scholars, students, and community members to conference and congregate together. These encounters build Indigenous research capability and capacity to self-determine and to critique the lived realities of our own world and to seek solutions that are fit for purpose within an Indigenous context. Additionally, the solutions may have wider benefits beyond Indigenous peoples (Vaioleti, 2013). It comes with an agenda to heal and emancipate ourselves from the oppressions we have suffered primarily from colonizing experiences (Hokowhitu et al., 2020).

Research Encounters and New Voyagers

As Indigenous peoples of the Pacific, our quest for new knowledge and excellence continues. The ancient wisdom and knowledge of our forebearers influences the encounters we have in our day to day lives to undertake new voyages in various research domains in a quest for solutions. For example, utilizing Pacifica informed methodology, Gillon (2020) engaged the metaphorical, specifically Moana-nui-a-kiwa as an informative navigational research pathway to inform her work, stating the following:

> The foundation of He Vaka Moana (A Pacific Seafaring vessel) lies within the ocean itself and our ancestors who navigated the vast Pacific Ocean purposefully, using ancestral knowledges, pedagogy, understandings and methods to travel the vastness that is Moana Nui a Kiwa in order to reach their goals. That ancestral knowledge is within us as Māori and Pasifika peoples. (p. 82)

The Indigenous research context is about conscientization and conceptualization to actively engage in scholarly and rigorous research that includes research methodologies and research methods where the research design and research tools are grounded on Indigenous knowledge (Fonua, 2020). Given the diversity of Indigenous peoples globally, this makes the research context multilayered and multifaceted (Anae, 2003). L.T. Smith (2006a, 2006b) has endeavored to identify and unpack the multifactorial layers to examine "from a researcher perspective what researching with marginalised groups might mean for researchers who are themselves from marginalised communities or marginalised in the work that they do" (p. 5). How then do we draw upon ancestral and culturally informed subjugated knowledge to overcome the burgeoning challenges of contemporary life struggles? The development of Indigenous methodologies is a demonstrated commitment to engage with culturally orientated knowledge to produce solutions for every day Indigenous struggles (Anae, 2003; Bishop, 1999; L.T. Smith, 2006a, 2006b).

The Politics of Healing

Developing Indigenous methodologies, methods, and educational pedagogy is a growing and emancipating discourse for healing and recovery that is occurring within the margins of colonized societies. L.T. Smith (2006a) stated, "These researchers work the borders, betwixt and between institutions and communities, systems of power and systemic injustice, cultures of dominance and cultures in survival mode, politics and theory, theory and practice" (p. 151). Epeli Hau'Ofa (2008) suggested, "Whatever their political situation may be, most educated people in the Pacific, like myself, are trying to redefine their cultural identities, or endeavouring to shed a kind of mentality bred under conditions of colonialism" (p. 3). Like other human beings, Indigenous and Pacific people have stories to tell about their lives (Ka'ili, 2005). Iseke (2013) considered Indigenous storytelling as a key focus that sustains communities and therefore is central to research. Narrative practice (Connelly & Clandinin, 1990; Moen, 2006) and sociocultural theory (Vygotsky, 1978) provide complementary approaches that describe and critique encounters within the social context. Vygotsky's (1978) human learning and development theories emphasize how people become who they are in socially constructed and culturally shaped contexts. Vygotsky's work was critical of the limitations of psychological theories that failed to consider phenomenon such as place and context in human development. According to Moen (2006),

> The social contexts individuals encounter are based on where they are at any particular point in time. As historical conditions are constantly changing, this also results in changed contexts and opportunities for learning and development. Thus, consciousness, or the human mind, cannot be considered as a fixed category. (p. 57)

A shift from Western mental health constraints with fundamental conceptual and empirical limitations is required (Rieger et al., 2020). This shift is needed to remove the harms of often-deficit-framed research reporting concerning colonized Indigenous populations who live with and suffer the consequences of forced dominance. Deficit-framed research reporting has led to a sociopolitical context that perpetuates a negative narrative and a negative consciousness concerning Indigenous peoples globally (Fernández-Llamazares & Cabeza, 2018; Iseke, 2013; L.T. Smith, 2006a; Wilson et al., 2019). Narrative research aligns with Indigenous custom providing the potential to rediscover and reclaim our stories of where we have come from, where we are now, and where we hope to be in the future (Fernández-Llamazares & Cabeza, 2018; Hokowhitu et al., 2020; Mikahere-Hall et al., 2021; Rieger et al., 2020).

Wilson et al. (2019) discussed the need for new knowledge to better reflect realities. *Hurihuri o Whakaaro me te Mahi: Transforming Thinking and Doing* (see Figure 17.2) is a theory of change asserted in their research work developed to transform violence against *wāhine Māori* (Māori women; see Wilson et al., 2019).

Wilson et al. (2019) suggested that "simply changing narratives and conversations is insufficient if different outcomes are to be achieved for wāhine Māori . . . Leadership is necessary for changing current unhelpful and obstructive pathways and practices" (p. 17). Indigenous critical research is providing new insights and that are emancipatory and consciousness raising.

The Past Is Present: Historical and Collective Trauma

Chronic mental health difficulties pester colonized and marginalized peoples. Understanding the complexities of trauma and meeting the challenges of people's lives with mental health problems has been an important focus for Indigenous people. Historical trauma theory was first introduced to recognize and explain the mental state of children of Holocaust survivors. Historical trauma

FIGURE 17.2. Hurihuri o Whatakaaro me te Mahi: Transforming Thinking and Doing

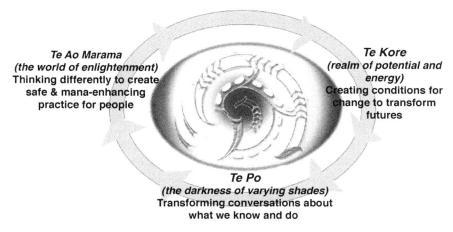

Note. From *E Tū Wāhine, E Tū Whānau: Wāhine Māori Keeping Safe in Unsafe Relationships* (p. 17), by D. Wilson, A. Mikahere-Hall, J. Sherwood, K. Cootes, and D. Jackson, 2019, Taupua Waiora Māori Research Centre, Auckland University of Technology. Copyright 2019 by Taupua Waiora Māori Research Centre AUT. Reprinted with permission.

is complex with enduring consequences experienced over time and across generations as well as held within a collective group with shared identity and shared histories (Evans-Campbell, 2008). Early clinical observations of children of Holocaust survivors began to emerge in the 1960s, which ultimately formed an extensive knowledge base (Kellermann, 2001). Earlier studies have since been utilized to better understand traumatology as it presents in other circumstances with different traumatized populations (Kellermann, 2001; Mohatt et al., 2014). A number of terms have been used to describe the notion of historical trauma (Campbell & Evans-Campbell, 2011). The terms include *intergenerational trauma, multigenerational trauma, historical trauma,* and *collective trauma*. To differentiate terms, Mohatt et al. (2014) identified three main characteristics of historical trauma:

> Historical trauma can be understood as consisting of three primary elements: a "trauma" or wounding; the trauma is shared by a group of people, rather than an individually experienced, the trauma spans multiple generations, such that contemporary members of the affected group may experience trauma-related symptoms without having been present for the past traumatizing event(s). (p. 128)

Mohatt et al. (2014) made the distinction that intergenerational trauma is familial and specific across generations without implying shared group experiences while collective trauma may not have features related to history or generational aspects. Brave Heart et al. (2011) considered cultural interventions as necessary to improve behavioral health, stating, "A long-term goal of historical trauma intervention practice is to reduce emotional suffering among Indigenous Peoples" (p. 282). Hall (2015) discussed the importance of shifting the cultural lens to advance mental health responsiveness to Indigenous people, suggesting that "self-determined Indigenous solutions that can aid in recovery . . . [require] urgent action" (pp. 173–174). Building on a traumagram model (Atkinson, 2002) and historical trauma theory (Brave Heart, 2003, 2011; Brave Heart & DeBruyn, 1998), Hall (2015) presented an intergenerational aspect within a Māori *whakapapa* (intergenerational family) context. Hall (2015) suggested that whakapapa transference is transmitted layer upon layer (generational layers) and can occur unconsciously:

> Trauma can be understood to have a whakapapa; this is where unresolved trauma remains nested in the whānau system, where underlying difficulties in everyday whānau life remain in the collective unconscious realities of whānau, hapū and iwi [family, extended family, extended community] life. (p. 72)

New and emerging concepts appear as people work to culturally define trauma and mental-health-related concepts specified within their immediate population groupings (Lawson-Te Aho, 2013). Homogenizing (Longmore, 2015) the mental health workforce runs the risk of elevating professionalism and qualifications at the expense of cultural differences and identity (Anae, 2003; Durie, 2005; Fairbairn-Dunlop, & Makisi, 2003). Indigenous peoples are developing culturally responsive interventions to resolve psychological suffering stemming from the past that is manifested in the present and increasingly recognized as historical trauma.

CASE ILLUSTRATION: NAVIGATING THE PERPLEXITIES

The following case illustration is provided by the first author (AMH) to highlight the implications of managing the intersecting quandaries of mental health and spiritual support. In this instance, referrals are managed by a hospital-based community mental health service. The services provide assessment, treatment, and clinical interventions for Māori adults, children, and families. The team members are multidisciplinary and include cultural advisers, contributing to the strength and importance of the Māori mental health team.

The case is descriptive to capture distinguishing aspects, and less detail is included to manage word limitations and to protect privacy. To summarize, the case includes financial disadvantage, addiction difficulties, social isolation, partner violence, trauma, and childhood exposure to adverse circumstances. The emphasis is on sensitively managing the spiritual dimensions of the case with cultural and nonjudgmental acceptance, steering away from unhelpful pathology. For this reason, the case is not presented using standardized global *DSM* case formulation. Names used are pseudonyms, and locations and sites have been obscured.

Ngā Āhuatanga: Presenting Problem

Mabel is a 34-year-old Māori woman who telephoned adult Māori Mental Health Services seeking support for herself and her children. Initial contact was made with the duty social worker, who undertook the initial family assessment. Mabel contacted Mental Health Services reluctantly and was reticent about seeking support, for she feared violent retribution from her partner and being misunderstood and diagnosed as crazy by a psychiatrist. For these reasons, she presented as hypervigilant, nervous, and cautious about who she engaged with and opened up to in her conversations. The social worker reported that Mabel was highly anxious and that her fears were escalated by both perceived and past threats to her life. Mabel's home-life situation was then at a point at which intense fear and desperation motivated her to make contact.

Mabel lived with her partner, Ty, and their three children: 8-year-old son, Billy; 4-year-old daughter, Wai; and 10-month-old baby boy, Tama. Ty has older children from a previous partner and has little or intermittent contact with them. Mabel reported that Ty is well entrenched in the culture of gang life and holds a senior position within the existing hierarchy. Family daily life appeared to be structured around Ty's control, temperamental mood swings, and expectations and demands. He has a history of severe violent offending, addiction problems, and incarceration. Mabel further reported living in fear of Ty and that he keeps Mabel and their children under a controlled, strict, and regimented routine. There was no telephone in the house, and Mabel relied on public transport. Mabel organized contact with Mental Health Services using the neighbor's telephone while Ty was at work. Mabel refused to leave the house to attend an appointment because she feared she would be seen in public either by Ty or any one of his gang associates. The social worker initiated a crisis home visit, coordinating this with the support of three Mental Health staff members who also attended. The team consisted of two cultural advisers, a nurse specialist, and the social worker. As a team, they attended two prearranged home visits. These visits were scheduled when Ty was at work and when 8-year-old Billy was at school. There was a concern that Billy has been forced to act as his father's informant. Present at the home visits were Mabel, her 10-month-old baby boy, and her 4-year-old daughter, Wai.

Āta Hāere: Proceeding With Respect

First, and to explain, the *Āta* concepts used in some of the level headings refer to respectful and considered engagement processes as described by Pohatu (2013). As articulated by Pohatu (2013) the Āta principles inform the way in which Māori allied health professionals—such as social workers, counselors, and psychotherapists—are engaging in practice in Aotearoa New Zealand.

To continue with the case illustration, the team observed interesting dynamics operating between Mabel and her daughter. Mabel was described as a slightly taller than average Māori woman, of athletic build, and with shoulder-length wavy dark brown hair. Mabel was casually dressed in denim jeans and a sweater and her appearance was described as clean and tidy. She had no obvious signs of physical injury, and she appeared anemic, as if lacking in color, and avoided eye contact. The team noted that Mabel presented as highly anxious, distressed, and agitated. They encountered setbacks as they attempted to fully understand what is going on and the underlying source of Mabel's distress. It became very clear that her 4-year-old daughter, Wai, controlled the dialogue that took place between Mabel and the Mental Health team. Mabel reported that her concerns were of a spiritual nature, activated by visions her daughter Wai was experiencing.

The team describe Wai as a clean and well-presented 4-year-old Māori girl of slight stature for her young age. Her hair was tied back from her face, her facial features appeared in proportion, and she had no obvious signs of physical or past injuries. Her skin was characteristically healthy in appearance, and her clothing was clean and appropriate. She was highly animated when she spoke, and she did this in a direct and authoritative manner. The team reported that Wai presented with a knowing and wisdom far beyond her chronological age. To quote, "It's as if we are talking to an older woman." Wai determined who could and could not enter the house and directed her mother during their visits while taking the lead in conversations. Wai did not appear to be overwhelmed or fazed by members of the team or adult authority. Wai was unwilling to share the details of the visions she has had, which are disturbing her mother. Likewise, her mother, Mabel, was unwilling to disclose details without Wai's permission. Wai was described by her mother as having very strong spiritual gifts, and there was a particular air of seriousness in Wai's demeanor.

At this point, the team discussed the possibility of bringing me on board as a member of the Child and Adolescent Mental Health team with the permission of Wai and Mabel. I was contacted, and the team briefed me on the peculiarities of the case and made arrangements for a home visit. The following events transpired thereafter.

Āta Kōrero: Setting the Terms of Engagement

When we arrived, Mabel met us at the door, and from the lounge, Wai beckoned us to come in. I could hear the maturity in her voice as she spoke. I was introduced to her, and I greeted her warmly while she intently observed and examined me. I was aware that her appraisal of me considered what is both seen and unseen by the naked eye, and I was not concerned by her observations. Wai invited me to sit down and we had a polite exchange, which helped to promote a warm rapport. I noted that the reports given by the team members were consistent with what I was seeing in the mother–child dyad, where Mabel allowed Wai to direct the proceedings. The cultural adviser suggested that we begin our meeting with *karakia* (prayers) and Wai agreed. When these were completed, the senior cultural adviser, who was also a kuia (female elder), was permitted to stay while the other team members were instructed by Wai to leave the room and wait outside the house. Wai's dialogue with me is best described as an interesting mix of both the naivety and curiosity of a young child and the insightfulness of a mature and wise adult. Essentially, the discussion was framed around *Ko wai Koe?* (who are you?) and *Ko wai au?* (who am I?), which is consistent with a Māori form of engagement. It is difficult to explain in English the nature of the exchange here except to say that Wai would communicate in a type of pidgin English. By this, I mean a broken and adapted form of English nuanced with Māori meaning. To summarize, the dialogue and introductions concluded with an acceptance of each other.

Wairangi: A Spiritual Manifestation

At this point, Wai told me this is her grandmother, pointing to a photograph on the wall, and she also said that I could meet her now. Wai's grandmother has been deceased for some time. Wai has never met her grandmother in the physical world; however, she went to some length to explain that her grandmother talks to her and watches over her. I acknowledged Wai's grandmother and her presence with us. During our exchanges, Wai's mother had been quietly present, listening in from the adjoining room. Wai then told her mother to come in and her tone toward her mother softened. Mabel entered the room and began to cry. Wai consoled her mother and reassured her, "It's okay, mummy." The *kuia* (female elder) also comforted Mabel while she was crying; her pain was heartfelt. As we sat with her, Wai explained, "It's okay mummy you can talk now;" offering reassurances. Mabel explained that Wai is spiritually gifted and for the past week she has been awakened by her daughter, who has come to check on her mother's safety in the middle of the night. Mabel also explained that she takes Wai's insights seriously.

The issue of pending death is a serious factor in this case where Wai has communicated an urgency for her mother to remove them all from the house, as death is imminent. As reported by Mabel, Wai has told her mother she must leave and take them away and has had visions of her father killing her mother. The family must leave the house within a specified time frame, and Wai counted, using her fingers, "one week and two weeks—not more."

Mabel then revealed to us the details of Wai's visions, and the perceptiveness provided by Wai was also compelling. The revelations included clear descriptions of events that took place some 18 years earlier and involved the murder of Mabel's father. Mabel testified that these events did take place and was adamant that she has never disclosed information and the circumstances involved in her father's murder to any of her children or her partner. According to Mabel, these events were too difficult for her to talk about.

Āta-Whakarongo: Deliberated Listening

Wai encouraged her mother to tell me what was happening in the family home and the way in which her partner, Ty, was treating her. Encouraged by Wai, Mabel explained experiences associated with partner violence, degradation, rape, and humiliation. She reported feeling trapped within the relationship and being financially dependent on Ty. Mabel was estranged from her own family and had considered the option of Women's Refuge; however, the likelihood of doing this within the local and wider region was untenable, as gang members know where many of the "safe" houses are located.

He Pūrākau Whakamamae: A Trauma Narrative of Pain and Suffering

Mabel explained that Wai's insights have triggered so many things for her, including flashbacks and the smell of blood, which sickened her. Mabel relayed her seemingly irrational fears of being ostracized by people if they were to find out the circumstances surrounding her father's death. Mabel reported that she deliberately distanced herself from her biological family to avoid a deep and overwhelming sense of shame and guilt that she associates with her perceived sense of failure to help her father. Paralyzed with fear, she witnessed her father die in a frenzied attack. Mabel reported that she loved her father and described him as a patient, loving, and caring man. Mabel was consequently separated from her own mother, who was charged and imprisoned for the murder of her father. Mabel described her mother as a harsh, cruel, and punitive mother who suffered the long-term effects of alcoholism. One evening in an alcohol-fueled rage, she repeatedly stabbed Mabel's father to death. Mabel felt certain that her deceased mother had communicated with Wai, sharing with her the history of past tragedies. There was a foreboding sense of familiarity as past pain and suffering were predicted to repeat themselves as revealed by Wai's insights.

A Problematic Diagnosis: Managing the Crisis

It is not possible for reasons of confidentiality and practicality to present in detail all the circumstances related to this *whānau* (family). Needless to say, it would be problematic to suggest that the core cultural spiritual beliefs of this case presentation can be culturally understood through a diagnostic lens. In terms of Mabel, we can consider adult psychopathology and family pathology to state the most obvious spouse or partner violence, physical and sexual and posttraumatic stress disorder, paranoia and depressive symptomology, and psychosocial difficulties. As clinicians, consider the deterioration and severity of Mabel's mental health and any dangers this may pose to her children. However, what is the suggested hypothesis to explain the triangular dynamic operating in the relationships between the deceased grandmother, daughter, and granddaughter that transcend the social environment? What are the protective functions that assist Mabel to overcome her fear of being misunderstood and diagnosed as crazy? Compliance with universal criteria and Western standards in mental health is problematic. Coates et al. (2006) illuminated the difficulties of mainstream practice, suggesting

> The essential problem with globalizing standards is that they assume that the Western approach should be treated as a universal perspective. Within this context, disagreements are generally couched in terms of cultural relativism versus universalism. Professionalizing trends define boundaries, serving to keep out those who do not conform. (p. 383)

Indigenous strengths-based approaches are developing in a manner that legitimizes Indigenous beliefs (see Coates et al., 2006). These approaches are not promoted at the expense of perceived professionalism; rather, they are relational and guided interventions. Returning to Mabel's family situation, there were no opportunities to provide ongoing psychotherapy support; managing the presenting crisis and prioritizing whānau safety was at the forefront. A coordinated safety plan was initiated with an urgent plan to relocate Mabel and her children to a temporary hotel accommodation and then on to a new city. Police were contacted to support the execution of the safety plan, as were emergency housing support, welfare, and mental health services and whānau support. Mabel and her children were successfully relocated, and the family was reported as doing well under the circumstances, adapting to the new changes in their lives. The removal of chronic external stressors related to severe partner violence assisted in reducing Mabel's distressing symptoms, enabling her to rebuild her life. The social worker passed on a short message of greetings and appreciation from Wai. Recognizing and accepting the spiritual elements of this case served to protect the family from further physical and mental health harm. However, Indigenous mental health workers often find themselves in the juxtaposition of regulated mental health practice and cultural beliefs. We are left to hold the tensions between Western conventions and our own spiritual values.

Wairua: Two Waters

In Māori philosophy, *Wairua* (spirit) refers to the spirit or spirituality; it involves perceptions and intuition. Wairua is distinctively intuitive and acknowledges that the soul exists beyond physical reality. Wairua has two composite parts: Wai (water) and *Rua* (two) to indicate a primary flow and fluidity emanating from a higher Atua (God l divinity) or esoteric divinity to the secondary physical world. *Matekite* (spiritual insight) is the Māori term that acknowledges one's intuitive spiritual abilities to see spiritually related manifestations both in the living and beyond the living. Matekite involves atypical insight and multisensory discernment that is *Hōhonu* (profound) in nature. Matekite is gaining recognition for its importance in Mental Health services in Aotearoa New Zealand (NiaNia et al., 2016). Wairua is central to every Māori model of health considered a critical construct of well-being (Lindsay et al., 2020). Māori Marsden (Marsden, 2003), recognized as a preeminent *tohunga* (specialist) of Māori philosophies, emphasized the centrality of spirituality. Endorsing and quoting Marsden (2003), Royal exclaimed the "ultimate reality is for Māori the reality of spirit" (p. 47). Spirituality is not unique to Māori; it is explained above in brief, from an Indigenous Māori perspective.

Te Wairua Tātou Tūhono: The Spiritual Water That Connects Us

Hurdle (2002) used *Ho'oponopono*, a native Hawaiian traditional healing approach, as a family conflict resolution intervention. Prayer and spirituality are core components of the Ho'oponopono approach. Duran (2006) spoke to the importance of soul wounds with American Indians and Native peoples. Ross (2010) raised the importance of traditional healing and spiritual traditions for Indigenous South Africans, while Kraft (2009) discussed the relevance of Sami Indigenous spirituality in Norwegian Sàpmi. Spirituality for Indigenous peoples is both healing medicine and linked to forms of social justice and self-preservation (Baskin, 2016). Spirituality is an ontological positioning concerning existence, belief, values, and meaning. It involves *tūhonotanga* connections to environment, relationships with people and places, and a universal omnipotence that transcends above all things physical (Mikahere-Hall et al., 2022). Kainga (home) discusses Māori environmental relational concepts that orientate psychotherapists toward a spiritually informed, holistic, and specific world view to inform their psychotherapy practice. Likewise, Indigenous psychologists in Aotearoa New Zealand are pushing for culturally nuanced and relevant psychologies (Groot et al., 2018). Effective treatments and interventions include ethnically and socially constructed responses. Capturing the spiritual beliefs and cultural nuances central to the individual and to the families that present for mental health support can be strengths based, adding value and meaning. In her doctoral work, Lawson-Te Aho (2013) theorized and discussed Māori suicide within the context of the Indigenous spirit and argued for therapies based on soul healing and indigenous determination. Lawson-Te Aho (2013) further considered colonizing degradation and damage:

> Māori suicide is theorised as an outcome of the wounding of the indigenous spirit as a result of complex trauma birthed during colonisation. The spirit is theorised

as the place where trauma and suffering take root in whakapapa (kinship). Whakapapa is theorised as the mechanism by which spiritual affliction is transferred inter-generationally manifesting in physical outcomes within and between generations. (p. 8)

Lawson-Te Aho and Liu (2010) suggested that Māori suicide is the physical manifestation of wounds encountered at the spiritual level. *Pūrākau* (narratives) gathered from whānau help to identify the root causes of pain, acts of trauma, and *hara* (violations) where whānau attachments have been severed as a consequence (Mikahere-Hall et al., 2022). *Whakataukī* (proverbs), *Oriori* (lullaby), and *mōteatea* (chants) are all traditional methods to support spiritual healing (Mikahere-Hall, 2020b). Spirituality can be thought of as soul healing, a social justice medicine for consequential colonial damage. Lawson-Te Aho (2014) emphasized the need to revisit trauma narratives and their histories as a starting point for healing.

CONCLUDING REMARKS

This chapter makes a stand for greater cultural congruency as a response to Indigenous people's mental health and well-being. We have positioned ourselves globally within Moana-nui-a-kiwa, acknowledging our connections to Oceania while maintaining our autonomy in the face of increasing homogeneity. We have traveled and traversed conversations from the margins of Indigenous solution-focused research methodologies and looked at the harmful impacts of colonization as destructive soul wounding, resulting in consequential trauma. The presented case study is a glimpse into the lives of whānau laiga (families) who are struggling on the fringes of society and the Indigenous mental health workers who support them. We have argued the need for greater recognition of spirituality as a soul healing social justice medicine. Further action is needed to validate and center the importance of spirituality in people's lives. Promoting spirituality as a core assessment and treatment component is a step toward inclusiveness. Wai and Wairua are Indigenous concepts that have the potential to provide navigational pathways in mental health healing and treatment. We began this discussion with karakia, and we conclude as we started:

Karakia Whakamutunga

Kia tau iho	Let the strength
Te tauwhirotanga	and serenity
O te wāhi ngaro	of our ancestors
E pai ai te nohotahi	guide us as we gather
Ā tinana, wairua hoki	in body and spirit
Werohia te manawa	with compassion
Ki te tao o aroha	for one another
Kia whakamaua kia tina	let it be realized
Hui e Tāiki e	for us all.

REFERENCES

American Psychiatric Association. (2013). *Diagnostic and statistical manual of mental disorders (DSM-5®)*.

Anae, M. (2003). O a'u/I: My identity journey. In P. Fairbairn-Dunlop & G.S. Makisi (Eds.), *Making our place: Growing up PI in New Zealand* (pp. 89–101). Dunmore Press.

Atkinson, J. (2002). *Trauma trails: Recreating song lines—The transgenerational effects of trauma in Aboriginal Australia*. Spinifex Press.

Barnes, H. M. (2000). Kaupapa Māori: Explaining the ordinary. *Pacific Health Dialog*, 7(1), 13–16.

Baskin, C. (2016). Spirituality: The core of healing and social justice from an Indigenous perspective. *New Directions for Adult and Continuing Education*, 2016(152), 51–60. https://doi.org/10.1002/ace.20212

Bishop, R. (1999). Kaupapa Māori Research: An indigenous approach to creating knowledge. In N. Robertson (Ed.), *Māori and psychology: Research and practice–The proceedings of a symposium sponsored by the Māori and Psychology Research Unit* (pp. 1–6). Māori & Psychology Research Unit.

Brave Heart, M. Y. H. (2003). The historical trauma response among natives and its relationship with substance abuse: A Lakota illustration. *Journal of Psychoactive Drugs*, 35(1), 7–13. https://doi.org/10.1080/02791072.2003.10399988

Brave Heart, M. Y. H., Chase, J., Elkins, J., & Altschul, D. B. (2011). Historical trauma among Indigenous Peoples of the Americas: Concepts, research, and clinical considerations. *Journal of Psychoactive Drugs*, 43(4), 282–290. https://doi.org/10.1080/02791072.2011.628913

Brave Heart, M. Y. H., & DeBruyn, L. M. (1998). The American Indian Holocaust: Healing historical unresolved grief. *American Indian and Alaska Native Mental Health Research*, 8(2), 56–78.

Campbell, C. D., & Evans-Campbell, T. (2011). Historical trauma and Native American child development and mental health: An overview. In M. C. Sarche, P. Spicer, P. Farrell, & H. E. Fitzgerald (Eds.), *American Indian and Alaska Native children and mental health: Development, context, prevention, and treatment* (pp. 1–26). Praeger/ABC-CLIO.

Coates, J., Gray, M., & Hetherington, T. (2006). An 'ecospiritual' perspective: Finally, a place for Indigenous approaches. *British Journal of Social Work*, 36(3), 381–399. https://doi.org/10.1093/bjsw/bcl005

Connelly, F. M., & Clandinin, D. J. (1990). Stories of experience and narrative inquiry. *Educational Researcher*, 19(5), 2–14.

Duran, E. (2006). *Healing the soul wound: Counseling with American Indians and other Native peoples*. Teachers College Press.

Durie, M. (2005). Indigenous knowledge within a global knowledge system. *Higher Education Policy*, 18(3), 301–312.

Evans-Campbell, T. (2008). Historical trauma in American Indian/Native Alaska communities: A multilevel framework for exploring impacts on individuals, families, and communities. *Journal of Interpersonal Violence*, 23(3), 316–338. https://doi.org/10.1177/0886260507312290

Fairbairn-Dunlop, P., & Makisi, G. S. (Eds.). (2003). *Making our place: Growing up PI in New Zealand*. Dunmore Press.

Fernández-Llamazares, Á., & Cabeza, M. (2018). Rediscovering the potential of indigenous storytelling for conservation practice. *Conservation Letters*, 11(3), e12398. https://doi.org/10.1111/conl.12398

Fonua, S. (2020). Lalanga ha kaha'u monu'ia: Helping science educators embed Indigenous knowledge, values, and culture in their courses for Māori and Pacific science student success. *MAI Journal*, 9(1), 49–58. https://doi.org/10.20507/MAIJournal.2020.9.1.6

Friesen, W., Blue, L., & Talo, R. (2016). *Pasifika festival representations and realities for the wellbeing of pacific peoples in Aotearoa/New Zealand: Soundscapes of wellbeing in popular music*. Routledge.

Gillon, A. (2020). Growing the fleet; views of the moana. *MAI Journal, 9*(1), 81–91.

Groot, S., Le Grice, J., & Nikora, L. (2018). Indigenous psychology in New Zealand. In *Asia-Pacific perspectives on intercultural psychology* (pp. 198–217). Routledge.

Haitana, T., Pitama, S., Cormack, D., Clarke, M., & Lacey, C. (2020). The transformative potential of Kaupapa Māori research and Indigenous methodologies: Positioning Māori patient experiences of mental health services. *International Journal of Qualitative Methods, 19*, 1–12. https://doi.org/10.1177/1609406920953752

Hall, A. (2012). Kāinga. *Ata: Journal of Psychotherapy Aotearoa New Zealand, 16*(1), 19–32.

Hall, A. (2015). *An indigenous Kaupapa Māori approach: Mother's experiences of partner violence and the nurturing of affectional bonds with tamariki* [Doctoral dissertation]. Auckland University of Technology. https://openrepository.aut.ac.nz/handle/10292/9273

Hall, A., Poutu, M., & Wilson, C. (2012). Waka Oranga: The development of an indigenous professional organisation within a psychotherapeutic discourse in Aotearoa New Zealand. *Psychotherapy and Politics International, 10*(1), 7–16. https://doi.org/10.1002/ppi.1255

Hau'Ofa, E. (2008). *We are the ocean: Selected works.* University of Hawaii Press.

Henry, E., & Pene, H. (2001). Kaupapa Māori: Locating indigenous ontology, epistemology and methodology in the academy. *Organization, 8*(2), 234–242. https://doi.org/10.1177/1350508401082009

Hokowhitu, B., Moreton-Robinson, A., Tuhiwai-Smith, L., Andersen, C., & Larkin, S. (Eds.). (2020). *Routledge handbook of critical Indigenous studies.* Routledge. https://doi.org/10.4324/9780429440229

Hurdle, D. E. (2002). Native Hawaiian traditional healing: Culturally based interventions for social work practice. *Social Work, 47*(2), 183–192. https://doi.org/10.1093/sw/47.2.183

Iseke, J. (2013). Indigenous storytelling as research. *International Review of Qualitative Research, 6*(4), 559–577. https://doi.org/10.1525/irqr.2013.6.4.559

Ka'ili, O. T. (2005). Tauhi va: Nurturing Tongan sociospatial ties in Maui and beyond. *The Contemporary Pacific, 17*(1), 83–114. http://doi.org/cxf7x9

Kellermann, N. P. (2001). Psychopathology in children of Holocaust survivors: A review of the research literature. *Israeli Journal of Psychiatry Related Science, 38*(1), 36–46.

Kraft, S. E. (2009). Sami indigenous spirituality: Religion and nation-building in Norwegian Sàpmi. *Temenos-Nordic Journal of Comparative Religion, 45*(2), 179–206.

Lawson-Te Aho, K. (2013). *Whāia Te Mauriora-In pursuit of healing: Theorising connections between soul healing, tribal self-determination and Māori suicide prevention in Aotearoa/New Zealand* [Unpublished doctoral dissertation]. Victoria University of Wellington. http://hdl.handle.net/10063/3086 [Google Scholar]

Lawson-Te Aho, K. (2014). The healing is in the pain: Revisiting and re-narrating trauma histories as a starting point for healing. *Psychology and Developing Societies, 26*(2), 181–212.

Lawson-Te Aho, K. (2017). The case for re-framing Māori suicide prevention research in Aotearoa/New Zealand: Applying lessons from indigenous suicide prevention research. *Journal of Indigenous Research, 6*(2017), 1.

Lawson-Te Aho, K., & Liu, J. H. (2010). Indigenous suicide and colonization: The legacy of violence and the necessity of self-determination. *International Journal of Conflict and Violence, 4*(1), 124–133.

Lindsay, N., Haami, D., Tassell-Matamua, N., Pomare, P., Valentine, H., Pahina, J., Ware, F., & Pidduck, P. (2020). The spiritual experiences of contemporary Māori in Aotearoa New Zealand: A qualitative analysis. *Journal of Spirituality in Mental Health, 24*(1), 74–94. https://doi.org/10.1080/19349637.2020.1825152

Longmore, M. (2015). Primary health care: Heartfelt messages. *Kai Tiaki: Nursing New Zealand, 21*(8), 40.

Marsden, M. (2003). *The woven universe: Selected writings of Rev. Māori Marsden.* Estate of Rev. Māori Marsden.

McWilliams, N. (1999). *Psychoanalytic case formulation*. Guilford Press.

Mikahere-Hall, A. (2017). Constructing research from an indigenous Kaupapa Māori perspective: An example of decolonising research. *Psychotherapy and Politics International, 15*(3), e1428.

Mikahere-Hall, A. (2020a). Tūhono Māori: Promoting secure attachments for Indigenous Māori children: A conceptual paper. *Ata: Journal of Psychotherapy Aotearoa New Zealand, 23*(2), 49–59.

Mikahere-Hall, A. (2020b). Tūhono Māori: A research study of attachment from an Indigenous Māori perspective. *Ata: Journal of Psychotherapy Aotearoa New Zealand, 23*(2), 61–76.

Mikahere-Hall, A., Morice, M. P., & Pye, C. (2020). Waka Oranga: The development of an Indigenous professional organisation within a psychotherapeutic discourse in Aotearoa New Zealand. *Ata: Journal of Psychotherapy Aotearoa New Zealand, 23*(2), 23–34.

Mikahere-Hall, A., Poutu, M., & Wilson, C. (2012). Waka Oranga: The development of an indigenous professional organisation within a psychotherapeutic discourse in Aotearoa New Zealand. *Psychotherapy and Politics International, 10*(1), 7–16.

Mikahere-Hall, A., Wilson, D., & Pou, P. (2022). *Tūhono Māori: Promoting secure whānau relationships for traumatised mokopuna* [Manuscript submitted for publication]. Taupua Waiora Research Centre, Public Health and Mental Health Research Institute Auckland University of Auckland, Auckland, New Zealand.

Moen, T. (2006). Reflections on the narrative research approach. *International Journal of Qualitative Methods, 5*(4), 56–69.

Mohatt, N. V., Thompson, A. B., Thai, N. D., & Tebes, J. K. (2014). Historical trauma as public narrative: A conceptual review of how history impacts present-day health. *Social Science & Medicine, 106,* 128–136.

Ngā Pou Arawhenua, Child and Youth Mortality Review Committee, & Suicide Mortality Review Committee. (2020). *Te Mauri—The life force. Rangatahi suicide report | Te pūrongo mō te mate whakamomori o te rangatahi*. Health Quality and Safety Commission.

NiaNia, W., Bush, A., & Epston, D. (2016). *Collaborative and indigenous mental health therapy: Tātaihono–stories of Māori healing and psychiatry*. Taylor & Francis.

Pohatu, T. W. (2013). Āta: Growing respectful relationships. *Ata: Journal of Psychotherapy Aotearoa New Zealand, 17*(1), 13–26. https://doi.org/10.9791/ajpanz.2013.02

Reeves, A., & Stewart, S. L. (2015). Exploring the integration of Indigenous healing and Western psychotherapy for sexual trauma survivors who use mental health services at Anishnawbe Health Toronto. *Canadian Journal of Counselling and Psychotherapy, 49*(1), 57–78.

Reid, P., & Robson, B. (2007). Understanding health inequities. In B. Robson & R. Harris (Eds.), *Hauora: Māori standards of health IV: A study of the years 2000–2005* (pp. 3–10). Te Rōpū Rangahau Hauora a Eru Pōmare.

Rieger, K. L., Gazan, S., Bennett, M., Buss, M., Chudyk, A. M., Cook, L., Copenace, S., Garson, C., Hack, T.F., Hornan, B., Horrill, T., Horton, M., Howard, S., Linton, J., Marin, D., McPherson, K., Rattray, J. M., Phillips-Beck, W., Sinclair, R., & Schultz, A. S. H. (2020). Elevating the uses of storytelling approaches within Indigenous health research: A critical and participatory scoping review protocol involving Indigenous people and settlers. *Systematic Reviews, 9*(1), Article 257. https://doi.org/10.1186/s13643-020-01503-6

Robson, B., Cormack, D., & Cram, F. (2007). Social and economic indicators. In B. Robson & R. Harris (Eds.), *Hauora: Māori standards of health IV: A study of the years 2000–2005* (pp. 3–10). Te Rōpū Rangahau Hauora a Eru Pōmare.

Robson, B., Purdie, G., & Cormack, D. (2006). *Unequal impact: Māori and non-Māori cancer statistics 1996–2001*. Ministry of Health.

Ross, E. (2010). Inaugural lecture: African spirituality, ethics and traditional healing– implications for indigenous South African social work education and practice. *South African Journal of Bioethics and Law, 3*(1), 44–51.

Smith, H., & Wolfgramm-Foliaki, 'E. (2020). Igniting the vä: Vä-kä methodology in a Māori Pasifika research fellowship. *MAI Journal, 9*(1), 15–25.

Smith, L. T. (2006a). Choosing the margins: The role of research in indigenous struggles for social justice. In N. K. Denzin & M. D. Giardina (Eds.), *Qualitative inquiry and the conservative challenge* (pp. 151–173). Left Coast Press.

Smith, L. T. (2006b). Researching in the margins: Issues for Māori researchers: A discussion paper. *Alternative: An International Journal of Indigenous Peoples, 2*(1), 4–27.

Smith, L. T. (2012). *Decolonizing methodologies: Research and indigenous peoples* (2nd ed.). Zed Books.

Stewart, S. L. (2008). Promoting Indigenous mental health: Cultural perspectives on healing from Native counselors in Canada. *International Journal of Health Promotion and Education, 46*(2), 49–56.

Turner, D. (2021). *Intersections of privilege and otherness in counselling and psychotherapy: Mockingbird*. Routledge.

Vaioleti, T. (2013). Talanoa: Differentiating the talanoa research methodology from phenomenology, narrative, Kaupapa Māori and feminist methodologies. *Te Reo, 56 & 57*, 191–212.

Vygotsky, L. S. (1978). *Mind in society: The development of higher psychological processes*. Harvard University Press.

Waitoki, W., Dudgeon, P., & Nikora, L. W. (2018). Indigenous psychology in Aotearoa/New Zealand and Australia. In S. Fernando & R. Moodley (Eds.), *Global psychologies* (pp. 163–184). Palgrave Macmillan.

Webber, M. (2019). Writing narratives of hope: An act of aroha. In S. Farquhar & E. Fitzpatrick (Eds.), *Innovations in narrative and metaphor* (pp. 119–132). Springer.

Wilkinson, R. G., & Pickett, K. E. (2009). Income inequality and social dysfunction. *Annual Review of Sociology, 35*, 493–511.

Wilson, D., Mikahere-Hall, A., Sherwood, J., Cootes, K., & Jackson, D. (2019). *E Tū Wāhine, E Tū Whānau: Wāhine Māori keeping safe in unsafe relationships*. Taupua Waiora Māori Research Centre, Auckland University of Technology.

SPIRITUALLY INTEGRATED PSYCHOTHERAPY FOR SPECIFIC PATIENT POPULATIONS

18

Spiritually Integrated Couple Therapy

Everett L. Worthington, Jr., Jennifer S. Ripley, Zhuo Job Chen, Vanessa M. Kent, and Elizabeth Loewer

Globally, most people adhere to some religion or profess spirituality (Pew Research Center, 2015). Even within the United States, many clients for mental health treatment are spiritual or explicitly religious, and many attend counseling because they have unhappy or failing long-term romantic relationships. Nearly 50% of marriage or marriage-like relationships struggle or fail over a lifetime. The relationships of people of faith are as vulnerable as others. Thus, they often seek counsel from a provider who also sacralizes the relationship. As a result, there is a strong, ongoing need for spiritually integrated couple therapy (SICT). Substantial differences likely exist between the types of people who seek SICT in lay counseling, clergy counseling, pastoral counseling, professional religiously identified couple therapy, and professional couple therapy from a nonreligious practitioner. Many variants of SICT exist. We focus on couple therapy per se even though perhaps more treatment occurs in spiritually integrated premarital, enrichment, and preventive approaches.

Couple therapists who offer SICT are responsive to their clients. In this chapter, we first outline reasons why some couples might prefer professional and others prefer clergy SICT. We then identify general approaches to SICT as well as common features of most SICT approaches. Next, we provide an illustrative case example, and finally, we summarize research on the effectiveness of SICT.

---

https://doi.org/10.1037/0000338-018
Handbook of Spiritually Integrated Psychotherapies, P. S. Richards, G. E. K. Allen, and D. K. Judd (Editors)
Copyright © 2023 by the American Psychological Association. All rights reserved.

Research on Christian-informed approaches is well developed, whereas research on approaches informed by other religions, whether Islam (Sauerheber et al., 2014) or Judaism (Cohen Davidovsky, 2019), is limited. Most evidence-based approaches to couple therapy are Christian. We did not find couple therapy research with Hindu- and Buddhist-informed approaches. Thus, reluctantly, we limit our discussion to Christian-informed approaches.

REASONS COUPLES MAY SEEK SPIRITUALLY INTEGRATED COUPLE THERAPY

One reason religious couples may seek a clergy member instead of a community professional for SICT is that they see marriage as a sacred relationship and might deem secular treatments incapable of dealing with, or insufficiently sensitive to, the sacred couple relationship. They might perceive that their religion values marital stability and commitment, as they do, but assume (often incorrectly) that secular therapists are more favorable toward divorce. Additionally, a couple might have theological beliefs that they do not think a professional would endorse—like "the man is head of the wife" (*New International Version Bible*, 1973/2011, Ephesians 5:23; 1 Timothy 3:1–16), or "God hates divorce" (Malachi 2:16). Even if the couples privately are comfortable with secular counseling, they might avoid it because they are concerned about criticism in their religious community or about the cost or availability of professional counseling. Therefore, they might seek pastoral or lay counseling (Tan, 2011) or marriage education classes in their churches.

Perceptions can thus result in different types of religious couples seeking counseling from clergy, secular professionals, or overtly religious or spiritual professionals. Different types of couple therapists, over time, come to see couples who have gravitated to their care. That selection effect might result in different types of couple therapists having different ideas about what the typical problems in couple therapy are, how to treat them, and how to use or not use the partners' spirituality with the counseling process. Fundamentally, couple therapists are responsive to their clients. They shape their treatments to meet clients' needs and wants.

HISTORY OF SICT

SICT does not have an original developer and defies succinct definition. Historically, family therapy emerged from religious pastoral counseling (Gurman, 2015). From its earliest days, couple therapy was adapted and combined with theology. Progressive or liberal theologies dominated the early development of SICT. Pastors who counsel or preach, theologians, and pastoral counselors employed such theologies. Theologically conservative pastors included their understanding of biblical principles or theology while theologically progressive pastors worked more from secular counseling approaches that they felt were congruent with their theology.

A major turn occurred when Christian psychotherapies emerged. At the very beginning, Christian psychotherapies largely drew on theologically progressive traditions (see Browning, 2006). More theologically conservative integration soon occurred. This involved biblical counselors like Adams (1970). Also, biblical counselors who combined evangelical Christian theology and cognitive and cognitive behavioral therapy, like Larry Crabb, brought to Christian psychotherapy and to SICT a "filter" model of integration. In that model, the integrator often used conservative evangelical Christian theology as a filter to decide which theories and methods were and were not consistent with the theology (Crabb, 1977).

In recent years, integration of psychology and Christian theology has broadened. One way of categorizing integrative approaches has been shown in *Psychology and Christianity: Five Views* (Johnson, 2010). These five views are a levels-of-explanation view (which treats theology and psychology as providing parallel explanations), an integration view (which treats theology and psychology as intermixed), a Christian psychology view (which treats fundamental theological truths as standards against which psychological findings are evaluated), a transformational psychology view (which is Christ centered and seeks to transform the person's spirit in addition to improving mental health), and a biblical counseling view (which roots psychological interventions in the Bible). These views are top-down approaches, beginning from theoretical perspectives to put theology and psychology together. That is, theoreticians formulated the approaches initially, and they were then applied to clients—usually whole cloth, though leaving open the possibility of modification due to usage with clients. More modern approaches take a bottom-up, client-informed view. For example, Neff and McMinn (2020) took a relational approach, arguing that most therapists' ideas are formed through personal interactions rather than theory. As therapists encounter religious people relationally, they apply psychological methods to problems within the relational context, integrating practical theology with clinical practice. The way clinicians treat SICT (Ripley et al., 2022) resembles Neff and McMinn's relational integration more closely than it resembles one of the discipline-driven *Five Views* approaches.

In couple therapy, this long history of seeking to create spiritually integrated approaches has manifested in several general approaches—all of which draw on therapists' personal practical theology. Many couples with relationship problems seek advice from public figures—such as book authors or media personalities—congregational pastors or lay counselors, faith-based popular seminars, or professional therapists.

APPROACHES TO SICT FROM PROFESSIONALS

When religious or spiritual couples seek professional therapy, they may desire SICT. However, different clinicians have different ways of conceptualizing SICT. The four basic approaches to SICT that follow represent different levels of integration of theology and psychology.

Relying on Couples to Do the Integration

Some practitioners claim that spiritual counseling is any counseling that is done by a couple therapist who is spiritual, regardless of how spirituality shows up (or doesn't) in counseling. The clinician essentially trusts the couple to do their own integration of psychology into their particular spiritual approach.

Psychodynamic, phenomenological, or narrative approaches do not initiate spirituality considerations. Most couples do not feel that spirituality has been addressed unless they bring it up directly. Sometimes therapists might hope that their clients will bring up religion in session or apply religion to their marriage on their own. Spiritual integration in such cases might occur in the mind of the provider more than in actual treatment. Thus, spiritual integration is thought to occur not through the therapist but rather in the client's life.

"Baptized" Secular Approach

Practitioners might employ a secular approach but, when they feel it is appropriate, "baptize" it with spiritual language, scriptural quotes, or religious justifications for interventions. Generally, this relies on a practitioner who is aware of, committed to, and knowledgeable about a particular religion's teachings and disciplines (Hook & Worthington, 2009). Clinicians thus attempt to direct couples toward resources from their faith depending on the therapist's implicit theology and clinical judgment. Emotion-focused couple therapy is an evidence-based treatment that does not have direct research on outcomes for spiritually integrated therapy but has case studies (Davidovsky, 2019) and clinical resources (Hawkins et al., 2020). The strength of this approach is indirect. It does not include specific randomized controlled trials. Both the voluminous research on the secular treatment and practical use by thousands of spiritual therapists, each of whom adapts the secular treatment to their personal theology, provide indirect evidence of effectiveness without direct efficacy research support. One downside is that because individuals spiritually baptize the approach, the effectiveness of the idiosyncratically baptized product is unable to be studied. A second downside, to carry the baptism analogy a step further, is that the amount of "water" (i.e., spiritual justification) used by the therapist could be anything from a drop on the forehead to total immersion.

Patchwork Quilt Integration of Evidence-Based Portions of Treatment

Third, the practitioner might create a practice that draws unsystematically from evidence. This approach could create a patchwork quilt of evidence-based techniques sewn together within the framework of the practitioner's clinical theory. Thus, a therapist might use brief interventions that are demonstrably effective but are not a self-contained couple treatment approach—such as Worthington's (2006) REACH Forgiveness intervention or Fincham's prayer intervention (Fincham & May, 2017). Even though the brief intervention is effective, the rest of the approach might not be. Alternatively, the therapist might choose components from evidence-based approaches but choose components that either are ineffective or not active contributors to therapy success, seem confusing to clients apart from the context of the original therapy, or clash with other aspects of the therapy. Or the therapist might draw from research evidence on how couples act outside of couple therapy—such as how healthy couples might communicate or resolve conflicts—and try to adapt those findings into untested interventions. However, findings from survey or even experimental research might not be causal.

Clinical Scientist–Created and –Tested, Evidence-Based, Whole-Cloth Approach

In a fourth approach to SICT, a theoretician creates, tests, and studies the components of an explicitly integrated approach drawing from an evidence-based psychological model with a recognized theology. An example is the Hope-Focused Couple Approach (Ripley & Worthington, 2014; Worthington, 2005), discussed within the case study. Nonetheless, this approach has weaknesses. First, practitioners might apply an approach that has been rigorously investigated in controlled research to their clients even though the model was developed for (and tested with) different clients. Second, the practitioner might tweak it to fit their clientele or personal beliefs and values, making its validity less certain. Third, the evidence is only as good as the scope of the studies supporting the method.

To What Degree Does Evidence Support Each of These Approaches?

Among these general approaches to spiritually accommodated couple therapy, only the whole-cloth approach has direct evidence supporting its efficacy. Little research supports its effectiveness. Two of the other three general approaches—baptizing secular approaches and patchwork quilt approaches—have evidence supporting them, but they have not been directly investigated as an entire approach. Therefore, the field really has little clear evidence of what might happen in couple therapy if a practitioner describes themselves as practicing spiritually integrated couple therapy.

COMMON FEATURES OF SICT

As we have demonstrated, SICT is not a single approach. Rather, it can mean different things to different practitioners. Moreover, offering spiritually integrative couple therapy can often feel like one has an entire lexicon of opportunities and offerings for couples, few of which will be actually employed. This difficulty is common to any therapy, where clients can only engage and change at a realistic pace. For therapists to engage with couples who desire to integrate their faith and relationship, they must understand how religion and spirituality can be both a hindrance to psychological and relational health and a path towards health. We next make some generalizations about SICT approaches.

Who Can Benefit From SICT?

In general, couples who are experiencing relational discord, conflict, and communication difficulties, but are still able to attend therapy conjointly, are major beneficiaries. Both partners do not have to be in full agreement on religious beliefs, values, and practices to benefit from therapy. Sometimes couples attend when one partner demands it and the other partner does not object. Some religious organizations will not provide couple therapy if the partners are not married, but most religious organizations do.

Theological and Theoretical Foundations of SICT

The general theological foundation of the approach in Christian communities is governed by the practitioner's assessment of the clients' practical theology. Importantly, though, therapists are not likely to agree to things they perceive as immoral or theologically wrong. Generally, therapists will work around aspects of clients' beliefs that are theologically inconsistent with their own faith tradition rather than confront and seek to convert. Like any secular approach, if the practitioner believes client behaviors to be immoral or illegal, they discuss this with clients and sometimes consult with peers to determine whether to treat or refer.

No agreed-upon theory guides the relationships and therapist behaviors in couple therapy. Rather, existing psychological theories are used. These have their own prescriptive approaches. Theology is married within and taken to be consistent with the secular approach. As we described earlier, this can range from therapists who use the secular theory without explicit mention of theology, to those who baptize the secular theory with their theology, to those who use explicitly evidence-based theories or interventions. In choice of both theology and theory of couple therapy, preferences of both couple therapist and couple are negotiated.

Ethical Issues Specific to SICT

There is no agreed-upon ethical statement for how SICT is practiced. It falls to couple therapists to draw from sources of ethics and morality. The first source consists of religious ethics. The second source draws on professional codes of ethics (e.g., American Psychological Association, American Counseling Association, American Association of Marriage and Family Therapy, American Association of Social Workers). The third source is guidelines by organizations of religious professionals who have articulated specific codes of ethics for their members. The American Association of Christian Counselors and the Christian Association for Psychological Studies have ethical standards for practicing psychological treatment using Christian principles. None of these specifically apply ethics to SICT.

A few ethical issues specific to SICT dominate the writing (see Ripley et al., 2022). One is whether marriage is among equals, with flexible roles, or within a theologically prescribed hierarchy with defined roles (Blankenhorn et al., 2003). Generally, the *zeitgeist* is favorable to egalitarian marriage. A second ethical issue centers on how much emphasis is given in marriage relationships to clearly unjust circumstances such as substance abuse. Third, ease of terminating relationships through divorce or break-up is addressed.

Additional ethical considerations concern competence in couple therapy. Most psychologists, counselors, and social workers are not trained in couple therapy or theology. Yet, in most general practices, more than half of cases involve intimate partner concerns (Gray & Cordova, 2018). It is likely that more than half these clients will be spiritual or religious (Pew Research Center, 2015). So, it is an ethical issue of competency whether a psychotherapist or counselor who was trained primarily in standard individual therapy can competently do couple therapy. Special considerations necessary for treating couples with different approaches to religion or spirituality make it more of concern that a therapist could do SICT—not just general couple therapy, or general integration—competently. Concerns exist in (a) useful assessment of religion and spirituality (R/S) issues, (b) treatment of those issues, and (c) staying sensitive to couple diversity.

Most psychotherapists disengage most of their own values from treatment of their patients. The difficulty in doing this in SICT is no different from doing it in other psychotherapy. However, if practitioners mostly see individuals, they simply might not be as experienced in dealing with the issues of couple therapy. Questions include: (a) Who is the client—the two individuals, the relationship, or an insurance company? (b) Can the couple therapist disengage from personal beliefs about the divorce, affairs, and the like? (c) How does the couple therapist treat secrets? (d) How does the couple therapist deal with attempts to triangulate God onto the side of one (or both partners)? (e) How might treating polyamorous, gay, or lesbian couples be similar to and different from treating straight couples? and (f) How does one deal with partners of radically different religious orientation from oneself (e.g., a couple in a cult)? Whereas these ethical dilemmas are solvable, a psychotherapist might have to make decisions in the moment or spend an extraordinary amount of time consulting.

Diversity Considerations

Diversity considerations in couple therapy add complexity with two people and the intersection of their backgrounds and identities. Clients may assign different salience to identities (e.g., race, religion) compared with each other or with the therapist. For some couples, both might share a religion and be at peace. For others, they might have spiritually charged, seemingly fight-to-the-death conflicts over religious issues, which the therapist might not even find important. Understanding client perspective on their spirituality and how it might intersect with other identities can be vital for many couples.

Religious differences can be challenging—especially if a couple therapist is similar in religion to one partner but dissimilar to the other. Religious beliefs, values, and practices are sacralized, which elevates partners' commitment to them. Unlike gender balance, the therapist's religion may be invisible or known to the couple. Therapists who advertise as spiritual may have to address this sacralized religious conflict more often than secular therapists.

Assessment Guidelines and Recommendations

Level 1 assessment—whether R/S is important to each client, and whether each client wishes to have R/S considered in therapy—is mandatory. Failure to do Level 1 assessment can be considered an ethical (competence) violation, especially if things do not work out well for the clients. However, unlike in individual therapy, the answers given by the partners about the importance of R/S to their lives and to couple therapy might differ, and who "wins" might be part of an ongoing power struggle that can triangulate the couple therapist. The answers to the Level 1 questions might need to be negotiated.

Beyond Level 1, Worthington (2005) recommended an up-front, full battery assessment taking an entire 1.5-hour session and a second session for feedback to the partners. He suggested that this assessment was vital to rapid progress in brief couple therapy. Whereas he used psychometrically sound couple satisfaction instruments, many of the other assessments were quick and not burdened by rigorous evidence supporting psychometric adequacy—though, importantly, they had face validity. Besides questionnaires to assess communication, conflict, and potential or actual couple violence, he had partners discuss two issues and record their discussion. One issue was something the partners perennially disagreed about, and the second issue (which served to lower the arousal) was an activity they enjoyed doing together.

Importantly, feedback from the assessments was provided in a session that negotiated whether to undertake couple therapy. The same written consultation report was given to each partner. At the end of the session, couples decided whether to begin couple therapy and how many sessions they would commit to.

Intervention Strategies and Techniques

SICT has many influential theories, the most common of which might be the hope-focused couple approach (HFCA; Hook et al., 2014; Ripley et al., 2022) and emotion-focused therapy (Ripley et al., 2022). These approaches have most commonly used a foundation of psychological theory and, to varying levels, added spiritual activities, integrative and religious practices, new religious perspectives on relational problems, and embedded therapy as part of a larger narrative towards spiritual growth. A fully spiritually integrated approach would align psychological, relational, and spiritual goals, selecting therapy activities and homework to further those goals.

Integrated interventions might attend to forgiveness, prayer, and grace. The HFCA counteracts power struggles and conflict by engaging couples in forgiveness. Forgiveness of their partner and their historical pain short-circuits control and conflict dynamics in the couple's relationship. Forgiveness is psychologically healthy for individuals, relationships, and spiritual growth and therefore a common activity in the HFCA. Another example would use prayer in emotion-focused therapy. Couples could access primary and secondary emotions as they employ healthy prayer for each other. The goal of prayer might be to express laments or negative emotions in a more healthful way through their attachment to God (if the attachment is healthy), patterned after Psalms. A third example would involve contemplating grace (or other religious virtues) in a couple's spiritual life, and then applying grace to their partner's weaknesses or persistent gridlocked problems. For clinicians who are versed in spirituality and couple therapy, an integrative couple therapy context provides many opportunities to engage spiritual activities and perspectives. The goal is simultaneous growth on multiple levels: individually, relationally, and spiritually.

Recommendations for Collaborating With Clergy

It is a joy to do professional counseling when clergy support those attempts. That has not always been the case in our experience. Because both clergy and therapists claim some authority over helping the couple, responsibility can be blurry and egos can easily get bruised. At times, clergy–therapist relationships seem competitive rather than collaborative. This is especially the case when clergy hold to theologies that are suspicious of professional counseling or therapists do not respect the counseling abilities of clergy.

It is often necessary to provide more feedback to referring clergy than one might provide to others who refer couples. We do not reveal details of actual therapy, but we might reveal some emphases of counseling (e.g., "We have been working to try to repair the marriage within the bounds of Christian marriage"). We also might suggest that clergy can help (e.g., "Thank you for referring the [couple's names]. I appreciate that you care for the people under your clerical care, and I hope you will keep encouraging the [names] to work on their marriage.").

CASE STUDY ILLUSTRATING TREATMENT PROCESSES AND INTERVENTIONS

In the case[1] described here, the therapist was a 35-year-old, biracial (Latina and White) counselor in private practice with in-depth training in emotion-focused couple therapy and HFCA therapy. She identified as a moderate, evangelical, charismatic Christian.

---

[1]Details, including names, in the case example have been altered to protect client confidentiality and therapist privacy.

The couple was seen in a private practice by telehealth at a Christian mental health practice, where about half the referrals come from churches in the region. The partners in the couple were married, African American, heterosexual, and in their early 50s. The wife attended a Black Baptist church with her large extended family. The husband attended occasionally. Both were professionals. The husband's career had not progressed as much as he wanted. They raised four grown children and have three grandchildren.

Presenting Problems and Concerns

The couple reported considering divorce. The husband was depressed due to aging, not reaching professional goals, and losing a parent to cancer. The wife was committed to the marriage, but she had withdrawn. She spent much of her time outside of work with friends and family and felt distant from her husband. For 2 years, the husband's nonacceptance of his aging affected their physical intimacy. He did not perceive his wife as supportive. This had caused a major rift in the relationship about the same time their youngest child moved out of the home. The couple had disengaged emotionally and sexually for about 2 years.

Client History

The couple had met and married after high school. They had their first child by age 25. Living in a rural, primarily African American community, they had been pillars of the community, with multiple civic and church leadership positions. Friends and family often relied on them for support, and they freely helped others, which was a primary basis of their marriage. The husband had a rift with church leadership and stopped attending in his 40s. He also withdrew from local government volunteer leadership. An underlying superficiality to the couple's intimate bond was exposed as they lost church and friends. Additional stressors of health, workplace, and losses were ignored, so the couple drifted further apart in their 40s.

Assessment and Diagnosis

The couple were interviewed for intake. They completed several face-valid relationship measures of dyadic trust, efficacy of their relationship, elements of their relationship, and relational satisfaction (for specific scales, see Ripley & Worthington, 2014). They also completed self-assessments of individual psychopathology. The husband met criteria for depression, but relationship distress appeared to be the primary cause. His loss of faith and rumination about offenses from previous church leaders contributed to his depressive symptoms. The wife had low relationship efficacy. Both were clinically dissatisfied and yet highly committed to the marriage, despite stating that they had considered divorce.

The Hope-Focused Couple Approach

For treatment, the therapist used the hope-focused couple approach, Christian version (HFCA-C; Ripley & Worthington, 2014). The HFCA-C is a semistructured, patient-responsive approach rather than driven by a rigid protocol. Couple therapists are encouraged to adapt it to clients and to use their own theoretical approach, using the HFCA-C as a metatheory. Hope is the focus. The approach is strategic with the strategy being to promote faith (e.g., trust in God, the counselor, themselves, and the counseling process), work (e.g., putting effort into the marriage), and love (e.g., valuing the partner).

Assessment, Feedback, and Treatment Planning

Each treatment plan is negotiated with the couple after an intensive assessment that uses pretreatment questionnaires plus a 1.5-hour interview and a 1-hour feedback session involving discussion of assessment results plus a treatment plan (as described previously). The couple determines whether they would enter treatment, and they and the therapist agree on a tentative (written) plan.

Conflict Resolution and Communication Training

Treatment proper often begins with the major perceived problem (or problems, if the partners disagree). Usually, that problem is conflict or the fallout from conflict, such as mutual coldness, disrupted sexual satisfaction, or constant arguing. Partners often want the therapist to declare them "winner" in power struggles or to negotiate compromises. However, the therapist wants to help couples resolve their own differences. The HCFA-C often teaches the Harvard Negotiation Project's method (Fisher et al., 2011). Partners look for the shared interests behind the often-incompatible positions they are arguing, thus yielding win-win solutions.

Couple therapists prefer different approaches to communication, such as emphasizing clarity of communicating verbally and nonverbally (semantics), stressing how to communicate (syntactics), or focusing on the implied meaning, usually in terms of power dynamics of communications (pragmatics). The HFCA-C accommodates all three approaches.

The content of disagreements fuel conversations. The therapist's goal is to use their own preference for a semantics, syntax, or pragmatics approach to teach and coach couples how to use the Harvard Negotiation Project method to resolve differences. Often, around half of all therapy sessions will need to promote better communication and conflict resolution.

The cause of a good marriage is the couple's willingness to form, maintain, grow, and repair a strong emotional bond. This goal can often be accomplished in part through training in communication and conflict resolution. Reducing strains on the emotional bond allows it to better be maintained and grow. Typically, partners know how to communicate, but they cannot do it consistently. Therapists therefore more often motivate and create conditions for people to consistently communicate well in spite of previous habits rather than teach new communication skills.

Closeness and Intimacy

After dealing with conflicts and communication, couples are typically ready to try to directly build closer emotional bonds. Building closer bonds will have been addressed all along, starting with positive-focused assessment, assigning conflict-free date nights (as conflict and communication are dealt with), and directing them to engage in enjoyable activities. Therapists might need to revisit conflict and communication if disagreements flare up, but it is important to move purposefully through a therapeutic program rather than allow the treatment to be merely crisis-driven responsiveness to the problem-du-jour.

Often, therapists create opportunities for couples to practice more intimacy by working to rearrange partners' time schedules to engage in more coaction, more intimacy, or more distancing, depending on their needs. During assessment and throughout therapy, therapists discern whether each partner needs more or less closeness for ideal intimacy, more or less coaction, or more or less alone time. However, now is the time to formulate plans and get the couple to experiment directly with new patterns of behavior leading to more emotional closeness.

Reconciliation and Forgiveness Following Transgressions

The last major aspect of couple therapy usually deals with forgiveness and reconciliation. Reconciliation involves restoring trust, which involves trustworthy behavior by both partners. Trust has usually been damaged by many large and small transgressions. The three steps to reconciling are discussion, detoxification, and devotion (Ripley & Worthington, 2014).

Discussion shows couples how to discuss the most hurtful past transgressions so they can also deal with future transgressions. Not every past hurt needs to be talked out, but some will require discussion. Offended partners are shown ways to make a good reproach (e.g., a request by the hurt partner for an explanation of why the other partner did something hurtful or offensive). Partners are shown not-so-good and better ways to respond to reproaches. The not-so-good methods are denying that one did wrong, refusing to take responsibility, blaming the partner, justifying one's acts, and making defensive excuses. Making good confessions helps the partner forgive. A good confession is guided by an acrostic, CONFESS. First, *confess* without excuse. Next, *offer* an apology that takes responsibility for wrongdoing and admits to regret, feelings of remorse, and a motivation to make things right. Then, *note* the other person's pain, which is to show that one not only recognizes what was done to hurt the partner but also describes the meaning of the hurt for the partner. After that, *forever* value the partner, which says that it is more important to resolve the wrongdoing than to save face. One can then *equalize*, meaning that one offers to make amends for the wrong that was done. Finally, the offender promises to try not to repeat the offense by *saying* "never again." Last, the offender *says*, "Can you forgive me?" Sometimes the partner who was hurt will spontaneously forgive, but more often with couples who seek counseling, the hurts are numerous and sometimes in the long past, so coaching partners to ask for forgiveness is helpful.

Detoxification of the bitterness and resentment from past hurts occurs in many ways. Forgiveness is not necessary for all. Some can be taken care of by restoring a sense of justice, relinquishing the hurt to God, forbearing, or accepting. Others will need forgiveness.

We teach REACH Forgiveness to couples. To learn the method, each partner chooses a hurt by someone else, before their relationship began. The therapist teaches the method (see Chapter 19, this volume, on REACH Forgiveness) and engages the partner as a support. Then, the second partner practices the method with the first partner in support. REACH Forgiveness can be applied to the most crucial hurts first. After being applied to some of the major hurts, the forgiveness begins to generalize to the relationship as a whole.

Devotion consists of building love and emotional closeness back into the relationship. This action is done early in couple therapy, and it is focused on when intimacy is addressed. After dealing with pent up unforgiveness after transgressions, it is important to again be more positive.

Consolidation of Gains and Termination

The partners will likely have dealt with most of their major issues by this time and might be approaching termination. As termination nears, the therapist initiates a conversation about whether and (if so) what other goals might need to be added to the treatment plan. When the couple does not want to add goals, the therapist drafts a tentative final assessment report before the penultimate session. In that session, the report is not discussed, but the therapist is alert to areas that cannot be accurately summarized on the final report. The report is completed between that session and the last scheduled session.

Between sessions, the couple is instructed to reflect on their treatment and come up with a creative way to commemorate their successes during therapy—a montage, song, art project, or something else. When the session convenes, the couple presents their commemoration, discusses treatment as a whole, and then—when each partner receives the written report—discusses the written feedback report from the therapist. The report contains a plan for their continued improvement at home and a schedule of future check-up appointments or phone calls.

Application of the HFCA-C to This Case

Treatment involved HFCA-C, as they both requested this approach. The therapist used a low-level spiritual integration (with few points of spiritual discussion) given the partners' differences in spiritual practices currently and the husband's disengagement from faith. His offenses from church leaders were blamed for his disengagement at first, although anger toward God for his health, losses, and job setbacks arose as insight developed. One thread of treatment responded to parallel disappointments with God, each other, and their church community. Treatment for this goal involved increasing empathy for each other, framing the wife's response to the husband as not engaging in the compassion that she wanted to convey, and validating the race-based stresses they face as an African American couple. Opening conversation about these disappointments created an opportunity for the couple to bond with each other, increasing trust. As they empathized with each other, the husband appeared to experience an increased sense of care and support from God. The wife spontaneously reported she felt the need to privately pray blessings on her husband daily, which increased her positive attributions.

The second thread of therapeutic work was in forgiveness. Both partners resisted forgiving early in treatment planning, when it was brought up as one option to address their offenses. Rigid Christian teachings that one "must" forgive appeared to be the primary channel of resistance as well as a well-defined defense of rumination about offenses. As treatment progressed, though, the therapist explained emotional forgiveness as different from decisional forgiveness. She wondered aloud whether the religious teaching to forgive was decisional, not emotional. As other relationship discussions and exercises took place in the first eight sessions, the therapist repeatedly noted how much pain their ruminations seemed to cause them both. By Session 8, enough trust was built in each other and the therapist to attempt forgiveness. The REACH Forgiveness DIY workbook was offered as homework and rejected. A winsome and noncoercive video series on forgiveness from a Black preacher (Michael Todd) was located, and the couple watched it. This helped break down barriers to engaging in forgiveness. The couple was able to apply the empathy they had practiced earlier in counseling to their offenses from church members and, finally, each other. They engaged in a humble exchange of apologies and forgiveness. The couple had reached 12 sessions at that point. Additional sessions to consolidate gains and "hold on" to forgiveness had to be cut short due to a sudden move out of state.

RESEARCH FINDINGS AND SUPPORT

The outcome and process research on SICT is limited. There are few studies of true SICT, although there are studies of prevention, enrichment, and preparation for marriage. Instead of outcome research (e.g., Ripley et al., 2021), we will focus on studies of processes in couple therapy. In one field study of Christian couple therapists in practice, Hook et al. (2014) examined religion and couple therapy among members of the American Association of Christian Counselors, typically highly religious and theologically conservative counselors and psychotherapists. Clients described the religious and nonreligious techniques that were used in couple therapy. Most religious techniques were used in about half the sessions. The religious commitment of clients was positively related to the number of religious techniques used within couple therapy. Clients improved over the first eight sessions of couple therapy in their relationship satisfaction and working alliance. Partners reported a high level of satisfaction with couple therapy.

Several prior studies of individual psychotherapy and counseling examined the use of religious techniques (e.g., Wade et al., 2007; Walker et al., 2004), but Hook et al. (2014) was the first reporting on couple therapy. In a meta-analysis of individual psychotherapy by Walker et al. (2004), religious therapists estimated that they dealt with forgiveness in 42% of cases, referred to Scripture in 39%, confronted sin in 33%, and used prayer in 29%. Hook et al. observed that in individual psychotherapy, religious therapists used religious techniques in between one third to one half of their sessions. They reported that clients said that couple therapy addressed forgiveness in 65.5% by Session 4 and in 82.3% by Session 8. Use of forgiveness more toward the end of couple therapy has been recommended in research on forgiveness (Worthington & Sandage, 2016). Forgiveness seems to be something that comes up after conflict and intimacy issues have been addressed. At least one partner reported discussing religious faith in 55% to 60% of the sessions, praying in session in 50% to 60% of the sessions, and quoting Scripture in 45% to 50% of the sessions.

Ripley et al. (2022) studied 108 clients from 29 community-based couple therapists (who advertised as Christian-accommodation therapists) completing over 402 sessions of SICT as usual. Similar to the findings of Hook et al. (2014), spiritually integrated interventions were tailored to the spirituality of the couple, focused largely on emotional experiences in treatment, and most frequently included the spiritual practices of prayer, hope, forgiveness, and encouraging people to consult their heart. Therapists usually used methods from several evidence-based interventions. Because highly distressed couples did not progress as rapidly as less distressed couples, therapists were advised to pay particular attention to those couples who seemed most troubled.

CONCLUSION

SICT is practiced in many forms—by lay counselors, clergy, pastoral counselors, and mental health professionals. Most of the studies have involved mental health professionals although sometimes a small minority of nonprofessional counselors have been included (see Hook & Worthington, 2009). Generally, the couple therapists who have been surveyed have drawn on existing therapies that are evidence-based or have incorporated techniques from evidence-based therapies. However, no research to date has identified what percentage of the therapy has referred to evidence-based treatments and what percentage has been therapists' use of homemade couple therapy and homemade integration of theology and spiritual techniques into their therapy. What we do know is that in community practice, therapists are indeed making some use of practices developed and investigated (and shown to be effective) by clinical scientists. Outcome research on SICT has shown it to be comparable to secular therapies when used with religious people. Occasionally, though, some of the highly religious people seem most resistant to SICT. We can only speculate that this might be due to hypervigilance to theological differences or to religious people waiting until their marriages are more severely disturbed prior to seeking help from a mental health professional. We nevertheless must point out that practitioners should remain especially alert when facing couples whose relationships are highly troubled, especially if they are also very religious. Overall, though, people who practice SICT can be as confident in their approach as if they applied a secular approach, and they are likely to match the value preferences of their clients more than if they applied secular approaches.

REFERENCES

Adams, J. (1970). *Competent to counsel.* Zondervan.

Blankenhorn, D., Browning, D., & Van Leeuwen, M. S. (2003). *Does Christianity teach male headship: The equal regards marriage and its critics.* Wm. Eerdmans & Co.

Browning, D. S. (2006). *Equality and the family: A fundamental practical theology of children, mothers, and fathers in modern society.* Wm. Eerdmans & Co.

Cohen Davidovsky, G. (2019). The Orthodox Jewish couple in therapy: Addressing religious conflict and confronting the Divine elephant in the room. *Clinical Social Work Journal, 47*(4), 353–362. https://doi.org/10.1007/s10615-018-0697-y

Crabb, L. J., Jr. (1977). *Effective Biblical counseling: A model for helping caring Christians become capable counselors.* Zondervan.

Fincham, F. D., & May, R. W. (2017). Prayer and forgiveness: Beyond relationship quality and extension to marriage. *Journal of Family Psychology, 31*(6), 734–741. https://doi.org/10.1037/fam0000331

Fisher, R., Ury, W., & Patton, B. (2011). *Getting to yes: Negotiating agreement without giving in.* Penguin.

Gray, T. D., & Cordova, J. V. (2018). Relationship concerns. In A. Maragakis & W. T. O'Donohue (Eds.), *Principle-based stepped care and brief psychotherapy for integrated care settings* (pp. 349–358). Springer International Publishing. https://doi.org/10.1007/978-3-319-70539-2_31

Gurman, A. S. (2015). The theory and practice of couple therapy: History, contemporary models, and a framework for comparative analysis. In A. S. Gurman, J. L. Lebow, & D. K. Snyder (Eds.), *Clinical handbook of couple therapy* (5th ed., pp. 1–22). Guilford Press.

Hawkins, J. M., McPhee, D. P., & Brown, C. C. (2020). Incorporating biopsychosocial-spiritual resources in emotionally focused couple therapy. *Contemporary Family Therapy, 42*(3), 217–227. https://doi.org/10.1007/s10591-019-09523-8

Hook, J. N., & Worthington, E. L., Jr. (2009). Christian couple counseling by professional, pastoral, and lay counselors from a protestant perspective: A nationwide survey. *The American Journal of Family Therapy, 37*(2), 169–183. https://doi.org/10.1080/01926180802151760

Hook, J. N., Worthington, E. L., Jr., Davis, D. E., & Atkins, D. C. (2014). Religion and couple therapy: Description and preliminary outcome data. *Psychology of Religion and Spirituality, 6*(2), 94–101. https://doi.org/10.1037/a0035412

Johnson, E. L. (2010). *Psychology and Christianity: Five views.* InterVarsity Press.

Neff, M. A., & McMinn, M. R. (2020). *Embodying integration: A fresh look at Christianity in the therapy room.* InterVarsity Press.

New International Version Bible. (2011). New International Version Bible Online. https://www.thenivbible.com/ (Original work published 1973).

Pew Research Center. (2015, April 2). *The future of world religions: Population growth projections, 2010–2050.* https://www.pewforum.org/2015/04/02/religious-projections-2010-2050/

Ripley, J. S., Solfelt, L., Ord, A., Garthe, R. C., Worthington, E. L., Jr., & Channing, T. (2021). Short- and long-term outcomes of Hope-Focused Couple Therapy. *Spirituality in Clinical Practice.* Advance online publication. https://doi.org/10.1037/scp0000286

Ripley, J. S., & Worthington, E. L., Jr. (2014). *Couple therapy: A new hope-focused approach.* InterVarsity Press.

Ripley, J. S., Worthington, E. L., Jr., Kent, V. M., Loewer, E., & Chen, Z. J. (2022). Spiritually incorporating couple therapy in practice: Christian-accommodated couple therapy as an illustration. *Psychotherapy, 59*(3), 382–391. https://doi.org/10.1037/pst0000411

Sauerheber, J. D., Nims, D., & Carter, D. J. (2014). Counseling Muslim couples from a Bowen family systems perspective. *The Family Journal, 22*(2), 231–239. https://doi.org/10.1177/1066480713514937

Tan, S.-Y. (2011). *Counseling and psychotherapy: A Christian perspective.* Baker Academic.

Wade, N. G., Worthington, E. L., Jr., & Vogel, D. L. (2007). Effectiveness of religiously tailored interventions in Christian therapy. *Psychotherapy Research, 17*(1), 91–105. https://doi.org/10.1080/10503300500497388

Walker, D. F., Gorsuch, R. L., & Tan, S. Y. (2004). Therapists' integration of religion and spirituality in counseling: A meta-analysis. *Counseling and Values, 49*(1), 69–80. https://doi.org/10.1002/j.2161-007X.2004.tb00254.x

Worthington, E. L., Jr. (2005). *Hope-focused marriage counseling: A guide to brief therapy.* InterVarsity Press.

Worthington, E. L., Jr. (2006). *Forgiveness and reconciliation: Theory and application.* Routledge.

Worthington, E. L., Jr., & Sandage, S. J. (2016). *Forgiveness and spirituality in psychotherapy: A relational approach.* American Psychological Association. https://doi.org/10.1037/14712-000

19

REACH Forgiveness in Couple, Group, and Individual Psychotherapy

Everett L. Worthington, Jr.

REACH Forgiveness is an intervention that is based on stress-and-coping theory and helps people forgive. It has numerous applications for communities, including promotion of community mental health and use in churches. In addition, REACH Forgiveness is useful in private practices, especially group practices. This intervention is also useful in hospital and medical settings, drug and alcohol rehabilitation settings, university counseling settings, criminal justice settings, and even for public physical and mental health. It can be used as a systemwide intervention within a church's awareness-raising campaign, and thus is ideal to promote clergy–clinician collaboration.

In this chapter, I summarize the REACH Forgiveness method and describe its development and use in individual psychotherapy, couple therapy, and group psychotherapy. I also show how it has been adapted for use in self-forgiveness, in Christian churches, and in public health applications. I present a case that shows how REACH Forgiveness is used in couple therapy that includes partner forgiveness and six steps to self-forgiveness, and I use out-of-session do-it-yourself (DIY) workbooks as supplements in forgiving another and oneself.

OVERVIEW OF THE INTERVENTION

REACH Forgiveness evolved from working with couples in therapy and individuals in groups rather than from a full-blown clinical protocol created theoretically. It was a collaborative effort with input from my graduate students,

https://doi.org/10.1037/0000338-019
Handbook of Spiritually Integrated Psychotherapies, P. S. Richards, G. E. K. Allen, and D. K. Judd (Editors)
Copyright © 2023 by the American Psychological Association. All rights reserved.

research findings, teaching, public speaking, theory, Christian and Hebrew scriptures, and academic (but more importantly) practical theology—all of which were sifted and shaken by my clientele, the patients of my students and supervisees, and the Christian environment in which I functioned. International speaking contributed to broad cultural awareness.

The method uses an acronym, REACH, to cue people's memories of the steps they can move through to forgive. "R" stands for *recall* the hurt. We have to face the offense rather than deny it. But we can't simply rehearse what a jerk we think the offender is or how damaged we feel we've been by the offense. We can make a decision to act more positively toward the offender, but we also need to "E," which can stand for *emotionally* replace the negative emotions with positive other-oriented ones like *empathy*, sympathy, compassion, or love for the offender. That is difficult and occupies the most time of any step. As we experience a transformation of emotion, we can choose to give an "A," *altruistic* gift of forgiveness, to the offender. It's altruistic because offenders do not deserve forgiveness. We forgive as a free gift. That leads to "C," a *commitment* to the forgiveness we have experienced. That commitment helps us "H," *hold* onto the forgiveness when we doubt. After the R step (*recall*), people are given the opportunity to make a decision to forgive, but most prefer to put it off until after moving through all five steps. At that point, decisional forgiveness is easier because the five steps have helped reduce the size of the injustice gap. The final aspect of the REACH Forgiveness method is to seek to broaden the application to other not-fully-forgiven events in the person's life, through *generalization*, *maintenance*, and *relapse prevention*. People are invited to review their relationships—with parents, siblings, teachers, friends, bullies, employers, work colleagues, people at church, and in avocational activities—and identify less-than-fully-forgiven events. Most people have no trouble identifying more than 10. Then they apply the REACH Forgiveness steps to 10 events. We got to be unforgiving, grudge-holding, and sometimes vengeful people by not forgiving one hurt at a time. Or in the case of a couple, we became unforgiving of our partner one hurt at a time. So, becoming a more forgiving person or a person who forgives the partner as a person (not just for one event) is achieved the same way we became unforgiving—forgiving one hurt at a time until we are ready to declare that we have forgiven the partner or that we are a more forgiving person.

The unspoken, and largely unanswerable, question involves the responsibilities for causing change using the REACH Forgiveness protocols. I personally believe that forgiveness is a collaborative process between us and God, through the (often unseen or unacknowledged work of the Holy Spirit). In that view, God's grace is at work at the divine level (and sometimes even the human level) and our effort is at work at the human level. This is best captured in Paul's statement: ". . . continue to work out your own salvation with fear and trembling, for it is God who works in you to will and to act in order to fulfill his good purpose" (*New International Version Bible*, 1973/2011, Philippians 2:12b–13). Sometimes Christians want to spiritualize the process of forgiveness, relying on God and believing that human effort is unnecessary. If they hold such beliefs, it increases their reliance on God, which is a good thing. Usually, though, they will not succeed with REACH Forgiveness groups or workbooks. The effort required seems too "works oriented." I believe that many are misunderstanding effort as earning. We certainly cannot earn God's favor, but that does not mean effort is not required. Many who see REACH Forgiveness as being too earning centered simply do not join the group or complete a workbook, viewing it as ill advised.

The key is to engage participants in emotionally evocative interventions. This is relatively easy to do in a therapeutic or group situation because the therapist guides the patient's attention along a route that will evoke a change in emotion and motivation. Progress is less certain in self-directed interventions. People are fairly easy to engage in workbook-centered exercises. The effect sizes for DIY workbook studies have actually been superior to effect sizes of group interventions of comparable duration. Internet-based interventions are a different beast. People are used to going to the internet for 5- to 10-minute YouTube clips, 18-minute TED Talks, or, at most, hour-long podcasts—not 7-hour interventions requiring several returns to a website. The difficulty in using such a time-intensive intervention on the web was demonstrated in a study by Nation et al. (2018), which had only a 29% completion rate. An effective internet intervention must be monitored closely by the website directors as part of the intervention. An internet intervention could be a series of hour-long or 30-minute podcasts that are highly engaging. People might "level up," as in game programs, whereby one receives acknowledgment of additional special status as one completes each level. In this model, one would level up by completing successive podcasts until the expert level is reached.

THEORETICAL FRAMEWORK FOR UNDERSTANDING FORGIVENESS

The stress-and-coping theory is the dominant theory of forgiveness (Worthington, 2006). According to this theory, offenses, hurts, and transgressions are ubiquitous. Each injustice creates a subjective amount of injustice called the *injustice gap* (Davis et al., 2016), which is adjusted as offenders and victims act in response to the injustice. For example, an offender denying responsibility for the offense increases the victim's injustice gap, but an offender's apology and amends making decrease it. When the victim says something to hurt the offender, that lowers the size of the victim's injustice gap (but likely creates an injustice gap for the offender). But if the victim empathizes, sympathizes, or expresses love for the offender, that narrows the victim's injustice gap.

Strelan (2020) evaluated the evidence supporting the theory as strong. The victim perceives the transgression as a stressor, which is appraised as to its threat potential and size of the injustice gap (Davis et al., 2016). Those appraisals, which are linked together, give rise to stress reactions. Unforgiveness is the emotional part of the stress reaction (Worthington, 2006), and motivations of avoidance and revenge are activated (McCullough et al., 1998). The victim selects among potential behavioral action tendencies to cope with the perceived stress by managing the problem (i.e., problem-focused coping), emotions (i.e., emotion-focused coping), and meaning (i.e., meaning-focused coping).

Victims can cope with an active injustice gap in many ways (Worthington, 2006). Paying back the offender or exacting revenge narrows the injustice gap. However, payback triggers a reciprocity cycle. The victim can also see justice done, seek justice, observe the offender get their "just desserts," or turn the matter over to God for divine retribution. The person can also inhibit negative responding by relinquishing the matter to God, forbearing, accepting and moving on, and using attributions that justify or excuse wrongdoing. The victim might also forgive. In fact, one can mix and match among the ways of dealing with injustice to reduce the injustice gap to zero.

There are two types of forgiveness. *Decisional forgiveness* (Davis et al., 2015) is endorsing a behavioral intention to forego revenge and treat the offender as a valued and valuable person. A person may make a decision to forgive and follow it for the rest of their life but be emotionally unforgiving each time they think about the offense. Unforgiveness is a complex emotion involving resentment, bitterness, anger, fear, hostility, and even hatred. This suggests that emotional forgiveness is another type of forgiveness. *Emotional forgiveness* is the emotional replacement of negative unforgiving emotions with positive other-oriented emotions (e.g., empathy, sympathy, compassion, love), which can be facilitated by other nonself-focused emotions like gratitude that one has been forgiven by others, hope, and humility. Emotional forgiveness can be stimulated by engaging people in emotionally involving forgiveness exercises. Exercises help people re-experience their relationship toward the offender, bringing more emotional equanimity within the relationship.

DEVELOPMENT AND APPLICATIONS OF REACH FORGIVENESS

Who Developed It?

I must give a great deal of credit to my graduate students and colleagues. I have reviewed the development of REACH Forgiveness in several sources (see Worthington & Sandage, 2016). Let me mention a few. While Don Danser and I initially developed a brief intervention to help people make a decision to forgive and Fred DiBlasio and I elaborated decisional forgiveness (Worthington & DiBlasio, 1990), Mike McCullough and I shaped that into a psychoeducational group intervention, first to decide to forgive, and later to seek emotional forgiveness, which was furthered by Steve Sandage. Jennifer Ripley later wanted to study forgiveness within the hope-focused couple intervention (Ripley & Worthington, 2014). Nathaniel Wade studied it in groups. I designed the REACH Forgiveness intervention into a DIY workbook, and Caroline Lavelock Bratney was a genius at turning interventions in humility, self-control, patience, and positivity into parallel DIY workbooks (Lavelock et al., 2017). Brandon Griffin did the same with the dual-process self-forgiveness intervention (Griffin et al., 2015).

What Treatment Settings Has It Been Used In and Found to Be Helpful?

Some forgiveness interventions are targeted at particular transgressions. Robert Enright has targeted his process model of forgiveness toward several applications, including teaching forgiveness in educational, medical, and psychotherapy settings. He has a general psychotherapeutic approach (Enright & Fitzgibbons, 2015), which he calls forgiveness therapy, and some general untargeted psychoeducation. I have taken a different tack. I have usually aimed at broad application in psychoeducational interventions and in individual, couple, and group treatments. This provides the general structure that allows the practitioner, in collaboration with the patient, to tailor the REACH Forgiveness model to specific problems.

I have targeted the REACH Forgiveness model to remain true to its Christian roots, explicitly tailoring the intervention to Christian groups (Lampton et al., 2005; Osei-Tutu et al., 2020; Stratton et al., 2008) or DIY workbooks for Christians (Greer et al., 2014). We have used randomized controlled trials (RCTs) to investigate its effectiveness specifically in Christian communities (Lampton et al., 2005; Osei-Tutu et al., 2020; Stratton et al., 2008; Toussaint et al., 2020). More research has been done on the secular version of REACH Forgiveness—as a group, couple, and workbook for individuals—than on the Christian-accommodated versions. The secular workbook has been used with Christians and with people of many faiths. It seems to work as well at helping people forgive when used in the secular form with committed Christians as it does in the adapted form. This is likely because people of faith going through the secular treatment still apply their faith—praying for the offender, seeking God's wisdom in how to act, following the norms of their local faith community, and searching the scriptures.

We welcome people of other faiths besides Christianity to engage with the REACH Forgiveness materials, which are offered free. They are encouraged to adapt the materials for their own faith or faith community, merely remembering to give credit to the source within the naming (e.g., REACH Forgiveness–Muslim Version, REACH Forgiveness–Buddhist Version). REACH Forgiveness can be adapted for particular cultural considerations as well (e.g., REACH Forgiveness–Collectivistic, REACH Forgiveness–Indonesian Culture).

What Types of Clinical Issues and Clients Has It Helped?

REACH Forgiveness has been efficacious for most people who struggle to forgive. Five psychoeducational group studies and one DIY workbook study support the Christian-integrated version. The secular version has been supported by at least 21 psychoeducational RCTs, two workbook RCTs, and one internet-based RCT. The secular version has worked with a Christian population (Toussaint et al., 2020), and the Christian version in a general population (Osei-Tutu et al., 2020).

Self-Forgiveness

REACH Forgiveness is a method of forgiving, and it can be used for self-forgiveness to deal with self-condemnation. Self-forgiveness can be more complicated than forgiving others because the action takes place within an individual who is at once the wrongdoer and the forgiver. Manipulating two points of view is psychologically complex. Also, wrongdoing might offend God (or whatever one holds to be sacred), a victim, observers, people indirectly affected, and oneself. There are usually responsible actions one must take before forgiving oneself. Moreover, self-forgiveness can be tied up with self-acceptance. People frequently can forgive themselves after taking appropriate responsibility and seeking to make repair for their wrongdoing, and yet still have trouble accepting that they are people flawed so deeply that they would do the wrong they've done.

Worthington (2013) proposed a six-step method for responsible self-forgiving. In Step 1, people make things right with the Sacred however is appropriate for them (e.g., confession to God or seeking to restore one's harmony with humanity through philanthropy if they felt they had done an act against humanity). In Step 2, they make things right with others affected (e.g., victims such as an abused child, observers of the wrongdoing such as a spouse, and people indirectly affected like other children and even child protection agencies). In Step 3, they make things right with their own psychology (e.g., through psychotherapy or self-insight). With the sense of responsibility appeased, they might (in Step 4) make a decision to forgive themselves and work through the REACH Forgiveness model applied to the self. Then they might turn attention to self-acceptance (Step 5), which is often a target for psychotherapy, especially in-depth psychotherapy approaches. Finally, in Step 6, they commit not to repeat the offense and to live as virtuously as possible. This model has been applied with general instances of self-condemnation. An RCT showed it to be effective for a 6-hour DIY workbook (Griffin et al., 2015). Also, Griffin et al. (2021) have applied REACH Forgiveness in veteran populations with people struggling with moral injury.

Untargeted Couple Treatment

Couples can seek improvement in their relationships in many areas, including better communication, better conflict resolution, more reconciliation, more forgiveness, and more positive responses to big stressors like affairs. I have taught couples to forgive any type of offense. I have not targeted treatments toward any specific type of problem such as affairs (see Baucom et al., 2009). In the most recent years, we have taught the REACH Forgiveness method to partners in conjoint (or individual) therapy aimed at couples' problems (Worthington & Sandage, 2016, 2017). Because guilt and shame arise when partners betray each other, we have applied the REACH Forgiveness model to forgiveness of both others and the self so partners may deal with their own guilt and seek to reduce the injustice gap regarding their partner's wrongdoing. Usually, we do not deal with forgiveness issues with couples until partners have worked on communication, conflict resolution, and intimacy. For most troubled couples, bringing up forgiveness too early opens conflict and, without steps to contain it, can flood the couple therapy with negative emotions.

Community Psychology

Another application has been to help people forgive others in their community through awareness-raising campaigns (Lampton et al., 2005; Stratton et al., 2008). Awareness is raised regarding (a) the definition of forgiveness as being of two types (decisional and emotional forgiveness); (b) the benefits of forgiving; and (c) the availability of resources to promote forgiveness if one wishes to forgive without the help of a psychotherapist or facilitator, including the idea that the amount of forgiveness likely depends on the time spent trying to forgive. These campaigns have been effective (Griffin et al., 2018). In one study, a forgiveness campaign occupied 2 weeks of a semester. On pre–post measures, 877 students (one third of the student body) reported improvements in forgiveness during and after the campaign relative to baselines. The students reported on which university-wide activities they participated in and how long they spent at each. The mean time of exposure to forgiveness was 2.5 hours. Recall that a linear relationship exists between the time spent trying to forgive and the amount of forgiveness, governed by the equation ES of $0.124 + 0.046 \times$ time, where ES is the effect size and time represents the exposure. Thus, a mean exposure of 2.5 hours yielded an average effect size of 0.237 *SD*s of change. That is a substantial change across a university campus.

Changing Religious Communities

The same types of community interventions have been done within Christian churches, although no RCTs have been conducted to date to see how empirically effective it can be. Awareness-raising guidelines have been offered online (https://www.evworthington-forgiveness.com). Worthington et al. (2020) reported on a program to train pastors in better preaching, especially preaching about forgiveness consistent with what the research shows to be true about forgiveness. After a week of instruction, the participants had more accurate knowledge of forgiveness, had more confidence in their knowledge, and had forgiven more than at the outset of the program. In follow-up surveys, they expressed more intentions to preach on forgiveness, preach a sermon series on it, conduct groups on forgiveness, and integrate it into their congregational life more.

GUIDELINES FOR IMPLEMENTING THE APPROACH

No special training or education is needed to lead REACH Forgiveness groups as long as group access is restricted so that people who are likely troubled are directed to psychotherapy. In one study in which undergraduate students were compared with counseling psychologists with a master's degree, the counselors had only marginally better outcomes from participants in their groups. Some guidelines are desirable, however. Group leaders should be selected for their sensitivity and ability to lead groups, experience leading groups, and familiarity with the REACH Forgiveness method. Leaders should have (1) completed a group themselves; (2) prepared to lead by going through a recorded and excerpted group led by Worthington (a 2-hour digest is available free on https://www.evworthington-forgiveness.com); (3) asked questions of experienced leaders on the recording; (4) worked through the group leader manual, highlighting or marking with sticky notes the transitions from one exercise to another; and (5) (for the first group) either co-led with or be supervised by an experienced group leader.

Diversity Considerations

It is difficult to make evidence-based diversity recommendations about the use of REACH Forgiveness. The research is mixed. In the United States, typically no differences have been found for gender or race and ethnicity across many investigations. Some researchers have specifically examined whether there is a need to accommodate REACH Forgiveness groups to culture or religion. For example, Lin et al. (2015) recruited college students born and raised in Virginia and foreign-exchange students and randomly assigned them in equal numbers to secular groups. No differences in forgiveness were found between participants in either condition. In Ghana, people were recruited from churches and assigned to Christian REACH Forgiveness small groups that were either accommodated to Ghanaian culture or not (Osei-Tutu et al., 2020). The Christian REACH Forgiveness groups were effective. Culturally adapting them made no difference in outcome. In largely Muslim Indonesia, the secular REACH Forgiveness method was adapted to the Indonesian collectivistic culture, and the groups were effective (Kurniati et al., 2020).

Relationship Establishment Guidelines

No particular relationship considerations have been formally identified. Group leaders, psychotherapists, couple therapists, and psychoeducational group leaders need the same qualifications as required to succeed in their respective type of therapy.

Assessment Measures

Assessment of forgiveness is well developed. Worthington et al. (2015) reviewed the assessment measures. They suggested that the Enright Forgiveness Inventory (EFI; Subkoviak et al., 1995) is the only forgiveness measure with sufficiently strong psychometric properties to allow for assessment in clinical uses for diagnosis and prognosis. However, many assessment instruments could be used to monitor progress. Thus, the EFI might be used at the beginning and end of psychotherapy to give a reliable picture of people's forgiveness. However, to track progress, clinicians might use the Transgression-Related Inventory of Motivations (TRIM; McCullough et al., 1998), which is the most-used instrument in research on forgiveness. TRIM has 18 items (McCullough et al., 2010) and is available publicly without cost. The estimated reliability of TRIM is still strong, although not as strong as the 60-item EFI.

Intervention Techniques and Strategies

Numerous exercises make up the psychoeducational group manuals and the DIY workbooks for REACH Forgiveness. In addition, for couples, Ripley and Worthington (2014) provided more than 80 interventions to promote couple harmony. Many of those are forgiveness exercises tailored for couples. DIY workbooks are ideal for patients to work through at their own pace.

The availability of (a) free DIY 7-hour and 2-hour interventions and (b) free participant and leader manuals for running psychoeducational groups increases clinicians' flexibility in treating people who need to forgive. Enright and Fitzgibbons (2015) aimed their treatment at forgiveness therapy, tailoring Enright's process forgiveness therapy to difficult-to-handle problems such as incest and alcoholism. When patients come to psychotherapy with a presenting problem of lack of forgiveness, this would be an excellent option. However, my clinical observation is that few patients seek solely forgiveness therapy. Also, insurance companies are unlikely to reimburse for a therapy not tied to a *Diagnostic and Statistical Manual of Mental Disorders* diagnosis (American Psychiatric Association, 2013). Instead, typically people present problems related to depression, anxiety, personality disorders, trauma, interpersonal problems, and the like. Then, within psychotherapy (or couple therapy), it becomes obvious to both the psychotherapist and patient that work on forgiving is needed. Forgiveness therapy is usually undertaken within general psychotherapy. Often, insurance limits the amount of time a patient can be seen in psychotherapy. Most practitioners treat depression, anxiety, trauma, or stress directly, which leaves few hours of psychotherapy that can be focused on forgiveness.

Good news. When it becomes obvious that forgiveness work is necessary, the psychotherapist could refer patients to groups. These could recur regularly in solo or group practices. In a group practice, many patients could be candidates for groups to deal with interpersonal problems—in which forgiveness is prominent. Practitioners can charge for groups, and patients can benefit from a 6-hour REACH Forgiveness group, which could produce an ES of $0.124 + 0.046 \times$ time (Wade et al., 2014), which is 0.400 *SD*s. The reduction in depression and anxiety that people realize (an ES of approximately 0.2 for both) is associated with forgiveness-group participation. The patient could make strong progress toward forgiving plus become less depressed and anxious by attending a forgiveness group. Even better news. The same gains are realized by having the patient complete a DIY workbook (https://www.evworthington-forgiveness.com) at home at no cost to the patient. Of course, the clinician receives no payment, yet financial gains for psychotherapists might be realized due to good will in providing patients with a cost-free DIY intervention. Such free help should increase the referral potential, too.

Recommendation for Collaborating With Clergy

The potential for collaborating with clergy is high. Usually, referrals flow from clergy to practitioner. Because many groups could be run in churches and workbooks could also be completed by patients on their own, clinicians might deed much of a patient's work on forgiveness to either a clergy member or lay counselor after psychotherapy or couple therapy is done.

The church-based forgiveness awareness-raising campaigns that were discussed earlier can ready people for groups and can alert some parishioners to their need for couple therapy or psychotherapy. Clinicians could assist clergy by training and supervising lay group leaders, consulting with pastors, or conducting groups (either pro bono or for pay by the church). In addition, Worthington et al. (2020) found a positive effect on clergy knowledge and confidence by providing workshops for clergy. Practitioners could organize workshops in the community for clergy or even conduct large-scale workshops for laypeople from numerous local churches.

CASE EXAMPLE ILLUSTRATING TREATMENT PROCESSES AND INTERVENTIONS

This example is a composite of people I have seen in individual and couple counseling and in group settings. Luis and Maria had been married for more than 19 years. Luis was an executive with an MBA. He met Maria when she was working her way through college by exotic dancing. Somehow they clicked. After a brief romance, they married. Maria quit dancing but continued college, and she graduated with a bachelor's degree in psychology a year after they married.

In their second year of marriage, both Luis and Maria had religious experiences in a large charismatic church. They began attending church when Maria had become pregnant about 7 months into their rocky, conflicted marriage. They had one child, a girl named Adriana.

Now age 17, Adriana had demanded a new car. Luis thought she should have it. Maria didn't. Luis bought one for Adriana anyway, which Maria took as a huge betrayal of trust. In retaliation, Maria forbade Adriana from driving it. So the conflict continued. Maria separated from Luis for 2 weeks and took Adriana with her, and Luis saw his act for the betrayal it was. He was counseled by the elders at his church to make amends and seek to reconcile the marriage. He felt guilty and ashamed, although this did not stop the conflict. Luis apologized to Maria, citing his fidelity to the elders' recommendation, and she moved back in. She claimed that Luis wasn't really sorry; he was just apologizing because the church said to. If anything, Luis's guilt over his betrayal heated up the conflicts as he attempted to "win" back his honor by winning arguments. It was clear to the couple therapist that this was only one issue that the couple was fighting over.

The couple therapist generally followed the hope-focused approach (Ripley & Worthington, 2014). After a thorough assessment using questionnaires on couple satisfaction, commitment, communication, conflict frequency and tactics, intimacy, and forgiveness, the partners were directed to have a brief discussion of a topic they frequently disagreed on. They had a heated in-session argument. In a feedback session, the therapist proposed a 20-week course of treatment.

Conflict negotiation was addressed first. Luis and Maria fought loudly and often. Their fights not only entailed loud shouting and cursing but had escalated to violence. Maria threw some dishes at Luis during one argument, and Luis restrained her, bruising her wrists. Luis and Maria had accumulated disagreements for 20 years. The therapist taught them the problem-solving approach from the Harvard Negotiation Project (Fisher et al., 2011). They identified their irreconcilable positions, and then sought to find the interests behind the positions, which might yield common ground. The method defused lots of anger and helped them resolve differences.

By Session 14, Luis and Maria were doing better. They were able to communicate less negatively and were having times that were positive. However, many hurtful past issues lurked in the background when they tried to resolve new conflicts. At the end of the session, the therapist approached the topic of forgiveness. They agreed to work on it in Sessions 15 and beyond. First, Maria still resented Luis's betrayal when he bought the car for Adriana. Maria said her most pressing concern was trying to forgive Luis for that betrayal. She also named Luis's restraint of her, which she found angering, humiliating, and disempowering. She felt that Luis was too controlling. He had, on several occasions, refused to give her money so she could purchase personal items. She said it felt as if he were treating her like a child.

Luis was disappointed with himself for purchasing the car for Adriana "out of spite." He identified no need to forgive Maria, describing himself as quick to anger but quick to let it go.

In Session 15, the couple therapist asked if Luis and Maria wanted to work on forgiveness. When they agreed, the therapist taught them REACH Forgiveness, which would be used for Maria's work forgiving Luis and Luis's work forgiving himself. Maria identified a hurt that occurred prior to meeting Luis. She described a time when her father had gotten drunk, come home, and forbidden her from going to the Valentine's dance that night because her mother caught her sneaking beer from the refrigerator. The therapist taught Maria the REACH Forgiveness model and how to apply it. Luis was appointed as Maria's emotional support.

At the end of the session, the couple therapist asked Luis and Maria to each complete at home a DIY workbook relevant to their problem. The therapist opened the REACH Forgiveness website (https://www.evworthington-forgiveness.com). They examined the workbooks and each chose the one most relevant to their problem. Maria chose to complete the 6-hour REACH Forgiveness DIY workbook concerning Luis's betrayal by purchasing the car for Adriana. Luis chose to complete the 6-hour Self-Forgiveness DIY workbook, which contained an application of the REACH Forgiveness method to self-forgiveness. If the partners both completed their workbook before the next meeting, then the three would meet. If either failed to complete the workbook, the appointment had to be rescheduled. Both partners were asked whether they were willing to complete the work. Both agreed to put in the 7 hours needed before the next appointment.

Session 16 was held 2 weeks later (Luis did not have time to complete the workbook during the first week). They discussed questions that arose as they completed the workbook. The couple therapist worked with Luis first because the therapist thought that Luis's feelings of regret, remorse, guilt, and shame might soften Maria's attitude. Luis confessed to difficulty completely forgiving and accepting himself as someone who could have been so manipulative. Feeling convicted, he had initiated a talk with Adriana during the week. He admitted to her that he had made a bad decision, apologized for the discord his decision had introduced between Adriana and Maria, and asked for Adriana's forgiveness.

After processing these events, the couple therapist turned to Maria's experience with forgiving Luis. She said that completing the workbook had helped. But Luis's admissions earlier in the session had helped the most. She also noted that tension with Adriana had eased during the week. She was ecstatic to find Luis's role in that. She expressed forgiveness. He, in turn, noted that it was easier to forgive himself now that he felt that both God and Maria had forgiven him.

The couple therapist invited each partner to review the workbook during the week—especially the end portion in which they had uncovered other relational transgressions that they had tried to forgive. Those would be addressed in the next session.

In Session 17, a few older incidents were discussed. Maria noted that the time Luis had restrained her during their argument was still troubling her. She was assigned to work through the 2-hour REACH Forgiveness DIY workbook on that incident. In Session 18, she was able to express forgiveness to Luis. They wrapped up in Session 19, constructing a physical metaphorical representation to what they learned in therapy. In Session 20, the couple therapist presented a written assessment report, and the couple terminated treatment, feeling that couple therapy had been successful.

EFFICACY OF REACH FORGIVENESS AND OTHER FORGIVENESS INTERVENTIONS

Among intervention studies, Enright's process model (Enright & Fitzgibbons, 2015) and the REACH Forgiveness model (Worthington, 2006) are far and away the most studied interventions to date. No head-to-head comparison between the two has yet been published. In a meta-analysis by Wade et al. (2014), Enright's process model was found to be equal to Worthington's in efficacy when length of intervention and severity of transgression were controlled. All other models were collapsed together and also did not differ from Enright's model with the same controls. Luskin's (2001) Forgive for Good model and Wade's process model (Wade et al., 2018) are in the second tier. Each has been compared head to head with REACH Forgiveness (Toussaint et al., 2020; Wade et al., 2018), and no differences in efficacy have been found. Other approaches, such as the Greenberg and Meneses (2020) model ensconced in emotionally focused couple therapy, the Baucom et al. (2009) model for forgiveness after affairs, and the DiBlasio and Benda (2008) decision-based forgiveness model, have a few studies supporting them. Other investigations were one-off studies.

In their meta-analysis of RCT intervention research, Wade et al. (2014) suggested additional conclusions. First, there was a linear relationship between the amount of time spent trying to forgive and the amount of forgiveness experienced. Second, the forgiveness interventions also stimulated reliable increases in hope and decreases in depression and anxiety. This is good news for a practitioner. Not only can the psychotherapist help make changes in a presenting problem—to increase forgiveness of a patient—but at least some mental health problems can be alleviated as well.

To date, more than 30 RCTs of REACH Forgiveness have been conducted. Recently, the intervention has been tested against a process-based group psychotherapy treatment (Wade et al., 2018) and Luskin's Forgive for Good treatment (Toussaint et al., 2020). Research on REACH Forgiveness is ongoing around the world. At present, a large project funded by the Templeton World Charity Foundation is examining a brief REACH Forgiveness workbook intervention in separate RCTs; there are at least 600 participants per site at six sites that have experienced high conflict or war (e.g., Hong Kong, Indonesia, Colombia, South Africa, and two sites in Ukraine). Each of these sites involves an RCT field experiment using the secular REACH Forgiveness model with highly traumatized participants. The six sites are combined in a preregistered RCT study testing the DIY workbook, which (after the study is done) will be available online in English (https://www.evworthington-forgiveness.com), Mandarin Chinese, Indonesian, Russian, Ukrainian, and Spanish—making it available without cost to about two thirds of the world population in their native language.

CONCLUSION

REACH Forgiveness is only one of many effective interventions to promote forgiveness. To date, no intervention has shown that it is more effective per hour than any other. REACH Forgiveness is clearly the pre-eminent Christian-accommodated forgiveness intervention. It is widely available without cost. It has enormous public health implications for use in churches, Christian colleges, and publicly available DIY workbooks. We cannot discount Rye and Pargament's (2002) finding that Christians who go through a secular REACH

Forgiveness group still pray for the person who harmed them, consult scripture regarding forgiveness, and practice spiritual disciplines as much as people who go through Christian-accommodated REACH Forgiveness groups. Thus, while this chapter has touted REACH Forgiveness, I commend *any* evidence-based forgiveness intervention for Christians to use.

REFERENCES

American Psychiatric Association. (2013). *Diagnostic and statistical manual of mental disorders* (5th ed.). https://doi.org/10.1176/appi.books.9780890425596

Baucom, D. H., Snyder, D. K., & Gordon, K. C. (2009). *Helping couples get past the affair: A clinician's guide*. Guilford Press.

Davis, D. E., Hook, J. N., Van Tongeren, D. R., DeBlaere, C., Rice, K. G., & Worthington, E. L., Jr. (2015). Making a decision to forgive. *Journal of Counseling Psychology, 62*(2), 280–288. https://doi.org/10.1037/cou0000054

Davis, D. E., Yang, X., DeBlaere, C., McElroy, S. E., Van Tongeren, D. R., Hook, J. N., & Worthington, E. L., Jr. (2016). The injustice gap. *Psychology of Religion and Spirituality, 8*(3), 175–184. https://doi.org/10.1037/rel0000042

DiBlasio, F. A., & Benda, B. B. (2008). Forgiveness intervention with married couples: Two empirical analyses. *Journal of Psychology and Christianity, 27*(2), 150–158.

Enright, R. D., & Fitzgibbons, R. P. (2015). *Forgiveness therapy: An empirical guide for resolving anger and restoring hope*. American Psychological Association. https://doi.org/10.1037/14526-000

Fisher, R., Ury, W., & Patton, B. (2011). *Getting to yes: Negotiating agreement without giving in* (3rd ed.). Penguin.

Greenberg, L. S., & Meneses, C. W. (2020). *Forgiveness and letting go in emotion-focused therapy*. American Psychological Association.

Greer, C. L., Worthington, E. L., Jr., Lin, Y., Lavelock, C. R., & Griffin, B. J. (2014). Efficacy of a self-directed forgiveness workbook for Christian victims of within-congregation offenders. *Spirituality in Clinical Practice, 1*(3), 218–230. https://doi.org/10.1037/scp0000012

Griffin, B. J., Cornish, M. A., Maguen, S., & Worthington, E. L., Jr. (2021). Forgiveness as a mechanism of recovery from moral injury. In J. M. Currier, K. D. Drescher, & J. Nieuwsma (Eds.), *Addressing moral injury in clinical practice* (pp. 71–86). American Psychological Association. https://doi.org/10.1037/0000204-005

Griffin, B. J., Toussaint, L. L., Zoelzer, M., Worthington, E. L., Jr., Coleman, J., Lavelock, C. R., McElroy, A., Hook, J. N., Wade, N. G., Sandage, S. J., & Rye, M. (2018). Evaluating the effectiveness of a community-based forgiveness campaign. *The Journal of Positive Psychology, 14*(3), 354–361. https://doi.org/10.1080/17439760.2018.1437464

Griffin, B. J., Worthington, E. L., Jr., Lavelock, C. R., Greer, C. L., Lin, Y., Davis, D. E., & Hook, J. N. (2015). Efficacy of a self-forgiveness workbook: A randomized controlled trial with interpersonal offenders. *Journal of Counseling Psychology, 62*(2), 124–136. https://doi.org/10.1037/cou0000060

Kurniati, N. M. T., Worthington, E. L., Jr., Widyarini, N., Citra, A. F., & Dwiwardani, C. (2020). Does forgiving in a collectivistic culture affect only decisions to forgive and not emotions? REACH Forgiveness collectivistic in Indonesia. *International Journal of Psychology, 55*(5), 861–870. https://doi.org/10.1002/ijop.12648

Lampton, C., Oliver, G., Worthington, E. L., Jr., & Berry, J. W. (2005). Helping Christian college students become more forgiving: An intervention study to promote forgiveness as part of a program to shape Christian character. *Journal of Psychology and Theology, 33*, 278–290. https://doi.org/10.1177/009164710503300404

Lavelock, C. R., Worthington, E. L., Jr., Elnasseh, A., Griffin, B. J., Garthe, R. C., Davis, D. E., & Hook, J. N. (2017). Still waters run deep: Humility as a master virtue. *Journal of Psychology and Theology*, 45(4), 286–303. https://doi.org/10.1177/009164711704500404

Lin, Y., Worthington, E. L., Jr., Griffin, B. J., Greer, C. L., Opare-Henaku, A., Lavelock, C. R., Hook, J. N., Ho, M. Y., & Muller, H. (2014). Efficacy of REACH Forgiveness across cultures. *Journal of Clinical Psychology*, 70(9), 781–793.https://doi.org/10.1002/jclp.22073

Luskin, F. M. (2001). *Forgive for good: A proven prescription for health and happiness*. HarperCollins.

McCullough, M. E., Luna, L. R., Berry, J. W., Tabak, B. A., & Bono, G. (2010). On the form and function of forgiving: Modeling the time-forgiveness relationship and testing the valuable relationships hypothesis. *Emotion*, 10(3), 358–376. https://doi.org/10.1037/a0019349

McCullough, M. E., Rachal, K. C., Sandage, S. J., Worthington, E. L., Jr., Brown, S. W., & Hight, T. L. (1998). Interpersonal forgiving in close relationships: II. Theoretical elaboration and measurement. *Journal of Personality and Social Psychology*, 75(6), 1586–1603. https://doi.org/10.1037/0022-3514.75.6.1586

Nation, J. A., Wertheim, E. H., & Worthington, E. L., Jr. (2018). Evaluation of an online self-help version of the REACH Forgiveness program: Outcomes and predictors of persistence in a community sample. *Journal of Clinical Psychology*, 74(6), 819–838. https://doi.org/10.1002/jclp.22557

New International Version Bible. (2011). New International Version Bible Online. https://www.thenivbible.com (Original work published 1973)

Osei-Tutu, A., Osafo, J., Anum, A., Appiah-Danquah, R., Worthington, E. L., Jr., Chen, Z. J., Cowden, R. G., & Nonterah, C. W. (2020). Is cultural adaptation needed beyond using Christian-accommodated REACH Forgiveness psychoeducational group intervention in Ghana? An efficacy study comparing a Christian-accommodated version against a version accommodated by Christian and cultural adaptations. *Spirituality in Clinical Practice*, 7(2), 73–88. https://doi.org/10.1037/scp0000215

Ripley, J. S., & Worthington, E. L., Jr. (2014). *Couple therapy: A new hope-focused approach*. InterVarsity Press.

Rye, M. S., & Pargament, K. I. (2002). Forgiveness and romantic relationships in college: Can it heal the wounded heart? *Journal of Clinical Psychology*, 58(4), 419–441. https://doi.org/10.1002/jclp.1153

Stratton, S. P., Dean, J. B., Nooneman, A. J., Bode, R. A., & Worthington, E. L., Jr. (2008). Forgiveness interventions as spiritual development strategies: Workshop training, expressive writing about forgiveness, and retested controls. *Journal of Psychology and Christianity*, 27(4), 347–357.

Strelan, P. (2020). The stress-and-coping model of forgiveness: Theory, research, and the potential of dyadic coping. In E. L. Worthington, Jr. & N. G. Wade (Eds.), *Handbook of forgiveness* (2nd ed., pp. 63–73). Routledge.

Subkoviak, M. J., Enright, R. D., Wu, C., Gassin, E., Freedman, S., Olson, L., & Sarinopoulos, I. (1995). Measuring interpersonal forgiveness in late adolescence and middle adulthood. *Journal of Adolescence*, 18(6), 641–655. https://doi.org/10.1006/jado.1995.1045

Toussaint, L. L., Griffin, B. J., Worthington, E. L., Jr., Zoelzer, M., & Luskin, F. (2020). Promoting forgiveness at a Christian college: A comparison of REACH Forgiveness and Forgive for Good methods. *Journal of Psychology and Theology*, 48(2), 154–165. https://doi.org/10.1177/0091647120911109

Wade, N. G., Cornish, M. A., Tucker, J. R., Worthington, E. L., Jr., Sandage, S. J., & Rye, M. S. (2018). Promoting forgiveness: Characteristics of the treatment, the clients, and their interaction. *Journal of Counseling Psychology*, 65(3), 358–371. https://doi.org/10.1037/cou0000260

Wade, N. G., Hoyt, W. T., Kidwell, J. E., & Worthington, E. L., Jr. (2014). Efficacy of psychotherapeutic interventions to promote forgiveness: A meta-analysis. *Journal of Consulting and Clinical Psychology, 82*(1), 154–170. https://doi.org/10.1037/a0035268

Worthington, E. L., Jr. (2006). *Forgiveness and reconciliation: Theory and application.* Brunner-Routledge.

Worthington, E. L., Jr. (2013). *Moving forward: Six steps to forgiving yourself and breaking free from the past.* WaterBrook/Multnomah.

Worthington, E. L., Jr., Cairo, A. H., Chen, Z. J., & Hicks, C. L. (2020). Changes after an educational intervention to teach about and promote forgiveness among seminarians and practicing clergy. *Journal of Psychology and Theology, 48*(3), 1–19. https://doi.org/10.1177/0091647120926488

Worthington, E. L., Jr., & DiBlasio, F. A. (1990). Promoting mutual forgiveness within the fractured relationship. *Psychotherapy: Theory, Research, & Practice, 27*(2), 219–223. https://doi.org/10.1037/0033-3204.27.2.219

Worthington, E. L., Jr., Lavelock, C., vanOyen Witvliet, C., Rye, M. S., Tsang, J.-A., & Toussaint, L. (2015). Measures of forgiveness: Self-report, physiological, chemical, and behavioral indicators. In G. J. Boyle, D. H. Saklofske, & G. Matthews (Eds.), *Measures of personality and social psychological constructs* (pp. 474–502). Elsevier Academic Press. https://doi.org/10.1016/B978-0-12-386915-9.00017-6

Worthington, E. L., Jr., & Sandage, S. J. (2016). *Forgiveness and spirituality in psychotherapy: A relational approach.* American Psychological Association. https://doi.org/10.1037/14712-000

Worthington, E. L., Jr., & Sandage, S. J. (2017). *Forgiveness in couple therapy* (Series IV—Relationships) [DVD]. American Psychological Association.

20

Search for Meaning

A Spiritually Integrated Approach for Treating Veterans With Posttraumatic Stress Disorder

Clyde T. Angel, John E. Sullivan, and Vincent R. Starnino

Posttraumatic stress disorder (PTSD) affects a significant proportion of individuals who serve in the military, particularly those who are deployed (up to 16%; Gates et al., 2012). This is not surprising considering the range of horrific events that can occur in war, including witnessing or experiencing devastating injury or being either directly or indirectly involved in killing (Starnino, Sullivan, et al., 2019). The psychosocial consequences associated with PTSD are well noted, with service members experiencing high levels of suicidality, substance abuse, relationship problems, unemployment, and co-occurring anxiety and mood disorders (Erbes et al., 2009). For some, this can result in a fracturing of one's meaning-making system, and a spiritual or existential crisis may ensue.

A holistic approach to trauma requires consideration and treatment based on a biopsychosocial-spiritual framework (Hatala, 2013). Observations from individuals treating victims of trauma have revealed that the spiritual component is often left untreated. Studies of proven psychotherapies in the treatment of trauma, especially evidence-based therapies (e.g., exposure therapy, cognitive processing therapy), have established clear results in reducing common symptoms related to PTSD (Steenkamp et al., 2015). However, many patients communicate that "something still isn't right."

This material is the result of work supported with resources from and the use of facilities at the Richard L. Roudebush Veterans Affairs Medical Center in Indianapolis, IN. The views expressed in this article are those of the authors and do not necessarily represent the views of the U.S. Department of Veterans Affairs.

https://doi.org/10.1037/0000338-020
Handbook of Spiritually Integrated Psychotherapies, P. S. Richards, G. E. K. Allen, and D. K. Judd (Editors)
Copyright © 2023 by the American Psychological Association. All rights reserved.

The Search for Meaning program is a co-led psychoeducational/processing group developed by Dr. Clyde Angel, a board-certified chaplain and licensed professional counselor, in collaboration with John Sullivan, a licensed clinical social worker. The initial protocol was the result of an organic process that arose from an 8-week group designed to help combat veterans discuss their spiritual woundedness. In 2014, Dr. Angel and Mr. Sullivan were invited to participate on a panel for a roundtable discussion at Indiana University–Purdue University Indianapolis, where they were joined by Dr. Vincent Starnino, associate professor of social work. The roundtable proved to be a springboard to further collaboration and research. The trio's first research project resulted in an expansion of the Search for Meaning intervention (10 weeks) and yielded full participant and facilitator manuals and published journal articles. This opened the door for further research, including a multisite study discussed later in this chapter.

The Search for Meaning program provides a group setting where trauma patients, many of whom carry a PTSD diagnosis, learn strategies and techniques that facilitate recovery and reintegration into their families and society. Although the intervention was created for military veterans initially, it has since expanded to other populations, including patients receiving palliative and hospice care, adolescents, and individuals with HIV/AIDS. Here, we share insights from our work with veterans.

THE SEARCH FOR MEANING TREATMENT APPROACH AND ITS THEORETICAL UNDERPINNINGS

Many patients were referred to the group while engaged in individual therapy. During individual sessions using either the cognitive processing therapy or prolonged exposure approaches, two things became evident. The first was that there were cognitive and behavioral issues that were being addressed and corrected. However, the patient was experiencing additional issues at a level and an intensity that cognitive and behavioral approaches were not reaching. One patient reported her dilemma this way: "I've been doing what you recommended. I have been thinking about my role in what happened differently and that helps. But I still feel shaken. I'm not the same person." Another patient said, "For me, trauma is like an earthquake and flashbacks are like aftershocks." The most common expression of the fact that interventions were missing the mark was stated succinctly as, "At my core, I'm not the same." These patients were not referring to their cognitions or behavior. They were talking about the impact of the trauma on their very being. Spouses and family members of traumatized veterans also provided feedback. They repeatedly observed that the veteran "isn't the same person who left for Iraq."

Therapists with extensive experience conducting group therapy would make a second discovery. They realized that the support a group provides, coupled with it being a crucible for learning and experiential processing, was a more powerful intervention than individual therapy alone. The manualized Search for Meaning program is presented in a psychoeducational/processing group setting. Leading a psychoeducational/processing group requires a skill set beyond simply conducting group therapy sessions. Therefore, coleaders of these groups were required to not only cover materials for a session, but time was made for processing issues related to content. Additionally, they had to allow for group discussion of the concepts being taught.

The Search for Meaning program addresses *spiritual wounding* and the means to treat and recover from this type of wounding in order for the treatment approach be truly holistic. The loss of a sense of self, disconnection from the self, is a spiritual issue. When patients report not knowing who they are or that they are not the same *person*, this is an existential issue. When co-occurring issues related to spiritual wounding are not addressed in the course of psychotherapy, the patient inevitably reports, "There is still something wrong."

Four Levels of Spiritual Wounding

The program recognizes that there are *levels of spiritual wounding*. The idea of levels of spiritual wounding emerged as a result of the second author's many years of working with traumatized veterans who were dealing with spiritual issues. Reference to *levels* of wounding emphasizes to the patient and clarifies for them the extent to which they have been affected. Of course, no one has to tell them that what they experienced was horrendous. In therapy, they learn the importance of processing the trauma event. And more than anything, they know that it is extremely difficult to give voice to their experiences. Explanation of the levels of wounding enhances their ability to communicate and process during the course of treatment.

The instructor begins by asking the group members to imagine someone hammering a nail. They miss the nail and hit their thumb. That is the trauma event. It is the first level of wounding. Now imagine they struck their thumb three more times, resulting in three deeper levels of wounding. The first blow results in flesh wounds and bruising. The next strike results in skeletal damage. With the third strike, there is nerve damage. We've heard the saying "Three strikes and you're out!" but this person administers a fourth blow. At this fourth level of wounding, they question their own sanity and even what kind of person they have become.

The trauma event itself is the first level of psychological wounding. It may or may not include physical wounding. Regarding the spiritual aspect of the human being, the trauma event is also the First Level of Spiritual Wounding. The instructor continues with an explanation of the process of experiencing a second, third, and fourth level of spiritual wounding. Wounding, that is, of the person's core, being, or essence—euphemisms for the soul.

At the Second Level of Spiritual Wounding, the person perceives the need to talk about what happened, but for most this is difficult. Too often, when the individual finally shares, the feedback they receive is at the very least not helpful and at worst detrimental, even when well meaning. The listener may explicitly express disbelief that the event(s) even occurred. When this is not the case, the traumatized person, being hypervigilant, may quickly pick up on the listener's body language or facial expression and perceive it as discounting what they are reporting. Being told to "suck it up" and "just forget about it" are examples of the most damaging response.

This bruising experience may become a basis for the Third Level of Spiritual Wounding. The person quickly learns they need to shut down in order to avoid more hammer strikes. They increase their isolation. The problem at this level of wounding is that the negative messages continue. This messaging is even more insidious because it is the traumatized person's self-talk. Their ruminations affect them emotionally. They may begin to *feel* incompetent, inferior, culpable, and even wicked or evil.

Movement from the third to fourth level is often subtle yet undeniably impactful. Here we are reminded of the most significant and distinguishing element of spiritual wounding—the *depth of wounding*. The concept of *depth* here is not simply deepness; it further refers to the profundity, intensity, gravity, and power of the impact. At the Fourth Level of Spiritual Wounding, there is a shift from *I feel* to *I am*:

- I *feel* incompetent to I *am* incompetent,
- I *feel* inferior to I *am* inferior,
- I *feel* culpable to I *am* culpable, or
- I *feel* wicked/evil to I *am* wicked/evil.

When the person questions the kind of person they have become and when the sense of *wickedness* and *evilness* transforms from "I *feel* wicked/evil" to "I *am* wicked/evil," this adaptation takes them beyond an emotional or cognitive disorder. This is spiritual wounding. It is at this point that the therapist is likely to hear the patient say, "I'm beyond help" and "I'm beyond forgiveness." This degree and/or depth of wounding and trauma requires the level of intervention that the Search for Meaning program provides, which is a spiritually integrated psychoeducational/processing group treatment approach.

Co-Occurring Issues Related to Spiritual Wounding, and the Use of Group Modality

In the remainder of this discussion of our treatment approach, we provide further insight into spiritual wounding, including co-occurring issues that many patients experience before they arrive at group. We also focus on group therapy as the modality of the Search for Meaning program. It was mentioned earlier that conducting a psychoeducational/processing group requires a special skill set. The program manuals contain a great deal of material as well as assignments. Absorbing and comprehending this volume of information is facilitated by a group process that involves modeling and experiential participation. This is a reason for naming one of the guidebooks, the *participant's manual*.

Through our work with veteran trauma patients, we identified nine co-occurring issues associated with spiritual wounding: (a) the shattering of trust, (b) struggle with meaning making, (c) loss of purpose, (d) feelings of disconnection and alienation (including from oneself and one's family, friends, or Higher Power), (e) moral and ethical struggles, (f) guilt issues, (g) shame, (h) unresolved grief, and (i) issues related to conscience. We discuss several of these issues next, and we provide a brief explanation of how they are addressed using a spiritually integrated group modality in order to show some of the advantages of this treatment approach when working with trauma patients. A more detailed description of the Search for Meaning protocol is provided in the next section, which describes the journey and processes and interventions.

The *shattering of trust* is unfortunately a common effect of trauma (Bell et al., 2019), and it is a co-occurring issue that most patients who join the Search for Meaning program have experienced, often as a result of feeling betrayed. In addition to not trusting others, it is not uncommon when asked to comment on *trust* and *trust issues* to hear patients report they no longer trust even themselves. What therapists need the most from patients is at the same time the most difficult for many of them to give—trust. Group norms and ethical guidelines, such as strictly preserving confidentiality, maintaining respectful boundaries, and honoring diversity, are necessary for engendering trust and therefore addressed early in the Search for Meaning program. Once a proper foundation is set, trust among group members and between patients and instructors grows as the weeks unfold.

Many patients who arrive at group do so having experienced long-standing *struggles with meaning making* and a *sense of purpose*. Trauma often forces questions about meaning to the forefront of one's conscience (Park, 2010). Core beliefs are tested. The same holds true for purpose. Patients may discover that they are quick to take the position that there is no purpose, concluding that life itself is no longer purposeful (Currier et al., 2015). The Search for Meaning program encourages patients to explore what they believe events they have experienced mean. Some may discover a need to adjust their understanding of meaning and purpose in life events and life itself—the group becomes a safe place to do this work.

Disconnectedness is strongly associated with spiritual wounding and may manifest as depression, PTSD, and a myriad of other psychological problems, although it is not always identified immediately as part of the etiology. Spirituality involves maintaining healthy connectedness (Spaniol, 2002), but this is rarely what is experienced by those with trauma symptoms. Instead, spiritual wounding is manifested in disconnection and alienation, including from one's family, friends, Higher Power, and self. Once again, the modality of group therapy and group dynamics is fertile ground and a safe place for healing. It provides a place for modeling and experiential learning of how to re-establish trust and also how to reconnect (Yalom & Leszcz, 2005). Patients come to trust one another by sharing and then experiencing positive feedback. Group encounters enhance reconnection. Chief among the lessons experienced and taught is the correlation between sharing and intimacy. As sessions progress, we often hear patients remark, "You know, I feel closer to the people in this group than to some of my closest relatives." This comment opens the door for the instructors to point out that by sharing tightly held, hidden secrets with the group, individuals felt a nearness to those with whom they shared. The more locked away the secrets, the richer the feelings of intimacy their sharing engenders. Honest sharing opens the door to intimacy with oneself and one's family, friends, and Higher Power. Given the affinity of spirituality and poetry, it is no surprise that this next quote is somewhat poetic. It validates that this is a spiritually integrated program: "I can see the light through the door of intimacy, the door that gets you out of the room with no doors, which is PTSD."

Another experience that is common among our patient population is the co-occurring issue of *moral injury* and its component parts of *guilt* and *shame* (Jinkerson, 2016). As mentioned earlier, spiritual wounding manifests as difficulty ascertaining meaning and purpose when experiencing life events, particularly those related to a trauma event. Moral injury occurs when one is involved in "an act of transgression that creates dissonance and conflict because it violates assumptions and beliefs about right and wrong and personal goodness" (Litz et al., 2009, p. 698). It is not surprising that horrific events associated with war can cause a person to feel as though their sense of right and wrong has been violated. For some, moral injury involves a sense of being betrayed "by someone who holds legitimate authority," typically a superior or leader in the military (Shay, 2014, p. 183). Moral injury and guilt, one of its component parts, combine to be perhaps the most disruptive to the therapeutic endeavor, since patients experiencing the effects of moral injury may have great difficulty staying in the moment. They can be trapped in the past or afraid of the future. Struggling to be fully present retards healing. Patients are unable to recognize and acknowledge the good things surrounding them that would provide positive counterpoints to their ongoing struggles.

Returning to lessons learned from the Four Levels of Spiritual Wounding, a significant point is reiterated, which is that the movement from the third to fourth level is concurrently imperceptibly subtle and extremely powerful. As it pertains to guilt, a person moves from feeling guilty about *something they have done* to feeling guilty for *who they are*, or at least whom they come to believe they are. The foremost spiritual leader of the Gelug school of Tibetan Buddhism, the Dalai Lama, describes this as "the second punch." The traumatic experience is the first punch, but the second punch occurs when we turn on ourselves and begin to identify our very essence with our feelings. The operative phrase here is "our very essence." When our very essence—being, self, soul—is impacted (wounded), this is what our program identifies as spiritual wounding. This gravity of wounding requires the spiritual intervention and the approach to treatment found in the Search for Meaning program.

The fourth level is also where toxic guilt becomes shame, another component part of moral injury. The group therapy modality is the optimal place to treat feelings of shame. Sharing with group members the behaviors and cognitions that produce shame is the perfect prescription. From the instructors, patients learn that it is its *hiddenness* that gives shame power over someone. Shame is like mushrooms—both thrive in the dark. Conversely, shame loses its grip when what had been hidden is exposed by sharing in group. The group becomes a safe setting where patients can work on the emotions of guilt and shame instead of these feelings working on them. Modeling of this flipping of the script is empowering. The patient who has been avoiding and isolating (hiding) out of fear that others will discover "who he or she truly is" has a radically different experience when they speak up in group. The most common feedback they receive is they are viewed as courageous and their openness is seen as admirable. Their willingness to expose what they had been hiding, coupled with the positive feedback they receive, is yet another modeling experience for the entire group and serves to encourage and motivate others.

Many patients who join the Search for Meaning program are carrying *unresolved grief*, including trauma-related grief. Many veterans are never given an opportunity to grieve, while others may find it too painful and avoid it (Pivar & Field, 2004). The Search for Meaning group modality offers a safe place for patients to engage in a healthy grieving process that involves the head, the heart, and the soul. Group members are told that involving the head relates to cognitive processes. Involvement of the heart relates to processing the emotion of grief. Reference to the soul involves spiritual interventions discussed throughout the program.

In all 10 sessions, group members are given assignments that are discussed at the beginning of the following session. For example, at the end of the session on grief, the instructor poses a challenging question to the group: "How can you use your intellect, emotion, and/or spirit to grieve?" Patients must answer this spiritually integrated question to participate in the group discussion. Success in doing this is related to what they have learned about spirituality and spiritual wounding in this program.

UNDERSTANDING THE JOURNEY—PROCESSES AND INTERVENTIONS

Search for Meaning is a 10-week journey designed to allow trauma victims to better understand how their traumatic experience has affected their spiritual well-being. Although the protocol has been manualized, it is designed to flow based on the sharing of information by the facilitators, and then allowing that information to be assimilated and responded to by the participants. After the first session, each subsequent session begins with a time for the participants to ask for clarifications and share insights related to the material presented. Group members, as the sessions progress, may return to topics discussed at any stage of the journey, much like one might process the different aspects of the grief journey. The following provides an overview of the process and nuances of leading individuals along the journey. Brief case examples are inserted throughout.

Building Trust: Trauma Shatters Trust (Week 1)

A critical element during the first session is to begin building trust. The first session has three distinct sections designed to start building trust. First is the opportunity to allow for introductions. Veterans are often reluctant to share, so they are asked to share when they served in the military, where they served, and the unit(s) they served with. It is also important for the group facilitators to share an introduction with an emphasis on sharing a part of oneself that reveals some level of vulnerability. Modeling by the facilitators is an important aspect of building trust in the group.

A second building block to establishing trust involves removing ambiguity, communicating a clear understanding about the goals of the group, and establishing clear boundaries. In addition to addressing issues of confidentiality, it is important to establish a clear understanding of diversity and acceptance of each individual's beliefs and worldviews. At the outset, group members are informed that all religious beliefs, and individuals with no religious beliefs, are welcomed. Participants are encouraged to focus on their own spiritual journey, utilize *I* language (*I think, I believe*) whenever they share their own religious perspectives, and avoid comments that imply what others "should believe." This is reinforced in the Search for Meaning participant's manual, which includes illustrations and sayings from multiple belief systems.

The third element in building trust is to set the course of the journey. A trip involves travel from Point A to Point B. The journey is what occurs once we arrive at the destination. A good example might be that the trip is to a favorite fly-fishing location, but the journey begins as we wade through the stream and seek possible locations where the fish await the gentle cast of the fly upon the water. At this junction, it is important to help the participants understand that this is *their* spiritual journey, and thus allows a moment for facilitators to differentiate between the concepts of *spirituality* and *religion*. For the purpose of this protocol, two brief definitions are shared:

> *Spirituality* is an aspect of humanity that refers to the way individuals seek and express meaning and purpose and the way they experience their connectedness to the moment, to self, to others, to nature, and to the significant or sacred. (Puchalski et al., 2009, p. 887)

> *Religion* is a collection of belief systems, cultural systems, and worldviews that relate humanity to spirituality and, sometimes, to moral values. Many religions have narratives, symbols, traditions and sacred histories that are intended to give meaning to life or to explain the origin of life or the universe. They tend to derive morality, ethics, religious laws or a preferred lifestyle from their ideas about the cosmos and human nature. (Jain, 2014, abstract)

At this juncture, we begin the process of helping participants understand the wound incurred by a traumatic experience. The concept of moral injury (discussed in further detail in the section on additional barriers to healing) finds its origin in writings from the field of psychology (e.g., Litz et al., 2009). The authors of this protocol, trained in the fields of counseling and theology, offer a slightly different terminology. Participants are introduced to the idea of spiritual wounding as a primary concept. Moral injury is treated as a subset of spiritual wounding, much like hospice care is a subset of palliative care. As stated earlier, moral injury tends to find its meaning around principles of right and wrong behavior and the goodness or badness of human character. In contrast, the concept of spiritual wounding includes moral injury but provides a larger umbrella to encompass the existential issues that arise with the human experience of traumatic events. These issues are often couched in the *why* questions and the struggle to understand human existence: "Why me? Why now? How does what happen fit into my existing belief system?"

Understanding spiritual wounding is captured in the concept of the *shattered soul*. The spiritual wounding occurs when an individual's belief or spiritual formation is compromised. The term *shattered soul* is used to illustrate this concept. An individual's spiritual formation begins at a very early stage in human development. This development is informed by family, teachers, friends, and the world at large. As individuals move from concrete to abstract thinking, typically during the early adolescent stage of development, they begin to form their own system of belief based on religious and other worldviews to which they have been exposed (Fowler & Dell, 2006). In some cases, an individual's spiritual formation may have been fractured during childhood and adolescence.

When sharing this concept in the group, the facilitators use the concept of a cup filled with one's beliefs. The individual (in this case, the combat veteran) is exposed to a trauma or series of traumas that shatters their belief system, with results similar to a car windshield being shattered into tiny pieces. Therefore, the process becomes that of rebuilding one's belief system utilizing a series of interventions.

An oft-repeated phrase used by members of the group when presented with the shattered soul concept is, "That is it!" There is often an expressed sense of clarity. Veterans at this point have said things like this: "I am not the same person I used to be" and "I am not who I was before." On one occasion, a veteran shared, "Chaplain, don't think I am crazy, but sometimes I feel like there are two different people living inside of me." What a great example of the dissonance that is occurring as a result of experiencing trauma.

At this point, the facilitator shares that the signature wound of PTSD is *shattered trust*. The question "Who or what do you trust?" is posed to the group. In a group of veterans diagnosed with PTSD, the resounding answer is, "No one, and not even me on a bad day."

For example, the chaplain was discussing the need to rebuild trust and a veteran said, "How do you do that? How do you rebuild trust?" The chaplain was somewhat caught off guard but responded,

> Well, you started rebuilding trust when you went to individual therapy and shared your story, and now you are here in this group sharing. That is a beginning of the path. So ultimately, you rebuild trust by your willingness to be

vulnerable. I mean by that, to be emotionally and spiritually vulnerable. That is tough, because the very life blood of PTSD is avoidance and the last thing you want to feel is vulnerable. But it is that willingness to risk being vulnerable that allows you to rebuild trust.

The facilitator will suggest that the goal of the participant's journey during the next 9 weeks is to begin to discover the process of moving from distress to contentment.

The first session ends with a time for the group to respond to these questions: "What are you seeking?" and "What are you hoping for during our time together?" Members of the group are encouraged to reflect on these questions during the week.

Redeveloping the Spiritual Formation: If the Spiritual Formation Is Shattered, Then It Must be Reformed (Week 2)

If life can be created, then it can be recreated. So if a spiritual formation is created, then it can be recreated. This is the next step in the journey. The concepts captured in this section are designed to counter ineffective thought patterns often developed as a result of trauma.

Taking responsibility in the moment and moving forward is the first foundational stone in recreating the spiritual formation. The participants are urged to "stop blaming and start taking responsibility." For many participants, this was framed in just admitting that the trauma has altered the way they perceive and live life. Taking responsibility is not about the trauma that occurred, but choosing not to avoid the consequences emotionally and spiritually that have manifested as a result of the trauma. A second foundational stone is understanding what we as humans can actually control. Attempting to control their surroundings, often exhibited by hypervigilance, contributes to anxiety and is counter to the search for peace and contentment. The question posed is "What can we really *control* in life?" It is important for participants to understand that they can *manage* many things—finances, relationships, parenting styles, work life, and so on. The truth presented is that the only thing we as individuals can control is the current moment and how we choose to react in the moment. Individuals are reminded that when we become fixated on the past, we become depressed; when we worry about the future, we become anxious. Contentment cannot exist if we are depressed or anxious. Understanding what we can actually control allows us to live in the moment.

A third foundational stone is learning "to be still and know." Spirituality is about *being*, not *doing*. This step aims to help the individual realize that human tendency often leads us to think we have to "do something" in order to be spiritual. Indeed, our spiritual convictions may indeed lead us to action, but it begins with being still and listening to ourselves, to the voices of others, and to what we perceive to be our Higher Power. The final stone in the foundation is helping the individual develop their own personal mantra. The group is introduced to the concept of mantras and the roles they play in helping individuals center themselves spiritually, especially in moments of increased anxiety. Examples of mantras are shared, and the facilitators may share their own mantras as examples.

As an example, one veteran was struggling to develop or discover his own mantra. Several weeks had passed. One day, he walked into the group and declared, "I found my mantra." He held up a cap with an embroidered frog and the letters F.R.O.G. on the front. He said, "This is my mantra: Fully Rely on God." This was a transformative moment for this individual, who began to make significant strides in his journey to contentment. As a former medic in a Marine unit, he had developed a sense of overresponsibility for life and death—this moment allowed him to let go of this unrealistic belief.

At this point, the participants are encouraged to reflect on the beliefs they held and how those beliefs were challenged, and even compromised, by the traumatic event(s) they experienced. For some, the belief(s) is readily identified; for others, it can be a process over time.

There was a veteran who often told the same story over and over about the children who died. The guilt had led to the veteran's addiction and had a profound effect on his physical, mental, social, and spiritual health. One day, the chaplain ventured to share an insight. He said, "I have heard you say, 'I would never hurt a child' when you discussed the abuse you experienced as a child. Is that the belief that was compromised in combat?" The veteran became tearful and slowly shook his head affirmatively. The chaplain happened to see this veteran a year later at the facility and was amazed at the veteran's physical appearance, his brightened demeanor, and his sense of calm.

It is imperative to help and encourage individuals to seek the source of the wounding related to the belief(s) that may have been compromised.

Veterans complete an exercise designed to lead them to examine their system of belief. Individuals can often maintain a series of beliefs that are actually conflicting. An example set forth as a framework are the concepts of law, mercy, and grace, simply defined as follows: Law is getting what we deserve. Mercy is not getting what we deserve. Grace is getting more than we deserve. The group discusses the concepts and how they can conflict our belief system based on various scenarios. Individuals are encouraged to discern what will be the bedrock or the guiding principle for their belief system.

The Anger Barrier (Week 3)

Any path to spiritual healing and peace must include helping individuals understand anger, dissect the effect of anger, and seek the source of their anger. Understanding anger begins with a differentiation between anger management and anger resolution. Two simple phrases are shared to help group members understand the two concepts:

- Anger management: *Be angry but don't do something stupid!*
- Anger resolution: *Make peace/reconcile the past event.*

Anger management is about managing our reactions and behavior when we feel and experience the emotion of anger. Anger resolution is about finding the source of our anger and making peace. Understanding anger begins with awareness of the anger continuum. The anger continuum is a concept introduced to help individuals identify the thoughts and words that represent their anger feelings. The group is asked to share their feeling words related to anger based on a continuum from 1 (*less angry*) to 10 (*most angry*). Group members will share various words, such as "upset," "irritated," "pissed off," or "frustrated." This exercise is important to help members track feelings of anger, manage responses, and avoid acting out behaviorally. Individuals often deflect anger by saying, "I am not angry, I am just upset" (or irritated, frustrated, and so on). To enable individuals to manage and ultimately resolve anger, they first must be aware of and own their feelings of anger at every level.

Five steps to identify and communicate anger effectively are reviewed in the group. These steps are as follows:

1. *Separate:* Remove oneself or attention away from the current irritant or trigger.
2. *Relax*: Take a few deep breaths and calm down.
3. *Ask yourself* two questions: "Why am I angry?" and "What am I feeling?"
4. *Clarify*: "When have I experienced this feeling in the past, and how can I get back to the moment?"
5. *Communicate*: Share what you are feeling in the moment.

To help the group understand the process, the facilitator will ask if anyone has experienced a moment of anger recently. With a room full of veterans with PTSD, we usually get multiple responses. The facilitator will choose an individual to share the event and ask, "What happened to make you angry?" The facilitator will then say, "Okay, that is the *why*. Now see if you can identify the feeling underneath the anger." This is often followed again by an explanation that we are treating anger as secondary and looking for the primary feeling that has triggered the anger. It can often be difficult for the individual to identify the feeling, and the group will often help.

Once the feeling is identified (e.g., *disrespected*), the facilitator will ask the veteran to remember and share the earliest time in their life that they have experienced a significant event that involved the same feeling (in this case, disrespect). Most often, the individual will go back to an event in childhood. The facilitator will ask the person if they are open to sharing the story. After they share their story, the facilitator will explain to the group the importance of exploring that single feeling from an early moment surrounding a significant event and moving forward to the current day. The goal is to list every key or significant event where the person has experienced that single feeling.

The homework for the week will be to identify emotions that trigger anger. The group members are asked to pause when they have an anger feeling (no matter where on the continuum it falls) and ask the two questions: "Why am I angry?" and "What am I feeling?" The purpose of this exercise is to identify feelings that most frequently trigger anger responses.

Identifying, Exploring, and Understanding the Roots of Anger: Getting Beyond the Tip of the Iceberg (Week 4)

Participants are encouraged to share feelings they have identified that frequently trigger their anger. Facilitators explain the cumulative aspect of anger related to a felt emotion:

> You feel disrespected and you experience anger. The first event was at a very young age. The wounding from that event is not reconciled or resolved. You experience another significant event where you feel disrespected and you wrap more anger around feeling disrespected. In time, you have wrapped 5, 10, 15, 20 . . . 40 years of anger around the feeling of disrespect. Now in the moment, someone cuts in front of you while driving or standing in a line, and you fly into a rage of anger. Those observing cannot understand the level of anger verses the event.

Group members are instructed to explore one or more feelings that they have identified as frequent triggers of anger. The goal is to mark all of the significant events in their life where they have felt that specific feeling (e.g., disrespected, abandoned, betrayed). Group members are given an example of how to chart the events on a timeline. This chart will be a tool used in a later session as part of the process of resolution, reconciliation, and peacemaking.

Vietnam veterans, almost to a person, express feeling disrespected. This group of veterans returned home to an angry and ungrateful nation based on the unpopularity of the war in Vietnam. One Vietnam vet said the following:

> Not long after returning home, I was standing in line at a hamburger joint. Some White guy came up to me and said, "You are in the wrong line." Needless to say, a fight broke out and the police showed up. They talked to the White guy, and they arrested me and took me to jail. That is my trauma, even more than what happened in Vietnam. I was a medic in Vietnam. I was helping people, didn't make any difference their color of skin. I thought that was part of what I was fighting for and then that happened!

Needless to say, this individual could recount many moments of disrespect prior to the moment described in this event and later in life. Yet this moment is significant because a belief that he held was compromised and shattered. He believed that the trauma and hardship of war would make a difference in how he would be treated as a person of color when he returned home. This is a prime example of trauma and the shattered soul.

The spiritual and moral wounding of trauma feeds the anger. It is essential to the healing process that the individual discover the roots of their anger, which are tied to significant life events that represent a fracturing of the soul. *A wound untreated never heals.*

Additional Barriers to Healing: Moral Injury, Guilt, and Shame (Week 5)

Moral injury, guilt, and shame each need to be addressed, otherwise they work to create a vicious cycle that leaves the individual stuck in depression and denial.

Guilt

It is important to understand that guilt is a natural feeling that stems from a person doing something that conflicts with their beliefs. The "check engine light" on a vehicle provides a simple illustration of how guilt operates. When the check engine light illuminates, it is simply a warning that something is wrong or is functioning improperly within the vehicle's system. So it is with guilt. When an individual experiences guilt, the feeling is an indication that something has been compromised in their system of beliefs. The issue of survivor's guilt is highlighted during the overall discussion of guilt.

Shame

Shame is guilt's twin. Yet it is important to understand that shame is distinct from guilt, in that it is related to the fear of being exposed. Fear of exposure is based on a deeper fear of how we may be perceived by others as less than, weak, or broken. The four levels of wounding mentioned earlier help provide insight into how guilt and shame distort the view of self.

Moral Injury

As mentioned previously, moral injury may occur as a violation of a held belief, through moral conflict, or through moral dissonance. Moral injury, understood in the simplest form, occurs when an individual engages in behavior or activity that the person feels is morally wrong. Dissonance conflict is slightly different because it involves a conflict with how the person sees the world. They may believe the world is a fair and just place or have faith that their Higher Power will protect innocents or those who are faithful. These are common worldviews that can be compromised during combat or other traumatic experiences (Hufford et al., 2010). Moral conflict, on the other hand, occurs when an individual has felt forced to engage in behaviors they view as wrong.

If sufficient trust has been achieved, individuals may decide to share an incident related to their personal guilt, shame, and moral injury. If this occurs, a palatable increase in trust and bonding will occur within the group. This event may foster strength for others to share in the group or to seek out the chaplain or the therapist to share a guilt, shame, or moral injury event that they have never shared with another person.

Here are some examples of things veterans share in the group:

- A veteran shares about being forced to execute a woman and her children by an officer while faced with the threat that he would be killed if he failed to execute the order.

- A veteran shares about making the decision to release a rocket on a truck moving toward a checkpoint. The veteran said, "I could see people sitting in the back of the box truck."

- A veteran shares about not firing on a civilian passenger vehicle that could have been a combatant and feeling guilty that his action could have cost a fellow servicemember their life in another event executed by this person.

- A veteran who operated a drone and could clearly see noncombatants among combatants and was ordered to release the munitions.
- A veteran shares about running over a local civilian with a vehicle and then laughing about it or discounting the worth of the person.

The wound of moral injury remains if any correlating shame is not addressed. Shame remains a monster in the dark, keeping one captive and wounded until it is exposed to the light of confession—thus the common idiom "Confession is good for the soul."

Grief: The Dark Night of the Soul (Weeks 6 and 7)

The need to grieve is often blocked by held resentment, guilt, and shame. Once those issues are addressed, the grief process may take a natural course. A basic understanding of grief, the ways people move through grief, and the ways they avoid grieving is important to the process of grief.

Grief is a normal response when a person loses someone or something important to them. The most common grief experience is the loss of another person in our life that we love and care for. Although the loss of a person we love is profound, there are a myriad of losses in life that have a significant effect, including the loss of pets, loss of employment, loss of relationships, loss of deeply held beliefs, or loss of self (esteem, confidence, pride). This is not an exhaustive list; ultimately, we can experience grief with the loss of anything we deem significant in our life. Although grief is a natural experience of any loss, grief often does not resolve unless we are intentional in the grief process.

Dr. Elisabeth Kübler-Ross (1969) developed what became known as common *stages of grief*. What is often missed in the popular presentation of the stages, however, is that they are not meant to be understood or to be followed in a direct line, and some may even be skipped. For example, a person may experience one stage, move on to a *later* stage, but find themselves back at the *earlier* stage once again. This is natural and appropriate. There are no *right* ways to grieve; these are just common descriptions of ways people process loss.

Individuals may become stuck in the grief process or what has been termed as *complicated grief*. Again, held resentments, unresolved guilt and shame, and denial may contribute to a person's inability to process grief naturally. Yet another contribution to unresolved grief is avoidance. Common patterns of avoiding grief may have one or a combination of causes, including postponing, displacing, replacing, minimizing, or somatizing grief. The consequences of avoiding grief may include the following: deterioration in relationships; chronic physical illness or pain; chronic depression, sleeping difficulties, or low-self-esteem; chronic anxiety, agitation, restlessness, or difficulty concentrating; and/or substance abuse. Another issue related to grieving is complicated grief. Grief is seldom simple, especially for people with spiritual and moral wounds.

Understanding the components of healthy grieving is important. A healthy grieving process will include the ability to mourn openly, confront loss, set no time limits, and express grief however is best for the individual. To reconcile a loss, the individual will need to come to terms with the loss, which will involve being deliberate and intentional with the realization that it involves intellect, emotion, spirit, and strong self-care.

Forgiveness: The Art of Letting Go (Week 8)

Dr. Angel, the originator of the Search for Meaning protocol, believes that understanding anger is the gate to healing, and forgiveness is the key to the gate. Forgiveness or letting go is the process that moves the individual to anger resolution and onto the path of healing. Held anger becomes resentment and as someone once said, "Holding on to anger is like drinking poison and hoping the other person dies."

Forgiveness is one of the hardest things for someone with spiritual wounds to do. Spiritual wounds are the result of something that has happened, and there is always a way for a person to blame themselves, another, or their Higher Power for what has occurred. Take, for example, someone who was abused as a child. This abuse may have had a lasting effect on their life. It would be natural for that person to feel angry with the person who abused them. In another example, a person may feel angry with themselves or their Higher Power for the harmful events that have occurred in their lives. These feelings will remain with the person and prolong their spiritual wounding until they can learn to forgive. In Christian scripture, there is a verse stating, "Love keeps no record of wrongs." This concept of love applies to the individual, those around them, and their Higher Power, and vice versa. Forgiveness is deciding not to keep a record of wrongs but deciding to love oneself and allow spiritual wounds to heal.

Forgiveness is a choice to stop investing today's emotions in yesterday's events. It is also choosing to live in the moment, instead of constantly allowing the past to influence the present. Some people are so focused on the causes of their wounds that they are unable to enjoy fully the lives they have now. In some cases, they may be angry with someone who is already dead. There is no way for them to have justice or closure with that person, yet their inability to forgive keeps that person's actions present in their lives now. They may feel betrayed by their Higher Power and thus cannot seek out a meaningful connection with their spiritual selves.

Forgiveness is intentional. A person has to make a conscious decision to forgive, literally marking the day that they decide to forgive others or themself. This is important when thoughts of the event may resurface—the individual can reflect back to the moment of a conscious decision to forgive and let go. Dr. Angel terms this the *ABCs of understanding forgiveness*. "A" looks at what forgiveness is not. For example, it is not "forgive and forget." It is not something that *just happens* with time. It is not something to be done out of a sense of obligation, nor is it grounded in guilt and shame. "B" examines when forgiveness is blocked by a focus on punishment. Holding a belief that is focused on punishment for wrongdoing (e.g., "I'm going to Hell") may serve as a block to forgiveness, especially self-forgiveness. "C" explores obstacles of forgiveness, such as the fear of one's actions being discovered by others or the sense that someone needs to be held accountable.

A veteran described a situation in which he was guarding a sector during a helicopter rescue. The helicopter was fired upon, and he returned fire, killing one of the combatants. Another combatant turned and ran. The veteran stated that he could have killed the other combatant, but he allowed him to run away. He never shared that story with anyone until now for fear of judgment by others, but also because of guilt that the one he let get away may have killed other American servicepeople in the future. Once he confessed, the veteran shared the story with his family. In the weeks that followed, the veteran shared amazing reports of healing, a sense of relief, and the ability to interact in ways he had been unable to for decades. He also reported improved relationships with family members.

The Whole Enchilada: Connecting All of the Parts and Continuing Self-Awareness (Weeks 9 and 10)

The final two sessions offer an opportunity to help the group members pull all of the elements of the Search for Meaning program together. The only way to increase trust is to reconnect with oneself, others, and one's Higher Power. Trust is one of the most fundamental parts of a person's life, and while it is difficult to trust again, it is not impossible.

It is important to understand the distinction between faith and trust. Often these terms are thought to be the same, but a simple example may help to clarify. We may have faith that a chair will hold us when we sit in it. This faith may be built on a series of beliefs and experiences. But it is only when we place our full weight on the chair that we can say absolutely that we trust the chair.

At the end of the day, it is the exercising of faith that leads to trust.

Exercising trust includes maintaining healthy boundaries. We are not suggesting that individuals drop all of their boundaries and begin telling strangers their most intimate secrets. Rather, we are saying that as participants show a willingness to engage with others, they can begin to understand who deserves their trust and that their safety is not as threatened as they believe it to be. They begin the process of learning how to trust and when trust is warranted.

Self-awareness and self-evaluation have been central in this 10-week journey. Therefore, continued self-awareness and self-evaluation are necessary for continued growth and healing. Participants have been provided a toolbox of exercises and knowledge to aid them in their continuing journey.

Individuals are welcome to return to the group. Individuals who have repeated the Search for Meaning protocol report learning new things about themselves each time they complete the sessions. Additionally, this journey may have revealed specific issues that the individual may want to address through individual counseling or other types of individual or group help.

They may just want to explore their faith more deeply and want to join a study group or speak with a religious leader. Facilitators help, when requested, through referrals or providing contact information for other professionals.

Group members are acknowledged for their courage and endurance. The journey toward contentment is continuous, and hopefully the experience of this group process has placed the individual on a path of healing toward the journey to peace and contentment.

It is priceless to be invited by others to journey with them on sacred ground.

RESEARCH FINDINGS AND SUPPORT

The authors have collaborated on several funded research projects focused on the Search for Meaning intervention. An initial study funded by Covenant Health was conducted to gather qualitative data from veterans about their experiences of spiritual wounding and coping as well as their opinions about the effect of participating in the Search for Meaning intervention. The study helped to establish a deepened understanding of how veterans experience spiritual wounding and provided preliminary qualitative evidence about the impact of the intervention. The study also contributed ideas for program improvement. For example, the Search for Meaning program was expanded from 8 to 10 weeks based on feedback received from participants. Several manuscripts have been published from this qualitative study (e.g., Starnino, Sullivan, et al., 2019; Starnino et al., 2020).

A second round of projects, funded by Indiana University, led the same researchers to develop written participant and facilitator manuals of the Search for Meaning intervention as well as to collect preliminary program evaluation data on 24 veterans (pre- and postgroup). The results from the program evaluation showed that those who participated had significantly improved PTSD scores, experienced less negative religious coping, and had reduced levels of spiritual injury (Starnino, Angel, et al., 2019).

Our most recent multisite study expands on our previous work. The study, which involved three Veterans Affairs sites, is part of the larger Enhancing Practice-Based Evidence for Spiritually Integrated Psychotherapies initiative funded by John Templeton Foundation and Brigham Young University. The overall goal of our multisite study was to test the efficacy of the 10-week Search for Meaning group intervention designed to treat military veterans diagnosed with PTSD. Eighteen separate cohorts (groups) of the Search for Meaning intervention were conducted across the three sites, with a total of 127 participants consenting and completing baseline surveys; 80 of these participants completed postintervention surveys. Our research team completed a pre–posttest analysis. The results showed a statistically significant improvement in scores for six of seven outcome measures used for the study, including (a) the Clinically Adaptive Multidimensional Outcome Survey, which measures a range of psychosocial-spiritual factors; (b) the Clinical Outcomes in Routine Evaluation–10, which measures psychological factors, including anxiety, depression, and trauma; (c) the Spiritual Injury Scale, which measures eight distinct spiritual struggles; (d) the Integration of Stressful Life Experiences Scale, which measures meaning making; (e) the PTSD Checklist for *DSM-5*, which measures PTSD symptoms; and (f) the Posttraumatic Growth Inventory, which measures posttraumatic growth. These results are encouraging and make a case for the use of spiritually integrated therapies for treating trauma. We are in the process of preparing manuscripts for publication.

FUTURE DIRECTIONS AND RECOMMENDATIONS

The Search for Meaning protocol is predicated on an understanding and acceptance of a biopsychosocial-spiritual framework. A secondary goal of the protocol is to bring together the fields of psychology and spiritual care to treat the whole person. The word *psychology* derives from the Greek meaning of *psyche*—the soul. Search for Meaning emphasizes the importance of treating the *soul* and *spirit* of trauma victims. Indeed, Search for Meaning seeks to put the soul back into psychological interventions for humans affected by trauma.

Search for Meaning was originally designed to be a chaplain-led protocol in collaboration with a mental health cofacilitator. Because of the unique aspects of spiritual wounding, it is recommended that the group be led by a board-certified chaplain. At a minimum, one of the cofacilitators will need to possess formal training related to pastoral care and theology.

In this chapter, we describe the Search for Meaning protocol as it was originally designed to address spiritual wounding related to veterans with a PTSD diagnosis. We have already taken steps to adapt the protocol for use with a broader range of individuals, including nonmilitary personnel. Recently, some of the language in the Search for Meaning protocol was revised to address individuals diagnosed with an irretractable illness or those who have been recommended for hospice care. The first cohort study will be conducted with individuals diagnosed with amyotrophic lateral sclerosis. We plan to conduct research with this population as well as a future study examining the efficacy of Search for Meaning with individuals who have experienced a traumatic event but do not necessarily experience symptoms rising to the level of a diagnosis of PTSD.

ADDITIONAL RESOURCES

Angel, C., Sullivan, J., & Starnino, V. R. (2017, July 31). At my core, I'm not the same: Spiritual injury and military trauma, Part I [Audio podcast episode]. In *InSocialWork Podcast Series*. University at Buffalo School of Social Work. https://www.insocialwork.org/episode.asp?ep=220

Angel, C., Sullivan, J., & Starnino, V. R. (2017, August 28). At my core, I'm not the same: Spiritual injury and military trauma, Part II [Audio podcast episode]. In *InSocialWork Podcast Series*. University at Buffalo School of Social Work. https://www.insocialwork.org/episode.asp?ep=222

REFERENCES

Bell, V., Robinson, B., Katona, C., Fett, A.-K., & Shergill, S. (2019). When trust is lost: The impact of interpersonal trauma on social interactions. *Psychological Medicine, 49*(6), 1041–1046. https://doi.org/10.1017/S0033291718001800

Currier, J. M., Holland, J. M., & Malott, J. (2015). Moral injury, meaning making, and mental health in returning veterans. *Journal of Clinical Psychology, 71*(3), 229–240. https://doi.org/10.1002/jclp.22134

Erbes, C. R., Curry, K. T., & Leskela, J. (2009). Treatment presentation and adherence of Iraq/Afghanistan era veterans in outpatient care for posttraumatic stress disorder. *Psychological Services, 6*(3), 175–183. https://doi.org/10.1037/a0016662

Fowler, J. W., & Dell, M. L. (2006). Stages of faith from infancy through adolescence: Reflections on three decades of faith development theory. In E. C. Roehlkepartain, P. E. King, L. Wagener, & P. L. Benson (Eds.), *The handbook of spiritual development in childhood and adolescence* (pp. 34–45). Sage.

Gates, M. A., Holowka, D. W., Vasterling, J. J., Keane, T. M., Marx, B. P., & Rosen, R. C. (2012). Posttraumatic stress disorder in veterans and military personnel: Epidemiology, screening, and case recognition. *Psychological Services, 9*(4), 361–382. https://doi.org/10.1037/a0027649

Hatala, A. R. (2013). Towards a biopsychosocial–spiritual approach in health psychology: Exploring theoretical orientations and future directions. *Journal of Spirituality in Mental Health, 15*(4), 256–276. https://doi.org/10.1080/19349637.2013.776448

Hufford, D. J., Fritts, M. J., & Rhodes, J. E. (2010). Spiritual fitness. *Military Medicine, 175*(8S), 73–87. https://doi.org/10.7205/MILMED-D-10-00075

Jain, S. (2014, July 5). Religion & its role and function in international law. *SSRN*. https://doi.org/10.2139/ssrn.2462687

Jinkerson, J. (2016). Defining and assessing moral injury: A syndrome perspective. *Traumatology, 22*(2), 122–130. https://doi.org/10.1037/trm0000069

Kübler-Ross, E. (1969). *On death and dying*. Macmillan.

Litz, B. T., Stein, N., Delaney, E., Lebowitz, L., Nash, W. P., Silva, C., & Maguen, S. (2009). Moral injury and moral repair in war veterans: A preliminary model and intervention strategy. *Clinical Psychology Review, 29*(8), 695–706. https://doi.org/10.1016/j.cpr.2009.07.003

Park, C. L. (2010). Making sense of the meaning literature: An integrative review of meaning making and its effects on adjustment to stressful life events. *Psychological Bulletin, 136*(2), 257–301. https://doi.org/10.1037/a0018301

Pivar, I. L., & Field, N. P. (2004). Unresolved grief in combat veterans with PTSD. *Journal of Anxiety Disorders, 18*(6), 745–755. https://doi.org/10.1016/j.janxdis.2003.09.005

Puchalski, C., Ferrell, B., Virani, R., Otis-Green, S., Baird, P., Bull, J., Chochinov, H., Handzo, G., Nelson-Becker, H., Prince-Paul, M., Pugliese, K., & Sulmasy, D. (2009). Improving the quality of spiritual care as a dimension of palliative care: The report of the Consensus Conference. *Journal of Palliative Medicine, 12*(10), 885–904. https://doi.org/10.1089/jpm.2009.0142

Shay, J. (2014). Moral injury. *Psychoanalytic Psychology, 31*(2), 182–191. https://doi.org/10.1037/a0036090

Spaniol, L. (2002). Spirituality and connectedness. *Psychiatric Rehabilitation Journal, 25*(4), 321–322. https://doi.org/10.1037/h0095006

Starnino, V. R., Angel, C. T., Sullivan, J. E., Lazarick, D. L., Jaimes, L. D., Cocco, J. P., & Davis, L. W. (2019). Preliminary report on a spiritually-based PTSD intervention for military veterans. *Community Mental Health Journal, 55*(7), 1114–1119. https://doi.org/10.1007/s10597-019-00414-8

Starnino, V. R., Sullivan, W. P., Angel, C. T., & Davis, L. W. (2019). Moral injury, coherence, and spiritual repair. *Mental Health, Religion & Culture, 22*(1), 99–114. https://doi.org/10.1080/13674676.2019.1589439

Starnino, V. R., Sullivan, W. P., Angel, C. T., & Davis, L. W. (2020). Like a blanket over a fire: Group work and spiritual repair in military trauma. *Families in Society, 101*(1), 95–109. https://doi.org/10.1177/1044389419862081

Steenkamp, M. M., Litz, B. T., Hoge, C. W., & Marmar, C. R. (2015). Psychotherapy for military-related PTSD: A review of randomized clinical trials. *JAMA, 314*(5), 489–500. https://doi.org/10.1001/jama.2015.8370

Yalom, I. D., & Leszcz, M. (2005). *The theory and practice of group psychotherapy* (5th ed.). Basic Books.

21

Spiritually Focused, Multiculturally Oriented Psychotherapy in the Criminal Justice Detention System

Jennifer Gafford, Courtney Agorsor, Don Davis, Joshua Hook, Cirleen DeBlaere, Sree Sinha, Jeremy Coleman, Emma Porter, and Jesse Owen

Correctional facilities are one of the largest mental health providers in the United States; as such, efforts are being made to increase the effectiveness of services, especially psychotherapy (Munetz et al., 2001; Steadman et al., 2009). Individuals with mental illness are disproportionately represented in the criminal justice system (Munetz et al., 2001; Steadman et al., 2009). Despite this disparity, there is scant empirical evidence about the efficacy of therapeutic services in detention centers. Morgan et al. (2012) conducted a meta-analysis with 26 studies on treatments, which included psychotherapy but was not exclusive to this modality, in detention centers. The meta-analysis included 1,649 clients (sample sizes ranged from 5 to 150). Although the overall treatment effects for detention center therapy studies were positive for mental health symptoms ($d = 0.87$) and criminality outcomes ($d = 0.42$), there was wide variation in the effect sizes of outcomes ($d = -1.57$ to 2.98). Sufficient data were not available to test moderators or process variables, leaving many unanswered questions about the change mechanisms. However, we suspect that religious and/or spiritual identity and attention to those beliefs and values could be important in the healing process during detention.

Religion or spirituality (R/S) is commonplace within correctional settings. R/S beliefs can create a way of making meaning in the lives of individuals who are incarcerated and may experience uncertainty and existential crises (Eytan, 2011). While data on religiosity in treatment are scarce, we can draw indirect evidence for the importance of spiritual themes in this setting from a Pew

---

https://doi.org/10.1037/0000338-021
Handbook of Spiritually Integrated Psychotherapies, P. S. Richards, G. E. K. Allen, and D. K. Judd (Editors)
Copyright © 2023 by the American Psychological Association. All rights reserved.

Research Center (2012) survey of chaplains. For example, chaplains indicated that converting to other religions in detention centers occurred "a lot" (26%) or "some" (51%). Also, 41% of respondents indicated that religious extremism was "very common" (12%) or "somewhat common" (29%) within their detention center. Most chaplains (73%) viewed religion-related programs as "absolutely critical" for successful rehabilitation and reentry. The reliance on chaplains and faith-based programs suggests an opportunity to examine the challenges of therapists working within these systems, in which a high degree of skill is needed to work effectively with R/S themes. Indeed, R/S can be used as a way of coping with the incarceration, finding purpose, gaining a sense of control, and encouraging empowerment (Maruna et al., 2006).

Worthington (1988) theorized that individuals with high R/S tend to view their world through an R/S lens. At higher levels of R/S commitment, it may be important that therapists honor R/S values in order to facilitate therapeutic alliances and outcomes (Worthington et al., 2003). R/S treatment approaches, when aligned with clients' beliefs, are shown to be beneficial in psychotherapy, as evidenced by positive effects for both psychological ($g = 0.74$) and spiritual outcomes ($g = 0.74$; Captari et al., 2018). For example, Owen et al. (2014) found that clients' rating of their therapists' cultural humility was a significant predictor of therapy outcomes only with clients for whom their cultural identity was most salient.

Although R/S may be significant for many people, research has indicated that many clinicians do not feel comfortable addressing issues of R/S in psychotherapy (Hage et al., 2006; Kellems et al., 2010). As with other disparities between the majority cultures represented by clinicians and those of the populations they may serve, a lack of personal familiarity or comfort discussing culture does not excuse the importance of these topics for clients. Because of their discomfort with R/S, clinicians may miss an opportunity to capitalize on the therapeutic benefits of individuals' religious or spiritual affiliations, especially in a correctional setting.

The Multicultural Orientation (MCO) framework, developed by Owen and colleagues, provides a way to integrate R/S themes throughout the therapy process, regardless of the clinician's theoretical orientation or personal R/S background (see Owen, 2013). The MCO framework helps clinicians process their own and their clients' identities in a way that can strengthen the therapy alliance and therapy outcomes. In this chapter, we apply the MCO framework explicitly to R/S to provide a lens for clinicians to capitalize on their client's R/S orientation as a means of facilitating conversation in the therapeutic process as well as promoting positive client outcomes within the context of incarceration.

MULTICULTURAL ORIENTATION FRAMEWORK

The MCO framework involves three primary pillars. First, *cultural humility* is the bedrock of developing a strong MCO (Hook et al., 2013). Cultural humility involves respect for and openness to the client's R/S identity. From the intake through termination, the therapist engages in behaviors that indicate openness to explore the client's R/S identity and how this identity is linked to the client's presenting problem and treatment. For instance, a therapist using the MCO framework would be more likely to be interested in and curious about what clients' R/S identity means in their life and how it might play a role in their healing process. The therapist also deemphasizes their own R/S perspective and instead honors and prioritizes the R/S perspective of the client. Openness to the other has been described as a core virtue of multiculturalism (Fowers & Davidov, 2006). Cultural humility also involves an interpersonal stance that is other oriented—rather than self-focused or morally superior—regarding the client's cultural background and experience.

The second pillar, *cultural opportunities*, involves taking the initiative to discuss the client's R/S perspective and integrate this perspective into therapy sessions (Owen, 2013; Owen et al., 2016). This begins in the intake, as the therapist asks the patient (a) about their R/S identity and commitment, (b) how these identities are related to the presenting problem, and (c) whether the client would like their R/S identities integrated into the therapy process. Throughout therapy, the therapist looks for opportunities to honor and discuss the client's R/S identities as they relate to the material in therapy.

Cultural opportunities arise when clients mention or introduce a cultural belief, value, or some other aspect of their cultural heritage. These moments provide natural chances for the therapist to transition to a deeper exploration of a client's cultural identity. Other times, the therapist may initiate cultural opportunities. For example, in a session in which a client describes the loss of a family member to suicide, the therapist might ask, "Sometimes when people face tragedy, they turn to religion or spirituality to cope. I am wondering if that is true for you?" In this example, the therapist relies on previous knowledge about grief and loss to create an opportunity for cultural exploration. What is innovative about this intervention is that the therapist does not make assumptions about the client's cultural worldview. If the question does not fit for the client, the therapist and client can move on to more relevant clinical material. But if it does fit, it may facilitate a discussion about a cultural identity that is important for the client.

Therapists have several decision points during therapy, and many of these involve deciding whether to engage in a discussion about the client's cultural background and identities. These choice points, which are guided by the therapist's MCO, can directly or indirectly communicate to the client that the therapist views the client's culture as an important aspect of the client's life that should be explicitly addressed in therapy. On the other hand, avoiding or moving away from a cultural opportunity can communicate that the client's cultural identity is unimportant or invalid.

Owen et al. (2016) found that clients had better therapy outcomes when they felt that their therapist attended to their cultural heritage and did not miss cultural opportunities. Moreover, cultural opportunities and cultural humility work in tandem during therapy sessions. Owen et al. found that the negative effects of missing cultural opportunities were mitigated when clients perceived their therapist to be more culturally humble. These findings suggest that maintaining a culturally humble stance can offset some cultural mistakes or missteps, as are wont to occur in any interpersonal or therapeutic relationship.

The third pillar, *cultural comfort*, involves the therapist's level of ease, smoothness, or calmness when discussing R/S material with the client (Owen, 2013). Here, the therapist is not awkward or uncomfortable; rather, they are able to have discussions about religion or spirituality in a natural, unforced manner that invites further exploration and discussion. In this way, MCO utilizes a process-cultural approach wherein the framework can be flexibly applied across contexts. Cultural comfort is expected to directly influence a therapist's likelihood of initiating cultural dialogue with a client, and it is also expected to relate positively to the quality of a discussion with a client about culture. For instance, therapists need to be able to tolerate discomfort that can arise when clients' R/S values may not align with their own views. Theoretically, without cultural comfort, therapists' attempts at engaging clients during cultural opportunities may not be fully realized. This element of the MCO framework also has empirical support, as Owen et al. (2015) found that therapists' cultural comfort partially accounted for racial and ethnic disparities in therapy outcomes within their caseloads (also see Pérez-Rojas et al., 2019).

The MCO approach for psychotherapy closely aligns with the contextual model of therapy (Wampold, 2001; Wampold & Imel, 2015). The contextual model espouses that therapists should be responsive to clients' belief systems about how change occurs. Wampold (2007) categorized three main belief systems: psychosocial (e.g., psychotherapy, social support, cultural rituals), spiritual/religious (e.g., prayer, sacraments, confession), or medical/technology (e.g., medication). It is posited that there are relational aspects of the therapeutic relationship (e.g., working alliance, therapeutic bond, agreement on goals and tasks for treatment), the need for a sound theory of change (e.g., rationale for how change occurs, R/S reasons, psychosocial reasons, or medical reasons), an agreed-upon rationale by the client and therapist, a ritual of activities that helps the client and therapist engage in an emotionally salient manner to address clients' distress, and the client's belief in the therapist's expertise (Wampold, 2007; Wampold & Budge, 2012; Wampold & Imel, 2015).

The MCO and the contextual model align with a long history of change from other fields, particularly R/S fields, which describe similar processes for faith healing. In regard to R/S beliefs, robust evidence suggests that many clients want spiritually oriented therapies and that these approaches work as well as secular therapies (Captari et al., 2018; Worthington et al., 2011). Accordingly, this chapter focuses on the application of the MCO framework related to R/S dimensions of client identities in psychotherapy within correctional settings. It should be noted that the reference to correctional settings here is inclusive of jails and prisons; while there are some differences in their characteristics (length of stay, availability of resources, training of officers) that can be substantial, the overall experience of incarceration is most relevant to the focus of this chapter.

The MCO framework is well aligned with intersectionality theories (see Crenshaw, 1991). Given that many underrepresented groups tend to be very religious, which can involve experiences of religious struggle or existential pain from hurts in religious communities or families, it would be impossible to develop "competence" to work with racial and ethnic diversity without having a fluency for working with R/S struggles as well as navigating religious systems. Nonetheless, a variety of studies on comfort with addressing R/S issues have revealed that many clinicians receive minimal training in R/S issues and report being poorly prepared to address R/S issues in their clinical work, despite their overall prevalence in the populations served (Oxhandler et al., 2019). In addition, it is important to acknowledge that clinicians themselves belong to salient cultural groups and that, although their theological commitments may provide opportunities for connection, they may also contribute to complex dynamics. Indeed, there can be a lot of diversity within any cultural identity and R/S experience; as such, it is important to recognize these differences and not assume connection or similarities.

Whereas many multicultural theories have focused on similar themes of openness and self-awareness, the MCO framework also describes expressions of MCO values within therapy dyads, which involve an inherent power dynamic. MCO clinicians explicitly look out for bids or opportunities by the client related to salient identities. The reason for doing this could be conceptualized differently, depending on the tradition. For example, from a psychodynamic perspective, clients are taking important risks when they disclose cultural information. In order to help the client develop a secure attachment with the therapist, it is important that the therapist show caring and responsive engagement toward these disclosures. In some cases, missing cultural opportunities might lead to alliance ruptures, which likewise require skill at repairing the relationship in order to maintain the emotional bond with the client and the overall success of therapy.

Clinicians working from an MCO perspective learn to track their degree of emotional comfort over time in cultural conversations. Discomfort itself is not necessarily a problem but more of a cue that something is happening within the process of the session. Indeed, clinicians should work on processing the origins of their discomfort with a supervisor or peer. The desire to avoid uncomfortable emotions is a natural instinct; as such, it is unlikely to help clinicians learn from the experience. Therefore, the MCO framework certainly provides language for the aspirational goals of multiculturalism included in the principles of autonomy, beneficence, and respect.

Some conceptual work has begun to elaborate on the MCO framework in order to include a view of the clinician within a larger system that puts assimilative pressure on therapists to conform to norms of White society (Moon & Sandage, 2019). A similar critique could also be applied for any system that, as part of the power dynamics, exerts the power to define good and evil, including the virtue of humility. From this viewpoint, therapists working from an MCO perspective will consider a dialectical tension between the commitment to care for clients with a simultaneous commitment to develop training and practice environments that promote flourishing in clinicians from marginalized groups.

Unfortunately, correctional settings are unique in the sense that they inherently carry cultural norms that contradict the tenets of psychotherapy and the pillars of MCO. Distrust, aggression, self-focused orientation, and protection are some examples of norms related to survival in correctional settings that could be prohibitive in psychotherapy if internalized by either the client or therapist. Following the three pillars of MCO in this space allows both the client and therapist to explore how their identities intersect with the culture of the correctional setting and thus how those intersections play out in the therapeutic relationship.

RELATIONSHIP ESTABLISHMENT GUIDELINES

At its core, the MCO framework is relationally oriented, with cultural humility at the foundation. As noted earlier, cultural humility has been defined using two main features: (a) an awareness of one's cultural limitations and (b) an other- and relationally oriented interpersonal stance (Davis et al., 2018; Hook et al., 2013). Thus, when engaging with clients using MCO, respect for a client's desire to address R/S topics is paramount. The therapist does not make assumptions about whether R/S or any other cultural identity is important to the client or whether R/S should be a topic of conversation integrated into the therapeutic process. Thus, when using MCO, the therapist asks questions about R/S in an open manner, letting the client lead the process.

The MCO process can be broached with any client, irrespective of their cultural background or R/S identity. However, the degree of depth with which therapists address aspects of R/S in therapy will differ based on the R/S identity and desires of the client. For clients who do not identify that R/S is salient (or for those who identify as R/S but this aspect of the client's cultural identity is not important in therapy), then it is key to not belabor additional questions regarding R/S. Alternatively, for clients who identify R/S as a salient cultural identity, the MCO process can be integrated throughout the course of therapy. For example, for many clients who are very strongly committed to a religion, religious categories inform how they view and experience all aspects of their life (Worthington, 1988). Thus, it is important to keep humility and respect in mind when establishing the relationship with the client. It is also important to ask questions about R/S but then let the client lead. After all, the client is the expert on their own experience, and this includes the extent to which R/S is integrated with the therapy process from beginning to end.

ASSESSMENT GUIDELINES AND RECOMMENDATIONS

There are research-based assessments for MCO based on client and external raters. Yet these research-oriented tools have not been validated for routine outcome monitoring over the course of therapy, at this point.[1] However, informal assessment at the beginning of therapy is critical for deciding how one might

---

[1] These assessments are free and available upon request from Dr. Jesse Owen (jesse.owen@du.edu).

integrate R/S themes and issues during the course of therapy. Interestingly, perhaps because a lot of information needs to be acquired during intake sessions and therapists often have limited time to address important clinical issues, therapists sometimes do not ask any questions about R/S. Given that R/S can often be an important source of support for individuals who are incarcerated, this is an unfortunate oversight. In other situations, aspects of one's R/S might contribute to the presenting problem or interfere with the therapy process. Thus, it is essential to ask questions about one's R/S identity and commitment during the intake session.

There is no one set of R/S questions that should be asked during the intake session. However, some suggestions include the following:

- Do you identify as religious or spiritual? If yes, how do you identify?
- What does religion or spirituality mean to you? How does it show up in your day-to-day life?
- How important is religion or spirituality to you? How much does it impact your life and decisions?
- Are you a part of a religious or spiritual community? How would you describe that community?
- What changes have you experienced in your religion or spiritual beliefs since being incarcerated? What about in your practices?
- How is your religion or spirituality a source of support for you?
- Have there been times when your religion or spirituality made your problems more difficult to manage?
- How might religion or spirituality be related to your presenting problem, or what we are planning to work on in therapy?
- What could be helpful to address in therapy related to your religious or spiritual issues?
- How has your religion or spirituality been impacted by being incarcerated?

It is also important to note that assessment does not end once the intake session is completed. Therapists should assess for R/S themes over the course of therapy. We discuss this further in the next section on intervention strategies and techniques, but linking what a client says to their R/S identity or commitments can be an important way to connect using cultural opportunities throughout the course of treatment.

INTERVENTION STRATEGIES AND TECHNIQUES

In what follows, we explore some different intervention strategies and techniques associated with the three pillars of the MCO model: cultural humility, cultural opportunities, and cultural comfort. First, cultural humility involves two key factors: (a) an awareness and acknowledgment of one's cultural limitations and (b) an other- and relationally oriented interpersonal stance. Cultural humility is more of a way of being than a list of intervention techniques, but we will review some therapist attitudes and behaviors that could be indicative of high versus low cultural humility.

In regard to being aware of and acknowledging one's cultural limitations, it is important for therapists to be honest and admit when they do not know something or are unfamiliar with something the client shares about their R/S background. Most clients understand that therapists cannot be experts in every type of R/S background, and they appreciate therapists who ask questions when they are uncertain. Asking questions and wanting to know more are important indicators of the second aspect of cultural humility: being other oriented rather than self-focused. This strategy conveys to clients that the therapist is interested in learning more about their background and connecting genuinely to the issues of importance to them. It also communicates to clients that R/S is an important aspect of identity and it is okay to discuss in therapy. On the other hand, making assumptions about the client and assuming knowledge are indicators of low cultural humility. It is also important for therapists to not place the burden on the client to "teach" them about their R/S identity. Rather, therapists should also be motivated to learn more about the specific R/S identity outside of the therapy room, including through consultation and supervision, external reading, and recognizing their limitations in knowing or understanding the R/S belief. In doing so, the therapist is building their knowledge and allowing the client to express how they enact their specific R/S beliefs. This is critical to keep in mind even if the therapist and client share R/S beliefs, as the assumption that two members of the same faith practice their religion in the same way is equally lacking in humility, characterized by orienting toward the specific client's beliefs and experiences.

Before selecting specific interventions, therapists might ask themselves the following questions:

- What do I know about the client's specific R/S orientation?

- How does the client relate to this R/S? For example, a client may align with the values of the Catholic religion but not participate in the practices of prayer or confession associated with the religion. If this is the case, the therapist would want to focus more on the values than the specific behaviors or practices.

- What assumptions do I have about the client's R/S orientation?

- What else do I need to know to better understand the client's R/S identity?

In asking these questions, therapists can better identify both the directions of treatment and specific interventions that may better serve the client.

Second, cultural opportunities involve initiating conversations or following up when a client makes a comment about something related to their R/S identity and beliefs. There are choice points in any session, in which the therapist can focus the discussion on symptoms or cultural identities. Clearly, the avoidance of R/S identity and beliefs is a clear example of a missed cultural opportunity. However, therapists should reflect on the reasons for such actions. Cultural discomfort and feelings of inadequacy are likely at the root of avoidance. However, therapists need cultural courage, self-compassion, and trust in the therapy process that they can engage in these conversations. For example, if the client shares about something that is often related to R/S (e.g., existential questions, grief/loss, anger at God), the therapist could create a link between the content that was shared, the client's R/S identity or commitments, and their psychological symptoms and/or presenting issue. The therapist simply offers it as an option and continues to let the client lead if they feel R/S is salient in their treatment.

Third, cultural comfort involves being relaxed and at ease when engaging in a discussion about a client's R/S identity, beliefs, or commitments. Similar to cultural humility, cultural comfort is more a way of being rather than a list of specific intervention strategies or techniques. Yet, at the heart of cultural comfort is the therapist's ability to (a) attune to their feelings in session, (b) regulate their affect, and (c) process their cultural comfort with supervisors and/or peers. In some forms of treatment, therapists might also use their emotional reactions in session through immediacy or interpretation techniques to enhance connection and healing.

A therapist with high levels of cultural comfort might approach a discussion of R/S in a relaxed, curious manner. The therapist might show comfort in their body language (e.g., sitting comfortably with their hands in their lap, not tapping their foot) and tone of voice (e.g., talking at a slow to moderate pace, not rushed). Cultural comfort could also be displayed by staying with the client and asking follow-up questions, rather than changing the subject because of one's discomfort. Cultural comfort is improved when therapists practice having discussions about R/S issues, both inside and outside of therapy. Indeed, therapists who embody more cultural humility and comfort will engage in activities outside of the therapy room to enhance their knowledge, comfort, and awareness. This way of being is, in and of itself, an intervention meant to more deeply understand the client as well as strengthen the therapeutic relationship.

RECOMMENDATIONS FOR COLLABORATING WITH CLERGY

Clergy often play an important role in jail settings, so it can sometimes be helpful for therapists to collaborate with clergy when treating their clients. There are several reasons why collaborating with clergy can be useful. First, the client may identify with an R/S background that the therapist knows little or nothing about. When this occurs, it can be difficult to discern how to work with the client's R/S beliefs and practices. Consulting with clergy can be a useful way to gain more information and resources for both the therapist and client. Second, the client may present with spiritual, in addition to psychological, problems or concerns. In this situation, working together with a clergy member can better meet the overall goals of treatment. Finally, sometimes treatment is time limited, while relationships with clergy can be ongoing.

In these situations, collaboration with clergy can often set the client up for a longer term source of support once the course of therapy ends.

McMinn et al. (2003) discussed a framework for therapist–clergy collaboration in which they distinguished between two levels of competence. Basic collaboration involved what we have been discussing—mutual respect and communication. Advanced collaboration involved shared values and a common language of R/S, which can serve as a foundation for more involved and bidirectional collaboration.

We have a few additional general recommendations for collaborating with clergy. First, it is important to build relationships and trust, especially within detention centers. Historically, mental health professionals and clergy have not always worked in tandem effectively (Hook et al., 2012), despite operating in similar spaces of human suffering and healing. They sometimes operate in separate spheres of influence, rarely engaging with each other in a meaningful way. Because of this, clergy may not have a high level of trust of mental health professionals (and vice versa). Thus, it can be helpful to get to know one another outside of the work setting, in order to work on building a trusting relationship. Also, like any relationship, a strong collaborative relationship can take time.

Second, consistent communication is key. When collaborating with clergy, it is important to discuss at the outset what the collaboration might look like. For example, a therapist may rely on clergy to help them understand specific religious traditions that might contribute to a client's reduction in distress. The therapist and clergy will want to address several questions regarding communication. What are the goals of the collaboration? If the client is meeting with both the therapist and a clergy member, are there any guidelines for what kinds of issues will be discussed with whom? Will the meetings have different goals? This type of conversation can be helpful in avoiding a situation in which the client has "two therapists." Finally, what kind of ongoing communication will be present? Will the therapist and clergy member meet regularly to discuss progress? What information does the client want shared with the clergy member, and what information does the client want to be kept private in each respective relationship? The collaboration serves to strengthen the work by both the therapist and chaplain and promote positive client outcomes.

CASE STUDY: JARVIS

The following case study[2] is taken from the larger research study described later in the chapter and illustrates the application of the MCO framework to psychotherapy within a correctional setting, with particular application to R/S as a diverse identity.

---

[2]Details, including names, in the case example have been altered to protect client confidentiality and therapist privacy.

Description of the Therapist

The therapist, Anika, was a 24-year-old, Asian American, bisexual cisgender woman and a nonspiritual atheist. At that time of the study, she held a master's degree in clinical mental health counseling, was in a doctoral program, and had been practicing for 3 years. Her therapeutic orientation was client centered but also integrated other therapeutic modalities.

Setting

The client was seen for individual counseling while being detained in the county jail. The jail was located in the western United States and houses individuals with a variety of security levels that dictate their access to privileges such as commissary, out time, and programming. Mental health services, including individual therapy, were accessible to all people who are incarcerated in the jails. All treatment was voluntary and could be requested at any time during a person's incarceration.

Client Demographic Characteristics

Jarvis was a 23-year-old, Black, heterosexual cisgender man and a Protestant Christian. Jarvis completed high school and was unemployed because of incarceration.

Presenting Problems and/or Concerns

Jarvis presented for counseling (a) to address his addiction to cocaine, depressive symptoms that included some passive suicidal ideation, and trauma as well as (b) to discuss his transition back to his life with his partner and children after being released.

Client History

Jarvis was one of three children. He reported having close relationships with his siblings and feeling protective of them. Jarvis's parents were never married, and he reported that he had very limited contact with his biological father. His mother married his stepfather when Jarvis was a teenager, and he reported having a strained relationship with him. He identified his stepfather's extramarital affairs as the primary source of discord. Jarvis had been engaged to his high school sweetheart for 2 years. He was serving a 60-day sentence for assault of his fiancé and a restraining order was in place. Jarvis believed that he and his fiancé would be able to reconcile once he was released from jail. Jarvis had two children from a prior relationship. He reported having intermittent contact with his daughter and son and desired to be a "good dad to my kids." Jarvis also reported that he had been sexually abused by a male family friend in his youth, and his family was aware of the abuse, but it was not discussed.

Jarvis moved multiple times across three states as a child and early adult with his family, which made developing and maintaining friendships difficult. He began using marijuana and alcohol as a teenager as a way of connecting with others. At around 20 years of age, Jarvis began using cocaine. Since developing an addiction to cocaine, he had not been able to maintain employment and had been arrested multiple times for "short stints" of a weekend or a few weeks.

He reported a history of anxiety, depressive symptoms, and suicidal ideation. Jarvis reported talking with therapists during his prior incarcerations but was not aware of any prior diagnoses. Jarvis identified as Christian with a strong Protestant Christian upbringing, and his R/S identity was very important to him. He also expressed an interest in the use of R/S interventions in counseling at intake. Beyond his clinical goals of addressing a history of sexual abuse and addiction to cocaine, Jarvis also stated that his spiritual goals upon release included finding a new church, connecting with a pastor, and being baptized.

Assessment and Diagnosis

Clinical interviewing was the primary form of assessment. The therapist conceptualized the client as having two primary clinical concerns. The first was helping Jarvis to process the sexual abuse he experienced as a child. He noted that he often had nightmares and experienced difficulty sleeping when memories of his abuse were activated. There seemed to be a connection between the abuse and Jarvis's anxiety, panic attacks, passive suicidal ideation, and unresolved feelings of anger. In particular, Jarvis expressed feeling confused and angry about the lack of protection provided by his mother and other adults in his family from the sexual abuse he experienced.

Secondary to his experiences of childhood sexual abuse, the therapist also noted Jarvis's distress from his addiction to cocaine. As a result of his addiction, Jarvis struggled to maintain employment or a residence. In addition, his addiction was a primary source of conflict between Jarvis and his fiancé. He had also engaged in petty crimes to support his cocaine addiction (e.g., theft), which accounted for his multiple short jail sentences. Therefore, the initial goals identified were to work on relapse prevention, anger management, and emotional regulation/coping around Jarvis's history of trauma.

During this course of counseling, Jarvis was diagnosed with posttraumatic stress disorder and severe cocaine use disorder. Mental health treatment was also supported by psychiatric medications. He generally took his medication as prescribed but also occasionally "cheeked" his medications, so monitoring of his prescription adherence was also an aspect of counseling and represented an additional area of management within the correctional setting. With regard to the client's R/S identity, Jarvis's Christian identity further provided him with a sense of purpose and hope. On multiple occasions, he stated that he believed "God has a plan for me."

Treatment Process and Outcomes

A total of six, 50-minute counseling sessions were conducted. Over the course of treatment, the client articulated for the first time that he perceived his addiction to be a significant problem and that he would like to enter a recovery facility. Support, psychoeducation about addiction and recovery, facilitation of insight, skill building related to self-control, and encouraging emotional expression were all effective interventions. R/S interventions were integrated throughout the therapy process and were particularly helpful with this client. Notably, the interventions were often client initiated and supported by the therapist. For instance, the client routinely discussed Bible scripture that he had reviewed since the prior session and the ways in which the themes of those passages fit with his current situation or concerns. He discussed the importance of his "devotional readings" to his connection with God and his greater purpose. Extending this intervention, the value of R/S bibliotherapy was discussed and Jarvis began to read books by Christian authors on the meaning of life and the role of God in one's life. To self-soothe, Jarvis requested crossword puzzles and coloring pages that incorporated Christian themes. Daily devotional journaling was also incorporated into Jarvis's practice and discussed in each session. Jarvis expressed that these readings and his journaling were helpful in clarifying the ways in which he could identify and stay connected with God's purpose for him after his release from jail. Therapy concluded with a reinforcement of the client's positive changes (e.g., establishing good sleep patterns, medication adherence, journaling practice, devotional reading practice, impulse-control skills, connecting with his emotions, and communicating with his fiancé and other interpersonal supports).

Multiple empirical indicators supported the effectiveness of these interventions. Jarvis's pre–post scores from intake to Session 6 suggested notable improvement in his psychological symptoms. The Clinically Adaptive Multidimensional Outcome Survey (CAMOS) was used to assess the client's level of distress, with scores from 1 to 6 indicating low to high distress (Sanders et al., 2018). His CAMOS scores on self-report measures of relational distress decreased from 3.67 to 1.00, and his overall psychological distress decreased from 5.00 to 1.00. In addition, the client rated the therapeutic alliance as high (4.83, on a 1–5 scale from low to high) and the therapist's level of positive cultural humility as high (4.85) at Session 3. Finally, the client's scores on spiritual distress also decreased from 2.00 to 1.00.

Therapist Commentary

The therapist's MCO was critical to the success of this case. A primary identity for this client was his R/S identity. As an atheist who rated R/S salience low, the therapist used an other-oriented stance to not only affirm the client's R/S identity but also to maximize the potential utility and effectiveness of R/S interventions in counseling. Moreover, being attuned to the client's R/S identities also meant that the therapist did not miss opportunities to explore the client's salient identity-related experiences as a Black Christian man. Indeed, the client rated the therapist low on missed cultural opportunities (1.60, on a 1–5 scale from low to high).

Concordant with the MCO framework, cultural humility was of critical importance in this case. The therapist needed to engage with the client related to R/S themes that were relevant to him, regardless of her own beliefs or familiarity with Protestant Christianity. A culturally humble stance was critical not only during intake but also throughout the treatment, which consisted of using emergent themes of R/S to support the client's short-term therapeutic goals as well as in service of his larger identities and life goals after release. By using MCO in support of establishing a strong therapeutic alliance, the therapist therefore engaged with openness regarding the client's perceptions of his own primary identities during intake, for example, and did not assume that his race and ethnicity was his primary identity. The therapist then incorporated Jarvis's spiritual identity as a source of strength throughout the course of treatment, continuing to attend to the client's relational and spiritual goals and orienting short-term goals in time-limited therapy toward the larger motivations in his life.

Beyond simply R/S themes, the intersectional salience of additional identities for both therapist and client needs to be considered. For example, as a non-Black person of color, the therapist additionally engaged with an MCO by taking a nonpresumptive stance in overly identifying with the client's experiences, instead allowing the client to share what identities were most salient to him and how his experiences as a Christian, a Black man, and a young father were integral to his success in therapy and his larger goals in life. Therefore, the therapist focused on seeking opportunities to discuss the identities most salient to Jarvis in the course of treatment. For example, the therapist followed the client's lead to discuss why it felt so important for him to be a present father in his children's lives because his own father was not present for him. At the same time, the therapist was also aware of the client's expressed preference for a female therapist based on his experiences of childhood sexual abuse as well as his present incarceration on charges related to gender-based violence. Being comfortable engaging in cultural topics related not only to religion and spirituality but also race and ethnicity, gender, age, and class is therefore critical throughout the process of engaging with MCO, particularly in an incarcerated setting. Furthermore, MCO can be incorporated in attending to R/S regardless of theoretical orientation and can support in the treatment of any presenting problems or diagnoses, including in posttraumatic stress disorder, substance abuse, and relational concerns as in the present case.

RESEARCH FINDINGS AND SUPPORT

This case study of Jarvis exemplifies one of many examples of the successful use of MCO in addressing R/S identities and cultural beliefs within settings of incarceration. This case study draws from the experiences in our larger study examining R/S themes in psychotherapy as well as therapy outcomes in two jails in a western city in the United States. As noted earlier, there is little empirical evidence documenting how often R/S themes arise in therapy in detention center settings, and whether the client or therapist is the initiator of these themes. In partnership with the John Templeton Foundation, we conducted a study within the jails that serve incarcerated adults in the city and county of Denver. These jails house both preadjudicated and postadjudicated individuals (for complete study details, see Coleman et al., 2022).

Participants

Participants included 22 therapists, whose age ranged from 23 to 36 years ($M = 25.7$, $SD = 3.02$). The majority of therapists (81.8%) identified as female (18.2% identified as male). In terms of race and ethnicity, therapists self-identified as Asian (13.5%), Hispanic (4.5%), Indian (4.5%), multiracial (9.0%), White (68.0%), or other (4.5%). In terms of religion/spirituality, the majority of therapists identified as atheist/nonreligious (41.0%), followed by Christian (27.0%), Jewish (9.0%), agnostic (9.0%), or spiritual (9.0%) or preferred not to answer (4.5%).

Client participants ($n = 138$) consisted of individuals incarcerated at the time of the study. They ranged in age from 18 to 51 years ($M = 35.4$, $SD = 11.23$). The majority of clients identified as male (73.9%), followed by female (21.0%), transgender (0.7%), genderqueer (0.7%), or other (0.7%) or declined to answer (3.0%). In terms of race and ethnicity, the majority of clients identified as White (26.1%), followed by Latinx/Hispanic (23.2%), multiracial (18.2%), African American/Black (18.1%), American Indian (3.6%), Asian (2.1%), or other (5.7%) or declined to answer (3.0%). The majority of client participants identified themselves as Christian (52.1%), followed by other (19.0%), atheist/nonspiritual or agnostic (9.3%), Jewish (5.8%), Muslim (5.1%), or Buddhist (2.2%) or declined to answer (6.5%).

Measures

Consistent with the overall project, we used two main outcome measures: Clinical Outcomes in Routine Evaluation–10 (Barkham et al., 2013) and CAMOS (Sanders et al., 2018). The Therapist Session Checklist was used to record the general focus of the session. This checklist also includes spiritual interventions that broadly fit within (a) affirmation of R/S beliefs (e.g., affirming belief in God, encouraged acceptance of God's love) and (b) discussion of virtues (e.g., gratitude, forgiveness), specific techniques (e.g., engaged in prayer with client, suggested bibliotherapy), and exploration (e.g., explored R/S doubts, explored questions and ultimate meaning). We also included MCO client-rated measures, including the Cultural Humility Scale (Hook et al., 2013) and the cultural (missed) opportunities approach (Owen et al., 2016).

Results

Notably, the pre–post change across the study was a medium- to large-sized effect for psychological distress ($d = 0.65$), a medium-sized effect for relationship distress ($d = 0.48$), and small-sized effect for spiritual distress ($d = 0.29$). Participants did not demonstrate reliable change on the remaining measures. Participants rated their therapists' cultural humility as relatively high ($M = 4.85$, $SD = 0.64$) and rated cultural (missed) opportunities as relatively low ($M = 1.99$, $SD = 0.64$). This suggests that overall the therapists were culturally oriented and attuned to the multiple cultural identities of their clients.

Some of the most common spiritual interventions endorsed in this study included, but were not limited to, the following: discussion of virtues (40%), exploration (25%), affirming of R/S beliefs (20%), and specific R/S techniques (e.g., praying with client; 9%). The results provide support that R/S interventions are infused in many therapy sessions along with other psychological interventions. Ultimately, this study demonstrated that clients experienced, on average, a decrease in psychological and relationship distress, as well as spiritual distress (although to a lesser degree than psychological and relationship distress), in jail settings.

FUTURE DIRECTIONS

This study and associated research provide the opportunity to gain a deeper understanding of types of R/S interventions utilized in a jail setting and the ways in which those interventions are used. Because of the critical need for mental health support in jail settings and the strong role that R/S plays in jail settings, it is integral for researchers to continue to examine how R/S interventions can best suit the needs of individuals who are incarcerated. There is a need for future research to examine what mechanisms of R/S therapy are most effective in decreasing distress—including psychological, relational, and spiritual—for incarcerated populations. Additionally, future studies may benefit from exploring the effect of clinicians specifically trained in R/S interventions tailored to this unique population's needs on individuals' treatment outcomes, owing to previous findings suggesting that interventions specifically tailored to jail settings have been most effective in decreasing recidivism (Morgan et al., 2012).

The MCO framework is a valuable tool for therapists to more deeply explore clients' inner lives and salient identities. In a setting such as a correctional facility that elicits existential and spiritual crises, the MCO can be particularly helpful in exploring the R/S domain in order to facilitate deeper connection and conversation between client and therapist. In doing so, the therapist can utilize the client's R/S orientation in a way that could ultimately facilitate positive client outcomes and more effective mental health treatment.

REFERENCES

Barkham, M., Bewick, B. M., Connell, J., & Cahill, J. (2013). The CORE-10: A short measure of psychological distress for routine use in the psychological therapies. *Counselling & Psychotherapy Research*, *13*(1), 3–13. https://doi.org/10.1080/14733145.2012.729069

Captari, L. E., Hook, J. N., Hoyt, W., Davis, D. E., McElroy-Heltzel, S. E., & Worthington, E. L., Jr. (2018). Integrating clients' religion and spirituality within psychotherapy: A comprehensive meta-analysis. *Journal of Clinical Psychology, 74*(11), 1938–1951. https://doi.org/10.1002/jclp.22681

Coleman, J., Drinane, J., Agorsor, C., Sinha, S., Freetly-Porter, E., DeBlaere, C., Davis, D., & Owen, J. (2022). *Cultural humility, cultural opportunities, and working alliance in a jail based psychotherapy setting* [Manuscript submitted for publication]. Department of Psychological Sciences, Augusta University.

Crenshaw, K. (1991). Mapping the margins: Intersectionality, identity politics, and violence against women of color. *Stanford Law Review, 43*(6), 1241–1299. https://doi.org/10.2307/1229039

Davis, D. E., DeBlaere, C., Owen, J., Hook, J. N., Rivera, D., Choe, E., Van Tongeren, D. R., Worthington, E. L., Jr., & Placeres, V. (2018). The multicultural orientation framework: A narrative review. *Psychotherapy, 55*, 89–100. https://doi.org/10.1037/pst0000160

Eytan, A. (2011). Religion and mental health during incarceration: A systematic literature review. *Psychiatric Quarterly, 82*(4), 287–295. https://doi.org/10.1007/s11126-011-9170-6

Fowers, B. J., & Davidov, B. J. (2006). The virtue of multiculturalism: Personal transformation, character, and openness to the other. *American Psychologist, 61*(6), 581–594. https://doi.org/10.1037/0003-066x.61.6.581

Hage, S. M., Hopson, A., Siegel, M., Payton, G., & DeFanti, E. (2006). Multicultural training in spirituality: An interdisciplinary review. *Counseling and Values, 50*(3), 217–234. https://doi.org/10.1002/j.2161-007X.2006.tb00058.x

Hook, J. N., Davis, D. E., Owen, J., Worthington, E. L., Jr., & Utsey, S. O. (2013). Cultural humility: Measuring openness to culturally diverse clients. *Journal of Counseling Psychology, 60*, 353–366. https://doi.org/10.1037/a0032595

Hook, J. N., Worthington, E. L., Jr., & Davis, D. E. (2012). Religion and spirituality in counseling. In N. A. Fouad, J. A. Carter, & L. M. Subich (Eds.), *APA handbook of counseling psychology, Vol. 2. Practice, interventions, and applications* (pp. 417–432). American Psychological Association. https://doi.org/10.1037/13755-017

Kellems, I. S., Hill, C. E., Crook-Lyon, R. E., & Freitas, G. (2010). Working with clients who have religious/spiritual issues: A survey of university counseling center therapists. *Journal of College Student Psychotherapy, 24*(2), 139–155. https://doi.org/10.1080/87568220903558745

Maruna, S., Wilson, L., & Curran, K. (2006). Why God is often found behind bars: Prison conversions and the crisis of self-narrative. *Research in Human Development, 3*(2–3), 161–184. https://doi.org/10.1080/15427609.2006.9683367

McMinn, M., Aikins, D., & Lish, R. A. D. (2003). Basic and advanced competence in collaborating with clergy. *Professional Psychology, Research and Practice, 34*(2), 197–202. https://doi.org/10.1037/0735-7028.34.2.197

Moon, S. H., & Sandage, S. J. (2019). Cultural humility for people of color: Critique of current theory and practice. *Journal of Psychology and Theology, 47*(2), 76–86. https://doi.org/10.1177/0091647119842407

Morgan, R. D., Flora, D. B., Kroner, D. G., Mills, J. F., Varghese, F., & Steffan, J. S. (2012). Treating offenders with mental illness: A research synthesis. *Law and Human Behavior, 36*(1), 37–50. https://doi.org/10.1037/h0093964

Munetz, M. R., Grande, T. P., & Chambers, M. R. (2001). The incarceration of individuals with severe mental disorders. *Community Mental Health Journal, 37*(4), 361–372. https://doi.org/10.1023/A:1017508826264

Owen, J. (2013). Early career perspectives: Therapist effects, cultural dynamics, and other processes in psychotherapy. *Psychotherapy: Theory, Research, & Practice, 50*, 496–502. https://doi.org/10.1037/a0034617

Owen, J., Adelson, J., Budge, S., Wampold, B., Kopta, M., Minami, T., & Miller, S. (2015). Trajectories of change in psychotherapy. *Journal of Clinical Psychology, 71*(9), 817–827. https://doi.org/10.1002/jclp.22191

Owen, J., Jordan, T., Turner, D., Davis, D., Hook, J., & Leach, M. (2014). Therapists' multicultural orientation: Cultural humility, spiritual/religious identity, and therapy outcomes. *Journal of Psychology and Theology, 42*(1), 91–98. https://doi.org/10.1177/009164711404200110

Owen, J., Tao, K., Drinane, J., Hook, J., Davis, D., & Foo Kune, N. (2016). Client perceptions of therapists' multicultural orientation: Cultural (missed) opportunities and cultural humility. *Professional Psychology, Research and Practice, 47*(1), 30–37. https://doi.org/10.1037/pro0000046

Oxhandler, H. K., Moffatt, K. M., & Giardina, T. D. (2019). Clinical helping professionals' perceived support, barriers, and training to integrate clients' religion/spirituality in practice. *Spirituality in Clinical Practice, 6*(4), 279–291. https://doi.org/10.1037/scp0000189

Pérez-Rojas, A. E., Bartholomew, T. T., Lockard, A. J., & González, J. M. (2019). Development and initial validation of the Therapist Cultural Comfort Scale. *Journal of Counseling Psychology, 66*(5), 534–549. Advance online publication. https://doi.org/10.1037/cou0000344

Pew Research Center. (2012). *Religion in prisons—A 50 state survey of prison chaplains.* Pew Research Center Religion & Public Life Project.

Sanders, P. W., Richards, P. S., & McBride, J. A. (2018). Development of the Clinically Adaptive Multidimensional Outcome Survey. *Psychotherapy Research, 28*(6), 925–939. https://doi.org/10.1080/10503307.2016.1277039

Steadman, H. J., Osher, F. C., Robbins, P. C., Case, B., & Samuels, S. (2009). Prevalence of serious mental illness among jail inmates. *Psychiatric Services, 60*(6), 761–765. https://doi.org/10.1176/ps.2009.60.6.761

Wampold, B. E. (2001). *The great psychotherapy debate: Models, methods, and findings.* Lawrence Erlbaum.

Wampold, B. E. (2007). Psychotherapy: The humanistic (and effective) treatment. *American Psychologist, 62*(8), 857–873. https://doi.org/10.1037/0003-066X.62.8.857

Wampold, B. E., & Budge, S. L. (2012). The 2011 Leona Tyler Award address: The relationship—and its relationship to the common and specific factors of psychotherapy. *The Counseling Psychologist, 40*(4), 601–623. https://doi.org/10.1177/0011000011432709

Wampold, B. E., & Imel, Z. E. (2015). *The great psychotherapy debate: The evidence for what makes psychotherapy work.* Routledge. https://doi.org/10.4324/9780203582015

Worthington, E. L. (1988). Understanding the values of religious clients: A model and its application to counseling. *Journal of Counseling Psychology, 35*(2), 166–174. https://doi.org/10.1037/0022-0167.35.2.166

Worthington, E. L., Jr., Davis, D. E., Hook, J. N., Miller, A. J., Gartner, A. L., & Jennings, D. J., II. (2011). Promoting forgiveness as a religious or spiritual intervention. In J. D. Aten, M. R. McMinn, & E. L., Worthington, Jr. (Eds.), *Spiritually oriented interventions for counseling and psychotherapy* (pp. 169–196). American Psychological Association.

Worthington, E. L., Jr., Wade, N. G., Hight, T. L., Ripley, J. S., McCullough, M. E., Berry, J. W., Schmitt, M. M., Berry, J. T., Bursley, K. H., & O'Conner, L. (2003). The religious commitment inventory-10: Development, refinement, and validation of a brief scale for research and counseling. *Journal of Counseling Psychology, 50*(1), 84–96. https://doi.org/10.1037/0022-0167.50.1.84

IV

MAINSTREAMING SPIRITUALLY INTEGRATED PSYCHOTHERAPIES

22

Training Opportunities and Resources for Spiritually Integrated Psychotherapists and Researchers

P. Scott Richards, Joseph M. Currier, Russell Siler Jones, Michelle Pearce, and Douglas Stephens

In this concluding chapter of the *Handbook of Spiritually Integrated Psychotherapies*, we describe training opportunities and other resources about spiritually integrated psychotherapy (SIP) that are available for graduate students, mental health practitioners, and researchers. We conclude the chapter by making five recommendations that we think will help accelerate the adoption of SIPs into mainstream mental health practice.

GRADUATE TRAINING IN RELIGIOUS AND SPIRITUAL COMPETENCIES

Several dozen mental health graduate programs have faculty with interests in the psychology of religion and spirituality (R/S;[1] Society for the Psychology of Religion and Spirituality, Division 36, n.d.). Faculty with such interests provide students with opportunities for mentoring and research in R/S aspects of diversity and treatment. Unfortunately, formal coursework that is required by

---

[1] "R/S" in this chapter can refer to "religion and spirituality," "religious and spiritual," "religious/spiritual," or "religion/spirituality."

The authorship order for Currier, Jones, Pearce, and Stephens was determined alphabetically. The section "Spiritual Competency Training in Mental Health Course" was written by Michelle Pearce. The section "ACPE SIP Program" was written by Russell Siler Jones. The section "Solihten Institute Training Program in SIP" was written by Douglas Stephens. The section "Bridges Institute for Spiritually Integrated Psychotherapies" was written by P. Scott Richards.

https://doi.org/10.1037/0000338-022
Handbook of Spiritually Integrated Psychotherapies, P. S. Richards, G. E. K. Allen, and D. K. Judd (Editors)
Copyright © 2023 by the American Psychological Association. All rights reserved.

academic institutions for graduate students in religious diversity and spiritual competencies in mental health treatment is less common. Although some graduate mental health training programs give attention to spiritual aspects of diversity and treatment competency, the majority do not (Oxhandler et al., 2015; Schafer et al., 2011; Vogel et al., 2013).

Spiritual and Religious Competencies Project for Graduate Education

In an effort to overcome these gaps in mental health education and training, the John Templeton Foundation recently awarded a 3-year grant (August 2021 to July 2024) for the Spiritual and Religious Competences Project (SRCP; for details, see https://www.spiritualandreligiouscompetenciesproject.com/). Focusing on the four professions providing most of the services in the United States (counseling, marriage and family therapy [MFT], psychology, and social work), the overarching goal for this interdisciplinary project is to improve mental health care and promote human flourishing by ensuring every mental health clinician in the United States possesses the basic awareness, knowledge, and skills to attend to clients' R/S in ethical and effective ways.

To this end, the SRCP team seeks to integrate R/S competency training in graduate and postgraduate training programs in five ways: (a) generating strategies and tools for defining, studying, and assessing R/S competencies; (b) establishing effective methods of promoting R/S competencies; (c) understanding graduate faculty views, experiences, supports, and barriers related to training R/S competencies across these disciplines; (d) synergizing diverse stakeholders with a commitment to promoting R/S competencies; and (e) fueling momentum for systemic and cultural changes in ways that R/S are addressed in mental health care beyond the funding period. These micro-, mezzo-, and macrolevel objectives are pursued across four subprojects.

Subproject 1: Strengthening Graduate Education in R/S Competencies

Given the omission of in R/S as a core area of diversity, identity, and psychosocial functioning in graduate education (Oxhandler et al., 2015; Schafer et al., 2011; Vogel et al., 2013), training needs to start in graduate education and continue throughout students' careers. In turn, a new generation of educators, supervisors, and clinicians who view R/S competence as the norm will enter their professions. Accreditation requirements and other issues preclude many graduate programs from developing a stand-alone course in R/S. Encouragingly, prior work in medical school training has demonstrated that teaching R/S content during required courses via an integrated modular manner represents a feasible and effective approach to promoting competence in this area (Puchalski & Larson, 1998; Puchalski et al., 2001).

Drawing on Pearce et al.'s (2019, 2020) Spiritual Competency Training in Mental Health (SCT-MH; details follow later in this chapter), Subproject 1 of the SRCP seeks to similarly strengthen coursework in mental health graduate education via a four-phase plan: (a) Enhance the SCT-MH program as standardized content (online and face-to-face) that can be incorporated into existing graduate-level courses; (b) implement the enhanced version of the SCT-MH program with 20 instructors at 20 institutions; (c) evaluate the efficacy, feasibility, and acceptability of the enhanced SCT-MH program with a large sample of graduate students; and (d) disseminate the enhanced SCT-MH program and all face-to-face teaching materials to other mental health graduate training programs. In so doing, the SRCP team aims to offer an effective, affordable, and feasible method of R/S competency training that can be readily implemented in required coursework across the four professions.

Subproject 2: Promoting Research in R/S Competencies in Clinical Training

Training mental health clinicians is usually a lengthy, sequential, and cumulative process in which coursework is more heavily emphasized at first. As a result, most graduate and postgraduate training programs use clinical supervision in practicum/internship settings as the signature pedagogy in fostering acquisition of clinical skills. R/S competency training is rarely included in clinical training in systematic or formal ways (Russell & Yarhouse, 2006), and there is a dearth of resources for addressing them in such settings. In turn, a lack of validated tools and methods hinder clinical training in R/S assessment, R/S integration in psychotherapy, and other possible competencies.

To address these gaps, the SRCP will partner with 12 to 15 clinician–scientists from the four professions via a request-for-funding-proposal approach. As of the writing of this chapter (December 2021), a large sample of letters of intent were received from a diverse group researchers, clinicians, and educations. Invitations for full proposals were offered in January 2022, and funding decisions are expected in the spring. By the end of Subproject 2, the SRCP team aims to catalyze research in R/S competencies and generate empirically supported resources, tools, and methods for equipping students and trainees with skills to address R/S dimensions of clients' lives. Looking ahead, pursuing these microlevel objectives will increase options for clinical training that practicum or internship programs could viably incorporate into supervision and didactics as well as synergize a community of clinician–investigators to hopefully collaborate with each other after the funding period.

Subproject 3: Understanding Faculty Views, Behaviors, and Needs Regarding Training in R/S Competencies

Graduate faculty perspectives on training in R/S are unknown across the professions of counseling, MFT, psychology, and social work. To date, surveys have been limited to a specific discipline or region, used assessments without established reliability/validity, and/or strictly relied on responses from program directors rather than individual faculty. Because of faculty's formative role in shaping clinicians' willingness and ability to attend to clients' R/S, it is critical to understand their orientation toward R/S competency training.

Focusing on the roughly 20,000 full-time graduate faculty members teaching in accredited programs across the four professions, Subproject 3 will obtain an interdisciplinary and national baseline assessment of their views, behaviors, and experiences with training students in R/S. In so doing, this survey will support these four mezzolevel objectives: (a) allow faculty to identify the current strengths and opportunities for improvement regarding R/S content delivery in graduate education; (b) provide a national data point to evaluate the long-term impact of the overall project; (c) coordinate dissemination of research findings, tools, and resources generated across the other three subprojects; and (d) invite a large subset of training faculty to reflect on the degree to which they include course content on R/S and offer tangible steps for how to integrate R/S in their work with students. In so doing, the SRCP team hopes that Subproject 3 will generate the most rigorous and comprehensive picture of the status of training of R/S in graduate education to date.

Subproject 4: Promoting R/S Competency Training for Mental Health Professionals—A Systems-Change Endeavor

The driving purpose of Subproject 4 is to shift the culture of training in mental health professions using a macrolevel approach informed by implementation and dissemination science. *Targeted systems-change* is a way of strategically transforming a system by identifying key stakeholders, assets, opportunities, challenges, and primary levers for change as well as involving stakeholders in creating shared solutions to the problem via a bottom-up, community-participatory approach.

To this end, the SRCP team will develop (a) an online platform to increase access to resources and tools to integrate R/S competencies for faculty, supervisors, and training directors; (b) an evidence map and data visualization map that demonstrate the impact of R/S competency training; (c) an open-access, practice-oriented book that will disseminate findings, resources, and tools generated across the four subprojects and others' work to support faculty, supervisors, and clinicians to integrate R/S competency training into their training activities; and (d) a road map for a systems-change approach to integrating R/S competencies into training. Leaving room for stakeholders to identify novel ideas and ways of enhancing the road map in (see Item d), other activities could be targeted. These activities might include working with professional associations to adopt R/S competency guidelines, including developments from psychology of R/S, into undergraduate and graduate-level textbooks; outreach to large mental health care delivery systems; advocacy for large funding organizations to increase funding on R/S competency training; and other activities that may accelerate access and adoption of R/S competency training.

CONTINUING EDUCATION OPPORTUNITIES FOR MENTAL HEALTH PRACTITIONERS

Continuing education (CE) opportunities about R/S aspects of diversity and treatment for licensed mental health practitioners have not been widely available during the past several decades, but fortunately, this is beginning to change (Pearce et al., 2019; Richards et al., 2015). In this chapter, we describe four training opportunities that are currently available for practicing mental health professionals: (a) SCT-MH online course, (b) ACPE (Association for Clinical Pastoral Education) SIP program, (c) Solihten Institute (SI) training program in SIP, and (d) Bridges Institute for Spiritually Integrated Psychotherapies (hereinafter, Bridges Institute) practice-research-training network training resources. These are not the only four training opportunities available for mental health practitioners, but they are of high quality.

SCT-MH Online Course

In response to the lack of graduate and postgraduate training for working with R/S issues in clinical practice, Pearce and colleagues developed the SCT-MH online course (Pearce et al., 2019), which is designed to assist mental health practitioners in developing basic competency and comfort in integrating R/S into treatment. Specifically, the course targets the 16 spiritual competencies—three items under "attitudes," seven under "knowledge," and six under "skills" (see Table 22.1)—identified in prior research as the minimum attitudes, knowledge, and skills mental health clinicians should have to be considered competent in this area (Vieten et al., 2013, 2016).

Designed to be multidisciplinary, the SCT-MH course focuses on core R/S competencies relevant to effective mental health care in general. As such, clinicians across all mental health fields can participate, including those in psychology, professional counseling, MFT, clinical social work, and psychiatry. It is designed to be relevant for all levels of training, from graduate students to seasoned clinicians.

Curriculum Development

The course curriculum was developed by the course directors (Michelle Pearce, one of the authors of this chapter, and Kenneth Pargament) using SIP and spiritual competency empirical and instructional materials. They also elicited feedback from more than 20 experts in the field. The curriculum content was carefully mapped to the 16 spiritual competencies the course directors sought

TABLE 22.1. Sixteen Spiritual and Religious Competencies for Mental Health Professionals

Competency	Competency item
Attitudes	1. Mental health professionals demonstrate empathy, respect, and appreciation for clients from diverse spiritual, religious, or secular backgrounds and affiliations.
	2. Mental health professionals view spirituality and religion as important aspects of human diversity along with factors, such as race, ethnicity, sexual orientation, socioeconomic status, disability, gender, and age.
	3. Mental health professionals are aware of how their own spiritual and/or religious background and beliefs may influence their clinical practice and their attitudes, perceptions, and assumptions about the nature of psychological processes.

(continues)

TABLE 22.1. Sixteen Spiritual and Religious Competencies for Mental Health Professionals (*Continued*)

Competency	Competency item
Knowledge	4. Mental health professionals know that many diverse forms of spirituality and/or religion exist and explore spiritual and/or religious beliefs, communities, and practices that are important to their clients.
	5. Mental health professionals can describe how spirituality and religion can be viewed as overlapping, yet distinct, constructs.
	6. Mental health professionals understand that clients may have experiences that are consistent with their spirituality or religion yet may be difficult to differentiate from psychopathological symptoms.
	7. Mental health professionals recognize that spiritual and/or religious beliefs, practices, and experiences develop and change over the life span.
	8. Mental health professionals are aware of internal and external spiritual and/or religious resources and practices that research indicates may support psychological well-being and recovery from psychological disorders.
	9. Mental health professionals can identify spiritual and religious experiences, practices, and beliefs that may have the potential to negatively impact psychological health.
	10. Mental health professionals can identify legal and ethical issues related to spirituality and/or religion that may surface when working with clients.
Skills	11. Mental health professionals are able to conduct empathic and effective psychotherapy with clients from diverse spiritual and/or religious backgrounds, affiliations, and levels of involvement.
	12. Mental health professionals inquire about spiritual and/or religious background, experience, practices, attitudes, and beliefs as a standard part of understanding a client's history.
	13. Mental health professionals help clients explore and access their spiritual and/or religious strengths and resources.
	14. Mental health professionals can identify and address spiritual and/or religious problems in clinical practice and make referrals when necessary.
	15. Mental health professionals stay abreast of research and professional developments regarding spirituality and religion specifically related to clinical practice and engage in ongoing assessment of their own spiritual and religious competency.
	16. Mental health professionals recognize the limits of their qualifications and competence in the spiritual and/or religious domains, including their responses to clients' spirituality and/or religion that may interfere with clinical practice so that they (a) seek consultation from and collaborate with other qualified clinicians or spiritual/religious sources (e.g., priests, pastors, rabbis, imam, spiritual teachers), (b) seek further training and education, and/or (c) refer appropriate clients to more qualified individuals and resources.

Note. Adapted from "Competencies for Psychologists in the Domains of Religion and Spirituality," by C. Vieten, S. Scammell, A. Pierce, R. Pilato, I. Ammondson, K. I. Pargament, and D. Lukoff, 2016, *Spirituality in Clinical Practice, 3*(2), pp. 92–114 (https://doi.org/10.1037/scp0000078). Copyright 2016 by the American Psychological Association.

to develop (Vieten et al., 2013). Table 22.2 shows the course content and competencies addressed in each module. Key topics include common stereotypes about R/S; the diversity of R/S forms and expressions; why it is important to address R/S in treatment; the importance of the therapist's own R/S attitudes, beliefs, and practices; how to assess R/S; how to help clients access R/S resources, and how to respond to R/S problems that arise in treatment.

The course directors used adult learning principles in the curriculum design, including opportunities for engagement with the material, short rather than lengthy videos, self-reflection, and a variety of activities and examples demonstrating the key concepts and their clinical application.

Description of SCT-MH Course

The SCT-MH course consists of eight modules that can be completed in an average of 60 minutes each (8–9 hours total). Each module is structured similarly. The module begins with a brief video introduction in which one of the course directors provides an overview of the module contents, and module objectives are listed beneath the video. Approximately three sections of content appear in each module; these sections consist of text, videos, case studies (text and video), audio recordings, self-reflection questions, and knowledge check questions. At the end of the course, participants are provided with a comprehensive reference and resource list.

The course is offered as an online asynchronous (prerecorded and self-paced) course rather than an in-person training to increase access, dissemination, and convenience. To house the course online, the course directors chose the online platform edX, which is the largest nonprofit and open-source provider of Massive Open Online Courses (commonly known as MOOC). In this platform, participants receive a structured, yet self-paced, learning opportunity with course content, readings, activities, and assessments. The course can be accessed anywhere at any time with an internet connection.

The following highlights what the eight training modules cover:

- *Module 1: Introduction and Orientation.* Participants are first introduced to the course goals and objectives. The instructors (Pearce and Pargament) define "spiritually integrated therapy," provide empirically based reasons for offering integrative care, explain what is needed to provide it, and outline challenges to this type of care.

- *Module 2: Understanding Spirituality.* The instructors define "religion" and "spirituality," challenge stereotypes, and introduce and compare the varieties of R/S. This module also provides a discussion of the development of spirituality over a life span.

- *Module 3: Guiding Principles for Spiritually Integrated Mental Health Care.* Participants learn how to navigate spirituality effectively and ethically in the therapeutic relationship, learn about the importance of respecting spiritual diversity, and learn about biases that can influence treatment and client outcomes.

TABLE 22.2. Training Program Modules and Spiritual Competencies

Training program module	Spiritual competencies, by number, addressed in the module
Module 1: Introduction and Orientation	#3: Being aware of your own beliefs (Attitudes) #10: Being aware of legal and ethical issues (Knowledge) #15: Staying up to date (Skill)
Module 2: Understanding Spirituality	#5: Understanding spirituality and religion as different but overlapping (Knowledge) #7: Recognizing spiritual development over the life span (Knowledge) #4: Learning about diverse beliefs and practices (Knowledge)
Module 3: Guiding Principles for Spiritually Integrated Mental Health Care	#1: Demonstrating empathy, respect, and appreciation (Attitude) #2: Appreciating religious and spiritual diversity (Attitude) #3: Being aware of your own beliefs (Attitude)
Module 4: Distinguishing Between Helpful and Harmful Types of Spirituality	#6: Knowing the difference between spirituality and psychopathology (Knowledge) #8: Learning about clients' spiritual and religious resources (Knowledge) #9: Recognizing harmful religious and spiritual involvement (Knowledge)
Module 5: Assessing Spirituality in Mental Health Care	#11: Working with religious and spiritual diversity (Skill) #12: Conducting a religious and spiritual assessment (Skill)
Module 6: Mobilizing Spiritual Resources	#8: Learning about clients' spiritual and religious resources (Knowledge) #13: Helping clients identify and access their religious and spiritual resources (Skill)
Module 7: Addressing Spiritual Problems	#9: Recognizing harmful religious and spiritual involvement (Knowledge) #14: Helping clients identify and deal with spiritual and religious problems (Skill) #16: Acknowledging your limits (Skill)
Module 8: Putting It All Together, Challenges, and Future Directions	#10: Developing awareness of legal and ethical issues (Knowledge) #15: Staying up to date (Skill) #16: Acknowledging your limits (Skill) #1–16: Summarizing and applying all 16 competencies

Note. Adapted from "A Novel Training Program for Mental Health Providers in Religious and Spiritual Competencies," by M. J. Pearce, K. I. Pargament, H. K. Oxhandler, C. Vieten, and S. Wong, 2019, *Spirituality in Clinical Practice*, 6(2), pp. 78–79 (https://doi.org/10.1037/scp0000195). Copyright 2019 by the American Psychological Association.

- *Module 4: Distinguishing Between Helpful and Harmful Types of Spirituality.* "Life-affirming" and "life-limiting" forms of spirituality are defined to show how R/S can be part of the solution or part of the problem in mental health treatment. Participants acquire the tools for distinguishing psychopathology from spiritual experiences.

- *Module 5: Assessing Spirituality in Mental Health Care.* Participants learn how to engage in spiritual assessment as a multistep process and are provided resources for engaging in various types of spiritual assessment.

- *Module 6: Mobilizing Spiritual Resources.* Guidelines for integrating spiritual resources are provided, followed by a discussion and examples on how therapists can cultivate and mobilize spiritual resources in therapy.

- *Module 7: Addressing Spiritual Problems.* This module outlines various types of spiritual problems and struggles as well as offers tools for effectively addressing spiritual problems in therapy.

- *Module 8: Putting it All Together, Challenges, and Future Directions.* Participants learn about ethical challenges of spiritually integrated care and several cutting-edge spiritually integrated approaches. Knowledge from all eight modules is then synthesized in a case study in which participants engage in hypothetical analysis, assessment, and treatment planning decision making.

Evaluation

Using a pre–post study survey design, Pearce et al. (2020) evaluated the SCT-MH course to determine its feasibility, helpfulness, and effectiveness for increasing competencies in spirituality and mental health care among mental health care professionals. The researchers evaluated the course with 169 participants from across a broad range of mental health disciplines who completed the course over a 4-week period. On completion, participants were awarded CE and continuing medical education credits. Participants completed a pre- and posttraining survey that evaluated their spiritual competency using measures assessing their attitudes, knowledge, and skills in the intersection of R/S and mental health. The researchers also collected qualitative data to evaluate program satisfaction.

Pearce and colleagues (2020) found that participating in SCT-MH led to statistically significant improvements in all measures of providers' attitudes, knowledge, and skills as they related to spirituality and mental health. Many participants also stated in their qualitative feedback that they were already using the information and skills in their work with clients, such as R/S assessment and R/S resources. Participants reported high satisfaction with both the content and online format of the training program; they also reported a decrease in perceived barriers to integrating R/S in practice. The number one barrier that was reduced was not being adequately trained in the integration of R/S into clinical practice.

Future Directions of the Course

A brief, evidence-based online training course can increase practitioners' comfort and competency levels in dealing with R/S issues in their clinical work. In doing so, the course helped to address the current gap between the clinical need and professional requirements for spiritual competency and the general lack of graduate training in this area. Pearce and her colleagues are currently working on adapting the SCT-MH online course to function as a hybrid (online and in-person), for-credit course for graduate students across mental health disciplines.

As far as the authors of this chapter know, this empirically driven, online course is the first of its kind, although we anticipate, and indeed hope, many other such training opportunities arise for clinicians at all stages of their training and career. These might include a course in advanced competencies in R/S and mental health, in-person workshops with experiential components, and practicum and internship experiences.

The SCT-MH course is available to the public on edX as a professional education course for a small fee. Those who complete the course are eligible for six CE credits sponsored by the American Psychological Association (APA). Interested individuals can find the course on the edX platform (see https://www.edx.org/) by searching for "spiritual competency training for mental health providers" or "spiritual competency training in mental health."

ACPE SIP Program

Founded in 1967, ACPE (see https://acpe.edu/) rebranded itself in 2017. Mindful of the spiritual and vocational diversity of its educators, students, and members, many of whom do not identify with the title of "pastor," the association changed its name to "ACPE: The Standard for Spiritual Care & Education." Under both names, and throughout its almost 60-year history, ACPE training has valued the power of a learning cohort and the action-reflection-action model of education. Through experiential practice, group and individual reflection, and group and individual supervision, participants in ACPE training programs learn to ground themselves deeply in their particular faith tradition or frame of meaning so they can help people in vulnerable moments of their lives draw on the spiritual resources they bring to such moments.

For the whole of its history, ACPE has offered training to persons exploring ministry and chaplaincy. Most ACPE training occurs in hospitals and health care settings, but there are programs in prisons, the U.S. military, homeless shelters, congregations, and community-based service settings. ACPE is a recognized specialized accreditor of the U.S. Department of Education, and there are currently more than 450 ACPE-accredited learning sites in the United States and across the globe. In 2019, ACPE began offering education and professional formation for psychotherapists. This expansion of ACPE's educational mission happened when it consolidated with a sister organization, the American Association of Pastoral Counselors (AAPC).

Like ACPE, AAPC was founded in the 1960s (1964). Its initial mission was to train ministers for the work of psychotherapy, but by the 2000s, AAPC was also training nonclerical psychotherapists who wanted to more effectively make engagement with spirituality a part of their practices. AAPC training stressed the value of the therapeutic relationship, therapists' use of self, and therapeutic presence; therapists' nonproselytizing attention to the spiritual worldview of their clients; therapists' deep reflection on their own spiritual and theological perspectives and how these shaped their understanding of their clients, themselves, and the therapeutic process; and, as with ACPE training, the importance of personal and professional formation, the power of the action-reflection-action model, and the value of ongoing learning in a community of colleagues and mentors.

The ACPE Spiritually Integrated Psychotherapy (SIP) Program (see https://acpe.edu/programs/spiritual-integrated-psychotherapy) is open to all helping professionals who want to explore the ways spirituality, religion, and the search for meaning affect their own lives, the lives of those they serve, and the practice of psychotherapy. Most participants in ACPE SIP training are licensed and prelicensed mental health professionals—counselors, social workers, marriage and family therapists, pastoral counselors, psychologists, psychiatrists, physician assistants, mental health nurse practitioners, addiction specialists, and more—as well as graduate students in those disciplines, but chaplains and clergypersons have also participated in trainings and found them relevant and helpful to the work they do.

The ACPE SIP Program offers three levels of training: (a) a 30-hour curriculum, offered as workshops for CE credit; (b) a postcurriculum consultation and certification process; and (3) ongoing ACPE SIP Communities of Practice in which connection, learning, and professional formation continue beyond the consultation and certification process. At each level, the ACPE SIP Program blends three emphases: (a) helping mental health providers recognize, appreciate, and make skillful therapeutic use of their clients' spirituality; (b) helping mental health providers recognize, reflect on, and make ethically appropriate use of their own spirituality; and (c) supporting mental health providers in personal integration, development of professional identity, and growth in a distinctive way of being.

The first level of training makes foundational training in SIP accessible to as many people as possible. The curriculum includes ten 3-hour courses, taught by an approved ACPE SIP trainer. Each course aims to increase participants' knowledge, skills, and personal formation, and each course uses a variety of learning methods: PowerPoint presentations; individual, small-group, and large-group reflection; and role plays and skill-building in practice groups. An overview of the 10 courses is presented in Table 22.3.

Course 1 introduces a biopsychosocial-spiritual understanding of human beings, connects a broad understanding of spirituality and religion to the work of psychotherapy, and locates the work of SIP within the codes of ethics of various therapy guilds. Courses 2 through 7 teach how to nourish implicit

TABLE 22.3. ACPE Spiritually Integrated Psychotherapy Program: Level 1 Courses

Course	Course title	Contact hours
1	Foundations and Ethics of Spiritually Integrated Psychotherapy	3
2	Developing Spiritual Conversations in Psychotherapy	3
3	Spiritual Assessment	3
4	Spiritual Interventions: Working with Spiritual Resources, Part 1	3
5	Spiritual Interventions: Working with Spiritual Resources, Part 2	3
6	Spiritual Interventions: Working With Harmful Spirituality and Religion	3
7	Spiritual Interventions: Working With Spiritual Struggles	3
8	Spirituality and Belief System of the Therapist	3
9	Spiritually Integrated Case Consultation, Part 1	3
10	Spiritually Integrated Case Consultation, Part 2	3
Total contact hours		30

Note. ACPE = Association for Clinical Pastoral Education.

and explicit spiritual conversation, how to assess for and work with clients' spiritual resources and spiritual struggles, and how to recognize and address the harmful impact spirituality and religion can sometimes have. Course 8 helps participants reflect on their personal spirituality: both the cognitive elements of their spirituality—their beliefs and values—and the embodied elements that manifest in therapeutic presence. Course 9 teaches participants how to write a spiritually integrated case conceptualization, and in Course 10, which happens in groups of three participants with an SIP trainer, participants bring a written conceptualization for consultation with a small group.

On completion of the 30-hour CE curriculum, some participants choose to begin a second level of training: a consultation process that leads to certification.

The second and third levels of the ACPE SIP Program provide an opportunity to apply and integrate at a more clinically concrete level the learnings from the 30-hour curriculum. In addition, this consultation portion of the training affords opportunities for participants to strengthen connections with colleagues and mentors as well as to deepen their journey of personal and professional formation. The second and third levels of training reflect ACPE's belief that high-quality therapists become competent therapists over time, in formative relationships, and they provide a community of ongoing learning and support for those who desire that level of connection.

In each consultation hour, consultees use the case conceptualization template introduced in Courses 9 and 10 to present their work. Consultation addresses the three emphases noted earlier: (a) helping therapists understand their clients' spirituality more fully; make use of their clients' spirituality as a resource for stabilization, growth, and healing; and help their clients find relief from or resolution of spiritual distress; (b) helping therapists draw on their own spirituality, in ethically appropriate ways, to understand their clients, themselves, and the therapeutic process; and (c) helping therapists deepen their experience of personal integration, professional identity, and therapeutic presence.

ACPE Certification in SIP requires 20 hours of consultation with an approved SIP trainer. At least 8 of the 20 hours happen in individual consultation. Twelve of the 20 hours can happen in small groups. The group consultation helps participants grow in competence and also in connection with others who value a spiritually integrated approach to psychotherapy. The ACPE SIP Program has identified 10 core competencies, and, at the end of each hour, consultant and consultee make record of the competencies addressed. These are the 10 ACPE SIP competencies:

1. appreciation for spiritual and religious diversity and ability to work across spiritual and religious difference
2. ability to work with clients holistically from a biopsychosocial-spiritual perspective
3. ability to integrate spirituality into psychotherapy in an ethically appropriate manner
4. ability to conduct a spiritual assessment
5. ability to help clients leverage healthy spiritual resources
6. ability to use a variety of spiritual interventions
7. ability to help clients work through spiritual struggles
8. ability to address harmful spirituality and religion in the context of psychotherapy
9. ability to articulate how the therapist's personal spirituality is a resource in understanding clients, themselves, and therapeutic process
10. ability to be aware of and make therapeutic use of spiritual countertransference

On completion of the 30-hour curriculum and 20 hours of consultation, participants who are fully licensed therapists are eligible for certification. The certification process concludes with a consultative peer review. Candidates prepare a case (using the template they learned in the 30-hour curriculum and that was used in their consultation process) and a brief personal statement. These written materials serve as the focus of conversation with a small group of peers and SIP trainers. The peer review recognizes and celebrates participants' learning thus far as well as their intention to continue engagement with a community of learning and support.

That ongoing learning and support happen in the third level of ACPE SIP training: the "community of practice." ACPE SIP communities of practice are containers for collegial connection that lasts well beyond the formal portion of SIP training. Communities of practice meet several times a year—for case consultation, CE events, practice management consultation, and informal networking—and are places of authentic professional friendship.

SIP Trainers

All three levels of the ACPE SIP Program are led by approved ACPE SIP trainers. These trainers are ACPE psychotherapists with the education, experience, training, and sense of calling to help other therapists develop the knowledge, skills, and way of being to integrate spirituality into the work of psychotherapy. They are the heart, soul, hands, and feet of ACPE's SIP Program.

ACPE maintains an application and training process for SIP trainers. Most of ACPE's initial cohort of SIP Trainers were persons previously certified at advanced levels (Fellow and Diplomate) by AAPC, but persons who earn the ACPE Certification in Spiritually Integrated Psychotherapy are also eligible to apply.

Before the coronavirus (COVID-19) pandemic, ACPE SIP trainings happened in person in communities where SIP trainers live and work. Since the pandemic, SIP trainings have been happening online by videoconference. This medium has allowed greater access to SIP trainings and helped persons in all parts of the United States connect with ACPE SIP trainings. Readers can visit the ACPE website (see https://acpe.edu/) find up-to-date information about the ACPE SIP Program and upcoming SIP trainings.

Plans for the Future

At the time of this writing, the ACPE SIP Program is more than a year old. There are 38 approved SIP trainers who offer training and consultation across the United States. Two persons have completed the consultation process, met with peer review committees, and completed certification. Many others have completed the 30-hour foundational training, and a good number of these have entered the consultation process. In their evaluations, participants have offered these comments:

- "I have been waiting for this training my entire professional life. Thank you."

- "This training has revolutionized my practice. I use something I learned in this training in every single session."

- "I am a pastoral counselor with over 50 years in the field. Since completing the ACPE SIP training, I am having more spiritually meaningful conversations with clients, and clients are doing deeper work at both conscious and unconscious levels."

- "I am a Muslim mental health therapist and woman of color. I serve clients from my own religion and from many other spiritual perspectives. The ACPE SIP training was a phenomenal program that provided a comprehensive foundation and practical skills for integrating spirituality and religion into counseling. I feel immense gratitude for the trainers as well as the participants for the fellowship that was created through the course of the program."

In addition to this anecdotal feedback, ACPE has begun conducting research into the efficacy of its SIP training. Scott Richards (editor of this *Handbook* and an author of this chapter), Peter Sanders (Richards's colleague at the Bridges Institute), and Russell Siler Jones (ACPE SIP program developer and an author of this chapter) are working with ACPE to conduct pre- and posttests with all training participants to measure the effectiveness of the ACPE SIP training in enhancing the attitudes, knowledge, and skills required of psychotherapists for the delivery of sensitive and competent spiritually integrated treatment. In addition, with a smaller number of participants, Richards, Sanders, and Jones will be conducting practice-based evidence (PBE) research to determine whether application of the attitudes, knowledge, and skills therapists learn during the ACPE SIP training improve treatment outcomes for their clients.

The ACPE SIP training curriculum is being translated into Korean. Samuel Lee, professor of pastoral counseling at Claremont School of Theology and an ACPE SIP trainer, has begun this meticulous work. Lee has introduced the ACPE SIP training to two counseling guilds in South Korea and is developing relationships to offer the training in South Korea soon.

The ACPE training curriculum is also being adapted and taught as a 3-hour elective course in several counseling-related graduate school programs. Students who engage the ACPE SIP material as part of their graduate training are also eligible to begin the consultation process as part of their internships. They cannot earn certification until after graduating and completing their state's requirements for licensure, but they can engage the program fully up to the point of certification.

ACPE (n.d.) names its organizational vision as this: "To create measurable and appreciable improvement in spiritual health that transforms people and communities in the US and across the globe" (*Vision* section). It adds that "we are more than just an association: we are a movement committed to the transformation of human suffering" (para. 4). The ACPE SIP Program is advancing this vision through the training and support of psychotherapists, and ACPE invites all who share this vision to connect with its community of learning.

Solihten Institute Training Program in SIP

The SI (https://solihten.org/) is an interfaith counseling network comprising more than 44 centers in 200 offices that provide 600,000-plus clinical hours every year. It recruits, accredits, connects, educates, and advances counseling centers that practice one of the most effective paths to healing: spiritually integrated therapy. Before 2019, it operated as Samaritan Institute, which was formed in 1972, when a physician joined together with two congregation clergy and a seminary professor in Elkhart, Indiana. Together, they formed a counseling resource that integrates what people believe into how they heal. For nearly half a century, this community of clergy, mental health professionals, and physicians has grown to serve a national collective of member centers that share a commitment to nurturing mind, body, spirit, and community.

The SI staff provide and facilitate several services for the SI network, including ongoing SIP training programs. Although a portion of the SI network's licensed psychotherapists are trained in and practice SIP, newer generations of psychotherapists within the network's centers had limited education and training in SIP from their graduate programs and postgraduate supervision toward licensure. This disparity represents the generational and experiential divide between therapists historically influenced by the AAPC (inclusive of theological education) and therapists who have become licensed following graduation within the past 20 years.

Furthermore, the newer clinicians were frequently unprepared to address these needs because of limited graduate curriculum and internship/residency experiences that often did not include studying spirituality and psychotherapy. This growing trend was problematic for centers intent on providing best practices in spiritually sensitive psychotherapy. It was from this realization that the SI staff chose to develop a user-friendly educational and training opportunity for all psychotherapists working nationally in the accredited counseling centers of the SI network.

Structured efforts at pilot project research through informal surveys and interviews with center executive directors of the SI network were started in 2017. Enough information was gleaned to warrant the development of a curriculum and faculty selection for a program starting in 2018. Faculty were invited from the senior ranks of SI centers based on clinical and supervisory experience, training in religion and spiritually oriented psychotherapy, factors of diversity in many forms, and reputation gleaned from those who had been taught by these faculty in many settings. (The formative work of Ken Pargament, encapsulated in his *Spiritually Integrated Psychotherapy* [Pargament, 2007], was a common knowledge thread for faculty.) The inaugural 10-month class of 24 persons began in fall 2018. The overall program effort is now in its annual third edition.

Philosophy of the SI Program in SIP

The SI program in SIP is built on key assumptions that parallel the mission of the SI and its accredited counseling centers:

- Psychotherapy and education services address the whole person: body, mind, spirit, and community.

- Psychotherapy services are available to all persons regardless of gender identity, race, religion or faith, socioeconomic status, sexual orientation, or ethnicity.

- The SI ministry is one that encourages equity and justice in all programs of counseling and psychotherapy within each network center's unique geographical circumstances.

The philosophy of the SI training programs is developed and maintained with these assumptions in mind. Therapists forge their craft over many years of practice, acquiring CE in best practices to hone their clinical abilities. That CE builds on the academic knowledge of graduate school as well as the learnings from 2 to 3 years postgraduate, prelicensure clinical supervision. It is rare that newer psychotherapists have had an organized program to guide their integration of clinical learning with their own spirituality development.

The SI program in SIP has two tracks, each of which has the embedded philosophy that the therapist's own psychological self-development is crucial to becoming a spiritually integrated psychotherapist. The first track, SIP, is designed for psychotherapists who have been state-licensed for 5 years or less. The curriculum for this program is concentrated in the integration of one or two key clinical theories (e.g., Kohut's self-psychology) with spiritual awareness and understanding. Cultural sensitivity and empathy are crucial skills developed using monthly seminars and monthly small case consultation groups (three therapists and a group supervisor). The SIP program lasts for 10 months, with a total of 30 CE credits. The faculty principally is cotaught by male and female supervisors.

ATSIP (Advanced Training in Spiritually Integrated Psychotherapy), the second track, is designed for more experienced psychotherapists who have actively practiced for several years beyond licensure. The curriculum covers religious influences and narratives in the therapist's family of origin and development of the Self, psychology of religions and faith development, how to conduct a spiritual assessment, healthy and unhealthy levels of spirituality, relational spirituality in psychotherapy with adults and couples, and religious traditions and cultural diversities. The ATSIP program has a monthly seminar and monthly small case consultation groups. All faculty are involved in each seminar, whereas each consultation group is led by one faculty member throughout the 11-month program (33 CE credits).

Cost for participants is made reasonable, with tuition assistance available to all. Access to the program is virtual, with additional in-person sessions when possible. Content of the programs is accessible and reflective of persons' spiritual experiences as therapists. Factors of equity and justice are part of the training to encourage deeper sensitivity to the cultural dynamics of clients who may be served by therapists in this training program. Faith development across religious traditions is explored in seminars and accompanying small consultation groups with actual clinical work of the trainees.

Each program applicant has had enough clinical experience to recognize some of the gaps in their learning about SIP. From that awareness, a discernment is made with the applicant by the faculty about which level program best suits the applicant: SIP (the basic program for therapists licensed 5 years or less) or ATSIP, a program best suited for clinicians with several years of postlicensed experience.

The training faculty work from the belief that all participants in seminars and consultation groups learn best by a multiplicity of techniques: experiential dialogue and reflection, written contemplation, virtual observation of group process, and assigned reading. The medium used has been a virtual video conference platform (Zoom), facilitating the accessibility for all and reduction of costs for travel and housing. The faculty come from a variety of educational and clinical experiences. They speak from varied religious traditions and convey learnings from their traditions consistent with the curricula. Ultimately, it is the connection each of these teachers develop with program participants that is at the heart of the program. The faculty relate openly and with great sensitivity with the trainees.

In the first 3 years of the SI programs in SIP, the faculty have been

- Christine Dietz, PhD, DMin, LCSW, Spiritual Director;
- Ellery Duke, PhD, LP, AAPC Fellow;
- Randy Hoedeman, PhD, LMFT, LPC, AAMFT [American Association for Marriage and Family Therapy] Supervisor;
- Russell Siler Jones, ThD, LPC, AAPC Diplomate;
- Percy Johnson, ThD;
- Carol Pitts, PhD, MDiv, LMFT, LPC, AAMFT Supervisor; and
- Douglas Stephens, ThM, EdD, LICSW, LMFT, AAMFT Supervisor.

Goals and Competencies of SIP

The goals and competencies of SIP are as follows:

- Participants develop an understanding and conversant ability to work with spirituality in client settings.
- Participants can define spiritual and spirituality in relation to the particular faith or religious circumstances for their clients.
- Participants are able to discuss their preferred clinical theory of therapy through the lens of spiritually oriented psychotherapy.
- Participants develop spiritual journaling as a skill to monitor their own spiritual journeys as they study psychotherapy.

Goals and Competencies of ATSIP

The goals and competencies of ATSIP are as follows:

- Participants develop and demonstrate an understanding of their family of origin history through the lenses of spirituality, religious tradition and symbolism, and differentiation of self-processes.
- Participants develop an understanding of psychology of religion, how religion can enhance or deter one's self-development (healthy or unhealthy spirituality), and the vital role that one's community plays in self object development.
- Participants develop a working knowledge of how SIP enhances their practice of individual and couples therapy.
- Participants develop an understanding of how to use spiritual assessment processes to deepen and enhance their therapy work with clients.
- Participants develop an appreciation and understanding of how cultural differences and diversities can deepen the work of SIP through faith traditions and practices as well as community inclusion in promoting improved mental health.

Participant Reviews and Responses

Since the start of the overall training program, there have been 46 participants in the ATSIP program and 11 in the SIP program. The feedback surveys and written comments have been supportive of the effort, with 86% stating that they were "very satisfied" in each question regarding their learning and their appraisal of the teaching. Of the participants, 12% averaged "satisfied in the questions," whereas 2% noted some areas of dissatisfaction in their responses to the postprogram questionnaire.

Meaningful growth of the overall program developed as participants asked for more active exchanges with faculty during each seminar. Shifting the Zoom platform features opened the direct dialogue such that all participants could directly question the faculty presenter as well as the other responding faculty. The open process and dialogue between participants and presenting faculty enhances the evolution of the program in real time.

The maintenance of the SI program in SIP can be done with relative financial ease because of the reasonable budget cost. It is anticipated that with more than 600 therapists practicing in just the SI network—aside from practitioners outside of the network who may wish to seek this program—the need for this creative effort will continue.

Bridges Institute for Spiritually Integrated Psychotherapies

In 2012, Richards (one of this chapter's authors) and colleagues organized and facilitated a think tank at Brigham Young University in Provo, Utah, for researchers, practitioners, and educators with an interest in bringing spiritually oriented therapies into the health care mainstream (Richards et al., 2015). Outstanding researchers, practitioners, and educators attended the think tank that represented seven academic institutions and 12 mental health treatment sites from around the United States. During the think tank, the participants agreed to create the Bridges practice-research-training network dedicated to bringing spiritually oriented treatment approaches into the health care mainstream. We named it "Bridges" because its mission is to build bridges between spiritual and secular approaches to psychotherapy and to help bridge the research–practice gap in the health care profession. Specific goals of Bridges include the following:

1. Seek grants to help fund collaborative research studies and to assist in developing training materials about spiritually oriented treatment approaches.

2. Conduct research studies about SIP treatment approaches.

3. Publish journal articles about SIPs in mainstream professional and scientific journals.

4. Publish books about SIP outcome and process research, practice, and training by respected mainstream scholarly publishers.

5. Mentor students in SIPs who will eventually teach and practice in universities, health care facilities, and school settings throughout North America.

6. Provide training opportunities in SIPs for professionals throughout the world so that through them, clients and students will have more access to counseling that affirms the values of faith and spirituality in therapeutic change and healing.
7. Seek media coverage about the research findings, publications, and other activities of *Bridges*, including news reports, magazine articles, and film documentaries. (Richards et al., 2015, p. 172)

The Bridges team achieved many of these goals. The team provided opportunities for practitioners, researchers, and educators throughout the world to connect and collaborate with one another in research, training, and practice. It obtained more than $3.9 million in grant funding from the John Templeton Foundation, which allowed the team to conduct research studies on SIPs with 19 research teams in more than 60 treatment clinics in various locations in the United States and eight other countries. The Bridges team also developed the Bridges assessment system, an online platform for collecting treatment process and outcome data on SIPs, and used it in the grant project. An extensive video library was created that consists of interviews with many of the leaders in the psychology of religion and spirituality in psychotherapy fields. And during a national capstone conference in March 2020, Bridges's 19 collaborating research teams shared preliminary findings from their studies (see https://bridgescapstoneconference.wordpress.com/).

Since the conclusion of the Templeton Foundation grant project in 2020, Richards and colleagues have continued our efforts to support and expand Bridges through research, publications, and the development of training materials for practitioners and researchers. We have formed the Bridges Institute for Spiritually Integrated Psychotherapies to continue the work initiated by the Bridges practice-research-training network. We did this because we know from our own experience that psychotherapists, researchers, and educators who have interests in spiritually integrated treatment face several potential challenges: feeling isolated—not having like-minded colleagues from whom they can get support, encouragement, and guidance; lacking opportunities for CE training about integrating spirituality into treatment; needing help in building and maintaining a niche (reputation and caseload) in the provision of spiritually integrated treatment; and lacking opportunities, expertise, and resources for conducting and publishing high-quality research on spiritually integrated treatment. We believe the Bridges Institute can help address these and other challenges.

For practitioners, these training opportunities and resources can be accessed through the Bridges Institute website (https://bridgesinstitutesip.com/):

- *CE webinars.* Basic and advanced training in SIP is provided via online webinars and other training curricula developed by clinicians and researchers with expertise in SIPs.

- *Video and print library.* A large video library offers interviews and presentations from leaders in the psychology of religion and spirituality in psychotherapy fields, religious leaders, and well-known public figures. The sizable print library offers articles, book chapters, and books about SIP.

- *Assessment system and research consulting.* The Bridges Institute maintains the Bridges assessment system, an online psychotherapy outcome and process research platform. Treatment sites, practitioners, and researchers may subscribe at discounted rates. This subscription provides access to the assessment system and training and support to help them implement the assessment system in their treatment facilities so they can monitor treatment processes and outcomes and/or collect data for research projects about spiritually integrated psychotherapies.

The most important mission and goal of the Bridges Institute is to ensure that individuals and families who desire spiritually sensitive, top-quality mental health treatment have access to such services regardless of their religious or spiritual preferences and geographic location. The Bridges Institute seeks to achieve this goal by promoting cutting-edge research on SIPs and by providing top quality training and CE opportunities for practicing mental health professionals. Bridges Institute staff believe in the great value of collaboration with colleagues from around the world and welcome and invite those with interests in mainstreaming SIPs into mental health care to participate in this important cause (Richards et al., 2015).

RECOMMENDATIONS FOR MAINSTREAMING SPIRITUALLY INTEGRATED PSYCHOTHERAPIES

We believe the *Handbook of Spiritually Integrated Psychotherapies* will be an excellent resource for practitioners, researchers, and educators about the practice of spiritually integrated mental health treatment. Hopefully, this handbook will help increase the availability of spiritually sensitive and competent mental health treatment for the many people in the world who need it. But by itself, we recognize that one book will not create the type of professional and systemic change that is needed if spiritually integrated psychotherapies are to be more widely adopted in mainstream mental health practice.

We have five recommendations for accelerating the adoption of SIPs into mainstream mental health practice: (a) expand the evidence-base about the processes and outcomes of treatment; (b) engage in collaborative, interdisciplinary research and training; (c) use technology more effectively to enhance collaboration, research, training, and practice delivery; (d) seek media coverage to inform and influence the public and professionals; and (e) educate leaders of accrediting bodies, licensing boards, health care insurance companies, religious organizations, and political parties.

Expand the Evidence Base

We think a more adequate evidence base about the processes and outcomes of SIPs is essential for successfully mainstreaming these approaches into mental health care practice. A stronger evidence base will provide more credibility and leverage for education and training efforts and outreach with academic institutions, accrediting bodies, policy makers, mental health educators, graduate students, and the public. A variety of research designs can help develop an evidence base concerning the effectiveness of mental health treatment (APA, Presidential Task Force on Evidence-Based Practice, 2006), including qualitative research, systematic case studies, single-case experimental designs, PBE designs, process-outcome studies, randomized clinical trials (RCTs), and meta-analytic reviews (APA, 2006). We think all of these research designs can help contribute to the evidence base about spiritually integrated psychotherapies.

One research design that we think can make especially valuable contributions to the evidence base about SIPs are PBE studies (Barkham et al., 2010; Castonguay et al., 2013). PBE designs are significantly different from the traditional RCTs but are complementary (Barkham et al., 2010). PBE studies focus on collecting data in a naturalistic setting that significantly increases their generalizability, a significant limitation of RCTs. In PBE studies, therapists do not have to follow a treatment manual or protocol but conduct treatment "as normal." In other words, they do not change how they normally practice psychotherapy, with the exception that they are asked to engage in routine outcome measurement to monitor therapist processes and client outcomes on a regular basis (e.g., every session) during the course of treatment (Barkham et al., 2010; Castonguay et al., 2013). Additional research designs can be combined within framework of PBE designs, if desired, including qualitative studies, systematic case studies, process studies, and even RCTs (Barkham et al., 2010). We think that PBE designs have much potential for providing rich insight into the processes and outcomes of SIPs (Richards et al., 2015).

Engage in Interdisciplinary Collaboration

Research studies that are read only by researchers will not change mental health practice. If practitioners help design and conduct the research studies, they will be more invested in sharing and implementing the findings because the studies will be more relevant to their work.

We also believe it is crucial to collaborate with mental health educators. By including mental health educators, we will ensure that training programs and CE opportunities are of higher quality and more widely available. Future generations of practitioners will have more opportunities to receive training about spiritual aspects of diversity and treatment so that these important issues are never again neglected in the mental health professions.

We also believe it is crucial to collaborate with clergy and other pastoral professionals. Clergy, chaplains, and pastoral counselors are frontline mental health workers in the sense that many people struggling with psychological and relationship problems first go to them for help (VanderWaal et al., 2012). Collaborating with clergy and pastoral professionals in research, training, and practice will enrich the field of SIP by making it more religiously and spiritually sensitive and relevant to the many people in the world who approach life from a religious and/or spiritual framework.

Use Technology Effectively

We think it is essential to use technology effectively to enhance collaboration, research, training, and practice delivery. The internet, video conferencing, mental health apps, smartphones, social media, and other technologies are expanding the public's access to mental health services and thus changing the way such services are provided and—hopefully—enhancing the effectiveness of treatment. Practitioners, supervisors, and educators who provide SIP services and training in these approaches also need to leverage modern technologies to enhance their effectiveness and increase the public's access to spiritually integrated treatment.

Seek Media Coverage

We believe it is crucial to use all forms of available media to inform and influence the public and professionals about the availability and effectiveness of spiritually integrated treatment approaches, including print, video, online, social media, radio, and television. By helping the public understand that spiritually sensitive and effective approaches to mental health care treatment are available, this will help increase the public demand for such services. As the public increasingly expects and demands access to these approaches, this will increase pressure on practitioners, educators and supervisors, accreditation bodies, and health care policy makers to ensure that such services are provided.

Educate Leaders

We think it is essential to educate leaders of accrediting bodies, licensing boards, health care insurance companies, religious organizations, and political parties about the need for spiritually competent mental health treatment. Current deficiencies and barriers to professional training in this domain also need to be confronted and corrected. Intervening systemically with leaders and organizations is challenging and not part of normal training for most mental health professionals, but many resources and professionals exist that can assist in this effort. As the evidence base supporting the effectiveness of spiritually integrated treatment approaches grows, and as training opportunities increase and more practitioners gain expertise, this will give researchers, practitioners, educators, and pastoral professionals credibility and leverage to influence leaders and organizations.

CONCLUSION

The spiritual lives of patients seeking help are just as important to them as their physical, mental, emotional, and relational lives. They want to be viewed, considered, and treated as whole individuals, and they deserve nothing less from professional psychotherapy providers. The inclusion of the spiritual in psychotherapy matters. We invite all mental health providers to consider their own spiritual beliefs and the potential negative impact and positive impact of those beliefs on clients. This work requires much self-awareness, self-honesty, and cultural sensitivity. We invite mental health providers to find their own way to include spirituality in helping themselves and in their efforts to help others.

Bringing spiritually integrated treatment approaches more fully into the mental health mainstream will require planning and effort by many professionals in the coming years. We acknowledge this need and invite researchers, academics, and mental health providers to continue the important work of research in the role of spirituality in psychotherapy and healing. We call on researchers and clinicians to continue to work together in cross collaboration so that the research–practice gap can be closed through implementation of study findings into clinical practice.

We are deeply involved in, and support, APA's (2006) evidence-based practice guidelines that affirm the value of clinical experience and a variety of research designs for advancing the field and improving treatment outcomes (Barkham et al., 2021; Richards et al., 2015). We invite others to collaborate with us in this effort so that we all might learn together, elevate the quality of treatment, and bless the lives of the souls we are honored to serve.

REFERENCES

ACPE. (n.d.). *About ACPE*. https://acpe.edu/about-acpe

American Psychological Association, Presidential Task Force on Evidence-Based Practice. (2006). Evidence-based practice in psychology. *American Psychologist, 61*(4), 271–285. https://doi.org/10.1037/0003-066X.61.4.271

Barkham, M., Hardy, G. E., & Mellor-Clark, J. (Eds.). (2010). *Developing and delivering practice-based evidence: A guide for the psychological therapies*. Wiley-Blackwell. https://doi.org/10.1002/9780470687994

Barkham, M., Lutz, W., & Castonguay, L. G. (2021). *Bergin and Garfield's handbook of psychotherapy and behavior change* (7th ed.). John Wiley & Sons.

Castonguay, L., Barkham, M., Lutz, W., & McAleavey, A. (2013). Practice-oriented research: Approaches and Applications. In M. J. Lambert (Ed.), *Bergin and Garfield's handbook of psychotherapy and behavior change* (6th ed., pp. 85–133). John Wiley & Sons.

Oxhandler, H. K., Parrish, D. E., Torres, L. R., & Achenbaum, W. A. (2015). The integration of clients' religion and spirituality in social work practice: A national survey. *Social Work, 60*(3), 228–237. https://doi.org/10.1093/sw/swv018

Pargament, K. I. (2007). *Spiritually integrated psychotherapy: Understanding and addressing the sacred*. Guilford Press.

Pearce, M. J., Pargament, K. I., Oxhandler, H. K., Vieten, C., & Wong, S. (2019). A novel training program for mental health providers in religious and spiritual competencies. *Spirituality in Clinical Practice, 6*(2), 73–82. https://doi.org/10.1037/scp0000195

Pearce, M. J., Pargament, K. I., Oxhandler, H. K., Vieten, C., & Wong, S. (2020). Novel online training program improves spiritual competencies in mental health care. *Spirituality in Clinical Practice*, 7(3), 145–161. https://doi.org/10.1037/scp0000208

Puchalski, C. M., & Larson, D. B. (1998). Developing curricula in spirituality and medicine. *Academic Medicine*, 73(9), 970–974. https://doi.org/10.1097/00001888-199809000-00015

Puchalski, C. M., Larson, D. B., & Lu, F. G. (2001). Spirituality in psychiatry residency training programs. *International Review of Psychiatry*, 13(2), 131–138. https://doi.org/10.1080/09540260124071

Richards, P. S., Sanders, P. W., Lea, T., McBride, J. A., & Allen, G. E. K. (2015). Bringing spiritually oriented psychotherapies into the health care mainstream: A call for worldwide collaboration. *Spirituality in Clinical Practice*, 2(3), 169–179. https://doi.org/10.1037/scp0000082

Russell, S. R., & Yarhouse, M. A. (2006). Training in religion/spirituality within APA-accredited psychology predoctoral internships. *Professional Psychology: Research and Practice*, 37(4), 430–436. https://doi.org/10.1037/0735-7028.37.4.430

Schafer, R. M., Handal, P. J., Brawer, P. A., & Ubinger, M. (2011). Training and education in religion/spirituality within APA-accredited clinical psychology programs: 8 years later. *Journal of Religion and Health*, 50(2), 232–239. https://doi.org/10.1007/s10943-009-9272-8

Society for the Psychology of Religion and Spirituality, Division 36. (n.d.). *Information on undergraduate and graduate programs with some focus on religion*. American Psychological Association. https://www.apadivisions.org/division-36/leadership/task-forces/student/graduate-programs

VanderWaal, C. J., Hernandez, E. I., & Sandman, A. R. (2012). The gatekeepers: Clergy involvement in referrals and collaboration with mental health and substance abuse professionals. *Social Work & Christianity*, 39(1), 27–51.

Vieten, C., Scammell, S., Pierce, A., Pilato, R., Ammondson, I., Pargament, K. I., & Lukoff, D. (2016). Competencies for psychologists in the domains of religion and spirituality. *Spirituality in Clinical Practice*, 3(2), 92–114. https://doi.org/10.1037/scp0000078

Vieten, C., Scammell, S., Pilato, R., Ammondson, I., Pargament, K. I., & Lukoff, D. (2013). Spiritual and religious competencies for psychologists. *Psychology of Religion and Spirituality*, 5(3), 129–144. https://doi.org/10.1037/a0032699

Vogel, M. J., McMinn, M. R., Peterson, M. A., & Gathercoal, K. A. (2013). Examining religion and spirituality as diversity training: A multidimensional look at training in the American Psychological Association. *Professional Psychology: Research and Practice*, 44(3), 158–167. https://doi.org/10.1037/a0032472

INDEX

A

AAPC (American Association of Pastoral Counselors), 432–433
ABCDE method, 174
ABC model, 174
ABCs of understanding forgiveness, 396–397
Aboulafia, Michael Binyamin, 273–274
Aboulafia Institute, 274
Absolutism
    and rational emotive behavior therapy, 174–176
    in religion, 178
Abuse
    anger and forgiveness following, 396
    prayer in Jewish psychotherapy for, 279
    spirituality in treatment approaches for, 113
    and spiritual struggles, 123, 128
Acceptance
    self-. *See* Self-acceptance
    in spiritually inclusive theistic treatment, 137
    of spiritual struggles, facilitating, 127
ACPE: The Standard for Spiritual Care & Education, 432
ACPE Spiritually Integrated Psychotherapy (SIP) program, 432–437
Adams, J., 349
Adaptive rational beliefs. *See* Rational beliefs (rBs)
Advanced Training in Spiritually Integrated Psychotherapy (ATSIP), 439–441

Affirming faith, 147
African American approach to psychotherapy, 6
African approach to psychotherapy, 6, 253, 260
Aggressive drives, 197, 198
Ainsworth, M. D., 58, 59, 60
Al-Bajuri, I., 198
Al-Balkhi, Abu Zayd, 202
Albert Ellis Institute, 173
The Albert & Jessie Danielsen Institute, 79, 81
Al-Ghazālā, Imam, 198
Al-Ghazali, A. H., 200, 202, 204
Ali Thanwi, Ashraf, 199
Al-Razi, Abu Bakr, 202
Al-Suhrawardi, S., 198, 200
American Association of Christian Counselors, 352–353, 360
American Association of Pastoral Counselors (AAPC), 432–433
American Psychiatric Association, 326, 373
American Psychological Association (APA), 109, 432
    APA Handbook of Psychology, Religion, and Spirituality, 6
    Ellis–Bergin debate before, 175, 177
    evidence-based practice guidelines of, 446
Angel, Clyde, 382, 396–397
Angelic drives, 197, 198

Anger
  anger management vs. anger resolution, 391–392
  and forgiveness, 396
  roots of, 393–394
Angha, Nader, 286, 288–289, 296
Angha, Sadegh, 287, 292
Anxiety(-ies)
  guilty, 179
  prayer practices for, 255
  REACH Forgiveness for, 373
  and religion/spirituality, 213
  and spiritual struggles, 123
  surface anxieties and depth anxieties, 85–86
Anxious attachment to God, 63–65
Aotearoa New Zealand, 326
APA. *See* American Psychological Association
APA Handbook of Psychology, Religion, and Spirituality (Sperry), 6
'Aql, 198
Argyle, M., 61
Arthur Kill Correctional Facility, 233
Asian approach to psychotherapy
  among Catholics, 253, 260
  spiritually integrated psychotherapy for East Asians, 319–320. *See also* Christian-Based Spiritually Integrated Psychotherapy for East Asians Research Initiative of Toronto (CSPEARIT)
Assessment
  Bridges system for, 442, 443
  in Christian-Based Spiritually Integrated Psychotherapy for East Asians Research Initiative of Toronto, 309–310
  in culturally informed therapy for schizophrenia, 37
  in Gestalt Pastoral Care, 238
  in Gospel-centered integrative framework for therapy, 216–217
  in hope-focused couple approach, 357
  in Multicultural Orientation framework, 408–409, 414
  in REACH Forgiveness, 372–373
  in relational spirituality model, 83–85
  with religious clients in rational emotive behavior therapy, 177
  in spiritually inclusive theistic treatment, 138, 150–151
  in spiritually integrated couples therapy, 354
  in spiritually integrated psychotherapy among Catholics, 254
  of spiritual struggles, 125–126
  in traditional Islamically integrated psychotherapy, 195, 201

Association for the Advancement of Gestalt Therapy, 110
ATG. *See* Attachment to God
Atheism, 3
ATSIP (Advanced Training in Spiritually Integrated Psychotherapy), 439–441
Attachment style
  in attachment theory, 58–59
  and attachment to God, 63–64
  changes in, 66–67
  and conduct disorder, 112
  and individuals' images of God, 216
  and relational development, 85, 86, 88
  religious beliefs and experiences related to, 64–65
Attachment system, 58
  activation of, 60–61
  assessment of, 83
  in relational spirituality model, 80, 88
Attachment theory, 57–58
  applied to psychotherapy, 66–67
  and psychology of religion, 216
  secure attachment in, 58–59
Attachment to God (ATG), 57–72
  and application of attachment theory to psychotherapy, 66–67
  and attachment style, 63–64
  case example of, 67–71
  and compensation pathway, 65–66
  and conduct disorder, 112
  and correspondence pathway, 64–65
Avarice, 196
Avoidant attachment to God, 63–66
Awaad, R., 20
Awfulizing
  as absolutistic, 175
  and rational emotive behavior therapy, 180
  scripture countering, 178, 179
Ayazi, M., 288
Ayvaci, E. R., 35

B

Bahadorani, N., 22
Balance, as goal of traditional Islamically integrated psychotherapy, 202–203
"Baptized" secular couples therapy, 350
Bar-Yoseph Levine, T., 99
Basic emotions (ihsas), in traditional Islamically integrated psychotherapy, 198, 199
Baucom, D. H., 377
Beal, D., 181
Beck, R., 63–64
Behavioral activation, 41
Behavioral change, in Gospel-centered integrative framework for therapy, 220

Behavioral health, and religion/spirituality, 34
Behavioral inclination (nafs), in traditional Islamically integrated psychotherapy, 198–199
Being, doing vs., 390
Beit-Hallahmi, B., 61
Belief(s)
 and attachment style, 64–65
 behavior vs., in Judaism, 268
 of being loved by God, 215
 cultural, 405
 in Indigenous peoples' spirituality, 338
 maladaptive irrational and adaptive rational, 173–176
 in religiosity gap, 35
 respect for and inclusive work with, 136–138
 SERT, 80, 81
 understanding, in culturally informed therapy, 44
Belief systems, types of, 406
Benda, B. B., 377
Benjamin, J., 86
Bergin, Allen, 175, 177
Biases, of clinicians, 170, 171
Bible
 Ellis on, 178
 emotion management concepts/principles from, 316, 317
 Gestalt Pastoral Care concepts from, 235, 236
 Gospel-centered integrative framework for therapy concepts from, 215, 219–221
 on human-level work, 366
 on Jesus' healing ministry, 236
 meditating on, 162–163
Bible Therapy, 278
Biblical counseling view, in Christian spiritually integrated psychotherapy, 349
Bio-psycho-social-spiritual models of treatment, 231, 381, 399
Birgegard, A., 61, 62, 65
Björgvinsson, Thröstur, 158
Blessed Are the Crazy (Lund), 36
Bloom, Dan, 102
Bockrath, M. F., 124
Body
 being present in the, 233
 and Ontological Model of the Human Psyche, 196, 198
 as quasithing, 105, 106
 in Sufism's physical dimension, 288–289
Book of Mormon, 179–181, 184
Bordin, E. S., 82
Boundaries, maintaining, 397
Bowlby, J., 58–61, 65, 67, 70, 216

Bozorgzadeh, S., 15–22, 296
Brave Heart, M. Y. H., 332
Breathing exercises, in Tamarkoz method, 295–296
Bridges assessment system, 442, 443
Bridges Consortium
 Gestalt Pastoral Care grant from, 245
 SPIRIT study funded by, 160, 167
Bridges Consortium for Spiritually Integrated Psychotherapy, Christian-based spiritually integrated psychotherapy in Canada and, 301
Bridges Institute for Spiritually Integrated Psychotherapies
 formation, 442
 goal of, 442, 443
 and Jewish psychotherapy in Israel, 271
 mission of, 443
 practice-research-training network, 442–443
 practice-research-training network of, 441–442
Brigham Young University (BYU)
 Bridges Consortium at, 245
 Bridges practice-research-training network at, 441–442
 Counseling and Psychology Services at, 179, 187–188
 Enhancing Practice-Based Evidence for Spiritually Integrated Psychotherapies, 398
 rational emotive behavior therapy at, 177, 180–186
 research studies at, 154
 think tank at, 441
Brown, C. A., 16
Brownell, P., 99, 101, 103
Buddhism, 3
Buddhist approach to psychotherapy, 6, 100
Buddhist mindfulness-based stress reduction and meditation, 113
Bugeja, T., 111
Building Spiritual Strength programs, 113
Building trust, in Search for Meaning program, 388–390
Burns, D., 316
BYU. *See* Brigham Young University

C

Campos, A. F., 111
Canada
 minority groups in, 301–302
 psychotherapy for East Asians in. *See* Christian-Based Spiritually Integrated Psychotherapy for East Asians Research Initiative of Toronto (CSPEARIT)
Cancer, 113, 121, 296

Case conceptualization, in traditional Islamically integrated psychotherapy, 205–206
Caspi, Yair, 273
Catholic Church, healing ministries in, 249
Catholics
 cultural diversity among, 252–253
 spiritually integrated psychotherapy among. *See* Spiritually integrated psychotherapy among Catholics (SIP-C)
CBT. *See* Cognitive behavior therapy
Center for Change, 153
CE opportunities. *See* Continuing education opportunities
Challenges, to mainstream implementation of spiritually integrated psychotherapies, 14
Chen, E. C., 20, 221–222
Child abuse
 anger and forgiveness following, 396
 and spiritual struggles, 123
Chinese Christian churches, 302
Chittister, J. D., 124
Christian approach to psychotherapy, 6, 349. *See also individual approaches*
Christian Association for Psychological Studies, 352–353
Christian-Based Spiritually Integrated Psychotherapy for East Asians Research Initiative of Toronto (CSPEARIT), 301–322
 assessment guidelines and recommendations for, 309–310
 case studies of, 312–318
 collaboration with clergy in, 311–312
 development of, 302–303
 diversity considerations in, 308
 intervention strategies and techniques in, 310–311
 need for, 301–302
 process and ethical guidelines for, 306–308
 relationship establishment guidelines or guiding principles for, 308–309
 research findings support for, 318–321
 theoretical and theological foundations of, 305–306
 treatment settings benefiting from, 303–304
 types of clients and clinical issues for, 304–305
Christian counseling, psychological distress and religious coping and, 113
Christianity, 3, 113
Christian psychology view, in Christian spiritually integrated psychotherapy, 349
CIT. *See* Culturally informed therapy
CIT-S (culturally informed therapy for), 37, 38

Clergy
 couples' choice of secular counselors vs., 348
 Gospel-centered integrative framework for therapy training for, 220–221
 mental health care from, 35–36
 mental health training for, 36
 need for collaboration with, 35. *See also* Collaboration
 personal counseling or psychotherapy for, 311
 referrals to mental health specialists by, 40
 sexual abuse by, 123
Clergy in Crisis program, 86–87
Clinicians. *See* Therapists
Coates, J., 337
Cognition ('aql), in traditional Islamically integrated psychotherapy, 198
Cognitive behavior strategies, in culturally informed therapy, 42
Cognitive behavior therapy (CBT)
 rational emotive behavior therapy as, 173. *See also* Rational emotive behavior therapy (REBT)
 SPIRIT protocol as. *See* SPIRIT (spiritual psychotherapy for inpatient, residential, and intensive treatment)
Cognitive restructuring, 161–162
Coleman, J., 25
Collaboration
 and boundaries in traditional Islamically integrated psychotherapy, 195
 in Christian-Based Spiritually Integrated Psychotherapy for East Asians Research Initiative of Toronto, 311–312
 in contemporary gestalt therapy, 105–106
 in culturally informed therapy, 35–36, 40–41
 in forgiveness, 366
 in Gestalt Pastoral Care, 241
 interdisciplinary, 444–445
 in Multicultural Orientation framework, 411–412
 in REACH Forgiveness, 374
 in relational spirituality model, 82, 86–87
 in religious/spiritual interventions, 35–36
 in spiritually integrated couples therapy, 355
 in spiritually integrated psychotherapy among Catholics, 253–254
Collective trauma, 332
Collectivism module, in culturally informed therapy, 42–43
College of Registered Psychotherapists of Ontario (CRPO), 306, 310

College students, spiritual struggles of, 121, 124, 128
Combat trauma, spirituality in treatment approaches for, 113. *See also* Search for Meaning program
Communication
　in culturally informed therapy, 45
　of divine grace, in Catholicism, 255
　in hope-focused couple approach, 357
　between religious and mental health providers, 39–40, 412
Community
　Islam's emphasis on, 204
　REACH forgiveness in, 371
Compassion, 289, 292
Compensation hypothesis, 65
Compensation pathway, 64–66
Competence/competency
　cultural, spirituality and religion as aspect of, 171
　diversity, 82, 83
　gaining, 8–9
　spiritual, graduate coursework in, 424–426
　spiritual, online program fostering, 129
　spiritual and religious, for mental health professionals, 427–430
　for spiritually inclusive psychotherapy, 139, 140
　in spiritually integrated couple therapy, 353
　training opportunities to develop, 14. *See also* Training
Complicated grief, 395
Conceptualization, in research, 329–330
Conduct disorder, 112
Confucianism, 3
Conscientization, in research, 329–330
Consenting to Grace (Norberg), 232
Contemporary gestalt therapy, 101–107
　experimental collaboration in, 105–106
　field perspective in, 104–105
　hermeneutic phenomenology in, 102–103
　as postsecular approach, 100, 106–107. *See also* Postsecular, spiritually integrated gestalt therapy
　relational process in, 103–104
Contextual model of therapy, 406
Continuing education (CE) opportunities, 426–443
　ACPE Spiritually Integrated Psychotherapy program, 432–437
　Bridges Institute for Spiritually Integrated Psychotherapies practice-research-training network, 441–443
　Solihten Institute training program in SIP, 437–441
　Spiritual Competency Training in Mental Health online courses, 427–432

Coping
　adaptive and maladaptive, 36
　and attachment security, 58
　and injustice gap, 368
　religious, during stressful times, 61
　in SPIRIT protocol, 161, 162
　and spiritual/religious themes, 161
Coral Gables UCC, 39–42
Core hurts, in system of self-redemption, 217–218
Correctional facilities, 403. *See also* Multicultural Orientation (MCO) framework
　cultural norms in, 407–408
　religion/spirituality in, 403–404
Corrective emotional experience, in Gospel-centered integrative framework for therapy, 222
Correspondence pathway, 64–65
Counselors. *See* Therapists
Counterfeit gods, 214
Countertransference issues, 309
Couple(s) therapy
　in Christian-Based Spiritually Integrated Psychotherapy for East Asians Research Initiative of Toronto, 318
　competence in, 353
　emotion-focused, 350
　hope-focused couple approach, 351, 354, 355, 357–360
　REACH Forgiveness in, 370–371. *See also* REACH Forgiveness
　with relational spirituality model, 78
　religious differences in, 354
　spiritually integrated, 349–351. *See also* Spiritually integrated couples therapy (SICT)
Covenant Health, 398
Covey, Stephen R., 146
COVID-19 pandemic, 123, 181, 436
Coyle, A., 17
Crabb, Larry, 349
Creativity, 289
Criminal justice detention system
　individuals with mental illness in, 403
　religion/spirituality in, 403–404
　spiritually focused, multiculturally oriented psychotherapy in. *See* Multicultural Orientation (MCO) framework
Crocker, S. F., 111
CRPO (College of Registered Psychotherapists of Ontario), 306, 310
Crumpler, C., 15–22
CSPEARIT. *See* Christian-Based Spiritually Integrated Psychotherapy for East Asians Research Initiative of Toronto
Cultural comfort, 406, 409, 411

Cultural competency, spirituality and religion as aspect of, 171
Cultural diversity
  among Catholics, 252–253
  in psychotherapy for incarcerated individuals. *See* Multicultural Orientation (MCO) framework
  and REACH Forgiveness, 372
  of relational dynamics in therapy, 82–83
  in spiritual intervention uses, 259–261
Cultural humility, 404–405, 408–410
Culturally informed therapy (CIT), 33–51
  case example of, 46–50
  collectivism module in, 42–43
  communication module in, 45
  feedback on, 41, 50–51
  framework for, 37–38
  future directions for, 51
  modifications for, 39–42
  need for collaboration in, 35–36
  preliminary data on outcomes of, 50–51
  problem solving module in, 45–46
  psychoeducation module in, 43–44
  for schizophrenia, 34, 37, 38
  spirituality module in, 44
  strengths of, 50
  treatment modules in, 42–46
Culturally informed therapy for (CIT-S), 37, 38
Culturally sensitive/responsive treatment
  and attending to spiritual concerns, 113
  in Christian-Based Spiritually Integrated Psychotherapy for East Asians Research Initiative of Toronto, 308
  for Indigenous peoples, 325–326, 332. *See also* Polynesian psychotherapies
Cultural opportunities, 405, 409–411
Cummings, J. P., 17
Currier, J. M., 17

D

Dalai Lama, 146, 386
Danser, Don, 368
Decisional forgiveness, 368, 371
Decision-based forgiveness model, 377
Declarative knowledge, 221
Deficit-framed research reporting, 330–331
Definitive/certain knowledge, 194
Demanding
  as absolutistic, 175
  and rational emotive behavior therapy, 179
  scripture countering, 178, 179
Demonic struggles, 120
Depression
  benefits of volunteerism for, 41–42
  prayer practices for, 255
  REACH Forgiveness for, 373
  and religion/spirituality, 213
  and spiritual struggles, 121, 123
  Tamarkoz method for, 296
Depth anxieties, 85, 86
Depth of wounding, 384
Despair, 214
Devotional practices, 252
Diagnostic and Statistical Manual of Mental Disorders (*DSM*; American Psychiatric Association), 326, 373
Dialectics
  in Jewish psychotherapies in Israel, 272–275, 280
  in relational spirituality model, 93–94
  in spiritually integrated psychotherapy among Catholics, 251, 259
DiBlasio, F. A., 368, 377
Dickie, G., 64
Dietz, Christine, 440
Difference, as diversity, 109–110
Differentiation system
  assessment of, 83–84
  in relational spirituality model, 80–81, 89–91
DiGiuseppe, Ray, 173
Disconnectedness, spiritual wounding and, 385–386
Dismissing attachment, 58–59
Disorganized attachment, 59, 80
Disputing maladaptive irrational beliefs, 175, 181, 182
Dissonance conflict, 394
Diversity
  among Catholics, 252–253
  in Christian-Based Spiritually Integrated Psychotherapy for East Asians Research Initiative of Toronto, 308
  in Gestalt Pastoral Care, 233, 237
  honoring, 137
  within Judaism, 268
  in postsecular, spiritually integrated gestalt therapy, 109–110
  racial and ethnic. *See* Multicultural Orientation (MCO) framework
  with REACH Forgiveness, 372
  in relational spirituality model, 81–83, 88
  religious, graduate coursework in, 424–426
  in SPIRIT study patients, 169
  spiritual, 3–4
  in spiritually inclusive theistic treatment, 136, 137
  in spiritually integrated couples therapy, 353–354
  of spiritual principles, 146
  in Sufi Psychology, 293
  of those experiencing spiritual struggles, 121
  in uses of spiritual intervention, 259–261

Divine calling, 250
Divine remembrance, 200
Divine spiritual struggles, 120, 162
Divine values, 251, 255
Doctrine and Covenants, 179, 180, 184
Doing, being vs., 390
Doubt-related struggles, 120
DSM (*Diagnostic and Statistical Manual of Mental Disorders*; American Psychiatric Association), 326, 373
Dual-factor mental health emphasis, 79
Dual-process self-forgiveness intervention, 368
Duggal, C., 17
Duke, Ellery, 440
Duran, E., 338
Dworsky, C. K. O., 18, 128

E

East Asians, spiritually integrated psychotherapy for, 319–320. *See also* Christian-Based Spiritually Integrated Psychotherapy for East Asians Research Initiative of Toronto
Eastern spiritual thought, in early gestalt therapy, 99–100
Educating leaders, 445
Effectiveness of treatment, with integrated spirituality, 8
EFT (emotionally focused therapy), 320
Electromagnetic forces, 292
Elkins, David N., 135
Ellis, Albert ("Al"), 173–175, 178, 188
Emotional bonds, in hope-focused couple approach, 358
Emotional experience
　corrective, in Gospel-centered integrative framework for therapy, 222
　self-defeating, absolutism in, 175, 176
　and therapy outcome, 188
Emotional forgiveness, 368
Emotional health
　ABCDE method for, 174
　as goal of spiritually inclusive theistic treatment, 137
　prayer practices for, 255
　and religion/spirituality, 34
Emotionally focused therapy (EFT), 320
Emotion-focused coping, 368
Emotion-focused couple therapy, 350, 354, 355, 377
Emotions
　biblical concepts/principles for managing, 316, 317
　reactive, in system of self-redemption, 217
　in traditional Islamically integrated psychotherapy, 198, 199
　uncomfortable, avoiding, 407

Empirical knowledge, 194
Enhancing Practice-Based Evidence for Spiritually Integrated Psychotherapies, 398
Enlightenment, 101, 106
Enright, R. D., 373, 376–377
Enright, Robert, 369
Environmental concerns, in psychotherapy with Indigenous peoples, 338
Envy, 196
Epicureanism, 174
Epistemology, Islamic, 193–194
Ethical Principles of Psychologists and Code of Conduct (American Psychological Association), 109
　General Principle E of, 109
Ethics
　and attending to spiritual concerns, 113
　for Christian-Based Spiritually Integrated Psychotherapy for East Asians Research Initiative of Toronto, 306–308
　in Gestalt Pastoral Care, 236–237
　in Gospel-centered integrative framework for therapy, 227
　in postsecular, spiritually integrated gestalt therapy, 109–110
　in relational spirituality model, 81, 94–95
　in spiritually integrated couples therapy, 352–353
　in spiritually integrated psychotherapy among Catholics, 251–252
　virtue ethics model, 94–95
European approach to psychotherapy, among Catholics, 253, 260
European Association for Gestalt therapy, 110
Evangelical Christian spirituality, mindfulness and, 113
Evidence-based practice guidelines (APA), 446
Evidence base for spiritually integrated psychotherapies, 444
Existential dimension
　in relational spirituality model, 80, 85–86
　in spiritual struggles, 120
　in spiritual wounding, 383
Existential perspective, 3
　in gestalt therapy, 100
　in rational-emotive philosophy, 174
Exline, J. J., 13, 18, 125, 127–128
Expansion and Contraction Within Being (Angha), 296
Experiential approach, in gestalt therapy, 100
Experimental psychology, 285

Experiments
　in contemporary gestalt therapy, 105–106
　in Gestalt Pastoral Care, 239–240
Extended self, 103–104

F

Fachler, Michal, 273
Faith
　in Christian-Based Spiritually Integrated Psychotherapy for East Asians Research Initiative of Toronto, 307
　trust vs., 397
Faith healing, 406
Faith imagination, in Gestalt Pastoral Care, 236, 240
Family/family-focused therapy, 348
　with relational spirituality model, 78
　with schizophrenia, 35, 37
Farrell, J. L., 36
Fear, R., 9
Fertile void, 111
Field(s)
　defined, 104
　gestalt theories about and of, 104–105
　of patient–therapist, 106–107
　potential research on, 111
"Filter" model of integration, 349
Fincham, F. D., 350
Fitzgibbons, R. P., 373, 376–377
Five R's, in Gospel-centered integrative framework for therapy, 219–220
FLC (Tyndale Family Life Centre), 303
Following the heart, 144–145
Forgive for Good model, 377
Forgiveness
　in gestalt therapy, 112
　in hope-focused couple approach, 355, 358–359
　meditating on, 163
　psychotherapeutic benefits of, 289
　scripture on, 179
　in Search for Meaning program, 396–297
　in Sufi Psychology, 292
　theoretical framework for understanding, 367–368
　types of, 368
Forgiveness interventions
　efficacy of, 376–377
　REACH. *See* REACH Forgiveness
　targeted, 369
Forgiveness therapy, 369
The Four Agreements (Ruiz), 146
Four Levels of Spiritual Wounding, 383–384
Francesetti, G., 99, 104, 105
Freedom to sin, 179
From, Isadore, 99

Frustration tolerance
　as absolutistic, 175
　and rational emotive behavior therapy, 180
　in scripture, 179
Fung, W. L. A., 23
Fusion of horizons, 103

G

Gestalt-consilient research, 111
Gestalt experiments, 239–240
Gestalt-hybrid research, 111
Gestalt Pastoral Care (GPC), 231–247
　assessment guidelines for, 238
　avoidance of analysis and interpretations in, 235
　case study of, 242–244
　collaboration with clergy in, 241
　diversity considerations in, 237
　ethical guidelines in, 236–237
　experiments in, 239–240
　faith imagination in, 240
　history of, 232
　intervention strategies and techniques in, 238–241
　personalized healing liturgies in, 240–241
　relationship establishment guidelines for, 237–238
　research findings and support for, 244–246
　theoretical and theological foundations for, 234–236
　treatment settings for, 232–233
　types of clients and clinical issues in, 233–234
Gestalt Pastoral Care Associates, 232, 233, 235, 237
Gestalt Reconsidered (Wheeler), 104
Gestalt-specific research, 111
Gestalt therapy, 99–101
　contemporary, 99, 101–107. *See also* Contemporary gestalt therapy
　current tensions within, 100–101
　Enlightenment thinking vs., 106
　forgiveness in, 112
　growth work in, 234–235
　as hermeneutic approach, 102
　as holistic approach, 234–235
　as humanistic, experiential approach, 100
　integration of spirituality with, 99–100. *See also* Postsecular, spiritually integrated gestalt therapy
　levels of research relevant to, 111
　as nonpathologizing modality, 238
　in pastoral care. *See* Gestalt Pastoral Care (GPC)

as phenomenological approach, 102, 103, 106, 235
spirituality in, 111
traditional vs. postsecular, spiritually integrated, 107
GHC. *See* Grace Health Centre
GIFT. *See* Gospel-centered integrative framework for therapy
Gillon, A., 329
God(s)
attachment to. *See* Attachment to God (ATG)
counterfeit, 214
divine remembrance of, 200
and forgiveness, 366–367
humans created in image of, 305
mental health and images of, 215–216, 255–256, 259
narrow representations of, 122–123
Protestant Christian concept of, 214–215
as safe haven, 60–61
as secure base, 61–62
terms referring to, 41
theistic religious conception of, 62
Goebert, D. A., 36
Gold, E., 99
Goldstein, Kurt, 104
Gonçalves, J. P., 34
Gospel-centered integrative framework for therapy (GIFT), 213–228
assessment in, 216–217
case study of, 224–227
clients' viability as candidates for, 216, 227, 228
empirical support for, 221–224
ethical considerations in, 227
intervention strategies and techniques in, 216–220
limitations of, 227–228
spiritual heart change process in, 218–220, 222
system of self-redemption in, 217–218
theological and psychological foundations of, 214–216
training clergy in, 220–221
GPC. *See* Gestalt Pastoral Care
Grace, 215, 220, 255, 355, 366
Grace Health Centre (GHC), 301, 302, 304. *See also* Christian-Based Spiritually Integrated Psychotherapy for East Asians Research Initiative of Toronto (CSPEARIT)
Graduate programs, 423–426
Granqvist, P., 59–62, 64–66, 71
Grasser, L. R., 22
Greenberg, L. S., 377
Grief
in Search for Meaning program, 395–396
unresolved, in spiritual wounding, 387

Griffin, B. J., 370
Griffin, Brandon, 368
Group therapy
in Christian-Based Spiritually Integrated Psychotherapy for East Asians Research Initiative of Toronto, 315–318
culturally informed therapy case example of, 46–50
Gestalt Pastoral Care in, 232
REACH Forgiveness in. *See* REACH Forgiveness
with relational spirituality model, 78
in Search for Meaning program, 381–399
SPIRIT protocol in, 157–171
Winding Road intervention in, 112, 128
Growth
emphasized in Gestalt Pastoral Care training, 232, 234
and self-transcendence, 251
and spiritually inclusive theistic treatment, 137, 142
from spiritual struggles, 124–125
Guilt
and rational emotive behavior therapy, 178–179
and REACH Forgiveness model, 370
in Search for Meaning program, 393–395
shame vs., 394
and spiritual wounding, 386–387
Gurak, K. K., 35, 38
Gurwitsch, A., 102
Gyalwa Rinpoche, 146

H

Hafner, Laurinda "Laurie," 39–41
Hagekull, B., 65–66
Halakha, 268, 269
Hall, A., 332
Hamlin, J. K., 197
Handbook of Religion and Health (Koenig), 33–34
Haque, A., 194–195
Harvard Medical School, 167
Hasidic Judaism, 279
Hau'Ofa, Epeli, 327, 330
Healing liturgies, in Gestalt Pastoral Care, 240–241
Healing prayer, in Gestalt Pastoral Care, 232, 236
Heart
following the, 144–145
in Ontological Model of the Human Psyche, 198
source of knowledge within, 288, 296. *See also* M.T.O. Sufi Psychology

spiritual heart change process in Gospel-centered integrative framework for therapy, 218–220, 222
  in Sufi Psychology, 289, 291
  in traditional Islamically integrated psychotherapy, 198, 200
Hedonistic drives, 197
Help-seeking process, 35
Henning-Geronasso, M. C., 111–112
Hermeneutic circle, 102
Hermeneutics, 102
Hindu approach to psychotherapy, 6
Hinduism, 3
Historical trauma, 331, 332
HIV/AIDS, spiritual struggles treatment and, 128
Hoedeman, Randy, 440
Holocaust survivors, 331, 332
Holy Spirit, 235, 255, 307, 366
Hook, J. N., 24, 360, 361
Ho'oponopono, 338
Hope, 289, 292
Hope-focused couple approach, 351, 354, 355, 357–360, 368
Horizons, in phenomenology, 103
Human divine subtle essence, 198
Humanistic perspective, 3
  in gestalt therapy, 100
  true self in, 310
Human psyche
  discernment of good and evil movements in, 259
  understanding, 285
Human Psyche, Ontological Model of the, 196–200
Human rating
  and rational emotive behavior therapy, 175, 180–181
  scripture countering, 178, 179
Human Rights Act (Canada), 308
Hurdle, D. E., 338
Hurihuri o Whakaaro me te Mahi: Transforming Thinking and Doing, 331
Hycner, R., 112
Hyperreligiosity, 161

I

iBs. *See* Irrational beliefs
Identity(-ies)
  collectivist vs. individualist, 42–43, 45–46
  in cultural humility, 404–405
  of educated people in the Pacific, 330
  Jewish, 268–270
  in M.T.O. Sufi Psychology, 286, 288, 289
  Polynesian, 326–329
  religious. *See* Religious identity/affiliation
  religious and spiritual beliefs integral to, 33
  spiritual, in Gospel-centered integrative framework for therapy, 217, 224
  spiritual beliefs and values tied to, 137. *See also* Religion/spirituality (R/S)
  in Sufi Psychology, 290
  in Sufism, 287
  of therapists, 407
Idolatrous strategies, in system of self-redemption, 218
Idols, 215, 219
Ignatius of Loyola, 249, 259
Ihsas, 198, 199
Incarcerated individuals, therapy with. *See* Multicultural Orientation (MCO) framework
Indiana University, 398
Indigenous peoples
  demand for mental health treatment interventions for, 326
  healing and liberation methodologies of, 329
  of the Pacific. *See* Polynesian psychotherapies
  spirituality for, 338
  storytelling among, 330
  traditions of, 3
Indigenous South Africans, 338
Individual therapy
  in Christian-Based Spiritually Integrated Psychotherapy for East Asians Research Initiative of Toronto, 312–314, 318
  Gestalt Pastoral Care in, 232
  REACH Forgiveness in. *See* REACH Forgiveness
  with relational spirituality model, 78
  for schizophrenia, 37
Infants
  attachment in, 216
  prosocial behaviors of, 197
  traumatized, 59
Injustice gap, 367–368
Institute of Psychology, Pontifical Gregorian University, 249–250
Integration view, in Christian spiritually integrated psychotherapy, 349
Integrity, 146–148
Interdisciplinary collaboration, 444–445
Intergenerational trauma, 332
Interpersonal struggles, 120, 162
Intersectionality theories, 406–407
Intersubjectivity system
  assessment of, 84
  in relational spirituality model, 81, 91–93
Interventions
  in Christian-Based Spiritually Integrated Psychotherapy for East Asians Research Initiative of Toronto, 318–319

culturally adapted, 37. *See also* Culturally informed therapy (CIT)
encouragement of forgiveness as, 112
in Gestalt Pastoral Care, 238–241
in Gospel-centered integrative framework for therapy, 214, 216–220
for historical trauma, 332
internet-based, 367
in Jewish psychotherapies in Israel, 271, 276–280
in M.T.O. Sufi Psychology, 292
in Multicultural Orientation framework, 409–411
in Polynesian psychotherapies, 338
in psychotherapy, 148, 149
in REACH Forgiveness, 367, 373
in relational spirituality model, 84–86
religious or spiritual, effect of therapist R/S on, 321
in Search for Meaning program, 387–398
in spiritually inclusive theistic treatment, 138, 140–145, 147–149, 151–152
in spiritually integrated couples therapy, 354–355
in spiritually integrated psychotherapy among Catholics, 254–256, 259–261
for spiritual struggles, 112, 128
as techniques, 106
that focus on religion/spirituality, 34–36
in traditional Islamically integrated psychotherapy, 203, 206–208
using terms "practice" or "invitation" in place of, 238
Intrapersonal struggles, 162
Intrapsychic struggles, 120
Intrinsic religiosity, 61
Irrational beliefs (iBs)
absolutism in, 174–176
finding rational antidotes to, 178
in rational emotive behavior therapy, 173, 174
religion as activating event for, 177–179
techniques for disputing, 181, 182
Islam, 3. *See also* Muslims
emphasis on community in, 204
Sufism in, 286–288, 293
Islamically integrated psychotherapy. *See* Traditional Islamically integrated psychotherapy (TIPP)
Islamic epistemology, 193–194
Islamic Sufism, 286–288, 293. *See also* M.T.O. Sufi Psychology
Israel
intertwining of state and religion in, 269
Jewish identities in, 268–270
New Age phenomena in, 269–270
religious identities in, 274–275
spiritually integrated psychotherapy in. *See* Jewish psychotherapies in Israel

J

Jacobs, L., 103, 110
Jacques, J. R., 66
Jain, S., 388
Jainism, 3
James, William, 199
Jankowski, P. J., 17
Jealousy, 196
Jensen, M. L., 78–79
Jesus (Christ)
gift of, 215
healing ministry of, 236
pastoral care rooted in ministry of, 232
spiritual disciplines of, 107
Jewish approach to psychotherapy, 6
Jewish identities, 268–270
Jewish psychotherapies in Israel, 267–281
attitude of universalism in, 275–276
case studies of, 276–280
field of, 270
founders of main schools of, 272–274
future research directions for, 281
heterogeneous religious identity in, 274–275
insights from research on, 274–280
integration of Jewish spirituality in, 274–275
and Jewish identities in Israel, 268–270
and Jewish religious tradition, 258
Jewish-spiritual tools used in, 276–280
mixed-methods research on, 270–272, 274–281
John of the Cross, St., 62
Johnson, Brad, 177
Johnson, E. L., 349
Johnson, Percy, 440
John Templeton Foundation, 14–15
Bridges Consortium SPIRIT project funded by, 160, 167
Bridges grant from, 442
CSPEARIT study funded by, 318
culturally informed therapy project funded by, 39
Enhancing Practice-Based Evidence for Spiritually Integrated Psychotherapies, 398
Gestalt Pastoral Care study funded by, 245
Spiritual and Religious Competences Project grant from, 424–426
Sufi Psychology study grant from, 29
Jones, Russell Siler, 436–437, 440
Jubis, R., 64
Judaism, 3, 268
divisions within, 268–269
Hasidic, 279
New Age phenomena in, 269–270
religious tradition in, 258

Justice
and forgiveness, 367–368
in kingdom of God, 250
in Polynesian psychotherapies, 338, 339
in relational spirituality model, 81–82, 88

K

Kaiser Permanente Hospital, 296
Keller, T., 214
Kennedy, D., 111
Keshavarzi, H., 10–20, 194–195
Khaldun, Ibn, 204
Khalil Center, New York, 195
Kim, E. E., 20, 221–222
Kincheloe, J. L., 194
Kirchmann, H., 66
Kirkpatrick, L. A., 59–61, 63–65, 216
Koenig, H. G., 33–34, 304, 305
Kopec, A. M., 181
Korean Christian churches, 302, 303
Kōrerotia, 328–329
Kornfield, J., 127
Kraft, S. E., 338
Krumrei, E. J., 36
Kübler-Ross, Elisabeth, 395
Kupor, D. M., 62
Kymalainen, J. A., 45

L

Latin American approach to psychotherapy, among Catholics, 252–253, 260
Latter-day Saints, 154, 177, 179–188
Lavelock Bratney, Caroline, 368
Lawson-Te Aho, K., 328, 338–339
Lea, T., 18
Leaders, educating, 445
Lee, R. G., 104
Lee, Samuel, 437
Levels-of-explanation view, in Christian spiritually integrated psychotherapy, 349
Levy, K. N., 66
Lewin, Kurt, 104
Lewis, C. S., 100
Licensing, 14
Life events, spiritual struggles and, 123
Lin, Y., 372
Linehan, M. M., 316
Listening
in Polynesian psychotherapy, 336
in spiritually inclusive theistic treatment, 144–145
Liturgies, in Gestalt Pastoral Care, 240–241
Liu, J. H., 339
Living Water Counselling Centre (LWCC), 301, 302, 304. See also Christian-Based Spiritually Integrated Psychotherapy for East Asians Research Initiative of Toronto (CSPEARIT)
Lomax, J. W., 123
Love
and forgiveness, 396
of God, 215, 219, 222
psychotherapeutic benefits of, 289
from spiritual communities, 219
in spiritually inclusive theistic approach, 147, 149
Lurianic Kabbalah, 272, 273
Luskin, F. M., 377
LWCC. See Living Water Counselling Centre

M

Mainstream psychotherapy
challenges of implementing spiritual approaches in, 14
spiritual approaches integrated in, 6
Maktab Tarighat Oveyssi Shahmaghsoudi, 286n1. See also M.T.O. Sufi Psychology
Maladaptive irrational beliefs. See Irrational beliefs (iBs)
Malony, H. N., 321
Mantras, 390–391
Maori, 326–328, 332, 333, 338–339. See also Polynesian psychotherapies
Marriage, 347, 353
Marriage-like relationships, 347
Maura, J., 16
May, R. W., 350
McCullough, Mike, 368
McDonald, A., 63–64
McLaughlin, M., 42
McLaren, P., 194
McLean Hospital, 158–160, 163, 164, 167–168
McMinn, M. R., 349, 412
MCO framework. See Multicultural Orientation framework
Meaning
in Indigenous peoples' spirituality, 338
need for, 213
search for, 121–123. See also Search for Meaning program
ultimate, struggles of, 121
Meaning-focused coping, 368
Meaning making, spiritual wounding and, 385
Media coverage, seeking, 445
Medical/technology belief system, 406
Meditation
in Christian-Based Spiritually Integrated Psychotherapy for East Asians Research Initiative of Toronto, 317
mindfulness-based, 113
neurobiological effects of, 199–200
in SPIRIT protocol, 162–163

in spiritually integrated psychotherapy among Catholics, 255
in Tamarkoz method, 295–296
Meditative approach to therapy, 15, 26
Menakem, Resmaa, 77, 78
Meneses, C. W., 377
Mental health
advanced by Muslim scholars, 193
Aotearoa New Zealand's inequities in, 328
of colonized and marginalized peoples, 331, 332
communication and self-assertiveness and, 45
correctional facilities services for, 403
culturally congruent treatment for Indigenous peoples, 325–326
dissemination of information on, 40
as goal of spiritually inclusive theistic treatment, 137
and God image/construct, 215–216
on health–wellness continuum in traditional Islamically integrated psychotherapy, 195, 196
help from clergy with, 35–36
and religion/spirituality, 33–34, 213
sacred moments promoting, 111
spirituality in, 231–232
and spiritual struggles, 123–125
Metaphysical heart (qalb), in traditional Islamically integrated psychotherapy, 198, 200
Mikahere-Hall, A., 327–328
Mikulincer, M., 66
Military service members, posttraumatic stress disorder in, 381
Mind–body synchronizations, 200
Mindfulness approach to therapy, 15, 26, 320
Mindfulness-based stress reduction and meditation approach, 113
Mindfulness exercises, in working with spiritual struggles, 127
Mission
of Bridges Institute for Spiritually Integrated Psychotherapies, 443
spiritual beliefs and values tied to, 137
Moana-nui-a-kiwa, 326–328
Modern/Zionist Orthodox Jews, 268, 269
Moen, T., 330
Mohammad, Prophet, 287
Mohammadi, M. R., 16, 66
Mohatt, N. V., 332
Mood disorders, spiritual struggles with, 121
Moral conflict, dissonance conflict vs., 394
Moral injury
concept of, 389–390
REACH Forgiveness with, 370
in Search for Meaning program, 393–395
and spiritual wounding, 386–387

Moral struggles, 120
Moré, C. L. O. O., 111–112
Morgan, R. D., 403
Movazeneh, 291, 295
M.T.O. Shahmaghsoudi School of Islamic Sufism, 286, 288, 291, 295
M.T.O. Sufi Psychology, 285–297
case illustration of, 293–294
diversity in, 293
and Islamic Sufism, 287–288
overview of, 288–289
process in, 290–292
research on, 295–296
Teacher and clinician in, 292–293
M.T.O. Tamarkoz, 295
Muhammad, Prophet, 196
Multicultural Orientation (MCO) framework, 403–418
assessment guidelines and recommendations for, 408–409
case study of, 412–416
collaborating with clergy in, 411–412
in criminal justice detention system, 403–418
future directions for, 418
intervention strategies and techniques in, 409–411
relationship establishment guidelines for, 408
research findings and support for, 416–418
Multigenerational trauma, 332
Murray-Swank, N. A., 18
Muslims
avoidance of psychotherapy services by, 112
psychotherapy approach of, 6. *See also* Traditional Islamically integrated psychotherapy (TIPP)
sources of knowledge for, 194
Mystical experiences, 199, 200, 252. *See also* M.T.O. Sufi Psychology

N

Nafs, 198–199
Naming spiritual struggles, 126–127
Nation, J. A., 367
Native American approach to psychotherapy, 6
Natural values, 251
Neff, M. A., 349
New Age spiritualities, 269–272, 274
New American Standard Bible, 107
New York Institute for Gestalt Therapy, 99
Nielsen, S. L., 19, 177, 178
Noller, P., 59
Noncorporeal attachment, 59–60
Nonreligious people, 3, 44
Norberg, T., 232, 233, 236, 238–241

Normalizing spiritual struggles, 126–127
Norms
  in correctional settings, 407–408
  pressure on therapists to conform to, 407
North Star, 291
Nouri, A., 294

O

Object relations theory, 215
O'Brien, M. E., 61
Ontical field, 105
Ontological Model of the Human Psyche, 196–200
Opening to Grace, 232, 241
Openness, in cultural humility, 404–405, 408
Organizational contexts of practice, 82
Original Sin, 215, 220
Orthodox Jews/Judaism, 269, 270, 273
Outcome research, 14
Owen, J., 404, 406

P

Pacifica mental health approaches/perspectives, 326
Pacific Islander approach to psychotherapy, 6. *See also* Polynesian psychotherapies
Paine, D. R., 17
Pargament, K. I., 13, 18, 61, 63, 111, 123, 125, 127–128, 158, 307, 377–378, 427, 438
Parlett, M., 104
Patchwork quilt integration, in couples therapy, 350–351
Paths of knowledge, in Caspi's approach, 273
PBE research. *See* Practice-based evidence research
Peace, in kingdom of God, 250
Pearce, M. J., 129, 424, 427, 431
The Pearl of Great Price, 179
Peck, M. Scott, 146
Perfectionism, 259
Perls, F. S., 99, 100, 234, 238
Perls, Laura, 99, 100
Permission, in spiritually inclusive theistic treatment, 143
Personal beliefs of therapist, staying true to, 9
Personalized healing liturgies, in Gestalt Pastoral Care, 240–241
Personhood, 305
Pew Research Center, 403–404
Phenomenological perspective, 102
  on fields, 104–105
  in gestalt therapy, 102, 103, 106–107, 235
  horizon in, 103

Philosophical perspective
  in gestalt therapy, 100
  in rational emotive behavior therapy, 174
Physical dimension of humans, in Sufism, 288–289
Physical health, religion/spirituality and, 33–34
Pickett, K. E., 328
Pitts, Carol, 440
Plante, T. G., 253
Politics of healing, in colonized societies, 330–331
Polynesian psychotherapies, 325–339
  case illustration of, 333–339
  Indigenous healing and liberation methodologies, 329–332
  Kōrerotia in, 328–329
  Moana-nui-a-kiwa identity, 326–328
Positive affect, religion/spirituality and, 213
Positive mental health emphasis, 79
Postsecular, 101
  phenomenal field relevant to, 105
  spiritually integrated psychotherapy as, 101
Postsecular, spiritually integrated gestalt therapy, 99–114
  case vignette of, 108–109
  and contemporary gestalt therapy theory, 101–107
  ethics and diversity in, 109–110
  guidelines for research and practice in, 110
  meaning of "postsecular" in, 101
  research on, 111–113
Posttraumatic stress disorder (PTSD), 381
  holistic approach to. *See* Search for Meaning
  spiritual struggles and symptoms of, 113
  suicidality among veterans with, 123
Power dynamics, in Multicultural Orientation framework, 407
Practice-based evidence (PBE) research, 250, 437, 444
Pragmatism, 174
Prayer
  as attachment to God, 60
  in culturally informed therapy sessions, 39
  in emotion-focused couple therapy, 355
  in Fincham's intervention, 350
  in Gestalt Pastoral Care, 232, 236, 240
  in Ho'oponopono approach, 338
  in Jewish psychotherapies in Israel, 278
  proximity seeking manifested in, 61–62
  as religious coping mechanism, 61
  in SPIRIT protocol, 163
  in spiritually integrated psychotherapy among Catholics, 254–256
  in Sufi Psychology, 291

Preoccupied attachment, 58, 65
Preparing to practice spiritually integrated psychotherapies, 8–13
Primary spiritual processes, in spiritually inclusive theistic treatment, 141–145
Primary spiritual struggles model, 124
Principle-based psychotherapy, 146
Principle-Centered Leadership (Covey), 146
Probabilistic/inferential knowledge, 194
Problem conceptualization, 35
    in culturally informed therapy, 37–38, 43–44
    in traditional Islamically integrated psychotherapy, 195, 201
Problem-focused coping, 368
Problem solving, in culturally informed therapy, 45–46
Procedural skills, 221
Process(es)
    in Christian-Based Spiritually Integrated Psychotherapy for East Asians Research Initiative of Toronto, 306–308
    in Gestalt Pastoral Care, 238–239
    in Gospel-centered integrative framework for therapy, 218–220, 222
    help-seeking, 35
    in M.T.O. Sufi Psychology, 290–292
    in Multicultural Orientation framework, 415
    in relational spirituality model, 81, 85–86
    in Search for Meaning program, 387–398
    with SPIRIT protocol, 164–165
    in spiritually inclusive theistic treatment, 141–145, 151–152
    in spiritually integrated psychotherapy among Catholics, 251–252, 254
    in traditional Islamically integrated psychotherapy, 200–204, 206–208
    using REACH Forgiveness, responsibilities for, 366–367
Process-cultural approach, 406
Process model of forgiveness, 369, 376–377
Protestant Christian tradition, 214–215
Prout, T. A., 113
Proximity seeking
    in attachment theory, 62
    in compensation hypothesis, 65
    manifested in prayer, 61–62
    in noncorporeal attachment, 60
Psalms, 162–163
Psychiatric problems
    caused by spirituality or religion, 165
    and spiritual struggles treatment, 128
Psychoeducation
    in culturally informed therapy, 43–44
    in REACH Forgiveness, 368–369, 372, 373
    in Search for Meaning program, 382, 383
    in SPIRIT protocol, 161, 167
    in traditional Islamically integrated psychotherapy, 201, 203, 206
Psychological distress, seeking of Christian counseling and, 113
Psychological problems
    conceptualization of, in culturally informed therapy, 35, 37–38, 43–44
    helping patients access spiritual resources for, 9–13
    in non-Western cultures, 252
    in Polynesian psychotherapy, 333–334
    solving, in culturally informed therapy, 45–46
    spirituality as contributor to, 7–8, 119–120
    and spiritual struggles, 123, 138–140
Psychology, 193–194
    defined, 399
    development of, 285
    of religion, 215–216
    as search for soul, 285, 399
    of Sufism, 286
Psychology and Christianity (Johnson), 349
Psychosocial belief system, 406
Psychospiritual balance, as goal of traditional Islamically integrated psychotherapy, 202–203
"Psychospiritual" language, 126
Psychotherapists. *See* Therapists
"Psychotherapy and Atheistic Values" (Ellis), 177
"Psychotherapy and Religious Values" (Bergin), 175, 177
PTSD. *See* Posttraumatic stress disorder
Puchalski, C., 388
Purpose, sense of, 122. *See also* Meaning and religion/spirituality, 213
    spiritual beliefs and values tied to, 137
    and spiritual wounding, 385

Q

Qalb, 198, 200
The Qur'an, 178, 196, 197

R

Randomized controlled trials (RCTs), 186, 369, 377
Rational beliefs (rBs)
    changing maladaptive irrational beliefs to, 175
    in rational emotive behavior therapy, 173, 174
    in scripture, 178
Rational emotive behavior therapy (REBT), 173–188
    and absolutism, 174–176, 178
    assessment with religious clients in, 177

and awfulizing, 180
and belief change, 175
CAPS REBTers, 187–188
case study of, 181, 182, 184–186
and demanding, 179
and frustration tolerance, 180
goal of, 174
and guilt, 178–179
and human rating, 180–181
integration of religion in, 173, 178–181
next steps for, 188
overview of, 174–177
religion and, 175, 177
research findings on, 186–187
and scripture as evidence, 179–181
techniques in, 181–183
Rational knowledge, 194
rBs. *See* Rational beliefs
RCS (Redeemer Counseling Services), 214, 227–228
RCTs. *See* Randomized controlled trials
REACH Forgiveness, 350, 365–378
assessment measures in, 372–373
case example, 374–376
collaborating with clergy in, 374
development of, 368
diversity considerations with, 372
efficacy of other forgiveness interventions and, 376–377
elements of, 366
in hope-focused couple approach, 359
implementation guidelines for, 371–374
intervention techniques and strategies in, 367, 373
overview of, 365–367
relationship establishment guidelines for, 372
theoretical framework for, 367–368
treatment settings benefiting from, 369
types of clinical issues and clients for, 369–371
Reactive emotions, in system of self-redemption, 217
REBT. *See* Rational emotive behavior therapy
Receiving, in Gospel-centered integrative framework for therapy, 219
Reconciliation, in hope-focused couple approach, 358–359
Re-Creating Your Life programs, 113
Redeemer Counseling Services (RCS), 214, 227–228
Redeemer Presbyterian Church, 220
Reflection
in Gospel-centered integrative framework for therapy, 220
in spiritually integrated psychotherapy among Catholics, 255
on spiritual struggles, facilitating, 127

Reist Gibbel, M., 18
Rejoicing, in Gospel-centered integrative framework for therapy, 219–220
Relational approach
in Christian spiritually integrated psychotherapy, 349
in contemporary gestalt therapy theory, 103–104
Multicultural Orientation framework as, 408
Relational beings, humans as, 305
Relational development systems, 80–81, 83–85
Relational ecologies of practice, 82, 83
Relational spirituality model (RSM), 77–95
assessment guidelines and recommendations for, 83–85
and attachment system, 88
background of, 78–79
case application of, 87–94
clinical contexts for, 79
clinical goal of, 78
collaborating recommendations for, 86–87
core values within, 77–78
dialectical balancing in, 93–94
and differentiation system, 89–91
diversity and justice considerations in, 81–82, 88
and intersubjectivity system, 91–93
intervention strategies and techniques for, 84–86
overview of, 79–86
process and ethical guidelines for, 81
relationship establishment guidelines for, 82–83
research findings and support for, 94–95
SERT dynamics in, 90–91
theoretical framework of, 80–81
Relational spirituality triangle, 86
Relationship establishment
in Christian-Based Spiritually Integrated Psychotherapy for East Asians Research Initiative of Toronto, 308–309
between clergy and therapist, 412. *See also* Collaboration
and contemporary gestalt therapy, 103, 106
in contemporary gestalt therapy theory, 103–104
in Gestalt Pastoral Care, 235, 237–238
in Multicultural Orientation framework, 407, 408
in Polynesian psychotherapy, 335
in REACH Forgiveness, 372
in relational spirituality model, 82–83
in spiritually inclusive theistic treatment, 151

in spiritually integrated psychotherapy among Catholics, 253–254
in traditional Islamically integrated psychotherapy, 200–202
Relaxation exercises, in Tamarkoz method, 295–296
Religion. *See also* Religion/spirituality
absolutism in, 178
Ellis on mental health and, 173, 175
integrated into rational emotive behavior therapy, 173, 178–181
Jews' varying beliefs about, 268
postsecular gestalt view of, 105–107
psychologists' training in, 5
psychology of, 215–216
and rational emotive behavior therapy, 175, 177
in relational spirituality model, 80
as significant in people's lives, 7
spirituality vs., 388
use of term, 33
Religion-accommodative REBT, 177
Religion-integrative REBT, 177
Religion/spirituality (R/S), 33
as both helpful and harmful, 79
and collaboration in therapy, 86
in correctional settings, 403–404. *See also* Multicultural Orientation (MCO) framework
God images in, 216
graduate program faculty with interests in, 423–426
health and, 33–34
interventions focusing on, 34–36. *See also* Culturally informed therapy (CIT)
and marriage or marriage-like relationships, 347
in meaning making, 213
in mental health, 213
mental health field attention to, 78
overlooked importance of, 44
themes of, 161
of therapist, therapy-related variables affected by, 320–321
Religiosity
of in Catholic Latin American clients, 253
in culturally informed therapy for schizophrenia, 38
of incarcerated individuals, 403–404
intrinsic, 61
Religiosity gap, 35
Religious coping
negative, intervention for, 112
and seeking of Christian counseling, 113
Religious identity/affiliation
and benefit of Tamarkoz method, 296
in correctional settings, 403–404, 408
in Israel, 274–275

of SPIRIT study patients and clinicians, 169–171
of those involved in Jewish psychotherapies in Israel, 274–275
Religious resources
in culturally informed therapy, 41–42
helping patients access, 9–13
Remembering, in Gospel-centered integrative framework for therapy, 219
Repenting, in Gospel-centered integrative framework for therapy, 219
Research designs, 444
Resilience
and mindfulness, 113
psychospiritual, 195
sacred moments promoting, 111
self-awareness as source of, 90
of therapist, 91, 113
in traditional Islamically integrated psychotherapy, 203–204
Respect
in cultural humility, 404–405, 408
in Polynesian psychotherapy, 334–335
in spiritually inclusive theistic treatment, 136, 137
Ribeiro, J. P., 111
Richards, P. Scott, 15, 18, 153, 249, 436–437, 441
Ripley, J. S., 24, 361, 368, 373
Rizzuto, A. M., 215–216
Robb, Hank, 178
Rogers, Carl, 310
Rosmarin, D. H., 19, 158–160, 162
Ross, E., 338
Rotenberg, Boaz, 273
Rotenberg, Mordechai, 272–273
The Rotenberg Institute—Center for Jewish Psychology, 273
Rothman, A., 17
Roubal, J., 101, 105, 238
R/S. *See* Religion/spirituality
RSM. *See* Relational spirituality model
Rūḥ, 198, 200
Ruiz, Don Miguel, 146
Rulla, L. M., 249, 250
Rumi, 291, 293–294
Rye, M. S., 377–378

S

Sacred (term), 80
Safe and effective use of self, 306, 309
Safe haven, God as, 60–61
Safran, J. D., 82–83
Salmanian, M., 112
Samaritan Institute, 437
Sami Indigenous spirituality, 338
Sandage, S. J., 17, 78–79, 368
Sanders, P., 18, 436–437

Satanic drives, 197
Scarred by Struggle, Transformed by Hope (Chittister), 124
Schizophrenia, culturally informed therapy for, 34, 37–38
Scripture
 added to rational emotive behavior therapy, 177, 178, 186–187
 Christian. *See* Bible
 Jewish, 268
 of Latter-day Saints, 179–186
Scripture as evidence
 in culturally informed therapy, 38
 and rational emotive behavior therapy, 179–181
Scrupulosity, 161
SCT-MH. *See* Spiritual Competency Training in Mental Health
Search for Meaning program, 381–399
 anger barrier in, 391–392
 building trust in, 388–390
 connecting parts of, 397–398
 continuing self-awareness in, 397–398
 examining roots of anger in, 393
 forgiveness in, 396–297
 future directions for, 399
 grief in, 395–396
 moral injury, guilt, and shame barriers in, 393–395
 processes and interventions in, 387–398
 redeveloping spiritual formation in, 390–391
 research findings and support for, 398–399
 and spiritual wounding, 383–387
 treatment approach and theoretical underpinnings of, 382–387
Secondary spiritual struggles model, 124
Secularism, 101, 270
Secular Jews, 268–269
Secular-religious Jews, 273
Secure attachment
 in attachment theory, 58–59
 in close relationships, 63
 to God, facilitating. *See* Attachment to God (ATG)
 in Multicultural Orientation framework, 407
 of relational spirituality, 80
Secure base
 God as, 61–62
 therapy relationship as, 67
Self
 contemporary gestalt view of, 103–104, 106
 negative views of, 222
 safe and effective use of, 306, 309
 true, 310

Self-acceptance
 in Gospel-centered integrative framework for therapy, 220, 224
 and self-forgiveness, 370. *See also* REACH Forgiveness
Self-assertiveness, 45
Self-awareness
 of clinicians, 78
 in Gestalt Pastoral Care, 234–235
 in Search for Meaning program, 397–398
 in traditional Islamically integrated psychotherapy, 202
Self-blame, 179
Self-defeating guilt, 178–179
Self-esteem, religion/spirituality and, 213
Self-evaluation, 397
Self-forgiveness, 370, 397
Self-images, 255–256, 259
Self-knowledge
 in Sufi Psychology, 290
 Sufism as discipline of, 287, 288. *See also* M.T.O. Sufi Psychology
Self-transcendence, in spiritually integrated psychotherapy among Catholics, 251, 255
Self-worth, in Protestant Christian tradition, 215
Seligman, Martin, 146
Sensory knowledge, 194
Separation distress, in attachment theory, 62–63
SERT dynamics. *See* Spiritual, existential, religious, theological dynamics
Service to others, 42
Sex offenders, spiritual struggles of, 123
Sexual abuse
 spirituality in treatment approaches for, 113
 and spiritual struggles, 123, 128
Shafranske, E. P., 17, 321
Shame, 217
 guilt vs., 394
 and REACH Forgiveness model, 370
 in Search for Meaning program, 393–395
 and spiritual wounding, 386–387
Shattered soul concept, in spiritual wounding, 389
Shattered trust, in spiritual wounding, 385, 389–390
Shaver, P. R., 65
Shepherd, Victor, 305
Shintoism, 3
Shupe, A., 62
SI (Solihten Institute), 437
SICT. *See* Spiritually integrated couples therapy
Significance, search for, 121–122. *See also* Meaning

Sikhism, 3
Sim, W., 13–21
Simon, W., 18
SIP. *See* Spiritually integrated psychotherapy
SIP-C. *See* Spiritually integrated psychotherapy among Catholics
SI (Solihten Institute) training program in SIP, 437–441
Situation, extending the self into, 103–104
Skills Training Manual for Treating Borderline Personality Disorder (Linehan), 316
SMHP (Spirituality and Mental Health Program), 158–160
Smith, L.T., 330
Smith, T. B., 186, 260
Social correspondence hypothesis, 65
Social health, religion/spirituality and, 34
Social justice considerations
 in relational spirituality model, 88
 in therapy with Indigenous peoples, 338
Solace for the Soul programs, 113
Solfelt, L., 24
Solihten Institute (SI), 437
Solihten Institute (SI) training program in SIP, 437–441
SOSR (system of self-redemption), 217–218
Soul, 112
 in Ontological Model of the Human Psyche, 198
 psychology as study of, 285, 399
 shattered, in spiritual wounding, 389
 in Sufism, 286, 293
South Pacific region. *See* Polynesian psychotherapies
Sperry, L., 6
SPIRIT (spiritual psychotherapy for inpatient, residential, and intensive treatment), 157–171
 case example of, 166–167
 description of SPIRIT study, 167–170
 development of, 157–160
 goal of, 165
 limitation of, 171
 next steps in using, 170–171
 treatment approach in, 160–163
 treatment implementation in, 163–166
Spirit (*rūḥ*), in traditional Islamically integrated psychotherapy, 198, 200
Spiritual, existential, religious, theological (SERT) dynamics, 80, 81, 90–91
Spiritual and Religious Competences Project (SRCP), 424–426
"Spiritual but not religious" identity, among Israeli Jews, 269
Spiritual bypass, 86
Spiritual companioning, in Gestalt Pastoral Care, 235

Spiritual Competency Training in Mental Health (SCT-MH)
 coursework plan based on, 424–425
 online courses for, 427–432
Spiritual connection, 138
 in spiritually inclusive theistic treatment, 138–140
 in traditional Islamically integrated psychotherapy, 200
Spiritual dimension of humans
 in Sufi Psychology, 290
 in Sufism, 289
Spiritual direction, 251–254
Spiritual discernment, 259
Spiritual diversity, 3–4
Spiritual dwelling, 79, 80
 assessment of, 83
 change process in, 85
Spiritual formation, redeveloping, 390–391
Spiritual illnesses, in traditional Islamically integrated psychotherapy, 195, 196
Spirituality. *See also* Religion/spirituality (R/S)
 as contributor to psychological problems, 7–8, 119–120
 in culturally informed therapy, 44
 defined, 7, 103, 111
 in gestalt therapy, 111
 in Ho'oponopono approach, 338
 for Indigenous peoples, 338
 integrated into treatment, 5
 Jewish, 274–275
 in mental health, 231–232
 postsecular gestalt view of, 105–107
 psychologists' training in, 5
 relational, 80. *See also* Relational spirituality model (RSM)
 relational definition of, 80
 relationship of psychotherapy to, 111, 112
 religion vs., 388
 in religious and non-religious traditions, 3
 as resource, 7
 as significant in people's lives, 7
 unaffiliated, 3
 use of term, 33
Spirituality and Mental Health Program (SMHP), 158–160
Spirituality & CBT group, 159–160
Spiritually inclusive theistic treatment, 135–154
 case report of, 150–152
 conceptual model for, 138–140
 described, 136
 encouraging spiritual practices and interventions in, 141, 148, 149
 facilitating primary spiritual processes in, 141–145

need for, 136–138
   spiritual pathways to recovery and healing in, 140–149
   teaching and modeling universal spiritual principles in, 141, 145–149
   treatment outcome findings for, 153–154
Spiritually integrated couples therapy (SICT), 347–362
   assessment guidelines and recommendations for, 354
   case study of, 355–360
   collaboration with clergy in, 355
   common features of, 351–352
   couples who can benefit from, 352
   differing professional approaches to, 349–351
   diversity considerations in, 353–354
   ethical issues specific to, 352–353
   history of, 348–349
   intervention strategies and techniques in, 354–355
   reasons for seeking, 348
   research findings and support for, 360–361
   theological and theoretical foundations of, 352
Spiritually Integrated Psychotherapy (Pargament), 438
Spiritually integrated psychotherapy (SIP)
   approaches to, 15–26. *See also individual approaches*
   challenges to mainstream implementation of, 14
   Christian approaches in, 349
   defining, 6–7
   elements of, 307
   gaining competency in, 8–9
   gap in field of, 78
   helping patients access spiritual resources in, 9–13
   helping patients address spiritual problems in, 13
   interdisciplinary approaches to, 78
   mainstreaming, 443–446
   as postsecular concept, 101
   preparing to practice, 8–13
   reasons for, 7–8
   recommendations for mainstreaming, 443–445
   relevance of, 170
   Richards' research on, 15
   staying true to one's own beliefs in, 9
   successful implementation of, 171
Spiritually integrated psychotherapy among Catholics (SIP-C), 249–261
   assessment guidelines and recommendations for, 254
   case study of, 256–259
   clients and client issues in, 250, 252–253
   and cultural diversity among Catholics, 252–253
   process and ethical guidelines for, 251–252
   relationship establishment and collaboration guidelines for, 253–254
   research findings and support, 259–261
   spiritual intervention strategies and techniques in, 254–256
   theoretical and theological foundations of, 251
   theoretical orientations in, 250
   treatment approach in, 250–251
Spiritually sensitive psychotherapist skills, 8–9
Spiritual pathways, in spiritually inclusive theistic treatment, 141–145
Spiritual principles, universally accepted. *See* Universal spiritual principles
Spiritual problems
   in correctional settings, 411–412
   helping patients address, 13
Spiritual psychotherapy for inpatient, residential, and intensive treatment. *See* SPIRIT
Spiritual/religious belief system, 406
Spiritual resources
   in culturally informed therapy, 41–42
   helping patients access, 9–13
   for Jewish psychotherapies in Israel, 277, 278
   in Polynesian psychotherapies, 339
   in spiritually inclusive theistic treatment, 140, 143
Spiritual seeking, 79, 80
   assessment of, 83
   change process in, 85
Spiritual struggles, 119–130
   assessment for, 83, 125–126
   case example of, 127–128
   consequences of, 123–125
   defined, 8, 113, 120
   facilitating acceptance of and reflection on, 127
   general dimensions of, 120
   in Gospel-centered integrative framework for therapy, 217
   naming and normalizing, 126–127
   as natural part of development, 122
   possibility of growth following, 124–125
   prevalence of, 121, 126
   in relational spirituality model, 80, 83
   roots of, 121–123
   in SPIRIT protocol, 162, 165–166
   in SPIRIT study group, 170
   in spiritually inclusive theistic treatment, 138, 140
   spiritual symptoms vs., 165
   as theme, 161
   in trauma survivors, 113

treatment programs for, 128
types of, 120–121
vulnerability to, 122–123
Winding Road intervention for, 112
Spiritual struggles models, 124
Spiritual symptoms, spiritual struggles vs., 165
Spiritual wounding, 383–387
co-occurring issues with, 384–387
depth of, 384
and forgiveness, 396. *See also* Search for Meaning program
levels of, 383–384
shattered soul concept in, 389
SRCP (Spiritual and Religious Competences Project), 424–426
Sriram, S., 17
Stages of grief, 395
Standards of Ethical Practice for Gestalt Pastoral Care (Gestalt Pastoral Care), 236–237
Starnino, V. R., 18, 25, 382
Steinberg, S. R., 194
Stephens, Douglas, 440
Stigma of psychological help, 252
Stoicism, 174
Storytelling, 330
Strange Situation, 58, 60
Strelan, P., 367
Stress
reduced by prayer, 255
Tamarkoz method for, 296
Stress-and-coping theory, 367
Stressors
and spiritual struggles, 123
transgressions as, 367–368
Stress reduction, mindfulness-based, 113
Struggles
spiritual. *See* Spiritual struggles
of ultimate meaning, 121
Substance use, religion/spirituality and, 213
Success in therapy, 310
Sufi Psychology, 287
conceptualization of the patient in, 289
research on, 295–296
Sufi Psychotherapy in, 290–294. *See also* M.T.O. Sufi Psychology
techniques used in, 290–292
Sufism
defined, 287
focus on soul in, 293
goal in, 288
human urge to know in, 292
importance of experience in, 287–288
Islamic, 286–288, 293. *See also* M.T.O. Sufi Psychology
psychology in, 286
Source of Life in, 289
Teacher in, 292
unique journeys in, 290

Suicidality
in Maori and Pacific Islanders, 328–329, 338–339
and religion/spirituality, 213
and spiritual struggles of veterans, 123
Sullivan, John, 382
Supernatural struggles, 120
Surface anxieties, 85–86
Suro, G., 16
Symbolic attachment, 59–60
System of self-redemption (SOSR), 217–218

T

Tamarkoz, 291, 295–296
Taoism, 3
Tarakeshwar, N., 18
Targeted systems-change, 426
Task analysis, 221
Taylor, Charles, 110
Taylor, P., 66
TCS (Tyndale Counselling Services), 303–304, 308
Teacher, in Sufism, 292
Techniques
in Christian-Based Spiritually Integrated Psychotherapy for East Asians Research Initiative of Toronto, 310–311
for disputing irrational beliefs, 181, 182
experiments vs., 106
in Gestalt Pastoral Care, 238–241
in Gospel-centered integrative framework for therapy, 216–220
interventions as, 106. *See also* Interventions
in Multicultural Orientation framework, 409–411
in rational emotive behavior therapy, 181–183
in REACH Forgiveness, 367, 373
in relational spirituality model, 84–86
in spiritually integrated couples therapy, 354–355
in spiritually integrated psychotherapy among Catholics, 254–256
in Sufi Psychology, 290–292
using terms "practice" or "invitation" in place of, 238
Technology, effective use of, 445
Tel-Aviv University, 273
Templeton spiritually integrative psychotherapy (TSIP) research, 186–187
Templeton World Charity Foundation, 377
Ten Days to Self-Esteem (Burns), 316
Teresa, Mother, 62
Teshuvah movement, 269
Theology, in relational spirituality model, 80
Theory formation, 194

Therapist–client working alliance, 82, 310. *See also* Relationship establishment
Therapists
  competency for, 8–9
  disengagement from personal values of, 353
  for Jewish psychotherapies in Israel, 270, 274–276
  lack of religious/spiritual training for, 36
  personal beliefs of, 9
  personal counseling for, 306
  salient cultural groups for, 407
  spiritual beliefs and practices of, 113, 129, 137
  spiritually sensitive, 8–9
  in Sufi Psychology, 292–293
  therapy-related variables affected by religiousness or spirituality of, 320–321
  for traditional Islamically integrated psychotherapy, 195
  training in religion and spirituality for, 5
Third space, 86
Thomas, M., 244–245
Thomas, M. J., 16, 66
Thomas, M. L., 35
Tillich, Paul, 100
TIPP. *See* Traditional Islamically integrated psychotherapy
Tisdale, T. C., 16, 66
Tocqueville, Alexis de, 214
Torah, 268
Toronto, Canada, 301–303
Toussaint, L. L., 24
Traditional Islamically integrated psychotherapy (TIPP), 193–208
  approach in, 194–195
  case conceptualization in, 205–206
  case illustration of, 204–208
  future implications for, 208
  health and wellness as continuum in, 195, 196
  intervention and change process in, 200–204, 206–208
  and Islamic epistemology, 193–194
  Ontological Model of the Human Psyche in, 196–200
  underlying assumptions and framework of, 195–196
Traditional Jews, 268–269, 273
Training, 423–443
  ACPE SIP program, 432–437
  Bridges Institute for Spiritually Integrated Psychotherapies practice-research-training network, 441–443
  in Christian-Based Spiritually Integrated Psychotherapy for East Asians Research Initiative of Toronto, 307, 309
  for clergy in mental health, 36
  continuing education opportunities, 426–443
  in Gestalt Pastoral Care, 232
  in Gospel-centered integrative framework for therapy, 220–221
  graduate programs, 423–426
  in Jewish psychotherapy, 273–275
  need for, 14
  perceived as authority, 309
  and REACH Forgiveness, 371
  in religion and spirituality, 5
  SCT-MH online courses, 427–432
  Solihten Institute training program in SIP, 437–441
  for SPIRIT protocol, 164
  Spiritual and Religious Competences Project, 424–426
  in Toronto, for faith integration in counseling, 303
Transference issues, 308
Transformational psychology view, in Christian spiritually integrated psychotherapy, 349
Transpersonal perspective, 3
Trauma
  historical, 331, 332
  holistic approach to, 381. *See also* Search for Meaning program
  spirituality in treating survivors of, 113, 381
  and spiritual struggles, 123
Traumatized infants, 59
Trier, K. K., 62
True self, 310
Trust
  building, 388–390
  faith vs., 397
  rebuilding, 397
  shattered, in spiritual wounding, 385, 389–390
  in therapist–clergy relationship, 412
Truth, in Islamic epistemology, 194
TSIP (Templeton spiritually integrative psychotherapy) research, 186–187
Tyndale Counselling Services (TCS), 303–304, 308
Tyndale Family Life Centre (FLC), 303
Tyndale Seminary, 303
Tyndale University, 301, 303. *See also* Christian-Based Spiritually Integrated Psychotherapy for East Asians Research Initiative of Toronto (CSPEARIT)

U

Ultra-Orthodox Jews, 268, 269, 273
Unaffiliated spirituality, 3
Unforgiveness, 367, 368

Universal human questions, 3
Universalism, in Jewish psychotherapies in Israel, 275–276
Universal spiritual principles
　popular attention to, 146
　in psychotherapy, 145
　in spiritually inclusive theistic treatment, 137, 138, 141, 144–149
　teaching and modeling, 141, 145–149
University of California, Berkeley, 296

V

Validation, 213, 220, 222
Values
　cultural, 405
　divine, 251, 255
　of heart vs. of brain, 291
　identity tied to, 137
　in Indigenous peoples' spirituality, 338
　in Multicultural Orientation framework, 407
　natural, 251
　of psychotherapists, disengagement from, 353
　in relational spirituality model, 77–78
　in spiritually integrated psychotherapy among Catholics, 251, 252
Verified reports of truth, 194
Veterans
　posttraumatic stress disorder in, 381. *See also* Search for Meaning program
　REACH Forgiveness with, 370
　spirituality in treatment approaches for combat trauma, 113
　spiritual struggles of, 123, 128
Vienna Circle, 100
Virtue(s), 84, 94
　and religion/spirituality, 213
　in spiritually integrated psychotherapy among Catholics, 250
　in traditional Islamically integrated psychotherapy, 203–204
Virtue ethics model, 94–95
Vision
　of ACPE, 437
　spiritual beliefs and values tied to, 137
Visualization, in Tamarkoz method, 295–296
Vocation, 250
Volunteerism, 41–42
Von Zweck, C., 102
Vulnerability, to spiritual struggles, 122–123
Vygotsky, L. S., 330

W

Wade, N. G., 24, 376–377
Wade, Nathaniel, 368
Wai, 326, 338, 339
Wairua, 337–339
Waka Oranga National Collective of Maori Psychotherapy Practitioners Aotearoa, 327–328
Walker, D. F., 361
Wampold, B. E., 406
Webber, R. D., 236
Weisman de Mamani, A., 16, 39, 42
Weisman de Mamani, A. G., 33
Well-being
　assessing, 84
　facilitating, in relational spirituality model, 79
　as goal of spiritually inclusive theistic treatment, 137
　and God as secure base, 61–62
　on health–wellness continuum in traditional Islamically integrated psychotherapy, 195, 196
　and prayer, 255
　and psychosocial functioning, 94
　from resolving spiritual concerns, 113
　sacred moments promoting, 111
Welwood, J., 86
Wheeler, G., 104
Whole-cloth approach to couple therapy, 351
Wilcox, L., 286
Wilkinson, R. G., 328
Willard, Dallas, 107
Wilson, D., 331
Winding Road intervention, 112, 128
Winnicott, D. W., 215
Wong, T.-Y., 23, 320
Woolfe, R., 9
Working alliance, 82, 310. *See also* Relationship establishment
Worthington, E. L., 404
Worthington, E. L., Jr., 24, 350, 354, 361, 370–374
Wundt, Wilhelm, 285

Y

Yale Baby Lab, 197
Yoga, 113

Z

Zahm, S., 99
Zoroastrianism, 3

ABOUT THE EDITORS

P. Scott Richards, PhD, is the founder of Bridges Institute for Spiritually Integrated Psychotherapies, a research and training institute. A retired professor of counseling psychology at Brigham Young University, he is past president and fellow of the Society for the Psychology of Religion and Spirituality (Division 36) of the American Psychological Association (APA) and is a fellow of APA's Society for the Advancement of Psychotherapy (Division 29). Among his six APA books about spirituality and psychotherapy is the best-selling citation classic *A Spiritual Strategy for Counseling and Psychotherapy* (with Allen E. Bergin; second edition, 2005). He was the principal investigator and project director of a $3.57 million grant from the John Templeton Foundation about the processes and outcomes of spiritually integrated psychotherapies, which was completed in 2020.

G. E. Kawika Allen, PhD, is an associate professor of counseling psychology at Brigham Young University. He has published more than 20 peer-reviewed research articles about Polynesian psychology and culture, the psychology of religion, and spiritual aspects of diversity. He is secretary of APA Division 45, the Society for the Psychological Study of Culture, Ethnicity and Race. He was a project codirector of the aforementioned grant from the John Templeton Foundation.

Daniel K Judd, PhD, is a retired professor and former dean of religious education at Brigham Young University with a doctorate in counseling psychology. He is a researcher, educator, psychologist, and pastoral leader. He was project codirector of the aforementioned grant from the John Templeton Foundation. Among the several books and numerous journal articles he has written about religion and mental health is his recent book *Let's Talk About Religion and Mental Health* (2021).